Barcelona

"All you've got to do is decide to go
and the hardest part is over.

So go!"

TONY WHEELER, COFOUNDER – LONELY PLANET

ISABELLA NOBLE, REGIS ST LOUIS

Contents

COVID-19

We have re-checked every business in this book before publication to ensure that it is still open after the COVID-19 outbreak. However, the economic and social impacts of COVID-19 will continue to be felt long after the outbreak has been contained, and many businesses, services and events referenced in this guide may experience ongoing restrictions. Some businesses may be temporarily closed, have changed their opening hours and services, or require bookings; some unfortunately could have closed permanently. We suggest you check with venues before visiting for the latest information.

Pont del Bisbe p71
A photogenic marble bridge in the Barri Gòtic.

La Pedrera p147
This Unesco-listed masterpiece is one of Gaudí's finest.

Gràcia &
Park Güell
(p172)

Camp Nou, Pedralbes &
La Zona Alta
(p204)

Barceloneta,
the Waterfront &
El Poblenou
(p117)

La Sagrada Família
& L'Eixample
(p138)

La Ribera &
El Born
(p97)

La Rambla &
Barri Gòtic
(p58)

El Raval
(p84)

Montjuïc, Poble Sec
& Sant Antoni
(p186)

Right: View
of Barcelona
from Park Güell
(p174)

WELCOME TO

Barcelona

I've been getting to know Barcelona since I was a teenager growing up in southern Andalucía. Like countless others, I'm bewitched by the golden beaches, jewel-like medieval architecture, Modernisme marvels and one-of-a-kind cuisine. But it's much more than the headline sights, Michelin stars and Mediterranean sun that pull me back. It's the village-vibe squares, neighbourhood markets and exquisitely tiled homes; gentle gegants (papier-mâché giants) bobbing through centuries-old streets; sprawling views from the pine-scented Collserola hills; and a quick cafè morphing effortlessly into a beautiful three-course lunch.

By Isabella Noble, Writer
🐦 @isabellamnoble 📷 isabellamnoble
For more about our writers, see p320

Barcelona's Top Experiences

1 ARCHITECTURAL MAGIC

Few cities are defined by their architecture to quite the same extent as Barcelona. A tangle of narrow medieval streets fills the ancient Ciutat Vella (Old City), beyond which the boulevards of L'Eixample reveal some of country's most inspiring buildings. More contemporary design awaits along the waterfront and northwest into the former industrial hub of El Poblenou.

Modernista Wonders

The weird and wonderful undulations of Antoni Gaudí's creations are echoed in countless Modernista flights of fancy across town. The gateway to these astonishing architectural works is the neighbourhood of L'Eixample, with Gaudí's La Pedrera and Casa Batlló (pictured right) or the unmissable La Sagrada Família (pictured left), still under construction 100 years after his death. p140

Other Eras

Barcelona's architectural riches travel well beyond Modernisme, whether you're wandering around the Museu Picasso (set in five contiguous medieval mansions in El Born), exploring the Catalan Gothic style of La Catedral (pictured above) or spinning into the future at El Poblenou's Torre Glòries. p126

Hot Hotels

Some of the city's most spectacular buildings happen to be fabulous hotels too, such as Gràcia's Hotel Casa Fuster, designed by Doménech i Montaner, or the unmissable Hotel Arts Barcelona (pictured above). p237

2 CUTTING-EDGE CUISINE

Barcelona has become one of the world's great culinary destinations. The city's most celebrated chefs blend traditional Catalan recipes with avant-garde cooking techniques to create deliciously inventive masterpieces. And the critics agree: the city has more than 20 Michelin-starred resstaurants. And no matter where you go (or what your budget is), you won't be far from a memorable meal.

Molecular Gastronomy

Leading the way on Barcelona's cutting-edge dining scene are Carles Abellán, who has elevated the humble tapa to high art in his sprinkling of restaurants; and contemporaries such as Jordi Vilà and Jordi Artal. Savour gastronomic works of art at deliciously original spots including Disfrutar (pictured left, p155), La Barra de Carles Abellán (p128), Lasarte (p155) and Cinc Sentits (p155). p37

Catalan Classics

Traditional Catalan cooking revolves around the gloriously fresh bounty of the surrounding landscape, and every neighbourhood bursts with options for uncovering local recipes, such as El Poblenou's Can Recasens. p130

Above left: Crema Catalana

Above right: Seafood tapas

3 INTO THE ART WORLD

The city shaped by Gaudí and his contemporaries is an endlessly lively art and design hub, home to some of Spain's most inspiring galleries and a rich creative heritage going back centuries. From the works of Pablo Picasso to anonymous medieval frescoes, art comes in many tantalising shapes.

Museu Picasso

Picasso lived in Barcelona between the ages of 15 and 23, and elements of the city undoubtedly influenced his pieces. Set across five El Born medieval mansions, the Museu Picasso (inner courtyard pictured below right) showcases perhaps the world's best collection of the master's early work. p99

J ENRIQUE MOLINA/ALAMY STOCK PHOTO ©

Montjuïc

Wander between unparalleled Catalan Romanesque frescoes at Museu Nacional d'Art de Catalunya (pictured above; p189), before exploring a temple to the great Catalan artist Joan Miró (p188). p191

MACBA

At the heart of El Raval's creative world, this packed collection of 20th-century artwork (pictured right) sprawls across a bold Richard Meier–designed building. p86

4 HIT THE TOWN

A whole different Barcelona springs to life as the sun sets, whether you're swilling Catalan wines in an elegant *vinoteca*, hunting down live-music gigs, sipping cocktails on a view-laden rooftop or dancing the night away at the clubs. Prepare by rounding up a few friends for a leisurely vermouth session.

El Born

Bar-hop from cocktail dens to live-music spots and convivial hang-outs around this leafy pocket of the old city, where Dr Stravinsky is a creative favourite. p111

El Raval

Some of Barcelona's finest historical bars and cocktail specialists line this buzzy corner of town, especially around Carrer de Joaquín Costa, where you'll find prize-winning Two Schmucks. p92

Gaixample

Wander up to the grid-like Eixample to party in Barcelona's lively LGBTIQ+ nightlife area. p158

Above: Plaça Reial by night (p66)

5 OUT IN THE OPEN

Refreshing natural spaces are another Barcelona jewel. The sun-drenched white-gold beaches and deep-blue Mediterranean sea make a fine backdrop for jogging, biking, strolling and swimming; or drink in the view from the water while kayaking, surfing, paddleboarding or kicking back on a sunset cruise. Pine-forested hills loom behind the city (perfect for hiking, running or mountain biking) and sloping Montjuïc offers endless explorations amid tangles of gardens.

KERT/SHUTTERSTOCK ©

ESME FOX/LONELY PLANET ©

Beach Bliss

The Mediterranean beckons from every corner of Barcelona, whether you fancy a quick dip at the Poblenou beaches or a day trip to the Garraf (pictured top left) or Maresme coasts. p123

Hill Hikes

Shady paths thread through 80 sq km of natural bliss in the Parc Natural de Collserola (pictured above left), which frames Barcelona's north. p208

Parks & Gardens

For a breath of fresh air, head up the hill to Montjuïc, explore landscaped Parc de la Ciutadella (pictured above right; p103), or wander around green Park Güell. p174

6 MARKET MARVELS

Mercat de Santa Caterina

With its remarkable undulating roof, the Mercat de Santa Caterina was designed by Enric Miralles and Benedetta Tagliabue. p104

Sant Antoni & Gràcia

The renovated iron-and-brick Mercat de Sant Antoni (pictured top left; p195) has thrown fresh energy into the surrounding neighbhourhood, while Gràcia's Mercat de la Llibertat remains a treasure trove of Catalan produce. p176

Mercat de la Boqueria

Though huge crowds at La Boqueria (pictured left) have made the world-famous market a victim of its own success, shoppers still wonder at its endless bounty. p64

Barcelonins are spoilt for choice when it comes to temples of temptation groaning with fresh produce, and market shopping is very much part of daily life here. Look beyond the famous headline-hitting addresses to unearth standout neighbourhood markets, many of which have been recently overhauled, with up-to-date design bringing a breath of fresh air to their ancient food-loving halls.

What's New

While concerns about overtourism and the issue of Catalan independence reached fever pitch in the years leading up to the COVID-19 pandemic, Barcelona – the city that gave birth to Gaudí and the ingenious creations of Modernisme – continues to break new ground, with ambitious projects bringing urban renewal.

Market Makeovers

Gràcia's 1892 Mercat de l'Abaceria Central (p185) is set to be the next long-established traditional market to be glammed-up to better gel with the modern-day city. It follows the astonishing success of the Mercat de Sant Antoni (p195) restoration project in 2018.

Vermouth Revival

The traditional Barcelona drink of vermouth (brandy-fortified wine) has experienced a dazzling revival over the last decade. New vermouth bars are opening all over town, and historical vermouth joints are more popular than ever. Catch *la hora del vermut* at Quimet i Quimet (p196) or Bodega La Peninsular (p126).

A New View

Over in El Poblenou, the boundary-pushing Torre Glòries (p126) is unveiling a sparkling-new viewing platform in 2022, with wraparound views from the building's top levels and an installation by Argentinian artist Tomás Saraceno set into its dome.

Neighbourhoods on the Up

The reopening of the local market and the arrival of a string of bars, cafes and boutiques have transformed residential Sant Antoni into one of the city's most fashionable neighbourhoods. The formerly industrial *barri* of El Poblenou continues to pull in creative minds, while the southernmost tip of La Barceloneta has seen a raft of restaurant openings. In L'Eixample,

WHAT'S HAPPENING IN BARCELONA?

Isabella Noble, Lonely Planet Writer

Wherever you wander across Barcelona, you'll spot pro-independence *estelades* (lone-star Catalan flags) and yellow-ribbon symbols of support for the politicians involved in Catalonia's 2017 referendum (which was judged illegal by Spain's constitutional court) and failed ensuing attempt to achieve independence. While the topic of Catalan separatism is on everyone's mind, worries about overtourism in Barcelona have sky-rocketed in recent years and, after the city came to a complete standstill during the COVID-19 pandemic, there's now a strong push to build back local tourism in a more responsible way.

But there's still plenty of positive excitement in Barcelona. The local commitment to innovation has hugely improved urban design, communications, transport and sustainability. The authorities are also busy pushing forward plans to recast Barcelona's tourism scene more sustainably, and several major architectural jewels, such as Gaudí's Casa Vicens in Gràcia and Bellesguard near Tibidabo, have recently been restored. Ambitious new hotels, restaurants and multiconcept ventures are popping up all over town, and the old industrial *barri* of El Poblenou continues its upward swing.

Passeig de Sant Joan is the latest foodie boulevard – try Chichalimoná (p156).

Luxury Hotels

Hot arrivals on Barcelona's blossoming top-end hotel scene over the last few years include Ian Schrager's Barcelona Edition (p236) in La Ribera, literary-inspired Sir Victor (p239) in L'Eixample, much-awaited Nobu Barcelona (p242) in untouristed Sants, Soho House's Little Beach House (p234) in seaside Garraf and **Kimpton Vividora** (https://kimptonvividorahotel. com/en/) in the Barri Gòtic.

A Contemporary Art Splash

Amsterdam's Moco Museum launched its second branch (p104) in Barcelona in late 2021, taking over El Born's former Palau dels Cervelló and filling it with a star-studded line-up of contemporary, modern and street art that includes Banksy, Warhol, Kusama, Basquiat and Dalí.

New & Improved Park Güell

Gaudí's fantastical Park Güell (p174) has undergone a host of ambitious renovations in recent years, including the creation of better kids' play areas and a biodiversity trail, and the addition of a shiny new shuttle bus from Alfons X metro stop to help spread the crowds.

Natural Wines

Drops crafted using organic, biodynamic, minimum-intervention techniques are taking Barcelona by storm. Hot favourites devoted to exclusively natural wines include L'Eixample's Bar Torpedo (p154) and Gresca (p153) (both by Rafa Peña), Can Cisa/Bar Brutal (p109) in La Ribera and La Violeta (p132) in La Barceloneta.

Cuca de Llum

In late 2021, Tibidabo (p210) celebrated the 120th birthday of its theme park with the launch of the much-anticipated Cuca de Llum funicular, which now lights up the mountain after dark and provides a fun-filled way to zip uphill.

Gastrobars

Not content to rest on their laurels, several well-established Barcelona restaurants

have launched intimate gastrobar spin-offs. Try Extra Bar (p178) in Gràcia, from the team behind much-loved La Pubilla, and Mediamanga (p155), by Mont Bar in L'Eixample.

Artisan Workshops

Artists, designers and craft-workers fuelling Barcelona's creative scene have thrown open their doors to those keen to learn the ropes – from flower-arranging sessions with superstar florist Alblanc (p136) to ceramics classes at Working in the Redwoods (p114) and clothing design with Lantoki (p95).

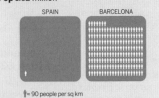

≈ 90 people per sq km

Need to Know

For more information, see Survival Guide (p267)

Currency
Euro (€)

Languages
Spanish, Catalan

Visas
Generally not required for stays of up to 90 days per 180 days; not required at all for members of EU or Schengen countries. Some nationalities need a Schengen visa.

Money
ATMs are widely available. Credit and debit cards are accepted in most hotels, shops, restaurants and taxis.

Mobile Phones
Local SIM cards can generally be used in unlocked European, Australian and North American phones (but may not be compatible with the Japanese system). Travellers with phones from within the EU have free roaming.

Time
Central European Time (GMT/ UTC plus one hour)

Tourist Information
Oficina d'Informació de Turisme de Barcelona Plaça de Catalunya (☑93 285 38 34; www.barcelona turisme.com; Plaça de Catalunya 17-S, underground; ☺8.30am-9pm; ⓂCatalunya)

Daily Costs

Budget: Less than €60
➡ Dorm bed: €15–40
➡ Set lunch: from €12
➡ Bicycle hire per hour: €5
➡ Tapas: €2 to €4 per tapa

Midrange: €60–200
➡ Standard double room: €80–170
➡ Two-course dinner with wine: from €25
➡ Guided tours and museum tickets: €15–40

Top end: More than €200
➡ Double room in boutique or luxury hotel: from €200
➡ Three-course meal at high-end restaurant: €80
➡ Concert tickets to Palau de la Música Catalana: around €45

Advance Planning

Three months before Book accommodation and reserve at popular restaurants.

One month before Check out reviews for theatre and live music, and book tickets.

One week before Book tickets for top sights like La Sagrada Família and the Museu Picasso. Browse the latest nightlife listings, art exhibitions and other events to attend while in town. Reserve spa visits and organised tours. Check for last-minute cancellations at top restaurants.

Useful Websites

Barcelona (www.barcelona. cat) Town hall's official site, with plenty of links.

Barcelona Turisme (www. barcelonaturisme.com) City's official tourism website.

Lonely Planet (www.lonely planet.com/barcelona) Destination information, hotel reviews and more.

Spotted by Locals (www.spot tedbylocals.com/barcelona) Insider tips.

Miniguide (https://miniguide. co) Style-conscious reviews and advice from locals.

Time Out Barcelona (www. timeout.com/barcelona) Great for restaurants and nightlife.

Foodie in Barcelona (www. foodieinbarcelona) Fab Barcelona food blog.

WHEN TO GO

July and August is peak tourist season. September is less busy and the sea still warm. For pleasant weather, but without the sea dips, come in May.

Barcelona

°C/°F Temp — Rainfall inches/mm

Arriving in Barcelona

El Prat airport Frequent *aerobuses* make the 30- to 40-minute run into town (€5.90) from 5.35am to 1.05am. Taxis cost €25 to €35.

Estació Sants Long-distance trains arrive at this large station near the centre of town, which is linked by metro to other parts of the city.

Estació d'Autobusos del Nord Barcelona's long-haul bus station is in L'Eixample, about 1.5km northeast of Plaça de Catalunya and a short walk from the Arc de Triomf metro station.

Girona-Costa Brava airport Sagalés runs direct bus services between Girona-Costa Brava airport and Barcelona's Estació d'Autobusos del Nord (€16, 1¼ hours).

Reus airport Hispano-Igualadina offers a bus service that runs between Reus airport and Barcelona's Estació d'Autobusos de Sants to meet flights (€16, 1¾ hours).

For much more on **arrival** see p268

Getting Around

The excellent metro can get you most places, with buses and trams filling in the gaps. Taxis are the best option late at night.

Metro The most convenient option. Runs 5am to midnight Sunday to Thursday, to 2am on Friday and 24 hours on Saturday. Targeta T-Casual (10-ride passes; €11.35) are the best value; otherwise, it's €2.40 per ride in Zone 1.

Bus Covers most of the city, especially where the metro doesn't. The hop-on, hop-off Bus Turístic, from Plaça de Catalunya, is handy on limited time.

Taxi You can hail taxis on the street (try La Rambla, Via Laietana, Plaça de Catalunya and Passeig de Gràcia) or at taxi stands, or book online/via app.

On foot Barcelona is generally best explored on foot.

For much more on **getting around** see p269

Sleeping

Barcelona's wonderful accommodation scene caters to all budgets, from sparkling contemporary hostels and family-owned guesthouses to boutique beauties, historical hotels and self-catering apartments. Book well ahead at any time.

Useful Websites

Booking.com and, controversially, Airbnb (p77) are of course popular accommodation-booking portals. Other options:

➡ **Aparteasy** (www.aparteasy.com)

➡ **Rent the Sun** (www.rentthesun.com)

➡ **Barcelona On Line** (www.barcelona-on-line.com)

➡ **Friendly Rentals** (www.friendlyrentals.com)

➡ **MH Apartments** (www.mhapartments.com)

➡ **Apartment Barcelona** (www.apartmentbarcelona.com)

➡ **Idealista** (www.idealista.com)

➡ **Lonely Planet** (www.lonelyplanet.com/spain/barcelona/hotels)

For much more on **sleeping** see p230

First Time Barcelona

For more information, see Survival Guide (p267)

Checklist

➡ Find out if you can use your phone in Spain and ensure you're up to date on potential roaming charges.

➡ Book accommodation ahead; Barcelona hotels fill up fast, especially in spring and summer.

➡ Check calendars to figure out which festivals to attend (or avoid!).

➡ Organise travel insurance.

➡ Look into restaurants and, if required (eg for Michelin-starred places), make reservations.

What to Pack

➡ Money belt

➡ Earplugs for noisy weekend nights

➡ Trainers or walking shoes

➡ Bathing suit

➡ Swim towel

➡ Sunglasses

➡ Sunscreen

➡ Hat

➡ Sandals

➡ Reading material (try page-turners by Carlos Ruiz Zafón or Manuel Vázquez Montalbán)

Top Tips for Your Trip

➡ Visit the top Gaudí sites and the Museu Picasso early in the morning or late in the day, to avoid the worst crowds.

➡ Wherever possible, book tickets online. This will allow you to bypass the queues, is often cheaper and guarantees you won't be turned away.

➡ Be mindful that many shops close during siesta time (generally 1pm to 4pm).

➡ Save time and money on public transport by purchasing a 10-ride T-Casual pass (p2710).

➡ Take advantage of great-value multi-course lunch menus.

➡ Overtourism in Barcelona is a serious concern; consider visiting outside peak season (November can be lovely) and staying outside the centre (such as in El Poblenou or La Zona Alta).

What to Wear

In Barcelona just about anything goes. That said, Catalans are fairly fashion-conscious and well dressed. If you're planning on going to upscale nightclubs, bring something stylish (sandals or sneakers are a no-go).

La Catedral advertises a policy of no admittance to those in baseball caps, sleeveless tops or shorts, and La Sagrada Família follows similar rules. The policy isn't always enforced, but it's best to be respectful.

Be Forewarned

➡ Violent crime is rare in Barcelona, but petty crime (bag-snatching, pickpocketing) is a major problem, especially along crowded La Rambla and the touristed city centre. Report thefts to the Guàrdia Urbana (p271).

➡ You're especially vulnerable when dragging luggage to/from hotels; make sure you know your route.

➡ Avoid walking around El Raval and the southern end of La Rambla late at night.

➡ Take nothing of value to the beach and don't leave anything unattended.

Money

There's no shortage of ATMs all over central Barcelona, including along Plaça de Catalunya, Via Laietana and La Rambla. You should be able to use international debit or credit cards to withdraw money in euros; there is often a charge (around 1.5% to 2%).

Major cards (MasterCard, Visa, Maestro, Cirrus) are accepted across Barcelona, though there may be a minimum spend of €5 or €10. When paying by credit card, photo ID is often required, even for chip cards (US travellers without chip cards can indicate that they'll give a signature).

Taxes & Refunds

Value-added tax (VAT) is a 21% sales tax levied on most goods and services. For restaurants and hotels it's 10%. Most restaurants include VAT in their prices; it's usually included in hotel room prices, too, but check when booking.

Tipping

➡ **Restaurants** Catalans typically leave 5% or less at restaurants. Leave more for exceptionally good service.

➡ **Taxis** Optional, but most locals round up to the nearest euro.

➡ **Bars** It's rare to leave a tip in bars, though small change is appreciated.

El Born (p97)

Etiquette

Barcelona is fairly relaxed when it comes to etiquette. A few basics to remember:

➡ **Greetings** Catalans, like other Spaniards, usually greet friends and strangers alike with a kiss on both cheeks, although two males rarely do this.

➡ **Eating and drinking** Waiters won't expect you to thank them every time they bring you something, but in more casual restaurants and bars they will expect you to keep your cutlery between courses.

➡ **Visiting churches** It is considered disrespectful to visit churches as a tourist during Mass and other worship services. Taking photos at such times is a definite no-no, as is visiting without dressing appropriately.

➡ **Escalators** Always stand on the right to let people pass, especially when using the metro.

Language

English is widely spoken in Barcelona. Even Catalans with only a few English words are generally happy to try them out. Learning a little Spanish will greatly enhance your experience, not least in your ability to converse with locals. It's even better if you can learn some Catalan.

There is English signage at most museums (though not all). Many restaurants have English-language menus, though simpler places may have them only in Spanish and Catalan.

Perfect Days

Day One

La Rambla & Barri Gòtic (p58)

 Head out early to explore the narrow medieval lanes of the Barri Gòtic, including the ancient Jewish **Call**, before the crowds arrive. Have a peek inside **La Catedral** – not missing its goose-filled cloister – and stroll through the picturesque squares of **Plaça de Sant Josep Oriol**, **Plaça Reial** and **Plaça Sant Just**, before uncovering Barcelona's ancient roots in the fascinating **Museu d'Història de Barcelona**. **La Rambla** and the **Mercat de la Boqueria** are both also most peaceful early in the morning.

 Lunch Cafè de l'Acadèmia (p74) does a terrific weekday lunchtime *menú*.

La Ribera & El Born (p97)

In the afternoon, wander over to El Born, which is packed with architectural treasures. Start with the majestic **Basílica de Santa Maria del Mar**, before heading over to **Carrer de Montcada** and the **Museu Picasso**, beautifully set inside conjoined medieval mansions. Be sure to allow time for wandering around El Born's boutiques and history-rich alleys.

Dinner Have tapas with *cava* at Bar del Pla (p109) and El Xampanyet (p111).

La Ribera & El Born (p97)

If you like, before a late dinner, catch a show at the **Palau de la Música Catalana**, one of the great Modernista masterpieces of Barcelona. Or swing by the architecturally fascinating **Mercat de Santa Caterina**. End the night with cocktails at **Bar Sauvage** on leafy Passeig del Born, or live music at **Farola**.

Day Two

La Sagrada Família & L'Eixample (p138)

 Start with a morning visit to **La Sagrada Família**, Gaudí's wondrous work in progress, where you've (hopefully) prebooked a guided tour or a trip up one of the spiralling towers. While in this part of L'Eixample, also visit the **Recinte Modernista de Sant Pau**, a lesser-known jewel of Modernisme, by Domènech i Montaner. You could also walk over to Passeig de Sant Joan, a buzzy boulevard that's on the up, with new bars, restaurants and the like.

Lunch Head to Tapas 24 (p156) for delectable contemporary tapas.

La Sagrada Família & L'Eixample (p138)

After lunch, explore more great Modernista buildings along **Passeig de Gràcia**; the three most famous creations make up the **Illa de la Discòrdia**, while lesser-known works lie dotted around nearby streets. Then visit one of Gaudí's houses – **Casa Batlló** or **La Pedrera** (again, prebooking helps!) If time and energy allow, L'Eixample is full of fabulous shopping, including local labels like **Avant**.

 Dinner Enjoy Catalan cooking at La Pubilla (p178) or Extra Bar (p178).

Gràcia & Park Güell (p172)

Walk or hop on the metro up to Gràcia and wander through its enchanting village-like streets, where cafes, bars, bookshops, galleries and boutiques await. The bars surrounding its pretty neighbourhood plazas come to life around sundown. Grab a vermouth at **La Vermu**, a cocktail at **Bobby Gin** or wines at **Viblioteca**.

PLAN YOUR TRIP PERFECT DAYS

La Rambla (p60)

La Catedral (p62)

Day Three

Barceloneta, the Waterfront & El Poblenou (p117)

 Time to take in the lovely Mediterranean. Start the day with a stroll, jog or cycle along the **Passeig Marítim**, where beach-facing restaurants and cafes provide refreshment. Wander through **Barceloneta**, stopping for a peek inside the **Mercat de la Barceloneta** and perhaps for pastries at **Baluard**.

> **Lunch** Go early to cram into tapas-tastic favourite La Cova Fumada (p126).

Barceloneta, the Waterfront & El Poblenou (p117)

 Afterwards, you could peel back the centuries on a journey into Catalan history at the **Museu d'Història de Catalunya,** or just relax at any of the nearby beaches (the sands northeast of the Port Olímpic near El Poblenou, such as **Platja del Bogatell**, are less touristed).

> **Dinner** Can Recasens (p130) is a magical, candle-lit restaurant in El Poblenou.

Barceloneta, the Waterfront & El Poblenou (p117)

After freshening up, make your way over to the up-and-coming neighbourhood of El Poblenou. Meander along cafe-dotted **Rambla del Poblenou** and its surrounding streets, where creative spots like plant-themed cafe **Espai Joliu** showcase the area's regeneration. Check out a local bar or two, like **Madame George** or **Balius**, or, if you still have energy, hit the dance floor at **Razzmatazz**.

Day Four

Montjuïc, Poble Sec & Sant Antoni (p186)

 Kick things off with a scenic **cable-car** ride up to Montjuïc, followed by a stroll past viewpoints and gardens to the **Museu Nacional d'Art de Catalunya**, perhaps via the scenic terrace cafe at **Salts Montjuïc**. Take in the magnificent Romanesque frescoes, vivid Gothic paintings and works by 17th-century Spanish masters.

> **Lunch** Palo Cortao (p197) is a charmer, or queue for Quimet i Quimet (p196).

Montjuïc, Poble Sec & Sant Antoni (p186)

After a taste of Montjuïc, wander down through the sloping neighbourhood of Poble Sec, sprinkled with cafes and bars. Hop across Avinguda del Paral·lel and spend a few hours knocking around recently trendy-fied Sant Antoni, checking out the wonderful **Mercat de Sant Antoni** and the bars, cafes and shops around partly pedestrianised **Carrer del Parlament**.

> **Dinner** Elisabets (p89) is a terrific Raval spot for Catalan cuisine.

El Raval (p186)

 Spend the evening soaking up Barcelona's bohemian side in multicultural El Raval. Browse record shops, vintage stores and one-of-a-kind boutiques, see the skaters and an exhibition at the **MACBA**, or watch an indie feature at the **Filmoteca de Catalunya**. Finish the night bar-hopping along **Carrer de Joaquín Costa**.

Month By Month

January

Barcelonins head to the Pyrenees for action on the ski slopes. School holidays run until around 8 January.

✵ Reis (Reyes)

On 5 January, children delight in the Cavalcada dels Reis Mags (Parade of the Three Kings), a colourful parade of floats, music and sweets, which runs up Avinguda del Marquès d'Argentera and Via Laietana. The Dia dels Reis Mags, on 6 January, is the main present-giving day.

February

Often the coldest month in Barcelona, February sees few visitors. Some of the first big festivals kick off, bringing abundant Catalan merriment amid the wintry gloom.

✵ Carnestoltes

Celebrated in February or March, Barcelona's carnival involves several days of fancy-dress balls, merrymaking and fireworks, ending on the Tuesday before Ash Wednesday. Over 30 parades happen around town on the weekend.

✵ Festes de Santa Eulàlia

Around 12 February this big winter festival (p45) celebrates Barcelona's first patron saint with a week of cultural events, including parades of *gegants* (papier-mâché giants), open-air art installations, theatre, *correfocs* (fire runs), *castells* (human castles) and the Llum BCN light festival in El Poblenou.

March

March brings longer, sunnier days, though still cool nights (lightjacket weather). There are relatively few tourists around and fairer hotel prices.

April

Spring arrives with a flourish, leading to Easter revelry and school holidays, but April showers can dampen spirits. Book well ahead for Easter trips.

✵ Setmana Santa

On Palm Sunday people line up to have their palm branches blessed outside La Catedral, while on Good Friday you can follow floats and hooded penitents in processions from the Església de Sant Agustí (Plaça de Sant Agustí 2), in El Raval. Sometimes falls in March.

✵ Dia de Sant Jordi

Catalonia honours its patron saint, Sant Jordi (St George), on 23 April). Traditionally men and women exchange roses and books – La Rambla and Plaça de Sant Jaume fill with book and flower stalls.

May

With sunny pleasant days and clear skies, May can be one of the best times to visit Barcelona. Lively *xiringuitos* (beach bars) open, gearing up for summer.

Top: *Castell* (p256)
Bottom: Pride Barcelona (p50)

☆ Primavera Sound

For one week in late May or early June, the open-air Parc del Fòrum stages an all-star line-up (p43) of international bands and DJs. There are also associated free open-air events at the Parc de la Ciutadella and Passeig Lluís Companys.

☆ Festival de Flamenco de Ciutat Vella

One of the best occasions to see great flamenco in Barcelona, this festival (p44) is held over four days in May at the Poble Sec's Teatre Mercat De Les Flors and other venues.

June

Visitor numbers (and hotel prices) soar as Barcelona plunges into summer. Live-music festivals and open-air events give the month a festive air.

✿ Festival Jardins Pedralbes

This summertime festival takes place in lovely gardens and stages big-name performers – many of them old-timers (Beach Boys, Sting, Blondie) from early June to mid-July.

✿ La Nit de Sant Joan

On 23 June locals hit the streets or hold parties at home to celebrate the Nit de Sant Joan (St John's Night), which involves drinking, dancing, bonfires and fireworks. In Spanish, it's called Verbenas de San Juan.

Pride Barcelona

Barcelona's Pride festival (p50) is a crammed program of culture and concerts over a couple of weeks, along with the traditional Pride march on Saturday, and raises awareness about issues affecting the LGBTIQ+ community.

☆ Sónar

Usually held in mid-June, Sónar (p43) is Barcelona's massive celebration of electronic music, with DJs, exhibitions, sound labs, record fairs and urban art.

July

Prices are high and it's peak tourist season, but July is a lively time to be in the city, with sunfilled beach days, openair dining and outdoor concerts.

☆ Festival del Grec

The major cultural event of the summer is a monthlong arts celebration (p43) with dozens of theatre, dance and music performances held around town, including at the Teatre Grec amphitheatre on Montjuïc.

August

The heat index soars; *barcelonins* leave the city in droves for summer holidays, as huge numbers of tourists arrive.

✩ Festa Major de Gràcia

Locals compete for the most elaborately decorated street in this popular weeklong Gràcia festival (p45) held around 15 August. There are also free outdoor concerts, street fairs and other events such as *correfocs* and *castells*.

✩ Festes de Sant Roc

For four days in midAugust, Plaça Nova in the Barri Gòtic becomes the scene of parades, *correfocs*, a market, traditional music and magic shows for kids.

September

After a month off, *barcelonins* return to work. Temperatures stay warm, making for fine beach days.

✩ Diada Nacional de Catalunya

Catalonia's national day curiously commemorates Barcelona's surrender on 11 September 1714 to the Bourbon monarchy of Spain, at the conclusion of the War of the Spanish Succession. Today it's a celebration of Catalan culture, but it has also become linked to the Catalan independence movement (there may be some disruption).

✩ Festes de la Mercè

Held around 24 September, the city's biggest party (p43) involves four days of concerts, dancing and street theatre. There are also *castells*, firework displays, a parade of *gegants*, and *correfocs*.

October

While northern Europe shivers, Barcelona enjoys mild October temperatures and sunny days. With the disappearance of summer crowds and lower accommodation prices, this is an excellent month to visit.

November

Cooler days and nights arrive, along with occasional days of rain and overcast skies. It's low season, but still a great month to visit.

December

As winter returns *barcelonins* gear up for the festive period, and the city is festooned with colourful decorations. Relatively few visitors arrive until Christmas, though.

✩ Nadal

Christmas Day (Navidad in Spanish) isn't Spain's main present-giving day, but a growing number of people do celebrate it. In Catalonia, the gift-filled *caga tió* (literally 'poop log') is opened on 24 December.

☆ New Year's Eve

On 31 December, Montjuïc's Font Màgica (p191) takes centre stage for the biggest Cap d'Any celebration in town. Crowds line up along Avinguda Reina Maria Cristina to watch a theatrical procession and audiovisual performance (plus *castells*), followed by fireworks at midnight.

With Kids

Barcelona is great for older kids and teens – the Mediterranean attitude means they are included in many seemingly adult activities, such as eating late meals at bars or restaurants. Babies will love the welcoming culture, and toddlers will be showered with attention.

arc d'Atraccions (p210), Tibidabo

WILLIAM HARLSBERRY/SHUTTERSTOCK©

Dining Out With Kids

Barcelona – and Spain in general – is superfriendly when it comes to eating with children. Locals take their kids out all the time and don't worry too much about keeping them up late. Spanish kids tend to eat the Mediterranean offerings enjoyed by their parents, but many restaurants have children's menus that serve up burgers, pizzas, tomato-sauce pasta and the like; some pla-ces even have a kids' *menú del dia*. Good local – and childproof – options are *truita de patates/tortilla de patatas* (potato omelette), *pa amb tomàquet/pan con tomate* (bread rubbed with tomato and olive oil) and *croquetes/croquetas* (croquettes).

Best Kid-Friendly Restaurants

La Nena

Fantastic for chocolate, this Gràcia cafe (p182) has a play area, and a toy and book corner.

Granja M Viader

No kid will be unimpressed by the luxuriously thick hot chocolate here (p93).

NEED TO KNOW

➡ **Supplies** Nappies (diapers), dummies, creams and formula can be bought at any of the city's many pharmacies and supermarkets. Nappies are cheaper in supermarkets.

➡ **Metro** Barcelona's metro is accessible and great for families with pushchairs. Be mindful of pickpockets.

➡ **Accessibility** The narrow streets of the Ciutat Vella, with their cobbles and unpredictable traffic, are less buggy-friendly than the rest of Barcelona.

➡ **Practicalities** Some restaurants and other venues have baby-changing tables, but certainly not all, and most places can rustle up a high chair. Many Spanish women breastfeed in public.

CITY TRAILS

For an insight into Barcelona aimed directly at kids, pick up a copy of Lonely Planet's *City Trails: Barcelona*. Perfect for children aged eight and up, it opens up a world of intriguing stories and fascinating facts about Barcelona's people, places, history and culture.

Pepa Tomate
With crayons and a tiny playground, this fun Gràcia tapas joint (p178) is a winner.

Granja La Pallaresa
A Gòtic favourite (p76) for crispy *xurros/churros* dipped in steaming chocolate.

Best Parks & Open Spaces

Parc de la Ciutadella
This super-central park (p103) has a zoo, a pond and a playground.

Parc d'Atraccions Tibidabo
A fabulous funfair (p210) with jaw-dropping views from atop Tibidabo.

Font Màgica
The light show (p191) below Montjuïc is guaranteed to make little ones shout 'Again!'

Parc Natural de Collserola
A huge pine-sprinkled park in the hills (p208) of northern Barcelona, with trails and picnicking possibilities.

Montjuïc
Ramble between gardens and viewpoints, and take kids to the fantastical Castell de Montjuïc (p191); some kids might love the thrilling cable-car ride up (for others there's a bus!)

Best Kid-Friendly Museums

CosmoCaixa
A fantastic science museum (p209) in the Zona Alta.

L'Aquàrium
One of Europe's largest aquariums (p121), with tank after tank of colourful fish and sharks gliding overhead.

Poble Espanyol
Families can travel through a mini-Spain (p192) together, with special child-oriented games and quests.

Museu Picasso
Older kids with a taste for the arts won't want to miss this outstanding museum (p99) in El Born.

Best Ways to See the City

By Bike
Barcelona has tonnes of bike tours and outlets (p270) that hire bicycles of all kinds.

By Cable Car
Travel up Montjuïc from Barceloneta beach through the air (p270).

Cuca de Llum
This new high-tech lightworm-like funicular, due to be ready in 2021, will make the journey up to Tibidabo (p210) all the more fun.

Best Shopping

Hibernian
This secondhand bookshop (p184) in Gràcia has a good English selection.

El Rei de la Màgia
A La Ribera cabinet of curiosities (p114) for all budding magicians.

Taller de Marionetas Travi
A small, enchanting shop full of handmade wooden and papier-mâché marionettes (p80), in the Gòtic.

Like a Local

Taking a local approach when it comes to eating, drinking and other amusements is the most rewarding way to experience Barcelona. Catalans are friendly, though they have seen their city taken over by tourists in recent years; you'll please barcelonins *if you learn a few words of Catalan.*

Sardana (p266) in front of La Catedral

MANEL VINUESA/GETTY IMAGES ©

When to Dine

In Barcelona, similar to elsewhere in Spain, meal times run late. Most restaurants don't open for dinner until 8.30pm or 9pm and close at midnight or 1am; peak dining time is around 10pm. Locals commonly have lunch between 1pm and 4pm. This is then followed by a long siesta (a loll on the beach or in one of the parks is a fine choice when the weather is pleasant). Locals aren't big on breakfast – a croissant and a *cortado* (espresso with milk) is a typical way to start the day.

Water & Wine

Lunch or dinner, wine is always a fine idea, according to most *barcelonins*. Many restaurants offer *menú del dia* (daily set menu) lunches that include a glass of red or white. If you become a regular, waiters may give you complimentary refills or even leave the bottle. Of course, you can also opt for another drink.

A word on water: no one drinks it straight from the tap (taste it and you'll know why). Order *agua mineral,* either *amb/con gas* (sparkling) or *sense/sin gas* (still). Sparkling Vichy water is a Catalan favourite.

Tapas

When hunger pangs arrive in the afternoon or early evening, locals head out for a pre-dinner tapa. This means heading to the local favourite for a bite of anchovies, sausage, squid, wild mushrooms, roasted peppers or dozens of other tempting morsels. Wine, *cava* and beer all make fine accompaniments.

Many tapas spots are lively stand-around-the-bar affairs; Vaso de Oro (p126), La Cova Fumada (p126), El Xampanyet (p111) and Bormuth (p106) are great, central places to start. When it's time for a change of scenery, *barcelonins* might make their way to dinner or just head to another tapas bar and skip the sit-down formality altogether.

Local Meal Spots

La Rambla is fine for a stroll, but no *barcelonin* would eat there. The same holds for Carrer Ferran and other tourist-packed streets in the Barri Gòtic. The Gòtic does, however, have some local-favoured gems, particularly on the narrow streets of the east side – such as Onofre (p75), Cafè de l'Acadèmia (p74) and Belmonte (p74). For a more authentic neighbourhood dining experience, browse the streets of El Born, Barceloneta, El Raval and Gràcia, or head over to Sant Antoni/Poble Sec or Poblenou.

Weekends

Many *barcelonins* head out of town at the weekends. That could mean skiing in the Pyrenees in winter, or heading up the Costa Brava in summer. Those that stick around might check out flea markets or produce markets, head to the beach or have an outing in the park. The parks are liveliest at weekends, when local musicians, picnickers, pop-up markets and playing children add to the city's relaxed air. Culture-craving locals might hit an art opening – those at Centre de Cultura Contemporània de Barcelona (p88) and MACBA (p86) are good fun – see a repertory film – Filmoteca de Catalunya (p94) has intriguing showings – or catch a concert, perhaps at JazzSí Club (p94) or Sala Apolo (p202).

The Sunday Feast

Sunday is typically the most peaceful day for Catalans, and a fine occasion for gathering with family or friends over a big meal. Lunch is the main event, and many restaurants prepare Sunday-only specials. Lots of places close on Sunday nights too, so it's worth lingering over a long multi-course lunch. A rich paella around La Barceloneta – try Can Ros (p128) or Red Fish (p130) – followed by a long leisurely stroll along the waterfront is always a hit.

Festivals & Other Events

One of the best ways to join in on local amusement is to come for one of the city's big festivals. During summer (June to August), Música als Parcs (www.barcelona.cat) puts on 30 or so open-air concerts at a dozen parks in Barcelona, and free concerts are held at various venues around the city. Another great open-air summer concert series is **Brunch in the Park** (https://barcelona.brunch-in.com/park; ☉Jul–mid-Sep).

For more local festivals, see Month by Month (p2).

Local Listings

Browse the latest art openings, film screenings, concerts and other events in the *Guía del Ocio* (www.guiadelocio.com), *Time Out Barcelona* (www.timeout.cat) or papers like *La Vanguardia* (www.lavanguardia.com) and *El Periodico* (www.elperiodico.com), some publish information in English as well as Catalan and Spanish. The council website (barcelonacultura.bcn.cat) also lists upcoming events, and local blogs and digital influencers can be a great resource for keeping up to speed.

See Need to Know (p16) for a list of local websites/blogs.

Football

FC Barcelona plays a prominent role in the city's imagination. Heading to a match at Camp Nou (p215) from September to May is the best way to catch a bit of Barcelona fever, but watching it on screen at a tavern can be just as much fun, depending on the crowd. For the most fervent fan base, head to Barceloneta, El Raval, Gràcia or Sarrià. The daily journal *Marca* (www.marca.com) gives the latest on sporting news.

Tickets can be bought at www.fcbarcelona.com, FC Botiga (p81) or tourist offices.

Sardana

The traditional Catalan folk dance *sardana* (p266) still attracts a small local following. On weekends aficionados gather in front of La Catedral for group dancing to a live 10-piece band. The action happens at 6pm on Saturday and 11am on Sunday, and lasts about an hour.

For Free

With planning Barcelona can be a surprisingly affordable place to travel. Many museums offer free entry on specific days, and some of the best ways to experience the city don't cost a penny – hanging out at the beach, and exploring fascinating neighbourhoods, gardens and parks.

Walking Tours

Numerous companies offer pay-what-you-wish walking tours. These typically take in the Barri Gòtic or the Modernista sites of L'Eixample. Recommended outfits include the following:

Discover Walks (www.discoverwalks.com)

Feel Free Tours (www.feelfreetours.com)

Runner Bean Tours (p82)

Barcelona Street Style Tour (p96)

Festivals & Other Events

Barcelona has loads of free festivals and events, including the Festes de la Mercè (p43) and the Festes de Santa Eulàlia (p24). From June to August, the city hosts

Música als Parcs (Music in the Parks; www.barcelona.cat), a series of over 40 open-air concerts held in different parks and green spaces around the city, featuring classical, blues and jazz groups. Popular venues include Parc de la Ciutadella (p103), Parc de Joan Miró (p195) and Parc de Turó (in Sant Gervasi). Check schedules online.

Sights

Entry to some sights is free on occasion, most commonly on the first Sunday of the month, while quite a few attractions are free from 3pm to 8pm on Sunday. Others are always free. The following are most likely to attract your attention:

Bunkers del Carmel (p179)

Mercat de Santa Caterina (p104)

Ajuntament (p65)

Palau de la Generalitat (p65)

Casa de l'Ardiaca (p63)

Centre d'Art Santa Mònica (p61)

Casa de la Barceloneta (p121)

Basílica de Santa Maria del Mar (p101)

Estadi Olímpic Lluís Companys (p194)

Col·lecció de Carrosses Fúnebres (p194)

Palau del Lloctinent (p69)

Temple d'August (p66)

Antic Hospital de la Santa Creu (p88)

Font Màgica (p191)

Porta de Mar (p69)

Espai Subirachs (p124)

Jardins de Mossèn Cinto de Verdaguer (p193)

Cementiri del Poblenou (p124)

Universitat de Barcelona (p148)

Palau de la Virreina (p61)

Under the Radar Barcelona

In recent years overtourism has become a serious concern for Barcelona, though the COVID-19 pandemic has slowed things down since early 2020. By exploring beyond the busy, tourist-driven pockets of town, you'll help build towards responsible tourism and a more sustainable environment for the local population, while uncovering all kinds of under-the-radar gems.

Apartments in El Poblenou (p123)

Less-Central Neighbourhoods

Staying in less-touristed, further-out Barcelona *barris* gives you the chance to tap into local life, support small neighbourhood businesses, explore quieter sights and gain a broader perspective of the city.

Barcelona is a city known for reinvention, but none of its neighbourhoods has seen a regeneration as dramatic as that of the unremarkable grid of streets around the splendid old Mercat de Sant Antoni (p195), west of El Raval. The tentative opening of a couple of contemporary cafes on Carrer del Parlament bloomed into a lively strip of bars, restaurants and shops, transforming Sant Antoni into one of the coolest spots in town.

Also increasingly appealing is the formerly industrial 'hood of El Poblenou, northeast of the centre, where ancient warehouses are being reimagined as creative tech and design hubs, cafes, boutiques, bars and more.

Smart Sarrià-Sant Gervasi in northwest Barcelona, peaceful northern Horta (with its garden labyrinth) and the Sants/Les Corts area west of the centre also make excellent bases, while Passeig de Sant Joan near La Sagrada Família is becoming an ever more popular gastronomic haunt.

Fun Alternatives

Whether you fancy gawping at architectural jewels, kicking back on the beach or heading out on a tapas crawl, there are plenty of thrilling alternatives to Barcelona's headline acts.

Get out into nature by going hiking and biking in the vast green expanses of the Parc Natural de Collserola (p208).

Beach lovers can swap always-busy Barceloneta to bask in the beauty of beaches further out of town, such as those along the Costa del Garraf or the Costa Maresme (p123), both easily accessible by public transport.

DIGITAL IMAGINATION/GETTY IMAGES ©

Hedge maze at Parc del Laberint d'Horta (p214)

If you're keen on Gaudí's work, visit some of his less-touristed creations, including Bellesguard (p216) near Avinguda Tibidabo.

Explore the peaceful Pedralbes area (p207) in northwest Barcelona, which reveals a 14th-century convent.

Sidestep the city centre for post-industrial El Poblenou (p119), which bursts with creative projects and has its own lovely strip of golden beaches.

Tap into buzzy Poble Sec, at the northern foot of Montjuïc, which brims with culinary deliciousness (p196).

Why not extend your stay and combine exploring Barcelona with a few other exciting nearby pockets of Catalonia? Beachy Sitges (p224), Roman Tarragona (p227) and lively Girona (p219) are among the jewels just a quick hop away by train.

Specialised Tours

A wonderful way to really get to know Barcelona (and support small-scale initiatives) is to join a local expert on an in-depth guided tour, with options covering all kinds of interests, from gastronomy to street art.

Devour Barcelona (p177) Fabulous neighbourhood-focused food tours.

Barcelona Architecture Walks (p116) Design-led itineraries with local architects.

Runner Bean Tours (p82) Thematic pay-what-you-wish tours.

Hidden City Tours (p274) Social enterprise collaborating with guides from the homeless community.

Barcelona Street Style Tour (p96) Donation-based street-art tours.

Bikini (toasted sandwich) with truffle and cured ham, Tapas 24 (p156), L'Eixample

Dining Out

Barcelona has a celebrated food scene fuelled by a combination of world-class chefs, superb markets and magnificent ingredients fresh from farms and the sea. Catalan culinary masterminds like brothers Ferran and Albert Adrià, and Carles Abellán have become international icons, reinventing the world of haute cuisine, while classic old-world Catalan recipes and creative international flavours continue to earn accolades.

New Catalan Cuisine

Avant-garde chefs have made Catalonia famous across the world for their food laboratories, their commitment to food as art and their mind-boggling riffs on the themes of traditional local cooking.

Here the notion of gourmet cuisine is deconstructed as chefs transform liquids and solid foods into foams, create 'ice cream' of classic ingredients by means of liquid nitrogen, freeze-dry foods to make concentrated powders and employ spherification to create unusual and artful morsels. This alchemical cookery is known as molecular gastronomy,

and invention is the keystone of this technique.

Diners may encounter olive oil 'caviar', 'snow' made of gazpacho with anchovies, jellified Parmesan turned into spaghetti, and countless other concoctions.

The dining rooms themselves also offer a reconfiguration of the five-star dining experience, with the setting playing a key part in the gastronomic experience. Restaurateurs generally aim to create warm and buzzing spaces, with artful design flourishes, and without the stuffiness and formality typically associated with high-end dining.

Top Chefs

Great chefs continue to redefine contemporary cuisine in Barcelona, although star chef Albert Adrià's restaurant empire sadly fell victim to the COVID-19 pandemic and he was forced to close his signature restaurants Tickets and Enigma in 2021. Michelin-starred chef Carles Abellán, creator of Suculent (p91), Tapas 24 (p156), La Barra (p128) and other headlining restaurants, playfully reinterprets traditional tapas with dishes like *melon amb pernil,* a millefeuille of layered caramelised Iberian ham and thinly sliced melon.

Another star of the Catalan cooking scene is Jordi Vilà, who continues to wow diners at Alkímia (p200) with reinvented Catalan classics. Other major players on the Catalan dining scene are Jordi Artal at Cinc Sentits (p155), Xavier Pellicer (p157) at his namesake restaurant, Albert Raurich at Dos Palillos (p235) inside the Casa Camper hotel, and the trio of Mateu Casañas, Oriol Castro and Eduard Xatruch at Disfrutar (p155).

The first (ever) to win a third Michelin star for Barcelona (in 2016), however, was Paolo Casagrande at Martín Berasategui's superb Lasarte (p155). He was followed in 2017 by Jordi Cruz at ABaC (p215).

Tapas Bars

Tapas, those bite-sized morsels of joy, are not a typical Catalan concept, but there are plenty of tapas bars here nonetheless. Most open earlier than restaurants – typically around 7pm – making them a good pre-dinner (or instead-of-dinner) option. Some open from lunch and stay open without a break through late-evening closing time. There are also plenty of wonderful Basque-style *pintxo* bars dotted around. Tapas bars are less formal than restaurants, and drinking is an essential component of the experience.

If you opt for *tapes*/tapas, it is handy to recognise some of the common items:

➡ **bombes/bombas** large meat-and-potato croquettes

➡ **boquerons/boquerones** white anchovies in vinegar – delicious and tangy

➡ **carxofes/alcachofas** artichokes

➡ **gambes/gambas** prawns, either *al all/al ajillo* (with garlic) or *a la plantxa/plancha* (grilled)

➡ **montadito** a sort of bread-chunk canapé, with delicious toppings

➡ **navalles/navajas** razor clams

➡ **patates braves/patatas bravas** potato

NEED TO KNOW

Price Ranges

The following price ranges represent the average cost of a main course:

€   less than €12

€€   €12–€20

€€€   over €20

Opening Hours

Most restaurants open from 1pm to 4pm and from 8.30pm to midnight.

Reservations

At midrange restaurants and simpler taverns you can usually turn up without booking ahead. At high-end restaurants, especially for dinner, make a booking. Some restaurants don't take bookings at all, in which case you'll need to arrive early to grab a table. Thursday to Saturday nights are especially busy.

Tipping

A service charge is rarely included in the bill. Catalans and other Spaniards are not overwhelming tippers, and 5% is generally considered plenty, though a little more is welcome if you are particularly happy.

Menú de Degustación

At high-end restaurants you can often get a *menú de degustación* – a tasting menu involving samples of different dishes. This can be a great way to get a broader view of what the restaurant does, at a fixed price.

chunks bathed in a slightly spicy tomato sauce, sometimes mixed with mayonnaise

➡ **pernil/jamón** cured Iberian ham

➡ **pop a feira/pulpo a la gallega** tender Galician-style boiled octopus with paprika

➡ **formatge/queso** cheese, with options from across the country

➡ **truita de patates/tortilla de patatas** potato-filled omelette; one with vegetables is a *truita de verdures/tortilla de verduras*

➡ **xampinyons/champiñones** mushrooms

Classic Catalan Cuisine

Traditional Catalan recipes showcase the great produce of the Mediterranean: fish, prawns, cuttlefish, clams, pork, rabbit, game, first-rate olive oil, peppers, tomatoes, loads of garlic. Classic dishes also feature

Eating by Neighbourhood

Gràcia & Park Güell
Classic-Catalan food, old-school bodegas, highly creative kitchens
(p177)

Camp Nou, Pedralbes & La Zona Alta
Neighbourhood tapas bars and restaurants; high-end favourites worth a trip
(p209)

La Sagrada Família & L'Eixample
Some of Barcelona's most fabulous and exclusive restaurants
(p152)

La Ribera & El Born
Wonderful tapas bars, Catalan kitchens and international-influenced cooking
(p106)

Plaça de Catalunya

Port Olímpic

El Raval
Boho-cool restaurants, classic cafes and tapas bars
(p89)

La Rambla & Barri Gòtic
Pocket-sized tapas bars, elegant taverns
(p72)

Barceloneta, the Waterfront & El Poblenou
Superbly fresh seafood, great tapas bars, creative cafes
(p126)

Montjuïc, Poble Sec & Sant Antoni
Inventive cafes, restaurants old and new, lively tapas bars
(p195)

Port de Barcelona

MEDITERRANEAN SEA

unusual pairings (seafood with meat, fruit with fowl) such as cuttlefish with chickpeas, cured ham with caviar, rabbit with prawns, or goose with pears.

Great Catalan restaurants can be found in nearly every Barcelona neighbourhood. The settings can be a huge part of the appeal, with candlelit medieval chambers in the Ciutat Vella and Modernista design in L'Eixample setting the stage for a memorable feast. Although there are plenty of high-end places in this city, foodie-minded *barcelonins* aren't averse to eating at humbler, less elegant places – which sometimes cook up the best meals.

Seafood Restaurants

Not surprisingly, Barcelona hosts a wealth of restaurants specialising in seafood. Barceloneta, which lies near the sea, is packed with eateries of all shapes and sizes doling out decadent paellas, cauldrons of bubbling molluscs, grilled catches of the day and other delights. Nearest the sea, you'll find pricier open-air places with Mediterranean views; plunge into the narrow lanes to find the real gems, including bustling family-run operations that serve first-rate plates at wonderfully down-to-earth prices.

Market Shopping

Barcelona has some fantastic food markets. The Mercat de la Boqueria (p64) is probably Spain's biggest, most famous and most touristed market, conveniently located just off La Rambla. That location comes at a price: these days it's usually very overcrowded, though *barcelonins* do still try to shop here early in the day, and temptations of all sorts still abound – plump fruits and veggies, freshly squeezed juices, artisanal cheeses, smoked meats, seafood and pastries. The best feature:

an array of tapas bars and food stalls where you can sample amazingly fresh ingredients cooked to perfection. Other great markets:

→ **Mercat de Santa Caterina** (p104)

→ **Mercat de Sant Antoni** (p195)

→ **Mercat de la Llibertat** (p176)

→ **Mercat de l'Abaceria Central** (p185)

→ **Mercat de la Concepció** (p165)

→ **Mercat de la Barceloneta** (p136)

→ **Mercat del Ninot** (p164)

Street-Food Markets

From health-focused, international-inspired lunch boxes and Spanish-Asian fusion tapas to Catalan classics given a contemporary kick, Barcelona's appetite for street food is seemingly insatiable. Keep an eye out for hit pop-up food markets including:

→ **Eat Street** (www.eatstreet.barcelona)

→ **All Those** (www.allthose.org)

→ **Van Van Market** (p130)

Vegetarians & Vegans

Vegetarians, and especially vegans, have traditionally had a hard time in Spain, but things are improving. In Barcelona a growing battery of vegetarian and vegan restaurants are saving the day, and many other places now offer meat-free options or adaptations. Be careful when ordering salads and soups, which may contain ham or tuna.

Catalan Specialities

STARTERS

→ **Calçots** Sweet and juicy spring onions cooked up on a barbecue, typically eaten with a *romesco*-like sauce (tomatoes, garlic, peppers), and celebrated with seasonal *calçotada* parties.

→ **Escalivada** Red pepper, aubergine and onion, grilled, cooled, peeled, sliced and served with an olive oil, salt and garlic dressing.

→ **Esqueixada** Salad of *bacallà/bacalao* (shredded salted cod) with tomatoes, red peppers, onions, white beans, olives, olive oil and vinegar.

→ **Pa amb tomàquet** Bread rubbed with tomato, olive oil and salt

MAIN COURSES

→ **Arròs a la cassola** Catalan paella, cooked without saffron

→ **Arròs negre** Rice cooked in black cuttlefish ink

→ **Bacallà a la llauna** Salted cod baked in tomato, garlic, parsley, paprika and wine

→ **Botifarra amb mongetes** Pork sausage with fried white beans

→ **Canelons/Canelones** Italian-influenced meat-stuffed pasta tubes in creamy sauce

→ **Cargols/Caracoles** Snails, often stewed with *conill/conejo* (rabbit) and chilli

→ **Fideuà** Similar to paella but with vermicelli noodles as the base. Often accompanied by *allioli* (pounded garlic with olive oil), which you can mix in as you wish

→ **Fricandó** Pork-and-vegetable stew

→ **Sarsuela/zarzuela** Mixed seafood cooked in *sofregit/sofrito* (fried onion, tomato and garlic sauce) with seasonings

→ **Suquet de peix** Fish-and-potato hotpot

DESSERTS

→ **Crema catalana** A cream custard with a crisp burnt-sugar coating

→ **Mel i mató** Honey and fresh cream cheese

MENÚ DEL DIA

The *menú del dia*, a full set meal with water or wine and usually several dish options, is a great way to cap prices at lunchtime. Menus start at around €11 (though prices typically rise in the most touristed parts of town) and can go as high as €25 for more elaborate offerings, and you will probably keep the same knife and fork throughout the meal. These days, all kinds of places offer a *menú*, from classic Catalan old-timers to fashionable vegan restaurants. Once your order is taken and the first course (which could range from a simple *amanida/ensalada rusa* – Russian salad thick with potatoes and mayonnaise – to an elaborate seafood item) is in place, you may find the level of service increases disconcertingly. Hovering waiters swoop like eagles to swipe your unfinished dish or lift your glass of wine, still tinged with that last sip you wanted to savour. Simply utter '*Encara no he terminat'/'Todavía no he terminado'* (I haven't finished yet) – you'll be flashed a cheerful smile and your waiter will leave you to finish in peace.

MATT MUNRO/LONELY PLANET ©

Above: *Pintxos* (Basque-style tapas)

Left: Quimet i Quimet (p196), Poble Sec

Lonely Planet's Top Choices

Disfrutar (p155) Consistently one of Barcelona's most talked-about, avant-garde restaurants.

Lasarte (p155) Barcelona's original three-Michelin-star restaurant.

Tapas 24 (p156) Carles Abellán crafts some of Barcelona's best tapas.

Bar Pinotxo (p74) La Boqueria's finest tapas bar: a celebration of Catalan cooking.

Best By Budget

€

Bar Central (p89) *Entrepans* (filled rolls), vermouth and coffee amid Raval gardens.

Little Fern Café (p129) Brunch sensation in Poblenou.

El Pachuco (p89) Queue-out-the-door taco spot in El Raval.

La Cova Fumada (p126) Barceloneta hole-in-the-wall with excellent tapas.

Tapas 24 (p156) Carles Abellán's signature glammed-up tapas.

Vaso de Oro (p126) Terrific tapas in a lively Barceloneta bar.

€€

Cafè de l'Acadèmia (p74) Catalan with a twist and terrific *menú* in the Barri Gòtic.

Bar Pinotxo (p74) La Boqueria's top tapas bar.

Pepa (p153) Divine, inventive tapas in an old Eixample bookshop.

Can Recasens (p130) An inviting Poblenou spot for a sumptuous feast.

La Vinateria del Call (p74) Wines paired with perfect sharing plates in the Gòtic.

Quimet i Quimet (p196) *Montaditos* (mini–open sandwiches) galore in Poble Sec.

€€€

Disfrutar (p155) Expect the unexpected – this is Catalan cooking at its most experimental.

Lasarte (p155) The ultimate eating experience, with three Michelin stars.

La Barra de Carles Abellán (p128) Seafood presented in myriad creative ways.

Mont Bar (p155) Home-grown ingredients become exquisite contemporary-Catalan cooking.

Best for Tapas

Quimet i Quimet (p1956) Mouth-watering morsels served to a standing crowd.

Bar Pinotxo (p74) Pull up a bar stool at this legendary Boqueria joint.

Tapas 24 (p156) Everyone's favourite gourmet tapas bar.

Pepa (p153) Natural wines meet ambitious bites in L'Eixample.

Belmonte (p74) Hidden-away Barri Gòtic bodega, home-grown produce.

Cañete (p91) Contemporary twists and Andalucian flourishes in El Raval.

Best for Catalan

Can Recasens (p130) Superb local cooking, romantic Poblenou setting.

La Pubilla (p178) Lightly creative Catalan classics opposite Gràcia's main market.

Cafè de l'Acadèmia (p74) High-quality dishes that never disappoint.

Cinc Sentits (p155) Jordi Artal's Michelin-starred cuisine highlights Catalan produce.

for a table at this so... joint with outstanding food.

La Pubilla (p178) Join the Gràcia crowd for Catalan breakfasts.

Elisabets (p89) Terrific home-style cooking and *menú* in El Raval.

Las Delicias (p177) A Sunday-morning classic, well located for a walk in Park Güell.

Best for Architecture

Els Quatre Gats (p76) Finely crafted interiors in a building where Picasso once supped.

La Dama (p155) French-inspired cuisine comes to L'Eixample's Modernista Casa Sayrach.

Bar Central (p89) Fabulous, fashionable cafe conversion of a 16th-century parish.

Bar Muy Buenas (p91) A 1920s Modernista dream, with super Catalan dishes.

El Asador de Aranda (p213) A beautiful spread of Modernista dining rooms.

Best for Vegetarians & Vegans

Green Spot (p127) Designer port dining room with dishes to match.

Sésamo (p89) Barcelona's finest veggie restaurant, tapas-style.

DINING OUT

...-rooted ... the Barri

... (p89) South ...nced vegan cooking ...y a young crowd.

... **& Kale** (p91) Vast, colourful ...ads and a truly creative approach.

Xavier Pellicer (p157) Vegetables get the gourmet star-chef treatment.

Best Lunch Specials

Cafè de l'Acadèmia (p74) Rich lunch specials and great Barri Gòtic atmosphere.

La Pubilla (p178) Gràcia's favourite *menú del dia*?

Elisabets (p89) A hugely popular home-style *menú* in El Raval.

La Cereria (p73) Fabulous vegetarian set lunches in the Gòtic.

Casa Delfín (p109) Lunch deals opposite the old Mercat del Born.

Best Dining with Views

Blue Spot (p128) Fairy-lit rooftop terrace by the sea.

Martínez (p195) Paella and tapas high up on Montjuïc.

Can Majó (p129) Elegant Barceloneta seafood joint with outdoor tables fronting the sea.

Red Fish (p130) Fantastic seafood to match delicious sea views.

Pez Vela (p129) Rice dishes by the Mediterranean.

Best for Brunch

Little Fern Café (p129) Organic produce, first-rate coffee, in Poblenou.

Federal (p198) Excellent Aussie-inspired brunches on a happening street.

Caravelle (p89) Serious coffee pairs with arty brunch dishes in El Raval.

Milk (p72) International brunchy bites until 4.30pm for the Gòtic crowds.

Can Dendê (p130) All-day brunches with Brazilian flair in El Poblenou.

Elsa y Fred (p106) Stylish La Ribera cafe serving weekend brunch.

Best for Late-Night Eating

Elisabets (p89) Raval neighbourhood favourite offering late-night dining on Friday.

El Pachuco (p89) There's often still a queue at 1am for the Raval taco stars.

Milk (p72) Pair inventive cocktails with international cooking well into the night.

Restaurant 7 Portes (p128) Paella and seafood sensations until 1am, by the port.

Can Cisa/Bar Brutal (p109) Late-night La Ribera dining on Catalan produce and natural wines.

Best for Market Dining

Bar Pinotxo (p74) Arrive early to snag a spot at this celebrated tapas bar in La Boqueria.

El Quim (p74) Another long-running star of La Boqueria.

Bar Joan (p107) Old-school meals and a relaxed neighbourhood feel in the Mercat de Santa Caterina.

El Tast de Joan Noi (p177) Super-fresh seafood tapas at Gràcia's Mercat de la Llibertat.

El Guindilla (p127) Grab an outdoor table and enjoy tasty lunch specials at this Mercat de la Barceloneta favourite.

Best for Desserts

Caelum (p76) Dine on sweet perfection in the pleasant cafe, or head downstairs for medieval atmosphere.

Granja Petitbo (p156) Sink into a leather armchair and devour a homemade cake at this rustic-chic cafe.

Escribà (p198) A household name in Barcelona for its beautiful pastries and other temptations.

Bar Open

Barcelona is a town for nightlife lovers, with an enticing spread of candlelit wine bars, old-school taverns, stylish lounges, magical cocktail hang-outs and kaleidoscopic nightclubs where the party continues until daybreak. For something a little more sedate, the city's atmospheric cafes and teahouses make a fine retreat.

Bars & Lounges

Barcelona has a dizzying assortment of bars where you can start – or end – the night. The atmosphere varies tremendously – candlelit, mural-covered chambers in the medieval quarter, antique-filled converted storefronts and buzzing Modernista spaces are all part of the scene. Of course, where to go depends as much on the crowd as it does on ambience – and whether you're in the mood to drink at the latest hot spot (try Sant Antoni), with the bohemian crowd (El Raval) or among young expats (Gràcia and El Born), you'll find a scene that suits in Barcelona.

Wherever you end up, keep in mind that eating and drinking go hand in hand in Barcelona (as in other parts of Spain), and some of the liveliest bars serve tapas as well as alcohol.

Wine, Cava & Cocktail Bars

A growing number of wine bars scattered around the city provide a showcase for the great produce from Spain and beyond. A big part of the experience is sharing a few platters of cheese and charcuterie and plenty of tapas. Bars serving mostly or even exclusively natural, organic and/or biodynamic wines are surging in popularity.

Cava bars tend to be more about the festive ambience than the actual drinking of *cava*, a sparkling white or rosé, most of which is produced in Catalonia's Penedès region. At the more famous *cava* bars you'll have to nudge your way through the garrulous crowds and enjoy your bubbly standing up. Two of the most famous are El Xampanyet (p111) in La Ribera and Can Paixano (p132) in Barceloneta.

The crafted-cocktail scene has exploded in recent years, with places like prize-winning Dr Stravinsky (p1101) in El Born, Gràcia's Bobby Gin (p180) and El Raval's Two Schmucks (p92) gaining international attention.

Vermouth

The Catalan wines and ambitious craft-beer bars are fabulous, of course, but the classic Barcelona drink is a hardy vermouth – red or white wine infused with botanicals and forti-fied with brandy.

Thought to have arrived in Catalonia in the mid-19th century, vermouth became a favourite of Barcelona's working class in the run-up to the civil war. It has experienced a dazzling revival over the last decade. Now, new vermouth bars are opening all over town; historical vermouth joints are more popular than ever; and creative artisan varie-ties are on the up. Join the *barcelonins* for *la hora del vermut* (the hour of vermouth), a super-sociable event typically around noon – and always accompanied by snacks, such as tapas of croquettes, anchovies and *patates braves*.

The perfect vermouth is usually served over ice with an olive or two and, sometimes, a slice of orange.

Drinks With a View

Barcelona has a handful of rooftop bars (p159) and hillside drinking spaces that pro-vide enchanting views over the city. Depend-ing on the neighbourhood, the vista may take in the rooftops of the Ciutat Vella (Old City),

NEED TO KNOW

Opening Hours

➡ **Bars** Typically open around 6pm and close at 2am (3am on weekends), though many are open all day.

➡ **Clubs** Open from midnight until 6am Thursday to Saturday.

➡ **Beach bars** 10am to around midnight (later on weekends), April to October.

When to Go

➡ Bars get lively around 11pm or midnight.

➡ Clubs don't start filling up until around 1.30am or 2am.

Getting In

Cover charges range from nothing to upwards of €20. Check club websites for details on joining guest lists and getting in more cheaply. You're also likely to pay less if you go early. In most cases the admission price includes your first drink. Bouncers have the last say on dress code and your eligibility to enter. If you're in a big group, break into smaller groups.

Guides for the Latest Nightlife

➡ **Time Out Barcelona** (www.timeout.com/barcelona)

➡ **Miniguide** (www.miniguide.es)

➡ **Xceed** (https://xceed.me)

➡ **Clubbingspain.com** (www.clubbingspain.com)

Bar-Hopping Hot Spots

➡ **Plaça Reial** Barri Gòtic

➡ **Carrer dels Escudellers** Barri Gòtic

➡ **Carrer de Joaquín Costa** El Raval

➡ **Carrer Nou de la Rambla** El Raval & Poble Sec

➡ **Carrer del Parlament** Sant Antoni

➡ **Platja de la Barceloneta** La Barceloneta

➡ **Carrer d'Aribau** L'Eixample

➡ **Plaça del Sol** Gràcia

➡ **Passeig del Born** El Born

➡ **Rambla del Raval** El Raval

➡ **Plaça de la Vila de Gràcia** Gràcia

➡ **Carrer de Blai** Poble Sec

the curving beachfront, or the entire expanse of the city centre with the Collserola hills and Tibidabo in the distance. Most of these drinking spots are perched atop high-end hotels, but they are not solely the domain of visiting foreigners. Late in the evening you'll find a mostly local crowd.

Beach Bars

During summer, small wooden beach bars, known as *xiringuitos* (*chiringuitos* in Spanish), open up along the strand from Barceloneta all the way up to Platja de la Nova Mar Bella. Here you can dip your toes in the sand and nurse a cocktail or munch a snack while watching the city at play against the backdrop of the deep-blue Mediterranean. Ambient sounds add to the laid-back environment. Some beachside bars also host big-name DJs and parties.

Clubs

Barcelona's *discoteques* (*discotecas*; clubs) are at their best from Thursday to Saturday; many open only on these nights. A surprising variety of spots lurk in the old-town labyrinth, ranging from plush former dance halls to grungy packed-out subterranean venues. A sprinkling of well-known clubs is spread over the classy parts of town, in L'Eixample and La Zona Alta.

At the Port Olímpic, a strip of noisy waterfront clubs and bars attract raucous crowds of tourists and a few locals, though at the time of writing there were plans to close these venues down (p133).

Cafes

Barcelona hosts a vibrant array of cafes and the third-wave coffee scene in particular is booming. You'll find charming teashops hidden on the narrow lanes of Barri Gòtic, bohemian hang-outs in the Raval, hipster haunts in L'Eixample and Modernista gems on La Rambla. While coffee, tea or perhaps *xocolata desfeta* (hot chocolate) are the main attractions, most places also serve snacks, while some serve beer, wine and cocktails.

Microbreweries

There's also a healthy line-up of local artisan beer brewers, especially in L'Eixample, Poble Sec and El Poblenou, plus pioneering BlackLab (p132) in the Port Vell, Barcelona's original brewhouse.

Drinking by Neighbourhood

Gràcia & Park Güell
Cocktail bars, vermouth and wine bars, buzzy squares
(p180)

Camp Nou, Pedralbes & La Zona Alta
High-end clubs, neighbourhood bars
(p215)

La Sagrada Família & L'Eixample
Student bars, cocktail lounges, LGBTQI+ bars/clubs
(p158)

La Ribera & El Born
Cava and wine bars, cool cafes, cocktail spots
(p111)

Plaça de Catalunya

Port Olímpic

El Raval
Bohemian hang-outs, small clubs, cocktail bars, cafes
(p92)

La Rambla & Barri Gòtic
Atmospheric bars, cafes, outdoor spots, clubs
(p76)

Barceloneta, the Waterfront & El Poblenou
Neighbourhood taverns, seaside bars, cafes, cocktail bars, touristy clubs
(p131)

Montjuïc, Poble Sec & Sant Antoni
Arty bars and cafes, open-air spots, clubs
(p200)

Port de Barcelona

MEDITERRANEAN SEA

Lonely Planet's Top Choices

Paradiso (p111) Glamorous, cavernous, speakeasy-style cocktail bar.

La Caseta del Migdia (p200) An open-air charmer, hidden high on Montjuïc.

Dr Stravinsky (p111) Crafted-cocktail wizardry amid El Born's alleys.

Two Schmucks (p92) Everyone's talking about this Raval cocktail den.

Best for Wine Lovers

Perikete (p131) Lively wine and tapas bar in Barceloneta.

Viblioteca (p182) A trendy Gràcia space famed for its wine (and cheese) selections.

Can Paixano (p132) Perfect tapas pair with house rosé in La Barceloneta.

La Vinya del Senyor (p111) Catalan wines in the shadow of Basílica de Santa Maria del Mar.

Best for Cocktails

Paradiso (p111) Walk through a fridge to this glam speakeasy.

Dr Stravinsky (p111) The place to linger over an avant-garde concoction.

Two Schmucks (p92) Pop-up cocktail bar turned Raval sensation.

Bobby Gin (p180) Beautifully mixed elixirs in Gràcia.

Hemingway (p159) Ambitious, expertly made creative cocktails in L'Eixample.

Bar Boadas (p77) An iconic drinking den going strong since the 1930s.

Best for Beer

Abirradero (p200) Creative microbrewery in Poble Sec.

BlackLab (p132) Barcelona's original craft brewer, by the waterfront.

La Cervecita Nuestra de Cada Día (p1343) A Poblenou brew bar for beer nerds.

Garage Beer Co (p158) Pouring its own brews in L'Eixample.

BrewDog (p160) Barcelona specials and classic international faves.

Best for Vermouth

Quimet i Quimet (p1956) House vermouth pairs with divine *montaditos* at this Poble Sec old-timer.

La Vermu (p182) Buzzy Gràcia favourite that makes its own vermouth.

Vermuteria del Tano (p182) Gràcia's residents gather for traditional-style vermouth hour.

Bar Calders (p202) Lively Sant Antoni hub with perfect vermouth.

Bodega La Peninsular (p127) Barceloneta fave for homemade vermouth and superb tapas.

Best Cafes

Bar Central (p89) Cafe of your dreams in a leafy, historic Raval building.

Nømad (p111) Barcelona's favourite home-grown roaster.

Little Fern Café (p129) Punchy brunches and third-wave coffee.

Federal (p72) Millennial vibes, Aussie-style brunches, solid coffee.

Caelum (p76) Gorgeous Barri Gòtic cafe with medieval ruins.

Best for Old-World Ambience

La Confiteria (p92) A 19th-century flavour infuses this Raval cocktail bar.

Raïm (p183) Old-fashioned Gràcia tavern with more than a hint of Havana.

Cafè de l'Òpera (p77) Serving opera-goers and passers-by for decades.

Bar Marsella (p92) History lives on in this 1820 watering hole.

Bar Pastís (p93) Atmospheric little bar with the warble of French cabaret tunes playing overhead.

Casa Almirall (p92) Step back into the 1860s inside this atmospheric drinking den.

Best for Dancing

Marula Café (p77) Barri Gòtic favourite for its lively dance floor.

La Terrrazza (p200) Party beneath palms in the Poble Espanyol.

Sala Apolo (p202) Gorgeous dance hall with varied electro, funk and more.

Moog (p94) Small Raval club that draws a fun, dance-loving crowd.

Antilla BCN (p159) The top name in town for salsa lovers.

Best for Views

La Caseta del Migdia (p200) Great hillside Montjuïc spot for a sundowner.

Mirablau (p215) The whole city stretches out beneath you from the foot of Tibidabo.

Martínez (p195) Drinking and dining with views on Montjuïc.

Alaire (p159) Rooftop Eixample bar overlooking Modernista masterpieces.

The Roof (p112) Admire Enric Miralles' Mercat de Santa Caterina over rooftop cocktails.

Best Bohemian Hang-Outs

Gran Bodega Saltó (p202) Poble Sec icon with psychedelic decor and an eclectic crowd.

Madame George (p133) Tiny, dramatically designed space with soulful DJs.

El Rouge (p200) Bordello-esque lounge with great people-watching.

Bar Marsella (p92) Historic absinthe bar that's seen them all.

Showtime

Barcelona teems with stages hosting all manner of entertainment from underground cabaret and comic opera to high drama and experimental performance. Dance companies are thick on the ground and popular local theatre companies, when not touring the rest of Spain, keep folks strapped to their seats.

Live Music

Almost every big international act has passed through Barcelona at some point, more often than not playing at Razzmatazz (p134), Bikini (p215), Sala Apolo (p202) or BARTS (p202), although there are also a number of other decent midsize venues. Many local gigs take place in institutions as diverse as CaixaForum (p191), La Pedrera (p147) and the Ateneu Barcelonès (p79), and at small locally loved venues such as Gràcia's Soda Acústic (p183), L'Eixample's Mediterráneo (p161) and Gran Bodega Saltó (p202) in Poble Sec. There are plenty of warm-weather music festivals, including **Sónar** (www.sonar.es; ⊘mid-Jun) and **Primavera Sound** (www.primaverasound.com; ⊘May-Jun).

Classical Music & Opera

Barcelona is blessed with a fine line-up of theatres for grand performances of classical music, opera and more. The two historic – and iconic – music venues are the Gran Teatre del Liceu (p79) and the Palau de la Música Catalana (p113), while the L'Auditori (p134) is the modern concert hall par excellence and home to the city's orchestra, the Orquestra Simfònica de Barcelona i Nacional de Catalunya (OBC).

The main season for classical music and opera runs from September to June, while in high summer you might find outdoor festivals or performances around town.

Dance & Theatre

Some fine local contemporary dance and theatre companies, along with international visiting companies, maintain a fairly busy performance programme across town. Look for leaflets at venues such as the Palau de la Virreina (p61) and watch theatre listings. For ballet and other big spectacles, you usually need to wait for acts to arrive from abroad. The summer **Festival del Grec** (http://grec.bcn. cat; ⊘Jul) is a month-long celebration of the performing arts.

Most local theatre is performed in Catalan or Spanish, although physical theatre is popular too. Keep your eyes peeled for any of the eccentric (if not downright crazed) performances of Barcelona theatre group **La Fura dels Baus** (www.lafura.com), which has won worldwide acclaim for its brand of startling, often acrobatic, theatre in which the audience is frequently dragged into the chaos. The company grew out of Barcelona's street-theatre culture of the late 1970s, and although it has grown in technical prowess and received great international attention, it has not abandoned the rough-and-ready edge of street performances.

SARDANA

In Barcelona the best chance you have of seeing people dancing the traditional *sardana* (Catalonia's national folk dance) is either at 6pm Saturday or 11am Sunday in front of La Catedral in the Barri Gòtic, or during festivals like **La Mercè** (www.barcelona.cat/merce; ⊘Sep).

NEED TO KNOW

Tickets

The easiest way to get hold of tickets for most venues throughout the city is through Eventbrite (www.eventbrite.es), Ticketmaster (www.ticketmaster.es) or, occasionally, Atrápalo (www.atrapalo.com).

Listings

➡ For exhibitions and other forms of entertainment, see Barcelona Metropolitan (www.barcelona-metropolitan.com), Time Out Barcelona (www.timeout.com/barcelona) and Miniguide (https://miniguide.co).

➡ The **Palau de la Virreina** (p61) cultural information office has oodles of information on theatre, opera, classical music and more.

➡ Good coverage of classical music is to be found on www.classictic.com.

When to Book

➡ Big names, festivals and events sell out quickly (especially at top venues such as the Palau de la Música Catalan), so it's best to book as far ahead as possible.

➡ At smaller music venues you can often just show up.

➡ Flamenco shows are easily booked once you're in town, but there's no harm in planning ahead.

➡ Accommodation prices sky-rocket during summer, when many of the most exciting shows and events come to town.

It is also performed sometimes in Plaça de Sant Jaume. For more information, contact the Agrupació Cultural Folklòrica de Barcelona (https://acfbarcelona.cat).

FLAMENCO

Seeing authentically good performances of this essentially Andalucian dance and music is tricky (though not impossible!). These days, Barcelona's few *tablaos* are generally tourist-oriented and often tacky. You can catch flamenco on Friday and Saturday at El Raval's JazzSí Club (p94), and often also at Farola (p113) in El Born and Paraigua (p79) in the Barri Gòtic. Keep an eye out for big-name performers at the Palau de la Música Catalana (p113) too.

The excellent **Festival de Flamenco de Ciutat Vella** (www.ciutatflamenco.com) is held in May. A series of concerts can also be seen, usually from April to July, as part of the **Barcelona Guitar Festival** (www.guitarbcn.com).

Cinemas

Outdoor cinema screens are set up in summer in the moat of the Castell de Montjuïc (p191; www.salamontjuic.org), on the beach and in El Fòrum. Foreign films with subtitles and original soundtracks are marked 'VO' *(versió original)* in movie listings.

Entertainment by Neighbourhood

➡ **La Rambla & Barri Gòtic** The Gran Teatre del Liceu, weekly *sardana* dances, music at El Paraigua, a few touristy flamenco *tablaos*.

➡ **El Raval** Great for theatre, jazz and flamenco at JazzSí Club, and all things film and arts at the Filmoteca de Catalunya.

➡ **La Ribera & El Born** Visit the spectacular Palau de la Música Catalana; Farola is a popular new live-music venture.

➡ **Poble Sec** For two of the best pop and rock venues, Sala Apolo and BARTS.

➡ **Barceloneta, the Waterfront & El Poblenou** Live gigs at Razzmatazz, Catalan theatre at the Teatre Nacional de Catalunya.

LA FURA DELS BAUS

Keep your eyes peeled for any of the eccentric (if not downright crazed) performances of Barcelona theatre group **La Fura dels Baus** (www.lafura.com), which has won worldwide acclaim for its brand of startling, often acrobatic, theatre in which the audience is frequently dragged into the chaos. The company grew out of Barcelona's street-theatre culture of the late 1970s, and although it has grown in technical prowess and received great international attention, it has not abandoned the rough-and-ready edge of street performances.

Lonely Planet's Top Choices

Palau de la Música Catalana (p113) This glittering Modernista gem, the city's traditional home for classical and choral music, is a multisensory delight.

Gran Teatre del Liceu (p79) Nineteenth-century style meets cutting-edge acoustics at Barcelona's elegant opera house.

Filmoteca de Catalunya (p94) This cinema and arts centre in El Raval also includes a film archive, bookshop and exhibition space.

Best for Live Bands

City Hall (p161) The perfect midsize venue for up-and-coming local and international acts.

Sala Apolo (p202) Cosy booths and a warm red glow give this hugely popular venue something special.

BARTS (p202) A key player on the live-music circuit, with superb sound and every mod con.

Bikini (p215) Hidden behind a shopping centre, Bikini still pulls in some great acts.

Farola (p113) Buzzing El Born sherry bar with daily live music.

Gran Bodega Saltó (p202) This traditional Poble Sec bodega hosts regular gigs.

Best for Classical Music

Palau de la Música Catalana (p113) A Modernista fantasy, where the fabulous interior can distract from the finest musician.

Gran Teatre del Liceu (p79) One of Europe's most splendid opera houses, built to impress.

L'Auditori (p134) Fiercely modern concert venue, with a resident orchestra.

Ateneu Barcelonès (p79) This elegant old library is hard to access if you're not a member – unless you catch one of its occasional concerts.

Best for Theatre

Teatre Nacional de Catalunya (p134) A neoclassical building hosting the best of Catalan theatre.

Teatre Romea (p95) Expect wacky (and not so wacky) versions of modern classics.

Teatreneu (p183) With three different stages, the Teatreneu dares to go where others dare not.

Sala Beckett (p134) Keep an eye on the alternative programming here.

Festival del Grec (p43) A summer performing-arts sensation.

Best for Jazz

JazzSí Club (p94) Small, lively, cramped Raval spot that's never less than fabulous fun.

Harlem Jazz Club (p79) Not just jazz, but also funk, blues, bossa nova and plenty more, in the Gòtic.

23 Robadors (p94) Excellent live jazz in a tiny Raval bar.

Best for Flamenco

JazzSí Club (p94) A tiny venue with impromptu jams and occasionally great performances.

Tarantos (p79) A cosy Gòtic basement affair, good for up-and-coming acts.

El Paraigua (p79) Weekend performances in a historical Gòtic basement.

Farola (p113) Sherries pair with live flamenco for Andalucian flavour in El Born.

Tablao Nervión (p113) A little bit touristy, but better than most for flamenco.

Best Local Festivals

Festes de la Mercé (p43) Catch *castells* (human castles), *gegants* (papier-mâché giants) and *correfocs* (fire runs) on the street, as well as dance, theatre and live music.

Festa Major de Gràcia (www. festamajordegracia.org; ⊘Aug) More summer concerts, *correfocs* and *castells* in the Gràcia neighbourhood.

Festes de Santa Eulàlia (http://lameva.barcelona.cat/ santaeulalia; ⊘Feb) Barcelona's first patron saint is celebrated with theatre, music, *castells* and parades of *gegants* and fire-runners.

Best for Cinema

Filmoteca de Catalunya (p94) The city's premier repertory cinema, with themed cycles and rock-bottom prices.

Cines Verdi (p183) Up-to-date releases, both commercial and less so.

Renoir Floridablanca (p202) Comfortable, modern cinema showing a good selection of recent films.

Treasure Hunt

Barcelona's creative side is on show with its vibrant, understated shopping scene. The Ciutat Vella, L'Eixample and Gràcia host a thick mantle of independent boutiques, historic shops, original one-off stores, gourmet corners, wine dens, designer labels and more, and in recent years a raft of young creatives have set up boutiques and workshops in happening spots like El Raval, El Born, Sant Antoni and Gràcia.

Design

Whether you are looking for homewares, gifts or decorations, you'll quickly realise that Barcelona is a stylish city – even the souvenirs have flair. High-end design shops are best found in L'Eixample and El Born, while arty places (where you'll find, among other things, quirky furniture, fashion and homewares with a difference) are scattered around El Raval, Sant Antoni, Gràcia and also El Born.

Boutique Barcelona

The heart of the Barri Gòtic has always been busy with small-scale merchants, but nowadays it's also the place for a more contemporary retail fix. Some of the most curious old shops, such as purveyors of hats, shoes and candles, lurk in the narrow lanes around Plaça de Sant Jaume. Once-seedy Carrer d'Avinyó has become a minor young-fashion boulevard. Antiques shops line Carrer de la Palla and Carrer dels Banys Nous.

La Ribera is nothing less than a gourmet's delight. Great old shops and some finger-licking newbies deal in speciality foodstuffs, from coffee and chocolate to roasted nuts. Amid such wonderful aromas, a crop of fashion and design stores – many of them flaunting Barcelona labels and designers – caters to the multitude of fashionistas in the *barri* (neighbourhood).

Gràcia is also full of quirky little shops, especially along Carrer de Verdi and Carrer de Bonavista, and you'll also find attractive boutiques in Sant Gervasi and Sarrià.

El Raval and Sant Antoni are fantastic for unique boutiques and artists selling their own creations (fashion, prints, curios), not to mention a buzzing vintage scene.

High-Street Chains

Everyone knows that across Europe (and further afield) Spain's chains rule the high street. This is the home of the ubiquitous Zara, Pull&Bear, Stradivarius, Bershka, Massimo Dutti, Uterqüe and Zara Home (in fact, all owned by one company, Inditex) – and sure enough, you'll find all of them dotted around Barcelona, along with fellow Spanish brands Mango and Desigual. Women's underwear is stylish and affordable at Oysho and Women's Secret. Bold Barcelona brand Custo (p115) is another favourite.

Department Stores

Spain's only surviving department store is El Corte Inglés (p162). An enormous fortresslike main branch towers over Plaça de Catalunya, covering all manner of things from books, music and food to fashion, jewellery, kids' clothes and toys, technology and homeware. There are smaller branches across town. French chain FNAC is another biggie, selling books, music, computers and mobile phones.

Vintage Fashion

El Raval is Barcelona's vintage-fashion hot spot, where irresistible old-time stores mingle with a colourful array of affordable, mostly secondhand boutiques. The central axis here is Carrer de la Riera Baixa, which plays host to '70s threads and military cast-offs. Carrer dels Tallers is also attracting a growing number of clothing and shoe shops (though music remains its core business). Small galleries, designer shops and arty bookshops huddle together along the streets running east of the MACBA towards La Rambla.

You'll also find a few vintage specialists in the Barri Gòtic, El Born and Sant Antoni.

Designers

The heart of L'Eixample, bisected by Passeig de Gràcia, is known as the Quadrat d'Or (Golden Square) and is jammed with all sorts of glittering shops. Passeig de Gràcia is a who's who of international shopping – you'll find Spain's own high-end designers like Loewe (p163) and Adolfo Domínguez (p165) mingling with Armani, Chanel, Gucci and the rest.

El Born, particularly Carrer del Rec, is big on cool designers in small, clean-line boutiques, and some Barcelona-based designs are also sold here. This is a great, atmospheric area if you have hours to browse.

If you're keen for local expertise, check out the high-end-fashion shopping tours run by Antiques & Boutiques (p82).

Markets

Barcelona's food markets are some of the best in Europe. Just think of the inviting, glistening, aromatic and voluptuous offerings to be savoured at the historical Mercat de la Boqueria (p64) or La Ribera's Mercat de Santa Caterina (p104) – though every neighbourhood has its own central market, and those in less touristed neighbourhoods are usually just as exciting as the traditional headliners. The Mercat de Sant Antoni (p195), which reopened in 2018, is a current favourite.

Several flea markets, like El Poblenou's Mercat dels Encants (p135), offer browsing, a local buzz and perhaps even a good bargain.

Shopping Malls

Barcelona has no shortage of shopping malls. One of the first to arrive was L'Illa Diagonal (p217), designed by star Spanish architect Rafael Moneo. The city's other emporia include **Centre Comercial Diagonal Mar** (Map p304; ☑93 567 76 37; www.diagonalmarcentre.es; Avinguda Diagonal 3; ⊙9.30am-10pm Mon-Sat Jun-Sep, 9am-9pm Mon-

NEED TO KNOW

Where to Go

For high fashion, design, jewellery and department stores, the principal shopping axis starts on Plaça de Catalunya, proceeds up Passeig de Gràcia and turns left into Avinguda Diagonal, along which it extends as far as Plaça de la Reina Maria Cristina. The densely packed section between Plaça de Francesc Macià and Plaça de la Reina Maria Cristina is an especially good hunting ground.

Sale Time

The winter sales start after Reis (6 January) and, depending on the shop, can go on well into February. The summer sales start in July, with shops trying to entice locals to part with one last wad of euros before they flood out of the city on holiday in August. Some shops prolong their sales to the end of August. Barcelona has also succumbed to the Black Friday sales craze around the last Friday in November.

Opening Hours

➡ In general, shops are open between 9am or 10am and 1.30pm or 2pm and then again from around 4pm or 4.30pm to 8pm or 8.30pm Monday to Friday. Many shops keep the same hours on Saturday, although some don't bother with the evening session.

➡ Large supermarkets, malls and department stores such as El Corte Inglés stay open all day Monday to Saturday, from about 10am to 10pm.

➡ Many fashion boutiques, design stores and the like open from about 10am to 8pm Monday to Saturday.

➡ A few shops open on Sundays and holidays, and the number increases in the run-up to key consumer holiday periods.

➡ Independent boutiques tend to have more reduced hours.

Sat Oct-May; Ⓜ El Maresme Fòrum), up by El Fòrum; **La Maquinista** (☑93 360 89 71; www.lamaquinista.com; Carrer de Potosí; ⊙9am-9pm Mon-Sat; 🚌42, Ⓜ Sant Andreu) in Sant Andreu; the waterfront Maremàgnum (p136); Centre Comercial de les Glòries (p136), in the former Olivetti factory; **SOM**

SHOP CLOSURES

From centuries-old candle-makers to family-owned hat shops going back decades and small-scale bakeries where scents waft down the street, Barcelona's traditional, historical, specialist shops are just as key to the city's soul as Gaudí's Modernista creations. Often flaunting elaborate facades known to everyone in town, many are also a feast of gorgeous tiling, stained glass and colourful signs, with a long artisan heritage.

Over the last few years, however, some of the city's best-known shops have been forced to close, in part due to customers favouring bigger brands but largely down to rising rents on what have become some of Spain's most expensive streets (and in some cases linked to growing numbers of tourist apartments pushing up prices – see p77). But it's certainly not all lost: in 2015, 228 stores across Barcelona were given a special preservation status, which essentially means that their original facades and interiors can't be altered; 32 of these now can't be changed in any way at all.

Visitors can show their support by shopping (not just taking photos) at long-established, much-loved Barcelona icons such as La Rambla's Escribà bakery (p80), hatmaker Sombrerería Obach (p80) and candle-producer Cererìa Subirà (p80) in the Barri Gòtic, or dried-fruit specialist Casa Gispert (p114) in El Born. A couple of historical drinking dens have been given special preservation status too, most notably Els Quatre Gats (p76) near the cathedral, and Casa Almirall (p92) and La Confiteria (p92) in El Raval.

Multiespai (📞93 276 50 70; www.sommul tiespai.com; Avinguda de Rio de Janeiro 42; ⏰9.30am-9pm Mon-Sat winter, to 10pm summer; Ⓜ Fabra i Puig), just off Avinguda Meridiana, 4km north of Plaça de les Glòries Catalanes; **Arenas** (p203) in Plaça d'Espanya; and **Gran Via 2** (📞93 259 17 62; www.gran via2.com; Gran Via de les Corts Catalanes 75; ⏰9.30am-9pm Mon-Sat; Ⓡ FGC Ildefons Cerdà) in L'Hospitalet de Llobregat.

Shopping Strips

Avinguda del Portal de l'Àngel This broad pedestrian avenue off Plaça de Catalunya is lined with high-street chains, shoe shops, bookshops and more. It feeds into Carrer dels Boters and Carrer de la Portaferrissa, characterised by stores offering light-hearted costume jewellery and youth-oriented streetwear.

Avinguda Diagonal This boulevard is loaded with international fashion names and design boutiques, suitably interspersed with cafes.

Carrer d'Avinyó Once a fairly squalid old-city street, Carrer d'Avinyó has morphed into a dynamic young fashion hub.

Carrer de la Riera Baixa & Carrer dels Tallers The Raval streets to scour for preloved threads.

Carrer del Consell de Cent The heart of the private art-gallery scene in Barcelona, between Passeig de Gràcia and Carrer de Muntaner.

Carrer del Petritxol Best for chocolate shops and art.

Carrer del Rec Another threads street, this one-time stream in El Born is lined with original boutiques, many of them by local designers, as are nearby Carrer del Bonaire and Carrer de l'Esparteria.

Carrer dels Banys Nous Along with nearby Carrer de la Palla, this is the place to look for antiques.

Passeig de Gràcia Barcelona's chic premier shopping boulevard, mostly given over to big-name international brands.

Carrer de Bonavista & Carrer de Verdi A sprinkling of intriguing boutiques in Gràcia.

Lonely Planet's Top Choices

Vila Viniteca (p113) Oenophiles unite at this wonderful wine shop.

Colmillo de Morsa (p183) Beautiful minimalist Gràcia-based fashion brand for women.

L'Arca (p79) Vintage so fabulous it's starred on the silver screen.

Flores Navarro (p164) A 24-hour floral wonderland in L'Eixample.

Grey Street (p95) Tempting trinkets crafted by local artists.

Best for Design & Craft

Grey Street (p95) Stylish homewares sourced from Spanish artists.

Teranyina (p95) The 'Spider's Web', so called for its intricate designs in textiles.

Working in the Redwoods (p114) Gorgeous earthy ceramics from natural materials.

Les Topettes (p95) A celebration of all things beautifully scented.

La Variété (p95) Home decor pieces made in collaboration with Thai artisans.

Best for Fashion

Colmillo de Morsa (p183) Elegant women's designs with a sustainable ethos, in Gràcia.

La Manual Alpargatera (p80) Shop the Barri Gòtic for *espardenyes* (espadrilles), just like Penélope Cruz.

Coquette (p115) Simple, beautiful designer clothes for women.

Bagués-Masriera (p162) Exquisite jewellery from a company with a long tradition.

Ozz Barcelona (p114) Slow fashion and avant-garde Barcelona designers, in El Born.

Avant (p162) A Modernista frontage conceals chic women's designer-wear.

Best Markets

Mercat de la Boqueria (p64) The quintessential Barcelona food market.

Mercat de Santa Caterina (p104) La Ribera's colourful alternative to La Boqueria.

Mercat de Sant Antoni (p195) Neighbourhood market that's back in business after a beautiful restoration.

Mercat dels Encants (p135) A sprawling flea market in a modern Poblenou building.

Mercat de la Barceloneta (p1365) Buzzy local food market near the sea.

Best for Souvenirs & Gifts

Les Topettes (p95) Creams, oils, perfumes and soaps that look every bit as tantalising as they smell.

Sabater Hermanos (p80) Divinely fragranced shop selling handmade soaps in pretty gift boxes.

MACBA (p86) El Raval's modern art museum sells colourful and covetable books and gifts.

La Nostra Ciutat (p96) Barcelona-themed prints, maps and totes designed by local artists.

Marsalada (p115) Original souvenirs include Barcelona-stamped tote bags.

Grey Street (p95) Pick up a locally hand-painted mug or two.

Best for Food & Wine

Casa Gispert (p114) The speciality is roast nuts at this Born old-timer, but you'll also find chocolate, conserves and olive oils.

Vila Viniteca (p113) A jaw-dropping cathedral of wines from Catalonia and elsewhere in Spain, tucked away in El Born.

Caelum (p76) Deliciously wicked sweet treats made by nuns, with a little tea room.

El Magnífico (p114) Barcelona's original coffee roastery, in El Born.

Escribà (p80) Pop behind the Modernista facade on La Rambla for divine chocolates and pastries.

Best for Vintage

L'Arca (p80) Ethereal gowns, often used for film sets, in the heart of the Barri Gòtic.

Mercat dels Encants (p135) Lively flea market for retro homewares and kitschy bric-a-brac.

Holala! Plaza (p95) Boho-chic Ibiza-inspired vintage fashion in El Raval.

Le Swing Vintage (p81) High-fashion pieces from the past.

LGBTIQ+ Barcelona

Barcelona has a vibrant LGBTIQ+ scene, with a lively array of bars, clubs, restaurants and even specialised bookshops in the 'Gaixample', an area of L'Eixample about five to six blocks southwest of Passeig de Gràcia around Carrer del Consell de Cent. Other LGBTIQ-focused venues are dotted around Sant Antoni and Poble Sec.

Local Attitudes

Spain is one of southern Europe's most LGBTIQ-friendly countries. Despite fierce opposition from the Catholic Church, Spain legalised same-sex marriage in 2005, becoming the fourth country in the world to do so and with strong support. Married same-sex couples in Spain can also adopt children.

As a general rule, Barcelona is a very open and accepting city (as is nearby Sitges), where LGBTIQ+ couples should feel comfortable arm in arm and are unlikely to raise eyebrows. Transgenderism, too, is increasingly accepted.

LGBTIQ+ Bars & Clubs

Barcelona's bar scene offers plenty of variety, with stylish cocktail bars, bear bars, beach bars and performance bars (with drag shows and other events) all part of the mix. Most cater to a largely male clientele.

As with all clubs in town, things don't get going until well into the early morning (around 2am), and most open only Thursday to Saturday nights. The bigger and better-known clubs, like Arena Madre (p158) and Arena Classic (p160) host top-notch DJs, multiple bars, dark rooms, drag shows and all kinds of other amusements. Many of the best clubs are dotted around the Gaixample (p160), while smaller venues await in El Raval.

Barcelona's Lesbian Scene

The lesbian bar and club scene is a little sparse compared to the gay scene, with more places catering to a mixed LGBTIQ+ crowd (and a few straights thrown in) than an exclusively lesbian clientele. The best-known proudly lesbian event is nightly Aire at Arena Classic (p160), and there are a couple of lesbian bars dotted around the Gaixample and Poble Sec.

Special Events

The LGBTIQ+ community from Barcelona and beyond takes centre stage during the annual, weeklong **Pride Barcelona** (www.pridebarcelona.org; ⊘late Jun-early Jul), which features concerts, drag shows, film screenings, art shows and open-air dance parties, and also raises awareness about issues affecting the community. It culminates with a festive parade along Carrer de Sepúlveda to Plaça d'Espanya, where the big events are held.

Also of note is the LGBTIQ+ film festival **Fire!!** (www.mostrafire.com), hosted by the Casal Lambda cultural centre in June. The hugely popular gay festival **Circuit** (https://circuitfestival.net) lands in Barcelona in August.

Sitges: Spain's LGBTIQ+ Capital

Barcelona has a busy scene, but the LGBTIQ+ capital of Spain is saucily hedonistic seaside Sitges (p224), 35km southwest of Barcelona and linked by frequent trains (45 minutes). This attractive town is a major destination on the international party circuit and hosts some fabulous LGBTIQ-oriented beaches. The community here takes a leading role in the raucous Carnaval celebrations in February/March, and Sitges also hosts its own Pride march in June.

Lonely Planet's Top Choices

Axel Hotel (p239) Stylish gay boutique hotel in the heart of the Gaixample.

Arena Classic (p160) Hosts Barcelona's top lesbian club night, Aire.

La Federica (p201) Lively Poble Sec bar for wines, cocktails, tapas and LGBTIQ+ events.

El Cangrejo (p94) Popular duo of LGBTIQ+ bars, with drag shows at the Raval branch.

Sitges (p224) All the fabulous fun in a gorgeous sea-hugging town outside Barcelona.

Best LGBTIQ+ Clubs

Arena Madre (p158) With striptease shows and pumping beats, it's always a fun night at Arena.

Arena Classic (p160) Buzzing LGBTIQ+ club with plenty of lesbian events.

El Cangrejo (p94) Dancing and drag shows in El Raval and the Gaixample.

Best Laid-Back Bars

La Monroe (p93) Stylish, low-key, all-welcoming bar in El Raval's Filmoteca.

La Chapelle (p161) Casual Gaixample spot for cocktails and a welcoming crowd.

La Federica (p201) Tasty wines, tapas and cocktails in Poble Sec, plus LGBTIQ+ events.

Punto BCN (p160) A two-level bar with a good mix of ages and creeds in the Gaixample.

Plata Bar (p158) Cocktails and glossy style at this corner gay bar.

Best Mixed Clubs

Arena Classic (p160) Fun, dance-loving crowds of all persuasions flock here.

La Terrrazza (p200) Open-air summer dance parties up on Montjuïc.

Arena Madre (p158) Pop, dance, house, reggaeton and more for all in the Gaixample.

Best LGBTIQ+Friendly Beaches

Platja de la Mar Bella (p119) A buzzing beach scene that's clothing optional at its southern tip.

Sitges (p225) Hop on a train to this LGBTIQ+ seaside favourite, with 17 golden beaches.

Best LGBTIQ+ Bookshops

Antinous (p164) Spacious bookstore with cafe in L'Eixample.

Cómplices (p81) Mix of lit and grit at this inviting bookseller.

Best LGBTIQ+ Stays

Room Mate Pau (p238) Stylish, budget-conscious hotel on the edge of the Barri Gòtic.

Axel Hotel (p239) Designer rooms, a sauna and a rooftop pool in the heart of the Gaixample; also has gay-friendly TWO in Sant Antoni.

NEED TO KNOW

LGBTIQ+ Organisations

Casal Lambda (Map p315; ☏93 319 55 50, WhatsApp ☏679 205204; www.lambda. cat; Carrer del Comte Borrell 22; ⊙5-9pm Mon-Sat; Ⓜ Barceloneta) An LGBTIQ+ social, cultural and information centre.

Useful Websites

➡ **Travel Gay** (www. travelgay.com) Global site with frequently updated Barcelona listings.

➡ **GaySitges** (www.gay-sitges.com) A site dedicated to this LGBTIQ+ friendly coastal town.

➡ **Patroc** (www.patroc. com) A European gay guide. Particularly good on upcoming events.

➡ **Time Out Barcelona** (www.timeout.com/barcelona) All the latest on bars, clubs, restaurants and more, including LGBTIQ+ listings.

➡ **Tilllate** (www.tilllate. es) Nightlife guide to regions around Spain, including Catalonia.

➡ **Miniguide** (https:// miniguide.co/lgbt) Fashionable Barcelona with LGBTIQ+ sections.

Anakena House (p238) Not LGBTIQ+ per se, but close to the Gaixample action.

Sitges (p224) A raft of LGBTIQ-friendly hotels at this beachy town outside Barcelona.

Active Barcelona

Mediterranean oceanfront and a rambling hilly park overlooking the city make fine settings for outdoor fun beneath the (generally) sunny skies of Barcelona. For a break from museum-hopping, cocktail-tasting and overindulging at tapas bars and Michelin-starred restaurants, Barcelona has all the antidotes – running, swimming, cycling, hiking, paddle-boarding, yoga or simply pumping fists in the air at a never-dull FC Barça match.

Walking, Hiking & Running

Barcelona's waterfront esplanade and beaches are perfect for an early-morning run or walk, before the crowds come out. Locals who want to log some serious miles take to the Parc Natural de Collserola (p208), which is laced with trails. Among the best is the Carretera de les Aigües, a 9km-long flat track from Tibidabo to the suburb of Sant Just Desvern, with superb views over the city. In central Barcelona, the most convenient spaces to walk and run are the gardens and parkland of Montjuïc or the smaller Parc de la Ciutadella.

If you want to jog while you're in town, but don't want to go alone, you can join others in a casual running club. Barcelona Casual Runners (www.meetup.com/barcelona-casual-runners) organises multiple midweek 10km runs, and longer events on weekends. The Hotel Brummell (p241) Running Club has Tuesday-night runs (at 8pm) around Montjuïc, departing from the hotel.

Cycling

Barcelona's long, enticing seafront makes a fine setting for a ride, with a bike lane separate from traffic and pedestrians (though you'll have to move slowly at peak times). The city itself has an extensive network of bike lanes, including along major streets like Passeig de Sant Joan, Carrer del Consell de Cent, Gran Via, Avinguda Diagonal and Ronda de Sant Pau/Carrer del Comte d'Urgell. Avid mountain bikers will want to make their way up to the vast Parc Natural de Collserola (p208), where rambling trails on a wooded massif overlook the city. Elsewhere, you can loop around the city on the 72km Ronda Verda (www.rondaverda.cat). There's also a wealth of cycling tours.

Swimming, Beaches & Water Sports

Among Barcelona's many draws is hitting the sun-soaked beach for a dip in the Mediterranean, though some of the best sands are outside the city centre (p123). You can also go paddle-boarding, surfing, kitesurfing, kayaking, windsurfing, sailing and even do SUP yoga, with classes and rental easily organised at most beaches. Up on Montjuïc, you can swim in the original 1992 Olympics pool at the Piscines Bernat Picorell (p203).

Football & Other Spectator Sports

Football in Barcelona has the aura of religion and, for much of the city's population, support of FC Barcelona (p256) is an article of faith. But the city also has another hardy (if less illustrious) side, RCD Espanyol. FC Barcelona is traditionally associated with Catalans and even Catalan nationalism, while Espanyol is often identified with Spanish immigrants from other parts of the country. The football season is August to May.

Beyond football, you might catch basketball games (October to June; the local team is FC Barcelona Bàsquet), the ASOBAL handball league (September to May or early June) and the spring professional tennis season, whose big event is the Barcelona Open in April.

Best Walking Tours

Devour Barcelona (p177) Tap into the Catalan-cooking scene on tapas-tastic strolls through Gràcia, Sant Antoni and more.

Wanderbeak (p116) Fabulous tapas-hopping walks and market visits, plus cooking classes.

Hidden City Tours (p82) Uncover an often-overlooked side to Barcelona with guides from its homeless community.

Barcelona Architecture Walks (p116) Join a team of local architects as you wander from medieval to modern.

Runner Bean Tours (p82) Entertaining Barri Gòtic and Modernisme itineraries.

Barcelona Street Style Tour (p96) Delve into Barcelona's street-art scene.

Best Cycling

Parc Natural de Collserola (p208) Mountain-biking through pine-scented hills.

Terra Bike Tours (p165) Adventurous itineraries outside Barcelona.

Seafront cycle (p125) Hire wheels and weave along the seafront.

Best Walking & Running

Montjuïc (p191) A handy, scenic setting for walking and running (and biking!).

Parc Natural de Collserola (p208) Join the *barcelonins* for a view-drenched mountain hike or jog.

Passeig Marítim de la Barceloneta (p121) This pedestrianised promenade is perfect for stretching the legs.

Best Language & Cooking Courses

Barcelona Cooking (p83) Hands-on cookery classes visiting La Boqueria.

Speakeasy (p165) Social Spanish-language school.

Wanderbeak (p116) Uncover the secrets to a classic paella.

Best Beaches

El Poblenou Platges (p119) A string of lovely gold-sand beaches stretching northeast from the centre.

Castelldefells (p123) Silky blonde sand and kitesurfing, southwest of Barcelona.

Platja de la Barceloneta (p121) Arrive early to savour this sunny old-timer without crowds.

Sitges (p224) Day trip southwest from Barcelona to Sitges' buzzing beaches.

Platja del Garraf (p123) Another gorgeous out-of-towner, with fishers' huts framing a sparkling bay.

Best Waterfront Fun

Molokai SUP Center (p136) Paddle or surf out into the Mediterranean.

Club Natació Atlètic-Barceloneta (p137) Warm and cool lap pools next to La Barceloneta.

Base Náutica Municipal (p136) Kayaking, windsurfing, kitesurfing, sailing and SUP from Platja de la Mar Bella.

Best Spas

43 The Spa (p136) Barcelona's most fabulously positioned spa at the luxe Hotel Arts.

Aire de Barcelona (p116) Beautiful historical El Born setting for baths and massages.

NEED TO KNOW

Football Matches

A match at Barça's Camp Nou (p206) can be breathtaking; the season runs from August to May, and tickets can be bought online, at tourist offices or at FC Botiga stores. If you can't make it to see Barça play, don't miss the Barça Stadium Tour & Museum.

Boat Tours

Several companies including Las Golondrinas (p137), Orsom (p137) and BCNaval Tours (p137) take passengers on short jaunts out on the water. These depart several times daily (with many more departures in the summer) from Moll de les Drassanes near the southern end of La Rambla. Avoid going on a windy day when seas can be rough. Various outfitters can arrange private boat trips, including Wanderbeak (p116), which offers fun yacht trips.

Soho House (p234) Signature Cowshed spa beneath Catalan vaulting.

Mandarin Oriental (p240) Massages, lap pool and more at this luxurious former bank.

Best Crafts & Fashion

Antiques & Boutiques (p82) Expert-led high-fashion tours around Barcelona.

Alblanc Atelier (p136) Craft beautiful floral arrangements in a stylishly boho space.

Working in the Redwoods (p114) Ceramics sessions using all-natural materials.

Amalia Vermell (p184) Jewellery-making workshops.

BORYANA MANZUROVA/SHUTTERSTOCK ©

Explore Barcelona

BARCELONA'S
TOP EXPERIENCES

Left: Park Güell (p174)

Neighbourhoods at a Glance

❶ La Rambla & Barri Gòtic p58

La Rambla, Barcelona's most famous pedestrian boulevard, is always a hive of activity, busy with tourists, locals and con artists (watch out!). The adjoining Barri Gòtic is packed with historical treasures – relics of ancient Rome, 14th-century Gothic churches and atmospheric cobblestone lanes lined with shops, bars and restaurants.

❷ El Raval p84

The once down-and-out district of El Raval is still seedy in parts, though it has seen remarkable rejuvenation in recent years, with the addition of cutting-edge museums and cultural centres. Other highlights include bohemian nightlife, one-of-a-kind shops and multicultural buzz.

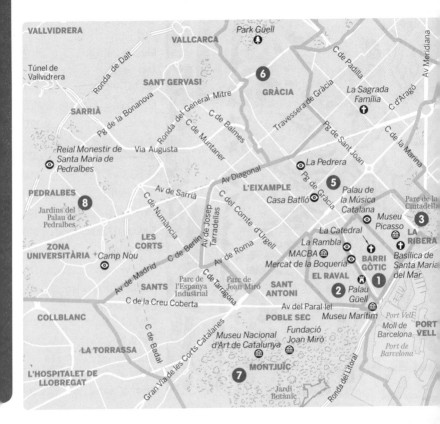

❸ La Ribera & El Born p97

This charming, busy medieval quarter hosts some of the city's liveliest tapas bars and most original boutiques, along with key sights such as the Museu Picasso, the awe-inspiring Basílica de Santa Maria del Mar, the artfully sculpted Palau de la Música Catalana and the leafy Parc de la Ciutadella.

❹ Barceloneta, the Waterfront & El Poblenou p117

Dramatically transformed since the 20th century, Barcelona's formerly industrial waterfront now boasts sparkling beaches, ultramodern high-rises and yacht-filled marinas. The gateway to the Mediterranean is the old-fashioned fishing quarter of Barceloneta, filled with seafood restaurants. To the northeast, post-industrial El Poblenou is a neighbourhood on the up, with a raft of creative design spaces.

❺ La Sagrada Família & L'Eixample p138

The elegant (traffic-filled) district of L'Eixample (pronounced 'lay-sham-pluh') is a showcase for Barcelona's great Modernista architecture, including Gaudí's unfinished masterpiece, La Sagrada Família, spread along broad boulevards. L'Eixample also has a celebrated dining scene, along with high-end boutiques and wildly diverse nightlife, including the buzzing LGBTIQ+ clubs of the 'Gaixample'.

❻ Gràcia & Park Güell p172

Gràcia was an independent town until the 1890s, and its narrow lanes and picturesque plazas still have a village-like feel. Well-worn cafes and bars, vintage shops and a smattering of multicultural restaurants make it a magnet for a young, largely international crowd. To its north lies Gaudí's outdoor Modernista storybook of Park Güell. Recently opened Casa Vicens is another Gaudí highlight.

❼ Montjuïc, Poble Sec & Sant Antoni p186

Best reached by soaring cable car, the hillside overlooking the port hosts some of the city's finest art collections, plus gardens, an imposing castle and fabulous views. Just below Montjuïc lie the lively tapas bars and sloping streets of Poble Sec, while the newly fashionable neighbourhood of Sant Antoni draws a stylish young crowd.

❽ Camp Nou, Pedralbes & La Zona Alta p204

Some of Barcelona's most sacred sights are situated within the huge expanse stretching northwest beyond L'Eixample: the medieval monastery of Pedralbes and the great shrine to Catalan football, Camp Nou. Other reasons to venture here are Tibidabo hill, the wooded trails of the Parc Natural de Collserola, and the untouristed former towns of Sarrià and Sant Gervasi.

NEIGHBOURHOODS AT A GLANCE

La Rambla & Barri Gòtic

Neighbourhood Top Five

❶ La Catedral (p62) Exploring the spectacular cloister, shadowy chapels and nooks and crannies of this magnificent Gothic masterpiece, before wandering around Barcelona's ancient Call (Jewish quarter).

❷ Museu d'Història de Barcelona (p67) Strolling through the subterranean ruins of Roman Barcino.

❸ Mercat de la Boqueria (p64) Feasting on tapas and weaving between fresh-produce stalls – early on!

❹ Museu Frederic Marès (p68) Discovering the strange and wondrous collections of a rich Catalan artist.

❺ La Rambla (p60) Rising early to take in Barcelona's liveliest street scene, with its flower stalls, historical sights and saunterers from every corner of the globe.

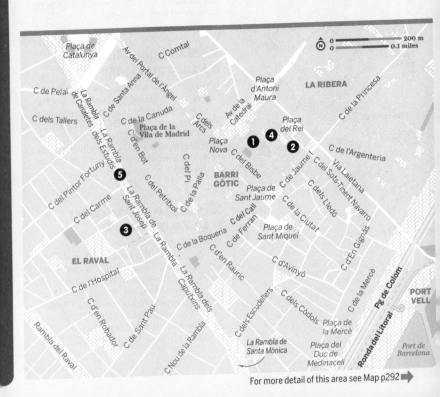

For more detail of this area see Map p292 ➡

Explore La Rambla & Barri Gòtic

La Rambla (p60) is Spain's most talked-about boulevard. It certainly packs a lot of colour into a short walk, with flower stands, historic buildings and the wonderful Mercat de la Boqueria (p64), alongside overpriced beers and tourist tat, and a ceaselessly changing parade of people from all corners of the globe. Once a river and sewage ditch on the edge of the medieval city, it still marks the southwest flank of the Barri Gòtic, the nucleus of old Barcelona. Come in the early morning to see it at its most peaceful.

You can easily spend several days exploring the Barri Gòtic. In addition to major sights, the tangle of narrow lanes and tranquil plazas conceal atmospheric shops, cafes and bars. There are swarms of tourists and some seriously overpriced restaurants, but the Barri Gòtic still retains plenty of local character.

Don't miss La Catedral (p62) and the smattering of Roman ruins inside the Museu d'Història de Barcelona (p67). Other highlights include the Barri Gòtic's many outdoor plazas and the narrow lanes of its ancient Call (Jewish quarter). Pretty, restaurant-lined Plaça Reial (p66) is the Gòtic's best-known square, but others like Plaça del Pi, Plaça de Sant Josep Oriol and tiny Plaça de Sant Just are also charming. By night, Barri Gòtic transforms into a maze of bars, clubs and restaurants.

Local Life

➤ **Market lunch** Don't miss the culinary scene at the Mercat de la Boqueria (p64) – either queue up and buy fresh produce, or let the local chefs shower you with Catalan delicacies at a stall.

➤ **Folk dancing** A growing number of young folks are now enjoying *sardana*, Catalonia's traditional folk dance. Join in at 6pm on Saturday and 11am on Sunday in front of La Catedral (p62).

➤ **Bar-hopping** Plaça Reial, Plaça de George Orwell and the narrow streets between the two are lively spots to take in the local Gòtic nightlife, as are Carrer Ample, Carrer d'en Gignàs and Carrer de la Mercè.

Getting There & Away

➤ **Metro** Key stops near or on La Rambla include Catalunya, Liceu and Drassanes. For the Barri Gòtic's east side, Jaume I and Urquinaona are handiest.

➤ **Bus** Airport and night buses arrive and depart from Plaça de Catalunya.

➤ **Taxi** Easiest to catch on La Rambla or Plaça de Catalunya.

Lonely Planet's Top Tip

For the best-value dining, make lunch your main meal. Many restaurants in the Barri Gòtic offer three-course meals for €12 to €16, including wine (even cheaper in less touristed parts of town).

LA RAMBLA & BARRI GÒTIC

 ## Best Historical Treasures

➤ Museu d'Història de Barcelona (p67)

➤ Plaça del Rei (p65)

➤ Temple d'August (p66)

➤ Via Sepulcral Romana (p71)

➤ Sinagoga Major (p69)

➤ Domus de Sant Honorat (p68)

For reviews, see p65.

Best Places to Eat

➤ Cafè de l'Acadèmia (p74)

➤ La Vinateria del Call (p74)

➤ Bar Pinotxo (p74)

➤ Belmonte (p74)

➤ El Quim (p74)

➤ Levante (p75)

For reviews, see p72.

Best Places to Drink

➤ L'Ascensor (p76)

➤ Bar Boadas (p77)

➤ Polaroid (p76)

For reviews, see p76.

TOP EXPERIENCE
STROLL DOWN FAMOUS LA RAMBLA

Barcelona's most famous street is both a tourist magnet (beware the pickpockets and con artists) and a window into Catalan culture. Flanked by plane trees, the middle of La Rambla is a broad pedestrian boulevard, always crowded with a wide cross-section of society. Though the busy tourist-centric scene won't appeal to everyone, a stroll here is pure sensory overload: churches, theatres and intriguing architecture mingle with souvenir hawkers and pavement artists.

DON'T MISS

➡ Església de Betlem
➡ Mercat de la Boqueria
➡ Mosaïc de Miró
➡ Flower market
➡ Gran Teatre del Liceu

PRACTICALITIES

➡ Map p292, C5
➡ ⓂCatalunya, Liceu, Drassanes

History

La Rambla takes its name from a seasonal stream (*ramal* in Arabic) that once ran here. From the early Middle Ages, it was better known as the Cagalell (Stream of Shit) and lay outside the city walls until the 14th century. Monastic buildings were then built (many were later destroyed) and, subsequently, mansions of the well-to-do from the 16th to the early 19th centuries. Unofficially, La Rambla is divided into five sections, which explains why many know it as Las Ramblas (Les Rambles in Catalan).

Horrific terrorist attacks in 2017, which killed 14 people, did little to diminish La Rambla's popularity with visitors or with the many hawkers, performers and living statues.

La Rambla de Canaletes

The initial stretch south from Plaça de Catalunya is named after the **Font de Canaletes** (Map p292; La Rambla; ⓂCatalunya), an inconspicuous turn-of-the-20th-century drinking fountain and lamppost, the water of which supposedly emerges from what were once known as the springs of Canaletes. Delirious football fans gather here to celebrate whenever the main home side, FC Barcelona, wins a cup or the league championship.

La Rambla dels Estudis

Running south from Carrer de la Canuda to Carrer de la Portaferrissa, La Rambla dels Estudis is named for the 15th-century university that once stood here. It was formerly home to a twittering bird market, which closed in 2010 after 150 years in operation.

Església de Betlem

Where La Rambla meets Carrer del Carme, this **church** (Map p292; ☏93 318 38 23; www.mdbetlem.net; Carrer d'en Xuclà 2; ◷8.30am-1.30pm & 6-9pm; ⓂLiceu) was constructed in baroque style for the Jesuits in the late 17th and early 18th centuries to replace a 15th-century church destroyed by fire in 1671. The church was once considered the most splendid of Barcelona's few baroque offerings, but anarchists torched it in 1936.

La Rambla de Sant Josep

From Carrer de la Portaferrissa to Plaça de la Boqueria, what is officially called La Rambla de Sant Josep (named after a now nonexistent monastery) is lined with flower stalls, which give it the popular alternative name La Rambla de les Flors. It's flanked on the west side by the buzzing Mercat de la Boqueria (p64), one of Europe's best-stocked produce markets.

Mosaïc de Miró

At Plaça de la Boqueria, where four side streets meet just north of Liceu metro station, you can walk all over a colourful 1976 pavement **mosaic** (Map p292; Plaça de la Boqueria; ⓂLiceu), with one tile signed by the artist, Miró. The mosaic's bold colours and vivid swirling forms are instantly recognisable to Miró fans, though plenty of visitors stroll right over it without realising. Miró chose this site as it's near the house where he was born on the Passatge del Crèdit.

Right next to the Mosaïc de Miró, a 12m-long engraved **memorial** commemorates the 14 victims of the 2017 terrorist van attack on La Rambla, with an anti-violence message inscribed in multiple languages.

Palau de la Virreina

A rare example of post-baroque architecture in Barcelona, the **Palau de la Virreina** (Map p292; ☎93 316 10 00; https://ajuntament.barcelona.cat; La Rambla 99; ⊙11am-8pm Tue-Sun; Ⓜ Liceu) FREE is a grand 18th-century rococo mansion (with some neoclassical elements) that now hosts rotating photography exhibitions.

Casa de Bruno Cuadros

Remodelled by Josep Vilaseca in 1883, the former Casa dels Paraigües (House of the Umbrellas) shop prominently advertised its wares with wall-mounted cast-iron parasols, Egyptian imagery and an ornate Chinese dragon adorning its exterior. It now houses a bank.

La Rambla dels Caputxins

La Rambla dels Caputxins, named after a former monastery, runs from Plaça de la Boqueria to Carrer dels Escudellers. The latter street is named for the potters' guild, founded in the 13th century, the members of which lived and worked here. On the western side of La Rambla is the Gran Teatre del Liceu (p79); to the southeast is the palm-shaded Plaça Reial (p66). Below this point La Rambla gets seedier, with the occasional strip club and peep show.

La Rambla de Santa Mònica

The final stretch of La Rambla widens out to approach the Mirador de Colom (p121) overlooking Port Vell. La Rambla here is named after the Convent de Santa Mònica, which once stood on the western flank of the street and has since been converted into the **Centre d'Art Santa Mònica** (Map p292; ☎93 316 28 10; http://artssantamonica.gencat.cat; La Rambla 7; ⊙11am-9pm Tue-Sat, to 7pm Sun Apr-Oct, 10am-8pm Tue-Sat, to 7pm Sun Nov-Mar; Ⓜ Drassanes) FREE, which hosts modern multimedia installations.

CIVIL WAR

Many writers and journalists headed to Barcelona during the Spanish Civil War, including British author George Orwell, who vividly described La Rambla gripped by revolutionary fervour in the early days of the war in his book *Homage to Catalonia*. Orwell spent three days holed up in the 1894 **Teatre Poliorama** (Map p292; ☎93 317 75 99; www.teatrepoliorama.com; La Rambla 115; Ⓜ Catalunya, Liceu) during street battles.

ESCAPING THE CROWDS

As one of the most touristed spots in Barcelona, there's no denying that La Rambla can feel a bit like a packed-out circus. Swing by first thing, around 8am, to enjoy this historic leafy boulevard with far fewer crowds. Alternatively, you could seek out some of the city's quieter *rambles* instead, such as Rambla del Raval (p88) or Rambla del Poblenou (p124).

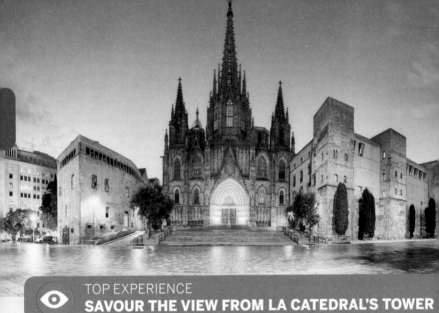

SAVOUR THE VIEW FROM LA CATEDRAL'S TOWER

Barcelona's central place of worship presents a magnificent image. The richly decorated main facade, dotted with gargoyles and the kinds of stone intricacies you would expect of northern European Gothic, sets it quite apart from other Barcelona churches. The facade was actually added from 1887 to 1890. The rest of the building dates to between 1298 and 1460.

The Interior

The interior is a broad, soaring space divided into a central nave and two aisles by lines of elegant, slim pillars. The cathedral was one of the few churches in Barcelona spared by the anarchists in the civil war, so its ornamentation, never overly lavish, is intact.

Coro

In the middle of the central nave is the exquisitely sculpted late-14th-century timber *coro* (choir stalls; €3; closed during worshipping hours). The coats of arms on the stalls belong to members of the Barcelona chapter of the Order of the Golden Fleece. Emperor Carlos V presided over the order's meeting here in 1519.

Cripta

A broad staircase before the main altar leads down to the crypt, which contains the 14th-century tomb of Santa Eulàlia, one of Barcelona's two patron saints and more affectionately known as Laia. The reliefs on the alabaster sarcophagus, executed by Pisan artisans, recount some of her tortures and, along the top strip, the removal of her body to its present resting place.

DON'T MISS

➡ The *claustre* and its 13 geese
➡ Views from the roof
➡ The crypt
➡ The *coro*
➡ The main facade

PRACTICALITIES

➡ Map p292, D3
➡ ☎ 93 342 82 62
➡ www.catedralbcn.org
➡ Plaça de la Seu
➡ €7, roof or choir €3, chapter house €2
➡ ⏱ worship 8.30am-12.30pm & 5.45-7.30pm Mon-Fri, 8.30am-12.30pm & 5.15-8pm Sat, 8.30am-1.45pm & 5.15-8pm Sun, tourist visits 12.30-7.45pm Mon-Fri, 12.30-5.30pm Sat, 2-5.30pm Sun
➡ Ⓜ Jaume I

Facades, Towers & Roof

Apart from the cathedral's main facade, its others are sparse in decoration, and the octagonal, flat-roofed towers are a clear reminder that, even here, Catalan Gothic architectural principles prevailed.

For a bird's-eye view (mind the poop) of medieval Barcelona, visit the roof and tower by taking the lift (€3) from the Capella dels Sant Innocents near the northeast transept.

Claustre

From the southwest transept, exit by the partly Romanesque door (one of the few remnants of the present cathedral's 11th-century predecessor). Next to the door are the coffins of Count Ramon Berenguer I and his wife Almodis, founders of the original Romanesque church. You'll then enter the leafy *claustre* (cloister), with its tinkling fountains and flock of 13 geese. The geese supposedly represent the age of Santa Eulàlia at the time of her martyrdom and have, generation after generation, been squawking here since medieval days. One of the cloister chapels commemorates 930 priests, monks and nuns martyred during the civil war.

Accessed from the northwest corner of the cloister, the **Capella de Santa Llúcia** is another of the few reminders of Romanesque Barcelona (although the interior is largely Gothic). It was originally the chapel for the adjacent Bishop's Palace.

Casa de l'Ardiaca

Outside, opposite the Capella de Santa Llúcia, the 16th-century **Casa de l'Ardiaca** (Arxiu Històric; Map p292; ☑93 256 22 55; https://ajuntament.barcelona.cat; Carrer de Santa Llúcia 1; ⊗9am-7.30 Mon-Fri, 10am-7.30pm Sat; Ⓜ Jaume I) FREE has housed the city's archives since the 1920s. The supremely serene courtyard is adorned with tilework by ceramicist Josep Roig, and was renovated by Lluís Domènech i Montaner in 1902. Domènech i Montaner also designed the distinctive postal slot, depicting swallows and a tortoise (representing swift truth and slow justice).

Palau Episcopal

Across Carrer del Bisbe from the cathedral's cloister exit is the 17th-century **Palau Episcopal** (Palau del Bisbat; Map p292; Carrer del Bisbe; Ⓜ Jaume I). Virtually nothing remains of the original 13th-century structure. The Roman city's northwest gate stood here and you can see the lower segments of the Roman towers that stood on either side of the gate at the base of the Palau Episcopal and Casa de l'Ardiaca.

LA RAMBLA & BARRI GÒTIC LA CATEDRAL

SANT CRIST DE LEPANT

In the first chapel (for prayer only) to the right of the main northwest entrance, the main crucifixion figure above the altar is Sant Crist de Lepant; it is said Don Juan's flagship bore it into battle at Lepanto and that the figure acquired its odd stance by dodging an incoming cannonball. Left from the main entrance is a 1433 marble baptismal font where, according to one story, six West Indies islanders brought to Europe by Columbus after his first voyage to the Americas were bathed in holy water.

VISITING LA CATEDRAL

Although technically it's free to go into La Catedral to pray, in practice if you go any time during tourist visiting hours, you'll need to pay. Otherwise, you can enter for free before 12.30pm (2pm on Sunday), though you'll have to pay to visit the choir stalls (€3), chapter house (€2) and/or roof (€3).

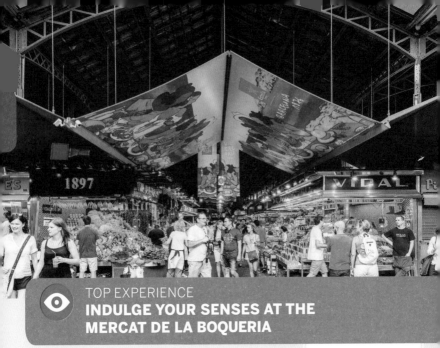

1897

TOP EXPERIENCE
INDULGE YOUR SENSES AT THE MERCAT DE LA BOQUERIA

Barcelona's most central fresh-produce market is one of Europe's greatest sound, smell and colour sensations. It's housed in an impressive Modernista-influenced building constructed from 1840 to 1914 on the site of the former Sant Josep monastery. La Boqueria may have taken a tourist-oriented turn in recent years, but towards the back you'll touch upon its soul: bountiful fruit, vegetables, sea critters, cheeses, meats...

There is believed to have been a market on this spot since 1217, and as much as La Boqueria has become a modern-day attraction, some *barcelonins* do still try to shop here (usually early on). What is now known as La Boqueria didn't exist until the 19th century. The iron Modernista gate was added in 1914.

Many of Barcelona's top restaurateurs also come here for their produce, though nowadays it's no easy task getting through the crowds to that slippery slab of sole or tempting piece of Asturian goat's cheese. The trick is to arrive early.

Whether you eat here or self-cater, don't miss the chance to try some of Catalonia's gastronomical specialities, such as *bacallà salat* (dried salted cod), *calçots* (a cross between a leek and an onion), *cargols* (snails), *peus de porc* (pig's trotters) or *percebes* (goose barnacles).

La Boqueria is dotted with a handful of vibrant, unassuming places to eat, many with charismatic owners at the helm. Try the wonderful *truites* (tortillas) at El Quim (p74) or anything at Bar Pinotxo (p74).

DON'T MISS

➡ Tucking in at the market bars

➡ Meeting local personalities like Quim (El Quim), Juanito (Bar Pinotxo) and Joan (La Llar del Pernil)

➡ The sparkling fish market

PRACTICALITIES

➡ Map p292, B4

➡ ☎93 318 20 17

➡ www.boqueria. barcelona

➡ La Rambla 91

➡ ⏰8am-8.30pm Mon-Sat

➡ Ⓜ Liceu

⊙ SIGHTS

LA RAMBLA   STREET
See p60.

LA CATEDRAL   CATHEDRAL
See p62.

MERCAT DE LA BOQUERIA   MARKET
See p64.

GRAN TEATRE DEL LICEU   ARCHITECTURE
Map p292 (☑93 485 99 00; www.liceubarcelona.cat; La Rambla 51-59; 45min tour adult/child €9/free; MLiceu) If you can't catch a night at the opera (p79), you can still take in the awe-inspiring architectural riches of one of Europe's greatest opera houses. Opened in 1847, the Liceu launched Catalan stars such as Josep (José) Carreras and Montserrat Caballé, and seats up to 2300 people in its grand auditorium. Standard 45-minute tours of classic spaces (the foyer, Saló dels Miralls and auditorium) run in Catalan, Spanish and English; check updated schedules online.

Fire virtually destroyed the Liceu in 1994, but technicians carefully reconstructed the 19th-century auditorium, with the latest in theatre technology and ceiling murals by Catalan artist Perejaume, by 1999.

The 45-minute tour leads through the grand foyer, with its thick pillars and sumptuous chandeliers, and up the marble staircase to the Saló dels Miralls (Hall of Mirrors). These both survived the fire. The latter was traditionally where theatre-goers mingled during intermission. With mirrors, ceiling frescoes, fluted columns and high-and-mighty phrases in praise of the arts, it exudes a typically neobaroque richness worthy of its 19th-century patrons. You are then taken up to the 4th-floor stalls to admire the restored theatre itself.

More in-depth tours include visits to the Cercle del Liceu (€16, one hour), a Modernista art collection with works by Ramon Casas, or through the inner workings of the stage and backstage work areas (€24, 80 minutes).

PLAÇA DEL REI   SQUARE
Map p292 (MJaume I) The courtyard of the Gothic former Palau Reial Major, this picturesque, almost entirely walled-in square is where the Reyes Católicos (Catholic Monarchs) are thought to have received Columbus following his first New World voyage.

Today, part of the palace houses a superb history museum (p67), with significant Roman ruins. The 14th-century Capella Reial de Santa Àgata (p68) and 16th-century Palau del Lloctinent (p69) overlook the square, as does the 1555 (off-limits) **Mirador del Rei Martí** lookout tower, now part of the Arxiu de la Corona d'Aragón.

PALAU DE LA GENERALITAT   HISTORIC BUILDING
Map p292 (http://presidencia.gencat.cat; Plaça de Sant Jaume; ⊘2nd & 4th weekends of month Sep-Jul; MJaume I) FREE The 15th-century Palau de la Generalitat opens through a monumental late-Renaissance facade with neoclassical leanings, designed by Pere Blai, but the masterful original Gothic entrance, the work of Marc Safont, sits on Carrer del Bisbe. The most impressive of its ceremonial halls is the muralled Renaissance Saló de Sant Jordi, named after Catalonia's patron saint. The Palau is visitable only on limited occasions (book online) – one-hour guided tours on the second and fourth weekends of the month, plus open-door days.

Normally you will enter at the north end from Carrer de Sant Sever. The first rooms you pass through are characterised by low vaulted ceilings. From here you head upstairs to the raised courtyard known as the Pati dels Tarongers, a modest Gothic orangery. The 16th-century Sala Daurada i de Sessions, one of the rooms leading off the patio, is a splendid meeting hall illuminated by huge chandeliers. The Renaissance Saló de Sant Jordi is still more imposing; its murals were added last century, and many an occasion of pomp and circumstance takes place here. Finally, you descend the staircase of the Pati Gòtic to leave by what was originally the building's main entrance.

The four Troyan granite pillars framing the modern-day entrance date back 1900 years to Roman times and were brought from Tarragona in the 16th century.

AJUNTAMENT   ARCHITECTURE
Map p292 (Casa de la Ciutat; ☑93 402 70 00; www.bcn.cat; Plaça de Sant Jaume; ⊘10am-2pm Sun; MJaume I) FREE Barcelona's town hall has been the seat of power for centuries. The Consell de Cent (the city's ruling council) first sat here in the 14th century, but the building has undergone many changes; only the original (disused) entrance on Carrer de la Ciutat retains its Gothic ornament.

The main 19th-century neoclassical facade is a charmless riposte to the Palau de la Generalitat (p65) opposite, though the interior is worth exploring. One-hour guided Sunday tours run in Catalan, Spanish and English (no bookings).

Inside, the Saló de Cent is the hall in which the town council once held its plenary sessions; the broad vaulting is pure Catalan Gothic and the *artesonado* (wooden ceiling of interlaced beams) demonstrates fine work. In fact, much of what you see is comparatively recent. The building was badly damaged in a bombardment in 1842 and has been repaired and tampered with repeatedly. The wooden neo-Gothic seating was added at the beginning of the 20th century, as was the grand alabaster *retaule* (altarpiece) at the back. To the right you enter the small Saló de la Reina Regente, built in 1860, where the Ajuntament now sits. To the left of the Saló de Cent is the Saló de les Croniques; the murals here recount Catalan exploits in Greece and the Near East in Catalonia's empire-building days.

PLAÇA REIAL   SQUARE

Map p292 (MLiceu) One of the most photogenic squares in Barcelona, and certainly its liveliest. Numerous restaurants, bars and nightspots lie beneath the arcades of 19th-century neoclassical buildings, with a buzz of activity at all hours. The lamp posts by the central fountain are Antoni Gaudí's first known works in the city.

ROMAN WALLS

From Plaça del Rei it's worth a detour to see the two best surviving stretches of Barcelona's **Roman walls** (Map p292; MJaume I), which once boasted 78 towers (as much a matter of prestige as of defence). One section is on the southern side of Plaça de Ramon Berenguer el Gran (p72), with the 14th-century Capella Reial de Santa Àgata (p68) atop. Another piece of wall sits towards the northern end of Carrer del Sots-Tinent Navarro, while more can be seen at the Porta de Mar archaeological site (p69).

The Romans built and reinforced these walls in the 3rd and 4th centuries CE, after the first attacks by Germanic tribes from the north.

The square was created on the site of a convent, one of several destroyed along La Rambla (the street was teeming with religious institutions) in the wake of the 19th-century Spain-wide disentailment laws that stripped the Church of much of its property.

BASÍLICA DE SANTA MARIA DEL PI   CHURCH

Map p292 (☑93 318 47 43; www.basilicadelpi.cat; Plaça del Pi; adult/concession/child under 8yr €4.50/3.50/free; ◷10am-6pm; MLiceu) Begun in 1320, on the site of a 10th-century Romanesque church, this striking 14th-century basilica is a classic of Catalan Gothic, with an imposing facade, a wide interior and a single nave. The simple decor in the main sanctuary contrasts with the gilded chapels and exquisite stained-glass windows that bathe the interior in ethereal light. The beautiful rose window – a brilliant 20th-century replica of the original – above the entrance is one of the world's largest.

According to legend, a 10th-century fisher discovered an image of the Virgin Mary in a *pi* (pine tree) that he was intent on cutting down to build a boat; struck by the vision, he instead built a little chapel, later to be succeeded by this Gothic church. A pine still grows in the square outside. The fourth chapel on the left is dedicated to the Mare de Déu de Montserrat (p223), while the sixth chapel on the left honours Sant Josep Oriol, who was parish priest from 1687 to 1702 (and was canonised in 1909).

Guided tours (€9), including the bell towers, run from Monday to Friday at noon, 1pm, 3pm, 4pm and 5pm and on Saturdays and Sundays at noon, 3.30pm, 4.30pm and 5.30pm. Occasional concerts are staged in the basilica and a couple of resident cats roam the garden.

TEMPLE D'AUGUST   RUINS

Map p292 (☑93 256 21 22; www.muhba.cat; Carrer del Paradís 10; ◷10am-2pm Mon, to 7pm Tue-Sat, to 8pm Sun; MJaume I) FREE Opposite the southeast end of La Catedral, narrow Carrer del Paradís leads towards Plaça de Sant Jaume. Inside No 10, an intriguing building with Gothic and baroque touches, are four columns and the architrave of Barcelona's main Roman temple, dedicated to Caesar Augustus and built to worship his imperial highness in the 1st century.

You are now standing on the highest point of Roman Barcino, Mont Tàber (a grand height of 16.9m).

TOP EXPERIENCE
TRAVEL BACK IN TIME AT MUSEU D'HISTÒRIA DE BARCELONA

One of Barcelona's most fascinating museums travels back to the very foundations of Roman Barcino. You'll stroll over the ruins of the old streets that flourished here following the town's founding by Emperor Augustus around 10 BCE. Equally impressive is the building itself, once part of the Palau Reial Major (Grand Royal Palace).

Enter through the 16th-century **Casa Padellàs**, just south of Plaça del Rei. Below ground lies a remarkable walk through 4 sq km of **excavated Roman and Visigothic Barcelona**. You'll see public laundries, dyeing shops, fish-preserve stores, a 6th-century public cold-water bath and a factory for making *garum* (a Roman paste of fish intestines, eggs and blood).

Next come the remnants of a 6th- to 7th-century church and necropolis, followed by winemaking stores. Ramparts then wind upward, past the remains of the gated patio of a Roman house and the medieval Palau Episcopal (Bishops' Palace). Don't miss the 14th-century foundations of Barcelona's Gothic cathedral.

You emerge in the **Saló del Tinell** (built 1359–70). It was here that the Reyes Católicos (Catholic Monarchs) heard Columbus' first reports of the New World. The finale is the Capella Reial de Santa Àgata (p68).

DON'T MISS
➡ Public laundry
➡ Winemaking stores
➡ Saló del Tinell
➡ Capella Reial de Santa Àgata

PRACTICALITIES
➡ Map p292, E3
➡ ☑93 256 21 00
➡ http://ajuntament.barcelona.cat/museu historia
➡ Plaça del Rei
➡ adult/concession/child €7/5/free, 3-8pm Sun & 1st Sun of month free
➡ ◷10am-7pm Tue-Sat, to 8pm Sun
➡ Ⓜ Jaume I

PLAÇA DE SANT JAUME   SQUARE
Map p292 (ⓂLiceu, Jaume I) In the 2000 or so years since the Romans settled here, the area around this often-remodelled square, which started life as the forum, has been the focus of Barcelona's civic life – and it's still the central staging area for Barcelona's traditional festivals. Facing each other across the square are the Palau de la Generalitat (p65), seat of Catalonia's regional government, on the north side and Barcelona's Ajuntament (p65) on the south.

BASILICA DE LA MERCÈ   CHURCH
Map p292 (☑93 315 27 56; www.basilicade lamerce.cat; Plaça de la Mercè 1; ◷9am-8pm; ⓂDrassanes) Raised in the 1760s on the site of its Gothic predecessor, following designs by architect José Mas Dordal, this baroque church is home to Barcelona's most celebrated patron saint. Though it was badly damaged during the civil war, what remains is quite a curiosity. The baroque facade facing the square contrasts with the Renaissance flank along Carrer Ample. Climb the steps behind the 1361 altar for a close-up view of the Virgin Mary statue for whom the church is named.

Guided tours (€8) run in Catalan or Spanish on Saturdays at 11am.

BASÍLICA DELS SANTS MÀRTIRS JUST I PASTOR   CHURCH
Map p292 (☑93 301 74 33; www.basilica santjust.cat; Plaça de Sant Just; ◷11am-2pm & 5-9pm Mon-Sat, 10am-1pm Sun; ⓂJaume I) This slightly neglected single-nave church, with chapels on either side of the buttressing, was built in 1342 in Catalan Gothic style on what is reputedly the site of the oldest parish church in Barcelona. Inside, you can admire some fine stained-glass windows, then climb the bell tower (closed Sunday) for knockout views across central Barcelona. In front of it, in a pretty little square that was used as a film set (a smelly Parisian marketplace) in 2006 for *Perfume: The Story of a Murderer,* is what's claimed to be the city's oldest Gothic fountain.

On the morning of 11 September 1924, Antoni Gaudí was arrested as he attempted to enter the church from this square to attend Mass. In those days of the dictatorship of General Primo de Rivera, it took little to ruffle official feathers, and Gaudí's refusal to speak Spanish to the overbearing Guardia Civil officers who had stopped him earned him the better part of a day in the cells until a friend came to bail him out.

There are guided tours (€10) at 11am, 12.30pm and 4.30pm Monday to Saturday; book online.

PLAÇA DE SANT JOSEP ORIOL SQUARE

Map p292 (Ⓜ Liceu) This small square flanking the majestic Basílica de Santa Maria del Pi (p66) is one of the prettiest in the Barri Gòtic, with its bars and cafes attracting buskers and artists and making it (and the surrounding streets) a lively place to hang out.

PLAÇA DE SANT FELIP NERI SQUARE

Map p292 (Ⓜ Jaume I, Liceu) Graced by leafy acacias, a trickling fountain and a baroque church, this small square still bears signs of the destruction it suffered during a 1938 bombing by the Franco-supporting Italian air force, in which 42 people were killed, most of them children (a school still operates here).

CAPELLA REIAL DE SANTA ÀGATA CHURCH

Map p292 (Plaça del Rei; ⊙10am-7pm Tue-Sat, to 8pm Sun; Ⓜ Jaume I) Accessed within the Museu d'Història de Barcelona (p67), this is the chapel of the old Gothic Palau Reial Major (Grand Royal Palace). Outside, a spindly bell tower rises from the northeast side of Plaça del Rei. Inside, all is bare except for the magnificent *techumbre* (decorated timber ceiling) and the 15th-century altarpiece, considered to be one of Jaume Huguet's finest surviving works.

DOMUS DE SANT HONORAT ARCHAEOLOGICAL SITE

Map p292 (☑93 256 21 22; http://ajuntament. barcelona.cat/museuhistoria; Carrer de la Fruita 2; adult/concession/child €2/1.50/free, 1st Sun of month free; ⊙10am-2pm Sun; Ⓜ Jaume I) These remains of a Roman *domus* (town house) and three small shops, unearthed in the mid-19th-century Casa Morell, lie close

---

TOP EXPERIENCE
ADMIRE THE PRIVATE COLLECTION AT MUSEU FREDERIC MARÈS

The wealthy Catalan sculptor, traveller and obsessive collector Frederic Marès i Deulovol (1893–1991) amassed one of the wildest collections of historical curios. Today, his astonishing displays of religious art and antiques (which he donated to the city) await inside this vast medieval complex, once part of the royal palace of the counts of Barcelona. A rather worn coat of arms on the wall indicates that the building was also, for a while, the seat of the Spanish Inquisition in Barcelona.

Frederic Marès' passion was medieval Spanish sculpture, huge quantities of which are displayed in the basement and on the ground and 1st floors. Among the most eye-catching pieces is a reconstructed Romanesque doorway with four arches, taken from a 13th-century country church in the Aragonese province of Huesca (in the basement).

The top two floors hold a mind-boggling array of knick-knacks, including medieval weaponry, ladies' fans and 19th-century daguerreotypes. Marès' wood-beamed former study and library is now crammed with sculptures, including some of his own. The shady courtyard is graced by the pleasant Cafè de l'Estiu (April to September).

DON'T MISS

➡ Aragonese Romanesque doorway
➡ Sculptures
➡ Marès' study
➡ Displays on the top two floors

PRACTICALITIES

➡ Map p292, D3
➡ ☑93 256 35 00
➡ www.museumares. bcn.cat
➡ Plaça de Sant Iu 5
➡ adult/concession/ child €4.20/2.40/free, 3-8pm Sun & 1st Sun of month free
➡ ⊙10am-7pm Tue-Sat, 11am-8pm Sun
➡ Ⓜ Jaume I

to the Roman forum, and the house owners were clearly affluent. In addition to providing an idea of daily Roman life, the site also contains six medieval grain silos installed during the period when this was the Jewish quarter, El Call (p73).

PALAU DEL LLOCTINENT ARCHITECTURE

Map p292 (Carrer dels Comtes; ⊙10am-7pm; Ⓜ Jaume I) **FREE** Flanking the Plaça del Rei, this 1550s palace was built as the residence of the Spanish *lloctinent* (viceroy) of Catalonia and later converted into a convent. From 1853 it housed the Arxiu de la Corona d'Aragón, with documents detailing the history of the Crown of Aragón and Catalonia, spanning the 12th to 20th centuries. The building opens through a peaceful courtyard, while an extraordinary 16th-century pine *enteixinat* (ceiling of interlaced beams with decorative insertions; *artesonado* in Spanish), sculpted like the upturned hull of a boat, sits above the main staircase.

Just off the stairs is the bronze 1975 Porta de Sant Jordi by Josep Maria Subirachs, depicting Sant Jordi and the dragon. Temporary exhibitions, usually related in some way to the archives, are often held here.

EL CALL HISTORIC SITE

Map p292 (✆93 256 21 22; http://ajuntament. barcelona.cat/museuhistoria; Placeta de Manuel Ribé; adult/concession/child €2/1.50/free, 3-7pm Sun & 1st Sun of month free; ⊙11am-2pm Wed, to 7pm Sat & Sun; Ⓜ Jaume I) Once a 14th-century house of the Jewish weaver Jucef Bonhiac, this small visitor centre is dedicated to the history of Barcelona's Jewish quarter, El Call (p73). Glass sections on the ground floor allow you to inspect Mr Bonhiac's former wells and storage space. The house, also known as the Casa de l'Alquimista (Alchemist's House), hosts a modest display of Jewish artefacts, including ceramics excavated around El Call, along with explanations and maps of the one-time Jewish quarter.

SINAGOGA MAJOR SYNAGOGUE

Map p292 (✆93 317 07 90; www.sinagogamayor. com; Carrer de Marlet 5; adult/child €3.50/free; ⊙10.30am-2.30pm & 3.45-6.30pm Mon-Fri, to 3pm Sun approx Nov-Mar, 10.30am-6.30pm Mon-Fri, to 3pm Sun approx Apr-Oct; Ⓜ Liceu) At the heart of the ancient Jewish Call (p73) lie the remains of what may well be the city's main medieval synagogue (though some historians cast doubt on the claim). Fragments

---

ⓘ MANIC MONDAYS

Some of central Barcelona's most popular sights shut their doors on Monday, but there are a growing number of exceptions, including:

➡ La Catedral (p62)
➡ Museu Picasso (p99)
➡ Basílica de Santa Maria del Mar (p101)
➡ Gran Teatre del Liceu (p65)
➡ Temple d'August (p66)
➡ Sinagoga Major

---

of medieval and Roman-era walls sit in the small vaulted space that you enter from the street, accompanied by tanners' wells installed in the 15th century. The second chamber has been spruced up for use as a synagogue.

WORLD BEGINS WITH EVERY KISS MURAL PUBLIC ART

Map p292 (Plaça d'Isidre Nonell; Ⓜ Jaume I, Catalunya) Created by Barcelona photographer Joan Fontcuberta for the 300th Diada Nacional de Catalunya (2014), this seductive mural depicts a kiss between two people. Up close, however, it's composed of thousands of tiny freedom-themed photos, which were sent in by readers of *El Periódico* newspaper and transferred on to tiny mosaics. Hidden down an alley opposite the cathedral, it's a popular photo spot.

PORTA DE MAR ARCHAEOLOGICAL SITE

Map p292 (✆93 256 21 22; http://ajuntament. barcelona.cat/museuhistoria; Carrer de Regomir 7-9; ⊙10am-1pm Tue & Thu, 5-8pm Wed, 10.30am-1.30pm Sat, closed Aug; Ⓜ Jaume I) **FREE** On the edge of the old Roman city, on the spot where the entry gate from the port once stood, further ruins of the 4th-century Roman wall (p66) have been uncovered next to the remains of some 1st-century thermal baths, all attached to the neo-Gothic Centre Cívic Pati Llimona. Next door is the 1503 Capella de Sant Cristòfol, patron of travellers and, since 1907, protector of automobiles!

COL·LEGI D'ARQUITECTES PUBLIC ART

Map p292 (https://arquitectes.cat; Plaça Nova; Ⓟ; Ⓜ Jaume I) Across from La Catedral your eye may be caught by what appear to be childlike

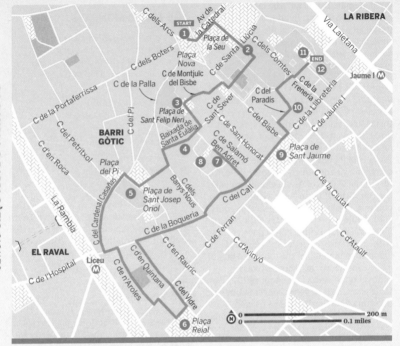

🏃 Neighbourhood Walk
Hidden Historical Treasures of the Barri Gòtic

START COL·LEGI D'ARQUITECTES
END PLAÇA DEL REI
LENGTH 1.5KM; TWO HOURS

Start with the three Picasso friezes on the ❶ **Col·legi d'Arquitectes** (p69) facing the cathedral square. After noting his signature style, wander through ❷ **La Catedral** (p62); don't miss the cloister with its flock of 13 geese. Leave the cathedral from the cloister and turn right, now within the former gates of the ancient fortified city, then turn left down narrow Carrer de Montjuïc del Bisbe into ❸ **Plaça de Sant Felip Neri** (p68), damaged by pro-Francoist bombers in 1938; a plaque commemorates the victims (mostly children).

Head south out of the square on to Baixada de Santa Eulàlia and turn right. On this slender lane, you'll spot a small ❹ **statue of Santa Eulàlia**, one of Barcelona's patron saints who suffered various tortures during her martyrdom. Make your way west to the looming 14th-century ❺ **Basílica de Santa Maria del Pi** (p66). Follow the curv-

ing road and zigzag down to ❻ **Plaça Reial** (p66), one of Barcelona's prettiest (and busiest) squares. Flanking the fountain are lamp posts designed by Antoni Gaudí.

Stroll north to Carrer de la Boqueria and turn left on Carrer de Salomó Ben Adret. This leads into El Call, once the heart of Barcelona's medieval Jewish quarter, until the bloody pogrom of 1391. The ❼ **Sinagoga Major** (p69), one of Europe's oldest, was discovered in 1996. Just north lie the remains of a 14th-century Jewish ❽ **weaver's house** (p69). Head across ❾ **Plaça de Sant Jaume** (p67) and turn left on Carrer del Paradís. You'll soon pass the unassuming entrance to the ❿ **Temple d'August** (p66): four Roman columns hidden in a small courtyard.

Your final stop is grand ⓫ **Plaça del Rei** (p65), where the Reyes Católicos (Catholic Monarchs) received Columbus following his first voyage to the Americas. The former palace today houses the superb ⓬ **Museu d'Història** (p67), with significant Roman ruins underground.

scribblings on the facade of the 1931 Col·legi de Arquitectes. It is, in fact, a giant public contribution by Picasso from 1962. The artwork, which represents Mediterranean festivals including Catalonia's *castellers* (human-castle builders), was much ridiculed by the local press when it was unveiled.

PONT DEL BISBE
BRIDGE

Map p292 (Carrer del Bisbe; ⓂJaume I) One of Barcelona's most-photographed pieces of architecture, this Gothic-style marble bridge links the Palau de la Generalitat (p65) with the Casa dels Canonges. Though appearing centuries old, it was in fact created in the 1920s by Modernista architect Joan Rubió i Bellver (who added the underside skull-and-crossbones when his plans for other buildings in the Barri Gòtic were turned down).

VIA SEPULCRAL
ROMANA
ARCHAEOLOGICAL SITE

Map p292 (☎93 256 21 22; www.muhba.cat; Plaça de la Vila de Madrid; adult/concession/child €2/1.50/free; ◷11am-2pm Tue, to 7pm Sun; ⓂCatalunya) A block east of the top end of La Rambla is a sunken garden where a series of Roman tombs from the 1st to 3rd centuries CE were uncovered in the 1940s, after a 1588 Carmelite convent was demolished. A small interpretation centre in Spanish and Catalan explores burial and funerary rites and customs; pieces of pottery (including a burial amphora with the skeleton of a three-year-old Roman child) accompany the display.

The burial ground stretches along either side of the road that once led northwest out of Barcelona's Roman predecessor, Barcino. As the burial ground sits in the open air, you can see the tombs at any time, even if it's closed.

GAUDÍ EXHIBITION
CENTER/MUSEU DIOCESÀ
MUSEUM

Map p292 (Casa de la Pia Almoina; ☎93 268 75 82; Plaça de la Seu 7; adult/concession/child under 8yr €15/12/free; ◷10am-8pm Apr-Sep, to 7pm Mar & Oct, to 6pm Nov-Feb; ⓂJaume I) Next to La Catedral, the Diocesan Museum hosts insightful exhibits on Gaudí including fascinating documentaries on his life and philosophy and the inspiration behind his whimsical creations. The building itself contains fragments of Barcelona's Roman wall, as well as elements from its days as

SQUARING UP TO THE PAST

The construction of most of the buildings at the port end of the Via Laietana was funded by 19th-century Cantabrian entrepreneur and philanthropist Antonio López y López, and a square here now bears his name. In recent years, however, it has emerged that some of his money was made from the slave trade. As a result, a statue of him was removed from the square in 2018 and there are plans under way to rename the square, very possibly as Plaça de Idrissa Diallo, for a 21-year-old Guinean immigrant who died in a local detention centre in 2012. In the meantime, activists have covered the street sign with a plaque in Diallo's honour.

an 11th-century almshouse and its later use as an ecclesiastical residence in the 15th century. Upstairs is a 1:25 model of what the completed Colònia Güell (p199) church would have looked like.

PALAU CENTELLES
ARCHITECTURE

Map p292 (cnr Baixada de Sant Miquel & Carrer dels Gegants; ⓂJaume I) A rare late 15th-century gem, the Palau Centelles is set around a fine Gothic-Renaissance courtyard adorned with later flourishes from the 18th and 19th centuries (you can wander in if the gates are open). Built on the site of a 13th-century predecessor, it now houses government offices.

ESGLÉSIA DE SANTA ANNA
CHURCH

Map p292 (Placeta de Ramon Amadeu; €2; ◷mass noon Mon-Fri, 7.30pm Sat & Sun; ⓂCatalunya) Part of a former monastery active from 1145 to the late 15th century, this Romanesque-origin church hidden away in plain sight stands out for its 15th-century Gothic cloister, with its rippling archways.

FONT DE SANTA ANNA
FOUNTAIN

Map p292 (Carrer de la Cucurulla; ⓂCatalunya, Jaume I) There's been a fountain on this spot since 1356, making Santa Anna the oldest in the city. The colourful ceramics were added in 1918 by Catalan artist Josep Aragay.

EDIFICI DE CORREUS ARCHITECTURE

Map p292 (www.correos.es; Plaça d'Antonio López; ⊙8.30am-9.30pm Mon-Fri, to 2.30pm Sat; Ⓜ Jaume I, Barceloneta) Designed by architects Josep Goday and Jaume Torres in the 1920s, Barcelona's main post-office building is filled with Noucentista paintings and crowned by a magnificent glass-and-steel dome.

PLAÇA DE RAMON BERENGUER EL GRAN SQUARE

Map p292 Watched over by some of the most substantial remains of Barcelona's Roman walls (p66), this square is dominated by a statue of count-king Ramon de Berenguer Gran, sculpted by Josep Llimona in 1880.

HASH, MARIHUANA & HEMP MUSEUM MUSEUM

Map p292 (☎93 319 75 39; www.hashmuseum. com; Carrer Ample 35; adult/child under 13yr €9/free; ⊙10am-10pm Mon-Sat, 11am-8pm Sun; Ⓜ Jaume I) One of the world's largest museums dedicated to all things cannabis-related opened to much fanfare in 2012. Set in the beautifully restored 16th-century Palau Mornau, exhibitions delve into the role the plant has played over the years, with 19th-century medicinal cannabis bottles, pulp film posters and consumer products made from hemp among the displays.

✖ EATING

First things first: skip La Rambla. Instead, venture off into the Barri Gòtic and your belly (and wallet) will be eternally grateful. Head for the northern half of the *barri* (neighbourhood) on the narrow streets around Carrer de les Magdalenes and between Plaça de Sant Jaume and the waterfront for old-time tapas bars as well as innovative newcomers. The busy Mercat de la Boqueria (p64) is also packed with food spots, and there are some great restaurants around Placeta de Manuel Ribé.

FEDERAL CAFE €

Map p292 (☎93 280 81 71; www.federalcafe.es; Passatge de la Pau 11; mains €7-10; ⊙9am-11pm Mon-Sat, to 5pm Sun; ☎; Ⓜ Drassanes) Brick-walled industrial-chic design, a sea of open MacBooks, stacks of design mags – this welcoming, queue-out-the-door branch of the Sant Antoni Federal (p197) mothership delivers outrageously popular Australian-inspired brunches in a calming glassed-in space overlooking a quiet square. It's known for creative dishes such as baked eggs with spinach and gruyère, avocado toast with carrot hummus and French toast with berry compote.

LA PLATA TAPAS €

Map p292 (☎93 315 10 09; www.barlaplata.com; Carrer de la Mercè 28; tapas €2.50-5; ⊙10am-3.15pm & 6.15-11pm Mon-Sat; Ⓜ Jaume I) Tucked away in a narrow lane near the waterfront, tile-walled La Plata is a humble, well-loved bodega that has served just four simple, perfect plates since launching back in 1945: *pescadito frito* (fried fish), *butifarra* (sausage), anchovies and tomato salad. Throw in the drinkable, affordable wines and vermouth, and you have the makings of a fine, popular tapas spot.

MILK INTERNATIONAL €

Map p292 (☎93 268 09 22; www.milkbarcelona. com; Carrer d'en Gignàs 21; mains €9-13; ⊙9am-2am Thu-Mon, to 2.30am Fri & Sat; ☎; Ⓜ Jaume I) Also loved for its crafted cocktails, Irish-run Milk rescues Barcelona night owls with morning-after brunches (until 4.30pm!). Arrive early or join the wait list for lemon-dusted avocado toast, banana pancakes, egg-white omelettes stuffed with *piquillo* peppers and other deliciously rich hangover-beating dishes. It's all served in a cosy lounge with ornate wallpaper, framed prints and cushioned seating.

The same team runs brunchy Marmalade (p94) in El Raval and Gigi von Tapas (p157) over in L'Eixample.

LA PACHUCA MEXICAN €

Map p292 (www.facebook.com/LaPachucaBcn; Carrer d'en Carabassa 19; mains €7-9; ⊙1.30pm-2am Tue-Sun; Ⓜ Jaume I, Barceloneta) This sister *taquería* to El Raval's forever-packed El Pachuco (p89) launched in 2019 and has been an instant hit. It's Mexican-owned and delivers its signature margaritas, mezcals and home-cooked, market-driven tacos and quesadillas with authentically delicious flair. The zingy guacamole makes a perfect sharing starter, then try the chicken-

EL CALL

One of the most atmospheric and interesting parts of the Ciutat Vella (Old City) to wander around is El Call (pronounced 'kye'), the medieval Jewish quarter that flourished here until a tragic pogrom in the 14th century. Today its narrow lanes conceal surprising sites including an ancient (alleged) synagogue (p69) unearthed in the 1990s, the remains of an old Jewish weaver's house (p69) (also, confusingly, known as El Call) and the fragments of a women's bathouse inside the basement of the cafe Caelum (p76). Some of the old city's most unusual shops are here, selling exquisite antiques, handmade leather products and even kosher wine, and the area's well-hidden dining rooms and candelit bars and cafes entice both *barcelonins* and visitors.

El Call (which probably derives from the Hebrew word *kahal*, meaning 'community') is a tiny area, and initially a little tricky to find. The boundaries of the original **Call Major** are roughly Carrer del Call, Carrer dels Banys Nous, Baixada de Santa Eulàlia and Carrer de Sant Honorat, while another pocket, the **Call Menor**, extended across the modern Carrer de Ferran as far as Baixada de Sant Miquel and Carrer d'en Rauric (and is believed to date from the mid-13th century).

Though a handful of Jewish families remained after the bloody pogrom of 1391, the subsequent expulsion of all Jews in the country in the 15th century put an end to the Jewish presence in Barcelona (which dated back to at least the 9th century). The present Església de Sant Jaume on Carrer de Ferran was built on the site of a synagogue.

Even before the pogroms of 1391, Jews in Barcelona were not exactly privileged citizens. As in many medieval centres, they were obliged to wear a special identifying mark on their garments and had trouble getting permission to expand their area as El Call's population increased (as many as 4000 people were crammed into the tiny streets of the Call Major).

and-*mole* tacos (with berry-and-chocolate sauce) or corn-truffle quesadillas. No bookings; cash only.

BAR CELTA GALICIAN €
Map p292 (📞93 315 00 06; www.barcelta.com; Carrer de Simó Oller 3; tapas €3-12; ⊘noon-midnight) Founded by a Galician couple in 1970, charmingly uncluttered Bar Celta shows off the northwestern region's famously seafood-tastic culinary riches with its house *pop a feira* (Galician-style octopus), now under the watch of the second and third family generation. Other traditional home-cooked goodies include salty *Padrón* peppers, *patates braves* (potatoes in a spicy tomato sauce) and giant wedges of tortilla.

There's another, newer **branch** (Map p300; 📞93 315 15 10; www.barcelta.com; Carrer de la Princesa 50; tapas €3-12; ⊘8.30am-midnight Mon-Fri, from 10am Sat, from noon Sun) in El Born.

ROCAMBOLESC ICE CREAM €
Map p292 (📞93 743 11 25; www.rocambolesc. com; La Rambla 51-59; ice cream €3-5; ⊘11am-12.30am Sun-Tue & Thu, noon-12.30am Wed & Sat, 11.30am-12.30am Fri) Step into the fantastical, candy-striped world of the multi-award-winning Roca brothers for Spain's most daringly divine ice cream, from rhubarb confit ice cream topped by flamed meringue to mandarin sorbet with a dusting of passionfruit flakes. The decor is inspired by the dessert trolley at Girona's world-renowned restaurant El Celler de Can Roca.

LA CERERÍA VEGETARIAN, VEGAN €
Map p292 (📞93 301 85 10; Baixada de Sant Miquel 3; mains €8-11; ⊘1-11pm Tue-Sat, to 6pm Sun; 📶🖋; ⓂJaume I) Black-and-white marble floors, a smattering of old wooden tables and ramshackle displays of musical instruments lend a bohemian charm to this warm vegetarian haunt that gets packed for its lunchtime *menú del día* (€12.50). Flavours change with the seasons, but expect dishes such as mushroom-stuffed courgettes, coconut curry with couscous and spinach-pumpkin lasagne. Vegan options too.

LA ALCOBA AZUL MEDITERRANEAN €
Map p292 (📞93 302 81 41; www.facebook.com/ LaAlcobaAzulBarcelona; Carrer de Salomó Ben

Adret 14; mains €6-10; ⊘12.30pm-late; 🛜; Ⓜ Jaume I) Peel back the centuries amid medieval walls, low ceilings, wooden floors and flickering candles in the heart of the old Jewish quarter. Grab a seat in the quaint square out front or slide into a table booth for excellent wines by the glass and punchy Spanish-Mediterranean tapas like goat-cheese-stuffed peppers, homemade hummus, curried squid and creative *torrades* (open toasted sandwiches).

BENEDICT — CAFE €

Map p292 (☑93 250 75 11; www.benedictbcn. com; Carrer d'en Gignàs 23; mains €10-11; ⊘9am-4pm Mon & Fri, to 4.30pm Tue-Thu, to 5pm Sat & Sun; 🛜; Ⓜ Jaume I) As the name suggests, brunch is the main event at friendly bistro-inspired Benedict, with eggs prepared every which way, savoury pancakes and even a full veggie fry-up. There's also a list of house-made burgers, salads, sandwiches and light bites like *patates braves*, Mexican-style plantain chips and fried green tomatoes with feta and strawberry marmalade.

XURRERIA — CHURROS €

Map p292 (☑93 318 76 91; Carrer dels Banys Nous 8; cone €1-2; ⊘7am-1.30pm & 3.30-8.15pm Mon, Tue, Thu & Fri, 7am-2pm & 4-8.30pm Sat, 7am-2.30pm & 4.30-8.30pm Sun; Ⓜ Liceu) It doesn't look much from the outside, but this brightly lit takeaway joint, which has been going since 1968, is Barcelona's top spot for paper cones of piping-hot *xurros* (*churros* in Spanish) – long batter sticks fried and sprinkled with sugar, best enjoyed dunked in hot chocolate.

★ CAFÈ DE L'ACADÈMIA — CATALAN €€

Map p292 (☑93 319 82 53; cafedelaacademia@ hotmail.com; Carrer dels Lledó 1; mains €10-20; ⊘1-4pm & 8-11pm Mon-Fri, closed Aug; 🛜; Ⓜ Jaume I) Smartly executed traditional Catalan dishes with the odd creative twist and excellent regional wines make this wood-beamed, stone-walled spot a packed-out local favourite, with tables also on Plaça de Sant Just. City-hall workers pounce on the lunchtime *menú del día* (€16 – or €12 at the bar!), which might mean pear and Parmesan salad, vegetable rice with Mahón cheese or grilled sole.

★ LA VINATERIA DEL CALL — SPANISH €€

Map p292 (☑93 302 60 92; www.lavinateriadel call.com; Carrer Salomó Ben Adret 9; raciones

€7-18; ⊘7.30pm-1am; 🛜; Ⓜ Jaume I) In a magical, rambling setting in the former Jewish quarter, this tiny candlelit jewel-box of a wine bar serves up divine Iberian sharing plates dancing from Galician-style octopus and cider-cooked chorizo to perfect *truites* (omelettes) and Catalan *escalivada* (roasted peppers, aubergine and onions). Spot-on service, super-fresh local ingredients and a wonderful selection of wines and artisan cheeses from across Spain.

★ BAR PINOTXO — TAPAS €€

Map p292 (☑93 317 17 31; www.pinotxobar.com; La Rambla 89, Mercat de la Boqueria; tapas €4-16; ⊘6.30am-4pm Mon-Sat; Ⓜ Liceu) Arguably La Boqueria's most brilliant tapas bar, standing strong since 1940. Ever-charming owner Juanito Bayén serves up superb Catalan classics: chickpeas with pine nuts and raisins, *cargols* (snails), smoky *escalivada*, soft baby squid with cannellini beans, or a quivering cube of caramel-sweet pork belly. Long-running and unpretentious, Pinotxo is also famous for its *forquilles* (traditional cooked breakfasts). Arrive early!

★ BELMONTE — TAPAS €€

Map p292 (☑93 310 76 84; Carrer de la Mercè 29; tapas €5-12; ⊘7pm-midnight Tue-Thu, 1-3.30pm & 7pm-midnight Fri & Sat; 🛜; Ⓜ Jaume I) 🗲 Run by two welcoming sisters, this tiny, down-to-earth rust-walled bodega in the southern Barri Gòtic whips up beautifully prepared Tarragona-style small plates rooted in home-grown ingredients from the family garden. Try the excellent *truita*, beautifully rich *patatons* (salted new potatoes) with *romesco* or sliced chillies and courgette carpaccio topped with olive oil and goat's cheese, plus the house-made vermouth (€2.75).

EL QUIM — TAPAS, CATALAN €€

Map p292 (☑93 301 98 10; http://elquimdela boqueria.com; La Rambla 89, Mercat de la Boqueria; tapas €3-5, mains €10-26; ⊘noon-4pm Mon & Wed, 8am-4pm Tue & Thu, 8am-5pm Fri & Sat; Ⓜ Liceu) This classic counter bar burrowed away in the Mercat de la Boqueria (p64) is ideal for traditional Catalan dishes such as fried eggs with baby squid (the house speciality) or *escalivada*. Daily specials star market-fresh seasonal produce, and might include artichoke chips or port-sautéed wild mushrooms, as well as outstanding egg dishes from owner Quim Márquez. No bookings.

LEVANTE
MEDITERRANEAN €€

Map p292 (☎93 858 26 79; www.bistrotlevante.com; Placeta de Manuel Ribé 1; mains €10-13; ⏲10am-midnight; ✈; ⓂJaume I) A snug, stylish and sunny space tucked into the old Call, Levante specialises in beautifully prepped sharing plates that delicately fuse Mediterranean and Middle Eastern flavours: spicy roast-carrot salad, coriander-infused shakshuka, zesty hummus with pomegranate, kumquats and pillowy pita. Polished-concrete floors and dangling plants grace the interior, and vegan and vegetarian options abound, as do natural wines and brunchy bites.

CAN CULLERETES
CATALAN €€

Map p292 (☎93 317 30 22; www.culleretes.com; Carrer d'en Quintana 5; mains €9-18; ⏲1.30-3.45pm & 8-10.45pm Tue-Sat, 1.30-4pm Sun; ✈; ⓂLiceu) Founded in 1786, Barcelona's oldest restaurant is still going strong, with visitors and locals alike flocking here for its rambling interior, old-fashioned tile-filled decor and enormous helpings of fuss-free traditional Catalan food. Dishes include fresh seafood, grilled meats, steaming stews and stuffed *canelons* (cannelloni), plus a fixed weekday lunch menu (€15 to €17).

RASOTERRA
VEGETARIAN, VEGAN €€

Map p292 (☎93 318 69 26; www.rasoterra.cat; Carrer del Palau 5; small plates €8-14, tasting menu €32; ⏲7-11pm Tue-Fri, 1-4pm & 7-11pm Sat & Sun; ✈✈; ⓂJaume I) ✈ Slow Food advocates at Rasoterra cook up first-rate vegetarian dishes in a Zen-like setting with tall ceilings, low-level jazz, and fresh flowers on minimalist-chic tables. The ambitious, globally influenced menu starring Catalan produce changes regularly and might feature mushroom *arròs negre* (black rice), purple-corn tacos with carrot chutney, or spicy veg curry with chickpea sorbet. Good vegan and gluten-free options too.

ONOFRE
SPANISH €€

Map p292 (☎93 317 69 37; www.onofre.net; Carrer de les Magdalenes 19; dishes €4-15; ⏲10am-4.30pm & 7.30pm-midnight Mon-Fri, noon-4.30pm & 7.30pm-midnight Sat, closed Aug; ✈; ⓂJaume I) Famed for its (good, affordable) Spanish wines, this snug modern restaurant, wine shop and deli has a strong local following. Beer-barrel tables and shelves stacked with olive oil and tinned seafood adorn a dimly lit room, while delicious dishes take in

herbed-cod carpaccio, garlic-baked prawns and original cheese platters. The weekday *menú* (€11.25) is excellent value.

PLA
FUSION €€

Map p292 (☎93 412 65 52; www.restaurantpla.cat; Carrer de la Bellafila 5; mains €16-20; ⏲6-11pm Mon-Thu, to 11.30pm Fri, 1-11.30pm Sat, to 11pm Sun; ✈; ⓂJaume I) One of the Barri Gòtic's long-standing favourites, Pla is a stylish, romantically lit medieval dining room where centuries-old original brick arches mingle with modern art. Skilled cooks churn out Catalan-rooted temptations such as chickpeas and basil hummus, grilled squid with red-pepper sauce, grilled duck breast with apple-and-beet purée or smoked aubergine infused with mint.

GRILL ROOM/BAR THONET
CATALAN €€

Map p292 (☎93 684 36 69; https://grillroom-barthonet.com; Carrer dels Escudellers 8; mains €8-16; ⏲noon-midnight) A Modernista frontage gives way to beautifully restyled interiors with green-leather stools, beamed ceilings and a marble bar at this updated-Catalan-cooking find, originally opened in 1902 as one of Barcelona's first vermouth bars. It's a friendly, relaxed, central spot for well-prepared dishes like *truita butifarra* (potato-and-sausage omelette), *escalivada* and meaty *canelons*, with a €15 set lunch.

BLACK REMEDY
CAFE €€

Map p292 (☎93 461 92 12; www.blackremedy.com; Carrer de la Ciutat 5; mains €9-14; ⏲9am-7pm Mon-Fri, from 10am Sat & Sun; ✈; ⓂJaume I) Local artisan beer? Check. Pulled-pork sandwiches? Check. Superb Barcelona-sourced coffee? Absolutely. An industrial-like space with floor-to-ceiling windows, mismatched furnishings and tiled floors, Black Remedy is the latest caffeine-fuelled spot to jump in on the slow transformation of the Barri Gòtic. Also does fresh pastries, cold-pressed juices, health-focused salads and all-day international-style brunch.

OCAÑA
INTERNATIONAL €€

Map p292 (☎93 676 48 14; www.ocana.cat; Plaça Reial 13; dishes €6-25; ⏲noon-2.30am Sun-Thu, to 3am Fri & Sat; ✈; ⓂLiceu) A flamboyant, elegantly designed multispace venture with high ceilings, chandeliers, plush furnishings and tables on Plaça Reial, Ocaña blends late-night carousing with serious eating. Cafe, restaurant and bar in one, it whips up everything from fabulous cocktails and Spanish wines (including vegan, biodynamic and natural) to burgers, seafood and rice dishes, plus tapas of tortilla, cheese, ham and home-smoked salmon.

KOY SHUNKA
JAPANESE €€€

Map p292 (☑93 412 79 39; www.koyshunka.com; Carrer de Copons 7; tasting menus €93-137; ⊙1.30-2.30pm & 8.30-10.30pm Tue-Sat; ⓂUrquinaona) Down a narrow lane north of La Catedral, chef Hideki Matsuhisa's Michelin-starred Koy Shunka opens a portal to sensational dishes from the East – mouth-watering sushi, sashimi, seared Wagyu beef and richly flavoured seaweed salads are served alongside inventive fusion specialities. Don't miss the tender signature tuna belly.

Most diners sit at the large wraparound counter, where you can watch the culinary wizardry in action. Set multicourse menus are pricey but well worth it for a truly extraordinary dining experience.

CECCONI'S
ITALIAN €€€

Map p292 (☑93 220 46 40; www.cecconisbarcelona.com; Passeig de Colom 20, Soho House; mains €12-30; ⊙noon-1am Mon-Sat, to midnight Sun; ⓢ☑; ⓂDrassanes, Barceloneta) Dressed with rust-red velvet sofas, black-and-white tiled floors and 19th-century vaulted brick ceilings, the exquisite signature restaurant at members-only Soho House (p234) welcomes all for smartly prepared cocktails and elegant yet unfussy northern-Italian cuisine straight from the open-plan kitchen (courgette frittata, burrata-and-avocado salad, pastas like *tonnarelli cacio e pepe*). If you book for Sunday brunch (€45; noon to 5pm), arrive hungry!

ELS QUATRE GATS
CATALAN €€€

Map p292 (☑93 302 41 40; www.4gats.com; Carrer de Montsió 3; mains €18-38; ⊙restaurant 1-4pm & 7pm-midnight, cafe 9am-1am; ⓂUrquinaona) Once the lair of Barcelona's Modernista artists, Els Quatre Gats is a stunning example of the movement, inside and out, with its colourful patterned tiles, geometric brickwork and wooden fittings designed by Josep Puig i Cadafalch. The local-focused cuisine (grilled meats, rice dishes, seafood tapas) isn't as thrilling as the setting, but you can just have coffee and a croissant.

DRINKING & NIGHTLIFE

Sidestep La Rambla and plunge into the lower end of the Barri Gòtic: Carrer dels Escudellers, Carrer Ample, Carrer d'en Gignàs, Carrer del Correu Vell and the area around Plaça Reial.

★CAELUM
CAFE

Map p292 (☑93 302 69 93; www.facebook.com/CaelumBarcelona; Carrer de la Palla 8; ⊙10am-8.30pm Mon-Thu, to 9pm Fri-Sun; ⓢ; ⓂLiceu) Centuries of heavenly Spanish gastronomic tradition collide at this exquisite medieval space in the heart of the city, which stocks sweets made by nuns across the country (including irresistible Toledo marzipan). The ground-floor cafe is a dainty setting for decadent cakes and pastries. In the stone-walled underground chamber, flickering candles cast a glow on the ruins of a medieval bathhouse.

L'ASCENSOR
COCKTAIL BAR

Map p292 (☑93 318 53 47; Carrer de la Bellafila 3; ⊙6pm-2.30am Sun-Thu, to 3am Fri & Sat; ⓢ; ⓂJaume I) Named after the lift (elevator) doors that serve as the front entrance, this clandestine drinking hideout – with its brick ceilings, vintage mirrors and marble-topped tables – gathers a faithful crowd for old-fashioned cocktails (from €7) and lively conversation against a soundtrack of up-tempo jazz and funk.

GRANJA LA PALLARESA
CAFE

Map p292 (☑93 302 20 36; Carrer del Petritxol 11; ⊙9am-1pm & 4-9pm Mon-Sat, 9am-1pm & 5-9pm Sun, closed Jul; ⓢ; ⓂLiceu) An old-school cafe filled with both locals and visitors, La Pallaresa specialises in crispy *xurros* for dipping in thick hot chocolate and whipped cream, and dates back to the 1940s. It also does impossible-to-resist pastries and *ensaïmades* (sweet pastry swirls dusted with icing sugar) from Mallorca.

POLAROID
BAR

Map p292 (☑93 186 66 69; www.polaroidbar.es; Carrer dels Còdols 29; ⊙7.30pm-2.30am Sun-Thu, to 3am Fri & Sat; ⓢ; ⓂDrassanes) For a dash of 1980s nostalgia, Polaroid is a blast from the past, with its wall-mounted VHS tapes, old film posters, comic-book-covered tables, action-figure displays and other kitschy decor. Not surprisingly, it draws

APARTMENTS & OVERTOURISM

While private apartments might seem a convenient and cost-effective accommodation choice, it's important to know that Airbnb and other apartment-rental agencies have been accused of contributing to Barcelona's overtourism problem and driving up prices (not to mention noise levels) for local residents. The Barri Gòtic, El Raval, La Barceloneta and El Born have been particularly affected. Barcelona's authorities stopped issuing new licences in 2014 and since 2016 have been firmly closing down unlicensed properties. Before booking your apartment, check whether it's licensed at www.fairtourism.barcelona.

a fun, unpretentious crowd who come for cheap *cañas* (draught beer), mojitos (from €6) and free popcorn.

SATAN'S COFFEE CORNER   COFFEE

Map p292 (☑666 222 599; www.satanscoffee.com; Carrer de l'Arc de Sant Ramón del Call 11; ☺9am-6pm Mon-Fri, from 10am Sat & Sun; ⓂLiceu, Jaume I) All ocean-blue walls, pounding beats and punk-inspired style, Satan's is firmly about the coffee (no wi-fi, no prams!). Local small-scale roaster Right Side provides regularly rotating signature brews, while snazzy snacks (€3 to €12) include rice-stuffed omelette, home-baked pastries, Japanese-influenced breakfasts and honey-roasted carrots with yoghurt.

BAR BOADAS   COCKTAIL BAR

Map p292 (☑93 318 95 92; www.boadascocktails.com; Carrer dels Tallers 1; ☺noon-2am Mon-Thu, to 3am Fri & Sat; ⓂCatalunya) One of Barcelona's oldest cocktail bars, Boadas is famed for its daiquiris. Amid old monochrome photos and a polished-wood bar, bow-tied waiters have been mixing unique, deliciously drinkable creations since Miguel Boadas opened it in 1933 – Miró and Hemingway both drank here. Miguel was born in Havana, where he was the first barman at the immortal El Floridita.

SALTERIO   TEAHOUSE

Map p292 (☑93 302 50 28; www.facebook.com/teteriasalterio; Carrer de Salomó Ben Adret 4; ☺noon-midnight; ☎; ⓂJaume I) Wafts of fresh mint greet you at this seductive teahouse tucked down a tiny lane in El Call. Salterio serves authentic Moroccan mint teas (€4), Turkish coffee and pots of milky, sweet spiced chai, between stone walls, candle-lit tables and swirls of incense. If hunger strikes, try the Mediterranean-style bites, like *sardo* (grilled flatbread with pesto, cheese or other toppings).

MARULA CAFÉ   BAR

Map p292 (☑93 318 76 90; www.marulacafe.com; Carrer dels Escudellers 49; cover €6-10; ☺11pm-5am Wed, Thu & Sun, to 6am Fri & Sat; ⓂLiceu) The Barri Gòtic outpost of a Madrid-born nightlife sensation, Marula transports you to the 1970s and the best in funk and soul. James Brown fans will think they've died and gone to heaven. It's not, however, a mono-thematic place: DJs slip in other tunes, from breakbeat to house, and there are regular live gigs. Samba and other Brazilian dance sounds also put in an appearance.

ČAJ CHAI   TEAHOUSE

Map p292 (☑93 301 95 92; www.cajchai.com; Carrer de Salomó Ben Adret 12; ☺10.30am-10pm Thu-Mon; ⓂJaume I) Inspired by Prague's bohemian tearooms, this bright and buzzing temple to steaming brews in the heart of the old Jewish quarter is a much-loved local haunt. Pick from around 200 teas from China, India, Korea, Japan, Nepal, Morocco and beyond, plus fresh cakes and pastries sourced from local bakers. Sound baths, tea ceremonies and tastings also happen; check online.

.CAFÈ DE L'ÒPERA   CAFE

Map p292 (☑93 317 75 85; www.cafeoperabcn.com; La Rambla 74; ☺8.30am-2.30am; ☎; ⓂLiceu) Opposite the Gran Teatre del Liceu, La Rambla's most traditional cafe has been operating since 1929 and remains popular with opera-goers. It's pleasant enough for an early-evening drink or, in the morning, coffee and croissants. Head upstairs for a seat overlooking the busy boulevard, and try the house speciality, the *cafè de l'Òpera* (with chocolate mousse).

EL RABIPELAO   COCKTAIL BAR

Map p292 (☑93 295 56 14; www.elrabipelao.com; Carrer de la Mercè 26; ☺7.30pm-2.30am Sun-Thu, to 3am Fri & Sat; ⓂBarceloneta, Drassanes) Super 'tropicocktails' (€6 to €10) are the thing from the team behind Barcelona's original Venezuelan good-time bar, a zingily patterned space in the southern Gòtic, with home-cooked *arepas* (stuffed maize cakes) and *cachapas* (maize cakes, usually with cheese) to soak up fresh-and-fruity mojitos and flamed mai tais. There are several branches around town, including in Gràcia (p182).

MACARENA CLUB
CLUB

Map p292 (📞93 301 30 64; www.macarenaclub.com; Carrer Nou de Sant Francesc 5; cover €5-10; ⏰midnight-5am Sun-Thu, to 6am Fri & Sat; Ⓜ️Drassanes) You won't believe this was once a tile-lined Andalucian flamenco musos' bar. Now it's a dark, intimate dance space: sit at the bar, meet people around you and then stand up for a bit of a shake to the DJ's electro and house offerings, all within about 5 sq metres.

MANCHESTER
BAR

Map p292 (📞627 733 081; www.facebook.com/manchesterbar; Carrer de Milans 5; ⏰6.30pm-2.30am Sun-Thu, to 3am Fri & Sat; 📶; Ⓜ️Liceu) A drinking den that has undergone several transformations over the years now treats you to the sounds of great Manchester bands, from Joy Division to Oasis to The Smiths, but probably not The Hollies. It has a pleasing rough-and-tumble feel, with tables jammed in every which way, and there's another branch in El Raval. DJs on Thursdays.

LA ISABELA
ROOFTOP BAR

Map p292 (📞93 552 95 52; www.hotel1898.com; La Rambla 109, Hotel 1898; ⏰noon-midnight; Ⓜ️Catalunya, Liceu) Overlooking La Rambla, this tucked-away roof-terrace bar at the elegant Hotel 1898 (p234) is a soothing haven of stripy sunloungers, sprinkled greenery and glorious 360-degree views. Take

---

TOP CAFES

••

Some of Barcelona's most atmospheric and original cafes lie hidden in the old cobbled lanes of the Barri Gòtic.

➡ Caelum (p76)

➡ Salterio (p77)

➡ Čaj Chai (p77)

➡ Satan's Coffee Corner (p77)

➡ Granja La Pallaresa (p76)

---

in the Barcelona skyline over a glass of *cava* (€7), a creative cocktail infused with herbs fresh from La Boqueria market (€15) or perhaps a bottle of ecological Penedès wine (€35).

LA TETERIA
CAFE

Map p292 (📞93 319 05 33; www.facebook.com/lateteriabarcelona; Baixada de Viladecols 2; ⏰10am-10pm Mon & Wed-Sat, 11am-10pm Sun; 📶; Ⓜ️Jaume I) Globally inspired options at this boho-feel corner include herbal teas, Turkish coffee, mango lassi and fresh juices, as well as home-baked cakes and vegetarian and vegan bites (€4 to €7) such as quiches, sandwiches, soups and salads. Gold-painted beams, white walls and a changing display of local artwork combine in a soothing space where youngish patrons often tap away on laptops.

KARMA
CLUB

Map p292 (📞93 302 56 80; www.karmadisco.com; Plaça Reial 10; club entry incl drink Fri & Sat €12; ⏰noon-5am Tue-Thu, to 6am Fri & Sat; Ⓜ️Liceu) A golden Barcelona oldie, tunnel-shaped Karma is small and gets quite tightly packed (claustrophobic for some) with a good-natured crowd of locals and out-of-towners. During the week there's mainstream indie music (and metal on Tuesdays), while on weekends DJs spin everything from rock to disco. The terrace bar on the Plaça Reial opens 11.30am until at least 1am daily.

BAR DEL PI
BAR

Map p292 (📞93 302 21 23; Plaça de Sant Josep Oriol 1; ⏰9am-11pm Wed-Mon; Ⓜ️Liceu) A welcome slice of old Barcelona in the thick of the Barri Gòtic, this friendly (admittedly touristed) split-level cafe-bar has been powering on since the 1920s and is now run by the fourth generation of the same family. Check-print floors, marble-topped tables and mirrors behind the bar create a traditional feel, while tapas (€2 to €5) include refreshingly fuss-free tortilla.

BOSC DE LES FADES
LOUNGE

Map p292 (www.facebook.com/BoscdelesFades; Passatge de la Banca 5; ⏰10am-1am Mon-Thu, to 2am Fri, 11am-2am Sat, to 1am Sun; Ⓜ️Drassanes) The 'Forest of the Fairies' is popular with tourists but offers a whimsical retreat from the busy Rambla nearby and has a wonderfully kitsch charm. Lounge chairs and lamp-lit tables are scattered around an indoor forest complete with trickling fountain and grotto. *Entrepans* (filled baguettes) and other snacks are served alongside wines, *cava*, cocktails and *combinats* (spirit with mixer; €7).

 ENTERTAINMENT

GRAN TEATRE DEL LICEU — THEATRE
Map p292 (☑902 787397; www.liceubarcelona. cat; La Rambla 51-59; tickets €15-250; ⓜLiceu) Barcelona's grand old opera house, skilfully restored after a fire in 1994, is one of the world's most technologically advanced theatres. Taking a seat in its grand auditorium, returned to all its 19th-century glory but with the very latest in acoustics, you'll time-travel to another age, or join a guided tour (p65) to explore its architectural beauty.

EL PARAIGUA — LIVE MUSIC
Map p292 (☑93 317 14 79; www.elparaigua. com; Carrer del Pas de l'Ensenyança 2; ⓢnoon-midnight Sun-Thu, to 3am Fri & Sat; ⓜLiceu) **FREE** A tiny chocolate box of dark-tinted Modernisme, the 'Umbrella' has been serving up drinks since the 1960s. But downstairs in the moody basement, travel from Modernisme to medieval amid 11th-century brick walls. Live bands – funk, soul, rock, blues, flamenco – regularly hold court on Friday and Saturday (check schedules online).

HARLEM JAZZ CLUB — JAZZ
Map p292 (☑93 310 07 55; www.harlemjazzclub. es; Carrer de la Comtessa de Sobradiel 8; tickets €8-12; ⓢ8pm-3am Sun & Tue-Thu, to 5am Fri & Sat; ⓜJaume I) This narrow, old-city dive is one of the best spots in town for jazz, as well as funk, Latin, blues and gypsy jazz, and attracts a mixed crowd that maintains a respectful silence during performances. Most concerts start at 10.30pm or 11pm; get in early if you want a seat in front of the stage.

SIDECAR — LIVE MUSIC, CLUB
Map p292 (http://sidecar.es; Plaça Reial 7; tickets from €6; ⓢ7pm-5am Thu, to 6am Fri & Sat; ⓜLiceu) Descend into the red-tinged, brick-vaulted bowels where just about any kind of live music could be on the agenda, from

UK indie through to country punk, though rock and pop lead the way. DJs take over later on. Upstairs at ground level you can get food (until midnight) or a few drinks (until 3am).

ATENEU BARCELONÈS — CLASSICAL MUSIC
Map p292 (☑93 343 61 21; www.ateneubcn.org; Carrer de la Canuda 6; ⓜCatalunya) Housed in the 1779 Palau Savassona, this historical private library and cultural centre (dating back more than 150 years) hosts a varied high-brow programme, from classical recitals to film screenings and literary readings.

TARANTOS — DANCE
Map p292 (☑93 301 75 64; www.tarantos barcelona.com; Plaça Reial 17; tickets from €17; ⓢshows 7.30pm, 8.30pm & 9.30pm Oct-Jun, plus 10.30pm Jul-Sep; ⓜLiceu) Since 1963, this basement locale has been the stage for emerging flamenco groups performing in Barcelona, with stars such as Antonio Gades and Maruja Garrido having graced the space. These days Tarantos is a mostly tourist-centric affair, with reliable half-hour shows three or four times nightly. Still, it's a good introduction to flamenco, and not a bad setting for drinks.

🛍 SHOPPING

The real shopping fun starts inside the labyrinth of the Barri Gòtic: young fashion on Carrer d'Avinyó, major chains on Avinguda del Portal de l'Àngel, some cute old shops on Carrer de la Dagueria...

★L'ARCA — VINTAGE
Map p292 (☑93 302 15 98; www.larca.es; Carrer dels Banys Nous 20; ⓢ11am-2pm & 4-8pm Mon-Sat; ⓜLiceu) Step inside this enchanting vintage boutique for beautifully crafted apparel from the past, mostly sourced from local homes: 18th-century embroidered silk vests, elaborate silk kimonos and 1920s shawls and wedding dresses, plus old-style earrings made by artisans in southern Spain. The incredible collection has provided fashion for films like *Titanic*, *Talk to Her* and *Perfume: The Story of a Murderer*.

LA MANUAL ALPARGATERA   SHOES

Map p292 (☑93 301 01 72; www.lamanualalpar gatera.es; Carrer d'Avinyó 7; ☺9.30am-8pm Mon-Fri, from 10am Sat; MLiceu) Stars from Salvador Dalí to Penélope Cruz and Jean Paul Gaultier have ordered a pair of *espardenyes* (espadrilles; rope-soled canvas shoes) from this famous shoe specialist, founded just after the Spanish Civil War. The roots of the simple design date back hundreds of years and originated in the Catalan Pyrenees, though La Manual also incorporates contemporary trends.

ESCRIBÀ   FOOD

Map p292 (☑93 301 60 27; www.escriba.es; La Rambla 83; ☺9am-9pm; ☎; MLiceu) Chocolates, dainty pastries and mouth-watering cakes can be nibbled behind the Modernista mosaic facade here or taken away for private, guilt-ridden consumption. This Barcelona favourite is owned by the Escribà family, a name synonymous with sinfully good sweet things. More than that, it adds a touch of authenticity to La Rambla.

SABATER HERMANOS   COSMETICS

Map p292 (☑93 301 98 32; Plaça de Sant Felip Neri 1; ☺10.30am-9pm; MJaume I) Handcrafted soaps and soap petals in seductive flavours like olive oil and *tarongina* (orange blossom) are the draw at this fragrant little shop. Varieties such as fig, cinnamon, grapefruit and chocolate smell good enough to eat, while sandalwood, magnolia, mint, cedar and jasmine add spice to any bathtub.

JOAN LA LLAR DEL PERNIL   FOOD

Map p292 (☑93 317 95 29; www.joanllardel pernil.com; Stalls 667-671, Mercat de la Boqueria; ☺8am-3pm Tue-Thu, to 7pm Mon & Fri, 7.30am-4pm Sat; MLiceu) This family-owned stall hidden away in the chaotic Mercat de la Boqueria (p64) sells some of the best *pernil* (cured Spanish-style ham; *jamón* in Castilian) and charcuterie in the city, much of which is sliced wafer-thin and presented in little cones as a snack by knowledgeable owner Joan. The speciality is *jamón ibérico de bellota*, sourced from free-roaming acorn-fed pigs.

CERERIA SUBIRÀ   HOMEWARES

Map p292 (☑93 315 26 06; https://cereriasu-bira.cat; Baixada de la Llibreteria 7; ☺10am-2pm & 4-8pm Mon-Sat Jun-Sep, 9.30am-1.30pm & 4-8pm Mon & Tue, 9.30am-8pm Wed-Sat Oct-May; MJaume I) Wafts of floral scents greet you at the oldest shop in Barcelona, whose interior has a beautifully baroque quality with a sweeping *Gone With the Wind*–style staircase. Cereria Subirà has been churning out candles since 1761 and at this address (originally a textiles outlet) since the 19th century.

ROBERTO & VICTORIA   JEWELLERY

Map p292 (www.roberto-victoria.com; Carrer dels Lledó 10; ☺11am-2pm & 4.30-8pm; MJaume I) Jeweller duo Roberto Carrascosa and Victoria Aroca handcraft exquisite, unique pieces in gold, silver, brass and semiprecious stones at their intimate, minimalist studio hidden away in the depths of the Barri Gòtic, combining avant-garde touches with classic design and reworking vintage jewels into contemporary 'cult jewellery'. The elegantly bold rings are bestsellers.

LA COLMENA   FOOD

Map p292 (☑93 315 13 56; www.pastisseriala colmena.com; Plaça de l'Angel 12; ☺9am-9pm; MJaume I) One of Barcelona's most ancient pastry shops, 1868-opened La Colmena is still run by the same family who acquired it in 1927 and produces its treats according to the original recipes. The Roig family sells many delicacies, but it's best known for its boiled sweets, pine-nut-encrusted *panellets* (almond cakes), meringues and *bolados* (18th-century powdered-sugar candy, flavoured with juice).

TALLER DE MARIONETAS TRAVI   TOYS

Map p292 (☑93 412 66 92; www.marionetastravi. com; Carrer de n'Amargós 4; ☺1-9pm Mon-Sat; MUrquinaona) Going strong since 1977, this atmospheric shop revolves around beautifully handcrafted marionettes, many of them made by owner Teresa Travieso herself. Don Quixote, Sancho Panza and other iconic Spanish figures make an appearance, as do unusual works from other parts of the world – including rare Sicilian puppets and pieces from Myanmar (Burma), Indonesia and beyond.

SOMBRERERÍA OBACH   HATS

Map p292 (☑93 318 40 94; www.sombrereria obach.es; Carrer del Call 2; ☺10am-2pm & 4-8pm Mon-Fri, 10am-2pm & 4.30-8pm Sat Oct-Jul, 10am-2pm & 4-8pm Mon-Fri, 10am-2pm Sat Aug-Sep; MJaume I) Since 1924 this family-owned beauty has been purveying all manner of headgear: hipsterish short-brimmed hats, low-key fedoras, elegant straw sun hats, a full-colour spectrum of *barrets* (berets)...

LE SWING VINTAGE
VINTAGE, CLOTHING

Map p292 (☑93 310 14 49; www.leswingvintage.com; Carrer dels Lledó 4-6; ◷11am-2pm & 4-8pm; ⓜJaume I) Specialising in haute-couture classics like Chanel, Dior, Givenchy and Yves Saint Laurent, collected from Paris and LA as well as Barcelona, this sparkling stone-walled boutique is a temple to designer vintage and neo-vintage fashion from the 1920s onwards, with new stock arriving weekly. One for serious fashionistas.

ELIURPÍ
HATS, CLOTHING

Map p292 (☑93 797 57 77; www.eliurpi.com; Baixada de Santa Eulàlia 3; ◷11.30am-2pm & 4.30-8pm Tue-Sat; ⓜJaume I) Founded by self-trained Catalan designer Elisabet Urpí and her photographer partner Nacho Umpiérrez, this whimsically stylish boutique is all about fabulous handmade women's hats (from around €190) created with mostly natural, locally sourced materials. Browse enormous maxi straw hats, silk campana hats, hats embroidered with florals or birds, and more. Fashion and handbag collections complement them.

ARTESANIA CATALUNYA
ARTS & CRAFTS

Map p292 (☑93 653 72 14; www.bcncrafts.com; Carrer dels Banys Nous 11; ◷10am-8pm Mon-Sat, to 2pm Sun; ⓜLiceu) A celebration of Catalan products, this nicely designed modern store is a great place to browse for one-of-a-kind pieces. You'll find jewellery inspired by Roman iconography (as well as works that reference Gaudí and Barcelona's Gothic era), plus pottery, fans, wooden toys, silk scarves, notebooks, housewares and much more.

CÓMPLICES
BOOKS

Map p292 (☑93 412 72 83; www.libreriacomplices.com; Carrer de Cervantes 4; ◷10.30am-8pm Mon-Fri, from noon Sat; ⓜJaume I) One of the most extensive LGBTIQ bookstores in the city has a mix of erotica in the form of DVDs and comics as well as books. It's a welcoming, resourceful place for all ages and orientations.

SALA PARÉS
ART

Map p292 (☑93 318 70 20; https://salapares.com; Carrer del Petritxol 5; ◷4-8pm Mon, 10.30am-2pm & 4-8pm Tue-Sat, plus 11.30am-2pm Sun Oct-May; ⓜLiceu) In business since 1877, this gallery has maintained its position as one of the city's leading purveyors of Catalan art, exhibiting a rich variety of works from the 19th century to the present. Increasingly it stocks more work from elsewhere in Spain and Europe. Check the website for upcoming art shows.

FC BOTIGA
GIFTS & SOUVENIRS

Map p292 (Carrer de Jaume I 18; ◷10am-9pm; ⓜJaume I) Need a Lionel Messi football jersey, a blue-and-burgundy ball, or any other football paraphernalia honouring what many locals consider to be the greatest team in the world? A convenient spot to load up without traipsing over to the stadium.

PAPABUBBLE
FOOD

Map p292 (☑93 268 86 25; www.papabubble.com; Carrer Ample 28; ◷10am-2pm & 4-8.30pm Mon-Fri, 10am-8.30pm Sat; ⓜJaume I) Born in Barcelona and now with branches around the world, this sweet shop beneath vintage signs feels like a step into another era. The speciality is pots of rainbow-coloured boiled lollies, just like some of us remember from corner-store days as kids. Watch the sticky sweets being made before your eyes.

PETRITXOL XOCOA
FOOD

Map p292 (☑93 301 82 91; www.petritxol.com; Carrer del Petritxol 11-13; ◷9.30am-9pm; ⓜLiceu) Tucked away along 'chocolate street' Carrer del Petritxol, this den of dental devilry tempts with ranks and ranks of original artisan bars in stunning designs, chocolates filled with sweet stuff, gooey pastries and more. It has a small cafe space, as well as branches scattered about town.

HOME ON EARTH
HOMEWARES

Map p292 (www.homeonearth.com; Carrer de la Boqueria 14; ◷9.30am-9pm Mon-Thu, to 9.30pm Fri & Sat, 10am-9.30pm Sun; ⓜLiceu) ✦ Launched by a well-travelled German-Danish couple, this soothing homewares haven stocks scented candles, yoga mats, woven baskets and other alluring trinkets sourced directly from artisans in Southeast Asia, working with all-natural recycled and recyclable materials wherever possible. The shop also sells jewellery crafted by Barcelona designers.

DRAP-ART
ARTS & CRAFTS

Map p292 (☑93 268 48 89; www.drapart.org; Carrer Groc 1; ◷11am-2pm & 5-8pm Tue-Fri,

THE SWEET LIFE

Barcelona has some irresistible temptations for anyone with a sweet tooth, especially around the Barri Gòtic. Chocolate lovers won't want to miss Carrer del Petritxol, home to several famous *granjas* (milk bars) that dole out cups of wonderfully thick hot chocolate, best accompanied by *xurros* (*churros* in Spanish); Granja La Pallaresa (p76) always draws a crowd.

At Christmas, specialist sweet stores fill with traditional *turrón*. You'll find this nougat treat year-round at stores in the city.

Other not-to-be-missed sinfully sweet spots include cafe Caelum (p76) for its delectable cakes and pastry shop La Colmena (p81), with its classic Catalan sweets, while El Raval's Chök (p96) lures fans with decadent doughnuts and cookies.

6-9pm Sat; Ⓜ Jaume I) 𝒫 A non-profit arts organisation runs this small gallery space devoted to wild designs made from recycled and reused products. Works change regularly, but might include sculptures, jewellery, handbags and other accessories from artists near and far, along with mixed-media installations. There's an annual exhibition at the Museu Marítim (p120).

FIRA DEL COL·LECTIU
D'ARTESANS D'ALIMENTACIÓ   MARKET
Map p292 (Plaça del Pi; ⊙11am-9pm Fri-Sun, 1st & 3rd week of month; Ⓜ Liceu) Once a fortnight, gourmands can sample homemade honeys, sweets, cheeses, oils and other edible delights at this Friday-to-Sunday artisan market on one of the Gòtic's most attractive squares.

MOSTRA D'ART   MARKET
Map p292 (Plaça de Sant Josep Oriol; ⊙11am-8.30pm Sat, 10am-2pm Sun; Ⓜ Liceu) On Saturdays and Sundays the Barri Gòtic is enlivened by a colourful art and craft market held beside the 14th-century Basílica de Santa Maria del Pi.

MERCAT DE
NUMISMÀTICA I FILATÈLIA   MARKET
Map p292 (Plaça Reial; ⊙9am-2.30pm Sun; Ⓜ Liceu) A relic of bygone Barcelona, in the shape of a dusty weekend stamp and coin collectors' market.

🏃 SPORTS & ACTIVITIES

HIDDEN CITY TOURS   CULTURAL, WALKING
(www.hiddencitytours.com; tour per person €21.50) 𝒫 Around 20% of Spain's homeless population lives in Barcelona, and this British-founded social enterprise trains up guides who have been part of the city's homeless community. Sensitive, insightful two-hour tours of the Barri Gòtic and El Raval (English, Spanish, German) are interwoven with the guides' own stories, showing a side of Barcelona unseen by most visitors. Book ahead; minimum two people.

RUNNER BEAN TOURS   WALKING
Map p292 (📞636 108 776; www.runnerbeantours.com; by donation; ⊙tours 11am & 4.30pm Mar-Oct, 11am Nov-Feb; 👬; Ⓜ Liceu) The brainchild of a Spanish-Irish couple, Runner Bean offers several daily thematic pay-what-you-wish tours with enthusiastic English-speaking local guides (it's best to book). The Gothic Quarter tour explores Barcelona's Roman and medieval history, visiting highlights of the Ciutat Vella (Old City); the Gaudí tour takes in the great works of Modernista Barcelona. All tours depart from Plaça Reial.

ANTIQUES & BOUTIQUES   SHOPPING
Map p292 (📞671 234 800, 607 653 817; www.antiquesandboutiques.com; Plaça de la Mercè 8; Ⓜ Drassanes) Fashion and interior designers

Lisa and Niki run private, tailored walking tours delving into Barcelona's fabulous, often-overlooked shopping and design scene, with a high-end focus. You might visit leather-bag artisans, local jewellery makers and couture boutiques in El Born and L'Eixample. Tours start from €300 for two people; book online.

BARCELONA COOKING COOKING

Map p292 (☑93 119 19 86; www.barcelona cooking.net; La Rambla 58, Principal 2; adult/child 5-13yr/child under 5yr €65/32.50/free, with market visit €78/39; 🛗; Ⓜ Liceu) Founded by three Galician friends, Barcelona Cooking hosts hands-on, four-hour culinary classes with bilingual chefs. Kick off with an expedition to the celebrated Mercat de la Boqueria, after which you'll be sizzling up a four-course meal (typically including paella), or try a wine-pairing class focused on traditional Catalan tapas. Thoughtful vegetarian, vegan and gluten-free adaptations on request. Book ahead.

FAT TIRE TOURS CYCLING, WALKING

Map p292 (☑93 342 92 75; www.fattiretours. com; Carrer de Marlet 4; adult/child from €28/26; ⊘ tours 11am, plus 4pm mid-Apr–early Oct; Ⓜ Jaume I, Liceu) This international outlet runs seven different guided bike tours, with a maximum of nine people per group. Options include four hours zipping around the Barri Gòtic, El Born and L'Eixample, exploring Montjuïc by e-bike and an after-dark spin with a tapas stop, as well as a few standard walking tours.

El Raval

Neighbourhood Top Five

1 **MACBA** (p86) Getting to grips with the occasionally challenging art collection and watching skaters perform their tricks out the front.

2 **Antic Hospital de la Santa Creu** (p88) Exploring this historic building, where Gaudí died, and relaxing under the trees in its elegant courtyard.

3 **Bars** (p92) Partaking in a glass of cloudy absinthe while admiring some lesser-known works of Modernisme such as Casa Almirall, or seeking out avant-garde cocktails at stylish new arrivals like Two Schmucks.

4 **Palau Güell** (p87) Walking around this artfully restored Gaudí-designed palace, with its colourful rooftop chimneys.

5 **Dinner time!** (p89) Diving into Barcelona's most multicultural food scene, from superb tacos at El Pachuco to classic Catalan at Elisabets.

For more detail of this area see Map p296 ➡

Explore El Raval

Long one of the most rough-and-tumble parts of Barcelona, El Raval has become so fashionable – in a grungy, inner-city way – that *barcelonins* have even invented a verb for rambling around it: *ravalejar*.

The northern half of El Raval is the best place to start exploring – this part of the *barri* (neighbourhood) has an almost respectable air about it. Spend a day wandering around the boutiques on the streets around Carrer del Pintor Fortuny, testing out experimental coffee spots along Carrer de Joaquín Costa and roaming the fascinating MACBA (p86).

Night-time is El Raval's forte, and not only because of all the illicit activities taking place under the shroud of darkness. This is where you will find some of Barcelona's more eccentric, on-trend and downright ancient bars and clubs.

The area between Carrer de l'Hospital and the waterfront – also known as Barri Xino – is where El Raval retains its dodgy flavour of yore, and you should watch your belongings carefully here. The national cinema and film archive, the Filmoteca de Catalunya (p94), has been relocated to just off the leafy Rambla del Raval (p88) in an attempt to change the face of this area of town. Despite its slight sleaziness, you shouldn't miss this part of El Raval – several fine old bars have stood the test of time on these streets.

If you're curious about the fabric of life in multicultural El Raval, take a stroll along Carrer de l'Hospital, home to the local mosque and numerous halal butchers' shops, cafes and barbers.

Local Life

→ **Vintage shops** El Raval is the epicentre of Barcelona's fascination with all things vintage – you'll find plenty of secondhand shops dotted around.

→ **Sugar rush** Locals swear that the best hot chocolate in town is to be had at Granja M Viader (p93).

→ **Bars: old and new** The streets of El Raval are sprinkled with bars (p90) beloved by *barcelonins*, from charming Modernista old-timers to up-to-the-minute cocktail lounges.

Getting There & Away

→ **Metro** El Raval is encircled by three metro lines. Línies 1, 2 and 3 stop at strategic points around the district, so nothing is far from a metro stop. The Línia 3 stop at Liceu and the Línia 2 stop at Sant Antoni are handy.

Lonely Planet's Top Tip

Some parts of El Raval still retain their seedy feel; as elsewhere in Barcelona, keep a close eye on your belongings and keep your wits about you after dark. For a spot of peace away from the noisy streets, head for the garden at the **Antic Hospital de la Santa Creu** (p88).

EL RAVAL

🍷 Best Places to Drink

→ Two Schmucks (p92)
→ La Confiteria (p92)
→ Casa Almirall (p92)
→ Bar Marsella (p92)
→ Nømad Every Day (p92)

For reviews, see p92. ➡

🍴 Best Places to Eat

→ Bar Central (p89)
→ El Pachuco (p89)
→ Cañete (p91)
→ Caravelle (p89)
→ Suculent (p91)
→ Elisabets (p89)

For reviews, see p89. ➡

🔒 Best Places to Shop

→ Les Topettes (p95)
→ Holala! Plaza (p95)
→ Lantoki (p95)
→ Teranyina (p95)

For reviews, see p95. ➡

TOP EXPERIENCE
ATTEND AN ART TALK AT MACBA

An extraordinary all-white, glass-fronted creation by American architect Richard Meier, opened in 1995, the MACBA (Museu d'Art Contemporani de Barcelona) has become the city's foremost contemporary art centre. The permanent collection features some 3000 pieces centred on three periods: post-WWII; circa 1968; and the years since the 1989 fall of the Berlin Wall, right up to the present day.

The emphasis is on Spanish and Catalan art from the second half of the 20th century, with works by Antoni Tàpies, Joan Brossa, Miquel Barceló and Joan Rabascall, among others. International artists, such as Paul Klee, Bruce Nauman, Alexander Calder, John Cage and Jean-Michel Basquiat, are also represented.

The temporary visiting exhibitions are almost always challenging and intriguing. MACBA's philosophy is to do away with the old model of a museum where an artwork is a spectacle and to create a space where art can be viewed critically, so the exhibitions are usually tied in with talks and events. This is food for the brain as well as the eyes.

The library and auditorium stage regular concerts, talks and events, all of which are either reasonably priced or free. The ground-floor cafe-restaurant Chichalimoná (p91) is great for coffee, a bite or a vermouth.

Outside, the spectacle is as intriguing as inside. While skateboarders dominate the space south of the museum (considered one of Europe's great skateboard locations), you may well find kids enjoying a game of cricket in Plaça de Joan Coromines.

DON'T MISS

→ The permanent collection of 20th-century Spanish and Catalan art

→ The fascinating temporary exhibitions

→ Richard Meier's extraordinary building

PRACTICALITIES

→ Museu d'Art Contemporani de Barcelona

→ Map p296, C3

→ ☎93 412 08 10

→ www.macba.cat

→ Plaça dels Àngels 1

→ adult/concession/child under 14yr €11/8.80/ free, 4-8pm Sat free

→ ⊙11am-7.30pm Mon & Wed-Fri, 10am-8pm Sat, 10am-3pm Sun & public holidays

→ Ⓜ Universitat

KAREN BLACK/GETTY IMAGES©

TOP EXPERIENCE
HEAR THE ORGAN IN PALAU GÜELL'S MUSIC ROOM

Built off La Rambla in the late 1880s for Gaudí's wealthy patron the industrialist Eusebi Güell, the Palau Güell is a magnificent example of the early days of the architect's fevered imagination. This extraordinary neo-Gothic mansion gives an insight into its maker's prodigious genius, and, though a little sombre compared with some of his later whims, it's a characteristic riot of styles (Gothic, Islamic, art nouveau) and materials.

After the civil war the police occupied the Palau and tortured political prisoners in the basement. The building was then abandoned, leading to long-term disrepair. It was reopened in 2012 after several years of refurbishment.

Visits begin on the ground floor, in what was once the coach house, and from there head down to the basement where the horses were stabled. Back upstairs you can admire the elaborate wrought iron of the main doors from the splendid vestibule, and the grand staircase lined with sandstone columns.

Up on the 1st floor is the main hall; central to the structure is the magnificent music room with its rebuilt organ (pictured) that is played during opening hours. The hall is a parabolic pyramid, each wall an arch stretching up three floors and coming together to form a dome. Off the music room is the Sala de Visites, with an exquisite *artesonado* (ceiling of interlaced beams with decorative insertions).

Above this main floor are the family rooms, some of which are labyrinthine or interlinked, and dotted with piercings of light, wrought-iron arabesques or grand, stained-glass windows. The view-laden roof is a tumult of tiled mosaics and fanciful design in the building's chimney pots.

DON'T MISS

➡ The music room
➡ The brick-arched basement stables
➡ The tiled chimney pots

PRACTICALITIES

➡ Map p296, G6
➡ ☎93 472 57 75
➡ www.palauguell.cat
➡ Carrer Nou de la Rambla 3-5
➡ adult/concession/child under 10yr incl audio guide €12/9/free, 1st Sun of month free
➡ ⏱10am-8pm Tue-Sun Apr-Oct, to 5.30pm Nov-Mar
➡ Ⓜ Drassanes

◉ SIGHTS

MACBA GALLERY
See p86.

PALAU GÜELL PALACE
See p87.

**ANTIC HOSPITAL
DE LA SANTA CREU** HISTORIC BUILDING
Map p296 (Former Hospital of the Holy Cross; Carrer de l'Hospital 56; ⊘9am-10pm; MLiceu) FREE
Behind the Mercat de La Boqueria stands the Gothic Antic Hospital de la Santa Creu, which was once the city's main hospital. Founded in 1401, it functioned until the 1930s, and was considered one of the best in Europe in its medieval heyday – it is famously the place where Antoni Gaudí died in 1926. Today it houses the **Biblioteca de Catalunya**, with its distinctive Gothic arches, and the Institut d'Estudis Catalans. The hospital's 15th-century former chapel, **La Capella** (Map p296; ⊘93 256 20 44; http://lacapella.barcelona; Carrer de l'Hospital 56; ⊘noon-8pm Tue-Sat, 11am-2pm Sun & public holidays; MLiceu) FREE, shows temporary exhibitions.

Entering from Carrer de l'Hospital, you find yourself in a peaceful courtyard garden. Up a sweep of stone steps is the members-only Catalan national library. Approaching the complex from Carrer del Carme or down a narrow lane from Jardins del Doctor Fleming (the little playground), you arrive at the entrance to the institute, which was once the 17th-century Casa de Convalescència de Sant Pau.

**CENTRE DE CULTURA CONTEMPORÀNIA
DE BARCELONA** GALLERY
Map p296 (CCCB; ⊘93 306 41 00; www.cccb.org; Carrer de Montalegre 5; adult/concession/child under 12yr €6/4/free, 3-8pm Sun free; ⊘11am-8pm Tue-Sun; MUniversitat) A complex of auditoriums, exhibition spaces and conference halls, the CCCB opened in 1994 in what was formerly an 18th-century hospice, the Casa de la Caritat. Its courtyard, with a vast glass wall on one side, is spectacular. With 4500 sq metres of galleries in four separate areas, the centre hosts a constantly changing programme of exhibitions, film cycles and other events.

**ESGLÉSIA DE SANT
PAU DEL CAMP** CHURCH
Map p296 (⊘93 441 00 01; www.santpaudelcamp.org; Carrer de Sant Pau 101; adult/concession/child under 14yr €5/4/free; ⊘10am-2pm & 3-6pm Mon-Sat, 10am-1pm Sun; MParal·lel) The best example of Romanesque architecture in Barcelona is the dainty little cloister of this small 11th- or 12th-century church, which was founded in the 9th or 10th century but later rebuilt. The cloister's 13th-century polylobulated arches, sitting atop intricately carved capitals, are unique in Europe. The church itself contains the tombstone of Guifré II, son of Guifré el Pelós, a 9th-century count considered the founding father of Catalonia.

INSTITUT D'ESTUDIS CATALANS COLLEGE
Map p296 (⊘93 270 16 20; www.iec.cat; Carrer del Carme 47; ⊘tours 10.30am, 11.30am & 12.30pm Tue & Thu; MLiceu) The Institute for Catalan Studies sits in the 17th-century Casa de Convalescència, once part of the Antic Hospital de la Santa Creu. The building, especially the entrance vestibule, is richly decorated with ceramic tiles. Visitors can peek at the courtyard, with its statue of St Paul, from the doorway, but to explore further in you'll have to book a guided tour (⊘93 170 17 97; www.sternalia.com; €8).

Up on the 1st floor at the far end is what was once an orange garden, now named after Catalan novelist Mercè Rodoreda.

RAMBLA DEL RAVAL STREET
Map p296 (MLiceu) This broad boulevard was laid out in 2000 as part of the city's plan to open up this formerly sleazy neighbourhood, with some success. Now lined with palm trees and terrace cafes, it hosts a craft market every weekend and is presided over by the glossy Barceló Raval (p234) hotel. Fernando Botero's 7m-long, 2m-tall bronze sculpture of a plump cat, **El Gat de Botero**, which stands near the bottom of the Rambla, is something of a Barcelona icon.

ⓘ ARTICKET

Barcelona's best bargain for art lovers is the **Articket BCN** (www.articketbcn.org; €35), which gives you entry to six museums for a fraction of what you'd pay if you bought individual tickets. The museums are the MACBA (p86), CCCB, Fundació Antoni Tàpies (p149), Fundació Joan Miró (p188), MNAC (p189) and Museu Picasso (p99).

EATING

El Raval's great-value dining scene roams across the globe. Timeless Barcelona classics are scattered across what was long the old city's poorest *barri*, while battalions of arty bars and restaurants dot the area around the MACBA and Carrer de Joaquín Costa. There are some great vegan and vegetarian dining spots, as well.

★ BAR CENTRAL
CAFE €

Map p296 (Carrer d'Elisabets 6; snacks €2-7; ⊙10am-9pm; MCatalunya) Launched in 2019 by the superstar foodie teams behind Barcelona hits Satan's Coffee (p77) and Xemei (p197), this fabulous tucked-away cafe-bar has taken over the palm-studded, ivy-wreathed courtyard and gardens and the priest's house of the 16th-century Casa de la Misericòrdia (a former orphanage). Classic coffees and vermouths accompany perfectly flaky croissants and delicate *entrepans* and salads. Find it via La Central bookshop (p96).

★ EL PACHUCO
MEXICAN €

Map p296 (www.facebook.com/pachucobcn; Carrer de Sant Pau 110; dishes €6-11; ⊙1.30pm-2am Mon-Thu, to 2.30am Fri-Sun; MParal·lel) Get to El Pachuco early or jump on the wait list – this tiny, narrow and deservedly popular *mezcalería/taquería* gets completely packed with a low-key, fashionable crowd. Exposed lightbulbs, dim lighting, bar stools and shelves cluttered with booze bottles and religious icons set the scene for first-rate tacos, quesadillas, guacamole and margaritas. There's a more spacious Barri Gòtic sister branch, La Pachuca (p72).

CARAVELLE
INTERNATIONAL €

Map p296 (☑93 317 98 92; www.caravelle.es; Carrer del Pintor Fortuny 31; mains €7-15; ⊙9am-5pm Mon, to midnight Tue-Fri, 10am-midnight Sat, 10am-5pm Sun approx May-Sep, reduced hours Oct-Apr; 🛜; MLiceu) Beloved of El Raval's stylish crowd and anyone with a discerning palate, this soulful little cafe-restaurant dishes up seasonally changing tacos like you've never tasted (cod, lime aioli and radish, roast pumpkin with frijoles) and creative international-style brunches that see queues snaking out the door. Coffee comes from Nømad (p92), while craft beers are home-brewed.

SÉSAMO
VEGETARIAN €

Map p296 (☑93 441 64 11; Carrer de Sant Antoni Abat 52; tapas €4-7, mains €9-14; ⊙7pm-midnight; 🛜🌱; MSant Antoni) Regularly lauded as one of the best veggie restaurants in the city, fun and cosy Sésamo transforms fresh, local ingredients into artful tapas: goat's-cheese salad, puff pastry filled with feta and spinach, mushroom croquettes and more. Most people go for the seven-course tapas menu (vegetarian/vegan €25/30, wine included, minimum two people). Nice touches include the home-baked bread and cakes.

ELISABETS
CATALAN €

Map p296 (☑93 317 58 26; Carrer de les Ramelleres 1; tapas €3-10, mains €8-10; ⊙7.30am-11.30pm Mon-Thu & Sat, to 1.30am Fri Sep-Jul, closed mid-Jul–mid-Aug; MCatalunya) Now just around the corner from its original location, this brilliant old neighbourhood restaurant, its walls dotted with radio sets, is known for its unpretentious, good-value cooking. The popular *menú del dia* (€12) changes daily, but you might also try *ragú de jabalí* (wild-boar stew), *mel i mató* (Catalan dessert of cheese and honey) or tempting classic-Catalan tapas like *fuet* (thin pork sausage).

VEGGIE GARDEN
VEGAN €

Map p296 (☑93 180 23 34; https://veggiegarden group.com; Carrer dels Àngels 3; mains €5-10; ⊙12.30-11.30pm; 🌱; MLiceu) Sit amid bright murals while charming staff serve a ridiculously good-value South Asian– and Mediterranean-influenced menu of plant-based thalis, curries, salads, veggie burgers, pastas and tapas to a young, woke crowd. There's a three-course, €9.25 *menú del dia*, plus another branch (p152) over in southern L'Eixample.

KASPARO
CAFE €

Map p296 (☑93 302 20 72; www.kasparo.es; Plaça de Vicenç Martorell 4; mains €7-12; ⊙9am-11pm or midnight Tue-Sat; 🛜; MCatalunya) This friendly terrace cafe, overlooking a traffic-free square and playground from beneath the arches, is a favourite with the neighbourhood parents and serves juices, tapas, quiches and salads, as well as more substantial dishes from around the globe and creative *entrepans* (filled sandwiches; perhaps with Brie, avocado and tomato).

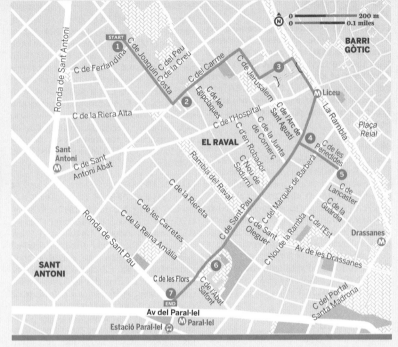

Neighbourhood Walk
Modernista Drinking & Dining in El Raval

START CASA ALMIRALL
END LA CONFITERIA
LENGTH 2KM; FIVE TO SIX HOURS

Long run by the Almirall family that opened it in the mid-19th century, the corner tavern **①Casa Almirall** (p92) preserves much of its Modernista decor, especially in the picture windows on to Carrer de Joaquín Costa and the counter and display cabinet.

Heading southeast, you'll recognise similarly sinuous curves as you reach welcoming **②Bar Muy Buenas** on Carrer del Carme. Launched as a milk bar in the late 19th century, it retains much of its original decoration: tiles, woodwork, a marble bar. It's a cosy place for a drink or a Catalan lunch.

Just off La Rambla, the **③Mercat de la Boqueria** (p64) dates to the 13th century, but it wasn't until 1840 that it was officially inaugurated on this site. In 1914 it was capped with a metal roof and given its charming wrought-iron, Modernista entrance sign.

A little south, on scruffy Carrer de Sant Pau, the **④Hotel España** (p235) is known above all for its dining rooms, part of the 1903 design by Lluís Domènech i Montaner. The bar features a magnificent alabaster fireplace designed by Eusebi Arnau.

While wandering around this part of El Raval, don't miss the **⑤Palau Güell** (p87), one of Gaudí's earlier big commissions. Not designed in his conventional Modernista style, it nonetheless has unmistakeable Gaudí touches.

Back on Carrer de Sant Pau, walk southwest past the Romanesque **⑥Església de Sant Pau del Camp** (p88) to lovingly restored **⑦La Confiteria** (p92), once a barber's shop and then a long-time confectioner's before becoming a bar in 1998. Most of the elements in the front section, including the facade, bar counter and cabinets, are the real deal.

A TU BOLA
MEDITERRANEAN €

Map p296 (☎93 315 32 44; www.atubolarest.
com; Carrer de l'Hospital 78; dishes €6-11; ⊘1pm-
midnight Mon & Thu, to 11pm Wed, to 1am Fri-Sun;
🖉; Ⓜ Sant Antoni) A snug brick-walled space
with just a few benches overlooking an
open kitchen, ATB delivers punchy street-
food flair with its seasonal, local-produce
menu of falafel-like bites. Enormous portions of sweet-potato, lentil or Caribbean-
style chicken 'balls' arrive with zesty cabbage salad, grilled pineapple or thick hummus. The €9.50 dish-with-bread-and-drink
deal is great value.

CHICHALIMONÁ
MEDITERRANEAN €

Map p296 (☎93 249 04 36; www.chichalimona.
com; Plaça dels Àngels 1, MACBA; tapas €2-7,
mains €7-11; ⊘8am-midnight Mon-Fri, from 9am
Sat & Sun) Tucked into the MACBA's (p86)
sunny ground floor, the latest branch of
Eixample-born Chichalimoná (p156) does
globally inspired brunches (with organic
eggs), roast-beef sandwiches, inventive
burgers and vermouth-time tapas like hummus, mussels and olives.

★CAÑETE
TAPAS €€

Map p296 (☎93 270 34 58; www.barcanete.
com; Carrer de la Unió 17; tapas €2-15, sharing plates €7-22; ⊘1pm-midnight Mon-Sat; 🛜;
Ⓜ Liceu) Epitomising the ongoing trend in
smartened-up versions of traditional tapas
bars, much-loved and always-busy Cañete
centres on a bustling open kitchen with
marble-topped bar. The long list of uber-
fresh tapas and *platillos* (sharing plates)
packs in modern twists (such as wild-tuna
tataki with seaweed) alongside traditional
favourites, including gooey tortilla and Andalucian classics like *boquerones* (anchovies) and *tortillitas de camarones* (shrimp
fritters).

SUCULENT
CATALAN €€

Map p296 (☎93 443 65 79; https://suculent.
com; Rambla del Raval 45; mains €11-18, tasting
menus €45-97; ⊘1-4pm & 8-11.30pm Wed-Sun;
🛜; Ⓜ Liceu) Part of celebrity chef Carles
Abellán's culinary empire, this old-style
bistro showcases the best of contemporary Catalan cuisine courtesy of El Bulli–
trained chef Toni Romero. From red-prawn
ceviche with avocado to steak tartare over
grilled bone marrow, only the finest ingredients make it into the smartly executed
creations.

BAR MUY BUENAS
CATALAN €€

Map p296 (☎93 807 28 57; http://muybuenas.
cat; Carrer del Carme 63; mains €9-15; ⊘1-
3.30pm & 8-11pm Mon-Thu, 1-4pm & 8pm-mid-
night Fri, 1pm-midnight Sat, 1-11.30pm Sun; Ⓜ Liceu) Modernista classic Muy Buenas has
been a bar since 1928, and wears its past
proudly with stunning and sinuous original
woodwork, etched-glass windows, old tiles
and a marble bar. Though the cocktails are
impressive, these days it's more restaurant
than bar, expertly turning out traditional
Catalan dishes such as *esqueixada* (salad
of shredded salted cod) and *fricandó* (pork-
and-vegetable stew).

There's a weekday *menú del dia* for €13,
and the bar opens all day until 12.30pm
(2am on Thursday and 3am on Friday and
Saturday).

FLAX & KALE
HEALTH FOOD €€

Map p296 (☎93 317 56 64; www.teresacarles.
com; Carrer dels Tallers 74b; mains €11-18; ⊘9am-
11.30pm Mon-Fri, from 9.30am Sat & Sun; 🛜🖉;
Ⓜ Universitat) Catalan chef Teresa Carles'
self-styled 'healthy flexitarian restaurant' is
a chic, sprawling, palm-dotted world where
80% of the menu is plant-based (20% comprises oily fish) and the all-round emphasis
is on nutrition. Raw, vegan and gluten-free
options abound; dishes wander from açai
bowls and red-quinoa pancakes to grilled-
aubergine ravioli and Panang red curry.
Head upstairs for the leafy terrace.

BACARO
ITALIAN €€

Map p296 (☎93 115 66 79; www.bacarobarce
lona.com; Carrer de Jerusalem 6; mains €13-25;
⊘1.30-4pm & 8.30pm-midnight Mon-Sat; Ⓜ Liceu) Widely considered one of Barcelona's
top Italian restaurants, Bacaro delivers
delicately crafted Venetian cuisine with
contemporary flair in a slender alley setting
just behind the Mercat de la Boqueria. It's a
warm, low-key yet stylish split-level spot in
which to tuck into beautiful seasonal plates
of, perhaps, wild-mushroom *passatelli* with
spinach pesto, smoked-mozzarella gnocchi
or Puglia burrata.

CERA 23
GALICIAN €€

Map p296 (☎93 442 08 08; www.cera23.com;
Carrer de la Cera 23; mains €12-17; ⊘7-11pm Mon-
Thu, 1-4pm & 7-11pm Thu-Sun; Ⓜ Sant Antoni) It's
easy to be won over by this good-natured
Galician place, set within the stone walls
of a century-old building, furnished with

eccentric touches like old alarm clocks and soundtracked by '80s bangers. Diners devour tastily modernised mains such as sea bass *en papillote*, Galician-style octopus and confit pork shoulder, with stellar cocktails including blackberry mojitos.

CASA LEOPOLDO
CATALAN €€

Map p296 (📞93 441 30 14; www.casaleopoldo.es; Carrer de Sant Rafael 24; tapas €4-15, mains €12-19; ⊘1-4pm & 8pm-late, closed Aug) Relaunched in 2017 by chefs Óscar Manresa and Romain Fornell, yet staying true to its classic roots, this charming El Raval old-timer has tile-patterned walls, bullfighting posters and smart white tablecloths. The kitchen showcases traditional Catalan favourites such as *cap i pota* (beef-and-chickpea stew) and oxtail in red wine, along with fried prawns, wild mushrooms and other deliciously uncomplicated tapas.

EN VILLE
SPANISH €€

Map p296 (📞93 302 84 67; www.envillebarcelona.es; Carrer del Doctor Dou 14; mains €13-19; ⊘1-4pm & 7.30-11.30pm; ⓂUniversitat) You'll want to come here for the divine decor – dramatic bouquets, oil paintings and antique details all around, in a 19th-century building – as much as the food. It's mostly, but not always, Spanish, and entirely gluten free, with dishes such as asparagus risotto, red-wine squid and spinach and camembert salad. Arrive early for lunch (*menú del dia* €15) to beat the queues.

🍷 DRINKING & NIGHTLIFE

★TWO SCHMUCKS
COCKTAIL BAR

Map p296 (📞635 396 088; www.facebook.com/schmuckordie; Carrer de Joaquín Costa 52; ⊘5pm-2am Sun-Fri, to 2.30am Sat; ⓂSant Antoni, Universitat) Originally a wandering pop-up bar, seriously edgy yet refreshingly unpretentious Swedish-run Two Schmucks has become one of Barcelona's (and Europe's) most talked-about cocktail bars, with ambitious owner-bartenders Moe and AJ sweeping multiple awards. Channelling a glammed-up dive-bar vibe, with recycled furniture and a fun friendly team, it mixes outstanding liquid concoctions like the signature Curry Colada (€9).

★LA CONFITERIA
BAR

Map p296 (📞93 140 54 35; www.confiteria.cat; Carrer de Sant Pau 128; ⊘7pm-2am Mon-Thu, 6pm-3am Fri & Sat, 5pm-2am Sun; 🛜; ⓂParal·lel) This evocative tile-covered cocktail hangout is a trip back to the 19th century. Until the 1980s it was a confectioner's shop, and though the original cabinets are now bursting with booze, the look barely changed with its conversion courtesy of one of Barcelona's foremost teams in nightlife wizardry. The scene these days is lively and creative (drinks €8 to €10).

CASA ALMIRALL
BAR

Map p296 (📞93 318 99 17; www.casaalmirall.com; Carrer de Joaquín Costa 33; ⊘4.30pm-1.30am Mon, 4pm-2.30am Tue & Wed, noon-2.30am Thu, noon-3am Fri & Sat, noon-12.30am Sun; 🛜; ⓂUniversitat) In business since 1860, this unchanged corner bar is dark and intriguing, with Modernista decor and a mixed clientele. There are some great original pieces in here, such as the marble counter, and the cast-iron statue of the muse of the Universal Exposition, held in Barcelona in 1888. Absinthe and vermouth star on the menu.

NØMAD EVERY DAY
COFFEE

Map p296 (www.nomadcoffee.es; Carrer de Joaquín Costa 26; ⊘8.30am-6.30pm Mon-Fri, 10am-7pm Sat & Sun; ⓂSant Antoni, Universitat) A seasonal roster of roasted-in-Barcelona beans combine with the latest caffeine tech at El Raval's branch of supersuccessful Nømad, founded by rockstar barista Jordi Mestre after a stint on London's coffee scene. Join the city's aficionados for a flat white, cold brew or Aeropress (coffees €2.50 to €5), surrounded by patterned floor tiles, minimal rust-red decor and a living wall.

Branches in La Ribera (p111) and Poblenou (p133).

BAR MARSELLA
BAR

Map p296 (📞93 442 72 63; Carrer de Sant Pau 65; ⊘6pm-2am Mon-Thu, 10pm-3am Fri, 6pm-2.30am Sat, 10pm-2.30am Sun; ⓂLiceu) Bar Marsella has been in business since 1820, and has served the likes of Dalí, Picasso, Gaudí and Hemingway. The latter was known to slump here over an *absenta* (absinthe) amid the tiled floors and glinting chandeliers. The bar still specialises in absinthe (€5), a drink to be treated with respect.

Your absinthe glass comes with a lump of sugar, a fork and a little bottle of mineral water. Hold the sugar on the fork, over your glass, and drip the water onto the sugar so that it dissolves into the absinthe, which turns yellow. The result should give you a warm glow.

BAR PASTÍS
BAR

Map p296 (☑634 031 527; www.facebook.com/barpastisraval; Carrer de Santa Mònica 4; ⊘7.30pm-2am Tue-Sun; ☎; ⓂDrassanes) A French-cabaret theme (with lots of Piaf on the stereo) pervades this tiny, cluttered classic, which has been going, on and off, since the end of WWII, when it was founded by a French exile. You'll need to be in before 9pm to have any hope of sitting at or getting near the bar. Frequent live performances usually include French *chanson*.

GRANJA M VIADER
CAFE

Map p296 (☑93 318 34 86; www.granjaviader.cat; Carrer d'en Xuclà 6; ⊘9am-1.15pm & 5-9pm Mon-Sat; ⓂLiceu) For over a century, people have been coming to this classically Catalan milk bar for hot chocolate ladled out with whipped cream (ask for a *suís*). The interior is delightfully old-fashioned, with marble-top tables and floor tiling. It also sells cheeses, cakes and charcuterie. In 1931, the Viader clan invented Cacaolat, a bottled chocolate milk drink with iconic label design.

LA MONROE
BAR

Map p296 (☑93 441 94 61; www.lamonroe.es; Plaça Salvador Seguí 1-9; ⊘noon-late; ☎; ⓂLiceu) Peer through the glass walls of this lively LGBTIQ-friendly hangout inside the Filmoteca de Catalunya (p94), and you'll spot long wooden tables, rickety chairs, leafy plants, industrial touches and a cobbled floor that mimics the square outside. Great cocktails and vermouth, a €12 *menú del dia* and delectable tapas (€4 to €12) like grilled Huelva prawns and Catalan *fuet* (thin pork sausage).

33 | 45
BAR

Map p296 (☑93 187 41 38; www.facebook.com/3345bar; Carrer de Joaquín Costa 4; ⊘5pm-2am Mon, 1pm-2am Tue-Thu, to 2.30am Fri & Sat, to 1.30am Sun; ☎; ⓂSant Antoni) A wonderfully low-key yet stylish bar on a street full of them, this busy industrial-chic place has excellent mojitos (€5 to €7), a fashionable crowd and a frequently changing exhibi-

OUT & ABOUT IN EL RAVAL

The shadowy side streets of El Raval are dotted with scores of bars and clubs, and despite its vestigial edginess, this is a great place to go out. You'll find super-fashionable cocktail spots alongside great old taverns that have been the hang-outs of the city's bohemia since Picasso's time. Studeny Carrer de Joaquín Costa is a treasure trove of bars old and new. The lower end of El Raval has a history of insalubriousness and the area around Carrer de Sant Pau retains its seedy feel: drug dealers, pickpockets and prostitutes mingle with nocturnal hedonists. Keep your wits about you at night.

tion of art on the walls. There are DJs most nights and cosy sofas for kicking back over coffee.

CARIBBEAN CLUB
COCKTAIL BAR

Map p296 (☑93 302 21 82; www.caribbeanclubbcn.com; Carrer de les Sitges 5; ⊘6pm-2.30am Tue-Sat; ☎; ⓂCatalunya) The dimly lit ship-like interior, with low wooden beams and cocktail shakers and literature displayed in glass cabinets, is just a taster at this elegant cocktail spot headed up by respected barman Juanjo González Rubiera. Caribbean rums steal the show (cocktails €9), while other tempting mixes include a delicate Gin Smash.

NEGRONI
COCKTAIL BAR

Map p296 (www.negronicocktailbar.com; Carrer de Joaquín Costa 46; ⊘7pm-2.30am Sun-Thu, to 3am Fri & Sat; ⓂUniversitat) Good things come in small packages, as this dark, teeny cocktail bar shows. The bold black decor lures in a largely student set for personalised cocktails, among them, of course, the celebrated negroni (€9), a Florentine invention with one part Campari, one part gin and one part sweet vermouth.

MARMALADE
BAR

Map p296 (☑93 442 39 66; www.marmaladebarcelona.com; Carrer de la Riera Alta 4-6; ⊘7pm-2am Mon-Thu, 10am-2.30am Fri & Sat, 10am-2am Sun; ☎; ⓂSant Antoni) The golden hues of this backlit bar and restaurant beckon seductively through the glass facade. There are various spaces, adorned in equally sumptuous styles: feathered lampshades, exposed brick, floral walls, pool table next to the bar. Cocktails (€6 to €9), both classic and innovative, are big business here, as is weekend brunch (€8 to €11).

Milk (p72) in the Barri Gòtic and L'Eixample's Gigi von Tapas (p157) are from the same team.

MOOG
CLUB

Map p296 (☑93 319 17 89; www.moogbarcelona.com; Carrer de l'Arc del Teatre 3; entry €5-10; ⊗midnight-5am Sun-Thu, to 5.30am Fri & Sat; MDrassanes) This fun and minuscule club is a standing favourite with the downtown crowd. In the main dance area, DJs dish out house, techno and electro, while upstairs you can groove to a blend of indie and occasional classic-pop throwbacks.

LA CONCHA
BAR, GAY

Map p296 (☑93 302 41 18; www.laconchadelraval.com; Carrer de la Guàrdia 14; ⊗5pm-2.30am Sun-Thu, to 3.30am Fri & Sat; 🛜; MDrassanes) This long-running bar is dedicated to groundbreaking 20th-century actress Sara Montiel: the walls groan with more than 250 photos of the sultry star surrounding an incongruous large-screen TV. La Concha used to be a largely gay and trans haunt, but anyone is welcome and bound to have fun – especially when the drag queens come out to play.

BETTY FORD'S
BAR

Map p296 (☑93 304 13 68; Carrer de Joaquín Costa 56; ⊗1pm-2.30am Tue-Fri, from 5pm Sat-Mon; 🛜; MUniversitat) This enticing corner bar near the MACBA is one of several standout stops along the student-jammed run of Carrer de Joaquín Costa. It puts together some nice cocktails and gets busy with an even mix of locals and foreigners, generally not much over 30. There's a decent line in burgers and soups, too.

EL CANGREJO
CLUB, GAY

Map p296 (www.facebook.com/elcangrejodelraval; Carrer de Montserrat 9; entry incl drink €10; ⊗11pm-3am Fri & Sat; MDrassanes) This altar to kitsch is a dingy dance hall that has transgressed since the 1920s, and for years starred the luminous underground cabaret figure Carmen de Mairena. It exudes a gorgeously tacky feel, especially with the 11.30pm drag shows. Due to its popularity with tourists, getting in is all but impossible unless you turn up early.

KENTUCKY
BAR

Map p296 (☑93 318 28 78; Carrer de l'Arc del Teatre 11; ⊗10pm-4am Thu-Sat; MDrassanes) Once a haunt of visiting US Navy boys, this exercise in Americana kitsch is the perfect way to finish an evening – if you can squeeze in. All sorts of odd bods from the *barri* and beyond gather here. An institution in the wee hours, Kentucky often stays open (unofficially) until dawn.

☆ ENTERTAINMENT

★FILMOTECA DE CATALUNYA
CINEMA

Map p296 (☑93 567 10 70; www.filmoteca.cat; Plaça de Salvador Seguí 1-9; adult/concession €4/3; ⊗screenings 5-10pm, ticket office 10am-3pm Tue-Fri, plus 4-9.30pm Tue-Thu & Sun, to 10pm Fri & Sat; MLiceu) Relocated to El Raval in 2012 as part of plans to revive the neighbourhood's cultural offerings, Catalonia's national cinema occupies a modern 6000-sq-metre building in the midst of the most louche part of El Raval. The films shown are a superior mix of classics and more recent releases, with frequent themed cycles.

In addition to two cinemas totalling 535 seats, the Filmoteca comprises a film library, a bookshop, La Monroe (p93) cafebar, offices and a dedicated space for exhibitions.

23 ROBADORS
LIVE MUSIC

Map p296 (www.23robadors.wordpress.com; Carrer d'en Robador 23; entry €5; ⊗8pm-3am; MLiceu) On what remains a sleazy Raval street in spite of gentrification in the area, this narrow little bar has made a name for itself with its shows and live music. Jazz is the name of the game, but you'll also hear live poetry, flamenco and plenty more.

JAZZSÍ CLUB
LIVE MUSIC

Map p296 (☑93 329 00 20; http://tallerdemusics.com; Carrer de Requesens 2; entry incl drink €6-12; ⊗8.30-11pm Mon & Thu, 7.45-11pm Tue & Wed, 8.45-11pm Fri & Sat, 6.30-10pm Sun; MSant Antoni) A cramped little bar run by the Taller de Músics (Musicians' Workshop) school and foundation, staging a varied programme that ranges from jazz jams to some good flamenco (Friday and Saturday). Thursday is Cuban night, Tuesday and Sunday are rock, and the rest are devoted to jazz and/or blues sessions. Some concerts are preceded by jam sessions.

TEATRE LLANTIOL
THEATRE

Map p296 (☏93 329 90 09; www.llantiol.com; Carrer de la Riereta 7; ⓂSant Antoni) At this small, charming cafe-theatre, which has a certain scuffed elegance and dates back to 1980, all sorts of stuff, from concerts and theatre to magic shows, is staged. The speciality, though, is stand-up comedy (occasionally in English).

TEATRE ROMEA
THEATRE

Map p296 (☏93 301 55 04; www.teatreromea. cat; Carrer de l'Hospital 51; ⊙box office 5.30pm to start of show Tue-Fri, from 4.30pm Sat & Sun; ⓂLiceu) Just off La Rambla, this 19th-century theatre was resurrected at the end of the 1990s and is one of the city's key stages for quality drama. It usually fills up for a broad range of interesting plays, often classics with a contemporary flavour, in Catalan and Spanish.

 ## SHOPPING

★LES TOPETTES
COSMETICS

Map p296 (☏93 500 55 64; www.lestopettes. com; Carrer de Joaquín Costa 33; ⊙4-9pm Mon, 11am-2pm & 4-9pm Tue-Sat; ⓂUniversitat) Globe-trotting products at this chic little temple to soap and perfume have been handpicked, by journalist Lucía and chef-interior designer Oriol, for their designs as much as for their qualities. You'll find gorgeously packaged scents, candles, soaps and creams from Diptyque, Cowshed and Hierbas de Ibiza, among others.

★GREY STREET
HOMEWARES

Map p296 (www.greystreetbarcelona.com; Carrer Peu de la Creu 25; ⊙11am-3pm & 4-9pm Mon-Sat; ⓂSant Antoni) Named for the Canberra home of Australian owner Amy Cocker's grandparents, this stylishly reimagined former perfume shop is decked with tempting trinkets, many of them crafted by local or Spanish artists – handpainted ceramic mugs and plant pots, fair-trade incense, tarot cards, patterned wall prints, handmade swimwear, vegan skincare and more.

HOLALA! PLAZA
FASHION & ACCESSORIES

Map p296 (☏93 302 05 93; www.holala-ibiza. com; Plaça de Castella 2; ⊙11am-9pm Mon-Sat;

ⓂUniversitat) Backing on to Carrer de Valldonzella, this Ibiza import is inspired by the Balearic island's long-established (and now somewhat commercialised) hippie tradition. Vintage clothes sourced from flea markets and reusable-fashion outlets across the globe are the name of the game, with lots of denim and vibrant colours on show, plus an eclectic exhibitions programme.

LANTOKI
FASHION & ACCESSORIES

Map p296 (www.lantoki.es; Carrer del Doctor Dou 15; ⊙11am-8pm Mon-Fri, from noon Sat; ⓂCatalunya, Liceu) 🛈 Designers Urko Martinez and Sandra Liberal handcraft their own minimalist women's fashion in this bright, breezy El Raval studio-boutique, which also flaunts pieces by other local creatives. The emphasis is on original, slow-fashion artisan collections, and there are also design-your-own-clothes workshops (around €40 to €90).

TERANYINA
ARTS & CRAFTS

Map p296 (☏93 317 94 36; www.textilteranyina. com; Carrer del Notariat 10; ⊙11am-3pm & 5-8pm Mon-Fri; ⓂCatalunya) Artist Teresa Rosa Aguayo runs this textile workshop in the heart of the artsy bit of El Raval. You can join workshops at the loom, admire some of the rugs and other pieces that Teresa has created and, of course, buy them.

LA VARIÉTÉ
HOMEWARES

Map p296 (☏93 519 83 51; www.lavariete.net; Carrer d'Elisabets 7; ⊙11am-3pm & 4-8.30pm Mon-Sat; ⓂCatalunya, Liceu) 🛈 Decorative pieces made from Chiang Mai wood, lampshades that reuse old bamboo lobster traps and handmade hanging terracotta plant pots are just a few of the tempting home-designed pieces at this calming interiors boutique, which collaborates directly with artists, craftspeople and farmers in Thailand.

FANTASTIK
ARTS & CRAFTS

Map p296 (☏93 301 30 68; www.fantastik.es; Carrer de Joaquín Costa 62; ⊙11am-1pm & 4-8.30pm Mon-Fri, 11am-3pm & 4-9pm Sat; ⓂUniversitat) Over 500 products, such as woodland dolls, tin robots, vintage posters and Mexican rubber tablecloths, fill this colourful shop, which sources its collection from countries including India, China, Morocco, Germany, Russia, Mexico and Japan. Perfect for all the things you don't need but can't live without.

EL RAVAL BOUTIQUES

Some of Barcelona's most original shopping is in El Raval. A handful of art galleries surround the MACBA, and there's a healthy secondhand and vintage clothes scene on Carrer de la Riera Baixa and around. Carrer dels Tallers is one of the city's main music strips, and local fashion designers and interior designers have set up workshops and boutiques all over the *barri*.

LA CENTRAL   BOOKS
Map p296 (⌘900 802109; www.lacentral.com; Carrer d'Elisabets 6; ⊙10am-9pm Mon-Sat; ⓂCatalunya) Built into what was originally a chapel, La Central stocks an impressive range of titles in various languages (including Barcelona guides) and a smart stationery line. It also has a fabulous garden cafebar (p89) out the back.

CHÖK   FOOD
Map p296 (⌘93 304 23 60; www.chokbarcelona.com; Carrer del Carme 3; ⊙9am-9pm; ⓂLiceu) Set inside an old chocolate-maker's store, with original wooden shelving and stained glass, Chök specialises in all things sweet, but especially doughnuts. These come in a huge array of colours and flavours, but there are also cookies, macarons and marshmallows, and a tiny space where you can sip a coffee. Various branches around town.

LA NOSTRA CIUTAT   ARTS & CRAFTS
Map p296 (⌘93 158 83 13; https://lanostraciutat.co; Carrer del Doctor Dou 11; ⊙11am-3pm & 4-9pm Mon-Sat; ⓂCatalunya, Liceu) The creative work of Catalan artists is the star at this jolly little shop with a few branches around the city centre. Pick up snazzy Barcelona-map prints by Idmary Hernandez, prints of iconic Modernista buildings by Daniella Ferretti, tote bags depicting city scenes and all kinds of beautiful stationery.

LA PORTORRIQUEÑA   COFFEE
Map p296 (⌘93 317 34 38; Carrer d'en Xuclà 25; ⊙10am-2pm & 5-8pm Mon-Fri, 9am-2pm Sat; ⓂCatalunya) Coffee beans from around the world, freshly ground before your eyes, have been the winning formula for this well-established store since 1902, though it also sells teas and all sorts of chocolate goodies. Carrer d'en Xuclà is also good for little old-fashioned food boutiques.

🏃 SPORTS & ACTIVITIES

Social enterprise **Hidden City Tours** (p83) runs excellent tours of El Raval (in Spanish, English or German), with guides who come from Barcelona's homeless community.

BARCELONA STREET STYLE TOUR   WALKING
(www.barcelonastreetstyletour.com; by donation) Highly entertaining, donation-based two-hour strolls around El Raval (10am, 4.45pm) and El Born/Barri Gòtic (2pm), delving into the history of Barcelona's street-art scene and its key artists. Tours are usually (not always) in English; book ahead online. Also does street-art workshops (from €26) and art-focused El Poblenou bike tours (€23 per person).

CRUISING BARCELONA   CYCLING
Map p296 (⌘93 011 03 11; www.cruisingbarcelona.com; Carrer de Jerusalem 32; tours adult €25, child €6-16; ⊙10am-8pm; 🚲) Handily based behind La Boqueria market, this friendly outfitter has three-hour bike tours in Spanish, English, German and Dutch, taking in El Raval, El Born, Barceloneta, the Arc de Triomf and Passeig de Gràcia. Also offers bike hire (from €9 per half day).

CICLOTOUR   CYCLING
Map p296 (⌘93 317 19 70; www.barcelonaciclotour.com; Carrer dels Tallers 45; tours €22; ⊙9.30am-9pm; ⓂUniversitat) This well-established team of multilingual guides runs one to four daily bike tours around the city's main sights, as well as e-bike jaunts up Montjuïc and evening tours visiting the Font Màgica. Check schedules online.

La Ribera & El Born

Neighbourhood Top Five

1 **Basílica de Santa Maria del Mar** (p101) Admiring the simplicity and beauty of this fine example of Catalan Gothic, built with help from local parishioners.

2 **Museu Picasso** (p99) Being introduced to the origins of Picasso's genius at this fascinating museum

spread across a series of interconnected palaces.

3 **Palau de la Música Catalana** (p102) Taking in a show or exploring on a tour of this marvellous Modernista concert hall.

4 **Bar-hopping in El Born** (p110) Tucking into old-school tapas and sipping

avant-garde cocktails amid El Born's buzz, maybe at award-winning Dr Stravinsky.

5 **Parc de la Ciutadella** (p103) Enjoying a stroll, having a picnic, taking a boat out on the lake and spotting the artworks.

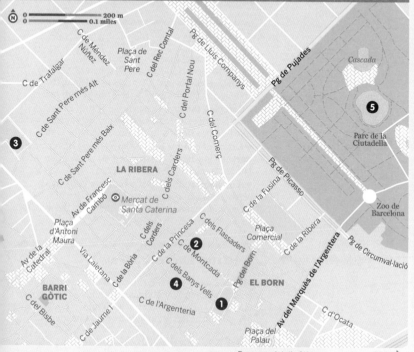

For more detail of this area see Map p300 ➡

Lonely Planet's Top Tip

Getting around Barcelona's many museums can be anything but cheap, so take advantage of free Sunday afternoons, when entry into many of the city's museums will cost you zilch!

🍷 Best Places to Drink

➡ Dr Stravinsky (p111)

➡ Paradiso/Pastrami Bar (p111)

➡ Nømad Coffee Lab & Shop (p111)

➡ Guzzo (p111)

➡ Bar Sauvage (p111)

For reviews, see p111.

✕ Best Places to Eat

➡ Casa Delfín (p109)

➡ Bormuth (p106)

➡ Euskal Etxea (p109)

➡ Can Cisa/Bar Brutal (p109)

➡ Cal Pep (p109)

➡ Bar del Pla (p109)

For reviews, see p106.➡

◉ Best Architecture

➡ Basílica de Santa Maria del Mar (p101)

➡ Palau de la Música Catalana (p102)

➡ Carrer de Montcada (p103)

➡ Museu Picasso

For reviews, see p113.➡

Explore La Ribera & El Born

La Ribera is widely used to refer to the area covered by the city council's rather long-winded appellation of Sant Pere, Santa Caterina i la Ribera. Below Carrer de la Princesa, the gentrified southern half is known as El Born, after Passeig del Born (p104), Barcelona's main drag from the 13th to the 18th centuries, now lined with bars and cafes. Capped at one end by the magnificent Gothic Basílica de Santa Maria del Mar (p101), it runs to the Born Centre de Cultura i Memòria (p104). With wonderful boutiques, bars, cafes and restaurants dotted all around, this area should be your first port of call, especially a stroll down Carrer de Montcada (p103), home to the Museu Picasso. Some visitors spend most of their time in El Born (and the adjacent Barri Gòtic), and many expats have settled in this part of town, which is also one of Barcelona's prime nightlife spots.

Northwest of Carrer de la Princesa, a tangle of narrow streets wiggles northward around the striking modern reincarnation of the locally loved Mercat de Santa Caterina (p104) and on towards the Modernista Palau de la Música Catalana (p102). Some good eating and drinking options have opened up in these narrow streets and slightly east near Plaça de Sant Pere, too. Via Laietana marks the southwest side of La Ribera, while the Parc de la Ciutadella (p103) – a rare green space in central Barcelona – closes off its northeastern flank.

Local Life

➡ **Market secrets** Locals get their produce at the Mercat de Santa Caterina (p104), where, in season, stand holders 'flavour' their eggs by stacking them up and placing truffles among them (divine soft-boiled!).

➡ **Catching the rays** Favourite local strip Passeig del Born is perfect for lazy Sunday-morning sunbathing on cafe terraces, or for sturdier drinks into the night.

➡ **A slice of culture** Join the largely local clientele for a weekend lunchtime classical concert at the Palau de la Música Catalana (p102).

➡ **Barcelona style** Shop at some of the city's most original fashion boutiques (p115), many of which have an ecoconscious ethos that also highlights the work of local designers.

Getting There & Away

Metro Línia 4 coasts down the southwest flank of La Ribera, stopping at Urquinaona, Jaume I and Barceloneta. Línia 1 also stops nearby, at Urquinaona and Arc de Triomf (the nearest stop for Parc de la Ciutadella).

SEE MANSIONS PACKED WITH PICASSOS

The setting alone, in five contiguous medieval stone mansions, makes Barcelona's Museu Picasso unique (and worth the queues). While the collection concentrates on Pablo Picasso's formative years – potentially disappointing lovers of his better-known later works – there is enough material from subsequent periods to showcase the artist's versatility and genius. Above all, you come away feeling that Picasso was the true original, always one step ahead of himself (let alone anyone else) in his search for new forms of expression.

History of the Museum

Allegedly it was Picasso himself who proposed the museum's creation in 1960, to his friend and personal secretary Jaume Sabartés, a Barcelona native. Three years later, the 'Sabartés Collection' was opened, since a museum bearing Picasso's name would have been met with censorship – Picasso's opposition to the Franco regime was well known. The Museu Picasso we see today opened in 1983. It originally held only Sabartés' personal collection of Picasso's art and a handful of other works, but the collection gradually expanded with donations from Salvador Dalí and Sebastià Junyer Vidal, among others. However, the largest part of the present collection came from Picasso himself. His widow, Jacqueline Roque, also donated 41 ceramic pieces and the *Woman with Bonnet* painting after Picasso's death.

Sabartés' contribution is honoured with Picasso's famous Blue Period portrait of him wearing a ruff (room B1).

DON'T MISS

→ *Las meninas* (The Ladies-in-Waiting)
→ *Retrato de la tía Pepa* (Portrait of Aunt Pepa)
→ *Ciència i caritat* (Science and Charity)
→ *Terrats de Barcelona* (Roofs of Barcelona)
→ *El foll* (The Madman)

PRACTICALITIES

→ Map p300, D5
→ 📞93 256 30 00
→ www.museupicasso.bcn.cat
→ Carrer de Montcada 15-23
→ adult/concession/under 18yr permanent collection & temporary exhibit €14/7.50/free, 6-9.30pm Thu & 1st Sun of month free
→ 🕙10am-5pm Mon, 9am-8.30pm Tue, Wed & Fri-Sun, to 9.30pm Thu
→ Ⓜ Jaume I

GETTING AROUND THE COLLECTION

The permanent collection is housed in the Palau Aguilar, Palau del Baró de Castellet and Palau Meca, all dating to the 14th century. The 18th-century Casa Mauri, built over medieval remains (even some Roman leftovers have been identified), and the adjacent 14th-century Palau Finestres, accommodate temporary exhibitions.

TOP TIPS

At €15, the Carnet del Museu Picasso annual pass is barely more expensive than a day pass, and allows multiple entries. There is a special desk for this at Carrer de Montcada 23.

Avoid queues by booking tickets online and choosing a time slot, or arrive first thing.

Admission is free on Thursday 6pm to 9.30pm and the first Sunday of the month.

The Collection

The collection, which includes more than 3500 artworks, is strongest on Picasso's earliest years, up until 1904, which is apt considering that the artist spent his formative creative years in Barcelona.

A visit starts with sketches and oils from his earliest years in Málaga and A Coruña (1893–5). What makes this collection truly impressive – one-of-a-kind among the world's many Picasso museums – is the way in which it displays Picasso's extraordinary talent at such a young age. Faced with the technical virtuosity of a painting such as the enormous *Ciència i caritat* (Science and Charity; room 3) or *Retrato de la tía Pepa* (Portrait of Aunt Pepa; room 2), it seems almost inconceivable that they could have been created by a 15-year-old. Some of his self-portraits and the portraits of his parents, which date from 1896, are further evidence of his precocious talent.

In rooms 5 to 7 hang paintings from his first Paris sojourn, while room 8 is dedicated to the earliest significant new stage in his development, the Blue Period. *Woman with Bonnet* is an important work from this period, as are the nocturnal blue-tinted views of *Terrats de Barcelona* (Roofs of Barcelona; room 8) and *El foll* (The Madman; often on loan).

Las Meninas Through the Prism of Picasso

From 1954 to 1962, Picasso was obsessed with the idea of researching and 'rediscovering' the greats, in particular Velázquez. In 1957 he made a series of renditions of Velázquez' masterpiece *Las meninas* (The Ladies-in-Waiting), now displayed in rooms 12 to 14. It is as though Picasso looked at the original Velázquez painting through a prism reflecting all the styles he had worked through until then, creating his own masterpiece in the process. This is a wonderful opportunity to see *Las meninas* in its entirety, in a beautiful space.

Ceramics

What is also special about the Museu Picasso is its showcasing of his work in lesser-known media. The last rooms contain Picasso's engravings and 42 ceramic pieces completed throughout the latter years of his unceasingly creative life. You'll see plates and bowls decorated with simple, single-line drawings of fish, owls and other animal shapes, typical for Picasso's daubing on clay. Room 16, meanwhile, displays portraits of his wife Jacqueline Roque from the 1960s.

TOP EXPERIENCE
CATCH A CONCERT IN A CATALAN GOTHIC CHURCH AT SANTA MARIA DEL MAR

At the southwestern end of Passeig del Born stands Barcelona's finest Catalan Gothic church, Santa Maria del Mar (Our Lady of the Sea). Begun in 1329, under the watch of architects Berenguer de Montagut and Ramon Despuig, the church is remarkable for its architectural harmony and simplicity. Famously, the parishioners themselves gave up their time to help construct the church, particularly the stevedores from the nearby port.

DON'T MISS

➡ The church's builders portrayed in memorial stone relief

➡ A live music performance

➡ El Fossar de les Moreres (next door)

PRACTICALITIES

➡ Map p300, E6

➡ ☑ 93 310 23 90

➡ www.santamariadel marbarcelona.org

➡ Plaça de Santa Maria del Mar

➡ guided tour €8.50-10

➡ ⊙ 9am-8.30pm Mon-Sat, 10am-8pm Sun, tours 1-5pm Sat, from 2pm Sun

➡ Ⓜ Jaume I

The Main Sanctuary

The pleasing unity of form and symmetry of the central nave and two flanking aisles owe much to the rapidity with which the church was built – a mere, record-breaking 54 years. The slender, octagonal pillars create an enormous sense of lateral space, bathed in the light of stained glass. The walls, side chapels and facades were finished by 1350 and the entire structure was completed in 1383.

Even before anarchists gutted the church in 1909 and again in 1936 (when it famously burned for 11 days straight), Santa Maria always lacked superfluous decoration. Absent are the gilded chapels that weigh heavily over so many Spanish churches, while the splashes of colour high above the nave are subtle – unusually and beautifully so. It all serves to highlight the church's fine proportions, purity of line and sense of space.

The Porters

During the construction, the city's *bastaixos* (porters) spent a day each week carrying across the stone required to build the church from royal quarries in Montjuïc. Their memory lives on in reliefs of them in the main doors and stone carvings elsewhere in the church, a reminder that Santa Maria was conceived as a people's church.

El Fossar de les Moreres

Opposite the church's southern flank, an eternal flame burns high over a sunken square. This was **El Fossar de les Moreres** (The Mulberry Cemetery; Map p300; Ⓜ Jaume I), where Catalan resistance fighters were buried after the siege of Barcelona ended in defeat in September 1714 during the War of the Spanish Succession.

Tours & Performances

From 1pm to 5pm (and 2pm to 5pm on Sundays), visitors must pay to enter and join a guided tour (€10), which takes in the main church, galleries and crypt. A separate tour zips you up to the towers and rooftop (€8.50). Musical performances occasionally take place; check the website or ask locally.

TOP EXPERIENCE
ATTEND A CLASSICAL OR CHORAL PERFORMANCE AT THE PALAU DE LA MÚSICA CATALANA

A fantastical symphony in tile, brick, sculpted stone; Unesco-listed, 2146-seat concert hall is a high point of Barcelona's Modernista architecture. It was built by Lluís Domènech i Montaner, with the help of some of the best Catalan artisans of the time, between 1905 and 1908, for the Orfeo Català musical society. It was conceived as a temple for the Catalan Renaixença (Renaissance).

Like a peacock, the *palau* shows off much of its splendour on the outside, and since 1990 it has undergone several major changes. Take in the principal facade with its mosaics, floral capitals and the sculpture cluster representing Catalan popular music. Wander inside the foyer and restaurant areas to admire the spangled, tiled pillars and clever use of natural light and stained glass, before climbing to the mosaic-adorned pillars gracing the front balcony outside the rest salon.

The showstopper, however, is the richly colourful auditorium, with its ceiling of blue-and-gold stained glass and a shimmering 1000kg skylight that looks like a giant, crystalline, downward-thrusting nipple. Above a bust of Beethoven on the stage towers a wind-blown sculpture of Wagner's Valkyries (Wagner was top of the Barcelona charts at the time the building was created), all accompanied by 18 Greek mythological muses. Tilted chandeliers look towards the sun-like skylight, like flowers.

Unless you're here for a show (p113), which is highly recommended, admission is by 55-minute guided tour in Spanish, Catalan, English, French or Italian; tickets can be bought ahead online.

DON'T MISS
➡ The main auditorium and its carved ceiling roses

➡ The principal facade's mosaics and columns

➡ The foyer and pillars in the restaurant

➡ A performance – day or night

PRACTICALITIES
➡ Map p300, A3

➡ ☎93 295 72 00

➡ www.palaumusica.cat

➡ Carrer Palau de la Música 4-6

➡ adult/concession/under 10yr €20/16/free

➡ ⊙guided tours 10am-3.30pm Sep-Jun, to 6pm Easter & Jul, 9am-6pm Aug

➡ Ⓜ Urquinaona

Controversies

The original Modernista creation did not meet with universal approval in its day. The doyen of Catalan literature, Josep Pla, did not hesitate to condemn it as 'horrible', but few share his sentiments today. Montaner himself was also in a huff and failed to attend the opening ceremony because of unsettled bills.

The *palau* was at the centre of a fraud scandal from 2009 to 2012, as its president, Fèlix Millet, admitted to having siphoned off millions of euros of funds; he and his partner Jordi Muntoll were ordered to repay the embezzled money to the *palau* and jailed for 9½ and 7½ years respectively in 2018.

⊙ SIGHTS

MUSEU PICASSO   MUSEUM

See p99.

**BASÍLICA DE SANTA
MARIA DEL MAR**   CHURCH

See p101.

**PALAU DE LA
MÚSICA CATALANA**   ARCHITECTURE

See p102.

CARRER DE MONTCADA   STREET

Map p300 (ⓂJaume I) Today running between the Romanesque Capella d'en Marcús and Passeig del Born, this medieval
high street (an early example of town planning) was driven towards the sea from the
road that in the 12th century led northeast
from the city walls. It became Barcelona's
most coveted address for the merchant
classes; the great mansions that remain
today mostly date from the 14th and 15th
centuries (several of them housing the Museu Picasso, p99).

PARC DE LA CIUTADELLA   PARK

Map p300 (Passeig de Picasso; ⊘10am-10.30pm;
🚼; ⓂArc de Triomf) Come for a stroll, a picnic, a lake boat ride, a tour of Catalonia's
parliament or to marvel at the swirling
waterfall-fountain in which Gaudí had a
hand. This is the city's most central green
lung, born in the mid-19th century on the
former site of the much-hated huge fortress
(La Ciutadella) on the eastern side of La
Ribera.

After the War of the Spanish Succession,
Felipe V razed a swath of La Ribera to build
the Ciutadella fortress, designed to keep
watch over Barcelona. It became a symbol
of everything Catalans hated about Madrid
and the Bourbon kings, and was later used
as a political prison. Only in 1869 did the
central government allow its demolition;
the site was turned into a park and adapted
for Barcelona's 1888 Universal Exposition
by Josep Fontserè.

The monumental **cascada** (waterfall; Map
p300; ⓂArc de Triomf) near the Passeig de Pujades park entrance, created between 1875
and 1881 by Fontserè with the help of an enthusiastic young Gaudí, is a dramatic combination of statuary, rugged rocks, greenery
and thundering water – all of it perfectly ar-

tificial. Topped by a golden statue of the Roman dawn goddess Aurora, it was inspired
by Rome's Trevi Fountain. The **bandstand**
opposite commemorates Sonia Rescalvo, a
trans performer murdered here in 1991 by a
group of neo-Nazis.

To the southeast, in what might be seen
as an exercise in black humour, the fort's
former arsenal now houses the **Parlament
de Catalunya** (Map p300; ✆93 304 65 00;
www.parlament.cat; ⓂArc de Triomf; 🆓. You
can join free 45-minute guided tours, in a
range of languages, with at least two days'
advance booking (online). The building is
only open for independent visiting on 11
September from 10am to 7pm. On show to
the public are the sweeping Escala d'Honor
(Stairway of Honour) and the several sol-
emn halls that lead to the Saló de Sessions,
the semicircular auditorium where parliament sits. In the lily pond at the centre
of the garden in front of the building is a
statue of a seemingly heartbroken woman, *Desconsol* (Distress; 1907), by Josep
Llimona.

The western Passeig de Picasso side of
the park is lined with several buildings
constructed for, or just before, the Universal Exhibition. The medieval-looking caprice at the top end, the **Castell dels Tres
Dragons** (Map p300; ⓂArc de Triomf), is the
most engaging (though it was closed for
renovations at research time). Domènech i
Montaner put the 'castle's' trimmings on a
pioneering steel frame. The coats of arms
are all invented and the whole building
exudes a teasing, playful air. It was used
as a cafe-restaurant during the Universal
Exhibition.

To the south is an elaborate greenhouse,
L'Hivernacle, followed by the former geology museum and L'Umbracle, a palm house.
On Passeig de Picasso itself lies Antoni
Tàpies' typically impenetrable 1983 **Homenatge a Picasso** (Map p300; ⓂArc de Triomf,
Jaume I): water runs down the panes of a
glass box full of bits of old furniture, steel
girders and ropes and sheets, surrounded
by a shallow pool.

Northwest of the park, Passeig de Lluís
Companys is capped by the Modernista
Arc de Triomf (Map p300; ⓂArc de Triomf),
designed by Josep Vilaseca as the exhibition's main entrance, with unusual earthy-
red Mudéjar-style brickwork; Josep Lli-

mona did the main reliefs. Just what the triumph was eludes us, especially since the exhibition itself was a commercial failure. It is perhaps best thought of as a bricks-and-mortar embodiment of the city's general fin de siècle feel-good factor.

PASSEIG DEL BORN STREET

Map p300 (Ⓜ Barceloneta, Jaume I) Framed by the majestic Basílica de Santa Maria del Mar and the former Mercat del Born, leafy Passeig del Born was Barcelona's main playground from the 13th to 18th centuries. It's a place in which to sit as much as to promenade, and it's here in this graceful setting beneath the trees that El Born's essential appeal is obvious – thronging people, brilliant bars and architecture from a medieval film set.

MOCO MUSEUM MUSEUM

Map p300 (Carrer de Montcada 25; https://moco museum.com; adult/child €13.50/free; ⊙10am-7pm Mon-Thu, to 9pm Fri-Sun) El Born's 16th-century Palau dels Cervelló has been reimagined as a dazzling creative space devoted to contemporary, modern and street art, courtesy of Amsterdam's independent Moco Museum, which opened its second branch in Barcelona in late 2021. Thought-provoking pieces by Kusama, Banksy, Warhol, Basquiat and Dalí feature among the carefully curated collection, set against gleaming white floors, soaring ceilings and mirrored walls.

BORN CENTRE DE
CULTURA I MEMÒRIA HISTORIC BUILDING

Map p300 (Ⓙ93 256 68 51; http://elborn culturaimemoria.barcelona.cat; Plaça Comercial 12; centre free, exhibition adult/concession/child under 16yr €4.50/3.15/free; ⊙10am-8pm Tue-Sun; Ⓜ Jaume I) Launched in 2013 as part of the events held for the tercentenary of the Catalan defeat in the War of the Spanish Succession, this cultural space is housed in the former Mercat del Born, a handsome 19th-century structure of slatted iron and brick designed by Josep Fontserè. Excavations in 2001 unearthed remains of whole streets (now exposed on the subterranean level) flattened to make way for the much-hated Ciutadella (citadel), with some sections dating back to Roman and Islamic times.

LA RIBERA & EL BORN SIGHTS

TOP EXPERIENCE
SHOP FOR PRODUCE AT MERCAT DE SANTA CATERINA

Come shopping for your tomatoes or pop in for lunch at this extraordinary-looking produce market, designed by forward-thinking architects Enric Miralles and Benedetta Tagliabue to replace its 19th-century predecessor. Completed in 2005 (sadly after Miralles' death in 2000), it's distinguished by its undulating, kaleidoscopic roof, suspended above bustling produce stands, restaurants, cafes and bars by twisting slender branches of what look like grey steel trees.

The multicoloured ceramic roof (with a ceiling made of warm, light wood) recalls the Modernista tradition of *trencadís* decoration (using a type of mosaic made from tile shards). Indeed, its curvy design, like a series of Mediterranean rollers, seems to plunge back into an era when Barcelona's architects were limited only by their (vivid) imaginations, and bears an uncanny resemblance to that of the Escoles de Gaudí at La Sagrada Família. The brightly coloured pattern is in fact from a photo of a fruit and veg stall, blown up to huge scale. The roof is perhaps best seen from The Roof bar (p111).

On the market's southern side you'll spot the excavated ruins of the monastery that existed on this spot between the 11th and 19th centuries.

DON'T MISS

➡ Old monastery ruins
➡ Eating at the market's cafe-bars
➡ The rippling roof

PRACTICALITIES

➡ Map p300, C4
➡ Ⓙ93 319 57 40
➡ www.mercatsanta caterina.com
➡ Avinguda de Francesc Cambó 16
➡ admission free
➡ ⊙7.30am-3.30pm Mon, Wed & Sat, to 8.30pm Tue, Thu & Fri, closed afternoons except Fri Aug
➡ Ⓜ Jaume I

On the ground floor, multilanguage panels give information about the ruins, and an exhibition space explains in greater depth the events surrounding the destruction of the area. You can wander into the building for free or join a 90-minute guided tour to walk among the ruins (€4, in English, Spanish or Catalan; check schedules online).

MONESTIR DE SANT
PERE DE LES PUELLES   CHURCH
Map p300 (☑93 26 80 742; www.benedictines santperepuelles.cat; Carrer de Lluís el Piadós 1; ⊙9am-1pm & 5-7.45pm Mon-Fri, 9am-1pm & 4.30-6.45pm Sat, 11am-1.15pm Sun; MArc de Triomf) It was around this much-remodelled Romanesque church, founded in 945, that settlement began in La Ribera. In 985 a Muslim force under Al-Mansur largely destroyed what was then a Benedictine convent, killing or capturing the nuns. Now overlooking a leafy square, the church was rebuilt in early medieval times and in the 20th century. The pre-Romanesque Greek-cross floor plan survives, as do some Corinthian columns (beneath the 12th-century dome) and a much-damaged Renaissance vault leading into a side chapel.

MUSEU DE CULTURES DEL MÓN   MUSEUM
Map p300 (☑93 256 23 00; http://museu culturesmon.bcn.cat; Carrer de Montcada 12; adult/concession/under 16yr €5/3.50/free, 3-8pm Sun & 1st Sun of month free; ⊙10am-7pm Tue-Sat, to 8pm Sun; MJaume I) Opening through a grand courtyard overlooked by an 18th-century staircase, the medieval Palau Nadal and the Palau Marquès de Liló host Barcelona's world cultures museum. Exhibits from private and public collections, including many from Montjuïc's Museu Etnològic (p192), travel through the ancient cultures of Africa, Asia, the Americas and Oceania. There are some fascinating finds, with displays spinning from Andean weaving, Ethiopian religious art and Papua New Guinean skull hooks to 17th-century Chola bronzes from Tamil Nadu in southern India.

There's a combined ticket (€12) with the Museu Etnològic on Montjuïc and the Museu Egipci (p151).

CAPELLA D'EN MARCÚS   CHURCH
Map p300 (☑93 310 23 90; Placeta d'en Marcús; ⊙10am-noon Mon-Fri, 10.30-11am Sat; MJaume I) Standing at the northern end of Carrer de Montcada, on the corner of Carrer dels Corders, this much-meddled-with Romanesque chapel was once a wayfarers' stop on the road northeast out of medieval Barcelona. Originally financed by wealthy bourgeois Bernat Marcús, it's one of the city's oldest churches, with a 17th-century subterranean crypt hidden below.

CASA DE LA SEDA   HISTORIC BUILDING
Map p300 (☑93 310 77 78; www.casadelaseda. com; Carrer de Sant Pere més Alt 1; adult/concession/child under 11yr €10/8/free; MUrquinaona) The headquarters of the Art of Silk Association is housed in a handsome 18th-century mansion covered in caryatid sgraffiti, overlooking Via Laietana. The richly adorned, silk-lined interior is accessible only once a month on Saturday by scheduled 45-minute guided tour, in English, Spanish and Catalan, which takes in rooms including the luxuriously appointed guild hall, various meeting spaces and the library, with 3000 documents exploring the guild's history back to the 16th century. Check schedules online.

FOTO COLECTANIA   GALLERY
Map p300 (☑93 217 16 26; http://fotocolectania. org; Passeig de Picasso 14; adult/concession/child under 14yr €4/3/free, 1st Sun of month free; ⊙11am-8pm Tue-Sat, to 3pm Sun; MArc de Triomf, Jaume I) Photography lovers should swing by this minimalist-design nonprofit foundation in El Born, which hosts thought-provoking, regularly changing exhibitions from across the globe and also works to bring Catalan and Spanish photography to the world. Some shows come from the foundation's extensive 3000-piece collection of more than 60 Spanish (especially Catalan) and Portuguese photographers from the 1950s onwards, though most are likely to be temporary exhibitions.

ARXIU FOTOGRÀFIC
DE BARCELONA   GALLERY
Map p300 (☑93 256 34 20; http://barcelona.cat/ arxiumunicipal/arxiufotografic; Plaça de Pons i Clerch 2, 2A; ⊙10am-7pm Mon-Sat; MArc de Triomf) FREE On the 2nd floor of the former Convent de Sant Agustí is the modest exhibition space of this photo archive, devoted to sharing photos of the city from the 1840s until the late 20th century. Exhibitions

come from its three-million-strong collection, sourced from professionals and amateurs alike.

MUSEU EUROPEU
D'ART MODERN MUSEUM

Map p300 (MEAM; ☑93 319 56 93; www.meam.es; Carrer de la Barra de Ferro 5; adult/concession/child under 10yr €9/7/free; ⊙11am-7pm Tue-Sun; MJaume I) Unravelling across three floors and a hushed courtyard within the handsome 18th-century Palau Gomis, around the corner from the Museu Picasso, this strictly representational collection showcases incredibly varied works mostly by young Spanish artists (the 'Modern' of the name simply means 'contemporary'). There are a few pieces from elsewhere in Europe, too, as well as changing exhibitions.

MUSEU DE LA XOCOLATA MUSEUM

Map p300 (☑93 268 78 78; www.museuxocolata.cat; Carrer del Comerç 36; adult/child under 7yr €6/free; ⊙10am-8pm Mon-Sat, 10am-3pm Sun mid-Jun–mid-Sep, 10am-7pm Mon-Sat, 10am-3pm Sun mid-Sep–mid-Jun; ☻; MArc de Triomf) Chocoholics have a hard time containing themselves at this museum dedicated to the fundamental cocoa-based foodstuff. Displays trace the origins of chocolate, its arrival in Europe and the many myths and images associated with it. Dotted among the informative panels and machinery used in chocolate production are large chocolate models of emblematic buildings such as La Sagrada Família. There are guided tours (€7.50), wine-and-chocolate pairings (€16) and a range of chocolate-fuelled activities for kids (book ahead online).

✖ EATING

El Born is peppered with great restaurants, cafes and tapas bars. You'll find avant-garde chefs playing with fusion and technology cheek by jowl with no-nonsense matrons serving up traditional Catalan comfort food, not to mention an increasing number of international offerings.

BORMUTH TAPAS €

Map p300 (☑93 310 21 86; www.facebook.com/bormuthbarcelona; Carrer del Rec 31; tapas €5-10; ⊙12.30pm-1.30am Sun-Thu, to 2am Fri & Sat; ☎; MJaume I) Clad in bare brick and recycled wood, lively, split-level Bormuth specialises

in homemade vermouth on tap, but also serves *cava*, artisan beers, Catalan wines and wonderful tapas. The kitchen whips up favourites from around Spain including tortilla, *pebrots del Padró* (fried green peppers), *espinacs a la catalana* (spinach with raisins and pine nuts) and *patates mojo picón* (potatoes in spicy red-pepper sauce).

CASA LOLEA TAPAS €

Map p300 (☑93 624 10 16; www.casalolea.com; Carrer de Sant Pere més Alt 49; tapas €4-14; ⊙9am-1am; ☎) Dangling strings of tomatoes and garlic, red-and-black-spot decor and whitewashed brick walls lend an air of Andalucian charm to this cheerful tapas-and-vermouth tavern. It's popular for its lightly creative breakfast *entrepans* (filled rolls) and classic-with-a-twist tapas like mushroom scrambles, just-cooked tortilla and platters of northern Spanish cheeses and cured ham. There are daily specials such as truffle risotto or octopus ceviche.

ELSA Y FRED INTERNATIONAL €

Map p300 (☑93 501 66 11; www.elsayfred.es; Carrer del Rec Comtal 11; tapas & brunch €4-10; ⊙8.30am-midnight Mon-Fri, from 9am Sat & Sun; ☎✐; MArc de Triomf) Named after an Argentinean film, Elsa y Fred feels like a cosy, old-school-glam living room, with a wooden fireplace, mirrored pillars and sink-down leather armchairs. The menu features gourmet tapas such as mandarin and orange salad with goat's cheese or grilled baby squid with yuzu emulsion. There's a €14.50 weekday set lunch, plus cakes, cocktails and weekend brunch (until 4pm!).

KOKU KITCHEN BUNS ASIAN €

Map p300 (☑93 269 65 36; www.kokukitchen.es; Carrer del Comerç 29; mains €9-11; ⊙1-4pm & 7.30-11.30pm; ☎✐; MBarceloneta) A stylish brick-walled space with scattered plants and communal tables, Koku serves delectable homemade bao stuffed with beef, pork or tofu, as well as dumplings, Vietnamese pho and fresh lemonade, sourcing most ingredients locally. The basement ramen-and-gyoza bar (closed lunch June to August) offers some of Barcelona's best steaming noodle bowls. On weekdays there's a great-value lunch *menú* (€13.50).

BRUNELLS 1852 CAFE €

Map p300 (☑93 653 64 68; www.brunells.barcelona; Carrer de la Princesa 22; dishes €3-8; ⊙9am-8pm; MJaume I) With coffee by locally

ESCAPING BARCELONA'S CROWDS

Barcelona's popularity as a tourist destination has sky-rocketed in recent years, and there's no denying that high-season crowds here can get the better of even the most carefree traveller – but explore beyond the busy city centre and you'll get to know *barris* (neighbourhoods) and *barcelonins* that few other visitors cross paths with.

Sarrià-Sant Gervasi (p212) This cluster of well-heeled former villages in northwest Barcelona is home to Gaudí's little-known Bellesguard (p217).

Parc Natural de Collserola (p208) Go hiking and biking amid bottle-green pines on the slopes of Tibidabo.

Pedralbes (p207) A serene 14th-century convent and several little-known Gaudí works await in one of Barcelona's quietest corners, in the city's northwest.

Horta (p214) This tranquil northern *barri* appeals with its pretty squares and romantic labyrinthine garden.

Beaches beyond Barcelona (p123) Join the *barcelonins* at unspoilt beaches just a short hop out of town.

El Poblenou (p119) Though this post-industrial *barri* is on the up, it remains a breath of fresh air away from the city-centre masses, with several beaches.

Sants & Les Corts Between the centre and Camp Nou, Sants has a restored 1913 market and the 2019-opened top-end hotel and restaurant Nobu (p242) hotel. Les Corts offers a few enticing bars around Plaça de la Concòrdia.

loved El Magnífico and deliciously flaky pastries by Canal Pastisseria (known for its prize-winning croissants), the beautifully stylish cafe behind these turquoise doors in El Born has become an instant hit. Classic Barcelona recipes and locally loved desserts star on the menu, which includes a tempting line-up of freshly baked croissants flavoured with mojito, passionfruit, mango and other goodies.

BAR JOAN   CATALAN €

Map p300 (☑93 310 61 50; Avinguda de Francesc Cambó 16, Mercat de Santa Caterina; menú del dia €12.50, tapas €3-5; ⏱7.30am-3.30pm Mon, Wed & Sat, to 5pm Tue, Thu & Fri; 🛜; Ⓜ Jaume I) A locally popular stop inside the Mercat de Santa Caterina (p104), old-school Bar Joan is known especially for its *arròs negre* (cuttlefish-ink rice) on Tuesdays and paella on Thursdays. It's a simple, friendly and good-value spot, serving only tapas, *entrepans* or the excellent-value *menú del dia*, with plenty of choice.

TANTARANTANA   MEDITERRANEAN €

Map p300 (☑93 268 24 10; www.gruposantelmo. com; Carrer d'en Tantarantana 24; tapas €5-10, mains €9-12; ⏱1pm-midnight; 🛜; Ⓜ Jaume I) All patterned tiled floors, marble-top tables and wooden beams, shoebox-sized Tantarantana attracts a lively crowd who make the most of the terrace tables in warmer months. Well-prepared, market-driven Mediterranean dishes and tapas swing from wild-mushroom risotto and citrusy deep-fried aubergines to cod with ratatouille. The lemon-meringue cake is divine.

MOSQUITO   ASIAN €

Map p300 (☑93 268 75 69; www.mosquitotapas. com; Carrer dels Carders 46; dishes €3-6; ⏱7-11pm Mon, 1-5pm & 7-11pm Tue-Sun) Hang out in El Born for a few days and you'll inevitably end up at this pint-sized, always-busy, unadorned spot devoted to great-value 'Asian tapas'. Catalan ingredients are worked into fragrant Vietnamese pho, salted edamame, Chinese dim sum, Japanese gyoza and the like, accompanied by craft beers or teas from Barcelona emporium Čaj Chai (p77). No bookings.

ESPAI MESCLADIS   MEDITERRANEAN €

Map p300 (☑93 319 87 32; www.facebook.com/ mescladis; Carrer dels Carders 3; dishes €3-8; ⏱10am-8.30pm; 🖊) Rainbow-coloured chairs and tables sit under medieval stone arches at this nonprofit social-project cafe-bar, which helps integrate immigrants to Barcelona. The North African–Mediterranean menu swings from hummus, tabbouleh and tagines to patates braves and zingy fresh lemonade, and there's a good value €12 set lunch on weekdays. Proceeds

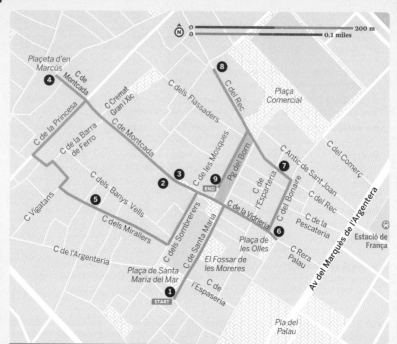

Neighbourhood Walk
Tapas & Bar-Hopping in El Born

START LA VINYA DEL SENYOR
END BAR SAUVAGE
DISTANCE 1.5KM; 4-5 HOURS

If there's one place that snapshots all that's irresistible about this city, it has to be El Born. This is where *barcelonins* and local ex-pats go for a real-deal Barcelona night out.

Most nights in El Born begin around the Basílica de Santa Maria del Mar and Passeig del Born, one of the prettiest little boulevards in Spain. Kick back over Catalan wines at elegant **1 La Vinya del Senyor** (p111), opposite the basilica.

Wander along Passeig del Born, then push through the crowd to order a *cava* and a few home-cooked tapas at **2 El Xampanyet** (p111), in business since 1929.

Having sampled Barcelona-style tapas, compare and contrast with the drool-worthy line-up of *pintxos* (Basque tapas) gracing the bar at **3 Euskal Etxea** (p107).

The detour to **4 Bar del Pla** on the northern limits of El Born is worth it for tapas with touches of originality.

Meander back south through narrow medieval alleys towards experimental **5 Dr Stravinsky** (p110), which mixes avant-garde cocktails from delicate homemade ingredients – it was voted one of the World's 50 Best Bars in 2019.

It can be difficult to snaffle a bar stool from which to order gourmet tapas at bois-terous **6 Cal Pep** – if it's full, order a drink and wait.

Hidden off Passeig del Born, **7 Farola** (p113) pulls in everyone from music-loving locals to fashionable twenty-somethings for its live gigs (from 9pm Thursday to Sunday), vinyl DJ sets and expertly selected sherries.

Zip over to **8 Bormuth** (p106), next to the old Mercat del Born, for homemade vermouth, Catalan wines and bubbly *cava*, plus a few divine Spain-spanning tapas.

Finish back on Passeig del Born at party-style **9 Bar Sauvage** (p111), which spotlights Latin American spirits and zingy street food. Don't blame us if you end up in the basement club...

help fund cooking courses for people on the fringes of society.

EL CASAL
FRENCH €

Map p300 (📞 93 268 40 04; www.elcasalcafe.com; Plaça Victor Balaguer 5; tapas €5-10; ⊕7am-4pm Mon-Wed, 7am-4pm & 6pm-midnight Thu & Fri, 6pm-midnight Sat; Ⓜ Jaume I) A French-run cafe serving excellent food at great prices in noisy but welcoming surroundings, adorned with *objets* from the motherland. The fixed lunch (€11.25) changes daily, but keep an eye out for the superior cauliflower cheese and authentically good tarte Tatin. Fuss-free breakfasts run until noon, and there are tapas and *xapatas* (ciabattas) throughout the day.

CAT BAR
VEGAN €

Map p300 (www.catbarcat.com; Carrer de la Bòria 17; mains €6-12; ⊕1-11pm Mon-Sat; 📶🍴; Ⓜ Jaume I) Reminiscent of a local student bar, this small joint serves the best vegan burgers in the city. The selection includes a spicy Mexican burger with jalapeños, a nut burger with pesto and spinach, and a hemp burger with pickles. There's also a range of artisanal vegan beers, plus vegan cakes.

BAR CELTA
GALICIAN €

Map p300 (📞 93 315 15 10; www.barcelta.com; Carrer de la Princesa 50; tapas €3-12; ⊕8.30am-midnight Mon-Fri, from 10am Sat, from noon SunMon-Sat) The newer Born branch of a beloved Barri Gòtic classic, delightfully old-school Bar Celta showcases Galician cuisine in all its simple, fresh beauty. The signature tapa is pop a feria (Galician-style boiled octopus), or you might try salt-dusted Padrón peppers, grilled prawns, deep-fried squid with a squeeze of lemon and wedges of tortilla carved from enormous wheels.

CASA DELFÍN
CATALAN €€

Map p300 (📞 93 319 50 88; www.casadelfinrestaurant.com; Passeig del Born 36; tapas €6-11, mains €12-20; ⊕noon-midnight Sun-Thu, to 1am Fri & Sat; 📶; Ⓜ Jaume I) One of El Born's culinary delights, Casa Delfín is everything you dream about Catalan-Mediterranean cooking in a traditional style. Lined with wine bottles inside, the service is spot on and creative presentation lends a contemporary touch. Menus change depending on market produce, but might offer salt-strewn *Padrón* peppers, plump anchovies

from L'Escala, big seafood paellas or *suquet dels pescadors* (Catalan fish stew) for two.

EUSKAL ETXEA
PINTXOS €€

Map p300 (📞 93 310 21 85; www.gruposagardi.com; Placeta de Montcada 1-3; pintxos €2, mains €12-26; ⊕bar 10am-12.30am Sun-Thu, to 1am Fri & Sat, restaurant 1-4pm & 7pm-midnight; 📶; Ⓜ Jaume I) Barcelona has plenty of Basque-style *pintxo* bars, but this stone-walled, tile-floored Born favourite is the real deal. Tempting *pintxos* are stacked up on the bar – from prawns topped with peppers to deep-fried goat's cheese with quince jam – or, if hot, handed around on trays (try the mushroom croquettes!). Sip *txakoli* (Basque white wine) or just-poured cider, and keep the toothpicks for your bill.

CAN CISA/BAR BRUTAL
SPANISH €€

Map p300 (📞 93 295 47 97, 93 319 98 81; www.cancisa.cat; Carrer de la Princesa 14; mains €11-20; ⊕7pm-1.30am Mon, 1-4pm & 7pm-2am Tue-Thu, 1pm-2am Fri & Sat Oct-Jun, 7pm-2am Mon-Thu, 1pm-2am Fri & Sat Jul-Sep; Ⓜ Jaume I) Can Cisa's elegant all-natural wines pair beautifully with Bar Brutal's innovative reimagining of fresh Catalan ingredients at this rowdy, fashionable wine-bar-restaurant venture from Barcelona culinary kings the Colombo brothers and team. Straight from the open kitchen, octopus with pak choi, watermelon-tomato salad and delicate artisan cheeses pull in a young, fun crowd until late. Wines are sourced from across Spain, Italy and France.

CAL PEP
TAPAS €€

Map p300 (📞 93 310 79 61; www.calpep.com; Plaça de les Olles 8; mains €10-20; ⊕7.30-11.30pm Mon, 1-3.45pm & 7.30-11.30pm Tue-Sat, closed last 3 weeks Aug; Ⓜ Barceloneta) It's getting a foot in the door of this legendary tapas and seafood restaurant that's the problem – queues spread out into the square. Most people are happy elbowing their way to the bar for some of the tastiest seafood tapas in town. Pep recommends *cloïsses amb pernil* (clams and ham), the *trifàsic* (calamari, whitebait and prawns) or the supersmooth tortilla.

BAR DEL PLA
TAPAS €€

Map p300 (📞 93 268 30 03; www.bardelpla.cat; Carrer de Montcada 2; tapas €4-11, mains €9-15; ⊕noon-11pm Mon-Thu, to midnight Fri & Sat; 📶;

MJaume I) A bright and buzzy favourite, with glorious Catalan tiling, a vaulted ceiling and bottles of wine lining the walls. At first glance, the tapas at informal Bar del Pla are traditionally Spanish, but the riffs on a theme display an assured touch of creativity. Try the ham croquettes, wasabi mushrooms, T-bone steak or rice of the day.

EL ATRIL   INTERNATIONAL €€

Map p300 (☑93 310 12 20; www.elatrilbarce lona.es; Carrer dels Carders 23; mains €8-18; ☺12.30-11.30pm Sun-Thu, to 12.30am Fri & Sat; ☺☑; MJaume I) Influenced by culinary flavours from all over the globe, rustic-modern El Atril delivers on both classic tapas (*patates braves*, Iberian ham boards, goat's-cheese salad drizzled with honey) and creative world-wandering plates like kangaroo tacos, mushroom risotto and tuna tartare with mango mousse. The cosy setting in what was once a convent or at sunny terrace tables adds to the appeal.

NAKASHITA   JAPANESE €€

Map p300 (☑93 295 53 78; www.nakashitabcn.com; Carrer del Rec Comtal 15; mains €10-22; ☺1-4pm & 8pm-midnight; ☺; MArc de Triomf) Brazil's particular immigration story means it has a tradition of superb Japanese food, and the Brazilian chef at Nakashita is no slouch, turning out excellent sashimi, maki rolls, softshell crab and *kakiage* (a mix of tempura). It's one of the top Japanese restaurants in Barcelona, with just a handful of tables – book if you can.

CUINES DE
SANTA CATERINA   MEDITERRANEAN, ASIAN €€

Map p300 (☑93 268 99 18; www.grupotra galuz.com; Mercat de Santa Caterina; mains €10-18; ☺9am-11pm Sun-Thu, to 11.30pm Fri & Sat; ☺☑; MJaume I) With a contemporary feel, open kitchens and a fun atmosphere, this multifaceted restaurant tucked into the Mercat de Santa Caterina wanders all over the globe. Tuck into classic rice dishes, chargrilled meats or the sushi bar, or go vegetarian with tofu-vegetable curry or pumpkin-filled ravioli. Breakfast *entrepans* and *revueltos* (scrambled eggs, usually with mushrooms or meat) are good too. No reservations, so you may have to queue.

PICNIC   BREAKFAST €€

Map p300 (☑93 511 66 61; www.picnic-restau rant.com; Carrer del Comerç 1; dishes €5-12; ☺10.30am-4pm Mon-Wed, 10.30am-4pm &

8-11.30pm Thu & Fri, 10.30am-5pm & 8-11.30pm Sat, 10.30am-5pm Sun; ☺☑; MArc de Triomf) Mismatched furniture, distressed-wood walls and scattered greenery set the buzzing scene at cosy, easy-going, Californian-Chilean–owned Picnic. It's one of Barcelona's brunch originals, which thoughtfully fuses the flavours of its owners' homelands. Try the delicate French toast, decorated with edible flowers and *dolç de llet*, or the punchy huevos rancheros, with a vodka-spiked (or just plain!) pink lemonade.

EL CHIGRE 1769   TAPAS €€

Map p300 (☑93 782 63 30; http://elchigre1769.com; Carrer dels Sombrerers 7; tapas €4-14, mains €10-16; ☺1-11.45pm Mon-Thu, from noon Fri & Sat; MJaume I) Part Asturian cider house and part Catalan *vermuteria* (vermouth bar), El Chigre brings elegant versions of classic dishes from both regions, devised by Asturian chef Fran Heras, to a stylishly revamped 18th-century building. Feast on potatoes with Cabrales sauce, Picos de Europa cheeses, Asturian *fabada* (bean-and-meat stew) or cured meats from the Pyrenees, all with *cava*, cider or house vermouth.

LLAMBER   ASTURIAN, CATALAN €€

Map p300 (☑933 19 62 50; http://llamber.com; Carrer de la Fusina 5; raciones €12-20; ☺9am-midnight; ☑) This favourite El Born hangout creatively fuses Catalan and Asturian flavours in a buzzy contemporary-design space with open-brick walls, dangling lamps and tall tables. *Pica pica* (snack) sharing plates wander from Iberian ham with tomato-rubbed bread to sautéed Pyrenees mushrooms and cheeses from Picos de Europa, or try sturdier dishes like artichoke rice with avocado-coriander emulsion. Great wine list, too.

LE CUCINE MANDAROSSO   ITALIAN €€

Map p300 (☑93 269 07 80; www.lecucinemanda rosso.com; Carrer de Verdaguer i Callís 4; mains €12-14; ☺1.30-4pm & 8-11.30pm Tue-Sat; MUr quinaona) This is Italian comfort food done to perfection, with seasonal market-fresh ingredients used in handed-down family recipes. The rotating menu includes lots of fresh pasta, as well as fish and meat dishes and homemade cakes. Antipasti can be vegetables or fresh cheese, such as wonderfully creamy *burrata* (made from mozzarella and cream), buffalo-milk mozzarella, or smoked *scamorza* and *provola* cheese.

FISMULER   MEDITERRANEAN €€€

Map p300 (☎93 514 00 50; www.fismuler.com; Carrer del Rec Comtal 17; tapas €4-17, mains €20-25; ⏱1.30-4pm & 8-11pm Sun-Wed, to 11.30pm Thu-Sat; ✍; Ⓜ Arc de Triomf) The brainchild of three ex El Bulli chefs, the minimalist-design Barcelona outpost of this Madrid-born market-based sensation is one of the city's hottest tickets. Daily-changing menus throw seasonal local produce into expertly executed, unpretentious Spanish–Mediterranean dishes: Delta de l'Ebre oysters, cod omelette, truffle-and-burrata salad or slow-cooked fennel seabass, followed by gooey cheesecake and with Catalan wines to start.

🍷 DRINKING & NIGHTLIFE

Bars line Passeig del Born and the web of streets winding off it and around the Basílica de Santa Maria del Mar, and the whole area has a lively party buzz. Some of Barcelona's best cocktail bars are dotted around El Born.

★**DR STRAVINSKY**   COCKTAIL BAR

Map p300 (☎93 157 12 33; www.drstravinsky.cat; Carrer dels Mirallers 5; ⏱6pm-2.30am; Ⓜ Jaume I) At this alchemist-inspired temple to crafted-cocktail wizardry, named one of the World's 50 Best Bars in 2019, mixologist Antonio Naranjo and team prepare knockout signature drinks (€8 to €13) using house-made gin, their own essential oils and other home-grown ingredients. Behind chilli-red doors, the centuries-old building has been reborn in lab-like, vintage-loving style, with herb jars and flasks on walls.

★**PARADISO/PASTRAMI BAR**   COCKTAIL BAR

Map p300 (☎639 310671; www.paradiso.cat; Carrer de Rera Palau 4; ⏱7pm-1.15am Sun-Thu, to 2.15am Fri & Sat; ☎; Ⓜ Barceloneta) A kind of Narnia-in-reverse, Paradiso is fronted by a snowy-white wardrobe-sized space, with pastrami sandwiches, pulled pork and other home-cured delights. But this is only the portal – step through the fridge door into a glam, sexy speakeasy guaranteed to raise the most world-weary of eyebrows, where highly creative, artfully prepared cocktails (€9 to €12) steal the show. Worth queueing for.

★**NØMAD CØFFEE LAB & SHOP**   COFFEE

Map p300 (☎628 566235; www.nomadcoffee. es; Passatge de Sert 12; ⏱8.30am-5pm Mon-Fri; Ⓜ Urquinaona) King of Barcelona's third-wave coffee scene, Nømad is known for its seasonally sourced, small-batch, Barcelona-roasted beans and experimental techniques. Owner and barista Jordi Mestre was inspired by his time in London and, at this snug, minimalist, lab-style cafe, it's all about coffee tastings and expertly poured espresso, flat whites, cold brews and Aeropress (€2 to €5).

GUZZO   COCKTAIL BAR

Map p300 (☎93 667 00 36; www.guzzorestau rante.es; Plaça Comercial 10; ⏱7-11.30pm Mon-Fri, 1-4pm & 7-11.30pm Sat & Sun; ☎; Ⓜ Jaume I) With good vibes any time of day, this old-school cocktail bar is run by much-loved Barcelona DJ Fred Guzzo, who is often at the decks spinning his delicious selection of funk, soul and rare groove. You'll also find frequent live-music acts, excellent mojitos (€8) and tasty homemade tapas like burrata fresh from Santa Caterina market.

BAR SAUVAGE   COCKTAIL BAR

Map p300 (☎93 832 51 84; https://barsauvage. com; Passeig del Born 13; ⏱7pm-3am; Ⓜ Jaume I) The ever-so-slightly more relaxed sister to party-hard Creps al Born across the road, this elegant good-time cocktail bar expertly knocks up original, fruity, herb-infused liquid mixes based on Latin spirits (€10 to €12), as well as Peruvian-Mexican street-food bites. Downstairs in the basement is a moody party lounge where DJs play.

LA VINYA DEL SENYOR   WINE BAR

Map p300 (☎93 310 33 79; www.facebook. com/vinyadelsenyor; Plaça de Santa Maria del Mar 5; ⏱noon-1am Sun-Thu, to 2am Fri & Sat; ☎; Ⓜ Jaume I) Relax on the terrace in the shadow of the Basílica de Santa Maria del Mar or crowd into the tiny bottle-lined bar. From Priorat to Languedoc, the wine list is as long as *War and Peace*, with 20 drops by the glass. Cheese platters and cold meats keep you going. There's an even more intimate space up the twirling staircase.

EL XAMPANYET   WINE BAR

Map p300 (☎93 319 70 03; www.elxampanyet. es; Carrer de Montcada 22; ⏱noon-3.30pm & 7-11pm Tue-Sat, noon-3.30pm Sun; ☎; Ⓜ Jaume I)

Nothing has changed for decades at chaotic El Xampanyet, one of Barcelona's best-known *cava* (sparkling wine) bars. It's usually packed, but plant yourself at the bar or grab a table against the decoratively tiled walls for a glass or three of the house *cava* and delicious homemade tapas such as tangy *boquerones* (anchovies) in vinegar or perfectly gooey tortilla.

CREPS AL BORN
COCKTAIL BAR

Map p300 (☑93 269 03 25; www.facebook.com/ CrepsalBorn; Passeig del Born 12; ⊙6pm-3am Mon-Fri, noon-4am Sat, noon-2am Sun; MJaume l) A rowdy, jam-packed and seriously fun party-loving cocktail bar, where people spill out onto Passeig del Born over wildly creative artisan cocktails (€10 to €12) and popular mojitos. The menu is decorated with street art; if you dare, try a gin-based Pez, infused with feta and mixed with vermouth and absinthe. Good crepes, too.

EL DISET
WINE BAR

Map p300 (☑93 268 19 87; www.facebook.com/ eldiset; Carrer Antic de Sant Joan 3; ⊙7pm-2am Mon-Thu, to 3am Fri, 1pm-3am Sat, 1pm-2am Sun; MBarceloneta,) Dealing almost exclusively in Catalan drops, El Disset is a sleek, candlelit wine, cocktail and tapas bar that also does tastings. Thin *torrades* (toasted bread) topped with, say, goat's cheese and stir-fried vegetables or tuna tataki and tapas of Catalan cheeses accompany glasses (€4 to €7) of Terra Alta, Montsant, Penedès, Priorat and more.

THE ROOF
ROOFTOP BAR

Map p300 (☑93 626 33 49; www.editionhotels. com; Avinguda de Francesc Cambó 14, Barcelona Edition; ⊙10.30am-midnight; MJaume l) This low-key-glam rooftop bar has fabulous horizon-reaching views across the Mercat de Santa Caterina's kaleidoscopic roof to the sea beyond. White-cushioned booths, rippling greenery and sprinkled lanterns set the chic tone for signature crafted cocktails (such as the pisco sour; €13), fresh juices and Latin-Asian fusion tapas, or just pop in for coffee. It's inside the swish Barcelona Edition (p236).

RUBÍ
BAR

Map p300 (☑671 441888; www.facebook.com/ RubiBarRestaurant; Carrer dels Banys Vells 6; ⊙7.30pm-2.30am Sun-Thu, to 3am Fri & Sat; ⚲; MJaume l) With its boudoir lighting, €4 mojitos and home-distilled gins, Rubí

is where the Born's cognoscenti head for a nightcap – or several. Push through the narrow, cosy space to the back, where you might just get one of the coveted tables. There's also superior bar food, from hummus and Vietnamese rolls to more traditional selections of cheese and ham.

BAR EL BORN
BAR

Map p300 (☑93 319 53 33; www.elbornbar.com; Passeig del Born 26; ⊙10am-2.30am Mon-Thu, to 3.30am Fri & Sat, noon-2.30am Sun; ⚲; MJaume l) Moss-green paintwork, marble tables and a black-and-white check-tiled floor mean a timeless look for this popular little cafe-bar, ideal for a morning coffee, an afternoon vermouth or an evening cocktail (€8). There's also Catalan wine (several of them organic or biodynamic).

CLUBHAUS
BAR

Map p300 (☑93 858 84 66; www.clubhaus.es; Avinguda del Marquès de l'Argentera 13; ⊙6pm-2.30am Mon-Thu, 5pm-3am Fri, 1pm-3am Sat, 1pm-2.30am Sun; MBarceloneta) Upstairs: graffiti-clad concrete walls, lively pool table, Mexican-style street food. Downstairs: table tennis, crafted cocktails, meaty American-inspired snacks, DJs from 11pm. Artsy multi-concept 2019 arrival Clubhaus keeps up the pace from coffee to brunch to espresso martinis to late-night karaoke. The focus is on homemade ingredients and a low-plastic ethos, with local artists' work on display.

BAR DE L'ANTIC TEATRE
BAR

Map p300 (☑93 315 23 54; www.anticteatre.com; Carrer Verdaguer i Callís 12; ⊙10am-11.30pm Mon-Thu, to midnight Fri, 5pm-midnight Sat, 5-11.30pm Sun; ⚲; MUrquinaona) There's often a queue for tables on the buzzy boho garden terrace at this relaxed community cafe-bar. It's set in the shade of a fig tree hidden away in a 17th-century building, down an alley opposite the Palau de la Música Catalana. Perfect for morning coffee, or beers and wine (€3) later on; proceeds go towards the Antic Teatre's cultural projects.

MUDANZAS
BAR

Map p300 (☑93 319 11 37; Carrer de la Vidrieria 15; ⊙10am-late; ⚲; MJaume l) This was one of the first bars to get things into gear in El Born and it still attracts a faithful crowd. With its chequered floor, marble-topped tables and vaulted brick ceiling, it's an attractive, lively place for a cocktail, coffee (from El Magnífico, p114) or perhaps a tapa. It also does a nice line in rum and malt whisky.

ABAIXADORS 10 BAR

Map p300 (☑93 160 03 83; www.facebook.com/abaixadors10; Carrer dels Abaixadors 10; ◷6pm-2am Tue-Thu, to 3am Fri & Sat) Part radio station, part DJ-led dance club, part gourmet cocktail bar from the La Confiteria group (which is behind some of Barcelona's best cocktail spots) – this neon-red-lit space set in a Modernista palace is now the permanent, year-round HQ of Barcelona's Primavera Sound (p43) alternative music festival. See the Facebook page for upcoming events.

BODEGA MAESTRAZGO WINE BAR

Map p300 (☑93 310 26 73; http://bodegamaestrazgo.com; Carrer de Sant Pere més Baix 90; ◷11am-3pm & 5-9.45pm Mon-Sat; Ⓜ Arc de Triomf) Going strong since 1952, this beautifully traditional, third-generation, stone-walled bodega sources thousands of interesting wines from across Catalonia, Spain and beyond. Wines by the glass change regularly, vermouth comes straight from the barrel and there are two-hour wine and *cava* tasting sessions (€45 to €90; book ahead; minimum two people), plus four-wine flights.

MAGIC CLUB

Map p300 (☑93 310 72 67; www.facebook.com/magicrockandrollclub; Passeig de Picasso 40; admission €12; ◷11pm-6am Thu-Sat; Ⓜ Barceloneta) While it sometimes hosts live acts in its sweaty basement, Magic is basically a straightforward, subterranean club blasting rock, indie, mainstream dance faves and Spanish pop. It's an established favourite on the scene, and queues can be long. Free Thursday and until 1.30am Friday and Saturday.

⭐ ENTERTAINMENT

⭐ PALAU DE LA MÚSICA CATALANA CLASSICAL MUSIC

Map p300 (☑93 295 72 00; www.palaumusica.cat; Carrer Palau de la Música 4-6; tickets from €15; ◷box office 9.30am-9pm Mon-Sat, 10am-3pm Sun; Ⓜ Urquinaona) A feast for both the eyes and ears, this Modernista confection (p102) doubles as the city's most traditional venue for classical and choral music,

though the wide-ranging programme also takes in flamenco, pop and – particularly – jazz. Just being here for a performance is an experience. Sip a pre-concert tipple in the foyer, its tiled pillars all a-glitter. Up the grand stairway, the main auditorium is a whirlpool of Modernista whimsy.

FAROLA LIVE MUSIC

Map p300 (☑663 332 643; www.farolabcn.com; Carrer del Rec 67; ◷6pm-2.30am Sun-Thu, to 3.30am Fri & Sat) From soulful jazz to foot-stomping flamenco, live music meets expertly crafted cocktails and a world of carefully curated sherries at lively Farola, hidden off Passeig del Born. Performances are 9pm Thursday to Sunday (upcoming shows listed online). There's also a smart Italian-influenced tapas menu of homemade hummus, local-cheese boards, and focaccia topped with, say, gorgonzola or Italian ham (€5 to €9).

TABLAO NERVIÓN DANCE

Map p300 (☑93 315 21 03; www.restaurantenervion.com; Carrer de la Princesa 2; show incl 1 drink €18, show & set dinner €30; ◷shows 8-10pm Wed-Sun; Ⓜ Jaume I) For admittedly tourist-oriented flamenco in a basement setting, this unassuming bar is cheaper than most and has good, professional offerings.

SHOPPING

The former commercial heart of medieval Barcelona is today still home to a cornucopia of old-style specialist food and drink shops – a feast of aroma and atmosphere. But these days they're joined by a raft of stylish fashion boutiques (particularly in El Born), many of them with a sustainable ethos that champions local artisans and designers.

⭐ VILA VINITECA FOOD & DRINKS

Map p300 (www.vilaviniteca.es; Carrer dels Agullers 7; ◷8.30am-8.30pm Mon-Sat; Ⓜ Jaume I) One of Barcelona's best wine stores (and there are a few...), Vila Viniteca has been hunting down the finest local and imported wines since 1932. There are year-round on-request tastings and a handful of bar tables, and on several November evenings it organises an almost riotous wine-tasting event at which cellars from across Spain present their young new wines.

EL MAGNÍFICO COFFEE

Map p300 (www.cafeselmagnifico.com; Carrer de l'Argenteria 64; ⊙10am-8pm Mon-Sat; Ⓜ Jaume I) All sorts of coffee beans, sourced seasonally from around the world, have been roasted at much-loved third-generation family-owned El Magnífico (which you'll spot all over town) since the early 20th century – and the aromas hit as soon as you walk in. Sample a cup on-site or wander over to the sleek Mag cafe (p111) on nearby Carrer de Grunyí.

CAPSULE FASHION & ACCESSORIES

Map p300 (www.capsulebcn.com; Carrer dels Banys Vells 21; ⊙noon-8pm Tue-Sat; Ⓜ Jaume I, Barceloneta) 🌿 Elegantly understated fashion and homewares sourced from small, sustainable, independent Spanish and international brands grace this tucked-away boutique. Capsule occupies a reimagined brick-walled stable and spotlights female artisans working with traditional techniques and organic materials. The gorgeous own-brand babucha-style raffia shoes are handmade by a women's cooperative in Morocco.

WORKING IN THE REDWOODS CERAMICS

Map p300 (☑93 301 66 63; www.working intheredwoods.com; Carrer de Lluís el Piadós 4; ⊙noon-8pm Mon-Sat; Ⓜ Arc de Triomf) Catalan designer Miriam Cernuda handcrafts beautiful, minimalist, earthy-toned bowls, mugs, vases and other ceramics from all-natural materials, inspired by the colours of the Costa Brava, at this soothing studio-workshop near the Arc de Triomf. There are also occasional ceramics classes (check online).

OZZ BARCELONA FASHION & ACCESSORIES

Map p300 (☑93 315 84 81; https://ozzbarcelona. com; Carrer dels Banys Vells 8; ⊙10.30am-9pm; Ⓜ Jaume I) Cutting-edge Barcelona designers take centre stage at slow-fashion-focused concept boutique and coworking space Ozz. Its handmade jewellery and bold clothing come courtesy of emerging, independent brands like Txell Miras, IKA, Ester Gueroa and Antonio Rodríguez.

CASA GISPERT FOOD

Map p300 (☑93 319 75 35; www.casagispert. com; Carrer dels Sombrerers 23; ⊙10am-8.30pm Mon-Sat; Ⓜ Jaume I) Wonderful, atmospheric, wood-fronted Casa Gispert has been toasting nuts and selling all manner of dried fruit since 1851. Pots and jars piled high on the shelves contain an unending variety of crunchy titbits: some roasted, some honeyed, all of them moreish. Your order is shouted over to the till, along with the price, in a display of old-world accounting.

EL REI DE LA MÀGIA MAGIC

Map p300 (☑93 319 73 93; www.elreidelamagia. es; Carrer de la Princesa 11; ⊙4-7.30pm Mon-Wed, 11am-2pm & 4-7.30pm Thu-Sat; Ⓜ Jaume I) Should you decide to stay in Barcelona and make a living as a magician, this rust-red world of make-believe is the place to buy levitation brooms, glasses of disappearing milk and decks of magic cards. The owners have been keeping locals both astounded and amused for almost 140 years.

HOFMANN PASTISSERIA FOOD

Map p300 (☑93 268 82 21; www.hofmann-bcn. com; Carrer dels Flassaders 44; ⊙9am-2pm & 3.30-8pm Mon-Sat, 9am-2pm Sun; Ⓜ Barceloneta, Jaume I) All painted wooden cabinets and sky-blue interiors, this bite-sized gourmet patisserie is linked to the prestigious Hofmann cooking school. Choose between jars of delicious jams, the prize-winning mascarpone-filled croissants (also in other flavours!) and more dangerous pastries, or an array of cakes and other sweet treats. Hofmann also has a cafe (p112) a few doors down.

CLAY HOMEWARES

Map p300 (www.clay-store.com; Carrer dels Banys Vells 11; ⊙noon-8pm Mon-Sat; Ⓜ Jaume I) Clay's organic beauty products and soothingly stylish homewares and lifestyle pieces are carefully collected by a trio of designer friends, from artisans around Spain and the Mediterranean. Finds might include delicate Andalucian pottery, handwoven straw baskets from La Palma or handblown Syrian glassware – all shown off in a centuries-old Born building.

NU SABATES
SHOES

Map p300 (☑93 268 03 83; www.nusabates.com; Carrer dels Cotoners 14; ☺noon-7pm Mon-Sat; ⓜJaume I) A modern-day Catalan cobbler has put together original handmade leather shoes for men and women (and a handful of bags and other leather items) in a friendly and stylish locale, enlivened by inspired musical selections. Personalised options available on request.

ETNIA
FASHION & ACCESSORIES

Map p300 (www.etniabarcelona.com; Carrer de l'Espasería 1-3; ☺10am-9pm Mon-Sat, noon-8pm Sun; ⓜJaume I, Barceloneta) Bold, art-world-inspired, Barcelona-designed glasses and sunnies are the stars at celeb-loved Etnia's flagship boutique, opposite the Basílica de Santa Maria del Mar.

COQUETTE
FASHION & ACCESSORIES

Map p300 (☑93 310 35 35; www.coquettebcn. com; Carrer de Bonaire 5; ☺11am-3pm & 5-9pm Mon-Fri, 11.30am-9pm Sat; ⓜBarceloneta, Jaume I) With its cut-back, industrial-chic designer look, this striking upmarket fashion boutique is attractive in its own right. Women can browse through casual, feminine wear by Spanish and international designers such as Masscob, Sur/Sac and Hoss Intropia.

CUSTO BARCELONA
FASHION & ACCESSORIES

Map p300 (☑93 268 78 93; www.custo.com; Plaça de les Olles 7; ☺noon-8pm Mon & Wed-Sat; ⓜBarceloneta, Jaume I) Avant-garde Barcelona brand Custo presents daring women's and men's collections each year on the international catwalks. The dazzling colours and cut of everything from dinner jackets to hot pants are for the uninhibited, and the psychedelic decor and casual atmosphere lend this store a youthful edge (there are several more around town).

OLISOLIVA
FOOD & DRINKS

Map p300 (☑93 268 14 72; Avinguda de Francesc Cambó 16, Mercat de Santa Caterina; ☺9.30am-3pm Mon-Wed, to 8pm Thu & Fri, to 3.30pm Sat; ⓜJaume I) Within the undulating-roofed Mercat de Santa Caterina (p104), this simple, glassed-in store is stacked with olive oils and vinegars from all over Spain, as well as Catalan wines. Taste some of the products before deciding. Some of the best olive oils come from southern Spain.

MARSALADA
GIFTS & SOUVENIRS

Map p300 (☑93 116 20 76; www.marsalada barcelona.com; Carrer de Sant Jacint 6; ☺10am-2pm & 4-7pm Mon-Sat; ⓜJaume I) For souvenirs with a difference, Marsalada has hand-printed tote bags in unbleached cotton, engravings and T-shirts. Each of these is emblazoned with a well-known Barcelona attraction, sketched in pen and ink and adorned with abstract colour mosaics.

SANS I SANS
DRINKS

Map p300 (☑93 310 25 18; www.sansisans.com; Carrer de l'Argenteria 59; ☺10am-8pm Mon-Sat; ⓜJaume I) Run by the owners of coffee-loving El Magnífico across the road, this exquisite tea shop stocks well over a hundred varieties of tea from around the world, along with pots, strainers and assorted other accessories.

LA BOTIFARRERIA
FOOD

Map p300 (☑93 319 91 23; www.labotifarreria. com; Carrer de Santa Maria 4; ☺9.30am-2.30pm & 5-8pm Mon-Sat; ⓜJaume I) Say it with a sausage! Although this delightful deli sells all sorts of goodies, the mainstay is an astounding variety of handcrafted sausages – the botifarra. Not just the regular pork variety either – these sausages are stuffed with anything from green pepper and whisky to apple curry.

EL BORN BOUTIQUES

The former commercial heart of medieval Barcelona is today still home to a cornucopia of old-style specialist food and drink shops – a feast of aroma and atmosphere. But these days they're joined by a raft of stylish fashion boutiques (particularly in El Born), many of them with a sustainable ethos that champions local artisans and designers.

🏃 SPORTS & ACTIVITIES

WANDERBEAK
FOOD & DRINK

(📞93 22 06 101; www.wanderbeak.com; Carrer del Comerç 29; group tour per person €79-99; ⊙9am-10pm; Ⓜ Jaume I, Barceloneta) Wanderbeak runs fun-filled, in-depth, small-group (maximum eight people) gastronomic experiences taking in Barcelona's history and foodie highlights; most dietary requirements are happily catered for on request, and there are cooking classes too. The signature Born to Eat tour leads you through El Born's buzzy lanes via three food stops and a relaxed wine-tasting session.

Private tours include Gourmet Gaudí (with Michelin-star dining), aperitifs out on a yacht, and day trips to Catalonia's *cava* wineries or the seafood-tastic Delta de l'Ebre.

BARCELONA ARCHITECTURE WALKS
ARCHITECTURE

(📞682 497208; https://barcelonaarchitecturewalks.com; Passatge de l'Hort de Velluters 5; 3hr tour €38; Ⓜ Arc de Triomf) A keen multilingual team of Barcelona-based architects and architecture professors, which leads carefully curated small-group, design-based itineraries around town. The signature Barcelona & Gaudí tour provides a crash course in all things Modernisme; Barcelona & The Market meanders through the Barri Gòtic's multilayered history and Enric Miralles' work; and Barcelona & The Future City tackles avant-garde architecture. Reservations essential.

BARCELONA GUIDE BUREAU
TOURS

Map p300 (📞93 315 22 61; www.barcelonaguidebureau.com; Casa de la Seda, Via Laietana 50; Ⓜ Jaume I) Barcelona Guide Bureau places professional guides at the disposal of groups for tailor-made tours of the city, with several languages catered for. It also offers a series of daily tours, from a five-hour highlights tour (adult/child €85/42) to a four-hour trip to Montserrat (adult/child €54/27).

AIRE DE BARCELONA
SPA

Map p300 (📞93 295 57 43; https://beaire.com; Passeig de Picasso 22; thermal baths €41-49; ⊙9am-11pm Sun-Thu, to midnight Fri & Sat; Ⓜ Arc de Triomf) With low lighting and relaxing wafting aromas, this basement spa within a converted 17th-century warehouse makes the perfect end to a day's exploring. Book ahead to spend 60 to 90 minutes sinking into hot, warm and cold baths, aromatherapy steam baths, a floatarium and more. Facials, exfoliations and massages (from olive-oil-infused rubs to floating-in-pool sessions) available, too.

Barceloneta, the Waterfront & El Poblenou

PORT VELL | BARCELONETA | PORT OLÍMPIC | EL POBLENOU | EL FÒRUM

Neighbourhood Top Five

❶ El Poblenou Platges (p119) Basking on these sun-kissed sandy beaches, before a dip in the glittering Mediterranean and a *xiringuito* lunch.

❷ Barceloneta Dining (p126) Hopping between this seaside *barri's* down-to-earth tapas bars (don't miss La Cova Fumada), or hunting down the perfect paella.

❸ Design in El Poblenou (p127) Wandering between creative cafes, forward-thinking boutiques and ambitious arts projects like Espacio 88 in this up-and-coming, formerly industrial neighbourhood.

❹ Museu d'Història de Catalunya (p122) Learning about the Romans, Moors, feudal lords and civil war freedom fighters, followed by drinks at the rooftop restaurant.

❺ Museu Marítim (p120) Stepping back in time in this fascinating Gothic shipyard and exploring Barcelona's rich maritime past.

For more detail of this area see Map p302 and p304 ➡

Lonely Planet's Top Tips

If you'd like to explore the sea and the mountains on the same day, take the **Telefèric del Port** (p121) cable car from Barceloneta's Torre de Sant Sebastià up to Montjuïc.

Over in El Poblenou, many (though not all) businesses close on weekends, so it's often best to visit midweek.

 Best Places to Eat

➡ La Barra de Carles Abellán (p128)
➡ Can Solé (p128)
➡ Minyam (p130)
➡ Oaxaca (p128)
➡ Can Recasens (p130)
➡ Little Fern Café (p129)

For reviews, see p126.➡

 Best Places to Drink

➡ Perikete (p131)
➡ Bodega Vidrios y Cristales (p131)
➡ Can Paixano (p132)
➡ BlackLab (p132)
➡ Espai Joliu (p132)

For reviews, see p131.➡

 Best Places to Shop

➡ Palo Market Fest (p134)
➡ Mercat dels Encants (p135)
➡ Noak Room (p135)
➡ Vernita (p135)

For reviews, see p134.➡

Explore Barceloneta, the Waterfront & El Poblenou

Barcelona's long, sun-drenched waterfront is a pleasant escape when you need a break from Gothic lanes and Modernisme. Heading northeast from the old city, you'll soon find yourself amid tempting seafood restaurants and waterfront bars, with a palm-lined promenade taking cyclists, joggers and strollers out to the white-gold beaches running 4km up to Parc del Fòrum in the modern El Fòrum (p124) area.

At the southern end of La Rambla, the transformed Port Vell, once an industrial wasteland, draws locals and tourists alike who come to stroll the peaceful pedestrian Rambla de Mar (p122).

Northeast of here, upmarket, open-air restaurants overlook a marina and one of the city's best museums for learning about the Catalan experience, the Museu d'Història de Catalunya (p122). Next on, the old fishing quarter of Barceloneta was laid out in the mid-18th century with narrow gridlike lanes criss-crossed with laundry in the breeze. Delve into the narrow lanes, which are dotted with festive tapas spots, old-fashioned seafood joints and bohemian bars.

Where Barceloneta abuts the water, you'll find open-air restaurants looking out over the promenade and the golden beaches beyond. Inland from these modern artificial beaches is the design and high-tech zone of post-industrial El Poblenou, which is transforming itself into one of Barcelona's most fashionable neighbourhoods with a wave of creative enterprises and stylish cafes, shops and restaurants.

Local Life

➡**Hang-outs** There are many great local haunts full of flowing *cava*, beer and great-value tapas: Vaso de Oro (p126), La Cova Fumada (p126) and Can Paixano (p132) are long-time favourites.

➡**Markets** Both Barceloneta (p136) and Poblenou (p136) have lively fresh-produce markets with a couple of cafe-bars.

➡**Beach action** From June to September, informal rustic bars known as *xiringuitos* dot the sands, doling out cold drinks and party vibes.

Getting There & Away

➡**Metro** Go to Drassanes (Línia 3) to reach Port Vell; Barceloneta (Línia 4) has its own stop. Línia 4 continues out to Ciutadella Vila Olímpica (the best stop for the Port Olímpic), El Poblenou, the city's northeastern beaches, and El Maresme Fòrum.

NITO/SHUTTERSTOCK ©

LAY A TOWEL ON EL POBLENOU PLATGES

A series of beautiful, broad, sandy golden beaches dotted with *xiringuitos* (seasonal beach bars) stretches northeast from the Port Olímpic marina. They're largely artificial, but that doesn't deter the millions of sunseekers and swimmers from descending in summer, especially for beach volleyball – and they're still quieter than the sandy strands closer to the city centre.

El Poblenou Area

First comes **Platja de la Nova Icària** (pictured; Map p304; V23, H16, Llacuna), the southernmost and busiest of El Poblenou's beaches, followed by lively **Platja del Bogatell** (Map p304; V25, H16, Llacuna), both with buzzy summer beach bars, good seafood restaurants and some volleyball action.

El Fòrum Area

Next along, **Platja de la Mar Bella** (Map p304; V31, H16, Poblenou) has a small nudist strip and some water sports and is popular with an LGBTIQ+ crowd. Locally loved **Platja de la Nova Mar Bella** (Map p304; V29, H16, Selva de Mar) has a bit of a watersports scene and leads into the new Front Marítim residential and commercial waterfront strip. It's part of the Diagonal Mar project in the Fòrum district, which is fronted by the last and easternmost of these artificial beaches to be created, **Platja del Llevant** (Map p304; V29, H16, Selva de Mar) (completed in 2006 and popular with dog walkers).

Activities

The main swimming season is from May to mid-September, when water temperatures can reach 24°C. On Platja de la Mar Bella you'll find Base Náutica Municipal (p137), which hires out water-sports equipment and offers lessons in everything from kayaking and windsurfing to catamaran sailing and stand-up paddleboarding.

DON'T MISS

➡ The vibrant bustle of Nova Icària & Bogatell beaches

➡ The fun seasonal beach bars

➡ Platja de la Mar Bella for an LGBTIQ+ scene

➡ A sunset seafront saunter

PRACTICALITIES

➡ Map p304, E3

➡ Ciutadella Vila Olímpica, Llacuna, Poblenou, Selva de Mar

The mighty Gothic Reials Drassanes (Royal Shipyards) are an extraordinary piece of civilian architecture. From here, Don Juan de Austria's flagship galley was launched to lead a joint Spanish-Venetian fleet into the momentous Battle of Lepanto against the Ottoman Empire in 1571. Today the broad arches shelter the Museu Marítim, one of Barcelona's most intriguing museums.

Royal Shipyards

The shipyards were, in their heyday, among the greatest in Europe. Begun in the 13th century and completed by 1378, the long, arched bays (the highest arches reach 13m) once sloped off as slipways directly into the water, which lapped the seaward side of the Drassanes until at least the end of the 18th century. Shipbuilding was later moved to southern Spain, and the Drassanes became a barracks for artillery.

Replica of Don Juan of Austria's Flagship

The centre of the shipyards is dominated by a full-scale replica (made in the 1970s) of Don Juan de Austria's 16th-century flagship. Slaves, prisoners and volunteers (!), at full steam, could haul this vessel along at 9 knots. They remained chained to their seats, four to an oar, at all times.

Here they worked, drank (fresh water was stored below decks, where the infirmary was also located), ate, slept and went to the loo. You could smell a galley like this from miles away.

Exhibitions

Fishing vessels, old navigation charts, models and dioramas of the Barcelona waterfront make up the rest of this engaging museum, which also spotlights Spain's epic history on the high seas through an expansive collection with multimedia exhibits. Intriguing temporary exhibitions are held too.

Ictíneo

In the courtyard, you can have a look at a life-size replica of the *Ictíneo I*, one of the world's first submarines. It was invented and built in 1858 by Catalan polymath Narcís Monturiol, and was operated by hand-cranked propellers turned by friends of Monturiol who accompanied him on dozens of successful short dives (two hours maximum) in the harbour. He later developed an even larger submarine *(Ictíneo II)* powered by a combustion engine that allowed it to dive to 30m and remain submerged for seven hours. Despite impressive demonstrations to awestruck crowds, he never attracted the interest of the navy and remains largely forgotten today.

Pailebot de Santa Eulàlia

The entrance fee also includes a visit to the **Pailebot de Santa Eulàlia** (Map p302; www. mmb.cat; Moll de la Fusta; adult/child €3/1, free with Museu Marítim ticket; ☻10am-8.30pm Tue-Fri & Sun, 2-8.30pm Sat Apr-Oct, 10am-5.30pm Tue-Fri & Sun, 2-5.30pm Sat Nov-Mar; Ⓜ Drassanes) – a 1918 three-masted schooner, restored by the Museu Marítim, which is moored along the palm-lined Moll de la Fusta promenade. You can see it perfectly well without going aboard; there's not an awful lot to behold below deck.

DON'T MISS

➡ The replica of Don Juan de Austria's flagship

➡ Temporary exhibitions

➡ *Ictíneo I*

➡ The courtyard cafe

PRACTICALITIES

➡ Map p302, A4

➡ ☎ 93 342 99 20

➡ www.mmb.cat

➡ Avinguda de les Drassanes

➡ adult/child €10/5, from 3pm Sun free

➡ ☻10am-8pm

➡ Ⓜ Drassanes

👁 SIGHTS

👁 Port Vell & Barceloneta

MUSEU MARÍTIM   MUSEUM

See p120.

L'AQUÀRIUM   AQUARIUM

Map p302 (☎93 221 74 74; www.aquariumbcn. com; Moll d'Espanya; adult/child €21/16; ⊙10am-9pm Easter & Jun-Sep, reduced hours Oct-May; 🚸; MDrassanes) It's hard not to shudder at the sight of a shark gliding above you, displaying its toothy, wide-mouthed grin – but this 80m shark tunnel is the highlight of one of Europe's largest aquariums. Jutting out into the port, Barcelona's aquarium is home to the world's best Mediterranean collection, as well as plenty of colourful fish from as far off as the Red Sea, the Caribbean and the Great Barrier Reef. A staggering 11,000 creatures of 450 species reside here.

Back in the shark tunnel, which you reach after passing a series of themed fish tanks with everything from bream to sea horses, various species of shark (white tip, sand tiger, black tip and sandbar) flit around you, along with a host of other critters, from flapping rays to creepy Mediterranean morays. The Planeta Aqua zone is host to a family of Humboldt penguins from Chile and a tank of rays and guitarfish, while Explora is a dedicated interactive children's area.

Underwater adventurers can cage dive (€150) in the main tank with the sharks, or scuba dive (€300) with a valid dive certificate.

**PASSEIG MARÍTIM
DE LA BARCELONETA**   WATERFRONT

Map p302 (MBarceloneta, Ciutadella Vila Olímpica) On Barceloneta's seaward side are the first of Barcelona's beaches, which get packed in summer. The broad 1.25km promenade from Barceloneta to the Port Olímpic is a favourite with strollers, runners and sun-seekers. Cyclists zip past on a separate path nearby.

TELEFÈRIC DEL PORT   CABLE CAR

Map p302 (www.telefericodebarcelona.com; Passeig de Joan de Borbó; 1 way/return €11/16.50; ⊙10.30am-8pm Jun-early Sep, shorter hours early Sep-May; 🚌V15, V19, MBarceloneta) First built for the 1929 Expo, this cable car strung across the harbour between La Barceloneta and Montjuïc provides an eagle-eye view of

the city. The cabins float between the Torre de Sant Sebastià (Barceloneta) – topped by a panoramic restaurant – and Miramar (Montjuïc), via the 107m-high Torre de Jaume I, every 10 minutes or so. The total 1292m journey takes seven minutes (but the cable car closes in windy weather).

PLATJA DE LA BARCELONETA   BEACH

Map p302 (MBarceloneta) Just east of its namesake neighbourhood, Barceloneta's main beach is a golden-brown strip of sand where, during warm months, pool-party promoters, mojito vendors and sarong sellers mingle with masses of sun-loving visitors and *barcelonins*. It's an iconic Barcelona spot, but can feel like a bit of a circus – perhaps better enjoyed very first thing or over a sunset stroll.

MIRADOR DE COLOM   VIEWPOINT

Map p302 (☎93 285 38 34; www.barcelona turisme.com; Plaça del Portal de la Pau; adult/child €6/4; ⊙8.30am-8.30pm; MDrassanes) High above the swirl of traffic navigating the roundabout at the southern end of La Rambla, Christopher Columbus keeps permanent watch, pointing vaguely out to the Mediterranean from this Corinthian-style iron column built for the 1888 Barcelona Universal Exposition. Zip up 60m in a lift for a bird's-eye view back up La Rambla and across Barcelona's ports. You can also enjoy a wine tasting afterwards in the cellar underneath (€8 for lift and wine).

PLATJA DE SANT SEBASTIÀ   BEACH

Map p302 (MBarceloneta) At the far southern end of the beach fronting La Barceloneta, this is a handy stretch of white-gold sand for a bit of sun and surf action when you need a quick break from the old city. There's a string of beach bars, restaurants and shops in front of the W Barcelona (p237).

PLATJA DE SANT MIQUEL   BEACH

Map p302 (MBarceloneta) Taking its name from the 18th-century church (p122) in nearby Barceloneta, this stretch of soft honey-gold sand fills with beachgoers when warm days arrive. Because of its proximity to the old city, the crowds are thicker here than at beaches further out.

CASA DE LA BARCELONETA   ARCHITECTURE

Map p302 (☎93 688 49 56; www.facebook.com/ lacasadelabarceloneta1761; Carrer de Sant Carles 6; ⊙10am-1pm & 4-9pm Tue & Thu, 4-9pm Wed & Fri, 10am-2pm & 4-8pm Sat; MBarceloneta)

FREE Devoted to the history and culture of the *barri* (with displays in Catalan), this tiny cultural centre occupies a brick-walled 1761 building that's a prime example of traditional Barceloneta architecture.

EL CAP DE BARCELONA
SCULPTURE

Map p302 (Passeig de Colom; MBarceloneta) An icon by the waterfront, this eye-catching 15m-high primary-coloured sculpture was designed by famous American pop artist Roy Lichtenstein for the 1992 Olympics.

L'ESTEL FERIT
SCULPTURE

Map p302 (Passeig Marítim de la Barceloneta; MBarceloneta) German artist Rebecca Horn's elegant *The Wounded Shooting Star* sculpture was commissioned for the 1992 Olympics and commemorates the old-fashioned shacks that once lined the beach. Popularly known as *els Cubs* (The Cubes), it's a time-honoured seaside meeting place.

ESGLÉSIA DE SANT MIQUEL DEL PORT
CHURCH

Map p302 (☑93 221 65 50; Plaça de la Barceloneta; ☺7am-1.30pm Mon-Fri, from 8am Sat; MBarceloneta) Dating from 1755, this sober baroque church was the first building completed in Barceloneta. Built low so that the cannon in the then Ciutadella fort could fire over it if necessary, it was damaged by Leftists in 1936 and restored in 1992. Its sculpture of St Michael (Sant Miquel) has attracted controversy for its depiction of the archangel as a bodybuilder.

RAMBLA DE MAR
WATERFRONT

Map p302 (off Passeig de Colom; MDrassanes) The city's authorities extended the world-famous La Rambla thoroughfare out into the sea in the early 2000s, connecting the city with the reclaimed port area of the Port Vell. Seeming to float above the water, it offers elevated marina views.

EDIFICI DE GAS NATURAL
ARCHITECTURE

Map p302 (Passeig de Salvat Papasseit; MBarceloneta) The work of Enric Miralles, completed in 2005, this shimmering glass waterfront office tower is only 86m (20 storeys) high, but remains extraordinary for its mirrored surface and weirdly protruding adjunct buildings, which could be giant glass cliffs bursting from the main tower's flank. It's the headquarters for the Naturgy energy company, so visitors can't go inside, but the exterior is still fascinating.

TOP EXPERIENCE
EXPLORE THE AGES AT MUSEU D'HISTÒRIA DE CATALUNYA

Within the revitalised 1880s **Palau de Mar** (Map p302; Plaça de Pau Vila; MBarceloneta), this excellent museum travels from the Stone Age through to the arrival of Modernisme in Catalonia and the Spanish Civil War (touching heavily on the cultural and political repression felt across Catalonia after the war) and into the 21st century.

It's a busy multimedia hotchpotch of dioramas, artefacts, videos, models, documents and interactive bits: all up, a thoroughly entertaining exploration of 2000 years of Catalan history. Signage is in Catalan, Spanish and English.

You'll see how the Romans lived, listen to Arab poetry from the time when the city was under Moorish rule, peer into the dwelling of a medieval family in the Pyrenees, try to mount a knight's horse or lift a suit of armour, and learn all about the Greek-then-Roman port of Empúries (on today's Costa Brava).

Afterwards, head upstairs to the first-rate rooftop restaurant **1881** (p128) and its attached terrace cafe-bar.

DON'T MISS
➡ Exhibits on the Spanish Civil War
➡ The chance to climb atop a knight's horse
➡ Rooftop restaurant 1881 and its sleek bar

PRACTICALITIES
➡ Map p302, C3
➡ ☑93 225 47 00
➡ www.mhcat.cat
➡ Plaça de Pau Vila 3
➡ adult/child €6/free, 1st Sun of month 10am-2.30pm free
➡ ☺10am-7pm Tue & Thu-Sat, to 8pm Wed, to 2.30pm Sun
➡ MBarceloneta

BEACHES BEYOND BARCELONA

Although Barcelona is a Mediterranean-hugging city, many of its most gorgeously enticing beaches lie outside the centre – but are still perfectly doable in a day trip.

Platja de Castelldefels Around 20km southwest of central Barcelona and beloved by kitesurfers, this beautiful long sweep of golden-blonde sand backed by dunes provides a blissful escape and is never too packed. Sunsets here are exquisite. Take *rodalies* train R2 from/to Passeig de Gràcia or Sants (€2.55, 35 minutes).

Sitges Spain's most famous LGBTIQ+ holiday town (p224), 35km southwest of Barcelona, has 17 fabulous beaches – from party-hard hang-outs to family-friendly beach-volleyball spots to relaxed naturist sands. Catch *rodalies* train R2 (€4.20, 40 minutes).

Platja del Garraf Tiny Garraf village, 30km southwest of Barcelona, trickles down to a sparkling teal bay and silvery sand beach framed by old whitewashed fishers' cottages with deep-green trim. Though these days it's less off-radar following the arrival of Soho House's Little Beach House (p234), there's still a local vibe. *Rodalies* train R2 goes here too (€3.50, 40 minutes).

Montgat Around 20km northeast of Barcelona, on the Costa del Maresme, Montgat is dotted with golden strands and just a quick train ride from Plaça de Catalunya (R1; €2.20, 20 minutes).

◉ Port Olímpic, El Poblenou & El Fòrum

EL POBLENOU PLATGES BEACH
See p119.

MUSEU DEL DISSENY
DE BARCELONA MUSEUM
Map p304 (☑93 256 68 00; www.museudel disseny.cat; Plaça de les Glòries Catalanes 37; adult/child €6/4, from 3pm Sun & 1st Sun of the month free; ◑10am-8pm Tue-Sun; ⓂGlòries) 🖊 Nicknamed *la grapadora* (the stapler), Barcelona's fascinating design museum lies inside a monolithic contemporary building with geometric facades and a rather brutalist appearance. Inside, it houses a dazzling collection of ceramics, fashion, decorative arts and textiles, and is a must for anyone interested in the design world, with plenty of temporary exhibitions, too.

Start at the top and work your way down. The 4th floor houses graphic arts focused on the post-Franco design boom and the arrival of the 1992 Olympics, including several Almodóvar film posters. The 3rd floor takes you through local fashion from the 1550s onwards. Among other highlights, you'll see a dramatically lit collection of 19th-century crinolines (cage-like frames worn as undergarments beneath dresses), displayed like rare sea creatures inside giant glass tubes, as well as 16th-century French ballgowns, 18th- and 19th-century corsets, and haute couture from the mid-20th century, including pieces by Spanish designer Cristóbal Balenciaga.

The 2nd floor is devoted to decorative arts, with a wildly varied collection that ranges from an elaborate 16th-century Brussels tapestry and antique jewel-encrusted pocket watches to ceramics by Picasso and Miró. The 1st floor houses Catalan product design from the 20th century – worth a quick peek for the furniture.

MUSEU CAN FRAMIS MUSEUM
Map p304 (☑93 320 87 36; www.fundaciovila casas.com; Carrer de Roc Boronat 116-126; adult/child €5/2; ◑11am-6pm Tue-Sat, to 2pm Sun, closed Aug & Sep; ⓂGlòries, Llacuna) Set in an 18th-century former textile factory surrounded by greenery, this contemporary gallery is a showcase for Catalan painting from the 1960s onwards. The galleries display around 300 works, arranged in thought-provoking ways – with evocative paintings by different artists (sometimes working in different time periods) creating fascinating intersections and collisions.

Highlights include the intricate, tapestry-style paintings of Victor Pérez-Porro, Gregori Iglesias' desolate black-and-white scenes, the dreamlike sequences of Perejaume, photographic portraits by Pedro Madueño, Agustí Puig's ethereal *Menines* (whose point of departure is Velázquez' iconic *Las meninas* created three centuries earlier) and luminous works by self-taught painter Xevi Vilaró.

RAMBLA DEL POBLENOU   STREET

Map p304 With its origins in the mid-19th century (when Poblenou's industrial boom kicked off), this leafy boulevard has long been the neighbourhood hub, sprinkled with tapas bars and restaurants, and flanked by a few Modernista buildings.

PEIX   SCULPTURE

Map p304 (Carrer de Ramon Trias Fargas 2; MCiutadella Villa Olímpica) With copper-hued stainless-steel scales sparkling at sunset, this 35m-tall, 56m-long fish sculpture at the foot of the swish Hotel Arts Barcelona (p237) looks poised for a dive into the deep-blue Mediterranean. It was designed by famed American-Canadian architect Frank Gehry in the run-up to the 1992 Olympics.

CEMENTIRI DEL POBLENOU   CEMETERY

Map p304 (☑93 225 16 61; www.cbsa.cat; Avinguda d'Icària; ☺8am-6pm; MLlacuna) FREE Just inland from Platja de Bogatell, Poblenou's cemetery dates from 1773. It was positioned outside the then city limits for health reasons; its central monument commemorates the victims of a yellow-fever epidemic that swept across Barcelona in 1821. It is full of bombastic family memorials, but an altogether disquieting touch is the sculpture *El Petó de la Mort* (The Kiss of Death), in which a winged skeleton kisses a young, kneeling, lifeless body.

PARC DEL CENTRE DEL POBLENOU   PARK

Map p304 (Avinguda Diagonal; ☺10am-sunset; MPoblenou) Barcelona is sprinkled with parks whose principal element is concrete,

---

REMEMBERING WAR VICTIMS
....

Buried beneath the concrete expanses, bathing zone and marina created in El Fòrum lies the memory of nearly 2000 people executed in the fields of Camp de la Bota between 1936 and 1952, most of them under Franco from 1939 onward. A commemorative sculpture, *Fraternitat* (Brotherhood; 1992), by Miquel Navarro, stands in Rambla de Prim. A 55m-long memorial mural, by Francesc Abad, recalling all 1706 victims, was installed on Plaça del Fòrum in 2019, marking 80 years since Nationalist troops attacked Barcelona.

---

and this 5-hectare creation by French architect Jean Nouvel, with its statuary and stylised metal seats, is no exception. However, the park's Gaudí-inspired walls are increasingly covered by rambling bougainvillea and, inside, around 1000 mostly Mediterranean trees, including 35 palm species, are complemented by thousands of aromatic bushes and plants. Nouvel's idea is that the trees, sustained by local groundwater, will eventually form a natural canopy over the park.

ESPAI SUBIRACHS   MUSEUM

Map p304 (☑93 541 52 77; www.subirachs.cat; Carrer Batista 6; ☺5-8pm Tue, Wed & Sat; MPoblenou) FREE In a building next to the town house in which he was born in 1927, this intimate exhibition is devoted to the late Josep Maria Subirachs. It highlights the artist's ever-evolving talents well beyond his best-known sculptural work on the Sagrada Família's Façana de la Passió.

EL FÒRUM   AREA

Map p304 (MEl Maresme Fòrum) Once an urban wasteland, this area has seen dramatic changes since the turn of the millennium, including sparkling buildings, open plazas and waterfront recreation areas. The most striking element is the eerily blue, triangular **Edifici Fòrum** building by Swiss architects Herzog & de Meuron, which houses the Museu Blau (p126).

MUSEU BLAU   MUSEUM

Map p304 (Museu de Ciències Naturals de Barcelona; ☑93 256 60 02; www.museuciencies.cat; Parc del Fòrum, Edifici Fòrum; adult/child €7/free, from 3pm Sun & 1st Sun of the month free; ☺10am-7pm Tue-Sat, to 8pm Sun; MEl Maresme Fòrum) Set inside the futuristic Edifici Fòrum, whose angular facades look like sheer cliff faces (with grand strips of mirror creating fragmented reflections of the sky), the sprawling Museu Blau takes visitors on a journey back in time and across the natural world. Multimedia and interactive exhibits explore topics such as the history of evolution, the earth's formation and the great scientists who have helped shaped human knowledge. There are also specimens from the animal, plant and mineral kingdoms, plus dinosaur skeletons.

PORT OLÍMPIC   MARINA

Map p304 (Moll de Mestral; MCiutadella Vila Olímpica) A busy marina built for the Olym-

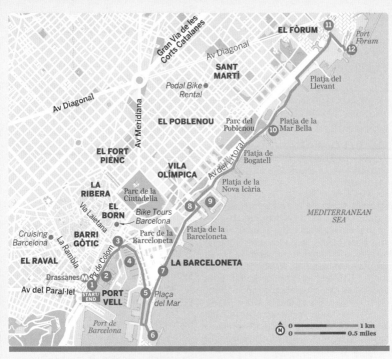

Cycling Tour
Barcelona's Waterfront

START/END PORT VELL
LENGTH 16KM RETURN; 1½ HOURS

Traversing Barcelona's ever-changing waterfront, this is a flat, safe ride along a dedicated bike path – though watch out for pedestrians (and potential building work!).

With the ① **Mirador de Colom** (p121) at your back, make your way northeast along the waterfront. Keep an eye out for the three-masted schooner ② **Pailebot de Santa Eulàlia** (p120), built in 1918. Another 400m up the road, you'll pass the colourful, 15m-high ③ **Cap de Barcelona** (p122) sculpture, created by American pop artist Roy Lichtenstein for the 1992 Olympics.

As you make your way along the ④ **marina**, you may have to dismount amid the throng of strollers and open-air restaurants. Hop back on and pedal south to the Plaça del Mar, which sports Alfredo Lanz' abstract 2004 sculpture ⑤ **Homenatge a la Natació** (Homage to Swimming; Map p302,

D5; Plaça del Mar; M Barceloneta). Around 600m south is Ricardo Bofill's instantly recognisable ⑥ **W Barcelona** (p237), nicknamed Hotel Vela (Sail Hotel).

Follow the crowds north, past ⑦ **L'Estel Ferit** (p122), which honours the traditional shacks that used to dot the beach and was installed by German artist Rebecca Horn for the 1992 Olympics.

Cycle another kilometre and you'll pass the copper-hued ⑧ **Peix sculpture**, designed by Frank Gehry, before arriving at the restaurant-lined ⑨ **Port Olímpic** (p126). Heading northeast from here you'll pass El Poblenou's lovely golden ⑩ **beaches** (p119), which fill with sunseekers in summer.

At the far northeast end, you'll find the ⑪ **El Fòrum** precinct, with two murals dedicated to the thousands executed here during the Franco years. El Fòrum's protected ⑫ **Zona de Banys** is a popular summer bathing spot. From here, head back to the Port Vell.

pic sailing events, the Port Olímpic is surrounded by bars and restaurants. An eye-catcher on the approach from Barceloneta is Frank Gehry's giant copper *Peix* (Fish) sculpture (p124). The area behind, dominated by twin tower blocks (the luxury Hotel Arts Barcelona (p237) and the Torre Mapfre office block), is the former Vila Olímpica living quarters for the Olympic competitors, which was later sold off as apartments.

MUSEU DE LA MÚSICA — MUSEUM

Map p304 (☑93 256 36 50; www.museumusica. bcn.cat; Carrer de Lepant 150; adult/child €6/free, 6-9pm Thu & 3-7pm Sun free; ⊘10am-6pm Tue, Wed & Fri, to 9pm Thu, to 7pm Sat & Sun; ⓂMarina) Some 500 instruments (less than a third of the full collection) are on show in this red-clad museum, housed on the 2nd floor of the administration building in L'Auditori (p134), the city's main classical music concert hall. Instruments range from a 17th-century baroque guitar, lutes and violins to Japanese kotos, Indian sitars, organs (some dating from the 18th century), pianos and a varied collection of drums and other percussion instruments from across Spain and beyond, along with phonographs and gramophones.

TORRE GLÒRIES — ARCHITECTURE

Barcelona's famously cucumber-shaped tower, Jean Nouvel's luminous Torre Glòries (formerly Torre Agbar) is among the most daring additions to the skyline since the first towers of La Sagrada Família went up. Opened in 2005, the 38-storey structure shimmers at night in shades of midnight blue and lipstick red. The building's top floors have been transformed into a viewing platform for visitors, due to open in 2022, with an installation by Argentinian artist Tomás Saraceno set into its dome.

EATING

Barceloneta's narrow lanes bristle with both good-natured, noisy tapas bars and upmarket seafood restaurants. Paella and its Catalan variant *fideuà* (with vermicelli noodles) are especially popular, and typically for a minimum of two diners. The Port Olímpic marina is lined with busy though underwhelming restaurants and tapas bars, while wonderful creative kitchens continue to pop up in post-industrial El Poblenou.

✕ Port Vell & Barceloneta

VASO DE ORO — TAPAS €

Map p302 (☑93 319 30 98; www.vasodeoro. com; Carrer de Balboa 6; tapas €3-10; ⊘11am-midnight, closed 3 weeks Sep; ⓂBarceloneta) Always packed, this narrow, old-school, tile-adorned bar gathers a high-spirited crowd, who come for fantastic tapas. Wisecracking, white-jacketed waiters serve plates of grilled *gambes* (prawns), *patates amanides* (Andalucian-style potato salad) or *solomillo* (sirloin) chunks. Want something a little different to drink? Ask for a *flauta cincuenta* – half lager and half dark beer.

LA COVA FUMADA — TAPAS €

Map p302 (☑93 221 40 61; Carrer del Baluard 56; tapas €3-12; ⊘9am-3.15pm Mon-Wed, 9am-3.15pm & 6-8.15pm Thu & Fri, 9am-1pm Sat; ⓂBarceloneta) The setting is decidedly frills-free, but this tiny, buzzing family-run tapas spot is something of a Barceloneta (and Barcelona) legend, with the queues to prove it. The secret? Mouth-watering *pop* (octopus), calamari, sardines, grilled *carxofes* (artichokes) and signature *bombes* (meat-and-potato croquettes with aioli) – all amazingly fresh and cooked in the open kitchen.

BODEGA LA PENINSULAR — TAPAS €

Map p302 (☑93 221 40 89; www.tabernaycafetin. es; Carrer del Mar 29; tapas €5-10; ⊘11.30am-midnight; ⓂBarceloneta) 🍴 At this traditional-style bodega with marble-topped tables, over three dozen artfully presented tapas pair with Catalan vintages and house-made vermouth. Adhering to the Slow Food ethos, ingredients are organic, seasonal and locally sourced; try the *mojama* (salt-cured, air-dried tuna), the renowned spicy *bombes* (meat-and-potato croquettes) with tangy aioli, or a giant wedge of tortilla. It's standing room only most nights.

CAN MAÑO — SEAFOOD €

Map p302 (Carrer del Baluard 12; raciones €4-15; ⊘8-11pm Mon, 8.15-11am, noon-4pm & 8-11pm Tue-Fri, 8.15-11am & 12.15-4pm Sat; ⓂBarceloneta) It may look like a dive, but you'll need to wait before being squeezed in at a packed table for a raucous night of *raciones* (full-plate-size tapas servings) over a bottle of cloudy white *turbio* (Galician wine) at this family-run stalwart. The seafood is fresh and abundant, with first-rate squid, prawns and fish served at rock-bottom prices. Cash only.

BITÁCORA
TAPAS €

Map p302 (☎93 319 11 10; Carrer de Balboa 1; tapas €4-13; ⊕9am-2.30am Mon-Fri, from 10am Sat & Sun; Ⓜ Barceloneta) Bitácora is a neighbourhood favourite for its congenial ambience and simple, well-priced tapas plates, which come in ample portions and have a splash of creativity. Top picks: *ceviche de peix* (fish ceviche), *calamarsets* (baby squid) and *gambes a la planxa* (grilled prawns). There's a small hidden terrace at the back.

NAP MAR
PIZZA €

Map p302 (☎93 007 36 39; www.facebook.com/nap.pizzeria; Carrer del Baluard 69; pizzas €6-10; ⊕1.30-4.30pm & 8pm-midnight Mon-Fri, 1pm-midnight Sat & Sun; 🛜🍴; Ⓜ Barceloneta) Though NAP (Neapolitan Authentic Pizza) has a couple of branches around town, this location footsteps from Platja de Sant Miquel makes elegant NAP Mar perfect for picking up a pizza to scoff on the beach. Fired in an Italian Stefano Ferrara woodburning oven, pizzas come with toppings such as speck, truffle cream and rocket, with plenty of veggie varieties available.

EL FILFERRO
TAPAS €

Map p302 (☎93 221 98 36; www.facebook.com/elfilferro.barceloneta; Carrer de Sant Carles 29; tapas €4-9, mains €7-11; ⊕10.30am-1am Tue-Sun; 🛜🍴♿; Ⓜ Barceloneta) One of the few Barceloneta restaurants where the focus isn't on seafood, cheerful Filferro has a loyal following for its good-value tapas, *entrepans* (filled rolls), salads and pasta. It has a warmly lit and eclectically furnished interior, or you can dine at outdoor tables on the square opposite (popular with families, as there's a playground just a few steps away).

BALUARD BARCELONETA
BAKERY €

Map p302 (☎93 221 12 08; http://baluardbarceloneta.com; Carrer del Baluard 38; snacks €1-4; ⊕8am-9pm Mon-Sat; Ⓜ Barceloneta) Fourth-generation Baluard serves some of the best freshly wood-fired breads in the city, along with filled baguettes perfect for picnics. It also bakes a range of tempting pastries, such as *xuixuixo* (deep-fried custard-filled pastries from Girona) and *bunyols* (doughnut-shaped pastries stuffed with cheese or jam), and tarts such as fig or wild berries. Also at L'Eixample's Praktik Bakery hotel.

ESPACIO 88

Hosting everything from yoga classes, pop-up boutiques and brunches to the (permanent) uberpopular SKYE (p133) coffee truck, this white-walled, concrete-floored **warehouse-like space** (Map p304; ☎93 356 88 18; www.espacio88.com; Carrer de Pamplona 88; ⊕9am-5pm Mon-Fri; Ⓜ Bogatell) embodies all that's wonderful about El Poblenou's post-industrial resurgence. The arts take centre stage, with dynamic events and exhibitions typically focusing on fashion, design, photography, architecture, food and film.

GREEN SPOT
VEGETARIAN €€

Map p302 (☎93 802 55 65; www.encompaniadelobos.com; Carrer de la Reina Cristina 12; mains €10-16; ⊕1pm-midnight Mon-Thu & Sun, to 2am Fri & Sat; 🍴; Ⓜ Barceloneta) Battered cauliflower with tamarind-and-mint sauce, quesadillas with kimchi and avocado, jackfruit tacos, and buckwheat pizza with cashew cheese and asparagus are among the deftly inventive vegetarian, vegan and gluten-free dishes available here. The food is presented in a stylish, minimalist dining room with beautiful whitewashed vaulted ceilings. Live music Tuesday and Thursday.

L'ÒSTIA
TAPAS €€

Map p302 (☎93 221 47 58; www.lostiabcn.com; Plaça de la Barceloneta 1; tapas €3-10, mains €6-16; ⊕11am-11pm; 🛜; Ⓜ Barceloneta) On a charming hidden square, this neighbourhood bar opens to a terrace facing Barceloneta's beautiful baroque church (p122). Tapas reflect the area's seafood-fired heritage but also come with fusion twists like seafood pappardelle, *truita* (potato omelette) with chorizo or marinated sardines with orange. Wines are primarily Catalan. A heated marquee sets up on the terrace in winter.

EL GUINDILLA
TAPAS, INTERNATIONAL €€

Map p302 (☎93 221 54 58; www.elguindillabarcelona.es; Plaça del Poeta Boscà 2; tapas €3-14, mains €11-15; ⊕9am-midnight; Ⓜ Barceloneta) Within the Mercat de la Barceloneta (p136), this popular modern-rustic place with cheery red decor and outdoor seating on a lively square serves international

BARCELONETA, THE WATERFRONT & EL POBLENOU EATING

breakfasts, good-value daily lunch specials and mains such as entrecot with *Padrón* peppers and goat's-cheese salad. It draws a tapas-sampling and beer-swilling crowd by night.

★LA BARRA DE CARLES ABELLÁN   SEAFOOD €€€

Map p302 (📞93 295 26 36; www.carlesabellan. com; Plaça de la Rosa dels Vents 1, W Barcelona; tapas €5-25, mains €18-36; ☺7-11am & 7-11.30pm Mon-Thu, 7-11am, 1.30-4pm & 7-11.30pm Fri & Sat, 7-11.30am & 1.30-4pm Sun; 🚌V15, V19, 🚇Barceloneta) Star Catalan chef Carles Abellán's stunning glass-encased, glossy-tiled restaurant (designed by favourite local interiorist Lázaro Rosa-Violán) celebrates seafood. Stellar tapas might include pickled octopus and *papas aliñás* (potato salad) with mackerel. Even more show-stopping are the mains: grilled razor clams with *ponzu* citrus sauce, squid filled with spicy poached egg yolk, and hake *kokotxas* (jowls) in a *pil pil* (garlic, chilli and oil) sauce.

★CAN SOLÉ   SEAFOOD €€€

Map p302 (📞93 221 50 12; www.restaurant cansole.com; Carrer de Sant Carles 4; mains €15-40; ☺1-4pm & 8-11pm Tue-Thu, 1-4pm & 8.30-11pm Fri & Sat, 1-4pm Sun; 🚇Barceloneta) Behind imposing wooden doors, this elegantly old-school restaurant with white-clothed tables, white-jacketed waiters and photos of celebrity customers has been serving terrific seafood since 1903. Freshly landed catch stars in traditional dishes such as *arròs caldòs* (rice broth with squid and langoustines) and 'grandmother'-style dishes like *zarzuela* (casserole with ground almonds, saffron, garlic, tomatoes, mussels, fish and white wine).

★OAXACA   MEXICAN €€€

Map p302 (📞93 319 00 64; www.oaxaca cuinamexicana.com; Pla de Palau 19; mains €14-28; ☺restaurant 1-4pm & 8pm-midnight, bar 1pm-midnight; 🖉; 🚇Barceloneta) 🍴 Menorcan chef Joan Bagur trained in Mexico for a decade under traditional cooks and has his own garden of Mexican plants, which supplies ingredients for outstanding culinary creations like chargrilled octopus and *cochinita pibil* (slow-roasted pork tacos). Hefty tables are made from Mexican hardwoods, original Mexican art lines the walls and there's alfresco seating under the arches.

RESTAURANT 7 PORTES   SEAFOOD €€€

Map p302 (📞93 319 30 33; https://7portes.com; Passeig d'Isabel II 14; mains €18-32; ☺1pm-1am; 📶; 🚇Barceloneta) Founded in 1836 as a cafe, then converted into a restaurant in 1929, 7 Portes has a grand setting beneath arches, and exudes an old-world atmosphere with its tiles, mirrors, beams and plaques naming luminaries – such as Orson Welles – who have passed through. Paella is the speciality (including one-person options), or try the *gran plat de marisc* ('big seafood plate').

1881   MEDITERRANEAN €€€

Map p302 (📞93 221 00 50; www.gruposagardi. com; Plaça de Pau Vila 3; mains €18-35; ☺10am-midnight; 🖉; 🚇Barceloneta) On the top floor of the Museu d'Història de Catalunya (p122), 1881 and its buzzing cocktail bar (open until 1am or 2am) have dazzling views over the waterfront. *Txuletón* (aged Basque beef) is a speciality, along with seafood fresh from the local docks, and Catalan and Basque wines. Swing by for sunset cocktails; the terrace transitions into a party space later on weekend nights.

CAN ROS   SEAFOOD €€€

Map p302 (📞93 221 45 79; www.canros.cat; Carrer del Almirall Aixada 7; mains €15-27; ☺1-4pm & 7-11pm Tue-Sun; 🚇Barceloneta) The fifth generation now leads this immutable seafood favourite, which first opened in 1908. In a restaurant where the decor is a reminder of simpler times, there's a straightforward guiding principle: juicy fresh fish cooked with a light touch, along with rich seafood rice dishes and *fideuà* (a paella-like fish and seafood noodle dish) with cuttlefish. Catalan wines, including organic options, accompany them.

BLUE SPOT   MEDITERRANEAN €€€

Map p302 (📞93 144 78 66; www.encompania delobos.com; Passeig Joan de Borbó 101, Edifici Ocean; mains €16-30; ☺1-4pm & 8-11pm; 🖉; 🚌V15, V19, 🚇Barceloneta) A subtle lobby unveils this exquisitely styled 8th-floor restaurant and cocktail bar, with leafy, fairy-lit indoor-outdoor design by renowned Brazilian architect Isay Weinfeld and unbeatable 360-degree views across Barcelona's seafront. Though really you're here for the setting, the creatively prepared, seasonal Mediterranean menu is good too: original pastas, seafood *arrossos* (rice dishes), locally sourced meats and fish straight from the open grill.

PEZ VELA
SEAFOOD €€€

Map p302 (☑93 221 63 17; https://grupotragaluz.com; Passeig del Mare Nostrum 19/21; mains €15-26; ◎12.30-11.30pm Sun-Thu, to midnight Fri & Sat; ☐V15, V19, Ⓜ Barceloneta) Basking in sparkling sea views, at the foot of the impossible-to-miss W Barcelona (p237), this beachy-glam *xiringuito* from the hugely popular Grupo Tragaluz couldn't feel more Barcelona. The menu revolves around freshly simmered *arrossos* (rice dishes) for sharing, from grilled-vegetable rice to squid-ink paella with artichokes, or try the wild fish of the day or one of the garden-fresh salads.

LA GAVINA
SEAFOOD €€€

Map p302 (☑93 221 05 95; www.lagavina.es; Plaça Pau Vila 1; mains €18-44; ◎noon-11.30pm; Ⓜ Barceloneta) The pick of the promenade-facing restaurants in the 19th-century edifice Palau de Mar (p122) is this swish white-tableclothed seafood specialist. It has been around (in different shapes) since 1930 and the interior is dominated by neon-lit glass-fronted wine cabinets containing over 300 Spanish and Catalan varieties. Swordfish in garlic and white wine, squid-ink paella, and seafood platters on shaved ice are highlights.

CAN MAJÓ
SEAFOOD €€€

Map p302 (☑93 221 54 55; www.canmajo.es; Carrer del Almirall Aixada 23; mains €15-36; ◎1-4pm & 8-11pm Tue-Sat, 1-4pm Sun; Ⓜ Barceloneta) On a square across from the beachfront promenade, with outdoor tables, smart white tablecloths and heat lamps in winter, 40-year-old Can Majó has a long and steady reputation for fine seafood, particularly its rice dishes (from shellfish paella to meaty mountain-style *arròs*) and bountiful *suquets* (fish stews). The bouillabaisse of fish and seafood is succulent.

BARRACA
SEAFOOD €€€

Map p302 (☑93 224 12 53; www.tribuwoki.com; Passeig Marítim de la Barceloneta 1; mains €19-28; ◎1-11.30pm; Ⓜ Barceloneta) 🌿 Opening to an elevated terrace, this buzzing space has mesmerising views over the Mediterranean – a key reference point in the all-organic dishes concocted here. Start off with a cauldron of chilli-infused clams, cockles and mussels or a platter of *Padrón*

peppers before moving on to the lavish rice dishes. Service is hit and miss.

✖ Port Olímpic, El Poblenou & El Fòrum

★ LITTLE FERN CAFÉ
CAFE €

Map p304 (☑93 808 93 17; www.littleferncafe.com; Carrer de Pere IV; dishes €6-10; ◎9am-5pm Mon, Thu & Fri, from 10am Sat & Sun; 🛜; Ⓜ Poblenou, Glòries) Worth a trip out to El Poblenou in itself, this beautiful Kiwi-Hungarian-owned cafe epitomises the area's newfound allure. White-brick walls, floor-to-ceiling windows and plants in terracotta pots form the backdrop to firmly original all-day-brunch bites fired by organic ingredients, such as fluffy corn fritters with smashed avocado and beetroot relish. There are also sunny mimosas, raft beers, and coffee by London-based Ozone.

MÉS DE VI
TAPAS €

Map p304 (☑93 007 91 51; www.mesdvi.cat; Carrer de Marià Aguiló 123; tapas €4-13; ◎7-11pm Mon, 1-4pm & 7-11pm Tue-Sat; Ⓜ Poblenou) At this buzzing wine bar, Catalan drops are accompanied by tapas dishes both inventive and delicious: courgette-pesto and burrata salad, pickled tuna belly with Peruvian yellow chilli, smoked mackerel with aubergine caviar, and lentil hummus mopped up with spelt crackers. Brick walls, timber tables and studded Chesterfield sofas give it a cosy ambience.

EL 58
TAPAS €

Map p304 (Le cinquante huit; ☑93 601 39 03; www.facebook.com/el58poblenou; Rambla del Poblenou 58; tapas €4-12; ◎1.30-11pm Tue-Sat, to 4pm Sun; Ⓜ Poblenou) This French-Catalan fave serves imaginative, beautifully prepared seasonal tapas: braised tuna with *romesco* sauce and asparagus, fried aubergines with honey and rosemary, sausage-and-chickpea stew, and local cheeses. Solo diners can take a seat at the marble-topped front bar. The back dining room with its exposed-brick walls, industrial light fixtures and original artworks is a lively place to linger over a long meal.

TIMESBURG POBLENOU
BURGERS €

Map p304 (☑93 328 51 88; www.timesburg.com; Carrer de Pujades 168; burgers €6-13; ◎1-4.30pm & 8.30-11pm, to midnight Fri & Sat; 🛜; Ⓜ Poblenou) Barcelona success story

Timesburg has a raft of locations, including this cavernous mezzanine in El Poblenou. Burger buns are stamped with its logo, and the 20 or so varieties include La Massimo (beef, Parmesan, sun-dried tomato, sunflower seeds, red onion) and La Maó (Mallorca sausage, Mahón cheese, honey mayo). Hand-cut fries are twice-fried in olive oil; sauces are homemade.

CAN DENDÊ   BREAKFAST €

Map p304 (☑646 325551; www.candende.com; Carrer de la Ciutat de Granada 44; dishes €5-13; ☺9am-4.30pm Mon, Thu & Fri, from 10am Sat & Sun; ⓂLlacuna) An eclectic crowd gathers at bohemian Brazilian-run Can Dendê in El Poblenou. All-day brunch is the culinary star here: you can tuck into eggs Benedict with smoked salmon, fluffy savoury pancakes or pulled-pork sandwiches, accompanied by a Bloody Mary or homemade pink lemonade by the jug, while watching the cooks in action and listening to Latin Tropicalia and American grooves.

SOPA BORONAT   VEGETARIAN, VEGAN €

Map p304 (☑93 309 56 76; http://sopa.vg; Carrer de Roc Boronat 114; 2-course menú del dia €10.50; ☺8am-7pm Mon-Fri, 10am-5pm Sat & Sun; ☑; ⓂGlòries, Llacuna) ✐ With branches in Madrid and Ubud (Bali), this bright and cheery contemporary cafe adorned with marine-life murals and big sharing tables does delicate meat-free menus fuelled by seasonal ingredients sourced from small local producers. There's a two-course weekday set lunch, along with organic coffee, lovely cakes (such as lemon-and-poppyseed or vegan carrot) and even yoga classes.

VAN VAN VAR   STREET FOOD €

Map p304 (☑93 024 00 83; www.vanvan market.com; Carrer de Pujades 27; mains €7-10; ☺9.30am-11pm Mon-Fri, noon-11.45pm Sat; ⓂBogatell) The vibing, shoebox-sized permanent outpost of hit street-food market **Van Van** (www.vanvanmarket.com) rustles up regularly changing themed menus devised by Barcelona's favourite food-truck chefs – locally sourced fried chicken or steaming ramen one week, creative vegan bowls or home-cooked falafel the next. There are also classic tinned tapas.

★MINYAM   SEAFOOD €€

Map p304 (☑93 348 36 18; www.facebook.com/minyamcisco; Carrer de Pujades 187; tapas €2-

10, mains €15-25; ☺1-11pm Tue-Thu, to 11.30pm Fri & Sat, to 5pm Sun; ⓂPoblenou) Billowing with smoke beneath a tajine-like metal lid, smouldering herbs infuse the rice of Minyam's signature Vulcanus (smoked seafood paella with squid ink). Tapas dishes at this stylish, contemporary El Poblenou restaurant are equally inventive and include asparagus fritters, oysters with sea urchin and lemon, prawn omelettes and fondue with truffle oil. There's a popular €12.50 *menú del dia*.

★CAN RECASENS   CATALAN €€

Map p304 (☑93 300 81 23; www.canrecasens. restaurant; Rambla del Poblenou 102; mains €8-21; ☺restaurant 8pm-1am, delicatessen 8.15am-1.30pm & 5pm-1am Mon-Fri, 8.15am-1.30pm Sat; ⓂPoblenou) One of El Poblenou's most romantic settings, century-old Can Recasens conceals a warren of warmly lit rooms full of oil paintings, flickering candles, fairy lights and fruit baskets. The food is outstanding, with a mix of salads, smoked meats, fondues, and open sandwiches topped with delicacies like wild mushrooms and Brie, *escalivada* (grilled vegetables) and Gruyère, or *sobrasada* (spicy cured sausage) with rosemary honey.

CAN FISHER   SEAFOOD €€

Map p304 (☑93 597 18 40; www.canfisher.com; Avinguda Litoral 64; mains €13-23; ☺12.30pm-1am; Ⓜ Vila Olímpica, Llacuna; 🐾☑) ✐ In a wonderfully scenic spot, on the seafront promenade overlooking Platja del Bogatell, Can Fisher is locally loved for its divine rice and seafood dishes, served in a beach-chic setting and prepared using fresh, organic, locally sourced ingredients. Paellas here are kept thin, letting the rice shine in the style of classic Costa Brava cooking - try the veggie-friendly grilled-mushroom paella, the black rice with cuttlefish or the wood-fired rice with scarlet shrimp.

RED FISH   SEAFOOD €€

Map p304 (☑93 171 68 94; www.redfishbcn. com; Moll de la Marina; tapas €2-12, mains €15-30; ⓂCiutadella Vila Olímpica) Bamboo chairs, swaying straw lamps, niftily repurposed paddle-boat tables – this chic beachy seafooder sits on its own tucked-away patch of blonde sand at the northwest end of Platja de la Barceloneta. Utterly fabulous Barcelona panoramas unfold as you tuck into superb, fresh rice dishes (like creamy lobster rice), clams in sherry or grilled turbot, or kick back over mojitos, vermouth and sharing platters.

LEKA

INTERNATIONAL €€

Map p304 (☑93 300 27 19; https://restaurante leka.com; Carrer de Badajoz 65; mains €7-16; ☺1pm-late Thu-Sat, to 5pm Sun-Wed; ☑; ⓂLlacuna) ☞ Cooking up vegetables from its own garden, organic meats sourced from responsible Pyrenees producers and seafood fresh from Barceloneta's markets or the Delta de l'Ebre, Leka gets crammed for its generous weekday lunch *menú* (€12). Creative vegetarian-friendly delights might include sweet-potato noodles with tofu, portobello burgers or creamy mushroom pasta, while other options swing from grilled entrecôte to herb-infused mussels.

AGUARIBAY

VEGETARIAN €€

Map p304 (☑93 300 37 90; www.aguaribay-bcn. com; Carrer del Taulat 95; mains €12-15; ☺10am-noon & 1-4pm Sun-Thu, 10am-noon, 1-4pm & 8-11.30pm Fri & Sat May-Oct, closed evenings Nov-Apr; ☑; ⓂLlacuna) ☞ Polished Aguaribay serves a small, well-executed à la carte menu by night: stir-fried rice noodles with crispy tofu and peanut sauce, green lasagne with goat's cheese, and seasonal vegetables with rich black rice, along with craft beers, biodynamic wines and fresh juices. Stop in for the daily lunch specials. All ingredients are organic; vegan and gluten-free options abound.

LA PICANTERÍA DE L'ESCRIBÀ

SOUTH AMERICAN €€

Map p304 (☑93 461 43 15; https://restaurants escriba.com; Carrer de Marià Aguiló 59; dishes €6-16; ☺12.30pm-1am Mon-Fri, from 1pm Sat & Sun; ⓂPoblenou) An elegant and imaginative marriage of Peruvian, Mexican, Brazilian and Japanese flavours awaits at this jazzy little number from Barcelona's famed Escribà (p80) clan. You might start with prawn gyoza or spicy nachos, before moving on to tuna tataki tacos, squid bao or sea bass ceviche. There are also some fabulous signature cocktails from the flower-adorned bar.

★XIRINGUITO ESCRIBÀ

SEAFOOD €€€

Map p304 (☑93 221 07 29; www.xiringuito escriba.com; Avinguda del Litoral 62; mains €18-26; ☺noon-10.30pm; ☑; ☐H16, V25, V27, ⓂLlacuna) The team behind Escribà (p198), which has been creating sweets since 1906,

is also in charge of one of Barcelona's most popular waterfront seafood restaurants. A whirl of busy waiters and bubbling paellas, this is one of few places in town that does one-person paella or Catalan *fideuà*, as well as delicious vegetarian-friendly mushroom paella. Finish off with Escribà pastries. Reservations recommended.

ELS PESCADORS

SEAFOOD €€€

Map p304 (☑93 225 20 18; www.elspescadors. com; Plaça de Prim 1; mains €15-40; ☺1-3.30pm & 7.45-11.30pm; ☎; ⓂPoblenou) On a picturesque square lined with low houses and long-established South American *bella ombre* trees, this quaint family restaurant continues to serve some of the city's best grilled fish and seafood-and-rice dishes. There are three dining areas inside: two are quite modern, while the main room preserves its old tavern flavour. On warm nights, try for a table outside.

☕ DRINKING & NIGHTLIFE

The northeastern end of the beach on the Barceloneta waterfront near the Port Olímpic takes on a balmy, almost Caribbean air in the warmer months (though many of the busy bar-clubs here were due to close down in 2020 – see p133). Further northeast, seasonal seaside beach bars draw a laid-back crowd in summer. Head inland for El Poblenou's cocktail lounges, brewpubs, and terrace bars along Rambla del Poblenou.

☕ Port Vell & Barceloneta

★PERIKETE

WINE BAR

Map p302 (☑93 024 22 29; www.gruporeini.com; Carrer de Llauder 6; ☺noon-1am; ⓂBarceloneta) Since opening in 2017, this fabulous wine spot has been jam-packed with *barcelonins* and visitors. Jabugo hams hang from the ceiling, vermouth barrels sit above the bar and wine bottles cram every available shelf space. There are over 200 varieties by the glass or bottle, accompanied by excellent tapas (€4 to €10) like made-to-order tortilla.

BODEGA VIDRIOS Y CRISTALES

WINE BAR

Map p302 (☑93 250 45 01; www.gruposagardi. com; Passeig d'Isabel II 6; ☺noon-midnight;

Barceloneta) In a history-steeped, stone-floored 1840 building, this atmospheric little jewel recreates an old-style neighbourhood bodega with tins of sardines, anchovies and other delicacies lining the shelves (and used in exquisite tapas, €3 to €15), house-made vermouth and a wonderful array of wines, including Andalucian *manzanilla* (sherry from Sanlúcar de Barrameda). A handful of upturned wine barrels let you rest your glass.

CAN PAIXANO
WINE BAR

Map p302 (La Xampanyeria; ☑93 310 08 39; www.canpaixano.com; Carrer de la Reina Cristina 7; ⊙9am-10.30pm Mon-Sat; Barceloneta) This lofty double-name *cava* bar has long been run on a winning formula: its own super-affordable bubbly rosé, served in elegant little glasses and combined with bite-sized *entrepans* and tapas (€2 to €4). It's usually packed, so elbowing your way to the bar can be a titanic struggle. There's another branch at El Poblenou's Mercat dels Encants (p135).

BLACKLAB
MICROBREWERY

Map p302 (☑93 221 83 60; www.blacklab.es; Plaça de Pau Vila 1; ⊙10.30am-2am daily Mar-Oct, 4-11pm Mon-Thu, 11.30am-1am Fri-Sun Nov-Feb; Barceloneta) Barcelona's first brewhouse opened in 2014 inside the 19th-century Palau de Mar (p122). Its taps feature 16 house-made brews, including saisons, double IPAs and dry stouts, and brewmaster Matt Boder is constantly experimenting. The kitchen sizzles up Asian-American bites (€4 to €10): burgers, dumplings, ramen. One-hour tours (€20; English/Spanish 5pm/6pm Sunday) take you behind the scenes, with a four-beer tasting.

ABSENTA
BAR

Map p302 (☑93 221 36 38; Carrer de Sant Carles 36; ⊙5pm-1am Mon & Wed, to 2am Thu, to 3am Fri, 1pm-3am Sat, to 1am Sun; Barceloneta) Decorated with old paintings, vintage lamps, check-tiled floors, stained-glass windows and curious sculptures, this whimsical drinking den specialises in absinthe, with 30 varieties available. (Go easy, though: the 50% to 90% alcohol content provides a kick!) It also has house-made vermouth and craft beers, if you'd prefer to sidestep the green fairy. There's been a bar here since the 1890s.

LA VIOLETA
WINE BAR

Map p302 (☑93 221 95 81; www.facebook.com/lavioletavinosnaturales; Carrer del Baluard 58; ⊙1-11pm; Barceloneta) A regularly changing line-up of natural wines (glasses €3.50 to €5.50), both Spanish and international, wanders into the spotlight at this cosy bar with terrace tables and mismatched wooden furniture. There are plenty of exciting Catalan picks (try the Conca de Barberà *albariño* blend), as well as lovingly made slow-food tapas (€6 to €10) starring market-fresh fish and home-grown vegetables.

LA DELICIOSA
BAR

Map p302 (☑93 309 12 91; www.panteabeach.com; Platja de Sant Miquel; ⊙9am-midnight Mar-Nov; ☎; Barceloneta) Bamboo fish and pots of herbs dangle from the ceiling at this barefoot-chic beach bar on Platja de la Barceloneta – a stylish setting for fresh juices, regional wines, G&Ts and imaginative cocktails (€11) amid upcycled decor. Soak it all up with sandwiches, burgers, black-bean nachos and tapas (dishes €3 to €12).

THE MINT
COCKTAIL BAR

Map p302 (Passeig d'Isabel II 4; ⊙7.30pm-2.30am Sun-Thu, to 3am Fri & Sat; Barceloneta) Named after the prized cocktail ingredient, this mojito-loving spot has an upstairs bar where you can peruse the first-rate house-infused gins (over 20 on hand, including creative blends like lemon grass and Jamaican pepper). Downstairs in the brick-vaulted cellars, red lights and driving beats create more of a night-out vibe.

BAR LEO
BAR

Map p302 (Carrer de Sant Carles 34; ⊙noon-9.30pm; Barceloneta) An almost entirely *barcelonin* crowd spills out into the street from Bar Leo, a hole-in-the-wall drinking spot plastered with images of late Andalucian singer Bambino, and with a jukebox mostly dedicated to flamenco. It's at its liveliest on weekends.

Port Olímpic, El Poblenou & El Fòrum

ESPAI JOLIU
CAFE

Map p304 (☑93 023 24 92; www.facebook.com/espaijoliu; Carrer Badajoz 95; ⊙9am-7pm Mon-Fri, 10am-3pm Sat; ☎; Llacuna) Inspired by its owner's time in Berlin, this charmingly stylish former carpenters' workshop is Barcelona's original plants-and-coffee concept cafe (much copied since). Potted plants, design mags and ceramics are sold up the front, while the peaceful cafe has recycled timber furniture, stone walls and exposed bulbs, and serves Barcelona-roasted Nømad coffee (€2 to €3) and organic cakes (try the gluten-free lemon-and-rosemary).

BALIUS COCKTAIL BAR

Map p304 (☑93 315 86 50; www.baliusbar. com; Carrer de Pujades 196; ⊙5.30pm-1.30am Mon-Wed, to 2.30am Thu, 5pm-3am Fri & Sat, 5pm-1.30am Sun; Ⓜ Poblenou) There's an old-fashioned jauntiness to this vintage-style cocktail den in El Poblenou, marked by its original-period exterior with tiles and gin bottles in the window. Staff pour classic cocktails (€8 to €10) as well as vermouths, and there's a small tapas menu (€3 to €7) of nachos, cheeses, *patates braves* and so on. Stop by on Sunday for live jazz around 8pm.

NØMAD ROASTER'S HOME COFFEE

Map p304 (www.nomadcoffee.es; Carrer de Pujades 95; ⊙9am-5pm Mon-Fri; Ⓜ Bogatell) Top barista Jordi Mestre's seasonal, fair-trade coffee beans (which you'll spot all over Barcelona) are roasted on-site at this uncluttered, beamed cafe-shop-and-workshop, which puts everyone's favourite caffeinated brew centre stage. From expertly served cold brews to perfect flat whites, coffee (€2.50 to €5) is serious (and experimental) business here.

MADAME GEORGE COCKTAIL BAR

Map p304 (www.madamegeorgebar.com; Carrer de Pujades 179; ⊙6pm-2am Mon-Thu, to 3am Fri & Sat, to 12.30am Sun; Ⓜ Poblenou) A theatrical elegance marks the interior of this small, chandelier-lit lounge just off the Rambla del Poblenou. Deft bartenders stir well balanced cocktails like the Lychee-tini (€9; vanilla-infused vodka, fresh lychees, homemade lychee liqueur and lime juice) in vintage glassware, while a DJ spins vinyl (mainly soul and funk) in the corner.

SKYE COFFEE COFFEE

Map p304 (☑699 542148; www.skye-coffee.com; Carrer de Pamplona 88; ⊙9am-1.30pm Mon-Wed, to 5pm Thu & Fri; ☎; Ⓜ Bogatell) Hang out at communal tables over single-origin flat whites and *cortados* (espressos with a drib-

ble of milk) inside the cavernous Espacio 88 (p127), an innovative space that's emblematic of the ongoing growth of this once-industrial neighbourhood. Beans are from Castelldefels roastery Right-Side; baristas brew them up inside a silver 1972 Citroën HY parked in the corner (coffees €2 to €4).

LA CERVECITA NUESTRA DE CADA DÍA CRAFT BEER

Map p304 (☑93 486 92 71; www.facebook. com/lacervecitanuestradecadadia; Carrer de Llull 184; ⊙11.30-2pm & 5.30-10.30pm Wed-Sat, 5.30-10.30pm Sun-Tue; Ⓜ Poblenou, Llacuna) Equal parts beer shop and craft-brew bar, minimal-decor La Cervecita has a changing selection of at least 15 unique beers on tap from around Europe and the US. You might stumble across a Catalan sour fruit beer, a rare English stout, a potent Belgian triple ale or half a dozen other draughts – plus many more varieties by the bottle.

ORVAL CAFE

Map p304 (www.facebook.com/orval.barcelona; Carrer de Buenaventura Muñoz 31; ⊙9am-7pm Mon-Fri, to 5pm Sat & Sun; ☎; Ⓜ Marina) Zingy homemade lemonade, Barcelona-roasted beans by Nømad (p133) (coffees €1.50 to €4), and divine cakes and pastries sourced from renowned bakeries around town pull coffee lovers to this off-radar corner just north of the Parc de la Ciutadella. Launched

---

PORT OLÍMPIC CLUB CLOSURES

The Port Olímpic has long been a popular nightlife hub, but the heaving clubs strung along it have become a growing source of conflict in recent years, with reports of robberies (often targeting tourists), disruptive drunken behaviour, some serious fights and even several deaths. The city is expected to close down most clubs (including legendary spots like Pacha, Opium, CDLC, Catwalk and Shôko), and turn the area's focus towards the sea, sailing and other outdoor activities, rather than after-dark antics, by creating more parks and pathways while also reducing traffic. At the time of writing, these changes had not yet come into effect.

mid-2019, with open-brick walls and potted plants tumbling out the door, Orval is the second outpost of El Poblenou's much-loved Espai Joliu (p133).

VAI MOANA
BAR

Map p304 (☎93 309 12 91; www.panteabeach.com; Avinguda del Litoral, Platja del Bogatell; ☺9am-late Mar-Nov; ☐H16, V25, V27, ⓂLlacuna) Candlelit tables, loungey beats and colourful cocktails bring a beachy Polynesian vibe to this easy-breezy *xiringuito* on Bogatell's lively, silky sands. Grab a glass of *cava* or Priorat wine, or a coconut-and-chilli mojito (€11), and watch the horizon morph into pink as the sun sets. It also does fresh juices, burgers, sandwiches and tapas (€4 to €12).

SYRA COFFEE
COFFEE

Map p304 (http://syra.coffee; Carrer de Pujades 100; ☺9am-6pm Mon-Fri; ⓂBogatell) 🍃 Local professionals and students pop into this sprawling minimalist-design space, with shared standing tables and a circular counter, for matcha lattes, or flat whites and cold brews made with Syra's signature seasonal, single-origin, sustainably sourced beans (coffees €2 to €3). Beans are roasted at owner Yassir Raïs' shop/roastery in Gràcia, where the original branch (p182) is.

EL TÍO CHÉ
CAFE

Map p304 (☎93 309 18 72; www.eltioche.es; Rambla del Poblenou 44; ☺10am-10pm Sun-Thu, to 1am Fri & Sat Apr-Oct, reduced hours Nov-Mar; ⓂPoblenou) First opened back in 1912 (in El Born), this local icon is famed for its *orxata* (*horchata* in Spanish), a sweet and refreshing, mildly grainy drink made of tigernut milk. Some love it, others less so, though you can also opt for other homemade beverages, along with sandwiches and ice cream.

⭐ ENTERTAINMENT

RAZZMATAZZ
LIVE MUSIC

Map p304 (☎93 320 82 00; www.salarazzmatazz.com; Carrer de Pamplona 88; tickets from €10; ☺hours vary; ⓂBogatell) Bands from far and wide occasionally create scenes of near-hysteria at Razzmatazz, one of the city's classic live-music and clubbing venues. Bands appear throughout the week (check online), while on weekends live music gives way to club sounds. Five different rooms, with offerings varying from night to night, in one huge postindustrial space attract people of all dance persuasions and ages.

The main space, RazzClub, is a haven for the latest international rock and indie acts. The Loft does techno, house and electro, while the Pop Bar offers anything from R&B to '80s hits. Lolita is the land of house, disco and electro, and upstairs in the Rex Room sounds range from hip-hop to dancehall.

L'AUDITORI
CLASSICAL MUSIC

Map p304 (☎93 247 93 00; www.auditori.cat; Carrer de Lepant 150; tickets vary; ☺box office 5-9pm Tue-Fri, 10.30am-1pm & 5-9pm Sat; ⓂMarina) Barcelona's modern home for the Orquestra Simfònica de Barcelona i Nacional de Catalunya, L'Auditori stages performances of orchestral, chamber, religious and other music. Designed by Rafael Moneo and opened in 1999, the main auditorium can accommodate more than 2000 concertgoers. The Museu de la Música (p126) is in the same building.

TEATRE NACIONAL DE CATALUNYA
PERFORMING ARTS

Map p304 (☎93 306 57 00; www.tnc.cat; Plaça de les Arts 1; tickets €10-29; ☺box office 4-7pm Wed, 5-8pm Thu & Fri, 3-8pm Sat, 3-6pm Sun; ⓂGlòries) The National Theatre of Catalonia hosts a wide range of performances, including dramas, comedies, musicals and dance in this ultra-neoclassical theatre designed by Barcelona architect Ricardo Bofill, which opened in 1996. Performances are in Catalan.

SALA BECKETT
THEATRE

Map p304 (☎93 284 53 12; www.salabeckett.cat; Carrer de Pere IV 228; tickets from €10; ☺box office 2hr before shows; ⓂPoblenou) One of the city's principal alternative theatres, the Sala Beckett doesn't shy away from challenging theatre, and stages an eclectic mix of productions in this lovely space in a 1920s building (also with a popular restaurant/vermouth bar, El Menjador de la Beckett). Performances are primarily in Catalan.

SHOPPING

PALO MARKET FEST
MARKET

Map p304 (☎93 159 66 70; https://palomarketfest.com; Carrer dels Pellaires 30; adult/child €4.50/free; ☺11am-9pm 1st Sun of month;

Ⓜ️Selva de Mar) One of the city's most loved events, festival-vibe Palo Market takes over an old Poblenou warehouse wreathed in flowers and greenery once a month. Local creatives – from up-and-coming fashion and jewellery designers to organic-cosmetics sellers and vintage experts – set up stalls alongside sizzling street-food trucks and lively vermouth bars, and there are also arty workshops.

MERCAT DELS ENCANTS MARKET

Map p304 (Fira de Bellcaire; 📞93 245 22 99; www.facebook.com/EncantsBarcelona; Plaça de les Glòries Catalanes; ☺9am-8pm Mon, Wed & Sat, 10am-5pm Fri & Sun; Ⓜ️Glòries) In a gleaming open-sided complex near Plaça de les Glòries Catalanes, the 'Market of Charms' is Barcelona's biggest flea market, and one of Europe's oldest, with its roots in medieval times. More than 500 vendors ply their wares beneath massive mirror-like panels. It's all here, from antique furniture to secondhand clothes. There's a lot of junk, plus the odd *ganga* (bargain).

Catch some behind-the-scenes action from 7.45am to 9.30am Monday, Wednesday and Friday, when the *subhastes* (auctions) take place.

NOAK ROOM ANTIQUES

Map p304 (📞93 309 53 00; www.noakroom.com; Carrer de Roc Boronat 69; ☺10.30am-2pm & 5-8.30pm Tue-Sat; Ⓜ️Llacuna) Lined with bold original works by Barcelona artists, this graceful showroom specialises in Scandinavian vintage furniture from the 1940s to 1970s, which has included pieces by Arne Jacobsen and Bruno Mathsson – all maintained in their original beauty. Owners Sara and Martin live between Barcelona and Sweden, so new pieces arrive all the time.

VERNITA CHILDREN'S CLOTHING

Map p304 (📞625 092341; www.facebook.com/vernitastudioshop; Carrer del Joncar 27; ☺10am-1.30pm & 6-8pm Tue-Sat; Ⓜ️Poblenou) Three mothers, Neli, Laura and Nacha, design and handmake children's clothing and accessories at this light, bright studio-boutique. Finds include animal-print cushions, backpacks, reusable napkins and snack boxes, as well as soft cuddly toys. They also offer sewing lessons for both adults and kids (English available).

WATERFRONT MARKETS

On weekends the Port Vell springs to life with markets selling a mix of antiques and contemporary art and crafts along the waterfront.

Mercat de Colom (Mercat de Brocanteria; Map p302; www.facebook.com/MercatdeColomBCN; Plaça del Portal de la Pau; ☺10am-8pm Fri-Sun Mar-Oct, 10am-8pm Sat & Sun Nov-Feb; Ⓜ️Drassanes) At the southern end of La Rambla; great for antiques and bric-a-brac.

Mercat de Pintors (Map p302; Passeig d'Ítaca; ☺10am-8pm Sat & Sun; Ⓜ️Drassanes) Art fair with paintings both collectable and forgettable, along the pedestrianised Rambla de Mar.

NOLLEGIU BOOKS

Map p304 (📞93 667 75 21; www.nollegiu.cat; Carrer Pons i Subirà; ☺10am-2pm & 5-8pm Mon-Sat, 10am-2pm Sun; Ⓜ️Poblenou) Within the turquoise-tiled former home of an old 20th-century neighbourhood shop, this inviting book specialist stocks Catalan and Spanish titles, along with translations of English-language works. Readings, performances and other events often happen.

ULTRA-LOCAL RECORDS MUSIC

Map p304 (📞661 017638; Carrer de Pujades 113; ☺4-8.30pm Mon-Fri; Ⓜ️Llacuna) Along an increasingly cool stretch of El Poblenou, this small, well-curated shop sells mostly used records from local and international artists, plus some re-releases and albums by current indie rock darlings. Vinyl aside, you'll find a smaller CD selection, zines and a few other curiosities.

MERCAT DE LA BARCELONETA MARKET

Map p302 (Plaça del Poeta Boscà 1-2; ☺7am-2pm Mon-Thu, to 8pm Fri, to 3pm Sat; Ⓜ️Barceloneta) Set in a modern glass-and-steel building fronting a long plaza in the heart of Barceloneta, this airy market has seasonal produce and seafood stalls, as well as several places where you can enjoy a sit-down meal, including popular El Guindilla (p128).

MERCAT DEL POBLENOU MARKET

Map p304 (http://mercatpoblenou.com; Plaça de la Unió; ☺8.30am-2pm Mon, 8.30am-2pm & 5-8.30pm Tue-Thu, 8.30am-8.30pm Fri, 8.30am-

3pm Sat; Ⓜ Poblenou) Designed in 1889 by Pere Falqués and originally a livestock market (though now sensitively remodelled), Poblenou's fresh-produce market bursts with Catalan cheeses, meats, fruit and veg, and has a couple of simple cafes and a supermarket.

SYSTEM ACTION
FASHION & ACCESSORIES

Map p304 (Ⓓ93 225 79 90; www.systemaction.es; Carrer de Pere IV 122; ⊙10am-7pm Thu-Sat; Ⓜ Llacuna) Though Barcelona-founded women's label System Action has shops across northeast Spain, its design headquarters are a few blocks south of this outlet store, in a former Poblenou ice factory. You'll find sustainably produced own-design basics at reasonable prices (especially when sales are on), including sweaters, skirts, dresses, scarves and shoes.

MAREMÀGNUM
SHOPPING CENTRE

Map p302 (www.maremagnum.es; Moll d'Espanya 5; ⊙10am-10pm; Ⓜ Drassanes) Created out of largely abandoned docks, this buzzing shopping centre is home to 72 stores including youthful Spanish chain Mango and Barcelona-based Desigual. Football fans will be drawn to the paraphernalia at FC Botiga.

CENTRE COMERCIAL DE LES GLÒRIES
SHOPPING CENTRE

Map p304 (www.glories.com; Avinguda Diagonal 208; ⊙9am-9pm Mon-Sat; Ⓜ Glòries) In the former Olivetti factory, this sprawling complex covers everything from fashion to sports and gifts, with all the usual suspects like Zara and Uniqlo, plus a huge supermarket and cinema. There are also around 40 places to eat, including well-known chains and fast-food restaurants.

SPORTS & ACTIVITIES

MOLOKAI SUP CENTER
WATER SPORTS

Map p302 (Ⓓ93 221 48 68; www.molokaisupcenter.com; Carrer de Meer 39; 2hr private SUP/surf lesson from €40/35, SUP/surfboard rental per hour €15/12; ⊙10am-6pm Tue-Sat, to 3pm Sun; Ⓜ Barceloneta) This respected outfit will give you a crash course in surfing or stand-up paddleboarding (SUP). In addition to two-hour beginner's classes, Molokai can help you improve your tech-

nique (in intermediate and advanced lessons – all in two-hour blocks); gear and wetsuits are included. If you'd rather just hire a board, staff can quickly get you out to sea.

ALBLANC ATELIER
ARTS & CRAFTS

Map p304 (www.alblancatelier.com; Carrer de Badajoz 90; workshop from €65; ⊙4.30-8pm Mon & Fri) Inspired by traditional Costa Brava *masies* (country houses), with soaring ceilings and Catalan vaults, this boho-chic space is the permanent home of favourite local florist Alblanc, whose gorgeously understated arrangements you've probably spotted at stylish stops around town. Three-hour flower-arranging workshops are hosted on Saturdays (in Spanish and/or English, maximum eight people); check upcoming dates online.

PEDAL BIKE RENTAL
CYCLING

Map p304 (Ⓓ93 300 45 06; https://pedalbikerental.cc; Camí Antic de València; 3hr tour per person €26; ⊙10am-7pm; Ⓜ Poblenou) Runs a range of two-wheel tours, including a jaunt around El Poblenou and a more challenging trip up to Park Güell and the Bunkers del Carmel viewpoint; also rents bikes (per day €14).

43 THE SPA
SPA

Map p304 (Ⓓ93 221 10 00; www.hotelartsbarcelona.com; Carrer de la Marina 19-21, Hotel Arts; 1hr treatment from €120; ⊙9am-10pm) Taking over the 43rd floor of the sky-spiralling Hotel Arts Barcelona (p237), this sleek spa offers hot tubs and open-air sun-soaking decks with jaw-droppingly beautiful views of Barcelona, along with steam rooms, saunas and ice fountains. Luxe treatments – like citrus scrubs and personalised facials – use local beauty brand Nature Bissé.

ORSOM
CRUISE

Map p302 (Ⓓ630 619615; www.barcelona-orsom.com; Moll de les Drassanes; tours adult/child from €15.50/13.50; ⊙hours vary; Ⓜ Drassanes) Operating year-round, Orsom's large sailing catamaran makes the 90-minute journey from the Port Vell to the Port Olímpic and back, with up to four departures daily. There's also a jazz cruise in the afternoon or early evening and a Sunday vermouth trip.

BASE NÁUTICA MUNICIPAL
WATER SPORTS

Map p304 (Ⓓ93 221 04 32; www.basenautica.org; Avinguda del Litoral, Platja de la Mar Bella;

2hr lessons from €40, equipment hire per hour from €15; ⊘9am-8pm; Ⓜ Poblenou) Just back from Platja de la Mar Bella, this established centre teaches the basics of kayaking, windsurfing, kitesurfing, catamaran sailing and stand-up paddleboarding. You can also hire equipment here. Prices for lessons are cheaper in groups of two or more. More in-depth multiday courses are also available.

LAS GOLONDRINAS CRUISE

Map p302 (☑93 442 31 06; www.lasgolondrinas.com; Moll de les Drassanes; adult/child port tour €7.70/2.80; Ⓜ Drassanes) Las Golondrinas offers popular cruises from its dock in front of the Mirador de Colom. The 40-minute excursion offers a quick overview of the port, while the 90-minute tour takes you out past Barceloneta and the beaches to El Fòrum and back. Both trips depart regularly throughout the day.

**CLUB NATACIÓ
ATLÈTIC-BARCELONETA** SWIMMING

Map p302 (☑93 221 00 10; www.cnab.cat; Plaça del Mar; day pass adult/child €13/7.40; ⊘6.30am-11pm Mon-Fri, 7am-11pm Sat, 8am-5pm Sun, to 8pm Sun mid-May–Sep; ☐V15, V19, Ⓜ Barceloneta) Operating since 1907, this athletic club has one indoor and two outdoor pools (one of these heated for lap swimming in winter). Admission includes the gym and spa.

BCNAVAL TOURS BOATING

Map p302 (☑93 443 60 50; www.barcelona navaltours.com; Moll de les Drassanes; 40/80min cruise €7.50/15; ⊘10.30am-8.30pm Apr–mid-Oct, to 5.30pm mid-Oct–Mar; Ⓜ Drassanes) From the dock near Mirador de Colom, BCNaval's boats run cruises including 75-minute trips out past La Barceloneta and the beaches and back. If you just want a peek at the area around the port, opt for a 40-minute excursion to the breakwater and back. Both run a few times a day.

BARCELONETA, THE WATERFRONT & EL POBLENOU SPORTS & ACTIVITIES

La Sagrada Família & L'Eixample

L'ESQUERRA DE L'EIXAMPLE | LA DRETA DE L'EIXAMPLE

Neighbourhood Top Five

1 La Sagrada Família (p140) Seeing history being made at Spain's most-visited monument and Gaudí's greatest legacy, begun in 1882 and still under construction to this day.

2 La Pedrera (p147) Wandering through this rippling Gaudí masterpiece and its superbly preserved early-20th-century apartment.

3 Casa Batlló (p146) Marvelling at the swirling, almost-alive facade of this Gaudí-designed home with wave-shaped window frames and balconies.

4 Fundació Antoni Tàpies (p149) Deciphering the fascinating contemporary art of leading 20th-century Catalan artist Antoni Tàpies.

5 Recinte Modernista de Sant Pau (p151) Admiring this lesser-known jewel of Modernisme, a Unesco-listed former hospital designed by Domènech i Montaner.

For more detail of this area see Map p306 and p310 ➡

Explore La Sagrada Família & L'Eixample

In the 1820s rows of trees were planted on either side of the road linking Barcelona and the town of Gràcia. The resulting Passeig de Gràcia is a strollers' boulevard now home to many of the city's most expensive shops, hotels and restaurants, but its show-stopping feature is the parade of Modernista architecture, the best of which – apart from La Sagrada Família – is clustered on or near it, including Antoni Gaudí's La Pedrera (p147) and Casa Batlló (p146). As you wander, be sure to always look up. Eating is at the high end (though set-lunch options and tapas bars are available for lower budgets), and the emphasis is on designer fashion, though there are some notable exceptions. Nightlife in this area tends to be student- and LGBTIQ-oriented, especially around the 'Gaixample'.

La Dreta (the Right) de L'Eixample, stretching from Passeig de Gràcia to increasingly fashionable Passeig de Sant Joan (now with its own line of trendy restaurants and bars), contains much sought-after real estate. Beyond it takes on a dowdier feel, even around La Sagrada Família (p140). L'Esquerra (the Left) de L'Eixample, running southwest from Passeig de Gràcia, changes character several times. The whole area between Carrer d'Aribau, Passeig de Sant Joan, Avinguda Diagonal and the Ronda de Sant Pere has been known since the early 20th century as the Quadrat d'Or (Golden Square) thanks to its extravagant architecture and grand houses; it's now the domain of high-end shops.

Local Life

→ **Student life** Join students from the Universitat de Barcelona (p148) at the string of unpretentious hangouts nearby on Carrer d'Enric Granados.
→ **Passeig de Sant Joan** Head over to this ever-more-popular boulevard for a smattering of contemporary bars and restaurants (p157) beloved by *barcelonins*.
→ **Say it with flowers** Walking around Flores Navarro (p164), a cathedral to colourful plant life, is quite a trip at 4am.

Getting There & Away

→ **Metro** Four metro lines criss-cross L'Eixample, three stopping at Passeig de Gràcia for the Illa de la Discòrdia. Línia 3 stops at Diagonal for La Pedrera, while Línies 2 and 5 stop at La Sagrada Família.
→ **Train** FGC lines from Plaça de Catalunya take you one stop to Provença, in the heart of L'Eixample.

Lonely Planet's Top Tip

Travellers interested in running the gamut of L'Eixample's Modernista gems might consider buying the Ruta del Modernisme pack (€12; www.rutadel modernisme.com). It includes a guide (in various languages) and discounted entry prices to major Modernista sights both in Barcelona and beyond.

Best Places to Eat
→ Lasarte (p155)
→ Disfrutar (p155)
→ Mont Bar (p155)
→ Auto Rosellon (p153)
→ Tapas 24 (p156)
→ Pepa (p153)
→ Cinc Sentits (p155)

For reviews, see p152.

Best Places to Drink
→ Les Gens Que J'Aime (p161)
→ Dry Martini (p158)
→ Milano (p158)
→ Satan's Coffee Corner (p161)
→ Hemingway (p159)

For reviews, see p158.

Best Places to Shop
→ Joan Múrria (p164)
→ Flores Navarro (p164)
→ Altaïr (p162)
→ Avant (p162)
→ Dr Bloom (p163)
→ Cacao Sampaka (p163)

For reviews, see p162.

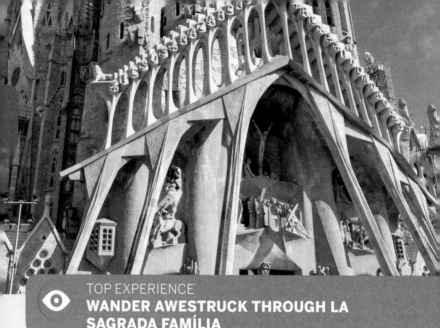

WANDER AWESTRUCK THROUGH LA SAGRADA FAMÍLIA

Antoni Gaudí's unparalleled, Unesco-listed La Sagrada Família inspires awe by its sheer verticality, and, in the manner of the medieval cathedrals it emulates, it's still under construction. Work began in 1882 and is hoped (perhaps optimistically) to be completed in 2026, a century after the architect's death (though the Covid-19 pandemic has inevitably delayed things). Unfinished it may be, but the cathedral attracts more than 4.5 million visitors a year and is Spain's most visited monument.

A Holy Mission

The Temple Expiatori de la Sagrada Família (Expiatory Temple of the Holy Family) was Antoni Gaudí's all-consuming obsession. Given the commission by a conservative society that wished to build a temple as atonement for the city's sins of modernity, Gaudí saw its completion as his holy mission. As funds dried up, he contributed his own, and in the last years of his life he was never shy of pleading with anyone he thought a likely donor. In all, he spent 43 years on La Sagrada Família.

Gaudí devised a temple 95m long and 60m wide, able to seat over 13,000 people, with a central tower 170m high above the transept (representing Christ) and another 17 of 100m or more. With his characteristic dislike for straight lines (there were none in nature, he said), Gaudí gave his towers swelling outlines inspired by the unusual peaks of the holy mountain Montserrat outside Barcelona, and encrusted them with a tangle of sculpture that seems an outgrowth of the stone.

DON'T MISS

➡ The apse, extraordinary pillars and stained glass
➡ Nativity Facade
➡ Passion Facade
➡ Schools of Gaudí & Museu Gaudí
➡ The crypt

PRACTICALITIES

➡ Map p310, E1
➡ ☎93 208 04 14
➡ www.sagradafamilia.org
➡ Carrer de la Marina
➡ adult/child €20/free
➡ ⊙9am-8pm Apr-Sep, to 7pm Mar & Oct, to 6pm Nov-Feb
➡ Ⓜ Sagrada Família

At Gaudí's death, only the crypt, the apse walls, one portal and one tower had been finished. Three more towers were added by 1930, completing the northeast (Nativity) facade. In 1936 anarchists burned and smashed the interior, including workshops and many of Gaudí's original plans and models. Work began again in 1952, but controversy has always clouded progress. Opponents of the continuation of the project claim that the computer models based on what little of Gaudí's plans survived the anarchists' ire have led to the creation of a monster that has little to do with Gaudí's plans and style. Love or hate what is being done, the fascination the building awakens is undeniable.

The Interior & the Apse

Inside, work on roofing over the church was completed in 2010. The roof is held up by a forest of innovative, extraordinary angled pillars. As the pillars soar towards the ceiling, they sprout a web of supporting branches, creating the effect of a forest canopy. Everything was thought through, including the shape and placement of windows to create the mottled effect one would see with sunlight pouring through the branches of a thick forest. The pillars vary in colour and load-bearing strength, from the soft Montjuïc stone pillars along the lateral aisles through to granite, dark-grey basalt and finally burgundy-tinged Iranian porphyry for the key columns at the intersection of the nave and transept. The stained glass, divided in shades of red, blue, green, yellow and ochre, creates a hypnotic, magical atmosphere when the sun hits the windows.

Nativity Facade

The northeastern Nativity Facade (Façana del Naixement) is the artistic pinnacle of the building, mostly created under Gaudí's personal supervision. With prior booking you can climb high up inside some of the four towers by a combination of lifts and narrow spiral staircases – a vertiginous experience. (Climbing the stairs is not recommended if you are pregnant or have cardiac or respiratory problems.) The towers are destined to hold tubular bells capable of playing complex music at great volume. Their upper parts are decorated with mosaics spelling out *'Sanctus, Sanctus, Sanctus, Hosanna in Excelsis, Amen, Alleluia'*. Asked why he lavished so much care on the tops of the spires, which no one would see from close up, Gaudí answered: 'The angels will see them.'

Continued on p144

A HIDDEN PORTRAIT

Careful observation of the Passion Facade will reveal a special tribute from sculptor Josep Maria Subirachs to Gaudí. The central sculptural group (below Christ crucified) shows, from right to left, Christ bearing his cross, Veronica displaying the cloth with Christ's bloody image, a pair of soldiers and, watching it all, a man called the evangelist. Subirachs used a rare photo of Gaudí, taken a couple of years before his death, as the model for the evangelist's face.

LA SAGRADA FAMÍLIA & L'EIXAMPLE LA SAGRADA FAMÍLIA

La Sagrada Família

A TIMELINE

1882 Construction begins on a neo-Gothic church designed by Francisco de Paula del Villar y Lozano.

1883 Antoni Gaudí takes over as chief architect, completes the ❶ **crypt** and plans a far more ambitious church to hold 13,000.

1909 The Escoles de Gaudí are completed.

1926 Gaudí dies; work continues under Domènec Sugrañes i Gras. Much of the ❷ **apse** and ❸ **Nativity Facade** is complete.

1930 ❹ **Bell towers** of the Nativity Facade completed.

1936 Construction interrupted by Spanish Civil War; anarchists destroy Gaudí's plans.

1939–40 Architect Francesc de Paula Quintana i Vidal restores the crypt and meticulously reassembles many of Gaudí's lost models, some of which can be seen in the ❺ **museum**.

1976 ❻ **Passion Facade** steeples completed.

1986–2006 Sculptor Josep Maria Subirachs adds sculptural details to the Passion Facade, amid much criticism for employing a style far removed from what was thought typical of Gaudí.

2000 ❼ **Central nave vault** completed.

2010 Pope Benedict XVI consecrates the church; work begins on a high-speed rail tunnel that will pass beneath the church's ❽ **Glory Facade**.

2016-2019 Work continues on the five central towers; the Passion Facade is completed in 2018.

2026 Projected completion date.

TOP TIPS

➡ The best light through the stained-glass windows of the Passion Facade bursts into the heart of the church in the late afternoon.

➡ Visit at opening time on weekdays to avoid the worst of the crowds.

➡ Head up the Nativity Facade bell towers for the views.

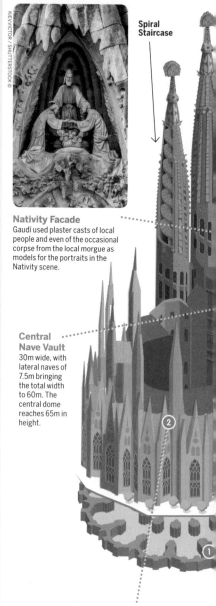

KIEV.VICTOR / SHUTTERSTOCK ©

Spiral Staircase

Nativity Facade
Gaudí used plaster casts of local people and even of the occasional corpse from the local morgue as models for the portraits in the Nativity scene.

Central Nave Vault
30m wide, with lateral naves of 7.5m bringing the total width to 60m. The central dome reaches 65m in height.

Apse
Building started just after the crypt in mostly neo-Gothic style. It is capped by pinnacles that show a hint of the genius that Gaudí would later deploy in the rest of the church.

Bell Towers
The towers of the three facades will represent the Twelve Apostles. Eight are completed. Lifts whisk visitors up one tower of the Nativity and Passion Facades (the latter gets longer queues) for fine views.

NIKADA / GETTY IMAGES ©

Completed Church
Along with the Glory Facade, six other towers remain to be completed. They will represent the four evangelists, the Virgin Mary and, soaring above them all over the transept, a 170m colossus symbolising Christ.

Glory Facade
This will be the most fanciful facade of all, with a narthex boasting 16 hyperboloid lanterns topped by cones that will look something like an organ made of melting ice cream.

Museu Gaudí
Jammed with old photos, drawings and restored plaster models that bring Gaudí's ambitions to life, the museum also houses an extraordinarily complex plumb-line device he used to calculate his constructions.

Escoles de Gaudí

Crypt
The first completed part of the church, the crypt is in largely neo-Gothic style and lies under the transept. Gaudí's burial place here can be glimpsed from the Museu Gaudí.

Passion Facade
See the story of Christ's last days from Last Supper to burial in an S-shaped sequence from bottom to top of the facade. Check out the cryptogram in which the numbers always add up to 33, Christ's age at his death.

YURY DMITRIENKO / SHUTTERSTOCK ©

Three sections of the portal represent, from left to right, Hope, Charity and Faith. Among the forest of sculpture on the Charity portal you can see, low down, the manger surrounded by an ox, an ass, the shepherds and kings, and angel musicians. Some 30 species of plant from around Catalonia are reproduced here, and the faces of the many figures are taken from plaster casts done of local people and the occasional one made from a corpse in the local morgue.

Directly above the blue stained-glass window is the archangel Gabriel's Annunciation to Mary. At the top is a green cypress tree, a refuge in a storm for the white doves of peace dotted over it. The mosaic work at the pinnacle of the towers is made from Murano glass from Venice.

To the right of the facade is the curious Claustre del Roser, a Gothic-style mini-cloister tacked on to the outside of the church (rather than the classic square enclosure of the great Gothic church monasteries). Once inside, look back to the intricately decorated entrance. On the lower right-hand side you'll notice a sculpture of a reptilian devil offering a worker a bomb. Barcelona was regularly rocked by political violence, and bombings were frequent in the decades prior to the civil war. The sculpture is one of several on the 'temptations of men and women'.

Passion Facade & Schools of Gaudí

The southwest Passion Facade (Façana de la Passió), on the theme of Christ's last days and death, was built between 1954 and 1978 based on surviving drawings by Gaudí, with four towers and a large, sculpture-bedecked portal – but was only officially completed in 2018. The late sculptor Josep Maria Subirachs (1927–2014) worked on its decoration from 1986 to 2006. He did not attempt to imitate Gaudí, instead producing angular, controversial images of his own. The main series of sculptures, on three levels, are in an S-shaped sequence, starting with the Last Supper at the bottom left, passing Christ's crucifixion in the top centre, and ending with Christ's burial at the top right. With prior booking you can travel up inside one of the Passion Facade's towers.

Immediately in front of the Passion Facade, the Schools of Gaudí (Escoles de Gaudí) make up one of the architect's simpler gems. Gaudí built this as a children's school in 1909, creating an original, undulating roof of brick that continues to charm architects to this day (and brings to mind Gaudí's masterpiece La Pedrera).

Glory Facade

The Glory Facade (Façana de la Glòria) will, like the others, be crowned by four towers – the total of 12 representing the Twelve Apostles. Gaudí wanted it to be the most magnificent facade of the church. Inside will be the narthex, a kind of foyer made up of 16 'lanterns', a series of hyperboloid forms topped by cones. Further decoration will make the whole building a microcosmic symbol of the Christian church, with Christ represented by a massive 170m central tower above the transept, and the five remaining towers under construction symbolising the Virgin Mary and the four evangelists.

VISITING

Although essentially a building site, the completed sections and museum may be explored at leisure. Guided 50-minute tours (adult/child €27/free) run in various languages; alternatively, book tickets with audio guides (€26/free). Enter from Carrer de la Marina. There are also tickets that include an audio guide and a trip (by lift and stairs) inside the towers on either the Nativity or Passion facades; these tower tours (€33/free) must be pre-booked online. It's best to pre-book all tickets online.

Hats, see-through clothing, low neck-lines and exposed backs/midriffs aren't permitted. Shorts and skirts must be at least mid-thigh; tops must cover shoulders.

Museu Gaudí & Crypt

Open at the same times as the church, the Museu Gaudí, below ground level next to the Passion Facade, meanders through interesting material on Gaudí's life and other works, as well as a re-creation of his modest office as it was when he died, and explanations of the geometric patterns and plans at the heart of his building techniques. You can see a good example of his plumb-line models that showed him the stresses and strains he could get away with in construction. A side hall towards the eastern end of the museum leads to a window above the simple crypt in which the genius is buried. The neo-Gothic crypt, where Masses are now held, can only be accessed from Carrer de Sardenya; it's the oldest part of the entire structure and largely the work of Gaudí's predecessor, Francisco de Paula del Villar y Lozano.

ADMIRE THE WHIMSY OF CASA BATLLÓ

One of Europe's strangest residential buildings, Casa Batlló (built 1904–06) is Gaudí at his fantastical best. From its playful facade and marine-world inspiration to its revolutionary experiments in light and architectural form (straight lines are few and far between), this apartment block is one of the most beautiful buildings in a city where the architectural stakes soar sky-high.

To Salvador Dalí, Casa Batlló's facade resembled 'twilight clouds in water'. Others see a more-than-passing resemblance to the impressionist masterpiece *Water Lilies* by Claude Monet. It's certainly exquisite and whimsical, sprinkled with fragments of blue, mauve and green tiles, and studded with wave-shaped window frames and mask-like balconies.

In the 1st floor's main salon, the ceiling twists into a whirlpool-like vortex around its sun-like chandelier; the doors, windows and skylights are dreamy waves of wood and coloured glass in mollusc-like shapes. The sense of light and space here is extraordinary thanks to the wall-length window onto Passeig de Gràcia.

Pass the interior courtyard (with its pale-blue cascading wave) to Casa Batlló's back terrace: a fantasy garden in miniature, opening on to an expansive L'Eixample patio. Flowerpots take on strange forms and the accumulation of more than 300 *trencadís* (broken ceramic pieces) have the effect of immersing you in a kaleidoscope.

With its twisting chimney pots so characteristic of Gaudí's structures, the roof is Casa Batlló's grand crescendo. It was built to look like the shape of an animal's back, with shiny scales – the 'spine' changes colour as you walk around. The eastern end represents Sant Jordi (St George) and the Dragon; one local name for Casa Batlló is the *casa del drac* (house of the dragon).

DON'T MISS

➡ The facade and balconies
➡ The swirling interior
➡ The dragon-back roof

PRACTICALITIES

➡ Map p306, G2
➡ ☎ 93 216 03 06
➡ www.casabatllo.es
➡ Passeig de Gràcia 43
➡ adult/child over 6yr €29/26
➡ ⊙9am-8pm, last admission 7pm
➡ Ⓜ Passeig de Gràcia

TOP EXPERIENCE
VISIT GAUDÍ'S MADCAP LA PEDRERA

In the top tier of Gaudí's achievements, this madcap Unesco-listed masterpiece, with 33 balconies, was built in 1905–10 as a combined apartment and office block. Formally called Casa Milà, after the businessman who commissioned it, it is better known as La Pedrera (the Quarry) because of its uneven grey stone facade, which ripples around the corner of Carrer de Provença.

Buy tickets online (saving €3 on most ticket types) for opening time to avoid the worst of the crowds, or a 'premium' ticket (adult/child €32/14), which allows you to skip the queue.

The Facade

When commissioned to design La Pedrera, Gaudí wanted to top anything else done in L'Eixample (including adding parking space – Pere Milà was one of the city's first car owners).

The natural world was one of the most enduring influences on Gaudí's work, and the building's undulating grey-stone facade evokes a cliff-face sculpted by waves and wind. The wave effect is emphasised by elaborate wrought-iron balconies that bring to mind seaweed washed up on the shore. The lasting impression is of a building on the verge of motion – a living building.

The Roof Terrace

Gaudí's blend of mischievous form with ingenious functionality is evident on the extraordinary rooftop, with its clusters of chimneys, stairwells and ventilation towers that rise and fall atop the structure's wave-like contours like giant medieval knights. Some are unadorned, others are decorated with *trencadís* (ceramic fragments) or even broken *cava* bottles. The deep patios, which Gaudí treated like interior facades, flood the apartments with natural light.

Espai Gaudí

One floor below the roof, with 270 gracious parabolic brick arches, the attic's Espai Gaudí feels like the fossilised ribcage of some giant prehistoric beast. At one point, 12 arches come together to form a palm tree. Note also the strange optical effect of the mirror and hanging sculpture on the eastern side. All this surrounds a modest museum dedicated to Gaudí's work.

El Pis de la Pedrera

Below the attic, the elegantly furnished apartment – Gaudí's vision of domestic bliss – is done up in the style a well-to-do family might have enjoyed in the early 20th century. The sensuous curves, rippling distribution and unexpected touches in everything from light fittings to bedsteads, from door handles to balconies, might seem admirable to us today, but not everyone thought so at the time.

The entire building's approach to space and light as well as its blurring of the dividing line between decoration and functionality are astounding. In the ultimate nod to flexible living, the apartment has no load-bearing walls: the interior walls could thus be moved to suit the inhabitants' needs.

DON'T MISS

➜ The marvellous roof
➜ The elegant apartment
➜ The wave-like stone facade

PRACTICALITIES

➜ Casa Milà
➜ Map p310, A4
➜ ☏ 93 214 25 76
➜ www.lapedrera.com
➜ Passeig de Gràcia 92
➜ adult/child 7-12yr from €25/14
➜ ⊙ 9am-8.30pm & 9-11pm Mar-Oct, 9am-6.30pm & 7-9pm Nov-Feb
➜ Ⓜ Diagonal

⊙ SIGHTS

⊙ L'Esquerra de L'Eixample

CASA BATLLÓ
ARCHITECTURE

See p146.

CASA AMATLLER
ARCHITECTURE

Map p306 (☏93 216 01 75; www.amatller.org; Passeig de Gràcia 41; adult/child 7-12yr 1hr guided tour €24/12, 40min multimedia tour €19/9.50; ☺10am-6pm; MPasseig de Gràcia) One of Puig i Cadafalch's most striking flights of Modernista fantasy, Casa Amatller combines Gothic window frames and Romanesque flourishes with a stepped gable borrowed from Dutch urban architecture. But the busts and reliefs of dragons, knights and other characters dripping off the main facade are pure caprice. The beautifully tiled pillared foyer and staircase lit by stained glass feel like the interior of some romantic castle. The building was renovated in 1900 for chocolate baron and philanthropist Antoni Amatller (1851–1910).

The 1st (main) floor, where Amatller and his daughter Teresa lived, has been converted into a museum, with period pieces and original furniture and decor; much of the furniture was also designed by Puig i Cadafalch, while artist Eusebi Arnau was also involved in the building. Amatller was a keen traveller and photographer; his absorbing shots of turn-of-the-20th-century Morocco are occasionally on show.

One-hour guided tours run in English at 11am, Catalan at noon and Spanish at 5pm; self-guided 40-minute visits, with a multimedia tablet, run every 30 minutes. All visits include a taste of Amatller chocolate at the end. It's free to wander into the foyer and admire the staircase and antique lift.

CASA LLEÓ MORERA
ARCHITECTURE

Map p306 (Passeig de Gràcia 35; MPasseig de Gràcia) Domènech i Montaner's 1905 contribution to the Illa de la Discòrdia (p151), with Modernista carving outside and a bright, tiled lobby in which floral motifs predominate, is perhaps the least odd-looking of the three main buildings on the block. It's now occupied by luxury fashion store Loewe (p163).

MUSEU DEL MODERNISME BARCELONA
MUSEUM

Map p306 (☏93 272 28 96; www.mmbcn.cat; Carrer de Balmes 48; adult/child €10/5; ☺10.30am-2pm & 4-7pm Mon-Fri, 10.30am-2pm Sat; MPasseig de Gràcia) Housed in a stuccoed, red-washed 1902 Modernista building by Enric Sagnier, this museum seems like a big Modernista-furniture showroom. Several pieces by Gaudí, including chairs from Casa Batlló and a mirror and chair from Casa Calvet, appear alongside a host of creations by his lesser-known contemporaries. The basement, which has mosaic-coated pillars, bare-brick Catalan vaults and metal columns, is lined with Modernista art, including paintings by Ramon Casas and Santiago Rusiñol, and statues by Josep Llimona and Eusebi Arnau.

UNIVERSITAT DE BARCELONA
ARCHITECTURE

Map p306 (☏93 402 11 00; www.ub.edu; Gran Via de les Corts Catalanes 585; ☺8am-8pm Mon-Fri; MUniversitat) FREE Although a university was first set up on what is now La Rambla in the 16th century, the present, glorious mix of (neo) Romanesque, Gothic, Islamic and Mudéjar architecture is a caprice of the 19th century (built from 1863 to 1871 by Ildefons Cerdà's friend Elies Rogent). Wander into the main hall, up the grand staircase and around the various leafy cloisters, and take a stroll in the rear gardens. The main 1st-floor hall is the Mudéjar-style Paraninfo.

CASA GOLFERICHS
ARCHITECTURE

Map p306 (☏93 323 77 90; www.golferichs.org; Gran Via de les Corts Catalanes 491; ☺10am-8pm Mon-Fri, to 2pm Sat; MRocafort) Designed by Joan Rubió i Bellver for businessman Macari Golferichs, this quirky 1901 Modernista villa is an oddity of another era on one of the city's busiest boulevards. Brick, ceramics and wood are the main building elements of the mansion, which displays a distinctly Gothic flavour. It came close to demolition in the 1970s but was saved by the local authorities and converted into a cultural centre. Opening times and prices vary depending on exhibitions, concerts and other activities.

MUSEU DEL PERFUM
MUSEUM

Map p306 (☏93 216 01 21; www.museudelperfum.com; Passeig de Gràcia 39; adult/child

TOP EXPERIENCE
SEE TÀPIES MASTERPIECES IN A MODERNISTA SETTING

The major collection of leading 20th-century Catalan artist Antoni Tàpies is housed inside this **Fundació Antoni Tàpies**, a Modernista building completed in the early 1880s. Tàpies died in February 2012, aged 88. Known for his esoteric work, he left behind a powerful range of typically complex paintings and a foundation intended to promote contemporary artists.

The building, designed by Domènech i Montaner for publishing house Editorial Montaner i Simón, combines a brick-covered iron frame with Moorish-inspired decoration. Tàpies crowned it with the meanderings of his own mind, a work called *Núvol i cadira* (Cloud and Chair) that spirals above like a storm.

Tàpies expressed a number of themes in his work, such as left-wing politics and humanitarianism, and art as alchemy or magic. He launched the Fundació in 1984, donating a large part of his own work. The collection spans the arc of his creations (with over 2000 works) and contributions from other contemporary artists. In the two main exhibition areas you can see an ever-changing selection of around 20 Tàpies works, from early 1940s self-portraits to grand items like *Jersei negre* (Black Jumper; 2008).

DON'T MISS

➡ Tàpies' swirling additions to the building's rooftop
➡ The main-gallery masterpieces

PRACTICALITIES

➡ Map p306, F2
➡ 93 487 03 15
➡ www.fundaciotapies.org
➡ Carrer d'Aragó 255
➡ adult/child €8/free
➡ 10am-7pm Tue-Thu & Sat, to 9pm Fri, to 3pm Sun
➡ M Passeig de Gràcia

€5/free; 10.30am-2pm & 4.30-8pm Mon-Fri, 11am-2pm Sat; M Passeig de Gràcia) At the back of the Barcelona-founded Regia perfume shop (p162), this museum tells the story of the scent world through the ages, with 5000 bottles of infinite shapes, sizes and histories. It shows oddities from ancient Egyptian and Roman scent receptacles (the latter mostly from the 1st to 3rd centuries CE) to classic eau de cologne bottles and advertising posters. Other items include ancient bronze Etruscan tweezers and little early-19th-century potpourri bowls made of fine Sèvres porcelain.

LA MODEL
HISTORIC BUILDING

Map p306 (www.lamodel.barcelona; Carrer d'Entença 155; 10am-7pm Mon-Sat, tours 5pm Fri, 11.30am & 5pm Sat; M Entença) FREE Over 100 years old, this imposing prison finally closed its doors to inmates in 2017, but has now reopened for tours and exhibitions. The entrance patio is open during the week, but 1½-hour tours of the interior (in Catalan or Spanish only) – during which

you'll see the exercise yard, cells and control room – are only available on Fridays and Saturdays.

PLAÇA DE CATALUNYA
SQUARE

Map p306 (M Catalunya) At the intersection of the old city and L'Eixample, busy Plaça de Catalunya is the city's central transport hub, both for buses and trains, and a convenient meeting point. A large square with impressive fountains and elegant statuary, it's filled with street sellers, tourists and families feeding pigeons.

PALAU ROBERT
GALLERY

Map p306 (93 238 80 91; http://palaurobert.gencat.cat; Passeig de Gràcia 107; 9am-8pm Mon-Sat, to 2.30pm Sun; M Diagonal) FREE The 1903-completed building that hosts Catalonia's regional tourist office (p274) also serves as an exhibition space, mostly for rotating Catalan-themed shows. In summer, concerts are occasionally held in the peaceful back gardens or main hall.

Neighbourhood Walk
Lesser-Known Modernisme in L'Eixample

START CASA SERRA
END PALAU MACAYA
LENGTH 3.5KM; ONE HOUR

Start at Josep Puig i Cadafalch's **①Casa Serra** (Can Serra; Map p306, E1; Rambla de Catalunya 126; ⓂDiagonal) (1903–08), where the architect let his imagination loose on a neo-Gothic whimsy with a central tower topped by a conical roof.

Around 400m east, **②Casa Comalat** (Map p310, A3; Avinguda Diagonal; ⓂDiagonal) is a striking twin-fronted building with vibrant tilework, created from 1909 to 1911 by Salvador Valeri (1873–1954). Note Gaudí's obvious influence on the main facade, with its wavy roof and bulging balconies. Head around the back to Carrer de Còrsega to see a more playful facade, with its windows stacked like cards and uneven wooden galleries.

Head 550m southeast to reach the 1912 **③Casa Thomas** (p165), one of Domènech i Montaner's earlier efforts – the floral motifs and reptile figurines are trademarks

and the massive ground-level wrought-iron decoration (and protection?) is magnificent.

Taking a 1km diversion southeast along Carrer del Bruc, you'll come to Gaudí's most conventional contribution to L'Eixample, **④Casa Calvet** (Map p310, D6; Carrer de Casp 48; ⓂUrquinaona, Tetuan), built in 1901 for textiles industrialist Pere Màrtir Calvet (it now houses a restaurant) and inspired by baroque.

Wander 1km north via Carrer de Girona, passing the Mercat de la Concepció (with cafe-bars), to **⑤Casa Llopis i Bofill** (Map p310, C3; Carrer de Bailén 113; ⓂVerdaguer), an interesting block of flats designed by Antoni Gallissà (1861–1903) in 1902. The graffiti-covered, oriental-inspired facade is particularly eye-catching, while the elaborate parabolic arches on the ground floor and wrought-iron balconies are typically Modernista. Just another 400m north stands Puig i Cadafalch's 1901 **⑥Palau Macaya** (p152), one of Barcelona's least-known Modernisme gems.

⊙ La Dreta de L'Eixample

LA SAGRADA FAMÍLIA BASILICA
See p140.

LA PEDRERA ARCHITECTURE
See p147.

**RECINTE MODERNISTA
DE SANT PAU** ARCHITECTURE
(☎93 553 78 01; www.santpaubarcelona.org; Carrer de Sant Antoni Maria Claret 167; adult/child €15/free, audio guide €4; ⊙9.30am-6.30pm Mon-Sat, to 2.30pm Sun Apr-Oct, 9.30am-4.30pm Mon-Sat, to 2.30pm Sun Nov-Mar; Ⓜ Sant Pau/Dos de Maig) Domènech i Montaner outdid himself as architect and philanthropist with the Modernista Hospital de la Santa Creu i de Sant Pau, renamed the 'Recinte Modernista' in 2014. Built between 1902 and 1930, it was long considered one of Barcelona's most important hospitals, but was repurposed into cultural centres, offices and a monument in 2009. A joint Unesco World Heritage Site together with the Palau de la Música Catalana (p102), the 27-building complex is lavishly decorated and each of its 16 pavilions unique.

Domènech i Montaner wanted to create an environment that would also cheer up patients, setting the hospital around a tranquil courtyard. The most richly adorned space is the **Pavelló de l'Administració**, with its lobby's domed pink-tiled ceiling and twirling staircase, and, upstairs, the **Sala Domènech i Montaner**, known for its soaring arched ceiling, fine tilework and stained-glass windows. Among artists who contributed pieces was the prolific Eusebi Arnau.

Guided 90-minute tours (adult/child €20/free) run in Catalan, Spanish, English and French.

CASA DE LES PUNXES ARCHITECTURE
Map p310 (Casa Terrades; ☎93 018 52 42; www.casadelespunxes.com; Avinguda Diagonal 420; adult/child €13.50/10, tour €20/16; ⊙10am-7pm; Ⓜ Diagonal) Puig i Cadafalch's 1905 Casa Terrades is known as the Casa de les Punxes (House of Spikes) because of its pointed tile-adorned turrets. Resembling a medieval castle, this former apartment block is the only fully detached building in L'Eixample, and opened to the public only in 2017. Visits (with multilanguage audio guide) take in its stained-glass bay windows, handsome iron staircase, hydraulic floors, pillars and arch-

ILLA DE LA DISCÒRDIA

The three houses on the block between Carrer del Consell de Cent and Carrer d'Aragó gave it the playful name **Illa de la Discòrdia** (Spanish: Manzana de la Discordia), meaning 'Apple (Block) of Discord'. Puig i Cadafalch's Casa Amatller (p148), Domènech i Montaner's Casa Lleó Morera (p148) and Gaudí's Casa Batlló (p146) were all renovated between 1898 and 1906 and show how eclectic a 'style' Modernisme was.

es with floral motifs, and rooftop. Guided midday tours run in Spanish (Saturday) and Catalan (Sunday).

Other options include an audio-guide tour with a glass of *cava* on the roof (€16).

MUSEU EGIPCI MUSEUM
Map p310 (☎93 488 01 88; www.museuegipci.com; Carrer de València 284; adult/child €12/5; ⊙10am-8pm Mon-Sat, to 2pm Sun Easter, Jun–mid-Sep & Dec, reduced hours rest of year; Ⓜ Passeig de Gràcia) Hotel magnate Jordi Clos has spent much of his life collecting ancient Egyptian artefacts, brought together in this private museum divided into thematic areas (the pharaoh, religion, funerary practices, mummification, crafts, eroticism etc). There are funereal implements and containers, statuary (such as a 300 BCE bronze representation of the cat goddess Bastet), jewellery (including a fabulous golden ring from the 6th or 7th century BCE), stonework and earthenware, and even a wood-and-leather bed dating to around 2800 BCE.

The basement exhibition area and library displays volumes including original editions of works by Howard Carter, the British Egyptologist who led the Tutankhamun excavations, and there's a cafe up on the rooftop.

A combined ticket with the Museu de Cultures del Món (p105) costs €12 (but isn't available online).

**BASÍLICA DE LA PURÍSSIMA
CONCEPCIÓ I ASSUMPCIÓ
DE NOSTRA SENYORA** CHURCH
Map p310 (www.parroquiaconcepciobcn.org; Carrer d'Aragó 299; ⊙8am-1pm & 5-9pm Mon-Sat, 8am-2pm & 5-9pm Sun, reduced hours Aug; Ⓜ Girona) One hardly expects a medieval

church on the grid-pattern streets of the late-19th-century Eixample, yet that is just what this is. Dating to the 14th century, the church was transferred stone by stone from the old centre in 1871–88. It has a pretty 15th- to 16th-century cloister with a peaceful garden and trickling fountain. Behind is a Romanesque-Gothic bell tower (11th to 16th century), from another old town church that didn't survive, the Església de Sant Miquel.

This is one of a handful of such old churches relocated to L'Eixample.

PALAU BARÓ DE QUADRAS ARCHITECTURE

Map p310 (https://casessingulars.com; Avinguda Diagonal 373; tour adult/child €10/free; ☉11am-1pm Wed; MDiagonal) Puig i Cadafalch redesigned this 1882 residential building in exuberant Gothic-inspired style, with two distinct facades, between 1902 and 1906. The main facade is most intriguing, with a soaring, glassed-in gallery; take a closer look at its emotive gargoyles and reliefs – the pair of toothy fish and sword-wielding knight clearly have the same artistic signature as Casa Amatller (p148). The only way to visit inside is by prebooked 45-minute Wednesday tour, in Catalan (noon), Spanish (1pm) or English (11am).

The eclectic interior is dominated by Moorish, Middle Eastern and East Asian themes, with an Andalucía-style patio.

PALAU MONTANER ARCHITECTURE

Map p310 (☎93 317 76 52; www.fundaciotapies. org; Carrer de Mallorca 278; adult/child €7/free; ☉by reservation; MPasseig de Gràcia) Though fascinating on the outside and made all the more enticing by its leafy gardens, this 1893 creation by Domènech i Montaner is especially spectacular on the inside. The interior is laden with sculptures (some by Eusebi Arnau), mosaics and fine woodwork; its central feature is a grand staircase beneath a broad, ornamental skylight. The Palau is only open by sporadic two-hour guided tour (€8; in Catalan), organised by the Fundació Antoni Tàpies (p149) (email reserves@ ftapies.com).

ESGLÉSIA DE LES SALESES CHURCH

Map p310 (Passeig de Sant Joan 90; ☉10am-1pm & 5-7pm Mon-Sat, 10am-2pm Sun; MVerdaguer) A singular neo-Gothic effort, this church is interesting because it was designed by Joan Martorell i Montells (1833–1906), Gaudí's

architecture professor. Raised in 1878–85 with an adjacent convent (badly damaged in the civil war and now a school), it offers hints of what was to come with Modernisme, with creative use of brick, mosaics and stained glass.

PALAU MACAYA PALACE

Map p310 (☎93 457 95 31; www.obrasocial lacaixa.org; Passeig de Sant Joan 108; ☉9am-8pm Mon-Fri; MVerdaguer) **FREE** The 1901 Palau Macaya is one of Barcelona's great yet least-known Catalan Modernisme gems. It was designed by architect Josep Puig i Cadafalch, who was also the master behind Casa Amatller (p148), Casa de les Punxes (p151) and Palau Baró de Quadras. The bright-white facade is impressive with its decorative windows and intricate paintwork, but the interior is where this palace really comes to life, with its grand entrance, open courtyard decked in colourful tiles and a delicately carved marble staircase.

 # EATING

Most of this huge area's many, enticing restaurants are concentrated in the Quadrat d'Or between Carrer de Pau Claris and Carrer de Muntaner, Avinguda Diagonal and Gran Via de les Corts Catalanes, though others are popping up further afield. L'Eixample's restaurants can be pricey, but you can still sample them at more budget-friendly prices if you head over for the *menú del dia* (daily set lunch menu).

✖ L'Esquerra de L'Eixample

VEGGIE GARDEN VEGAN €

Map p306 (☎93 304 39 53; https://veggie gardengroup.com; Gran Via de les Corts Catalanes 602; mains €5-10; ☉12.30-11pm; 🖉; MUniversitat) Indian thalis, spiced-seitan wraps, Nepalese momos and tofu burgers wedged between home-baked bread are among the plant-based Mediterranean and South Asian deliciousness cooked up at this mural-filled fave. It also does vegan tapas, raw dishes and a brilliant-value three-course *menú del dia* (€9.25). There's another branch (p89) near the Raval's MACBA.

COPASETIC
MEDITERRANEAN €

Map p306 (☑93 532 76 66; www.copasetic barcelona.com; Carrer de la Diputació 55; mains €6-13.50; ⊗10.30am-midnight Tue & Wed, to 1am Thu, to 2am Fri & Sat, to 5.30pm Sun; ☎⁂; MRocafort) ✔ Styled with 1920s vintage inspiration, Catalan-Greek-owned cafe Copasetic has a fun, friendly vibe and a seasonal menu that holds plenty for everyone, whether your thing is eggs Benedict, a wildberry tartlet or a fat, juicy burger. There are lots of vegetarian, gluten-free and organic options, superb weekend brunches and weekday lunch *menús* (€11 to €12.50).

CREMERIA TOSCANA
GELATO €

Map p306 (☑93 539 38 25; www.cremeriatos cana.es; Carrer de Muntaner 161; gelato €3-6; ⊗1pm-midnight Mon-Thu, to 1am Fri, noon-1am Sat, noon-midnight Sun Apr-Oct, reduced hours Nov-Mar; MHospital Clínic) At the most authentic gelato outlet in town, all flavours are natural (and most gluten-free) and fruit arrives fresh every day. Along with classic Italian choices by cone or tube such as creamy *stracciatella* and wavy hazelnut *nocciola* are more unusual offerings like goat's cheese with caramelised fig, pear and chocolate or plum and pink grapefruit.

CHARLOT CAFÈ
CAFE €

Map p306 (☑93 451 15 65; www.facebook.com/ CHARLOTCAFEBCN; Carrer d'Aribau 67; dishes €6-14; ⊗8.30am-10pm Mon-Thu, to 3am Fri, 7pm-3am Sat; ☎⁂; MUniversitat, ⓕFGC Provença) Movie stills and posters, from *Breakfast at Tiffany's* to *Pulp Fiction*, line the walls at Charlot. Get a morning kick-start with a truffled tortilla (Spanish omelette) or eggs baked in Iberian ham, or drop by for lunch (sautéed quinoa salad; burgers with hand-cut fries) or dinner (duck with blackberry sauce). Craft beers and cocktails like burnt-pineapple caipirinhas go all day long.

★PEPA
TAPAS €€

Map p306 (☑93 611 18 85; www.pepapla.cat; Carrer d'Aribau 41; sharing plates €7-18; ⊗5-11pm Sun-Thu, 1-11.30pm Fri & Sat, closed 2 weeks Aug; ⁂; MUniversitat) ✔ An old bookshop graced by original check-tiled floors and exposed-brick walls is the setting for this outstanding venture from the team behind El Born's beloved Bar del Pla (p109). Don't miss the mushroom carpaccio with strawberries and wasabi vinaigrette, or, in season, the fabulous eggs with truffle and chips. Desserts – like flambeed berries – are just as exquisite, while wines are natural, organic and/or biodynamic.

★AUTO ROSELLON
INTERNATIONAL €€

Map p306 (☑93 853 93 20; www.autorosellon. com; Carrer del Rosselló 182; breakfasts €4-9, mains €10-15; ⊗8am-1am Mon-Wed, to 2am Thu & Fri, 9am-2am Sat, 9am-midnight Sun; ☎⁂; MDiagonal, ⓕFGC Provença) ✔ With cornflower-blue paintwork and fresh produce on display, Auto Rosellon works mostly organic ingredients sourced from small producers and its own garden into creative dishes like avocado toast with feta, cauliflower doused in kale pesto, *gnudi* pasta with baked pumpkin, and slow-roasted-pork tacos. Homemade juices, lemonade and cakes are exceptional, and there are natural wines, cocktails and craft beers.

The €16 lunchtime *menú* is popular.

PARKING PIZZA
PIZZA €€

Map p306 (☑93 633 96 45; www.parkingpizza. com; Carrer de Londres 98; mains €11-15; ⊗1-4pm & 8-11pm Sun-Thu, to midnight Fri & Sat, closed 12-25 Aug; ⁂; ⓕFGC Provença) In this garage-style space, you're likely to be sharing a long unvarnished wooden table, squeezed in on a cardboard-box stool, but that's half the fun. Wood-fired pizzas arrive loaded with toppings like creamy burrata stracciatella or earthy black truffle, while tempting starters include a superb red-quinoa salad with avocado and a poached egg.

There's another branch (p156) on ever-trendier Passeig de Sant Joan.

LA CUINA D'EN GARRIGA
SPANISH €€

Map p306 (☑93 250 37 00; https://lacuinaden garriga.com; Carrer d'Enric Granados 58; mains €9-20; ⊗1-11pm Wed-Sun; ☎⁂; ⓕGFC Provença) ✔ Tomatoes dangle above the open kitchen at this cheerful bistro-style spot with brightred trim and checkered marble floors, popular with lunching *barcelonins*. Seasonal, organic farm-to-table menus highlight small, mostly local producers in creatively plated dishes like pea-and-mint hummus (served in a jar), grilled aubergine dressed with *romesco* sauce, fresh fish of the day or grilled *costella* (T-bone steak) for sharing.

BESTA
FUSION €€

Map p306 (☑93 019 82 94; https://bestabar celona.com; Carrer Aribau 106; dishes €5-20; ⊗1-3.30pm Mon, 8-10.30pm Thu, 1-3.30pm & 8-10.30pm Fri-Sat, 1-3.30pm Sun) The fruits of both the Atlantic and Mediterranean infuse the ambitious, weekly-changing menu devised by a Galician-Catalan chef duo at this hot Eixample arrival, with tall tables by the bistro-inspired bar and a rotation of crafted cocktails. Fresh seafood stars in creative, boundary-pushing dishes, which might include Betanzos-style tortilla topped with octopus, fennel with honeyed goat's cheese and seaweed or squid with jalapeños.

GRESCA BAR
CATALAN €€

Map p306 (☑93 451 6193; Carrer de Provença 230; sharing plates €7-16; ⊘1.30-4pm & 8.30-10.30pm; ✒; ☒FGC Provença) ✐ From the team behind smart restaurant Gresca (with whom it shares an open-plan kitchen), this elegant gold-and-green wine and tapas bar is a whispered-about local hit. Chef Rafa Peña specialises in thoughtful, ambitious reinterpretations of quality seasonal produce, combined with exclusively natural wines. Try leeks with burrata, veal sweetbreads or a *bikini* with mushrooms or pork loin and Comté cheese.

You can also try Peña's culinary creations until late in gourmet-sandwich style at nearby green-clad **Bar Torpedo** (Map p306; ☑93 858 37 60; www.facebook.com/bartorpedo; Carrer d'Aribau 143; sandwiches €7-8; ⊘7pm-2.30am Tue & Wed, to 3am Thu-Sat; ☒) ✐, where the natural wines continue.

LA BODEGUETA PROVENÇA
TAPAS €€

Map p306 (☑93 215 17 25; www.provenca. labodegueta.cat; Carrer de Provença 233; tapas €6-15, mains €10-16; ⊘7am-1.45am Mon-Fri, 8am-1.45am Sat, 1pm-12.45am Sun; ☎; ☒FGC Provença) The 'Little Wine Cellar' offers classic tapas presented with a touch of class, from *calamars a l'andalusa* (lightly battered squid rings) to *cecina* (dried cured veal meat). The speciality is *ous estrellats* ('smashed eggs') – a mix of scrambled eggs, potato and meats like *chistorra* (fast-cured sausage). Pair with a Ribera del Duero wine or *caña* (small beer). Lunchtime *menús* are €16.

CERVESERIA CATALANA
TAPAS €€

Map p306 (☑93 216 03 68; Carrer de Mallorca 236; tapas €4-14; ⊘8am-1.30am Mon-Fri, from 9am Sat & Sun; ☒FGC Provença) The 'Catalan Brewery' is perfect for a morning coffee and croissant, or tapas and *montaditos* (bread with toppings) at lunch or dinner. Sit at the bar, on the pavement terrace or in the back restaurant. The variety of hot tapas, salads and other snacks draws a well-dressed crowd of locals and visitors. It's usually rammed; no reservations.

EL VELÓDROMO
TAPAS, MEDITERRANEAN €€

Map p306 (☑93 430 60 22; www.moritz.com; Carrer de Muntaner 213; tapas €3-13, mains €10-24; ⊘1pm-1am; ☒Hospital Clínic) The restoration of this history-steeped literary tavern by Barcelona brewer Moritz brought back a wonderfully atmospheric establishment. Stop in for an aperitif and tapas or more substantial dishes such as salmon with caramelised cabbage or a giant two-person entrecôte, from a menu devised by acclaimed chef Jordi Vilà. The spectacular high-ceilinged space retains many of its original art deco fittings.

CERVESERIA BRASSERIA GALLEGA
GALICIAN €€

Map p306 (☑93 419 94 77; Carrer de Casanova 238; mains €8-20; ⊘1.30-4pm & 9pm-midnight Mon-Sat, closed Aug; ☎; ☒Hospital Clínic) You could walk right by this modest establishment without giving it a second glance, but it's usually chock-full of *barcelonins* enjoying plates of abundant Galician classics. The fresh *pop a feira* (Galician-style octopus) starter marks this place as a cut above the competition. The setting is simple, the meat dishes succulent and the *fideuà* (a noodle-based Catalan dish similar to paella) flavoursome.

TAKTIKA BERRI
PINTXOS €€

Map p306 (☑93 453 47 59; www.facebook.com/ taktikaberri; Carrer de València 169; pintxos €4-15, mains €12-28; ⊘1-4pm & 8.30-11pm Mon-Fri, 1-4pm Sat, closed early-late Aug; ☒Hospital Clínic) Reservations are essential at Taktika Berri, which teems with smartly dressed local diners who come for some of the best *pintxos* (Basque tapas) in town. Morsels like blood sausage, gooey tortilla or *bacallà* (salt cod) with potato gratin are snapped up as soon as they arrive fresh from the kitchen, so keep your eyes peeled.

PACO MERALGO
TAPAS €€

Map p306 (☑93 430 90 27; http://restaurant pacomeralgo.com; Carrer de Muntaner 171; tapas €3-15; ⊘1pm-midnight; ☒Hospital Clínic) ✐ *Patates braves*, cod fritters, courgette flowers with mozzarella, grilled Palamós prawns, sautéed squid with Santa Pau beans and, just sometimes, lunchtime paella are among the exquisite seasonal tapas at this strikingly contemporary *alta taberna* ('haute tavern'). Only the freshest, top-quality local ingredients are used. Dine at tall tables or at the pale-wood bar.

CU-CUT! SPANISH €€

Map p306 (☑93 027 06 36; www.cu-cut.cat; Carrer d'Enric Granados 68; mains €9-14; ☺noon-2am; ⒭FGC Provença) Named after a popular early-19th-century Catalan satirical magazine, Cu-Cut! is a beautiful beamed tavern with a large covered porch, a timber bar and a long, romantically lit dining room. There are dishes from all over Spain and further afield, including Galician-style *pop a feira* (octopus with paprika), roast Iberian pork and prawn tagliatelle, plus a €13 weekday lunch *menú*.

CAFÉ SAN TELMO CAFE €€

Map p306 (☑93 439 17 09; www.gruposantelmo.com; Carrer de Buenos Aires 60; mains €9-15; ☺8.30am-1am Mon, to 2am Tue & Wed, to 3am Thu & Fri, 9.30am-3am Sat, 9.30am-1am Sun; ☺✆; Ⓜ Hospital Clínic) Framed by big windows, this stylish corner cafe serves hearty breakfasts, tapas, burgers, salads, sandwiches (such as roast beef and mustard or Milanese chicken with tomato and Brie) and the like. It's also a popular after-work spot, with a great list of gin and tonics.

★LASARTE MODERN EUROPEAN €€€

Map p306 (☑93 445 32 42; www.restaurantlasarte.com; Carrer de Mallorca 259; mains €52-70; ☺1.30-3pm & 8.30-10pm Tue-Sat; Ⓜ Diagonal) One of Barcelona's preeminent restaurants – and its first to gain three Michelin stars (in 2016) – Lasarte is overseen by lauded chef Martín Berasategui and headed up by Paolo Casagrande. From Duroc pig's trotters with Jerusalem artichoke to squid tartare with kaffir consommé, this is seriously sophisticated, seasonally inspired cookery, served in an ultra-contemporary dining room by staff who could put the most overawed diners at ease. For an all-out dining extravaganza, order the 12-course tasting menu (€245).

★DISFRUTAR EUROPEAN €€€

Map p306 (☑93 348 68 96; www.disfrutar barcelona.com; Carrer de Villarroel 163; tasting menus €155-195; ☺2.15pm & 8-9.15pm Mon-Fri; ✆; Ⓜ Hospital Clínic) Two-Michelin-star Disfrutar ('Enjoy') is among the city's finest restaurants. Run by alumni of Ferran Adrià's game-changing El Bulli, nothing is as it seems, such as black and green olives that are actually chocolate ganache with orange-blossom water. The Mediterranean-inspired decor is fabulously on point, with latticed brickwork and trademark geometric ceramics from Catalan design team Equipo Creativo, and service is faultless.

★CINC SENTITS CATALAN €€€

Map p306 (☑93 323 94 90; www.cincsentits.com; Carrer d'Entença 60; tasting menus €99-119; ☺1.30-2.30pm & 8.30-9.30pm Tue-Sat; ✆; Ⓜ Rocafort) ✐ Enter the realm of the 'Five Senses' to indulge in jaw-dropping eight- or 11-course tasting menus of small, experimental dishes concocted by chef Jordi Artal (no à la carte, although dishes can be tweaked on request). The use of fresh local produce, such as Costa Brava line-caught fish and top-quality Extremadura suckling pig, is key at this Michelin-star address.

★MONT BAR BISTRO €€€

Map p306 (☑93 323 95 90; www.montbar.com; Carrer de la Diputació 220; tapas €4-10, mains €15-30; ☺1-4pm & 7-11.30pm Wed-Mon; ☺✆; Ⓜ Universitat) ✐ Named for the owner's Val d'Aran hometown, this stylish space with black-and-white floors, pine-green booths and bottle-lined walls offers next-level cooking fired by organic, seasonal ingredients, many of them home-grown. Exquisite tapas (like corn-and-jalapeño crisp-bread and oyster with mandarin tiger's milk) precede superb small-plate mains, such as celery risotto with truffle, and show-stopping desserts. Stunning wines (over 250) span all price points. Reservations recommended.

Next door **Mediamanga** (Map p306; ☑93 832 56 94; www.mediamanga.es; Carrer d'Aribau 13; sharing plates €10-30; ☺1-4pm & 7-11.30pm; ✆; Ⓜ Universitat) ✐, by the same team, delivers similarly spectacular Catalan-inspired cuisine, such as truffled chicken risotto, scallop ceviche and kimchi-smoked prawns.

LA DAMA EUROPEAN €€€

Map p306 (☑93 209 63 28; www.la-dama.com; Avinguda Diagonal 423-425; mains €22-30; Ⓜ Diagonal, ⒭FGC Provença) Diagonal's 1917 Modernista Casa Sayrach has been reborn as a graceful multiroom gastro space filled with grand-yet-homey lounges, sparkling mirrors, floral-patterned wallpaper and rich velvet touches. Perfectly executed dishes wander around northern Spain, France and Italy, with a few other international hints: pork ribs with vegetable cream, squid-ink carbonara, sole meunière for two. There's also a fine cocktail bar.

SPEAKEASY
INTERNATIONAL €€€

Map p306 (☏93 217 50 80; www.drymartiniorg. com; Carrer d'Aribau 162; mains €18-30; ⊙8-11.30pm Mon-Sat; ℝFGC Provença) This clandestine restaurant lurks behind Dry Martini (p158): you'll be shown a door through the open kitchen to the 'storeroom', lined with hundreds of bottles of backlit, quality tipples. Tempting options might include Iberian suckling pig or mushroom-and-king-prawn ravioli in a creamy Parmesan sauce. Dark decor, a few works of art, low lighting and light jazz complement the smooth service.

✕ La Dreta de L'Eixample

★ TAPAS 24
TAPAS €

Map p310 (☏93 488 09 77; www.carlesabellan. com; Carrer de la Diputació 269; tapas €4-12; ⊙9am-midnight; ☏; MPasseig de Gràcia) Hotshot chef Carles Abellán runs this basement tapas haven known for its gourmet renditions of old faves, including the *bikini* (toasted ham-and-cheese sandwich, here with truffle and cured ham), freshly cooked tortilla and zesty lemon-infused *boquerones* (anchovies). You can't book, but it's worth the wait. For dessert, try the creamy *payoyo* cheese. Before 1pm, pop in for superb *entrepans* (filled rolls) and omelettes.

There are also branches at Camp Nou (p210) and Diagonal (p209).

GRANJA PETITBO
MEDITERRANEAN €

Map p310 (☏93 265 65 03; www.granjapetitbo. com; Passeig de Sant Joan 82; mains €5-11; ⊙8.30am-11.30pm Mon-Fri, 10am-midnight Sat, 10am-11.30pm Sun; ☏✍; MGirona) High ceilings, battered leather armchairs, creative flower arrangements and soaring windows set the scene in this sunny little corner cafe, beloved of fashionable locals and young families. As well as an all-day parade of homemade cakes, freshly squeezed juices and terrific coffee, there are burgers, salads, pastas and Buddha bowls, along with a brunch menu, all made with local produce.

ENTREPANES DÍAZ
SANDWICHES, TAPAS €

Map p310 (☏93 415 75 82; www.facebook.com/ entrepanesdiaz; Carrer de Pau Claris 189; sandwiches €6-10, tapas €3-10; ⊙1pm-midnight; MDiagonal) Gourmet sandwiches, from roast beef to suckling pig or the favourite

crispy squid with squid-ink aioli, are the highlight at this sparkling old-style bar, along with sharing plates of Spanish specialities such as sea urchins, prawn fritters or blood-sausage croquettes. Service is especially charming; black-and-white photos of Barcelona line the walls.

HAWKER 45
ASIAN €€

Map p310 (☏93 763 83 15; www.hawker45. com; Carrer de Casp 45; mains €10-16; ⊙1-4pm & 8-11pm Mon-Sat; ✍; MTetuan) Taking its cues from an Asian hawkers market, chef Laila Bazahm's aromatic restaurant sizzles up Asian–Latin American street-food dishes such as spicy Malaysian squid laksa, Indonesian lamb satay, Indian tandoori carrots and Thai green veg curry with avocado. Dine at the long, red bar overlooking the open kitchen or in the postindustrial dining space with bare beams and wall murals.

The six-course tasting menu (€35) can be paired with craft beers (€42) or Asian-inspired cocktails (€60), and there's also a lunchtime *menú del dia* (€12 to €15).

CHICHALIMONÁ
MEDITERRANEAN €€

Map p310 (☏93 277 64 03; www.chichalimona. com; Passeig de Sant Joan 80; mains €12-17; ⊙9.30am-1am Tue-Thu, to 2am Fri & Sat, to 5pm Sun; ☏; MGirona) Bright, bustling Chichalimoná is a favourite along ever-more-fashionable Passeig de Sant Joan. Steak tartare with chipotle, spicy chicken tacos, basil-and-mascarpone ravioli or vegetable spring rolls dipped in coconut sauce might be among the original dishes, along with vermouth-hour bites like olives, hummus and squid. Weekend brunches star organic eggs. There's another branch at El Raval's MACBA (p91).

PARKING PIZZA
PIZZA €€

Map p310 (☏93 541 80 11; www.parkingpizza. com; Passeig de Sant Joan 56; mains €11-15; ⊙1-4pm & 8-11pm Sun-Fri, to midnight Sat; ✍; MTetuan) A sprawling warehouse with cardboard-box chairs, big sharing tables and an open-plan kitchen, buzzing Parking Pizza cooks up outrageously popular wood-fired pizzas topped with the likes of black truffle and egg or smoked salmon with mascarpone, plus perfect rigatoni with salvia and gorgonzola. Also here is the smaller **Parking Pita**, with gorgeously spiced falafel wraps, roast cauliflower and zingy hummus.

CAN KENJI
JAPANESE €€

Map p310 (📞93 476 18 23; www.cankenji.com; Carrer del Rosselló 325; mains €9-14; ⏱1-3.30pm & 8.30-11.30pm; Ⓜ Verdaguer) The chef of this understated little *izakaya* (Japanese tavern), on the southeastern fringes of Gràcia, gets his ingredients fresh from the city's markets, with traditional Japanese recipes receiving a Mediterranean touch. Choices include udon noodles sautéed with squid and clams, or tuna *tataki* (lightly grilled meat) with *salmorejo* (Córdoba-style cold-tomato soup), plus various lunch-menu deals.

XAVIER PELLICER
VEGETARIAN, VEGAN €€

Map p310 (📞93 525 90 02; www.xavierpellicer. com; Carrer de Provença 310; mains €9-15; ⏱1-3.30pm & 8-10.30pm Tue-Sat; 📷; Ⓜ Diagonal) 🅟 Creatively spiced, delicately grilled or sizzlingly stir-fried – beautifully fresh, organic local vegetables leap into the spotlight at top chef Xavier Pellicer's extremely popular 'healthy kitchen', just off upper Passeig de Gràcia. *Platillos* (shared plates) might include spicy roasted celery with dates or potatoes with wild mushrooms. Wines are organic, biodynamic and/or natural, and the interior features walnut wood, exposed stone and an open kitchen.

The attached El Menjador dining space offers a smarter, more gastronomic take, with nine-course vegan (€95), vegetarian (€115) and omnivore (€145) tasting menus.

CAN PIZZA
PIZZA €€

Map p310 (📞93 436 40 43; http://canpizza. eu; Passatge de Simó 21; pizzas €9-15; ⏱1-4pm & 8-11pm; 📷; Ⓜ Sagrada Família) Born in the unlikely area of El Prat de Llobregat near the airport, uberpopular Can Pizza has landed in Barcelona with this warehouse-like, industrial-feel outpost just around the corner from La Sagrada Família. Snappy service and hot-red styling set the tone for slow-cooked pizzas made with 72-hour-fermented dough, starring local or 100% Italian ingredients, such as the Vaya Trufa, sprinkled with truffle.

EMBAT
MEDITERRANEAN €€

Map p310 (📞93 458 08 55; http://embatrestau rant.com; Carrer de Mallorca 304; mains €11-21; ⏱1-3.45pm Mon-Wed, 1-3.45pm & 8.30-11pm Thu-Sat; Ⓜ Verdaguer) Enthusiastic young chefs turn out beautifully presented, market-fuelled dishes in this light-filled, Scandi-chic setting. Menus change weekly: indulge perhaps in artichokes with cured ham and aubergine puree or green-pea soup sprinkled with goat's cheese, followed by smooth boletus ravioli or cod in sabayon cream.

GIGI VON TAPAS
TAPAS €€

Map p310 (📞93 246 90 28; http://gigivontapas. com; Carrer de la Marina 189; dishes €6-9; ⏱9am-4pm & 6pm-midnight; 📷; Ⓜ Tetuan, Glòries) At this punchy tapas bar, bold flavours and creative presentation collide in delicious contemporary Spanish-international sharing plates like crunchy tofu doused in black-bean sauce or quinoa risotto topped with ricotta, lemon gel and leek-dusted asparagus. Dine at the marble-topped bar amid open-brick walls and straw bull heads, or out on the street. Homemade vermouth, Catalan wines and artisan cocktails, too.

CASA ALFONSO
SPANISH €€

Map p310 (📞93 301 97 83; www.casaalfonso.com; Carrer de Roger de Llúria 6; tapas & sandwiches €4-15, mains €13-23; ⏱8am-1am Mon-Fri, from 1pm Sat; 📶; Ⓜ Urquinaona) In business since 1934 (and a tanning warehouse before that), Casa Alfonso is perfect for morning coffee, breakfast or tapas at the long marble bar. Wood-panelled and festooned with old photos, posters and swinging hams, it attracts a faithful local clientele at all hours for its *flautas* (thin filled baguettes), hams, cheeses, homemade desserts, and grilled-meat mains.

MR KAO
DIM SUM €€

Map p310 (📞93 445 25 88; www.misterkao.com; Carrer de València 271; dim sum €3-4, mains €10-30; ⏱12.30-3.30pm & 8.30-11.30pm Tue-Sat, 12.30-3.30pm Sun; Ⓜ Passeig de Gràcia) Within the grand Hotel Claris, this elegant Shanghai-style dim sum restaurant serves top-flight dumplings. They're not cheap, but every bite is a joy; the *jiao zi* with pig's trotters are especially good, as are the *siu mai* with langoustines and trout roe. More substantial dishes include Peking duck and noodles with wild mushrooms, poached egg and truffles.

PATAGONIA BEEF & WINE
SOUTH AMERICAN €€€

Map p310 (📞93 304 37 35; www.patagoniabw. com; Gran Via de les Corts Catalanes 660; mains €20-38; ⏱1.30-3.30pm & 7-11pm Mon-Thu, to 11.30pm Fri & Sat, to 10.30pm Sun; 📶; Ⓜ Passeig de Gràcia) This stylish restaurant delivers on its promise of an Argentinian meat-fest. Start with *empanades* (meat-stuffed pastries), then head for a hearty main, such as a juicy beef *medallón amb salsa de múrgoles* (medallion in morel-brandy sauce), the 350g *bife de chorizo* (sirloin strip) or Brazilian *picanha* (rump). Choose from five sides to accompany your pound of flesh.

🍷 DRINKING & 🍸 NIGHTLIFE

Noisy Carrer de Balmes is thronged with a young crowd. Bars lining Carrer d'Aribau roughly between Avinguda Diagonal and Carrer de Mallorca range from elegant cocktail bars to '60s retro joints; few get going much before midnight and most are closed or empty from Sunday to Wednesday. On and around Carrer del Consell de Cent and Carrer de la Diputació is the heart of the 'Gaixample' (p160), filled with LGBTIQ+ bars and clubs (mostly male-oriented).

🍷 L'Esquerra de L'Eixample

DRY MARTINI   BAR
Map p306 (☎93 217 50 72; www.drymartiniorg. com; Carrer d'Aribau 162-166; ☺1pm-2.30am Mon-Thu, 1pm-3am Fri, 6.30pm-3am Sat, 6.30pm-2.30am Sun; ᘰFGC Provença) Waiters make expert cocktail suggestions, but the house drink, taken at the gleaming wooden bar or on one of the plush green banquettes, is always a good bet – an expertly mixed martini (over a million are thought to have been served here). Dry Martini is a smart, dimly lit, old-style space, with bottle-filled cabinets and original artwork.

MILANO   COCKTAIL BAR
Map p306 (☎93 112 71 50; www.camparimilano. com; Ronda de la Universitat 35; ☺1pm-4am, hours can vary; ᘰCatalunya) Subtly signed from street level, this gem of hidden Barcelona nightlife is a subterranean old-school cocktail bar with red-velvet banquettes and glass-fronted cabinets, presided over by white-jacketed waiters. Live music (Cuban, jazz, blues, flamenco, swing) plays nightly (schedules online); DJs take over after 11pm. Fantastic cocktails include the rum-infused Hemingway and seven different Bloody Marys (€10 to €15).

ARENA MADRE   CLUB, GAY
Map p306 (☎93 487 83 42; www.grupoarena. com; Carrer de Balmes 32; cover incl drink €10-12; ☺12.30-5am Sun-Thu, to 6am Fri & Sat; ᘰPasseig de Gràcia) Popular with a hot young crowd, Arena Madre is one of the top LGBTIQ+ clubs in town (though these days it can be quite mixed). Mainly pop, dance and house music, with a striptease show on Monday, drag shows on Tuesday and Wednesday, a Thursday reggaeton night, and live shows throughout the week.

GARAGE BEER CO   CRAFT BEER
Map p306 (☎93 528 59 89; www.garagebeer.co; Carrer del Consell de Cent 261; ☺noon-midnight Sun-Thu, to 3am Fri & Sat; ᘰUniversitat) One of the original craft-beer bars to pop up in Barcelona, Garage brews its own in a space at the bar and at its out-of-town brewery, and offers around 10 styles at a time. The Ocata (a delicate session IPA) and Soup (a more robust IPA) are always on the board; other favourites include Circus Tears (an Imperial stout).

MONKEY FACTORY   COCKTAIL BAR
Map p306 (☎93 270 31 16; www.facebook.com/ monkeyfactorybcn; Carrer de Còrsega 234; ☺6.30pm-3am Tue-Sat; ᘰFGC Provença) DJs spin on weekends at this high-spirited venue, but it's positively hopping from early on most nights, often hosting language-exchange sessions. Funky Monkey (triple sec, gin, lime and egg white), Chimpa Sour (cardamom-infused pisco sour) and Chita Tai (rum, lime, cacao, triple sec and almond syrup) are among the inventive cocktails mixed up behind the green-neon-lit bar.

PLATA BAR   GAY
Map p306 (☎93 452 46 36; www.platabar.com; Carrer del Consell de Cent 233; ☺8pm-2am Mon, Thu & Sun, to 1.30am Wed, to 3am Fri & Sat; ᘰUniversitat) Summer seats on the corner terrace of this wide-open bar attract guys hopping between the area's gay bars. Inside, metallic horse-saddle stools are lined up at the bar and high tables, the music is a mix of dance and trance, and bartenders whip up eye-popping cocktails including fabulous passionfruit mojitos (€16).

EL CANGREJO   CLUB, GAY
Map p306 (www.facebook.com/elcangrejoeix ample; Carrer de Villarroel 86; ☺11pm-3am Fri & Sat; ᘰUrgell) With shimmering walls and

chandeliers, tightly packed El Cangrejo brings a taste of its kitschy original Raval sibling (p94) to the Gaixample. Chart-topping Spanish and international hits keep things busy.

ALAIRE ROOFTOP BAR

Map p306 (☎93 445 00 00; www.condesde barcelona.com; Passeig de Gràcia 73, Condes de Barcelona; ◷noon-midnight Sun-Wed, to 2am Thu-Sat; ⓂPasseig de Gràcia) From the Condes de Barcelona hotel lobby, a sparkling glass lift zips up to this sleek 8th-floor roof-terrace bar with soul-stirring views across Passeig de Gràcia and La Pedrera. Sunsets are exquisite, particularly over a *cava* (€8) or Penedès wine (€7). It gets packed with a stylish young crowd of locals and visitors; you can book only if dining (mains €10 to €16).

ANTILLA BCN CLUB

Map p306 (☎93 451 45 64; www.antillasalsa. com; Carrer d'Aragó 141; cover incl drink Fri & Sat €10; ◷10pm-4am Wed, 11pm-5am Thu, 11pm-6am Fri & Sat, 7pm-2am Sun; ⓂUrgell) *The* salsateca in town, this is the place to come for Cuban *son*, merengue, salsa and a whole lot more, across a couple of spaces. The free bachata (Wednesday 10pm and Thursday 11pm) and salsa (Wednesday 11pm) classes are popular.

HEMINGWAY COCKTAIL BAR

Map p306 (☎93 129 67 93; http://heming waybcn.com; Carrer de Muntaner 114; ◷4pm-2.30am Sun-Thu, to 3am Fri & Sat; ⓂHospital Clínic) There's often a queue at the door for a table at this intimate, speakeasy-style basement cocktail den with a tiny front terrace. International whiskies, rare gins and lightly imaginative cocktails crafted with fresh-pressed citrus juices are owner-barista Luca Izzo's specialities; try the best-selling gin-based Montgomery (infused with ginger and Earl Grey tea; €12) or a classic G&T (€12).

The team also runs Old Fashioned (p182), another brilliant cocktail spot in Gràcia.

BIERCAB CRAFT BEER

Map p306 (☎644 689045; www.biercab.com; Carrer de Muntaner 55; ◷noon-midnight Mon-Thu, to 2am Fri & Sat, 5pm-midnight Sun; 🛜; ⓂUniversitat) Beneath an artistic wooden ceiling installation resembling a forest of giant matchsticks, this brilliant craft-beer bar has 30 brews from around the world rotating on its taps. Burgers to accompa-

ny them are made from Wagyu beef and named for Barcelona neighbourhoods. Pop into its adjacent shop to choose from another 500 bottled varieties kept cold in fridges.

COSMO CAFE

Map p306 (☎93 105 79 92; www.galeriacosmo. com; Carrer d'Enric Granados 3; ◷10am-10pm; ⓂUniversitat) 🌿 Set on a pedestrian strip just behind the university, this cool cafe–cultural space has bicycles hanging from high, white walls and bright, splashy murals, and even makes a feature of its fire hose. Along with fresh juices, hot chocolate, teas and pastries, it serves arty brunches and Nømad (p133) coffee, not to mention beer and wine. All ingredients are sourced within 100km.

Cosmo also runs Cafè Cometa (p198) in Sant Antoni.

TERRAZA DEL PULITZER ROOFTOP BAR

Map p306 (☎93 481 67 67; www.hotelpulitzer. es; Carrer de Bergara 8, Hotel Pulitzer; ◷6-11pm daily May-Oct, noon-sunset Sat & Sun Nov-Apr; ⓂCatalunya) An intimate terrace wreathed in jasmine and other greenery, gazing out onto Plaça de Catalunya with Montjuïc and Barceloneta in the distance, the Hotel Pulitzer's mellow rooftop is a favourite summer hang-out. There's live pop, funk and electronica on Wednesday, while respected DJs play Thursday to Saturday. Perfect for a well-mixed cocktail (€12).

HIDDEN ALFRESCO BARS

L'Eixample's elegant streets conceal an array of hidden-away, view-laden open-air bars and cafes beloved by *barcelonins*, many of them within swish hotels but open to all. Some of our favourites:

➜ Alaire, at Condes de Barcelona

➜ Jardí del Alma (p239), at Alma

➜ Batuar Terrace (p239), at Cotton House

➜ Jardí Diana (p239), at El Palace

➜ Terraza del Pulitzer, at Hotel Pulitzer

➜ The Rooftop (p240), at Sir Victor

➜ La Dolce Vitae (p240), at Majèstic Hotel & Spa

THE GAIXAMPLE

The area just north of Gran Via de les Corts Catalanes and to the west of Rambla de Catalunya is popularly known as the 'Gaixample', for its proliferation of LGBTIQI+ bars, clubs and restaurants. Some of the best include Arena Madre (p158), Arena Classic, with lesbian events, Punto BCN and El Cangrejo (p159), though several old favourites are also in adjoining neighbourhoods, such as Metro (p202) in Sant Antoni.

PUNTO BCN
GAY

Map p306 (📞93 451 91 52; www.grupoarena.com; Carrer de Muntaner 65; ⏰6pm-2.30am Sun-Thu, to 3am Fri & Sat; 🅼Universitat) A big bar over two levels with a slightly older crowd, Punto gets busy on Friday and Saturday nights with its blend of Spanish pop and dance. It's a friendly early stop on a night out at the gay bars.

ARENA CLASSIC
GAY & LESBIAN

Map p306 (📞93 487 83 42; www.grupoarena.com; Carrer de la Diputació 233; cover incl drink Fri & Sat €6-12; ⏰11pm-3am Thu, to 6am Fri & Sat; 🅼Passeig de Gràcia) Spinning pop hits from all decades, Arena Classic has a spacious dance floor and attracts a fun LGBTIQ+ crowd. There are various lesbian nights, including popular event Aire from 11pm to 2am nightly, though in practice the crowd is often fairly mixed.

QUILOMBO
BAR

Map p306 (📞606 144272; www.facebook.com/quilombo.pub; Carrer d'Aribau 149; ⏰9pm-2.30am Mon-Thu, 8.30pm-3am Fri & Sat; 🆁FGC Provença) Some formulas just work, and this place has been working since the 1970s. Set up some guitars in the table-packed back room, add some cheapish preprepared mojitos and plastic tubs of nuts, and let the punters do the rest. They pour in, creating plenty of *quilombo* (fuss). Live music plays most nights from 11pm and impromptu parties are common.

BREWDOG BARCELONA
CRAFT BEER

Map p306 (📞93 488 59 79; www.brewdog.com; Carrer de Casanova 69; ⏰noon-midnight Thu-Mon; 🅼Urgell) Spain's first branch of beloved Scottish artisan-beer label BrewDog is set within a boldly reimagined early-20th-century bank, with 20 taps on the go. The classic Punk IPA and hoppy Dead Pony Club are among the house brews, and there are limited-edition Barcelona-only picks plus national and international guest brands, on draft or by bottle. Bites include hearty burgers (€10).

CELLARER
WINE BAR

Map p306 (📞93 451 72 33; www.facebook.com/CELLARERWINEBAR; Carrer de Mallorca 211; ⏰6pm-1am Mon-Sat; 🆁FGC Provença) A terrific, friendly little stone-walled spot for South American–style tapas and unusual wines, where local regulars linger over the likes of *patates braves* and meat-stuffed *empanadas* paired with carefully curated drops from across Catalonia, Cantabria, Galicia and elsewhere in northern Spain.

CITY HALL
CLUB

Map p306 (📞660 769865; www.cityhallbarcelona.com; Rambla de Catalunya 2-4; cover incl drink from €10; ⏰midnight-5am Mon-Thu, to 6am Sat; 🅼Catalunya) A long corridor leads to the dance floor of this venerable and popular club, located in a former 19th-century theatre. Music styles, from house and techno to reggaeton, change nightly; check the agenda online. It's also a live music venue.

LA FIRA
CLUB

Map p306 (📞682 323714; www.facebook.com/lafiraprovenza; Carrer de Provença 171; entry incl drink €16; ⏰11pm-5am Thu, to 5.30am Fri & Sat; 🆁FGC Provença) Wander in past crazy mirrors, penny slot machines and other ancient fairground attractions from Germany, as well as futuristic furniture like glowing cuboid stools. Music at La Fira swings wildly from house through to '90s hits and Spanish pop classics, but it's known for its popular Thursday reggaeton night. With 150 spirits on hand, it claims to offer 500 different shots.

BACON BEAR BARCELONA
GAY

Map p306 (📞93 431 00 00; www.facebook.com/baconbearbar; Carrer de Casanova 64; ⏰6pm-2.30am Sun-Thu, to 3am Fri & Sat; 🅼Urgell) The music cranks up on weekends at this busy big bar for burly gay folk.

LA CHAPELLE
GAY

Map p306 (☏93 453 30 76; Carrer de Muntaner 67; ⏰4pm-2am Sun-Thu, to 2.30am Fri & Sat; Ⓜ Universitat) A typical long, narrow Eixample bar with white-tiled walls, La Chapelle houses a plethora of crucifixes and niches that far outdo what you'd find in any other 'chapel'. This is a relaxed gay meeting place that welcomes all.

🍷 La Dreta de L'Eixample

★ LES GENS QUE J'AIME
BAR

Map p310 (☏93 215 68 79; www.facebook.com/lesgensquejaime.pub; Carrer de València 286; ⏰6pm-2.30am Sun-Thu, 7pm-3am Fri & Sat; Ⓜ Passeig de Gràcia) Atmospheric and intimate, this basement relic of the 1960s follows a deceptively simple formula: chilled jazz music in the background, minimal lighting from an assortment of flea-market lamps, classic cocktails, and a cosy, cramped scattering of red-velvet-backed loungers around tiny dark tables. Tarot readings are also thrown into the mix.

SATAN'S COFFEE CORNER
COFFEE

Map p310 (https://satanscoffee.com; Gran Via de les Corts Catalanes 700, Casa Bonay; ⏰7am-6pm; Ⓜ Tetuan) Home-baked pastries and Japanese-inspired, street-food-style bites (€3 to €12) pair with devilishly delicious seasonal beans at this white-walled speciality cafe tucked into the chic Casa Bonay (p239). The coffee is sourced and roasted by favourite local producer Right Side. There's another branch (p77) in the Barri Gòtic.

EL VITI
BAR

Map p310 (☏93 633 83 36; www.elviti.com; Passeig de Sant Joan 62; ⏰noon-midnight Sun-Thu, to 1am Fri & Sat; 🛜; Ⓜ Girona) Along fashionable Passeig de Sant Joan, modern-rustic El Viti ticks all the nouveau-tavern boxes – black subway tiles, soaring ceilings, open-brick walls, marble-top tables and a barrel of artisan vermouth on the bar. Inventive tapas (€4 to €11) take in smoked-aubergine croquettes, Castilian cheeses and squid with own-ink mayo.

THREE MARKS
COFFEE

Map p310 (https://threemarkscoffee.com; Carrer d'Ausiàs Marc 151; ⏰8.30am-6pm Mon-Wed & Fri, to 4pm Thu, 10am-3pm Sat & Sun; Ⓜ Marina) Catalan-Italian-owned by, yes, three Marks, this is a split-level stripped-back speciality-coffee corner with a cosy neighbourhood vibe, whitewashed walls and a few decorative succulents, on the untouristed Poblenou side of L'Eixample. Flat whites and espresso (€2 to €3) made with beans from roasters in Madrid and Barcelona arrive on bright-red trays in handle-free mugs, to go with creative sandwiches (€6.50).

CAFÈ DEL CENTRE
CAFE

Map p310 (☏93 488 11 01; Carrer de Girona 69; ⏰9.30am-midnight Mon-Fri, noon-midnight Sat; 🛜; Ⓜ Girona) Travel back to the 19th century at this charmingly old-world cafe, in business since 1873. The mahogany bar extends down the right side as you enter, fronted by marble-dressed tables and wooden chairs. It exudes an almost melancholy air by day but gets busy at night, when live jazz piano plays.

☆ ENTERTAINMENT

CITY HALL
LIVE MUSIC

Map p306 (☏660 769865; www.cityhallbarcelona.com; Rambla de Catalunya 2-4; Ⓜ Catalunya) This former 19th-century theatre is the perfect size and shape for live music, holding a crowd of around 500 and with a varied line-up. The acoustics are great and the layout means everyone gets a good view of the stage. It's also home to a nightclub. Check schedules and prices online.

MEDITERRÁNEO
LIVE MUSIC

Map p306 (El Medi; www.elmedi.net; Carrer de Balmes 129; ⏰10.30pm-3am; 🚆 FGC Provença) A range of free, quality live music is staged nightly at this student favourite. Order a beer and enjoy the free nuts at one of the tiny tables while waiting for the next act to tune up at the back.

TEATRE TÍVOLI
THEATRE

Map p310 (☏93 215 95 70; www.grupbalana.com; Carrer de Casp 8; ⏰box office 5-8pm, plus 90min before shows; Ⓜ Catalunya) Dating from 1919, this grand theatre has three storeys of boxes and a generous stage hosting a fairly rapid turnover of drama and musicals. Concerts also take place; Bruce Springsteen, Elvis Costello and Radiohead have all played, and the Royal Shakespeare Company made its Spanish debut here in 1984.

SHOPPING

See the Shopping in the Quadrat d'Or walking tour for a spin around some of Passeig de Gràcia's shiniest boutiques.

L'Esquerra de L'Eixample

ALTAÏR BOOKS

Map p306 (☎93 342 71 71; www.altair.es; Gran Via de les Corts Catalanes 616; ☺10am-8.30pm Mon-Sat; ☏; MCatalunya) Enter a travel wonderland at this extensive bookshop, founded in 1979, which has enough guidebooks, maps, travel literature and other works to induce a severe case of itchy feet. There's also a helpful travellers' noticeboard and cosy downstairs cafe.

AVANT FASHION & ACCESSORIES

Map p306 (☎93 300 76 73; www.theavant.com; Carrer d'Enric Granados 106; ☺10.30am-8.30pm Mon-Fri, to 2.30pm Sat; MDiagonal, ☒FGC Provença) Taking inspiration from the world of dance and cultures around the globe, *barcelonin* designer Silvia Garcia Presas creates her elegant women's dresses, shirts, shoes and other pieces working directly with local producers. The boutique setting is a chicly white, classically Modernista building.

REGIA COSMETICS

Map p306 (☎93 216 01 21; www.regia.es; Passeig de Gràcia 39; ☺9.30am-9pm Mon-Fri, 10.30am-9pm Sat; MPasseig de Gràcia) In business since 1928, Barcelona-born Regia stocks Spanish and international fragrance and beauty brands, along with Diptyque candles. It also has its own line of bath products, and a perfume museum (p149) out the back.

LA CENTRAL BOOKS

Map p306 (www.lacentral.com; Carrer de Mallorca 235; ☺10am-9pm Mon-Fri, from 10.30am Sat; MPasseig de Gràcia, Diagonal, ☒FGC Provença) An excellent multilingual bookshop with titles stocked amid lovely old tiled floors and a speciality cafe run by Satan's Coffee Company (p161), with a sunny back terrace.

EL CORTE INGLÉS DEPARTMENT STORE

Map p310 (☎93 306 38 00; www.elcortein-gles.es; Plaça de Catalunya 14; ☺9.30am-9pm Mon-Sat; MCatalunya) Spain's only

Local Life
Shopping in the Quadrat d'Or

While visitors to L'Eixample do the sights, *barcelonins* go shopping in the Quadrat d'Or (Golden Square), the grid of streets either side of Passeig de Gràcia. This is Barcelona at its most fashion and design conscious, which also describes a large proportion of L'Eixample's residents. All the big names are here, alongside the boutiques of local designers who capture the essence of Barcelona cool.

❶ Lurdes Bergada

You could spend an entire day just along Passeig de Gràcia, but detour for a moment to **Lurdes Bergada** (Map p306; ☎93 218 48 51; www.lurdesbergada.es; Rambla de Catalunya 112; ☺10.30am-8.30pm Mon-Sat; MDiagonal), run by mother-and-son designer team Lurdes Bergada and Syngman Cucala. Their classy men's and women's fashions using natural fibres have attracted a cult following.

❷ Mauri

Few bakeries have such a long-established pedigree as **Mauri** (Map p306; ☎93 215 10 20; www.pastelerias mauri.com; Rambla de Catalunya 102; pastries €3-7; ☺8am-midnight Mon-Fri, 9am-midnight Sat, 9am-4.30pm Sun; MDiagonal). Ever since it opened in 1929, this grand old pastry shop and teahouse has dazzled its regular customers with spectacular sweets, chocolate croissants, feather-light *ensaïmades* (Balearic-style sweet buns) and gourmet delicatessen items.

❸ Purificación García

Spanish designer **Purificación García's** (Map p306; ☎93 496 13 36; www.purificacion garcia.com; Carrer de Provença 292; ☺10am-8.30pm Mon-Sat; MDiagonal) collections are breathtaking as much for their breadth as anything else. You'll find all kinds of fashion over this shop's two floors, from light summer dresses to men's ties and jeans.

❹ Bagués-Masriera

In harmony with its location, inside the Modernista Casa Amatller (p148), the team from **Bagués-Masriera** (Map p306; ☎93 216 01 74; www.bagues-masriera.com;

Above: Loewe

Passeig de Gràcia 41; ⏱10am-8.30pm Mon-Fri, 11am-8pm Sat; ⓂPasseig de Gràcia) have been chipping away at precious stones and moulding metal since the 19th century. Many of the pieces here have a flighty, Modernista influence.

❺ Loewe

Loewe (Map p306; ☎93 216 04 00; www.loewe.com; Passeig de Gràcia 35; ⏱10am-8.30pm Mon-Sat, noon-8pm Sun; ⓂPasseig de Gràcia) is one of Spain's leading and oldest luxury fashion stores, founded in 1846. While bags and suitcases in every conceivable colour of butter-soft leather are the mainstay, there is also a range of clothing, shoes, sunglasses, silk scarves and jewellery. This branch is in the Casa Lleó Morera (p148).

❻ Cacao Sampaka

Chocoholics will be convinced they have died and passed on to a better place at sleek **Cacao Sampaka** (Map p306; ☎93 272 08 33; www.cacaosampaka.com; Carrer del Consell de Cent 292; ⏱9am-9pm Mon-Sat; ⓂPasseig de Gràcia). Load up on every conceivable flavour (rosemary, perhaps, or curry?) or head for the cafe, where you can have a classic *xocolata* (hot chocolate) and munch on exquisite chocolate cakes, tarts and sandwiches. The bonbons make good presents.

❼ Dr Bloom

A new collection comes out every month at bright local brand **Dr Bloom** (Map p306; ☎93 315 41 89; www.drbloom.es; Rambla de Catalunya 30; ⏱10am-9pm Mon-Sat; ⓂPasseig de Gràcia), which designs and makes all its own pieces in Barcelona. The label's dresses, tops, jumpers, shawls, bags and more channel bold prints and colours no matter the season.

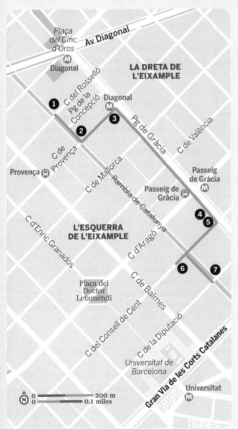

AN OUTLET OUTING

For the ultimate discount-designer overdose, head 35km northeast of central Barcelona for some outlet shopping at **La Roca Village** (☑93 842 39 39; www.larocavillage.com; Santa Agnès de Malayanes; ⊙10am-10pm), a village that has been given over to consumer madness. Among a long line of Spanish and international fashion boutiques, you'll find reduced-price clothes, shoes, accessories and designer homewares.

The Village runs a Shopping Express bus from Passeig de Gràcia (adult/child €10/5, 30 to 45 minutes); check schedules online. Alternatively, take the hourly Sagalés (p268) Shopping Bus (adult/child €10/6, 40 minutes) from Carrer de Casp 34 in L'Eixample (just north of Urquinaona metro).

remaining department-store chain stocks everything you'd expect, from computers to cosmetics and high fashion to homewares. Fabulous city views extend from the top-floor restaurant. Nearby branches include one on **Avinguda Diagonal** (Map p306; ☑93 493 48 00; www.elcorteingles.es; Avinguda Diagonal 471; ⊙9.30am-9pm; Ⓜ Hospital Clínic).

MERCAT DEL NINOT   MARKET
Map p306 (☑93 323 49 09; www.mercatdelninot.com; Carrer de Mallorca 133-157; ⊙9am-8pm Mon-Fri, to 2pm Sat; ☎; Ⓜ Hospital Clínic) A gleaming, modern neighbourhood market, on the site of a 19th-century open-air predecessor, the Mercat del Ninot sells mostly meat and fish and also has a couple of cafebars where you can grab a tortilla sandwich or seafood tapa. It reopened in 2015 after a five-year makeover.

ANTINOUS   BOOKS
Map p306 (☑93 301 90 70; www.antinouslibros.com; Carrer de Casanova 72; ⊙11am-2pm & 5-8pm Mon-Sat; Ⓜ Universitat) A relaxed, spacious LGBTIQ+ bookshop in the Gaixample, with titles in various languages.

🔒 La Dreta de L'Eixample

★FLORES NAVARRO   FLOWERS
Map p310 (☑93 457 40 99; www.floristeriasnavarro.com; Carrer de València 320; ⊙24hr; Ⓜ Girona) You never know when you might need flowers, and this vast, packed-to-the-rafters florist never closes. Established in 1960, it has two spaces on Carrer de València, and is worth a visit just for the

bank of colour and wonderful fragrance, from sky-blue roses to tiny cacti.

★JOAN MÚRRIA   FOOD & DRINKS
Map p310 (Queviures Múrria; ☑93 215 57 89; www.murria.cat; Carrer de Roger de Llúria 85; ⊙10am-2pm & 5-8pm Tue-Sat; Ⓜ Girona) Ramon Casas designed the 1898 Modernista shopfront advertisements at this culinary temple of speciality foods from around Catalonia and beyond. Artisan cheeses, Iberian hams, caviar, canned delicacies, olive oils, smoked fish, *cavas* and wines, coffee and loose-leaf teas are among the treats in store.

LAIE   BOOKS
Map p310 (☑93 318 17 39; www.laie.es; Carrer de Pau Claris 85; ⊙9am-9pm Mon-Fri, from 10am Sat; ☎; Ⓜ Urquinaona) Laie has novels and books on architecture, art and film in English, French, Spanish and Catalan, as well as a terrific all-day upstairs cafe where you can examine your purchases or browse through the newspapers over quiches, cakes and *entrepans*.

MERCAT DE LA CONCEPCIÓ   MARKET
Map p310 (☑93 476 48 70; www.laconcepcio.cat; Carrer d'Aragó 313-317; ⊙8am-8pm Tue-Fri, to 3pm Mon & Sat early Sep–mid-Jul, 8am-3pm Mon-Sat mid-Jul–early Sep; Ⓜ Girona) Dating from 1888 (though remodelled in 1998), the iron-clad Mercat de la Concepció has around 50 stalls selling food, flowers, wine and more, including three on-site bars.

CUBIÑÁ   HOMEWARES
Map p310 (☑93 476 57 21; www.cubinya.es; Carrer de Mallorca 291, Casa Thomas; ⊙10am-2pm & 4.30-8.30pm Mon-Sat; Ⓜ Verdaguer) Even if interior design doesn't ring your bell, it's worth a visit to this century-old world

of furniture, lamps and just about any home accessory imaginable, just to see the Domènech i Montaner building, **Casa Thomas** (Map p310; Carrer de Mallorca 293; Ⓜ Verdaguer), that it lives inside. Admire the enormous and whimsical wrought-iron decoration at street level before heading inside to marvel at the brick columns and intricate timber work.

ADOLFO DOMÍNGUEZ   FASHION & ACCESSORIES

Map p310 (www.adolfodominguez.com; Passeig de Gràcia 32; ⊙ 10am-9pm Mon-Sat; Ⓜ Passeig de Gràcia) One of the stars of Spanish prêt-à-porter, this label produces classic men's and women's garments from quality materials. Encompassing anything from regal party gowns to kids' outfits (which might have you thinking of British aristocracy), the broad range generally has a conservative air, with elegant cuts that make no concessions to rebellious urban ideals.

NORMA COMICS   BOOKS

Map p310 (☑ 93 244 84 23; www.normacomics.com; Passeig de Sant Joan 7-9; ⊙ 10.30am-8.30pm Mon-Sat; Ⓜ Arc de Triomf) Norma stocks a huge range of comics, both Spanish and international – everything from Tintin to out-there sci-fi comics, along with figurines, clothing, mugs and other merchandise.

🏃 SPORTS & ACTIVITIES

SPEAKEASY   LANGUAGE

Map p306 (☑ 93 342 71 97; www.speakeasybcn.com; Ronda de la Universitat 7; Ⓜ Universitat) A friendly Spanish-language school next to the university, popular for its small-group classes and social calendar (Sitges trips, street-art tours). Courses cater to all levels. An intensive 20-hour course, over four weeks, costs €129 per week.

TERRA BIKE TOURS   CYCLING

Map p310 (☑ 93 416 08 05; www.terrabiketours.com; Carrer de València 337; 1-day self-guided tour from €12, 1-day guided tour from €50; ⊙ 10am-2pm & 4-8pm Mon-Sat; Ⓜ Verdaguer) This outfit offers a wide range of cycling tours (guided or self-guided, with preloaded GPS) from one day to one week. Options include mountain biking in the Parc Natural de Collserola, Montserrat or the Pyrenees, and road-biking tours between Barcelona and Girona via La Garrotxa or the Costa Brava. Bike hire starts at €17 per day.

DON QUIJOTE   LANGUAGE

Map p306 (☑ 923 26 88 60; www.donquijote.org; Carrer de Mallorca 27; Ⓜ Entença) A reputable Spanish-language school with branches across the country; offers private and small-group lessons, plus accommodation and optional excursions. An intensive 20-class course, for example, costs €155 to €175 per week.

CATALUNYA BUS TURÍSTIC   BUS

Map p310 (☑ 932 80 58 05; www.catalunyabusturistic.com; Plaça de Catalunya; excursions €50-80; Ⓜ Catalunya) Offers a range of day trips from Barcelona, including excursions to Montserrat, Figueres, Penedès wine country, and the Vall de Núria (in the Pyrenees), with multilingual guides.

BARCELONA BUS TURÍSTIC   BUS

(☑ 93 298 70 00; www.barcelonabusturistic.cat; adult/child 1-day pass €30/16, 2-day pass €40/21; ⊙ 9am-8pm mid-Apr-Oct, to 7pm Nov-mid-Apr) This hop-on, hop-off service covers three circuits linking all major tourist sights. The main Blue (Plaça de Catalunya–Camp Nou via Passeig de Gràcia and La Sagrada Família) and Red (Plaça de Catalunya–Parc de la Ciutadella via Montjuïc and Port Vell) routes take two hours each.

Antoni Gaudí & Modernisme

Barcelona's architectural gift to the world was Modernisme, a flamboyant Catalan creation that erupted in the late 19th century. Modernisme was personified by the visionary work of Antoni Gaudí, a giant in the world of architecture. Imaginative creations by Gaudí and his contemporaries have filled Barcelona with dozens of masterpieces.

A Blank Canvas

In the 1850s, a rapidly growing city fuelled by industrialisation meant notoriously crowded conditions in the narrow streets of the Ciutat Vella, Barcelona's old quarter. In 1869 the architect Ildefons Cerdà was commissioned to design a new district: L'Eixample (El Ensanche in Spanish; the Expansion).

Cerdà drew wide boulevards on a gridlike layout and envisioned neighbourhoods with plenty of green space – an objective that city planners unfortunately overruled amid the rampant land speculation of the day. With a blank slate before them, and abundant interest from upper-class residents eager to custom-design a new home, architects were much in demand. What developers could not have predicted was the calibre of those architects.

Antoni Gaudí

Leading the Modernista way was Antoni Gaudí. Born in Reus to a long line of coppersmiths, Gaudí was initially trained in metalwork. In 1878, when he obtained his architecture degree, the school's headmaster is reputed to have said, 'Who knows if we have given a diploma to a nutcase or a genius. Time will tell.'

The Book of Nature

As a young man, what most delighted Gaudí was being outdoors, and he became fascinated by the plants, animals and geology beyond his door. This deep admiration for the natural world would heavily influence his designs. 'This tree is my teacher,' he once said. 'Everything comes from the book of nature.' Throughout his work, Gaudí sought to emulate the harmony he observed in the natural world, eschewing the straight line and favouring curvaceous forms and more organic shapes.

The spiral of a nautilus shell can be seen in staircases and ceiling details, and tight buds of flowers in chimney pots and roof ornamentation, while undulating arches evoke a cavern, overlapping roof tiles mimic the scales of an armadillo and flowing walls resemble waves on the sea. Tree branches, spider webs, stalactites, honeycombs, starfish, mushrooms, shimmering beetle wings and many other elements from nature – all were part of the Gaudí vernacular.

Gaudí's Creations

The architect's work is an earthy appeal to sinewy movement, but often with a dreamlike or surreal quality. The private Casa Batlló (p146) is a fine example

1. L'Eixample 2. Lizard fountain, Park Güell (p174)

in which all appears a riot of the unnaturally natural – or the naturally unnatural. Not only are straight lines eliminated, but the lines between real and unreal, sober and dream-drunk, good sense and play are all blurred.

Gaudí seems to have particularly enjoyed himself with rooftops. At the **Palau Güell** (p87) he created all sorts of fantastical, multicoloured tile figures, as chimney pots resembling oversized, budlike trees that seem straight out of *Alice in Wonderland*. Over at **La Pedrera** (p147), his other-worldly tile-patterned rooftop chimneys take on the appearance of medieval knights.

La Sagrada Família

Gaudí's masterpiece was **La Sagrada Família** (p140),which he took over on from Francisco de Paula del Villar y Lozano in 1883; in it you can see the culminating vision of many ideas developed over the years. Its massive scale evokes the grandeur of Catalonia's Gothic cathedrals, while organic elements foreground its harmony with nature.

The church is rife with symbols that tangibly express Gaudí's Catholic faith through architecture: 18 bell towers symbolise Jesus, the Virgin Mary, the four evangelists and the 12 apostles. Three facades cover Jesus's life, death and resurrection. Even its location is relevant: the Nativity Facade (p141) faces east, where the sun rises; the Passion Facade (p144) depicting Christ's death faces west, where the sun sets.

GAUDÍ OFF THE BEATEN TRACK

Bellesguard (p217), La Zona Alta

Casa Vicens (p176), Gràcia

Col·legi de les Teresianes (p209), Sant Gervasi

Palau de Pedralbes & Pavellons Güell (p208), Pedralbes

Portal Miralles (p212), Sarrià

1. Nativity Facade (p141), La Sagrada Família 2. Casa Vicens (p176)

Gaudí: A Catholic & a Catalan

Gaudí was a devout Catholic and a Catalan nationalist. In addition to nature, Catalonia's great medieval churches were a source of inspiration to him. He took pride in utilising the building materials of the countryside: clay, stone and wood.

In contrast to his architecture, Gaudí's life was simple. With age he became almost exclusively motivated by stark religious conviction, and he devoted much of the latter part of his life to what remains Barcelona's call sign – La Sagrada Família.

In 1926 he was struck down by a tram while taking his daily walk to the Sant Felip Neri church. Wearing ragged clothes with empty pockets – save for some orange peel – Gaudí was initially mistaken for a beggar and taken to a nearby hospital where he was left in a pauper's ward; he died two days later. Thousands attended his funeral, forming a half-mile procession to La Sagrada Família, where he remains buried in the crypt.

Much like his famous work in progress, Gaudí's story is far from over. In March 2000 the Vatican decided to proceed with the case for canonising him, and pilgrims already stop by the crypt to pay homage to him.

Lluís Domènech i Montaner

Although overshadowed by Gaudí, Lluís Domènech i Montaner (1850–1923) was one of the great masters of Modernisme. He was a widely travelled man of prodigious intellect, with knowledge of subjects from mineralogy to medieval heraldry, as well as being an architectural professor, a prolific writer and a nationalist politician. The question of Catalan identity and how to create a national architecture consumed Domènech i Montaner, who designed more than a dozen large-scale works in his lifetime.

The exuberant, steel-framed **Palau de la Música Catalana** (p102) is one of his masterpieces. Adorning the facade are elaborate Gothic-style windows, floral designs (Domènech i Montaner also studied botany) and sculptures depicting characters from Catalan folklore and the music world, as well as everyday citizens of Barcelona. Inside, the hall leaves visitors dazzled with delicate floral-covered colonnades, radiant stained-glass walls and ceiling, and a rolling, sculpture-packed proscenium referencing the epics of musical lore.

His other great masterpiece is the Hospital de la Santa Creu i de Sant Pau; now known as the **Recinte Modernista de Sant Pau** (p151), it boasts sparkling mosaics on the facade and a stained-glass skylight that fills the vestibule with golden light (like Matisse, Domènech i Montaner believed in the therapeutic powers of colour).

Josep Puig i Cadafalch

Like Domènech i Montaner, Josep Puig i Cadafalch (1867–1956) was a polymath; he was an archaeologist and an expert in Romanesque art as well as one of Catalonia's most prolific architects. As a politician – and later president of the Mancomunitat de Catalunya (Commonwealth of Catalonia) – he was instrumental in shaping the Catalan nationalist movement.

One of his many Modernista gems is the **Casa Amatller** (p148), a rather dramatic contrast to Gaudí's Casa Batlló next door. Here the straight line is very much in evidence, as is the foreign influence (the gables are borrowed from the Dutch). Blended with playful Gothic-style sculpture, Puig i Cadafalch designed a house of startling beauty and invention.

Another pivotal work by Puig i Cadafalch is the 1896 Casa Martí, today better known as **Els Quatre Gats** (p76). It is one of Barcelona's earliest Modernista-style buildings, with Gothic window details and whimsical wrought-iron sculpture.

Materials & Decorations

Modernista architects relied on artisan skills that have now been all but relegated to history. There were no concrete pours (contrary to what is being done at La Sagrada Família today). Stone, unclad brick, exposed iron and steel frames, and the copious use of stained glass and ceramics in decoration, were all features of the new style – and indeed it is in the decor that Modernisme is at its most flamboyant.

The craftspeople required for these tasks were the heirs of the guild masters and had absorbed centuries of know-how about just what could and could not be done with these materials. Forged iron and steel were newcomers to the scene, but the approach to learning how they could be used was not dissimilar to that adopted for more traditional materials. Gaudí, in particular, relied on these old skills and even ran schools at La Sagrada Família's workshops to keep them alive.

1. La Sagrada Família (p140) 2. Palau de la Música Catalana (p102) 3. Casa Amatller (p148)

Gràcia & Park Güell

Neighbourhood Top Five

1 **Park Güell** (p174) Meandering along winding paths amid the wild sculptures, mosaics and columns of Gaudí's open-air wonderland, high above the city.

2 **Casa Vicens** (p176) Admiring the curious interplay of brick, chequerboard patterns and Moorish elements on this Unesco-listed castle-mansion – Gaudí's first commission.

3 **Mercat de la Llibertat** (p176) Shopping for delectable local specialities (and sampling them too) at the neighbourhood's emblematic market, dating from the 19th century.

4 **Bunkers del Carmel** (p179) Escaping up to this hilltop former anti-aircraft battery for fabulous 360-degree city panoramas.

5 **Tapas and squares** (p181) Wandering between Gràcia's many charming squares and dipping into locally loved tapas spots such as Bar Bodega Quimet.

For more detail of this area see Map p312 ➡

Explore Gràcia & Park Güell

Once a separate village north of L'Eixample, and an industrial district famous for its republican and liberal ideas, Gràcia was incorporated into the city of Barcelona in 1897, despite staunch opposition from residents. The neighbourhood retains its distinct character today – with a boho feel, it's home to artists, local luminaries and young families.

Start the day by exploring Gaudí's Park Güell (p174), then move south down into central Gràcia – about a 15-minute walk, or a short hop on the metro's Línia 3 (Fontana stop) to Carrer Gran de Gràcia.

Plunge into Gràcia's narrow streets and small plazas, and the bars and restaurants on and around them. The liveliest are Carrer de Verdi, where you'll find wonderful cafes, bars and shops; Plaça del Sol, a raucous square populated by cool bars; Plaça de la Vila de Gràcia, dotted with cafes and restaurants; family-friendly Plaça de la Revolució de Setembre de 1868; and tree-lined Plaça de la Virreina, a particularly lovely square overlooked by an 1884 church in which Gaudí is said to have had a hand. Gràcia's squares are sunny and relaxed for breakfast or lunch, and lively at night with scenesters enjoying a drink alfresco, and there are some great restaurants and cocktail bars in the neighbourhood.

If time allows, make your way west from Park Güell to the Bunkers del Carmel (p179) for some of the finest city views.

Local Life

→**Independent shops** Wander up Carrer de Verdi and along Travessera de Gràcia for an insight into what Gràcia does best: one-off boutiques and original food shops on people-filled streets.

→**Markets** The 19th-century Mercat de la Llibertat (p176) is a neighbourhood jewel, but it's not the only historic market here. Also seek out the Mercat de l'Abaceria Central (p185).

→**Old-time bars** Gràcia still has plenty of tapas bars that have been around forever – Bar Bodega Quimet (p177) and La Vermuteria del Tano (p182) are classics.

Getting There & Away

→**Metro** Línia 3 (Fontana stop) leaves you halfway up Carrer Gran de Gràcia and close to a network of busy squares. To enter Gràcia from the northern side, take Línia 4 to Joanic.

→**Foot** Strolling northwest along Passeig de Gràcia from Plaça de Catalunya is a lovely way to reach the neighbourhood. The 1.5km walk takes around 25 minutes.

Lonely Planet's Top Tip

A wonderful way to take in Gràcia's atmosphere is from a cafe or restaurant on one of its many squares. Arrive after dusk and watch as the place comes to life in the post-work hours.

 ### Best Places to Drink

→ Bobby Gin (p180)
→ El Ciclista (p180)
→ SlowMov (p180)
→ Elephanta (p180)
→ El Rabipelao (p182)

For reviews, see p180.→

Best Places to Eat

→ La Pubilla (p178)
→ Berbena (p178)
→ Les Tres a la Cuina (p177)
→ Extra Bar (p178)
→ Con Gracia (p180)
→ La Panxa del Bisbe (p178)

For reviews, see p177.→

 ### Best Places to Shop

→ Colmillo de Morsa (p183)
→ Casa Atlântica (p184)
→ Family Beer (p184)
→ Fromagerie Can Luc (p184)
→ Amalia Vermell (p184)
→ Bodega Bonavista (p184)

For reviews, see p183.→

GRÀCIA & PARK GÜELL

TOP EXPERIENCE
TAKE IN THE CITY VIEWS FROM PARK GÜELL

Park Güell – around 1km north of Gràcia – is where Gaudí turned his hand and imagination to landscape gardening. It's a surreal, enchanting place where the Modernista's passion for natural forms really took flight, to the point where the artificial almost seems more natural than the natural.

A City Park

Park Güell originated in 1900, when Count Eusebi Güell bought the tree-covered hillside of El Carmel (then outside Barcelona) and hired Gaudí to create a miniature city of houses for the wealthy, surrounded by landscaped grounds. The project was a commercial flop and was abandoned in 1914 – but not before Gaudí had created, in his inimitable manner, steps, a plaza, two gatehouses and 3km of roads and walks. In 1922 the city bought the estate for use as a public park, which became a Unesco World Heritage site in 1984 (along with several other Gaudí works). The idea was based on the English 'garden cities', much admired by Güell, hence the spelling of 'Park'.

Much of the park is still wooded, but it's laced with pathways. The best views are from the cross-topped **Turó de les Tres Creus** (Turó del Calvari) in the southwest corner.

Plaça de la Natura, Banc de Trencadís & Sala Hipóstila

Arriving via the park's main eastern entrance, you'll reach a broad open space, the **Plaça de la Natura**, whose centrepiece is the **Banc de Trencadís**, completed in 1914. Curving

DON'T MISS

➡ The Sala Hipóstila's stone forest

➡ The undulating, tiled Banc de Trencadís with views across the city

➡ The artist's life at the Casa-Museu Gaudí

➡ Learning about Modernisme and Gaudí's building methods at the Casa del Guarda

PRACTICALITIES

➡ Map p312, C1

➡ ☎ 93 409 18 31

➡ www.parkguell. barcelona

➡ Carrer d'Olot 7

➡ adult/child €10/7

➡ ⊙ 8am-9.30pm May-Aug, to 8.30pm Apr, Sep & Oct, to 6.15pm Nov–mid-Feb, to 7pm mid-Feb–Mar

➡ 🚌 H6, D40, V19, Bus Güell, Ⓜ Lesseps, Vall-carca, Alfons X

sinuously around the perimeter, this multicoloured tiled bench was designed by one of Gaudí's closest colleagues, architect Josep Maria Jujol (1879–1949). To the west of the square extends the **Pòrtic de la Bugadera** (the Laundry Room Portico), a gallery where the twisted stonework columns and roof give the effect of a cloister beneath tree roots – a motif repeated in several places in the park.

With Gaudí, however, there is always more than meets the eye. The giant Plaça de la Natura was designed as a kind of catchment area for rainwater washing down the hillside. The water is filtered through a layer of stone and sand, and drains down through the columns below to an underground cistern.

Beneath the square, steps guarded by a much-photographed mosaic dragon/lizard lead to the **Sala Hipóstila** (the Doric Temple, pictured). This forest of 86 stone columns – some leaning like mighty trees bent by the weight of time – was originally intended as a market, with its tiled ceilings and Catalan vaults. On the east side of the Sala Hipóstila are the lavender-scented **Jardins d'Àustria**.

Casa del Guarda

Just inside the (southern) Carrer d'Olot entrance, which sits below the Sala Hipóstila and is immediately recognisable by the two Hansel-and-Gretel gatehouses, stands the Casa del Guarda. This typically curvaceous former porter's home hosts a display on Gaudí's building methods and the history of the park. There are superb views from the top floor (and often long queues to get in).

Casa-Museu Gaudí

Near the park's eastern entrance lies the spired dusty-pink **Casa-Museu Gaudí** (Map p312; ☏93 208 04 14; https://sagradafamilia.org; Park Güell, Carretera del Carmel 23a; adult/child €5.50/free; ⏰9am-8pm Apr-Sep, 10am-6pm Oct-Mar; ☐V19, H6, D40, Bus Güell, Ⓜ Lesseps, Alfons X, Vallcarca), where Gaudí lived for almost the last 20 years of his life (1906–26). Furniture and ironwork he designed (including pieces that once lived in La Pedrera, Casa Batlló, Casa Calvet and Colonia Güell) are displayed along with other memorabilia, with information in Catalan, Spanish and English. The house, with its rippling tiled floors, was built in 1904 by Francesc Berenguer i Mestres as a prototype for the 60 or so houses originally planned here.

ACCESS, ADMISSION & TOURS

A Bus Güell shuttle (15 minutes; included in pre-bought tickets) was introduced in 2019, zipping visitors from Alfons X metro stop (Línia 4) to the park's eastern entrance on Carretera del Carmel. Arriving by this route, you'll enter the park's core from the top, at the Banc de Trencadís.

The park is extremely popular and an entrance fee is imposed on the central 'restricted' area containing most of its attractions. Access is limited to 400 people every half-hour – book ahead online. The rest of the park is free and doesn't require reservations. One-hour guided tours in multiple languages take place year-round and cost €12 (plus park admission); pre-book online. Private guided tours cost €45 per person (plus admission) and require at least two people.

TAKE A BREAK

Before or after making the trip up to the park, stop off at La Panxa del Bisbe (p178) in upper Gràcia for deliciously creative tapas and good wines.

SIGHTS

PARK GÜELL PARK, ARCHITECTURE
See p174.

ESGLÉSIA DE SANT JOAN CHURCH
Map p312 (☑93 237 73 58; Plaça de la Virreina; ⏰8am-12.45pm & 4-8pm, hours vary; Ⓜ Fontana, Joanic) Construction on this striking church began in 1878 and was completed in 1884. It was designed by Francesc Berenguer i Mestres, Gaudí's protégé, but it's believed by some that the interior chapel is the work of Gaudí himself (the jury is still out, however). What is certain is that Gaudí regularly worshipped here. Much of the church was damaged during the 1909 Setmana Tràgica and again in 1938, though the chapel survived unscathed, and rebuilding wrapped up in 1951.

MERCAT DE LA LLIBERTAT MARKET
Map p312 (☑93 217 09 95; www.facebook.com/elmercatdelallibertat; Plaça de la Llibertat 27; ⏰8.30am-8pm Mon-Fri, to 3pm Sat; Ⓜ Fontana, Ⓡ FGC Gràcia) Opened in 1888, the 'Market of Liberty' was covered in 1893 by Francesc Berenguer i Mestres (1866–1914), Gaudí's long-time assistant, in typically fizzy Modernista style, employing generous whirls of wrought iron. Despite a considerable facelift in 2009, it remains emblematic of Gràcia: full of life and fabulous fresh produce, and with tapas spots like El Tast de Joan Noi.

G EXPERIÈNCIA MUSEUM
Map p312 (☑93 285 44 40; www.gaudiexperiencia.com; Carrer de Larrard 41; adult/child €9/7.50; ⏰9.30am-7pm Apr-Sep, 11.30am-5pm Oct-Mar; Ⓜ Lesseps) A fun-filled Disney-style look at the life and work of Barcelona's favourite son Gaudí, just a stone's throw from Park Güell. There are models of Gaudí's buildings and whizz-bang interactive exhibits and touchscreens (in multiple languages), but the highlight is the stomach-churning 4D augmented reality experience in a tiny screening room with moving chairs (not recommended for children under six or anyone with back or heart issues).

TOP EXPERIENCE
ADMIRE THE TILEWORK AT CASA VICENS

A Unesco-listed masterpiece, this angular, turreted 1885-completed private house was Gaudí's inaugural commission, when the architect was aged just 30, created for stock and currency broker Manuel Vicens i Montaner. Tucked away west of Gràcia's main drag, the richly detailed facade is awash with ceramic colour and shape, including distinctive marigold tiling, and opened to the public in 2017. You're free to wander through in your own time, but one-hour guided tours (in Catalan, Spanish, English and French) bring the building to life.

As was frequently the case, Gaudí sought inspiration for Casa Vicens from the past, in this case the rich heritage of building in the Mudéjar-style brick, typical in parts of Spain reconquered from the Moors by the Christians (and created by Arabs and Berbers allowed to remain in Spain post-reconquest) – note the tinkling fountain overlooking the gardens, and the plant motifs in stucco and papier-mâché in the 1st-floor bedrooms.

The renovated building is accessible for visitors with limited mobility (including wheelchairs). Temporary exhibitions are mounted alongside permanent displays covering the building's history, and the attractive garden cafe is by the respected Hofmann culinary clan.

DON'T MISS

➜ Dazzling exterior tilework
➜ The Hofmann courtyard cafe
➜ Bedroom decor

PRACTICALITIES

➜ ☑93 547 59 80
➜ www.casavicens.org
➜ Carrer de les Carolines 20-26
➜ adult/child €16/12, guided tour per person additional €4
➜ ⏰10am-8pm Apr-Sep, 10am-3pm Mon, 10am-7pm Tue-Sun Oct-Mar, last admission 1hr 20min before closing
➜ Ⓜ Fontana

EATING

Spread across this busy quarter are all sorts of enticing dining options, from simple tapas bars to top-class seafooders. Gràcia is loaded with international cuisines, many of which are good value, while several classic Catalan taverns continue to have a strong local following. Devour Barcelona (☎944 58 10 22; www.devourbarcelonafoodtours.com; tours €79-119) runs excellent food tours around Gràcia.

LES TRES A LA CUINA · MEDITERRANEAN €

Map p312 (☎637 990078; www.lestresalacuina. com; Carrer de Sant Lluís 35; 2-/3-course menú €8.50/10; ◷1-4pm Mon-Fri; ☀; ☒Joanic) Fresh local ingredients are thrown into creative, health-focused, home-cooked mixes at this eco-aware deli-restaurant, with compostable tableware and daily-changing menus that might mean delicately dressed fig-and-goat's-cheese salad, mango-and-cucumber soup or spiced chickpeas with fragrant rice. It's mostly takeaway, with neighbours popping in, but there's a communal table if you want to eat in.

BAR BODEGA QUIMET · TAPAS €

Map p312 (☎93 218 41 89; Carrer de Vic 23; tapas €3-12; ◷10am-midnight Mon-Fri, noon-4pm & 6.30pm-late Sat & Sun; ☒Fontana) A relic from a bygone age, now lovingly managed by a pair of brothers, this is a delightfully atmospheric spot, with old bottles lining the walls, marble tables, tiled floors and a burnished wooden bar backed by house-vermouth barrels. The lengthy tapas list specialises in *conserves* (canned seafood), but also turns out cheese platters and fresh anchovies and octopus.

NOU CAN CODINA · CATALAN €

Map p312 (☎93 457 44 13; www.facebook.com/ cancodina; Carrer del Torrent de l'Olla 20; tapas €2-7, mains €8-12; ◷noon-11pm; ☒Diagonal) Founded back in 1931, this vintage bar (one of the oldest in Gràcia) has been spruced up into a buzzy all-day tapas stop. Order a house-made vermouth or Moritz beer and snack on bite-sized delights like spinach-and-goat's-cheese croquettes and *patates braves*, platters of cheeses from northern Spain and the Balearics, or heartier plates such as entrecôte with chips and *Padrón* peppers.

EL TAST DE JOAN NOI · TAPAS €

Map p312 (☎635 706429; www.facebook.com/ eltastdejoannoi; Plaça de la Llibertat 27, Mercat de la Llibertat; tapas €4-15; ◷9am-5pm Tue-Fri, to 3pm Sat, closed Aug; ☒Fontana, ☒FGC Gràcia) At this fuss-free tapas counter within the 19th-century Mercat de la Llibertat, chef Paco González, who trained at swish Gràcia seafood restaurant Botafumeiro (p179), works up gloriously fresh tapas using ingredients from the next-door fish stall. Dishes change with the day's catch, but favourites to try include tuna in walnut vinaigrette, grilled prawns or seafood 'meatballs'.

LA PEPITA · TAPAS €

Map p312 (☎93 238 48 93; www.lapepitabcn. com; Carrer de Còrsega 343; tapas €5-14; ◷1pm-midnight; ☀; ☒Diagonal) The walls are scrawled with messages from past diners at this busy-busy place with a long marble bar, great G&Ts and vermouth on tap. The lightly creative cooking takes in artichoke hummus, roast octopus, homemade desserts and the signature *pepitas* – open sandwiches topped with, perhaps, spinach and courgette or beef and mashed potato. Catalan wines and a €13 set lunch.

LAS DELICIAS · SPANISH €

Map p312 (☎93 429 22 02; www.barrestaurante delicias.com; Carrer de Mühlberg 1; tapas €5-13, mains €9-15; ◷10am-4pm & 7-10.30pm Tue-Thu, 10am-4pm & 8-11pm Fri & Sat; ☒24) This welcoming hillside restaurant in El Carmel makes a fine add-on to an afternoon exploring the nearby Park Güell or Bunkers del Carmel. There's a decent selection of tapas as well as heartier grilled meat and seafood dishes. Standouts include classics such as *pop a feira* (Galician-style octopus), cured Iberian ham and fluffy paella. It's 1km northeast of Park Güell.

CAFÈ CAMÈLIA · VEGETARIAN €

Map p312 (☎93 415 36 86; Carrer de Verdi 79; mains €8-10; ◷10am-5pm Mon, to midnight Tue-Sat; ☀; ☒Fontana) A peaceful spot for set lunches, cakes and El Magnífico (p114) coffee, this pastel-pink, check-floor vegetarian cafe has a world-wandering menu of well-executed dishes – pumpkin cannelloni, green tofu curry, watermelon gazpacho, hummus, or veggie brochettes with satay sauce. The three-course lunch menú (€10.50) is popular.

.IT ITALIAN €

Map p312 (☏93 461 92 71; www.facebook.com/puntoitsocial; Carrer del Topazi 26; mains €7-12; ⊙9.30am-midnight Mon-Fri, noon-4pm & 7pm-midnight Sat, closed 2 weeks Aug; ☎🖐; 🅼Fontana) Pizza bases at .IT ('Italian Tradition') are made from Caputo flour and fermented for 35 hours before being baked in a 400°C wood-fired oven. There's a creative range of antipasti (fried courgette flowers, meat-stuffed olives, aubergine 'meatballs'), plus rotating fresh pastas, homemade bread and a great-value one-dish lunch deal (€7 to €8). The huge salads are a meal in themselves.

★LA PUBILLA CATALAN €€

Map p312 (☏93 218 29 94; www.lapubilla.cat; Plaça de la Llibertat 23; mains €10-18; ⊙8.30am-5pm Mon, to 11.30pm Tue-Sat; 🅼Fontana) Hidden away behind a peachy-pink door by the Mercat de la Llibertat, La Pubilla special-ises in hearty *'esmorzars de forquilla'* ('fork breakfasts') beloved by market workers and local residents. There's also an outra-geously popular daily three-course *menú* (€16), which stars seasonal produce and Catalan dishes such as baked cod, or roast pork cheek with chickpeas; book ahead or arrive early.

BERBENA MEDITERRANEAN €€

Map p312 (☏93 801 59 87; www.berbenabcn.com; Carrer de Minerva 6; set 4-dish menu €16.50; ⊙7.30-11pm Mon & Sat, 1-3.30pm & 7.30-11pm Tue-Fri; 🖐; 🅼Diagonal) 🍃 Tucked away off busy Diagonal, Berbena special-ises in ambitiously prepared, beautifully presented seasonal dishes from the open-plan kitchen. The daily-changing *menú* starts with home-baked bread, accom-panied by a main such as zestily dressed burrata with pumpkin and sides of tortilla or chilled green-vegetable soup. It's a tiny, minimalist-modern space, with seats in the window and coffee from neighbouring roaster SlowMov (p180).

EXTRA BAR TAPAS €€

Map p312 (☏93 218 29 94; www.lapubilla.cat; Carrer Torrent de l'Olla 79; raciones €5-13; ⊙6.30pm-midnight Tue-Thu, to 1am Fri, noon-3.30pm & 7.30pm-1am Sat; 🅼) At this lively pint-sized tapas bar, the team behind much-loved La Pubilla serves simple yet highly memora-ble local-rooted *platillos* (sharing plates) alongside a carefully curated selection of Spanish wines by the glass. Seasonal flavours and fresh local ingredients fuel weekly-changing menus with a few Asian influences, which might feature lime-laced squid tacos, terrific croquettes or made-to-order omelettes.

LA PANXA DEL BISBE TAPAS €€

Map p312 (☏93 313 70 49; Carrer del Torrent de les Flors 158; tapas €9-14, tasting menus €30-38; ⊙1.30-3.30pm & 8.30pm-midnight Tue-Sat; ☎🖐; 🅼Joanic) With its local buzz and art-fully minimalist interior, the 'Bishop's Bel-ly' is a pleasant surprise in upper Gràcia, delivering creative tapas that earn high praise from both *barcelonins* and visitors. Feast on provolone-stuffed courgette flow-ers, grilled octopus with capers and celery, or Iberian ham with melon and mint. The wine list includes excellent picks from Cata-lonia and elsewhere in Spain.

LLURITU SEAFOOD €€

Map p312 (☏93 855 38 66; www.lluritu.com; Carrer del Torrent de les Flors 71; dishes €5-15; ⊙1-4pm & 7.30-8.30pm Wed & Thu, to 12.30am Fri & Sat, noon-11.30pm Sun; 🅼Joanic) From salted sardines to king prawns and razor clams, perfectly grilled, unadorned bites fresh from the ocean are the order of the day at this self-styled *desenfadada* (casual) seafood restaurant, decorated with tile-patterned floors and a marble bar. Prized ingredients for the short, select menu are sourced from all along the Spanish coast but especially Catalonia.

LES FILLES CAFE €€

Map p312 (☏93 787 99 69; www.lesfillesbarcelona.com; Carrer de Minerva 2; mains €12-17; ⊙9am-11pm Mon-Fri, from 10am Sat & Sun; 🖐; 🅼Diagonal) 🍃 Both gorgeous design space and buzzing garden cafe-restaurant, Les Filles is adorned with pine-green booths, vases of fresh flowers and jazzy cushions and rugs. Rooted in fresh, seasonal fla-vours and organic ingredients, dishes take a health-focused turn, with options like wild-salmon pasta, quinoa bowls, creative breakfasts and cold-press juices from the owners' Loup & Filles line.

PEPA TOMATE TAPAS €€

Map p312 (☏93 210 46 98; www.pepatomategrup.com; Plaça de la Revolució de Setembre de 1868 17; tapas €6-12; ⊙9am-midnight Mon-Fri, from 10am Sat, from 11am Sun; 🚰; 🅼Fontana) Dressed in jolly reds, this casual tapas spot with a few coveted terrace tables keeps busy at all hours. Fresh produce from the local mar-

BUNKERS DEL CARMEL

For magnificent 360-degree Barcelona views, head to the El Carmel neighbourhood (under a kilometre east of Park Güell) and up the Turó de la Rovira hill to the **Bunkers del Carmel** (Turó de la Rovira; Map p312; ☑93 256 21 22; https://ajuntament.barcelona.cat; Carrer de Marià Labèrnia; ⊘museum 10am-2pm Wed, to 3pm Sat & Sun; ⬚V19, 22, 24) `FREE` viewpoint. Above the weeds and dusty hillside, you'll find old concrete firing platforms where students and visitors gather, especially at sunset. The platforms were part of anti-aircraft battery during the Spanish Civil War; postwar, it was a shanty town until the early 1990s, and it has lain abandoned since then.

There's a small information centre/museum inside the bunkers themselves; placards give an overview of what once stood here. Buses run here from central Barcelona; from the nearest bus stop in El Carmel, it's a 10-minute (600m) walk east to the viewpoint.

ket is front and centre on the wide-ranging menu, with elegantly presented dishes such as fried green tomatoes, baked aubergine with goat's cheese, grilled asparagus dressed with burrata and almonds, or *patates braves* with a kick.

BAR BUT
TAPAS €€

Map p312 (☑93 360 71 28; http://barbut.es; Carrer de Bonavista 8; platillos €7-12, mains €11-14; ⊘9am-late Mon-Fri, from 10am Sat & Sun; ⓂDiagonal) Upcycled furniture blends with sprinkled plants and whitewashed-brick walls at this enticing neighbourhood cafe-restaurant, with its distinctive open-window seating and well-prepared slow-cooked *platillos* (sharing plates), including truffled Brie, anchovies from L'Escala and cured Iberian ham. There's also a popular three-course lunch *menú* for €13.50.

DIÀNIA
VALENCIAN €€

Map p312 (☑93 707 66 72; Carrer de Mozart 20; mains €10-15; ⊘noon-midnight Tue-Sat, to 5pm Sun; ⓂDiagonal) Culinary-minded twins Roger and Jordi Mascarell bring a taste of central Valencia to this cosy, uncluttered tavern decked out with old-fashioned chairs and marble tables in the heart of Gràcia. The traditional-style menu revolves around good-value paellas (including a veggie-friendly option), but also does *fideuà* (a Catalan dish similar to paella) and *arròs a banda* (rice cooked in fish broth). Book ahead for weekends.

CHIVUO'S
BURGERS €€

Map p312 (☑93 218 51 34; www.chivuos.com; Carrer del Torrent de l'Olla 175; burgers €9-14; ⊘1pm-midnight; ⓂFontana) Burgers and craft beers make a fine pair at this buzzing den. A mostly local crowd comes for huge burgers (including a mushroom veggie and a Philly cheese steak) with house-made sauces – best ordered with fluffy, golden-fried chips. Mostly Catalan and Spanish brews, including excellent offerings from Barcelona-based Catalan Brewery, Napar and Garage Beer.

CAFÉ GODOT
INTERNATIONAL €€

Map p312 (☑93 368 20 36; www.cafegodot.com; Carrer de Sant Domènec 19; mains €9-15; ⊘10am-1am Mon-Fri, 11am-2am Sat & Sun; ⓢ; ⓂFontana) Godot is a tasteful, relaxing bistro-style space of exposed stone, timber, mirrors and tiles, with arched windows overlooking the street. It has an extensive menu: from white-wine-steamed mussels and slow-cooked cod to aubergine-and-onion-stuffed ravioli. Weekend brunch features avocado toast, fluffy pancakes and build-your-own omelettes, with *cava* and cocktails.

CAL BOTER
CATALAN €€

Map p312 (☑93 458 84 62; www.facebook.com/restaurantcalboter; Carrer de Tordera 62; mains €8-15; ⊘9am-noon & 1-4pm Mon-Wed, 9am-noon, 1-4pm & 8-11pm Thu, 9am-noon, 1-4pm & 9pm-midnight Fri & Sat; ⓂJoanic) Families and high-spirited groups of pals are drawn to this classic for *cargols a la llauna* (sautéed snails), *botifarra* (Catalan sausage) with beans, roast lamb and other Catalan specialities, rustled up amid marble tables and green-washed doors. The €12.50 three-course *menú* is good value, and you might also stumble across curious *mar i muntanya* (sea and mountain) combinations such as pig trotters with prawns.

BOTAFUMEIRO
SEAFOOD €€€

Map p312 (☑93 218 42 30, Whatsapp 662 669337; www.botafumeiro.es; Carrer Gran de Gràcia 81; mains €22-55; ⊘noon-1am; ⓂFontana) A wonderfully smart world of Galician seafood,

Botafumeiro has long been a magnet for VIPs visiting Barcelona. It's a good place to try *percebes* (goose barnacles), often considered the ultimate fruit-of-the-sea delicacy. You can bring the price down by sharing a marine *mitges racions* (large tapas plates), followed by mains like baked spider crab, shellfish paella or charcoal-grilled wild hake.

ROIG ROBÍ
CATALAN €€€

Map p312 (☑93 218 92 22; www.roigrobi.com; Carrer de Sèneca 20; mains €21-36; ⏱1.30-4pm & 8.30-11.30pm Mon-Fri, 8.30-11.30pm Sat, closed 2 weeks Aug; Ⓜ Diagonal) ⏺ At this long-running altar to refined traditional cooking, the seasonally changing menu serves as a showcase for beautifully presented creations with local and organic ingredients. Dishes may include sautéed wild mushrooms to start, followed by outstanding seafood rice dishes, salt-baked market-fresh fish or slow-roasted Pyrenees lamb. Book ahead for a table on the vine-draped back patio.

CON GRACIA
FUSION €€€

Map p312 (☑93 238 02 01; www.congracia.es; Carrer de Martínez de la Rosa 8; tasting menus €65, with wine €95; ⏱7-11pm Tue-Sat; Ⓜ Diagonal) This teeny hideaway (seating about 20 in total) is a hive of originality, producing delicately balanced, seasonally inspired Mediterranean cuisine with Asian touches. On offer is a regularly changing surprise tasting menu or a set 'traditional' one (both six courses), with dishes such as pasta stuffed with pumpkin and cod, or wild-duck magret. Book ahead.

IPAR-TXOKO
BASQUE €€€

Map p312 (☑93 218 19 54; www.ipartxoko.es; Carrer de Mozart 22; mains €20-25; ⏱1.15-3.30pm & 9-10.45pm Tue-Sat, 1.15-3.30pm Sun, closed Aug; Ⓜ Diagonal) Inside this Basque restaurant the atmosphere is warm and traditional. Hefty wooden beams hold up the vaulted ceiling, and the bar serves terrific tapas. Traditional cooking from northern Spain includes a massive grilled *txuleta* (T-bone steak), rich squid in its own ink and curiosities like *kokotxes de lluç* (grilled heart-shaped hake jowls).

The wine list is daunting, but kind-hearted owner Miguel is on hand to explain everything – in English, too.

DRINKING & NIGHTLIFE

★BOBBY GIN
COCKTAIL BAR

Map p312 (☑93 368 18 92; www.bobbygin.com; Carrer de Francisco Giner 47; ⏱5pm-2am Sun-Thu, to 3am Fri & Sat; 🛜; Ⓜ Diagonal) With over 80 varieties, this whitewashed stone-walled bar is a haven for gin lovers, and arguably Barcelona's top spot for a perfectly mixed, artfully garnished, goblet-sized G&T. Try an infusion-based concoction (€10 to €12), such as citrus-infused Nordés, or a cocktail like the L'Aperitiu Modernista, with cardamom bitters and thistle liqueur.

EL CICLISTA
COCKTAIL BAR

Map p312 (☑93 368 53 02; www.elciclistabar. com; Carrer de Mozart 18; ⏱7.30pm-2am Mon-Thu, to 3am Fri & Sat; Ⓜ Diagonal) As the name suggests, this elegant little cocktail bar is Barcelona's original cycle-themed boozy hang-out – expect bike-wheel chandeliers and tables, handlebar pieces, and bicycle frames on the walls. Among the list of classic cocktails is an excellent selection of gin and tonics, as well as plenty of flavoured mojitos. There's often live music on Thursdays or Fridays.

SLOWMOV
COFFEE

Map p312 (☑93 667 27 15; www.slowmov.com; Carrer de Luis Antúnez 18; ⏱8.30am-3pm Tue-Fri, 10am-2pm Sat; 🛜; Ⓜ Diagonal) ⏺ SlowMov founders Carmen and François work directly with coffee producers to responsibly source their seasonal, single-origin beans, which are roasted on-site at this light-flooded cafe with original floral-tiled floors, shared tables and local artwork. Laptop workers gather for flat whites (€2.50), coffee events are organised, and organic wines, coffees, oils and jams line the shelves.

ELEPHANTA
COCKTAIL BAR

Map p312 (☑93 237 69 06; www.elephanta.cat; Carrer del Torrent d'En Vidalet 37; ⏱6pm-1.30am Mon-Thu, to 3am Fri & Sat, to 12.30am Sun; 🛜; Ⓜ Joanic) Off Gràcia's main drag, this petite cocktail bar has an old-fashioned feel, with plush green banquettes, art-lined walls and a five-seat bar with vintage stools. Gin (€8 to €12) is the drink of choice, with citrusy, botanical and classic dry options, including a selection of Catalan gins. Snacks include hummus, *empanades* and *torrades* (toast with toppings; €3 to €5).

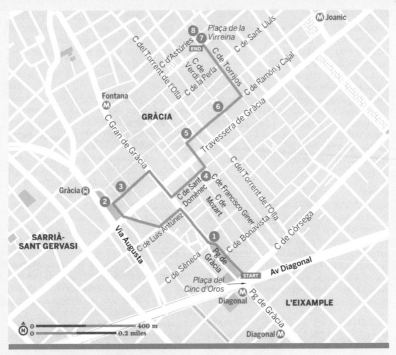

Neighbourhood Walk
Gràcia's Village Squares

START DIAGONAL METRO STATION
END PLAÇA DE LA VIRREINA
LENGTH 2KM; 50 MINUTES

From Diagonal metro station, head through Passeig de Gràcia and up Carrer Gran de Gràcia into Gràcia proper, where you'll find a grand Modernista edifice now turned hotel, **1 Casa Fuster** (p241), designed by Domènech i Montaner.

A little northwest, the **2 Plaça de Gal·la Placídia** (Map p312, A6; ℝFGC Gràcia) recalls the brief sojourn of the Roman empress-to-be Galla Placidia, captive and wife of the Visigothic chief Athaulf in the 5th century.

Just northeast, **3 Plaça de la Llibertat** (Map p312, A5; ℝFGC Gràcia) is home to a bustling Modernista produce market, along with a couple of great little restaurants. The market was designed by Gaudí's protégé, Francesc Berenguer, who was busy in this part of town despite never having been awarded a diploma as an architect.

Meandering east, you'll find the popular **4 Plaça de la Vila de Gràcia** (Map p312, B5; ℝFontana, Diagonal, ℝFGC Gràcia), which was until 2009 named after the mayor under whom Gràcia was absorbed by Barcelona, Francesc Rius i Taulet. It's fronted by the local town hall (designed by Berenguer), and at its heart stands the 1862 Torre del Rellotge (Clock Tower), long a symbol of Republican agitation.

Just north lies the rowdiest of Gràcia's squares, **5 Plaça del Sol** (Map p312, B5; ℝFontana), where bars and restaurants come to life on long summer nights. The square was the scene of summary executions after an uprising in 1870, and, during the civil war, an air-raid shelter was installed.

Nearby, the busy, elongated **6 Plaça de la Revolució de Setembre de 1868** (Map p312, C4; ℝFontana, Joanic) commemorates the toppling of Queen Isabel II, a cause of much celebration in this working-class stronghold.

Pleasant terraces adorn the leafy, pedestrianised **7 Plaça de la Virreina** (Map p312, B3), presided over by the 19th-century **8 Església de Sant Joan** (p176).

EL RABIPELAO
COCKTAIL BAR

Map p312 (☑93 182 50 35; www.elrabipelao.com; Carrer del Torrent d'En Vidalet 22; ☺7pm-1.30am Mon-Thu, to 3am Fri & Sat, 1-4.30pm & 7pm-1.30am Sun; ⓂJoanic) With DJs spinning salsa beats, occasional live music and a covered back patio, El Rabi is a celebratory space. Silent films play, red-washed walls are decorated with vintage photos, and there's a colourful mural above the bar. Gins, Caribbean rums and tropical cocktails (€6 to €10) like mojitos and caipirinhas pair with Venezuelan snacks such as *arepas* (filled cornbread patties).

ONNA
COFFEE

Map p312 (☑93 269 48 70; http://onnacoffee.com; Carrer de Santa Teresa 1; ☺9am-7pm Wed-Mon; ⓂDiagonal) Cold brews, flat whites and even your classic *cafè amb llet* (€1.50 to €4) are artfully crafted with beans from inland Costa Rica at laid-back Onna. Inside, marble-top tables mingle with black-and-white murals. Choose from Aeropress, Chemex and other innovative caffeine creations.

VIBLIOTECA
WINE BAR

Map p312 (☑93 284 42 02; www.viblioteca.com; Carrer de Vallfogona 12; ☺7pm-midnight; ⓂFontana) A glass cabinet piled high with ripe cheese (over 50 varieties), sourced from small-scale European producers, entices you into this small, white, cleverly designed contemporary space. The real speciality at Viblioteca, however, is wine, and you can choose from 150 mostly local labels, many of them available by the glass.

OLD FASHIONED
COCKTAIL BAR

Map p312 (☑93 368 52 77; www.facebook.com/oldfashionedbcn; Carrer de Santa Teresa 1; ☺5pm-2am Mon & Sun, noon-2am Tue-Thu, noon-3am Fri, 5pm-3am Sat; ⓂDiagonal) At this moody, shoebox-sized Gràcia hang-out, creative mixologists smartly outfitted in braces rustle up wildly original reinventions of the classic old fashioned, as well as a never-ending line-up of G&Ts.

Sister cocktail bar Hemingway (p159) in L'Eixample is also a huge hit.

SYRA COFFEE
COFFEE

Map p312 (http://syra.coffee; Carrer de la Mare de Déu dels Desamparats 8; ☺8am-7pm Mon-Fri, from 9am Sat, from 10am Sun; ⓂJoanic) ✐ A loyal crowd of regulars swings by teensy check-floored Syra for takeaway coffees (€2 to €3), accompanied by delicate Moroccan pastries, cookies and doughnuts. Its coffees are brewed with seasonal, single-origin, sustainably produced beans roasted at its shop just up the street. Syra also has a Poblenou branch (p134).

LA VERMU
BAR

Map p312 (☑695 925012; www.facebook.com/lavermubcn; Carrer de Sant Domènec 15; ☺6.30pm-midnight Mon-Thu, 12.30pm-12.30am Fri-Sun; ⓇFGC Gràcia) House-made *negre* (black) and *blanc* (white) vermouth (€2 to €3), served with a slice of orange and an olive, is the speciality of this stylish neighbourhood spot. The airy space with exposed timber beams, red trim and industrial lighting centres on a marble bar. Vermouth aside, it also has a small, stellar wine list and smartly presented tapas.

LA NENA
CAFE

Map p312 (☑93 285 14 76; https://la-nena-chocolate-cafe.business.site; Carrer de Ramón y Cajal 36; ☺8.30am-10.30pm Mon-Fri, from 9am Sat & from 9.30am Sun; 👶; ⓂFontana) At this delightfully chaotic cafe, indulge in cups of *suïssos* (rich hot chocolate) served with heavy homemade whipped cream and *melindros* (spongy sweet biscuits), desserts, cakes and a few savoury dishes (including crêpes). The place is filled with old-fashioned photos, toys and board games.

LA VERMUTERIA DEL TANO
BAR

Map p312 (☑93 213 10 58; www.facebook.com/VermuteriaTano; Carrer de Joan Blanques 17; ☺9am-9pm Tue-Fri, noon-4pm Sat & Sun; ⓂJoanic) Scarcely changed in decades, with barrels on the walls, old fridges with wooden doors, vintage clocks and marble-topped tables, this corner vermouth bar is a favourite local gathering point. Its house-speciality Perucchi is served traditionally with a glass of carbonated water. Tapas are also classic: most dishes use ingredients from tins (anchovies, smoked clams, cockles, pickled octopus). Cash only!

EL SABOR
BAR

Map p312 (☑674 988863; www.facebook.com/elsaboracuba; Carrer de Francisco Giner 32; ☺10pm-3am; ⓂDiagonal) This home of *ron y son* (rum and sound) has been going since 1992. A mixed crowd of Cubans and fans of the Caribbean island come to drink mojitos and shake their stuff in this diminutive, good-humoured locale. Stop by on Wednesdays at 9pm for a free two-hour salsa lesson.

BAR CANIGÓ   BAR

Map p312 (✆93 213 30 49; www.barcanigo.com; Carrer de Verdi 2; ⏰10am-2am Mon-Fri, from 8pm Sat; Ⓜ Fontana) Now run by the third generation of owners, this corner bar overlooking Plaça de la Revolució de Setembre de 1868 is an animated spot to sip a house vermouth or an Estrella beer around rickety marble-top tables, as people have done here since 1922. Earlier on, it's ideal for coffee paired with a *bikini* (toasted cheese-and-ham sandwich).

CHÂTELET   COCKTAIL BAR

Map p312 (✆93 284 95 90; Carrer de Torrijos 54; ⏰6pm-2.30am Mon-Thu, to 3am Fri, noon-3am Sat, to 2.30am Sun; Ⓜ Joanic) A popular meeting point in the 'hood, Chatelet has big windows for watching the passing people parade and a buzzing, art-filled interior with decorative surf boards that sees a wide cross-section of Gràcia society. Blues and old-school American soul play in the background. The cocktails (from €4) are excellent, and there's brunch on weekends.

RAÏM   BAR

Map p312 (Carrer del Progrés 48; ⏰8pm-2am Tue-Thu, to 3am Fri & Sat; Ⓜ Diagonal) Open for over a century, Raïm is alive with black-and-white photos and paraphernalia of Cubans and Cuba. It's like being in a bar in Old Havana, with weathered wooden chairs around marble tables, old fashioned clocks, and wood-framed mirrors hanging on the walls. It pulls in a friendly, garrulous crowd for first-rate mojitos, excellent rums and live music.

14 DE LA ROSA   BAR

Map p312 (www.14delarosa.com; Carrer Martínez de la Rosa 14; ⏰10am-1am Mon-Thu, to 2am Fri, to midnight Sat; Ⓜ Diagonal) At this fun, smart cocktail bar with vintage style (tiled floors, marble bar), wines are all natural and from Catalonia, while subtly creative cocktails (€5 to €10) are crafted by a former mixologist from London's Chiltern Firehouse. A few Andalucian sherries and, in the mornings, good strong espresso round things out.

NOU CANDANCHÚ   BAR

Map p312 (✆93 237 73 62; Plaça de la Vila de Gràcia 9; ⏰9am-2am Sun-Thu, to 3am Fri & Sat; Ⓜ Fontana) One of the liveliest spots on Plaça de la Vila de Gràcia, long-time favourite Nou Candanchú is good for both breakfast coffee and *torrades* (topped toast), and drinks and tapas such as pumpkin tortilla later on. *Barcelonins* flock to its sunny terrace.

 # ENTERTAINMENT

LA MURIEL   GALLERY

Map p312 (Carrer de Verntallat 30; ⏰9am-11pm Wed & Thu, to midnight Fri, noon-midnight Sat, to 11pm Sun; Ⓜ Lesseps) **FREE** Set in a stylishly converted garage, this forward-thinking multipurpose space encompasses a cultural centre, a restaurant and an events area, hosting stand-up comedy, changing exhibitions, live music on weekends and even podcast-recording sessions.

SODA ACÚSTIC   LIVE MUSIC

Map p312 (✆93 016 55 90; www.soda.cat; Carrer de les Guilleries 6; tickets free-€5; ⏰8.30pm-2.30am Wed, Thu & Sun, 9pm-3am Fri & Sat; Ⓜ Fontana) One of Gràcia's most innovative performance spaces, this low-lit modern venue stages an eclectic line-up of bands, artists and jams: jazz, world music, Balkan swing, Latin rhythms and plenty of experimental, not-easily-classifiable musicians all receive their due.

TEATRENEU   THEATRE

Map p312 (✆93 285 37 12; www.teatreneu.com; Carrer de Terol 26; Ⓜ Joanic) This lively theatre experiments with all sorts of material, from monologues to social comedy, and also screens films. Aside from the main theatre, two cafe-style spaces serve as intimate stage settings for small-scale productions. Most performances are in Catalan or Spanish.

CINES VERDI   CINEMA

Map p312 (✆93 238 79 90; www.cines-verdi.com; Carrer de Verdi 32; tickets from €8; Ⓜ Fontana) A neighbourhood icon in the heart of Gràcia, this five-screen cinema shows art-house and blockbuster films in their original language, as well as films in Catalan and Spanish. It's close to lots of local restaurants and bars for pre- and post-film fun.

 # SHOPPING

★ COLMILLO DE MORSA   FASHION & ACCESSORIES

Map p312 (www.colmillodemorsa.com; Carrer de Vic 15; ⏰11am-2.30pm & 4.30-7pm Mon-Fri, 11am-2.30pm Sat; ®FGC Gràcia) Javier Blanco and Elisabet Vallecillo, who have made waves at Madrid's Cibeles Fashion Week, showcase their Barcelona-made women's designs at this flagship boutique-workshop filled with delicate dresses, jumpsuits and shirts in soothing tones. Fabrics are sustainably produced using nontoxic dyes, and they've also opened the floor to other up-and-coming local labels.

CASA ATLÂNTICA
CERAMICS

Map p312 (☑93 382 18 88; www.casaatlantica. es; Carrer de la Llibertat 7; ⊗noon-8.30pm Mon-Sat; ⓂDiagonal) 🍃 The delicate basketry and beautiful custom-designed bowls, mugs, plant pots, vases and other ceramics dotting this charming studio-boutique are created by Galician artisans Belén and Lester, who collaborate with small-scale, family-owned village workshops across Galicia and Portugal to keep traditional crafts alive. Their work graces popular venues around town.

FAMILY BEER
DRINKS

Map p312 (☑93 219 29 88; www.family-beer.com; Carrer de Joan Blanques 55; ⊗5-8.30pm Mon, 10am-2pm & 5-8pm Tue-Sat; ⓂJoanic) Around 200 varieties of local and international craft beers and ciders pack out the fridges at Peio and Sílvia's store. It also has brewing kits and books, runs regular brewing workshops (three hours €45) and hosts free demonstrations of cheese-making and cookery using beer, as well as 'meet the brewer' tastings.

FROMAGERIE CAN LUC
CHEESE

Map p312 (☑93 007 47 83; www.canluc.es; Carrer de Berga 4; ⊗5-9pm Mon, 10am-2.30pm & 5-8.30pm Tue-Sat; ☒FGC Gràcia) At any given time, this inviting shop stocks 150 varieties of European cheese. Catalan favourites are the speciality, though you'll also spot a selection from France, Italy, the Netherlands, Switzerland and Britain. Welcoming, expert staff provide guidance. Wines, condiments, crackers and cheese knives are available too, along with gourmet picnic hampers (€25 to €100) and tasting sets.

AMALIA VERMELL
JEWELLERY

Map p312 (☑655 754008; www.amaliavermell. com; Carrer del Planeta 11; ⊗5-9pm Mon-Thu, 10.30am-2.30pm & 5-9pm Fri & Sat, hours vary; ⓂFontana) Striking geometric jewellery made from high-quality materials such as sterling silver is handcrafted right here in the atelier by designer-owner Pamela Masferrer, who also offers long-term jewellery-making workshops. Browse for pendants, necklaces, bracelets and rings, as well as vibrant homeware pieces and dresses by Barcelona brands.

BODEGA BONAVISTA
WINE

Map p312 (☑93 218 81 99; www.facebook.com/ bodegabonavistabcn; Carrer de Bonavista 10; ⊗10am-2.30pm & 5-9pm Mon-Fri, noon-3pm & 6-9pm Sat; ⓂFontana) An excellent little neighbourhood bodega, Bonavista endeavours to seek out great wines at reasonable prices. The stock is mostly from Catalonia and elsewhere in Spain, but there's also a well-chosen French selection. The Bonavista also doubles as a deli, with some especially good cheeses. You can sample wines by the glass, along with cheeses and charcuterie, at the in-store tables.

HIBERNIAN
BOOKS

Map p312 (☑93 217 47 96; www.hibernianbooks. com; Carrer de Montseny 17; ⊗4-8.30pm Mon, 10.30am-8.30pm Tue-Sat; ⓂFontana) Barcelona's biggest secondhand English bookshop stocks thousands of titles covering all sorts of subjects, from cookery to children's classics. There's a smaller collection of new books in English, too.

AMAPOLA
VEGAN SHOP
FASHION & ACCESSORIES

Map p312 (☑93 010 62 73; www.amapolavegan shop.com; Travessera de Gràcia 129; ⊗5-8.30pm Mon, 10am-2pm & 5-8.30pm Tue-Sat; ⓂFontana) 🍃 A shop with a heart of gold, Amapola proves that you need not toss your ethics aside to get stylish clothing and accessories. You'll find sleek leather alternatives for wallets, handbags, messenger bags, belts and boots by Matt & Nat, and elegant vegan scarves by Barts. Pieces are hand-picked by owner Raquel and many are locally made.

BE
GIFTS & SOUVENIRS

Map p312 (☑93 218 89 49; www.bethestore.com; Carrer de Bonavista 7; ⊗10am-9pm Mon-Fri, from 10.30am Sat; ⓂDiagonal) With several branches around town, Be is a fun place to browse for clothes, accessories and all kinds of trinkets. You're likely to find Fjällräven Kånken backpacks, leather handbags, yoga mats, stylish Happy Socks, portable record players, cookery books, sneakers (Vans, Pumas, old-school Nikes) and gadgets (including richly hued Pantone micro speakers and Polaroid digital cameras).

SURCO
MUSIC

Map p312 (☑93 218 34 39; www.facebook.com/ surcobcn; Travessera de Gràcia 144; ⊗10.30am-2pm & 5.30-9pm Mon-Sat; ⓂFontana) Going strong since the 1970s, Surco is an obligatory stop for music lovers, especially fans of vinyl. You'll find loads of new and used records and CDs here, with a mix that includes Tom Waits, Mishima (a Catalan indie pop band), Calexico and more.

REKUP & CO
HOMEWARES

Map p312 (☑694 472297; www.rekupandco.com; Carrer de Verdi 63; ⊙11am-2pm & 5-9pm Tue-Sat; ⓂFontana) ✦ Self-trained French designer Emmanuel Wagnon recasts recycled timbers and metals to create individual works of art that are functional too: chairs, tables, shelves, mirrors and lamps. International shipping can be arranged.

LADY LOQUITA
FASHION & ACCESSORIES

Map p312 (☑93 217 82 92; www.ladyloquita. com; Travessera de Gràcia 126; ⊙11am-2pm & 5-8.30pm Mon-Sat; ⓂFontana) ✦ At this chic little shop you'll find locally made, organic-cotton summer dresses and tops by Barcelona's own Tiralahilacha (including for kids), evening wear by Japamala and handmade jewellery by Barcelona design label Klimbim. There are also whimsical odds and ends, like dinner plates with dog-people portraits and digital prints on wood by About Paola.

FORN FORTINO
FOOD

Map p312 (☑93 237 38 73; http://fornfortino. com; Travessera de Gràcia 126; ⊙7.30am-9pm Mon-Fri, from 8am Sat; ⓂFontana) ✦ In business since the 1920s, this family-run operation turns out delectable freshly baked breads and pastries using traditional artisan techniques, locally sourced organic flour and, often, wheat alternatives.

PICNIC
FASHION & ACCESSORIES

Map p312 (☑93 016 69 53; www.facebook.com/ picnicstorebcn; Carrer de Verdi 17; ⊙11am-9pm Mon-Fri, 11am-2.30pm & 5-9pm Sat; ⓂFontana) This tiny, beautifully curated concept store has many temptations: stylish unisex sneakers by Spanish brand Barqet, jazzy tops from Basque label Loreak Mendian and Barcelona-born Behulah, and locally made Ölend backpacks. Other finds include animal-print ceramics for the home, small-scale art prints and fashion mags.

MA.LU.MA
FASHION & ACCESSORIES

Map p312 (☑93 189 10 22; www.facebook.com/ malumashop; Carrer de Santa Tecla 2; ⊙11am-2pm & 5-8pm Mon-Sat; ⓂDiagonal) Small Spanish women's fashion labels such as Loreak Mendian and Tiralahilacha are the thing at Ma.lu.ma, an intimate boutique with a couple of branches around town. Pick from breezy summer dresses, bold jackets, floppy straw hats and wow-factor handbags.

NOSTÀLGIC
PHOTOGRAPHY

Map p312 (☑93 368 57 57; www.nostalgic.es; Carrer de Goya 18; ⊙10.30am-2pm & 5-8pm Mon-Fri, 11am-2.30pm Sat; ⓂFontana) In a calming space with exposed-brick walls and wooden furniture, Nostàlgic specialises in all kinds of modern and vintage photography equipment, from camera bags and tripods for the digital snappers to rolls of film and quirky Lomo cameras. There's also a decent collection of photography books.

MERCAT DE L'ABACERIA CENTRAL
MARKET

Map p310 (☑93 213 62 86; www.mercatabaceria. cat; Passeig de Sant Joan 168; ⊙8am-2.30pm & 5-8.30pm Mon-Thu, to 8.30pm Fri, to 3pm Sat; ⓂJoanic) Having relocated in 2019 to Passeig de Sant Joan while its original 1892 iron-and-brick structure (on Travessera de Gràcia) undergoes major restoration works, this is an atmospheric place to browse for fresh produce, cheeses, bakery items and more, or grab a quick bite on the cheap.

SPORTS & ACTIVITIES

CASA PROTEA
ARTS & CRAFTS

Map p312 (☑93 002 28 64; www.casaprotea.com; Carrer de Ramón y Cajal 124; workshops €50-60; ⊙11.30am-2.30pm & 5-8.30pm Tue-Sat; ⓂJoanic) Succulents, cacti and terracotta pots overflow from this chic little studio, where self-styled plant collectors Pancho and Jesús run creative, floral-focused small-group workshops that might range from ceramics and plant printing to tea ceremonies and making natural cosmetics. Check schedules online.

Montjuïc, Poble Sec & Sant Antoni

MONTJUÏC | SANT ANTONI | POBLE SEC

Neighbourhood Top Five

1 **Museu Nacional d'Art de Catalunya (MNAC)** (p189) Dedicating a day to the world's most important collection of early-medieval art in the Romanesque halls, followed by a masterpiece-filled stroll through six centuries of Catalan art.

2 **Fundació Joan Miró** (p188) Viewing brilliant works from an art-world giants inside the light-filled galleries designed by Josep Lluís Sert.

3 **Sant Antoni stroll** (p195) Wandering between vintage-chic coffee shops, stylish boutiques, creative tapas bars and a reimagined 19th-century market in this revitalised neighbourhood.

4 **CaixaForum** (p191) Catching a ground-breaking art exhibition in a Modernista former factory.

5 **Cable-car views** (p192) Gazing out over the sea and city on a high-flying cable-car ride between Barceloneta and Montjuïc.

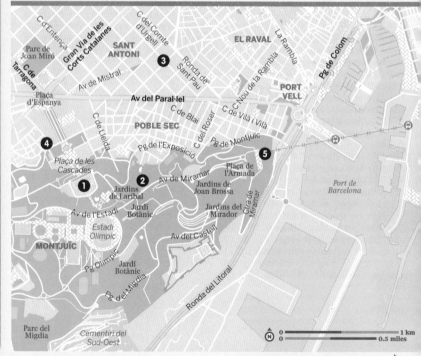

For more detail of this area see Map p314

Explore Montjuïc, Poble Sec & Sant Antoni

The culture-packed hill of Montjuïc hosts some outstanding art institutions and a formidable castle (p191), as well as the bulk of the installations left over from the 1992 Olympic games. Throw in various parks and gardens and you have the makings of an extremely full couple of days. Visit at night to check out the spectacle of the Font Màgica (p191), theatres and nightclubs.

You can approach Montjuïc from Plaça d'Espanya on foot and take a series of escalators from the west side of the Palau Nacional up to Avinguda de l'Estadi. Alternatively, you can get a cable car (p270) across from Barceloneta and/or up to the Castell de Montjuïc. Otherwise, explore on foot, along the numerous forest paths that zigzag through gardens.

The tree-lined streets of of working-class Poble Sec spread down the north face of Montjuïc, revealing some of Barcelona's most creative bars and restaurants. Cross busy Avinguda del Paral·lel to reach Sant Antoni, a formerly humdrum neighbourhood that's become the epicentre of Barcelona hipsterdom, particularly along Carrer del Parlament.

Local Life

→ **Hang-outs** Lined with tapas bars, most with outdoor seating on the pedestrian lane, Carrer de Blai (p196) draws a student crowd.

→ **Nightlife** Join the dance party at iconic Sala Apolo (p202), catch a concert at BARTS (p202) or see an avant-garde performance at Hiroshima (p202).

→ **Cafe culture** Head to Carrer del Parlament (and neighbouring streets) in Sant Antoni for fab drinking and dining openings.

Getting There & Away

→ **Metro** Montjuïc's closest metro stops are Espanya, Poble Sec and Paral·lel; Sant Antoni has its own metro stop.

→ **Bus** Bus 150 loops from Plaça d'Espanya to Castell de Montjuïc. Bus 55 runs across town via Plaça de Catalunya past the Museu d'Arqueologia de Catalunya to the Parc Montjuïc funicular station.

→ **Funicular** From the Paral·lel metro station, pick up the funicular (www.tmb.cat; single ticket €2.20; ⏱7.30am-10pm Mon-Fri, 9am-10pm Sat & Sun Apr-Oct, 7.30am-8pm Mon-Fri, 9am-8pm Sat & Sun Nov-Mar) railway to Parc Montjuïc station.

→ **Cable car** There are two cable cars up to Montjuic, including the Telefèric del Port from Barceloneta (p270).

Lonely Planet's Top Tip

The Arqueoticket is a special pass, available at tourist offices and participating museums for €14.50, that allows entry into the Museu d'Arqueologia de Catalunya (MAC) (p191), the Museu Egipci (p151), the Born Centre de Cultura i Memòria (p104) and the Museu d'Història de Barcelona (p67) – a substantial saving.

Best Places to Eat

→ Quimet i Quimet (p196)
→ Agust Gastrobar (p196)
→ Mano Rota (p197)

For reviews, see p195.

Best Places to Drink

→ La Caseta del Migdia (p200)
→ Abirradero (p200)
→ Bar Calders (p201)
→ El Rouge (p200)
→ La Mari Ollero (p201)

For reviews, see p200.

◉ Best Art Collections

→ Museu Nacional d'Art de Catalunya (MNAC) (p189)
→ Fundació Joan Miró (p188)
→ CaixaForum (p191)

For reviews, see p191.

TOP EXPERIENCE
RELAX IN THE SCULPTURE GARDEN AT FUNDACIÓ JOAN MIRÓ

Joan Miró, the city's best-known 20th-century artistic progeny, bequeathed this art foundation to his home town in 1971. The light-filled buildings, designed by close friend and architect Josep Lluís Sert (who also built Miró's Mallorca studios), are crammed with seminal works, from Miró's earliest timid sketches to paintings from his last years.

Sert's Temple to Miró's Art

Sert's shimmering white temple to one of Spain's artistic luminaries is considered one of the world's most outstanding museum buildings. The architect designed it after spending many of Franco's dictatorship years in the USA as head of the School of Design at Harvard University. The foundation rests amid the greenery of the mountains and holds the greatest single collection of Miró's work, including around 220 of his paintings, 180 sculptures, some textiles and more than 8000 drawings spanning his entire life. Only a small portion is ever on display, interspersed with courtyards, water features and olive trees.

The Collection

The thoughtfully positioned exhibits give a broad impression of Miró's artistic development. Just inside the entrance, on the main level, you'll find Sala 1, the Sala Joan Prats, with works spanning the early years until 1919. Here you can see how the young Miró moved from relative realism towards his own unique style that uses primary colours and morphed shapes symbolising the moon, the female form and birds.

Sala 2, the Sala Pilar Juncosa (named after his wife), covers the years 1925–68 – his surrealist years. Sala 3 contains masterworks from the 1960s and 1970s, such as *Personatge Davant del Sol*. Salas 5, 6 and 7 host a selection of the private Katsuta collection of Miró works from 1914 to 1971. Sala 9 exhibits some more major paintings and bronzes from the 1960s onwards, including the famed 1970s *antipintura* works.

Next up, Sala 11 holds *Tapís de la Fundació*, a giant tapestry in Miró's trademark primary colours. You'll then pass *Mercury Fountain (Font de Mercur)* by Alexander Calder, a rebuilt work that was originally created for the 1937 Paris Fair and represented Spain at the Spanish Republic's Pavilion. Basement room 13 (Espai 13; €3) is a small space for temporary exhibitions.

Upstairs, Sala 14 contains a video on the artist's life, while Sala 16, called *Homenatge a Joan Miró* (Homage to Joan Miró), is dedicated to works by his contemporaries, such as Henry Moore, Antoni Tàpies, Eduardo Chillida, Joan Brossa and Fernand Léger. The museum library (with reduced hours) contains Miró's personal book collection.

The Garden

Outside on the eastern flank of the museum lies the Jardí de les Esculptures, a small garden with various pieces of modern sculpture. The green areas surrounding the museum, together with the garden, are perfect for a picnic.

DON'T MISS

➡ Sert's architectural design
➡ Masterworks in Rooms 3 and 9
➡ Early works (Sala 1) and Miro's move to surrealism (Sala 2)
➡ The sculpture garden

PRACTICALITIES

➡ Map p314, E4
➡ ☏93 443 94 70
➡ www.fmirobcn.org
➡ Avinguda de Miramar
➡ adult/child €13/free, multimedia guide €5
➡ ◷10am-8pm Tue-Sat, to 3pm Sun Apr-Oct, 10am-6pm Tue-Sat, to 3pm Sun Nov-Mar
➡ ☐55, 150, ⛟from Paral·lel

ENJOY THE ROMANESQUE FRESCOES IN THE PALAU NACIONAL

The spectacular neo-baroque silhouette of the Palau Nacional (Museo Nacional D'Art de Catalunya) can be seen on Montjuïc's slopes from across the city. Built for the 1929 World Exhibition and restored in 2005, it houses a vast collection of mostly Catalan art spanning the early Middle Ages to the early 20th century. The high point is the unique collection of extraordinary Romanesque frescoes.

Romanesque Masterpieces

The MNAC's Romanesque art collection is considered the most important concentration of early medieval art in the world. Rescued from neglected country churches across northern Catalonia (particularly the Pyrenees) in the early 20th century, the collection consists of 21 frescoes, wood-carvings and painted altar frontals (low-relief wooden panels that were the forerunners of the elaborate altar-pieces of later churches). The insides of several churches have been recreated and the frescoes – in some cases fragmentary, in others extraordinarily complete and alive with colour – have been placed as they were when in situ.

The first of the two most striking frescoes, in Sala 7, is a magnificent image of Christ in Majesty done around 1123. Based on the text of the Apocalypse, we see Christ enthroned with the world at his feet. He holds a book open with the words *Ego Sum Lux Mundi* (I am the Light of the World) and is surrounded by the four Evangelists. The images were taken from the apse of the Església de Sant Climent de Taüll in the Vall de Boí in northwest Catalonia.

DON'T MISS

➡ Romanesque pieces

➡ Gothic artworks

➡ The Cambò Bequest and Thyssen-Bornemisza collections

➡ 1930s Spanish Civil War posters

PRACTICALITIES

➡ MNAC

➡ Map p314, D4

➡ ☏93 622 03 60

➡ www.museunacional.cat

➡ Mirador del Palau Nacional, Parc de Montjuïc

➡ adult/child €12/free, after 3pm Sat & 1st Sun of month free, audio guide €4, rooftop viewpoint only €2

➡ ⊙10am-8pm Tue-Sat, to 3pm Sun May-Sep, 10am-6pm Tue-Sat, to 3pm Sun Oct-Apr

➡ 🚌55, Ⓜ Espanya

THE FRESCO STRIPPERS

The Stefanoni brothers, Italian art restorers, brought the secrets of *strappo* (stripping of frescoes from walls) to Catalonia in the early 1900s. The Stefanonis would cover frescoes with a sheet of fabric, stuck on with a glue made of cartilage. When dry, this allowed the image to be stripped off the wall and rolled up. For three years the Stefanonis roamed the Pyrenean countryside, stripping churches and sending the rolls back to Barcelona, where they were eventually put back up on walls to reflect how they had originally appeared.

TOP TIPS

If you're on a museum mission, you can save money by purchasing the Articket BCN (p88), a €35 pass that provides admission to six museums (including the MNAC).

Be sure to take in the fine city view from the **terrace** (Map p314; Passeig de Santa Madrona 39-41; ☐55) just in front of the museum, which draws crowds around sunset.

Another fine viewpoint is the museum's roof terrace (included in admission, or €2 for the rooftop only).

Nearby in Sala 9 are frescoes done around the same time in the nearby Església de Santa Maria de Taüll. This time the central image taken from the apse is of the Virgin Mary and Christ Child. These images were not mere decoration but tools of instruction in the basics of Christian faith for the local medieval population, typically illiterate, ignorant, fearful and in most cases eking out a subsistence living. These images transmitted the basic personalities and tenets of the faith and were accepted at face value by most.

The Gothic Collection

Opposite the Romanesque collection on the ground floor is the museum's Gothic art section, with Catalan Gothic painting and works from other Spanish and Mediterranean regions. Look out especially for the work of Bernat Martorell in Sala 32 and Jaume Huguet in Sala 34. Among Martorell's works figure images of the martyrdom of St Vincent and Santa Eulàlia. Huguet's *Consagració de Sant Agustí,* in which St Augustine is depicted as a bishop, is dazzling in its detail.

Renaissance & Baroque

Next you pass into the 2018-launched Renaissance & Baroque gallery, which exhibits some 300 Spanish and international pieces spanning the 16th to 18th centuries, including works by Diego Velázquez, Francisco de Zurbarán, Josep de Ribera, Francisco Goya, Tiepolo, Rubens, El Greco and Canaletto. Incorporated into this section are two eclectic and excellent private collections, the Cambò Bequest by Francesc Cambó and the Thyssen-Bornemisza collection on loan to the MNAC by Madrid's Museo Thyssen-Bornemisza.

Modern Catalan Art

Up on the next floor, beyond a beautiful domed hall, the collection turns to modern art, mainly but not exclusively Catalan. These galleries are arranged thematically: Modernisme, Noucentisme, Art and the Civil War and so on. Among the many highlights: an early Salvador Dalí painting, *Retrat del meu pare* (Portrait of My Father), Juan Gris' collage-like paintings, the brilliant portraits of Marià Fortuny, and 1930s call-to-arms posters against the Francoist onslaught (nearby you'll find photos of soldiers and bombed-out city centres). There are also works by Modernista painters Ramon Casas and Santiago Rusiñol, as well as Catalan luminary Antoni Tàpies.

Also on show are items of Modernista furniture and decoration, which include chairs by Gaudí and a mural by Ramon Casas (the artist and Pere Romeu on a tandem bicycle) that once adorned the legendary bar and restaurant Els Quatre Gats.

 SIGHTS

With its splendid museums, galleries and gardens, the challenge in the Montjuïc area is planning: there's far too much to see in one day, and distances can be great.

⊙ Montjuïc

MUSEU NACIONAL
D'ART DE CATALUNYA   MUSEUM
See p189.

FUNDACIÓ JOAN MIRÓ   GALLERY
See p188.

CASTELL DE MONTJUÏC   FORTRESS
Map p314 (☑93 256 44 40; https://ajuntament. barcelona.cat; Carretera de Montjuïc 66; adult/ child €5/3, after 3pm Sun & 1st Sun of month free; ☺10am-8pm Mar-Oct, to 6pm Nov-Feb; ᗺ150, ᗺTelefèric de Montjuïc, Castell de Montjuïc) Enjoying commanding views over the Mediterranean, this forbidding fortress dominates the southeastern heights of Montjuïc. It dates, in its present form, from the late 17th and 18th centuries, though there's been a watchtower here since 1073. For most of its dark history, it has been used as a political prison and killing ground. Anarchists were executed here around the end of the 19th century, fascists during the civil war and Republicans after it – most notoriously Republican Catalan president Lluís Companys in 1940.

The castle is surrounded by pines, palms and a network of ditches and walls; as you wander the walls, its strategic position over the city and port becomes clear. A multilanguage exhibition space off the sprawling **Pati d'Armas** explains the history of the site, with archaeological finds from prehistoric days to its role as medieval beacon and its later days as a strategic bastion. Most interesting (and disturbing) is the exhibition devoted to the imprisonments, trials and executions that happened here.

One-hour **guided visits** (adult/child €9/7 including entrance) in various languages visit otherwise off-limits areas such as the cistern and the dungeons, where graffiti etched into the walls by 19th-century prisoners was recovered in 2018.

The views over the sea, port and city below are the best part of making the trip up here; around the seaward foot of the castle is an airy walking track, the **Camí del Mar**, which offers breezy views of the city and sea.

CAIXAFORUM   GALLERY
Map p314 (☑93 476 86 00; www.caixaforum.es; Avinguda de Francesc Ferrer i Guàrdia 6-8; adult/ child €4/free, 1st Sun of month free; ☺10am-8pm year-round, to 11pm Wed Jul & Aug; ᗰEspanya) The La Caixa building society prides itself on its involvement in (and ownership of) art, in particular all that is contemporary. The bank's premier expo space in Barcelona hosts part of its extensive global collection, as well as fascinating temporary international exhibitions, in the completely renovated former Casaramona factory, an outstanding brick Modernista creation by Josep Puig i Cadafalch. From 1940 to 1993, the building housed the First Squadron of the police cavalry unit.

The major international exhibitions are the key draw, though portions of La Caixa's own collection of 800 works of modern and contemporary art also go on display occasionally. Musical recitals are sometimes held here too, especially in the warmer months. In the courtyard where the police horses used to drink is a steel-and-glass tree designed by Japanese architect Arata Isozaki, who led the building's 2002 renovation.

FONT MÀGICA   FOUNTAIN
Map p314 (Avinguda de la Reina Maria Cristina; ☺every 30min 9.30-10.30pm Wed-Sun Jun-Sep, 9-10pm Thu-Sat Apr, May & Oct, 8-9pm Thu-Sat Nov-Mar; ᗰEspanya) 🎣FREE Originally created for the 1929 World Exposition, this huge colour-lit fountain has again been a magnet since the 1992 Olympics, shimmering on the long sweep of Avinguda de la Reina Maria Cristina to the grand Palau Nacional. With a flourish, the 'Magic Fountain' erupts into a feast of musical, backlit aquatic life; it's a unique 15-minute night performance in which the water can look like seething fireworks or a mystical cauldron of colour.

On hot summer evenings especially, this spectacle (repeated several times) mesmerises onlookers. On the last evening of the September Festes de la Mercè (p43) and on New Year's Eve, the particularly beautiful displays feature fireworks. Eco initiatives include the use of groundwater and LED lights.

MUSEU D'ARQUEOLOGIA
DE CATALUNYA   MUSEUM
Map p314 (MAC; ☑93 423 21 49; www.macbarce lona.cat; Passeig de Santa Madrona 39-41; adult/ child €6/free; ☺9.30am-7pm Tue-Sat, 10am-2.30pm Sun; ᗺ55, ᗰPoble Sec) Occupying

CABLE CARS

The quickest and most scenic route from the beach to the mountain is via the Telefèric del Port (p270) cable car, which runs between the Torre de Sant Sebastiá in Barceloneta and the Miramar stop on Montjuïc. From the Parc Montjuïc cable car station on northern Montjuïc, the separate **Telefèric de Montjuïc** (Map p314; www.teleferic demontjuic.cat; Avinguda de Miramar 30; adult/child 1 way €8.40/6.60; ⊙10am-9pm Jun-Sep, to 7pm Mar-May & Oct, to 6pm Nov-Feb; ☐55, 150) whizzes you up to the Castell de Montjuïc (p191) via the mirador (lookout point).

the 1929 World Exhibition's Graphic Arts Palace, this intriguing archaeology museum covers both Catalonia and cultures from across Spain. There's good material on the Balearic Islands (including 5th- to 3rd-century BCE statues of Phoenician goddess Tanit from Ibiza) and the Greek and Roman city of Empúries (Emporion), as well as the region's prehistoric inhabitants. Don't miss the 53,200-year-old human jaw found near Sitges, or the beautiful Roman mosaic depicting Les Tres Gràcies (The Three Graces), unearthed in the 18th century.

Other notable items range from copies of pre-Neanderthal skulls to jewel-studded Visigothic crosses. The Roman finds upstairs were mostly dug up in and around Barcelona, including fine mosaics like the one of Bellerophon and the Chimera.

POBLE ESPANYOL   CULTURAL CENTRE

Map p314 (☑93 508 63 00; www.poble-espanyol.com; Avinguda de Francesc Ferrer i Guàrdia 13; adult/child €14/7; ⊙9am-8pm Mon, to midnight Tue-Thu & Sun, to 3am Fri, to 4am Sat; ☐13, 23, 150, ⓜEspanya) Welcome to Spain! All of it! This 'Spanish Village' is an intriguing scrapbook of Spanish architecture built for the local-crafts section of the 1929 World Exhibition. You can meander from Andalucía to Galicia in the space of a couple of hours, visiting surprisingly good to-scale copies of Spain's characteristic structures. The 117 buildings include restaurants, cafes, bars and clubs, and craft shops and workshops (for glass artists and other artisans), as well as souvenir stores.

Enter from beneath a towered medieval gate from Ávila, flanked by two Catalan *gegants* (papier-mâché giants). Inside on the right, an information office has free maps and a worthwhile multimedia guide (€3.50; leave a €20 deposit). Straight ahead from the gate is the Plaza Mayor (Town Sq), surrounded by mainly Castilian and Aragonese buildings; it sometimes hosts summer concerts. Elsewhere you'll find an Andalucian *barri* (neighbourhood), a Basque street, Galician and Catalan quarters, and even a Catalan Romanesque monastery (at the eastern end).

There's also an excellent multimedia exhibition of some of Spain's most popular festivals, including Buñol's La Tomatina (a giant tomato fight in Valencia) and Semana Santa (Holy Week) in Andalucía.

Spare time for the **Fundació Fran Daurel** (Map p314; ☑93 423 41 72; www.fundaciofran daurel.com; ⊙11am-8pm Jun-Sep, 10am-6.30pm Mon, to 7pm Tue-Sun Oct-May), an eclectic collection of more than 300 works of art, including sculptures, prints, ceramics and tapestries by modern artists ranging from Picasso and Miró to more contemporary figures such as Miquel Barceló, as well as a sculpture garden.

Children's groups can participate in the two-hour Joc del Sarró (€6.50; multiple languages), in which kids go around the *poble* seeking answers to various mysteries.

MUSEU ETNOLÒGIC   MUSEUM

Map p314 (☑93 256 34 84; www.barcelona.cat; Passeig de Santa Madrona 16; adult/child €5/free, from 3pm Sun & 1st Sun of month free; ⊙10am-7pm Tue-Sat, to 8pm Sun; ☐55) Delving into Catalonia's rich heritage, Barcelona's ethnology museum presents an intriguing permanent display from its 70,000-object collection, with multilanguage panels. Exhibits cover origin myths, religious festivals, folklore, and the blending of sacred and secular. There are several *gegants*, including depictions of King Jaume I and Queen Violant, and a dragon (you'll have to imagine the spewing burning embers it emits) and devil costumes used in *correfocs* (fire runs), which still figure prominently in Catalan festivals.

The collection also has instruments and archive images of traditional dances from the Catalan Pyrenees, plus accoutrements of bygone days showcasing the region's

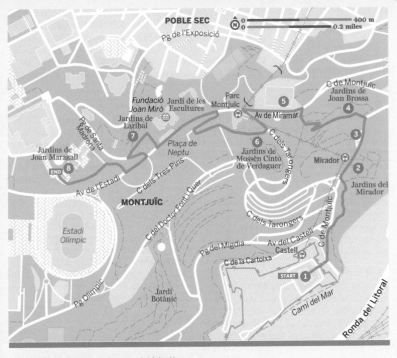

POBLE SEC

Pg de l'Exposició

N 0 | 400 m
0 | 0.2 miles

Fundació Joan Miró
Jardí de les Escultures
Parc Montjuïc
Av de Miramar
Jardins de Joan Brossa
Jardins de Laribal
Pg de Santa Madrona
Plaça de Neptú
Jardins de Mossèn Cinto de Verdaguer
C dels Tarongers
Mirador
Jardins del Mirador
Jardins de Joan Maragall
END
Av de l'Estadi
C dels Tres Pins
MONTJUÏC
C del Doctor Font i Quer
C dels Tarongers
Estadi Olímpic
C de Montjuïc
Pg del Migdia
Av del Castell
Castell
Jardí Botànic
Pg Olímpic
C de la Cartoixa
START
Camí del Mar
Ronda del Litoral

Neighbourhood Walk
Montjuïc's Gardens & Panoramas

START CASTELL DE MONTJUÏC
END JARDINS DE JOAN MARAGALL
LENGTH 3KM; 1½ HOURS

Get the cable car to hilltop **1 Castell de Montjuïc** (p191) for stupendous views over the city and sea; don't miss the sea-facing trail behind the fortress.

A short stroll northeast down the Camí del Mar pedestrian trail leads to another inspiring viewpoint at the **2 Jardins del Mirador** (Map p314, G5; www.barcelona.cat; Carretera de Montjuïc ⊙10am-sunset) **FREE**, opposite the Mirador cable car station.

Immediately downhill, **3 Plaça de la Sardana** (Map p314, G5; Carrer de Montjuïc; ⊠150) is decorated with a sculpture of people engaged in the classic Catalan folk dance after which the square is named. To its left lie the charming landscaped **4 Jardins de Joan Brossa** (Map p314, G4; www.barcelona.cat; Plaça de la Sardana; ⊙10am-sunset) **FREE**, with fine views from the site of a former amusement park, now covered in Mediterranean species from

cypresses, cedars and pines to olive trees and large-fan palms. Take a break at nearby tapas bar **5 Salts Montjuïc** (p200).

Head west and cross Carrer dels Tarongers to the painstakingly laid out **6 Jardins de Mossèn Cinto de Verdaguer** (Map p314, F5; www.barcelona.cat; Avinguda de Miramar 30; ⊙10am-sunset; ⊠55, 150) **FREE**, with tulips, water lilies and lotus flowers.

Dropping away 500m further west, just beyond the Fundació Joan Miró, the soothing terraced gardens of the 1922-opened **7 Jardins de Laribal** (Map p314, E5; www.barcelona.cat; Passeig de Santa Madrona 2; ⊙10am-sunset; ⊠55) **FREE** are linked by paths, stairs and wisteria-clad walkways. Pretty sculpted watercourses take inspiration from Granada's Alhambra.

Continue 300m or so west to reach the little-visited, weekend-only **8 Jardins de Joan Maragall** (Map p314, D5; www.barcelona.cat; Avinguda dels Montanyans 48; ⊙10am-3pm Sat & Sun; MPlaça Espanya) **FREE** for ornamental fountains, photogenic sculptures and a neoclassical palace (the Spanish royal family's residence in Barcelona).

blacksmiths, winemakers, weavers, fishers, apothecaries, shepherds, potters, toymakers and even *saurí* ('diviners'; those tasked with finding water and hidden things). International finds include a couple of magnificently carved 19th-century doorways from South India.

JARDÍ BOTÀNIC
GARDENS

Map p314 (www.museuciencies.cat; Carrer del Doctor Font i Quer 2; adult/child €3.50/free, after 3pm Sun & 1st Sun of month free; ☉10am-8pm Jun-Aug, to 7pm Apr, May, Sep & Oct, to 6pm Feb & Mar, to 5pm Nov-Jan; ☐55, 150) Dedicated to Mediterranean flora, these hillside gardens have a collection of some 40,000 plants and 1500 species, including many that thrive in areas with a climate similar to that of the Mediterranean, such as the Canary Islands, North Africa, Australia, California, Chile and South Africa.

L'ANELLA OLÍMPICA
AREA

Map p314 (Olympic Ring; ☑93 426 20 89; www.estadiolimpic.cat; Avinguda de l'Estadi; ☉8am-8pm May-Sep, 10am-6pm Oct-Apr; ☐13, 23, 150) FREE The group of installations built for the main events of the 1992 Olympics includes the Piscines Bernat Picornell (p203), where the swimming and diving

events were held (now open to all), and the 60,000-capacity **Estadi Olímpic** (Map p314; ☑93 426 20 89; www.estadiolimpic.cat; Passeig Olímpic 15-17; ☉8am-8pm May-Sep, 10am-6pm Oct-Apr; ☐13, 23, 150) FREE, which can be visited when not in use for sporting events or concerts.

CEMENTIRI DE MONTJUÏC
CEMETERY

(Cementiri Nou; Cementiri del Sud-Oest; ☑93 484 19 99; www.cbsa.cat; Carrer de la Mare de Déu de Port 56-58; ☉8am-6pm; ☐21, 107) FREE On the seaward hill to the south of L'Anella Olímpica, this huge cemetery dating from 1883 stretches down Montjuïc's southern slopes, combining elaborate architect-designed tombs for rich families and small niches for the rest. The graves of numerous Catalan artists, including Joan Miró, and politicians rest here. At the southern entrance stands the **Col·lecció de Carrosses Fúnebres** (☉10am-2pm Sat & Sun) FREE, filled with late-18th-century to mid-20th-century hearses. Check online for guided visits (Spanish and Catalan).

MUSEU OLÍMPIC I DE L'ESPORT
MUSEUM

Map p314 (☑93 292 53 79; www.museu olimpicbcn.cat; Avinguda de l'Estadi 60; adult/child €6/free; ☉10am-8pm Tue-Sat, to 2.30pm

---

GOING UNDERGROUND: REFUGI 307

Barcelona was the city most heavily bombed by Franco's air forces during the Spanish Civil War, and as a result it developed more than 1300 air-raid shelters. Now overseen by the Museu d'Història de Barcelona (MUHBA), the city's **307th refuge** (Map p314; ☑93 256 21 00; http://ajuntament.barcelona.cat; Carrer Nou de la Rambla 175; tour adult/child €3.50/free; ☉tours 10.30am, 11.30am & 12.30pm Sun; ⓂParal·lel), one of its best preserved, was dug under a fold of northern Montjuïc by local citizens from 1937 to 1939. Compulsory tours (reservations essential) run on Sunday only: English at 10.30am, Spanish at 11.30am and Catalan at 12.30pm.

Over two years, the web of tunnels was slowly extended to 200m, with a theoretical capacity for 2000 people. Sleeping overnight in the shelter was not allowed – when raids were not being carried out work continued on its extension. Vaulted to displace the weight above the shelter to the clay brick walls (the porous clay allowed the bricks to absorb the shock waves of falling bombs without cracking), the tunnels were narrow and winding. Coated in lime to seal out humidity and whitewashed to relieve the sense of claustrophobia, they became a second home for many Poble Sec inhabitants – and today remain a testament to Barcelona's resilience.

When the civil war ended, Franco extended the *refugi* while considering entering WWII on Hitler's side. When he decided not to join the war, many shelters including 307 were largely abandoned. In the tough years of famine and rationing during the 1940s and 1950s, families from Granada took up residence here. Later on, an enterprising fellow grew mushrooms here for sale on the black market.

Sun Apr-Sep, 10am-6pm Tue-Sat, to 2.30pm Sun Oct-Mar; 🚃13, 55, 150) At this information-packed interactive sporting museum, you wander down a ramp that snakes below ground level and is lined with multimedia displays on the history of sport and the Olympic Games. The timeline starts with the ancients and runs all the way up to a Dalí-stamped swimsuit worn by the Spanish synchronised swimming team at the 2004 Athens Olympics. Visitors also get the chance to run against US sprint champion Carl Lewis in a simulator.

PAVELLÓ MIES
VAN DER ROHE   ARCHITECTURE
Map p314 (📞93 215 10 11; www.miesbcn.com; Avinguda de Francesc Ferrer i Guàrdia 7; adult/child €5/free; ⏱10am-8pm Mar-Oct, to 6pm Nov-Feb; Ⓜ Espanya) Designed in glass, steel and various marbles in 1929 by Ludwig Mies van der Rohe (1886–1969) for the World Exhibition, this curious work of artful simplicity is emblematic of the Modernisme movement, and has inspired several generations of architects. It was removed after the show and reconstructed only in the 1980s, after been consistently referred to as one of the key works of modern architecture. That said, unless you're an avid architecture fan, there isn't much to see beyond the building's exterior.

PLAÇA D'ESPANYA   SQUARE
Map p314 (Ⓜ Espanya) The whirling roundabout of Plaça d'Espanya, distinguished by its so-called Venetian towers (vaguely reminiscent of the bell tower in Venice's St Mark's Square), was built for the 1929 World Exhibition and is the junction of several major thoroughfares.

JARDINS DE MOSSÈN
COSTA I LLOBERA   GARDENS
Map p314 (www.barcelona.cat; Carretera de Miramar 38; ⏱10am-sunset; 🚡Teleféric del Port, Miramar) FREE Above the thundering traffic of the main B10 road to Tarragona, the seafacing Jardins de Mossèn Costa i Llobera have a good collection of tropical, desert and high-mountain plants – including a veritable forest of cacti (Europe's largest collection), with some species reaching over 5m in height.

⊙ Sant Antoni

MERCAT DE SANT ANTONI   MARKET
Map p314 (📞93 426 35 21; www.mercatdesantantoni.com; Carrer del Comte d'Urgell 1; ⏱8am-8.30pm Mon-Sat; Ⓜ Sant Antoni) Just beyond the western edge of El Raval, this glorious iron-and-brick market was originally completed in 1882, but reopened in 2018 with 250 stalls following a nine-year renovation job. It's a great place to stock up on seasonal produce or grab a bite in between browsing the fashion, textiles and homewares stalls. Also on display are the remains of a piece of the Roman Via Augusta and a 1st-century-CE mausoleum, as well as a ruined 17th-century defensive wall, all uncovered during restoration works.

A secondhand-book market takes place out front on Sunday mornings.

PARC DE JOAN MIRÓ   PARK
Map p314 (Carrer de Tarragona; ⏱10am-sunset; Ⓜ Tarragona) FREE This palm-filled park is worth a look for its massive phallic 1980s Miró sculpture, **Dona i ocell** (Woman and Bird), whose red, yellow, blue and green tiles were added by Miró's collaborator Joan Gardy Artigas.

✖ EATING

Made up mostly of parks and gardens, Montjuïc has limited eating options. In Poble Sec, however, you'll turn up all sorts of inventive eating and drinking spots, from historic taverns offering Catalan classics to smart, new-wave eateries. Equally creative Sant Antoni is the place for boundary-pushing new openings.

✖ Montjuïc

MARTÍNEZ   SPANISH €€€
Map p314 (📞93 106 60 52; www.martinez barcelona.com; Carretera de Miramar 38; mains €20-35; ⏱1-11pm; 🚃150, 🚡Teleféric del Port, Miramar) With a fabulous panorama over the port, stylish Martínez is a standout among Montjuïc's lacklustre dining options. The terrace is ideal for warm-day lunches of the

CARRER DE BLAI

Carrer de Blai in Poble Sec is packed with busy tapas and *pintxo* (Basque tapas) bars, both classic and contemporary, where you can feast on bite-sized batches of deliciousness at around €1 or €2 a piece – from chunks of perfectly gooey tortilla to king prawns with *piquillo* peppers.

signature rice dishes. There are also oysters, calamari, fresh market fish and other seafood hits, plus cured ham and grilled meats. It's a fine spot for drinks too: the bar stays open until 1.30am or 2.30am.

✕ Poble Sec

★ QUIMET I QUIMET   TAPAS €

Map p314 (☎93 442 31 42; www.quimetquimet. com; Carrer del Poeta Cabanyes 25; tapas €4-10, montaditos €3-4; ☉noon-4pm & 8-10.30pm Mon-Fri, closed Aug; Ⓜ Paral·lel) Now led by its fourth generation, family-run Quimet i Quimet has been passed down since 1914. There's barely space to swing a *calamar* (squid) in this bottle-lined, standing-room-only place, but it's a treat for the palate. Try delectable made-to-order *montaditos* (tapas on bread), such as salmon with Greek yoghurt or tuna belly with sea urchin, with a house wine or vermouth.

LA PLATILLERIA   TAPAS €

Map p314 (☎93 463 54 01; www.facebook.com/ laplatilleria; Carrer del Roser 82; tapas €4-9; ☉7.30-11.30pm Mon & Wed-Fri, 12.30-4pm & 7.30-11.30pm Sat & Sun; Ⓜ Poble Sec) Lovingly prepared tapas that change depending on the day's seasonal produce are the draw at this tucked-away spot in upper Poble Sec. Classic crowd-pleasers such as *pa amb tomàquet* (bread rubbed with tomato, olive oil and salt) and *patates braves* put in an appearance alongside more creative contemporary sharing plates.

SPICE   CAFE €

Map p314 (☎93 624 33 59; www.spicecafe.es; Carrer de Margarit 13; dishes €3.50-5; ☉11am-8pm Tue-Sun; ☎; Ⓜ Poble Sec) Run by friendly English-speaking staff, this delightful independent cafe has earned a following for its delicious home-baked treats, including

ricotta-and-cinnamon cheesecake, gluten-free orange-and-cardamom loaf, and divine carrot cake often lauded as Barcelona's best. Along with excellent coffees, there are loose-leaf teas and homemade sodas to enjoy at cute tiled tables and cushioned booths.

ELS SORTIDORS DEL PARLIAMENT   TAPAS €

Map p314 (☎600 600600; Carrer del Parlament 53; raciones €5-14, ☉5-11pm Mon, Wed & Thu, 1-11pm Fri-Sun; Ⓜ San Antoni) A rustic-modern space filled with barrel tables, concrete floors and open-stone walls, this former motorbike workshop in Sant Antoni is popular for its house vermouth, Catalan wines (you can even buy a bottle at shop prices plus corkage!) and fuss-free raciones, from cheese platters, tinned seafood and cured meats to quail-egg omelette with truffle oil.

★ AGUST GASTROBAR   BISTRO €€

Map p314 (☎93 162 67 33; www.agustbarcelona. com; Carrer del Parlament 54; mains €16-24; ☉7pm-midnight Mon-Thu, 2-4pm & 7pm-midnight Fri-Sun; ☎; Ⓜ Poble Sec) Set up by two French chefs (one of whom trained under Gordon Ramsay), Agust occupies a fabulous mezzanine space with timber beams, exposed brick and textured metro tiles. Scallops gratinéed with asparagus and prawn-and-avocado stuffed cannelloni are savoury standouts, with housemade vermouth and inventive cocktails alongside. Desserts include the extraordinary 'el cactus' (chocolate-crumble soil, mojito mousse, lemon sorbet), in a terracotta pot.l

BENZINA   ITALIAN €€

Map p314 (☎93 659 55 83; www.benzina.es; Passatge Pere Calders 6; mains €16-21; ☉8pm-midnight Wed & Thu, 1.30-5.30pm & 8pm-midnight Fri-Sun; ☎; Ⓜ Poble Sec, San Antoni) ✿ A stylishly converted mechanic's garage sets the tone for Sant Antoni's favourite Italian restaurant, a New York-inspired hangout where the vibe is lively, the cocktails punchy and the food flawless. Creative plates by chef Nicola Valle swing from wild-boar cannelloni and potato-herb ravioli to grana padano croquettes with truffle mayo, all fusing local and Italian ingredients.

BAR SECO   TAPAS €€

Map p314 (☎933 29 63 74; Passeig de Montjuïc 74; tapas €5-10; ☉9am-6pm; ☎; Ⓜ Paral·lel) ✿ Local, sustainably sourced produce and a

Slow Food ethos infuse the original tapas at this sunny, peach-pink corner spot, where you can dig into organic scrambled eggs, citrusy tabbouleh, salmon or tuna tartare and *patates braves* with rich homemade sauce, or home-baked cakes. It's also great for coffee, cocktails and vermouth, with palm-cloth tables on the square opposite.

MANO ROTA
FUSION €€

Map p314 (🖉93 164 80 41; www.manorota.com; Carrer de la Creu dels Molers 4; mains €13-20; ⊕8-11.30pm Mon, 1-3.30pm & 8-11.30pm Tue-Sat; Ⓜ Poble Sec) Exposed brick, aluminium pipes, industrial lighting and recycled timbers set a pleasingly contemporary tone for inspired bistro cooking at Mano Rota ('broken hand', a Spanish idiom for consummate skill). Asian, South American and Mediterranean flavours meet in fusion temptations such as Thai-inspired coconut-laced *suquet* (Catalan fish stew), monkfish tagine or shiso-leaf quesadillas. The 12-course tasting menu is decent value at €65.

PALO CORTAO
TAPAS €€

Map p314 (🖉93 188 90 67; www.palocortao.es; Carrer Nou de la Rambla 146; medias raciones €7-10; ⊕8pm-1am Tue-Fri, 1-5pm & 8pm-1am Sat & Sun; Ⓜ Paral·lel) Chicly contemporary and welcoming Palo Cortao is renowned for its beautifully executed seafood and meat *raciones* with hints of Andalucía, accompanied by Jerez sherry and other elegant Spanish wines. Highlights include truffled-chicken cannelloni, fried aubergines with honey and miso, delicate cheese plates, and tuna tataki with *ajo blanco*. Dine at the long bar or seated in the intimate restaurant, amid draped greenery.

LASCAR 74
PERUVIAN €€

Map p314 (🖉93 017 98 72; www.lascar.es; Carrer del Roser 74; mains €9-14; ⊕7-11.30pm Mon-Fri, 2-4.30pm & 7-11.30pm Sat & Sun; Ⓜ Paral·lel) At this self-styled 'ceviche and pisco bar', oyster shooters with *leche de tigre* (the traditional ceviche marinade) are served alongside exquisite Peruvian ceviche as well as renditions from Thailand, Japan and Mexico, and Hawaiian-style poke or veg bowls. Pisco sours are the real deal, frothy egg white and all. It's a modern space with open-brick walls, white tiles and mood lighting.

CASA DE TAPAS CAÑOTA
TAPAS €€

Map p314 (🖉93 325 91 71; www.casadetapas. com; Carrer de Lleida 7; tapas €5-15; ⊕1-4pm & 7.30pm-midnight Tue-Sat, 1-4pm Sun; Ⓜ Poble Sec) This friendly, unfussy old-timer serves affordable, nicely turned out tapas plates. Seafood is the speciality, with rich razor clams, garlic-fried prawns and tender octopus. Wash it down with a refreshing bottle of *albariño* (a Galician white). Book ahead for weekends. The Iglesias family also runs traditional seafood spot Rías de Galicia next door and Japanese-fusion Espai Kru, just upstairs.

XEMEI
VENETIAN €€

Map p314 (🖉93 553 51 40; www.xemei.es; Passeig de l'Exposició 85; mains €16-25; ⊕1.45-3.30pm & 8.45-11pm, closed 2 weeks Aug; Ⓜ Poble Sec) Everyone's favourite Italian, Xemei ('Twins' in Venetian) is a wonderful, authentically delicious slice of Venice in Barcelona, named for its twin Venetian owners Stefano and Max Colombo. To the accompaniment of gentle jazz and vintage-inspired design, you might try a light burrata salad or Venetian-fish platter, followed by *bigoli* pasta in anchovy-and-onion sauce, squid-ink spaghetti, grilled octopus or seasonal risotto.

CASA XICA
FUSION €€

Map p314 (🖉93 600 58 58; www.facebook.com/ casaxicabarcelona; Carrer de la França Xica 20; sharing plates €5-15; ⊕8.30-11pm Mon, 1.30-11pm Tue-Sat; Ⓜ Poble Sec) On the parlour floor of an old house, Casa Xica is a casual, artfully designed space where elements of various Asian cuisines are fused with fresh Catalan ingredients. Owners Marc and Raquel lived and travelled extensively in Asia, and their creativity is beautifully expressed in dishes like stir-fried noodles with scallops, prawn gyoza and catfish tacos.

PIZZA DEL SORTIDOR
PIZZA €€

Map p314 (🖉93 173 04 90; www.lapizzadelsor tidor.com; Carrer de Blasco de Garay 46; pizza €7-14; ⊕7.30pm-midnight Tue-Thu, 1-4pm & 7.30pm-1am Fri-Sun; 🖥🍴; Ⓜ Poble Sec) Dive into this rock-loving Poble Sec pizzeria for delicious thin-crust pizza with toppings like goat's cheese or prosciutto, served piping hot from the wood-burning oven. It's utterly pretension-free – cardboard plates, no utensils, cheap beer in plastic cups. But that's half the fun, especially after the complimentary shot of limoncello. Cash only. Expect queues for €8 pizzas on Tuesday and Wednesday.

TAVERNA CAN MARGARIT
CATALAN €€

Map p314 (☑93 441 67 23; Carrer de la Concòrdia 21; mains €10-15; ⊘8.30pm-midnight Mon-Sat; Ⓜ Poble Sec) For decades this former wine store has been dishing out dinner to often raucous groups. Traditional Catalan cooking is the name of the game. Surrounded by aged wine barrels, take your place at old tables and benches and perhaps order the signature *conill a la jumillana* (fried rabbit with garlic, onion and herbs).

LA BELLA NAPOLI
PIZZA €€

Map p314 (☑93 442 50 56; www.bellanapoli.es; Carrer de Margarit 14; mains €10-24; ⊘1.30pm-midnight; Ⓜ Paral·lel) From the simple margherita to the more complex *tartufo* with gorgonzola and black truffles, delicious pizzas at this busy long-established Italian specialist are done the way they make them in Naples. There are also meaty mains and delicate homemade pastas.

✖ Sant Antoni

FEDERAL
CAFE €

Map p314 (☑93 187 36 07; www.federalcafe.es; Carrer del Parlament 39; mains €7-12; ⊘8am-11.30pm Mon-Thu, to midnight Fri, 9am-midnight Sat, 9am-5.30pm Sun; 🖥🍴; Ⓜ Sant Antoni) On Sant Antoni's main stretch, which now teems with cafes, Australian-founded Federal was the trailbazer, with its expertly crafted coffee (including flat whites) and superb creative brunches ranging from avocado toast with carrot hummus to baked eggs. Later in the day, try veggie burgers or grilled salmon with soba noodles. Head to the breezy roof terrace or grab a cushioned window seat.

BAR RAMÓN
TAPAS €

Map p314 (☑93 325 02 83; http://barramon.dudaone.com; Carrer del Comte Borrell 81; tapas €5-12; ⊘8.30-11.30pm Mon-Thu, 2-4pm & 8.30-11.30pm Fri & Sat; Ⓜ Sant Antoni) A much-loved Sant Antoni haunt, Bar Ramón is a lively blues-filled joint opposite the market. Old photos of American musical R&B legends (and a few guitars) line the walls – a fine backdrop for tapas like tender slices of cured ham, grilled prawns and house-speciality *jabuguitos* (chorizo cooked in

cider with Cabrales-cheese sauce). It fills up fast, so reserve ahead.

SANT ANTONI GLORIÓS
TAPAS €

Map p314 (☑93 424 06 28; www.facebook.com/SantAntoniGlorioso; Carrer de Mansó 42; dishes €4-12; ⊘1-11pm Tue-Sat, 1-3pm Sun; Ⓜ Poble Sec) Launched by neighbourhood chef Fran Manduley, this smartly updated Sant Antoni bodega with oversized mirrors, wine-barrel tables and bottle-lined walls pulls in a local crowd. Tapas are unpretentious and expertly prepared, including vegetable-stuffed omelettes and charcuterie platters of truffled mortadella with Catalan cheeses. Vermouth-hour snacks include cod fritters and *patates braves*.

ESCRIBÀ
PASTRIES €

Map p314 (☑93 454 75 35; www.escriba.es; Gran Via de les Corts Catalanes 546; pastries €2-7; ⊘9am-9pm; Ⓜ Urgell) The Escribà family carries forward a tradition (since 1906) of melting *barcelonins'* hearts with remarkable pastries and chocolate creations. Seasonal treats include the Easter *bunyols de xocolata* (little round pastry balls filled with chocolate cream). There's another branch (p80) in a Modernista setting on La Rambla.

JUICE HOUSE
HEALTH FOOD €

Map p314 (☑93 117 15 15; www.thejuicehouse.es; Carrer del Parlament 12; dishes €5-12; ⊘10am-4.30pm Mon-Wed, to 11.30pm Thu-Sat, to 7.30pm Sun; 🍴; Ⓜ Poble Sec) Rustic wood tables, exposed bulbs and fresh-cut flowers evoke a Zen-like vibe at this warm health-focused cafe. Caribbean, Mediterranean and Asian flavours combine in thoughtfully prepared dishes rooted in fresh local produce, such as superfood bowls, cheese boards or salmon in coconut-vermouth sauce. Oat-and-chia pancakes, açaí fruit bowls and oven-baked eggs make fine breakfasts.

CAFÈ COMETA
CAFE €

Map p314 (http://cafecometa.com; Carrer del Parlament 20; dishes €5-7; ⊘9am-10pm Mon-Wed, to 11pm Thu-Sun; 🖥; Ⓜ Poble Sec) A colourful, cosy cafe with mismatched furniture, paintings climbing the walls, a vintage-style kitchen and a bar covered in posters announcing fun cultural events around town. Cometa does speciality coffee, home-baked cakes, fresh juices and tasty sandwiches made with artisan breads for its trendy devotees. It also runs several other

COLÒNIA GÜELL

Apart from La Sagrada Família, Gaudí's last big project was the creation of a utopian textile workers' complex for his magnate patron Eusebi Güell at Santa Coloma de Cervelló, 14km west of central Barcelona. Gaudí's main role at **Colònia Güell** (☑93 630 58 07; www.gaudicoloniaguell.org; Carrer Claudi Güell, Santa Coloma de Cervelló; adult/concession €8.50/6.50; ⊙10am-7pm Mon-Fri, to 3pm Sat & Sun May-Oct, 10am-5pm Mon-Fri, to 3pm Sat & Sun Nov-Apr; ☒FGC lines S3, S4, S8, S9 to Colònia Güell) was to create the church. Work began in 1908, but the idea fizzled out eight years later and Gaudí only finished the crypt – the Unesco-listed monument is still a working church, and key to understanding what the master had planned for his magnum opus, La Sagrada Família.

The mostly brick-clad columns that support the ribbed vaults of the church ceiling are inclined at all angles in much the way you might expect trees in a forest to lean. That effect was deliberate, but also grounded in physics. Gaudí worked out the angles so that their load would be transmitted from the ceiling to the earth without the help of extra buttressing. Similar thinking lay behind his plans for La Sagrada Família, whose Gothic-inspired structure would tower above any medieval building, without requiring a single buttress. Gaudí's hand is visible down to the wavy design of the pews. The primary colours in the curvaceous plant-shaped stained-glass windows are another reminder of the era in which the crypt was built.

There are guided midday tours (adult/concession including admission €12/9.50) of the Colònia and crypt on Saturday in Spanish and Sunday in Catalan; book ahead. In a five-room display with audiovisual and interactive material, the history and life of the industrial colony and the story of Gaudí's church are told in colourful fashion.

Near the church spread the brick houses designed for the factory workers, which are still inhabited today. A short stroll away, the 23 factory buildings of a Modernista industrial complex, idle since the 1970s, were brought back to life in the early 2000s, with shops and businesses moving into the renovated complex.

cafes around town, including Cosmo (p159) in L'Eixample.

MANSO'S CAFE
CAFE €

Map p314 (☑93 348 63 46; www.facebook.com/mansoscafe; Carrer de Mansó 1; snacks €2-6; ⊙7.30am-7pm Mon-Sat, from 8.30am Sun; ☒Poble Sec) Dangling plant baskets and kitchen utensils adorn this cosy little cafe loved for its fresh home-baked pastries, especially its Nordic-style cinnamon buns, as well as its own quiches, salads and sandwiches and seasonal coffee.

FÀBRICA MORITZ
GASTROPUB €€

Map p314 (☑93 426 00 50; www.moritz.com; Ronda de Sant Antoni 41; tapas €4-10, mains €8-18; ⊙8.30am-1.30am Sun-Thu, to 2am Fri & Sat; ☒Sant Antoni) In a building redesigned by architect Jean Nouvel, with a menu created by chef Jordi Vilà of Michelin-starred Alkímia (p200) (also on the premises), the popular Moritz brewery restaurant offers pan-European gastropub fare such as gourmet sandwiches, wood-oven-baked eggs, fish and chips, frankfurters with sauerkraut and *flammkuchen* (Alsatian-style

pizza). The adjacent wine bar does tapas, vermouth and beer tastings.

CASA DORITA
TAPAS €€

Map p314 (☑93 853 91 95; http://casadorita.com; Carrer de Tamarit 142; dishes €5-15; ⊙9.30am-4.30pm & 8.30-11.30pm Tue-Sat, 10am-4pm Sun; ☑; ☒Sant Antoni) Deliciously uncomplicated *cuina de mercat* (market cuisine) based on quality seasonal ingredients is the thing at Casa Dorita, which honours a long line of female family cooks. Breads come from a neighbourhood baker, cheeses and eggs from local farmers, and every Thursday there's lunchtime paella or *fideuà* (a Catalan dish similar to paella). A handful of tables dot the pavement terrace.

BODEGA SEPÚLVEDA
CATALAN €€

Map p314 (☑93 323 59 44; www.bodegasepulveda.com; Carrer de Sepúlveda 173; tapas €6-16, mains €9-20; ⊙8pm-12.30am Mon, 1.30-4.30pm & 8pm-12.30am Tue-Fri, 1.30-4.30pm & 8pm-1am Sat; ☒Universitat) Still owned by the same family, this venerable tavern has been in business since 1952. The dizzying range of dishes mixes traditional Catalan faves like *cap i pota* (stew made with bits of the calf you don't want to think about) with more surprising options such as courgette carpaccio draped in cod and Parmesan, accompanied by excellent Catalan and other Spanish wines.

BAMBALINA
MEDITERRANEAN €€

Map p314 (☑93 423 73 76; Avinguda del Paral·lel 142; mains €8-15; ☺1-4pm & 8-11pm; ☎📶; ⓜPoble Sec) Shelves filled with wine bottles line the walls of this cavernous red-hued space, which turns out smart, seasonal contemporary Mediterranean cuisine like slow-cooked Iberian pork, truffle risotto and salt-baked lamb with potato confit. Two-course lunch menus (€11.45) and varied dinner menus (€21 or €25) are fantastic value.

ALKÍMIA
CATALAN €€€

Map p314 (☑93 207 61 15; www.alkimia.cat; Ronda de Sant Antoni 41; mains €26-47, tasting menu €138; ☺1.30-3.30pm & 8-10.30pm Mon-Fri; ⓜUniversitat) Inside the innovatively redesigned Fàbrica Moritz (p198) brewery, amid tile-patterned floors and shimmering white surfaces, culinary alchemist Jordi Vilà creates refined Catalan dishes with a twist that have earned him a Michelin star: potato-and-truffle soufflé, wild fish of the day in shellfish stew, mushrooms with caramelised cabbage and carrot toffee, and other seriously original visions.

DRINKING & NIGHTLIFE

Montjuïc's has a sprinkling of bars and clubs but the most popular districts for nightlife are currently Poble Sec and neighbouring Sant Antoni where a trendy, buzzing and ever-growing array of chic cafes, creative bars, busy clubs, avant-garde boutiques and new-wave restaurants attract a young, stylish and in-the-kow crowd. .

🍷 Montjuïc

★LA CASETA DEL MIGDIA
BAR

Map p314 (☑617 956572; www.lacaseta.org; Mirador del Migdia; ☺8pm-1am Wed-Fri, noon-1am Sat & Sun Apr-Sep, noon-sunset Sat & Sun Oct-Mar; ☐150) The effort of getting to what is, for all intents and purposes, a simple *xiringuito* (summer snack bar) perched atop

Montjuïc's seaward slopes, is worth it. Gaze out on the Mediterranean over a beer or soft drink by day. As sunset approaches, the atmosphere changes, as reggae, samba and funk waft out over the hillside. Food is fired on outdoor grills.

Walk west along the dirt track below the walls of the Castell de Montjuïc or follow Passeig del Migdia – look for signs to the Mirador del Migdia.

SALTS MONTJUÏC
BAR

Map p314 (☑616 893356; www.saltsmontjuic. com; Avinguda de Miramar 31; ☺10am-midnight Sun-Wed & Thu, to 1am Fri & Sat; ☐55, 150) Overlooking Montjuïc's municipal pools (with a €25 evening swim-and-dine deal available!), this all-day terrace bar from the team behind much-loved La Caseta del Migdia enjoys exquisite views across town. Grab a vermouth or *cava* (both €3.50) and a few tapas such as *patates braves*, squid-in-ink croquettes and cured-ham *montaditos*.

LA TERRRAZZA
CLUB

Map p314 (☑687 969825; http://laterrrazza.com; Avinguda de Francesc Ferrer i Guàrdia 13, Poble Espanyol; cover €10-15; ☺midnight-6.30am Thu-Sat May-Sep; ☐13, 23, 150, ⓜEspanya) Come summer, this re-created Balearic-style mansion attracts squadrons of beautiful people, locals and visitors alike, for a full-on night of music (mainly house, techno and electronica), cocktails and vaguely Ibiza vibes. It's set partly under the stars, inside the Poble Espanyol (p192) complex.

🍷 Poble Sec

★ABIRRADERO
MICROBREWERY

Map p314 (☑93 461 94 46; www.abirradero.com; Carrer de Vilà i Vilà 77; ☺noon-midnight Sun-Thu, to 2am Fri & Sat; ☎; ⓜParal·lel) Barcelona is spoilt for choice with craft breweries, and this bright, buzzing space is one of the best. There are 40 of its own beers rotating on the taps, including IPAral·lel (a double IPA), Imperial Choco-Icecream-Cookies Stout, and Trigotopia. Tapas, sharing boards and burgers are standouts from the kitchen (dishes €5 to €14). You'll occasionally catch live jazz and blues here.

EL ROUGE
BAR

Map p314 (☑634 127581; www.facebook.com/elrougebar; Carrer del Poeta Cabanyes 21; ☺9pm-2.30am Wed-Thu & Sun, to 3am Fri & Sat;

☎; Ⓜ Paral·lel) Decadence is the word that springs to mind in this bordello-red lounge-cocktail bar, with acid jazz, drum and bass, and other sounds drifting in the background, and drinks at €7 to €14. The walls are covered in heavy-framed paintings, dim lamps and mirrors, and no two chairs are alike. You can sometimes catch DJs, risqué poetry soirées, cabaret shows, jam sessions or even tango dancing.

LA FEDERICA
BAR

Map p314 (☑93 600 59 01; www.facebook.com/barlafederica; Carrer de Salvà 3; ⊘7pm-1am Tue, to 2am Wed & Thu, to 3am Fri & Sat; Ⓜ Paral·lel) With weekend parties, rotating art exhibits, vintage decor and jazzy geometric-print walls, La Federica has become a favourite of the local LGBTIQ+ scene. Thoughtfully prepared artisan tapas like tortilla and Catalan cheeses accompany well-mixed G&Ts, creative cocktails and Spanish wines.

REDRUM
BAR

Map p314 (☑670 269126; www.facebook.com/tacosredrum; Carrer de Margarit 36; ⊘6pm-1am Wed & Thu, to 2am Fri & Sat, to 12.30am Sun; Ⓜ Poble Sec) Redrum's craft brews and cocktails (€5 to €9, including punchy margaritas) are complemented by Mexican street food (€6 to €10), especially excellent tacos, nachos and ceviche. It has a brightly coloured interior and friendly service.

TINTA ROJA
BAR

Map p314 (☑93 443 32 43; www.tintaroja.cat; Carrer de la Creu dels Molers 17; ⊘8pm-midnight Wed, 8.30pm-2am Thu, to 3am Fri & Sat, shorter hours Aug; Ⓜ Poble Sec) A succession of nooks and crannies, dotted with flea-market finds and dimly lit in violets, reds and yellows, makes Tinta Roja an intimate spot for a craft beer, cocktail or glass of Argentinean wine. There are also tango classes and shows in the back, featuring anything from actors to dancers to acrobats (check schedules online).

SALA PLATAFORMA
CLUB

Map p314 (☑93 329 00 29; www.salaplataforma.com; Carrer Nou de la Rambla 145; cover incl drink €8-13; ⊘10pm-6am Thu-Sat, from midnight Sun; Ⓜ Paral.lel) With two adjoining if smallish dance spaces, Plataforma feels like a clandestine location in an otherwise quiet residential street. Inside this friendly, straightforward, long-established dance dive, you'll find popular '80s grooves, timeless rock,

reggaeton and occasional live bands – plus drum and bass on Thursday.

MALEVO
BAR

Map p314 (☑93 137 57 70; www.facebook.com/malevobar; Carrer de Margarit 52; ⊘8pm-midnight Mon, to 1am Tue-Thu to 2am Fri & Sat; Ⓜ Poble Sec, Paral·lel) This joyful bar feels a bit like a lost cabin in the woods with its wood-panelled walls, tiled floors and old sporting photos. Once you've wedged yourself alongside a tiny table, you can join the young soul- and blues-loving crowd over inexpensive *empanades* and vermouth. Bands also occasionally play.

🍷 Sant Antoni

BAR CALDERS
BAR

Map p314 (☑93 329 93 49; Carrer del Parlament 25; ⊘5pm-2am Mon-Thu, to 2.30am Fri, 11am-2.30am Sat, 11am-12.30am Sun; Ⓜ Poble Sec) Neighbourhood fave Bar Calders bills itself as a wine bar, with a range of Catalan drops gracing its selection (glasses €2 to €4). At weekends it's unbeatable as an all-day cafe, tapas and vermouth bar, and its outdoor tables on a tiny pedestrian lane have become the go-to meeting point for Sant Antoni's boho set.

LA MARI OLLERO
WINE BAR

Map p314 (☑93 327 84 85; www.lamariollero.com; Carrer de Calàbria 5; ⊘noon-midnight, hours can vary; Ⓜ Poble Sec) With red-brick walls and marble tables, elegant La Mari Ollero brings a buzzy contemporary spin and a jolly Andalucian touch to the classic Catalan *vermuteria*. Wines (glasses €3 to €5) come from the south (including sherry-style Montilla-Moriles) as well as Catalonia and elsewhere

MONTJUÏC, POBLE SEC & SANT ANTONI DRINKING & NIGHTLIFE

HOT SPOTS

The area of Poble Sec (literally 'Dry Town'!) and neighbouring Sant Antoni is the hot destination of the moment, with a burgeoning array of chic cafes, creative bars, busy clubs, avant-garde boutiques and new-wave restaurants. It seems now everyone wants to live in this once-sleepy corner of Barcelona, and the area draws young, stylish crowds.

in northern Spain. Tapas (€1 to €6) combine flavours from Barcelona and Córdoba (*patates braves, salmorejo,* and so on).

HORCHATERIA SIRVENT   CAFE

Map p314 (📞93 441 27 20; www.turronessirvent.com; Carrer del Parlament 56; ⊙9am-11pm; MSant Antoni) Along with ice cream, *granissat* (iced fruit crush) and *turrón* (nougat), this old-school parlour has served *barcelonins'* favourite *orxata/horchata* (tiger-nut drink; €2 to €4) since 1926 – the best you'll try without having to catch the train down to this drink's spiritual home, Valencia.

 ## ENTERTAINMENT

SALA APOLO   LIVE MUSIC

Map p314 (📞93 441 40 01; www.sala-apolo.com; Carrer Nou de la Rambla 113; club incl drink from €15; ⊙concerts from 8pm, club from midnight; MParal·lel) Red velvet dominates and you feel as though you're in a movie-set dance-hall scene at this fine old theatre turned club and concert hall. 'Nasty Mondays' are aimed at a diehard, never-stop-dancing crowd. Earlier in the evening, concerts take place here and in 'La 2', a smaller auditorium downstairs – everything from local bands and burlesque shows to big-name international acts.

BARTS   LIVE PERFORMANCE

Map p314 (Barcelona Arts on Stage; 📞93 324 84 92; www.barts.cat; Avinguda del Paral·lel 62; MParal·lel) BARTS has a solid reputation for its innovative line-up of urban-dance troupes, electro swing, psychedelic pop, circus acrobatics and other shows. Its smart design combines a comfortable midsized auditorium with excellent acoustics. Hours and ticket prices vary; check online.

GRAN BODEGA SALTÓ   LIVE MUSIC

Map p314 (📞93 441 37 09; www.bodegasalto.net; Carrer de Blesa 36; ⊙6pm-1am Mon-Thu, noon-3am Fri & Sat, noon-midnight Sun; MParal·lel) The ranks of barrels and classic tapas menu give away this century-old bar's history as a traditional bodega. Now, after a little homemade psychedelic redecoration with mismatched lamps, figurines and old Chinese beer ads, it's a magnet for an eclectic barfly crowd and gets busy during live-music sessions (usually 8pm Thursday, 1pm and 8pm Friday to Sunday, but check online).

HIROSHIMA   LIVE PERFORMANCE

Map p314 (📞93 315 54 58; www.hiroshima.cat; Carrer de Vilà i Vilà 65; ⊙6-11pm Wed-Sun; MParal·lel) Set in a former elevator factory, this creative lynchpin hosts emerging and avant-garde musicians, dancers and performing artists. There are two stages (seating 130 and 250 people) and a lively ground-floor bar where you can grab a drink after the show. For unconventional performances, this is a good place to look.

TEATRE MERCAT DE LES FLORS   DANCE

Map p314 (📞93 256 26 00; www.mercatflors.cat; Carrer de Lleida 59; ⊙box office 2hr before show; 🚇55) Next door to the **Teatre Lliure** (Map p314; 📞93 289 27 70; www.teatrelliure.com; Plaça de Margarida Xirgu 1; ⊙box office 9am-8pm, plus 2hr before performance; 🚇55), and together known as the Ciutat de Teatre (Theatre City), this spacious modern stage is Barcelona's top venue for local and international contemporary dance acts.

RENOIR FLORIDABLANCA   CINEMA

Map p314 (www.cinesrenoir.com; Carrer de Floridablanca 135; MSant Antoni) With seven screens, this cinema shows a mix of quality art-house flicks and blockbusters.

 ## SHOPPING

Shopping options are fairly limited among these neighbourhoods. Sant Antoni offers the best exploring for shoppers, with a famed food market, and secondhand shops and galleries sprinkled on its tree-lined streets. The streets near Carrer del Parlament are the best place to roam.

POPCORN STORE   FASHION & ACCESSORIES

Map p314 (www.facebook.com/popcornstorebcn; Carrer Viladomat 30-32; ⊙11am-3pm & 4.30-8.30pm Mon-Sat) Cutting-edge Barcelona women's labels at this pink-patterned boutique mean asymmetrical tops, jackets and dresses, bold prints and delicate lace. Men will find stylish shirts, trousers and belts from Italian and other European designers.

LLIBRERIA CALDERS BOOKS

Map p314 (☑93 442 78 31; www.facebook.com/lacalders; Passatge de Pere Calders 9; ☺10am-9pm Mon-Fri, 11am-9pm Sat, 11.30am-7pm Sun, closed Sun Aug; Ⓜ Poble Sec) Spread across what was once a button factory, this lively bookshop and literary hub stocks both secondhand and brand-new titles in a stylish concrete-covered space, and puts an emphasis on local authors.

BRAVA FASHION & ACCESSORIES

Map p314 (www.bravafabrics.com; Carrer del Parlament 25; ☺11am-9pm Mon-Fri, 11am-3pm & 4-9pm Sat & Sun; Ⓜ Poble Sec) 🖉 Inspired by travel and the arts, fair-trade Barcelona-born label Brava works exclusively with Catalan and other Spanish and Portuguese ateliers, and uses only sustainable materials to craft its stylishly minimalist men's and women's fashion. Finds include fun shirts and blouses in millennial-beloved prints such as avocados and bicycles.

ARENAS SHOPPING CENTRE

Map p314 (☑93 289 02 44; www.arenasdebarcelona.com; Gran Via de les Corts Catalanes 373-385; ☺10am-10pm Mon-Sat Jun-Sep, 9am-9pm Mon-Sat Oct-May; Ⓜ Espanya) Housed within an old 1900-built bull ring (bullfighting ceased in 1977), Las Arenas is one of the city's best malls, converted by Italian-British architect Lord Richard Rogers in 2011. The exterior still features the original arched windows and Moorish-inspired designs, while inside it's sleek and modern, with high-street stores. The open-air rooftop offers spectacular city views and several restaurants.

SPORTS & ACTIVITIES

MY FAVOURITE THINGS TOURS

(☑637 265405; www.myft.net; tours per person from €30) Offers tours (with no more than 10 participants) based on numerous themes: street art, shopping, food, movies, musical journeys and forgotten neighbourhoods are among the options, and there are tours of Poble Sec and Sant Antoni. Other activities include flamenco and salsa classes, cooking workshops, and bicycle rides in and out of Barcelona. Book online.

PISCINES BERNAT PICORNELL SWIMMING

Map p314 (☑93 423 40 41; www.picornell.cat; Avinguda de l'Estadi 30-38; adult/child €12.50/7.50, nudist hours €6.85/4.80; ☺6.45am-midnight Mon-Fri, 7am-9pm Sat, 7.30am-4pm Sun; ☐13, 150) Admission to Barcelona's official Olympic pool on Montjuïc also includes use of the complex's fitness room, sauna, Jacuzzi, steam bath and track. The outdoor pool, with incredible panoramic city views, has reduced hours outside summer and closes in December and January. Nudist-only swimming times are 9.15pm to 11pm Saturday and 4.15pm to 6pm Sunday October to May.

Camp Nou, Pedralbes & La Zona Alta

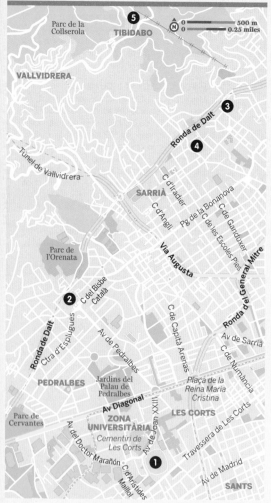

Neighbourhood Top Five

1 **Camp Nou** (p206) Reliving the great moments of FC Barcelona, one of the world's legendary football teams, at the multimedia museum – or, better yet, cheering along at a live game.

2 **Reial Monestir de Santa Maria de Pedralbes** (p207) Wandering around the 14th-century cloister and admiring exquisite medieval murals.

3 **CosmoCaixa** (p209) Getting a feel for the Amazon (tropical downpour and all) and travelling through Earth's evolution at warp speed at this excellent science museum.

4 **Bellesguard** (p217) Gazing upon Gaudí's imposing, medieval-like masterpiece, with its crenellated walls, stained glass and ornate ironwork.

5 **Tibidabo** (p210) Escaping up to this forested mountain for awe-inspiring views and an old-fashioned amusement park – or hiking and running along its protected trails.

For more detail of this area see Map p317 and p318 ➡

Explore Camp Nou, Pedralbes & La Zona Alta

Few visitors make the journey to this vast area (north of L'Eixample and west of Gràcia) due to its relative remoteness and the longer distances between its scattered attractions. But venture here and you'll uncover some intriguing sights and explore Barcelona off the usual tourist paths.

Framing the north end of La Zona Alta (the High Zone) are the Collserola hills, mostly protected by the rugged, pine-sprinkled Parc Natural de Collserola (p208). Looming Tibidabo hill (512m) is the most recognisable landmark, with the towering Basílica del Sagrat Cor (p210) visible from all over the city. Tibidabo marks Barcelona's highest point, and its old-fashioned amusement park and panoramic views are the big attraction.

South of Tibidabo (in northwest Barcelona) sits Sarrià (p212), a wealthy neighbourhood of brick streets, tiny plazas and medieval buildings. Another area well worth exploring is **Sant Gervasi**, immediately east of Sarrià, with its upmarket restaurants and bars and village-like feel. West of Sarrià, upmarket Pedralbes has a mix of high-end gated residences and boxy apartment buildings, peaceful streets and manicured gardens, as well as the atmospheric 14th-century monastery (p207). Just south of Pedralbes lies the great shrine to Catalan football, Camp Nou (p216), home of FC Barcelona.

Local Life

→ **Outdoor pursuits** Head to the hills to join *barcelonins* running, hiking, mountain biking and picnicking in the sprawling Parc Natural de Collserola (p208).

→ **Nightlife** Les Corts' Plaça de la Concòrdia is a charming spot for drinks and tapas at bars such as El Maravillas (p215).

→ **Village days** The picturesque narrow lanes of old Sarrià (p212) are idyllic for a stroll, stopping for a gourmet meal on the leafy terrace at Vivanda (p211).

Getting There & Away

→ **Metro** Línia 3 is handy for the Parc del Laberint d'Horta (Mundet), and Camp Nou and Palau de Pedralbes (Palau Reial).

→ **Train** FGC trains are good for getting close to sights in and around Tibidabo and the Parc Natural de Collserola.

→ **Funicular** The Funicular de Vallvidrera and Funicular del Tibidabo normally run up to Tibidabo, though the latter was closed for renovations at research time.

→ **Tram** T1, T2 and T3 serve the area's southwest. The long-running *tramvia blau* from Avinguda del Tibidabo to Plaça del Doctor Andreu was closed at the time of research for modernisation works.

Lonely Planet's Top Tip

Making the most of these scattered neighbourhoods requires some advance planning. Transport links are limited and many of the attractions here have varied opening hours; check before travelling.

Best Places to Eat

→ Aspic (p211)

→ La Balsa (p213)

→ Via Veneto (p213)

→ Tapas 24 (p209)

→ Vivanda (p211)

For reviews, see p209. ➡

Best Places to Drink

→ El Maravillas (p215)

→ Gimlet (p215)

→ Mirablau (p215)

For reviews, see p215. ➡

Best Parks & Gardens

→ Parc Natural de Collserola (p208)

→ Parc del Laberint d'Horta (p214)

→ Jardins del Palau de Pedralbes (p208)

→ Parc de la Creueta del Coll (p208)

For reviews, see p208. ➡

JOIN BARCELONA FC FANS AT CAMP NOU

While nothing compares to the excitement of attending a live match, the Barça Stadium Tour & Museum is a must for football fans. On a visit to FC Barcelona's hallowed home ground (guided or self-guided), you'll get an in-depth look at the club, starting with a museum filled with multimedia exhibits, trophies and historical displays, followed by a tour of the stadium.

Camp Nou Experience Museum

Tours begin in FC Barcelona's high-tech museum, where massive touchscreens allow visitors to explore arcane aspects of the legendary team. You can also watch videos of artful goals. Displays delve into the club's history, its social commitment and connection to Catalan identity, and in-depth stats of on-field action. Sound installations include the club's anthem (with translations in many languages) and the match-day roar of the crowds.

The museum's highlights are the photo section, the goal videos and the views out over the stadium. You can admire the golden boots (in at least one case literally) of great goal-scorers of the past and learn about the legends who have played for the club over the years, including Diego Maradona, Ronaldinho, László Kubala and many others. A special area is devoted to Argentine Lionel Messi, considered one of the greatest footballers playing the game today.

The Stadium

Gazing out across Camp Nou is an experience in itself. The stadium, built in 1957 and enlarged for the 1982 World Cup, is one of the world's biggest, holding almost 100,000 people. After major renovations wrap up in August 2023 (the stadium will remain open throughout), Camp Nou will have a capacity of 106,000. The club has a membership of 143,000.

Tours take in the visiting team's dressing room, then head out through the tunnel and on to the edge of the pitch. You'll also get to visit the press room. Set aside at least 1½ hours. A Players Experience ticket (adult/child €149/99) allows you to visit the FC Barcelona dressing room and includes two free photos, a virtual experience and a leaving gift.

Getting Tickets

Tickets to FC Barcelona matches are available at Camp Nou, online (through FC Barcelona's official website), and through various city locations, including the main Plaça de Catalunya tourist office (p272) and FC Botiga stores. Tickets can cost anything from €39 to upwards of €400, depending on the seat and match. On match day the ticket windows are open at **gate 9** (Map p318; Avinguda de Joan XXIII; ⏱9.15am-7.30pm in season, 9.45am-6.30pm Mon-Sat, to 2.30pm Sun out of season, 9.15am–kick-off match days; Ⓜ Palau Reial) and gate 14 from 9.15am until kick-off. Tickets for matches with Real Madrid sell out years in advance.

If you attend a game, go early so you'll have ample time to find your seat (this stadium is massive) and soak up the atmosphere.

You will almost definitely find scalpers lurking near the ticket windows. They are often club members and can sometimes get you in at a significant reduction. Don't pay until you are safely seated.

DON'T MISS

➡ Hearing the rousing anthem sung before FC Barcelona takes the field

➡ The museum's footage of the team's best goals

➡ A tour of the stadium

PRACTICALITIES

➡ Map p318, C8

➡ ☎ 902 189900

➡ www.fcbarcelona.com

➡ Gate 9, Avinguda de Joan XXIII

➡ adult/child 4-10yr self-guided tour €29.50/23.50, guided tour €45/37

➡ ⏱ 9.30am-7.30pm mid-Apr–mid-Oct, 10am-6.30pm Mon-Sat, to 2.30pm Sun mid-Oct–mid-Apr

➡ Ⓜ Palau Reial

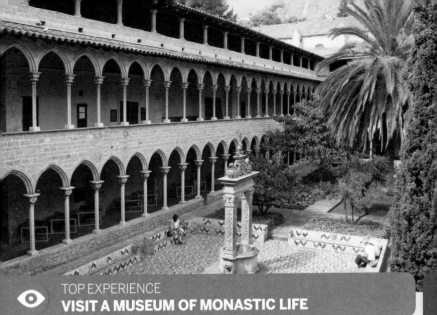

TOP EXPERIENCE
VISIT A MUSEUM OF MONASTIC LIFE

Founded in 1327, the serene convent Reial Monestir de Santa Maria de Pedralbes is now a museum of monastic life (the few remaining nuns have moved into more modern neighbouring buildings). Full of architectural treasures, it stands in a residential area that was countryside until the 20th century, and which remains a divinely quiet corner of Barcelona.

The convent's architectural highlight is the large, elegant, three-storey cloister, a jewel of Catalan Gothic, built in the early 14th century. Following its course to the right, stop at the first chapel, the Capella de Sant Miquel. Ferrer Bassá, one of Catalonia's earliest documented painters, created its (now restored) murals in 1346. Nearby is the ornamental 14th-century grave of Queen Elisenda, who founded the convent. Unusually, it's divided in two: the cloister side shows her dressed as a penitent widow, while the other part, an alabaster masterpiece inside the adjacent church, depicts her dressed as queen.

Strolling around the ground floor of the cloister, you can peer into the restored refectory, kitchen, stables, stores and a reconstruction of the infirmary, as well as the tiled cistern. Eating in the refectory must not have been a whole lot of fun, judging by the exhortations of *Silentium* (Silence) and *Audi Tacens* (Listen and Keep Quiet) written on the walls. Opening off the refectory is the Claustre dels Gats, named for its cat flap into the kitchen. Upstairs is a grand hall that was once the *dormidor* (sleeping quarters); its tiny night cells have long since been removed. Today a modest collection of the monastery's art, especially Gothic devotional works, graces this space.

DON'T MISS

➡ Ferrer Bassá's murals

➡ The three-storey Gothic cloister

➡ The refectory's admonishing inscriptions

PRACTICALITIES

➡ Map p318, B5

➡ ☎93 256 34 34

➡ http://monestir pedralbes.bcn.cat

➡ Baixada del Monestir 9

➡ adult/child €5/free, from 3pm Sun & 1st Sun of month free

➡ ⏰10am-5pm Tue-Fri, to 7pm Sat, to 8pm Sun Apr-Sep, 10am-2pm Tue-Fri, to 5pm Sat & Sun Oct-Mar

➡ 🚌H4, V5, 63, 68, 75, 78, 🚇FGC Reina Elisenda

◉ SIGHTS

CAMP NOU MUSEUM
See p206.

**REIAL MONESTIR DE SANTA
MARIA DE PEDRALBES** MONASTERY
See p207.

PARC NATURAL DE COLLSEROLA PARK
Map p318 (☑93 280 35 52; www.parcnatural
collserola.cat; Carretera de l'Església 92; ⊙Cen-
tre d'Informació 9.30am-3pm, Can Coll 9.30am-
2.30pm Sun & holidays Sep–mid-Jun; ℝFGC Baixador de Vallvidrera, ℝFunicular de Vallvidrera)
🖉 *Barcelonins* needing an easy escape
from the city seek out this protected pine-
scented 80-sq-km park. It's a great place
to hike, run and bike, and has a smattering of country chapels (some Romanesque),
the ruined 14th-century Castellciuro castle
in the west, various lookout points and, to
the north, the grand 15th-century Can Coll
farmhouse, now an environmental education centre. Pick up maps from park information centres such as the Carretera de
l'Església 92 headquarters (near Baixador
de Vallvidrera FGC station).

Opposite the information centre, you
can learn about one of Barcelona's great
19th-century writers, Jacint Verdaguer, at
the **Vil·la Joana** (Map p318; ☑93 256 21 00;
https://ajuntament.barcelona.cat; Carretera de
l'Església 104; adult/child €2/free; ⊙10am-2pm
Thu, to 7pm Sat, Sun & holidays; ℝFGC Baixador
de Vallvidrera), where he spent his final days.

**JARDINS DEL PALAU
DE PEDRALBES** PARK
Map p318 (Avinguda Diagonal 686; ⊙10am-9pm
Apr-Oct, to 7pm Nov-Mar; ⓂPalau Reial) `FREE`
Sculptures, fountains, citrus trees, bamboo
groves, fragrant eucalyptus, towering cypresses and bougainvillea-covered nooks
lie scattered along the paths criss-crossing
the small, enchanting gardens of the **Palau
de Pedralbes** (closed to the public). Among
the little-known treasures here are a vine-
covered parabolic pergola and a gurgling
fountain of Hercules (buried in thick veg-
etation before being rediscovered in 1984),
both designed by Antoni Gaudí (the fountain's bust is a re-creation). At the park's
northeast end stand the Gaudí-designed
Pavellons Güell gatehouses.

The Palau, in whose original renovations
Gaudí also had a hand, belonged to Eusebi
Güell (Gaudí's patron) until he donated it
as a royal residence in 1918; it was later
rebuilt in its current Noucentista incar-
nation. Past guests include King Alfonso
XIII, the president of Catalonia and General Franco.

PAVELLONS GÜELL ARCHITECTURE
Map p318 (☑93 317 76 52; Avinguda de Pedralbes
7; ⓂPalau Reial) Created by Gaudí for the
Finca Güell, as the Güell estate attached to
today's Palau de Pedralbes was then called,
these stables and porter's lodge were built
between 1884 and 1887, when Gaudí was
strongly impressed by Islamic architecture.
One of the most eye-catching features is
the fantastical wrought-iron dragon gate
on Avinguda de Pedralbes. You can usually peer inside on guided visits, though
the Pavellons were closed for renovations at
research time and not expected to reopen
until 2024.

FUNDACIÓ SUÑOL GALLERY
Map p318 (☑93 496 10 32; www.fundaciosunol.
org; Carrer de Mejía Lequerica 14; adult/child
€4/2; ⊙11am-2pm & 4-7pm Mon-Fri, 4-8pm 1st
Sat of month; ⓂLes Corts) Rotating exhibitions of portions of this private collection
of mostly 20th-century art (some 1300
works in total) offer anything from Man
Ray's photography to sculptures by Alberto
Giacometti. You're most likely to run into
Spanish artists – anyone from Picasso to
Jaume Plensa – along with a sprinkling of
international works.

**PARC DE LA
CREUETA DEL COLL** PARK
(Passeig de la Mare de Déu del Coll 77; ⊙10am-
9pm Apr-Oct, to 7pm Nov-Mar; ♿; ℝV19, 22,
119, ⓂPenitents) A favourite with families,
this refreshing palm-studded park centres
on a meandering summer lake-pool for
splashing in, and has swings, showers and
a snack bar. It's set inside a deep former
quarry crater, adorned by Eduardo Chillida's enormous concrete sculpture *Elogio
del agua* (In Praise of Water), suspended
on one side.

Enter from Carrer Mare de Déu del Coll,
1km east of Penitents metro station.

OBSERVATORI FABRA OBSERVATORY
Map p318 (☑93 327 01 21; www.fabra.cat; Carretera del Observatori; night observation €15-25;
⊙night observation by reservation Fri & Sat Oct-

TOP EXPERIENCE
EXPERIENCE AN AMAZONIAN STORM AT COSMOCAIXA

One of the city's most popular family-friendly attractions, this science museum is a favourite with kids (and kids at heart). The single greatest highlight is the recreation of more than 1 sq km of flooded **Amazon rainforest** (*Bosc Inundat*). More than 100 species of Amazon flora and fauna (including anacondas, colourful poisonous frogs, and capybaras) prosper in this unique, living diorama in which you can even experience a tropical downpour.

In another original section, the **Mur Geològic**, seven great chunks of rock (90 metric tons in all) have been assembled to create a 24m-long wall showing different geological processes.

Exhibits cover many fascinating areas of science, from fossils to physics, and from the alphabet to outer space. Interactive exhibits such as the 3D **Planetari** (Planetarium) cost extra. Various guided tours are available.

Outside, you can stroll through the extensive Plaça de la Ciència, whose modest garden flourishes with Mediterranean flora.

DON'T MISS

➡ A tropical storm in the Amazon
➡ The geological wall
➡ The Planetarium

PRACTICALITIES

➡ Museu de la Ciència
➡ Map p318, D2
➡ ☑93 212 60 50
➡ www.cosmocaixa.com
➡ Carrer d'Isaac Newton 26
➡ adult/child €6/free, guided tours from €3, planetarium €4
➡ ⊙10am-8pm
➡ ☐V15, V13, 196, 123, ☐FGC Avinguda Tibidabo

May; ☐FGC Avinguda Tibidabo) Inaugurated in 1904, this Modernista observatory 415m above sea level on Tibidabo is still a functioning scientific foundation. On certain evenings visitors can observe the stars through its grand old telescope; check the website for schedules. Observations must be pre-booked; English-language visits are on Saturday nights.

From mid-June to mid-September, **Sopars amb Estrelles** (Map p318; ☑93 327 01 21; www.sternalia.com; Carretera del Observatori; meal & observatory packages €73-126; ⊙8.15-11.45pm Tue-Sun Jun–early Oct; ☑ ☑) offers an evening of high-end dining and astronomy here.

CENTRE CÍVIC CAN DEU   CULTURAL CENTRE
Map p318 (☑93 410 10 07; http://ajuntament. barcelona.cat; Plaça de la Concòrdia 13; ⊙9am-10pm Mon-Sat, 10am-2pm Sun, closed Aug; ☐Numància) Set in a handsome late-19th-century neo-Gothic mansion designed by Eduard Mercader i Sacancha, this cultural centre stages concerts, exhibitions and workshops throughout the year. Its cafe opens to a peaceful plaza.

COL·LEGI DE LES TERESIANES   ARCHITECTURE
Map p318 (Carrer de Ganduxer 85-105; ☐FGC Les Tres Torres) Built in 1889 for the Order of St Teresa, this striking, fortress-like Gaudí creation has exposed-brick pillars and steep catenary arches, each of which is unique. It functions as a school and the interior is closed to the public.

 EATING

Dining in this area tends to be both a culinary treat and a genuinely local experience. Some of Barcelona's best kitchens are here, often with sweeping views to match.

TAPAS 24   TAPAS €
Map p317 (☑93 858 93 29; www.carlesabel lan.com; Avinguda Diagonal 520; tapas €4-12; ⊙7.45am-midnight Mon-Fri, from 9am Sat & Sun; ☐Diagonal) Barcelona's favourite chef Carles Abellán brings his signature up-market twist on classic tapas to this neon

TIBIDABO: GARDENS OF EARTHLY DELIGHTS

Framing the north end of the city, the pine-forested mountain of **Tibidabo** (Map p318), which tops out at 512m, is the highest peak in Serra de Collserola. Much of its gorgeous green surrounding expanses are protected within the 80-sq-km Parc Natural de Collserola (p208), which is a delight to hike, run and cycle through (as many *barcelonins* do). Tibidabo gets its name from the devil, who, trying to tempt Christ, took him to a high place and said, in Latin: '*Haec omnia tibi dabo si cadens adoraberis me*' ('All this I will give you if you fall down and worship me').

Aside from the natural park's peaceful shaded paths and the superb views from the top of Tibidabo, highlights of a trip out here include an old-fashioned amusement park, the **Parc d'Atraccions** (Map p318; ☑93 211 79 42; www.tibidabo.cat; Plaça de Tibidabo 3-4; adult/child €28.50/10.30; ☉Mar-Dec, hours vary; 🖳; 🚍T2A, T2C); the 288m-high **Torre de Collserola** (Map p318; ☑93 406 93 54; www.torredecollserola.com; Carretera de Vallvidrera al Tibidabo; adult/child €5.60/3.30; ☉noon-2pm Sat & Sun Mar-Dec, hours can vary; 🚍111, 🚋Funicular de Vallvidrera) telecommunications tower, designed by Sir Norman Foster and accessed by prebooked 25-minute tour; and the looming 20th-century **Basílica del Sagrat Cor de Jesús** (Map p318; ☑93 417 56 86; https://tibidabo.salesianos.edu; Plaça de Tibidabo; lift €4; ☉11am-6pm; 🚍T2A, T2C), which has some Modernista influences.

At the time of writing, the long-running *tramvia blau* and the Tibidabo funicular railway – which combined linked the FGC Avinguda Tibidabo train station with the top of Tibidabo via Plaça del Doctor Andreu – were out of action for restoration works. A shiny, new modern funicular is due to launch in 2021; check online for updates. In the meantime, a replacement shuttle, the T2C 'Funibús', runs from Plaça Kennedy (outside Avinguda Tibidabo station) to Plaça de Tibidabo atop the hill (€12.70 including amusement park admission, 20 minutes, every 15 to 30 minutes from 10.30am during park and/or viewing platform opening hours). Alternatively, the T2A 'Tibibús' runs from Plaça de Catalunya to Plaça de Tibidabo (€3, 30 minutes, every 20 to 30 minutes from 10am until 30 minutes after park closure on Saturday, Sunday and other park opening days).

Bus 111 runs between Tibidabo and Vallvidrera, passing in front of the Torre de Collserola.

corner cafe (which remains slightly quieter than its Eixample original, p156). Top picks are the sensational *bikini* toastie (made with truffle and cured ham), just-cooked tortilla, lemon-marinated anchovies and creamy Andalucian *payoyo* cheese. No bookings.

Over at Camp Nou there's another **branch** (Map p318; ☑618 478461; www.carlesabellan.com; Carrer Arístides Maillol 12; tapas €4-12; ☉9am-9pm; 🚇Palau Reial).

PINHAN
CAFE €
Map p317 (☑625 227811; www.facebook.com/pinhancafe; Parc del Turó; dishes €5-15; ☉10am-8.45pm; 🖳; 🚍T1, T2, T3 Francesc Macià) Like a secret little garden in leafy Parc del Turó, this stylish food-truck-inspired cafe serves light Mediterranean meals (hummus, creative salads, grilled halloumi, local-cheese platters) along with home-baked cakes, tempting breakfasts, cocktails and smooth rose-petal lemonade, at sunny tables sprinkled between the palms.

CHENNAI MASALA DOSA
SOUTH INDIAN €
Map p318 (☑935 176 176; www.facebook.com/Chennaimasaladosa; Carrer de Galileo 326; dishes €7-10; ☉1-4pm & 8-11pm; 🖳; 🚇Les Corts) For a splash of authentically delicious South Indian spice, seek out this popular spot near Les Corts' Plaça de la Concòrdia. Omelettes arrive loaded with chillis, classic southern idlis (steamed lentil cakes) are served with spiced sambar and the show-stealing, wafer-thin dosas (lentil pancakes) are stuffed with everything from red-chilli chutney to paneer to potato masala. Punch starters include pakora and puffy vadas.

5° PINO
CATALAN €
Map p318 (☑93 252 22 81; www.quintopino.es; Passeig de la Bonanova 98; tapas €2-10; ☉8am-1.30am; 🖳; 🚍FGC Sarrià) While exploring Sarrià, it's worth detouring a few blocks east to this charming cafe-restaurant, which is a favourite local spot for tasty sandwiches, salads, tortillas, drinks, and tapas like *patates braves* and guacamole

with nachos. It's on a busy road, though the pine-shaded terrace is still a pleasant spot for a bite, and there's a lively buzz.

SANTAMASA
INTERNATIONAL €

Map p318 (☑93 676 35 74; www.santamasa restaurant.com; Carrer Major de Sarrià 97; dishes €7-12; ⊙9.30am-midnight; ☒FGC Reina Elisenda) Next to Sarrià's pretty 18th-century church, Santamasa is an enticing spot for a light meal at any time of day, with red-brick arches and rustic-chic style. The menu is wide-ranging, with a mix of creatively topped *pizzetes* (small pizzas), salads, open-faced sandwiches, fondue, burgers, and good sharing appetisers such as hummus, cheeses and guacamole. There's a €15 lunch *menú* on weekdays.

LA FERMATA DE SARRIÀ
PIZZA €

Map p318 (☑93 315 84 02; www.lafermata. es; Carrer Major de Sarrià 2-4; pizza slices €2-4; ⊙11am-11pm; ⏍; ☐66,130, ☒FGC Sarrià) 🍴 Pizza slices are sold by weight at this little industrial-style Sarrià pizzeria run by a Rome-trained chef. They're made with organic flour and come with 150 varieties of classic and Catalonia-inspired toppings. It's perfect for picking up takeaway, but there's also a handful of tables on the pavement, where you can stop for coffee too. Leftover food goes to local charities.

LA BURG
BURGERS €

Map p318 (☑93 205 63 48; www.laburg.com; Passeig de Sant Joan Bosco 55; burgers €7-13; ⊙1-4pm & 8-11.30pm Mon-Wed, 1-4pm & 8pm-midnight Thu, 1.30-4.30pm & 8pm-midnight Fri-Sun; ☎; ☐V7, ☒FGC Sarrià) 🍴 Catalan wines by the glass or bottle accompany sleek La Burg's gourmet burgers made from organic, farm-to-table ingredients. Cheese lovers should try La Quesos (with Emmental, Gouda and Brie); other standouts include La Sarrià (porcini mushrooms, fried egg and black truffle shavings). Buns are handmade; gluten-free options are available.

FOIX DE SARRIÀ
BAKERY €

Map p318 (☑93 203 04 73; www.foixdesarria. com; Plaça de Sarrià 12-13; pastries €2-5; ⊙8am-9pm; ☒FGC Reina Elisenda) Since 1886 this swish pastry shop has been selling the most exquisite cakes, sweets, chocolates, wines and cheeses. You can stock up for later or grab a stool to sip tea, coffee or hot chocolate while sampling little lime or mango cakes and other baking wizardry. There's

another nearby branch on Carrer Major de Sarrià.

BAR TOMÀS DE SARRIÀ
TAPAS €

Map p318 (☑93 203 10 77; www.eltomasdesar ria.com; Carrer Major de Sarrià 49; tapas €2-8; ⊙noon-4pm & 6-10pm Mon-Sat; ☒FGC Sarrià) Many *barcelonins* swear Bar Tomàs is the best place in the city for *patates braves,* served with its house-speciality garlic aioli or spicy tomato sauce. Despite the fluorescent lights and low-key service, folks from all walks of life pile in, particularly for lunch on weekends. Fried artichokes, Cantabrian anchovies and other bites also hit the spot.

FLASH FLASH
SPANISH €

Map p317 (☑93 237 09 90; www.flashflashbar celona.com; Carrer de la Granada del Penedès 25; dishes €7-12; ⊙1pm-1.30am; ⏍; ☒FGC Gràcia) Styled with monochrome murals and an all-white interior, Flash Flash has a fun, kitschy pop-art aesthetic that harks back to its opening in 1970. Fluffy tortillas are the speciality, with more than 50 varieties ranging from black-truffle and cheese to sweet garlic, as well as massive bunless burgers.

★ASPIC
CAFE €€

Map p317 (☑93 200 04 35; www.aspic.es; Avinguda de Pau Casals 24; dishes €10-20; ⊙9am-midnight Tue-Sat, to 4pm Sun; ☎⏍; ☐T1, T2, T3 Francesc Macià) At the flagship cafe of this Barcelona caterer, luxury ingredients – smoked salmon, premium charcuterie and cheeses, high-grade olive oils, carefully chosen Spanish wines – step into the spotlight in stunning seasonal soups, creative market-based salads and dishes like wild sea bass with garlic. The attached deli is perfect for picking up a gourmet picnic to eat in nearby Parc del Turó.

VIVANDA
CATALAN €€

Map p318 (☑93 203 19 18; www.vivanda.cat; Carrer Major de Sarrià 134; tapas €4-14, sharing plates €10-22; ⊙1.30-3.30pm & 8.30-11pm Tue-Sat, 1.30-3.30pm Sun; ⏍; ☒FGC Reina Elisenda) Diners are in for a treat with the knockout menu conceived by acclaimed Catalan chef Jordi Vilà, who also runs Sant Antoni's Alkímia (p200). Delicate tapas and *platillos* (sharing plates) showcase the freshest seasonal fare, from artisan cheeses to vegetable ravioli and oven-baked wild fish with potatoes. Hidden behind a reincarnated

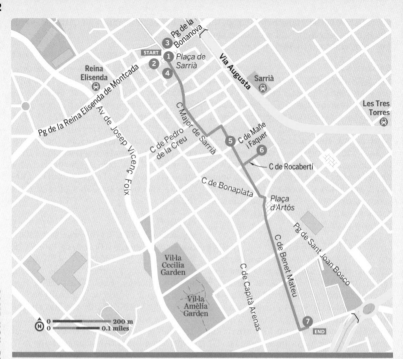

Neighbourhood Walk
A Wander Through Old Sarrià

START PLAÇA DE SARRIÀ
END PORTAL MIRALLES
LENGTH 1.3KM; ONE HOUR

The old centre of elegant, affluent Sarrià is a largely pedestrianised haven of peace, with cosy squares, upmarket homes and slender streets. Founded in the 13th or 14th century and incorporated into Barcelona only in 1921, the neighbourhood unravels around sinuous, sloping Carrer Major de Sarrià, today a mix of old and new, with a sprinkling of shops and restaurants.

At the street's top (north) end is pretty **1 Plaça de Sarrià** (from where Passeig de la Reina Elisenda de Montcada leads west to the medieval Monestir de Pedralbes). Buses such as 68 and V7 pass by here. Looming over the square, the **2 Església de Sant Vicenç de Sarrià** dates to the 18th century but sits on the site of a Romanesque predecessor.

Opposite the square is exclusive pastry shop **3 Foix de Sarrià** (p211), where you

can stop for coffee or a hot chocolate. As you begin to meander south along Carrer Major de Sarrià, duck into **4 Plaça del Consell de la Vila**, which is overlooked by the whitewashed town hall.

Continue 200m down Carrer Major de Sarrià, then take a left (east) to leafy, colourful **5 Plaça de Sant Vicenç de Sarrià**, where a handful of cafe-restaurants awaits.

Head south again before turning left (east) on to Carrer de Rocabertí, at the end of which is the **6 Monestir de Santa Isabel**, with a neo-Gothic cloister. Built in 1886 to house Clarissan nuns, whose order first set up in El Raval in the 16th century, it was abandoned during the civil war and used as an air-raid shelter.

From here, wander 600m south along Carrer de Benet Mateu to the 1902 **7 Portal Miralles** on Passeig de Manuel Girona. A little-visited, minor Gaudí creation, this undulating wall and gateway is adorned with (faded) white *trencadís* and topped with sunshields made from concrete tiles set into a metal framework.

Sarrià home, the tree-shaded terrace has winter heat lamps, blankets and broths.

CERVECERIA SAN FERNÁNDEZ SPANISH €€

Map p317 (Casa Fernández; ☑93 201 93 08; www.drymartiniorg.com; Carrer de Santaló 46; tapas €4-12, mains €9-20; ⊙1-5pm & 8pm-midnight Mon-Sat, noon-midnight Sun; ☑FGC Gràcia) The family team behind gracefully old-school L'Eixample bar Dry Martini (p158) is in charge at this smart, lively, long-running spot decorated with local artwork. With tables on the pavement or inside amid hot-red walls and jazzy murals, it's ideal for elegantly yet unfussily prepared Catalan cuisine – Padrón peppers, L'Escala anchovies, *patates braves*, fried eggs with home-cooked chips – and creative international bites.

CAFÉ TURÓ MEDITERRANEAN €€

Map p317 (☑93 200 69 53; http://romain fornell.com/restaurantes/cafe-turo; Carrer del Tenor Viñas 1; tapas €4-12, mains €8-19; ⊙8am-11.30pm Mon-Fri, from 9am Sat & Sun; ☑T1, T2, T3 Francesc Macià, ☑FGC Muntaner) Framed by red awnings, with vivid crimson walls brightening the low-lit interior, this Parisian-feel cafe by acclaimed chef Romain Fornell has year-round seating on the pavement opposite the Parc del Turó – ideal for catching some sun over a morning coffee, afternoon glass of wine or evening cocktail. Tempting bistro plates and tapas include Padrón peppers, quiches, light salads and seafood tagliatelle.

CASA JOANA CATALAN €€

Map p318 (☑93 203 10 36; https://restaurant casajoana.negocio.site; Carrer Major de Sarrià 59; tapas €5-11, mains €9-20; ⊙1-3.45pm & 9-10.30pm Mon & Thu-Sat, 1-3.45pm Tue & Wed; ☑FGC Sarrià) Daily-changing market-fresh produce is transformed into subtly inventive contemporary Catalan meals at this bustling fave on Sarrià's sloping main street, with pine-green tiles and a spruced-up antique-style interior. Cheese boards, anchovies from L'Escala, mushroom or cured-ham croquettes and other tapas accompany hearty mains like grilled cod or beef carpaccio. Lunch is a €12.95 *menú del dia*.

AJOBLANCO CATALAN €€

Map p317 (☑93 667 87 66; www.ajoblancores taurant.com; Carrer de Tuset 20; tapas €7-19, mains €14-20; ⊙12.30-11pm Mon-Wed, to 2am Thu, to 3am Fri & Sat; ☑; ☑FGC Gràcia) This

beautifully designed, dimly lit bar and restaurant serves a mix of classic and creative tapas plates that go nicely with the imaginative cocktails and Catalan wines. Sip a house vermouth while digging into the €15 set menu, or dishes such as stir-fried squid, tuna tataki with avocado cream and Galician chops in spiced-radish sauce. DJs play Thursday to Saturday.

EL ASADOR DE ARANDA SPANISH €€

Map p318 (☑93 417 01 15; www.asadordearanda. net; Avinguda del Tibidabo 31; tapas €6-16, mains €19-25; ⊙1-11pm; ☑; ☑FGC Avinguda Tibidabo) Occupying the 1913 Casa Roviralta, a striking Modernista creation by Joan Rubió i Bellver, with stained-glass windows, Moorish-style brick arches and elaborate ceilings, El Asador de Aranda is known for its succulent roast lamb and suckling pig straight from the wood-fired clay oven (service is hit and miss). Book ahead, especially for the landscaped terrace, or pop in for vermouth and tapas.

BANGKOK CAFE THAI €€

Map p318 (☑93 339 32 69; www.facebook.com/bangkokcafebarcelona; Carrer d'Evarist Arnús 65; mains €9-14; ⊙8-11pm Mon-Thu, 1-3.30pm & 8-11pm Fri-Sun; ☑Plaça del Centre) If you're craving Thai cuisine, it's well worth making the trip out to Les Corts for this small, buzzing place with an open kitchen, photos of the Thai royals, blackboard specials and an oversized chandelier. It serves up authentically delicious spicy green papaya salad, red curries, noodle stir-fries and other standouts.

★LA BALSA MEDITERRANEAN €€€

Map p318 (☑93 211 50 48; www.labalsarestau rant.com; Carrer de la Infanta Isabel 4; mains €21-28; ⊙1.30-3.15pm & 8.30-10.30pm; ☑; ☑FGC Avinguda Tibidabo) With its grand ceiling and scented gardens surrounding a main terrace dining area, La Balsa is one of the city's premier dining addresses, founded in 1979. The seasonally changing menu mixes traditional Catalan flavours and creative expression: suckling pig with apple and cardamom, scallops with cabbage and Iberian pork loin, for example. Lounge over a cocktail at the bar before dinner.

★VIA VENETO GASTRONOMY €€€

Map p318 (☑93 200 72 44; www.viavenetobar celona.com; Carrer de Ganduxer 10; mains €30-48; ⊙1-4pm & 8-11.45pm Mon-Fri, 8-11.45pm

PARC DEL LABERINT D'HORTA

Laid out in the late 18th century by Italian engineer Domenico Bagutti for Joan Antoni Desvalls, the Marquès d'Alfarràs i de Llupià, this carefully **manicured park** (www.barcelona.cat; Passeig del Castanyers 1; labyrinth adult/child €2.25/1.50, Wed & Sun free; ⊙10am-8pm Apr-Oct, to 6pm Nov-Mar; ⓂMundet) at the foot of the Collserola hills remained a private family idyll until the 1970s. The highlight is the central cypress-hedge *laberint* ('labyrinth' in Catalan). Other paths meander past a lake, waterfalls, a neoclassical pavilion and a false cemetery (inspired by 19th-century romanticism). It's a 20-minute ride on metro *línia* 2 from Plaça de Catalunya.

Scenes of the film *Perfume: The Story of a Murderer* were shot in the gardens. Combine a visit with lunch at nearby Can Cortada.

Sat, closed Aug–mid-Sep; ⒭FGC La Bonanova) Salvador Dalí was a regular at this high-society, Michelin-starred restaurant after it opened in 1967, and you can still dine at his favourite table. Oval mirrors, orange-rose tablecloths and fine cutlery set the stage for intricate dishes such as oyster-and-crayfish tartare, *suquet de peix* (Catalan fish stew) and the signature roast duck for two. The cellar has over 1800 Spanish wines.

HISOP
MEDITERRANEAN €€€

Map p317 (☑93 241 32 33; www.hisop.com; Passatge de Marimon 9; mains €21-28; ⊙1.30-3.30pm & 8.30-11pm Mon-Fri, 8.30-11pm Sat; ⓂDiagonal) Black, white and burgundy dominate the decor at this elegant Michelin-starred restaurant just off the beaten path, with Catalan chef Oriol Ivern at the helm. The wine list is impressive and the service immaculate, while seasonal menus are works of art that might feature Ebro Delta duck tartare, hake with liquorice and jalapeños, or coconut *caldereta de llamàntol* (lobster stew).

CAN TRAVI NOU
CATALAN €€€

(☑93 428 03 01; www.gruptravi.com; Carrer de Jorge Manrique 8; mains €15-30; ⊙1-4pm & 8-11pm; ⓂMontbau) A romantic 17th-century farmhouse-mansion wrapped in bougain-villea, with scattered dining areas, is the setting at Can Travi Nou, 4km north of Gràcia in Horta. The warm colours, grand-father clock and rustic air create a magical ambience for dining on Catalan specialities such as sautéed mushrooms, slow-roasted pork and seafood casseroles. Book ahead.

CAN CORTADA
CATALAN €€€

(☑93 427 23 15; www.cancortada.com; Avinguda de l'Estatut de Catalunya; mains €13-29; ⊙1-4pm & 8-11pm; ⓯; ⓂMundet, Valldaura) The setting and hearty welcome make this 11th-century Horta estate (still graced by the remains of a defensive tower) worth the excursion to northern Barcelona. Grilled meats dominate, though there are also seasonal dishes like salted artichokes fired up on the grill and *calçots* (spring onions) in winter. Reserve a table in the former cellars or on the garden terrace.

HOFMANN
MEDITERRANEAN €€€

Map p317 (☑93 218 71 65; www.hofmann-bcn.com; Carrer de la Granada del Penedès 14; mains €30-40; ⊙1.30-3.30pm & 8.30-11pm Mon-Fri, 8.30-11pm Sat; ⒭FGC Gràcia) Trainee chefs from the celebrated Hofmann (p114) culinary school (and their instructors) run the kitchen here. Dishes are generally elegant seasonal renditions of classic Mediterranean food (suckling pig with crunchy citrus fruit; bluefin tuna loin with spicy vegetables and pesto), followed by such delicious desserts that some people prefer a starter and two sweets, skipping the main course altogether.

ABAC
GASTRONOMY €€€

Map p318 (☑93 319 66 00; https://abacbarcelona.com; Avinguda del Tibidabo 1; tasting menus €190-210, with wine €280-330; ⊙1.30-3pm & 8.30-10pm; ⒭FGC Avinguda Tibidabo) Led by celebrated chef Jordi Cruz, this triple-Michelin-starred restaurant housed in an 1890 mansion (p242) offers one of Barcelona's most memorable dining experiences (also one of its priciest). The experience begins with an aperitif on the terrace. Expect creative, mouth-watering perfection in dishes like grilled seaweed bread, blue crab with caviar and oysters with green-apple ceviche. Reservations essential.

DRINKING & NIGHTLIFE

Drinking in this area is often upmarket (and prices can rise accordingly), whether you sample the bars and clubs around Carrer de Marià Cubí (and surrounding streets) or try the bars around Tibidabo.

EL MARAVILLAS
COCKTAIL BAR

Map p318 (☑93 360 73 78; www.elmaravillas. cat; Plaça de la Concòrdia 15; ⊙noon-midnight Sun-Tue, to 1am Wed, to 2am Thu, to 3am Fri & Sat; ⓂLes Corts, ☑T1, T2, T3 Numància) Overlooking Les Corts' peaceful Plaça de la Concòrdia, El Maravillas is an escape from the crowded Ciutat Vella (Old City), filled with tiled floors, marble-top tables and mirrored walls. Andreu Estríngana, one of Spain's top mixologists, and team concoct creative cocktails (€7 to €12) named for celebrated sports players. Spanish wines and easy-drinking vermouths are other drinks of choice.

GIMLET
COCKTAIL BAR

Map p317 (☑93 201 53 06; www.drymartiniorg. com; Carrer de Santaló 46; ⊙6pm-1am Mon-Wed, to 2.30am Thu, to 3am Fri & Sat; ☑T1, T2, T3 Francesc Macià, ☑FGC Muntaner) Under the watch of the talented folk behind popular restaurant Cerveceria San Fernández (p213) next door, and Dry Martini (p158) in L'Eixample, red-dressed, stylishly updated Gimlet is one of Barcelona's oldest cocktail bars. Dry martinis and, of course, gimlets are the signature drinks. There are also cocktail-making workshops.

MIRABLAU
BAR

Map p318 (☑93 418 58 79; www.mirablaubcn. com; Plaça del Doctor Andreu; ⊙11am-3.30am Mon-Wed, to 4.30am Thu, 10am-5am Fri & Sat, 10am-2.30am Sun; ☑196, ☑FGC Avinguda Tibidabo) Views over the entire city from this balcony bar, restaurant and club at the base of the Funicular del Tibidabo make up for sometimes patchy service. The bar is renowned for its impressive gin selection (€12 to €15). Wander downstairs to the tiny dance space, which opens at 11.30pm; in summer you can step out onto the even smaller terrace for a breather.

MARCEL
BAR

Map p317 (☑93 209 89 48; Carrer de Santaló 42; ⊙7.30am-1am Mon-Thu, 7.30am-3am Fri & Sat, 9.30am-midnight Sun; ☑FGC Muntaner) A busy, classic Sant Gervasi meeting place, Marcel has an old-world feel, with a wood bar, black-and-white floor tiles, high windows and uncomplicated tapas like tortilla. Customers inevitably spill out onto the footpath, where there are also a few tables.

CAFÉ BERLIN
BAR

Map p317 (☑93 200 65 42; www.cafeberlinbar celona.com; Carrer de Muntaner 240; ⊙9am-1.30am Mon-Wed, to 2.30am Thu, to 3am Fri, 10.30am-3am Sat; ⓂHospital Clínic, Diagonal) This elegant corner bar offers views over Avinguda Diagonal, with a cluster of tables outside on the ground floor and designer lounges downstairs. Service can be harried, but the location is excellent for starting an uptown night before kicking on to nearby clubs, and there are plenty of cocktails, G&Ts and tapas on the go.

BIKINI
CLUB

Map p318 (☑93 322 08 00; www.bikinibcn.com; Avinguda Diagonal 547; cover incl 1 drink €15; ⊙midnight-6am Thu-Sat; ⓂMaria Cristina) This old star of the Barcelona nightlife scene has been keeping the beat since 1953. Every possible kind of music gets a run, from reggaeton to 1980s disco, depending on the night and the space you choose. Get on the guest list to get in for free.

SUTTON
CLUB

Map p317 (☑667 432759; www.suttonbarcelona. com; Carrer de Tuset 13; admission incl drink €20; ⊙midnight-5.30am Wed & Thu, midnight-6am Fri & Sat; ⓂDiagonal, ☑FGC Gràcia) With mainstream sounds on the dance floor and some hopping house in a side bar, this glossy, neon-adorned club inevitably attracts just about everyone pouring in and out of the nearby bars at some stage of the evening. The main dance floor gets packed with a fashionable crowd. Even with reservations, the bouncers can be tough.

⭐ ENTERTAINMENT

CAMP NOU
FOOTBALL

Map p318 (☑902 189900; www.fcbarcelona. com; Carrer d'Arístides Maillol; ⓂPalau Reial) The massive stadium of Camp Nou ('New Field' in Catalan) is home to the legendary FC Barcelona. Attending a game amid the roar of the loyal crowds is an unforgettable experience; the season runs from August to

BELLESGUARD

An entrancing work that combines Gothic and Modernista elements, this lesser-known **Gaudí masterpiece** (Map p318; ☑93 250 40 93; www.bellesguardgaudi.com; Carrer del Bellesguard 20; adult/child 8-18yr €9/7.20; ⊙10am-3pm Tue-Sun; ⊠FGC Avinguda Tibidabo) was rescued from obscurity and opened to visitors in 2013. Built between 1900 and 1909, the private residence (still owned by the Guilera family) has a castle-like appearance with crenellated walls of stone and brick, narrow stained-glass windows, elaborate ironwork, gorgeous gardens and a soaring turret topped by a colourfully tiled Gaudían cross, along with spectacular city views. There's been a manor here since the 1400s.

One-hour guided tours in Catalan, Spanish and English run on Saturday and Sunday (€16; book ahead). At other times, you can visit the building's interior and the grounds with a multilingual audioguide.

Bellesguard is a 1.4km walk west of Avinguda Tibidabo train station, though several buses pass nearby (196, 123, V13, H2). Check schedules before making the trek out – it's sometimes closed for private events.

May. Alternatively, get a taste of all the excitement at the interactive Barça Stadium Tour & Museum (p206).

LUZ DE GAS
LIVE MUSIC

Map p317 (☑93 209 77 11; www.luzdegas. com; Carrer de Muntaner 246; entry from €15; ⊙midnight-6am Wed-Sat; ⓜDiagonal, Hospital Clínic, ⓗT1, T2, T3 Francesc Macià) Set in a grand former theatre, this club stages concerts ranging through rock and soul to salsa, jazz and pop several nights a week. From about 2am, the place turns into a club that attracts a well-dressed crowd with varying musical tastes, depending on the night.

🛍 SHOPPING

Plenty of trendy little boutiques are scattered around La Zona Alta.

CATALINA HOUSE
HOMEWARES

Map p317 (☑93 140 96 39; www.catalinahouse. net; Carrer d'Amigó 47; ⊙10.15am-2pm & 5-8pm Mon-Fri, 10.30am-2pm Sat; ⓗFGC Muntaner) After its decade-long success on the Balearic island of Formentera, Catalina House now has a second branch in Barcelona's Sant Gervasi. Sustainable materials such as linen, cotton, stone, glass, terracotta and oil-treated recycled timbers are used in stylish Mediterranean designs for the home including cushions, tableware, vases, clocks, sculptures and furniture.

COQUETTE
FASHION & ACCESSORIES

Map p317 (☑93 414 51 06; https://coquettebcn. com; Carrer dels Madrazo 153; ⊙10.30am-2.30pm & 4.30-8.30pm Mon-Wed & Fri, 10.30am-8.30pm Thu, 10.30am-2.30pm Sat; ⓗFGC Muntaner) A minimalist-chic world of Catalan, other Spanish and international designerware, Coquette showcases elegant women's pieces with a timeless Parisian edge, from brands such as Sur/Sac, Hoss Intropia, Masscob and Ball Pagès. There's another branch (p115) in El Born.

DR BLOOM
FASHION & ACCESSORIES

Map p318 (☑93 252 32 99; www.drbloom.es; Plaça de Sarrià 14; ⊙10.30am-2pm & 4.30-8pm Mon-Fri, 10.30am-2pm & 5-8pm Sat; ⓗFGC Reina Elisenda, FGC Sarrià) Just off Sarrià's main square, this cheery boutique designs and creates its own bright, boldly styled pieces in Barcelona. Finds include lovely vibrant patterned jumpers, floaty summer dresses and rainbow-coloured handbags. There are other branches around town, including in L'Eixample (p163).

MERCAT DE GALVANY
MARKET

Map p317 (www.mercatgalvany.es; Carrer de Santaló 65; ⊙7am-2.30pm Mon-Thu & Sat year-round, to 8pm Fri approx Sep-May; ⓗFGC Muntaner) Opened in 1927, Galvany is one of the city's most beautiful markets, with a brick facade and glass- and cast-iron interior. Over 80 stalls sell an enticing variety of bakery items, fresh produce and deli goods, and there's also a low-key cafe.

UKKA FASHION & ACCESSORIES

Map p317 (☎661 919710; www.ukka.es; Carrer de Laforja 122; ☺10.30am-2pm & 5-8.30pm Mon-Fri, 10.30am-2pm Sat; ☒FGC Muntaner) Founded in 1995, Ukka makes its bohemian-inspired women's fashion and accessories (including scarves, hats and eye-catching jewellery) at its Barcelona factory and sells them exclusively in this chic little terracotta-floored Sant Gervasi boutique.

FC BOTIGA MEGASTORE GIFTS & SOUVENIRS

Map p318 (www.fcbarcelona.com; Gate 9, off Avinguda de Joan XXIII; ☺10am-8pm, to kick-off match days; ⓂPalau Reial) This sprawling three-storey shop at Camp Nou has footballs, shirts, scarves, socks, wallets, bags, footwear – pretty much anything you can think of – all featuring FC Barcelona's famous red-and-blue insignia.

L'ILLA SHOPPING CENTRE

Map p318 (☎93 444 00 00; www.lilla.com; Avinguda Diagonal 557; ☺9.30am-10pm Mon-Sat Jun-Sep, to 9pm Oct-May; ⓂMaria Cristina) One of Barcelona's best and biggest shopping centres, with high-end boutiques, high-street favourites and a mesmerising spread of eateries.

LABPERFUM COSMETICS

Map p317 (☎93 298 95 12; www.labperfum. com; Carrer de Santaló 45; ☺10am-2.30pm & 5-8.30pm Mon-Sat; ☒FGC Muntaner) This tiny shop looks like an old apothecary, with pretty glass bottles of extraordinary fragrances (for men and women) made in-

house, beautifully packaged and lined up on the shelves. You can also buy scented candles, soaps and creams.

ORIOL BALAGUER FOOD

Map p318 (☎93 201 18 46; www.oriolbalaguer. com; Plaça de Sant Gregori Taumaturg 2; ☺9am-2.30pm & 4-9pm Mon-Fri, 8.30am-2.30pm & 4-9pm Sat, 8.30am-2.30pm Sun; ☒FGC La Bonanova) Magnificent cakes, sweets, ice cream, chocolates and other sweet creations tantalise in this museum-like shop.

PASTISSERIA NATCHA FOOD

Map p317 (☎93 430 10 70; www.natcha.cat; Avinguda de Sarrià 45; ☺8am-9pm Mon-Sat, 8.30am-8.30pm Sun; ⓂHospital Clínic) Pastisseria Natcha has been tempting *barcelonins* with chocolates and custom-made cakes since 1958.

🏃 SPORTS & ACTIVITIES

RITUELS D'ORIENT SPA

Map p317 (☎93 419 14 72; www.rituelsdorient.com; Carrer de Loreto 50; baths per 45min €29, treatments from €21; ☺11am-9pm Tue, Wed & Sun, to 10pm Thu-Sat; ⓂHospital Clínic) Resembling a Moroccan fantasy, with dark woods, window grilles, candle lighting and ancient-looking stone walls, Rituels d'Orient is a wonderfully relaxing setting for luxuriating in a hammam and indulging in a massage, body scrub, facial or hand and foot treatments.

Day Trips from Barcelona

Girona p219
A splendid cathedral, a maze of narrow cobbled streets and Catalonia's finest medieval Jewish quarter, plus outstanding dining.

Montserrat p223
Catalonia's most important shrine is in this spectacularly sited mountain monastery, also home to Europe's oldest choir and superb walks.

Sitges p224
The Costa Daurada's sizzling summer-fun queen: tantalising nightlife and food scenes, golden-white beaches, an evocative old town.

Penedès Wine Country p226
Sample Spain's Champagne-like *cava* and favourite wines on a spin around the history-rich, architecturally fascinating bodegas.

Tarragona p228
Some of Spain's most extensive Roman ruins await alongside a beautiful medieval core and cathedral in this ancient port city.

Girona

la Llibertat 1; ⊙9am-8pm Mon-Fri, 9am-2pm &
4-8pm Sat Apr-Oct, 9am-7pm Mon-Fri, 9am-2pm
& 3-7pm Sat Nov-Mar, 9am-2pm Sun year-round)

Explore

Northern Catalonia's largest city, Girona is a jewellery box of museums, galleries and Gothic churches, strung around a web of cobbled lanes and medieval walls. Reflections of Modernista mansions shimmer in the Riu Onyar, which separates the walkable historic centre on its eastern bank from the gleaming commercial centre on the west. With Catalonia's most diverse nightlife and dining scene outside Barcelona, Girona makes a delicious distraction from the coast.

The Roman town of Gerunda lay on the Via Augusta from Gades (now Cádiz) to the Pyrenees. Taken from the Muslims by the Franks in the late 8th century, Girona became the capital of one of Catalonia's most important counties, falling under the sway of Barcelona in the late 9th century. Girona's wealth in medieval times produced many fine Romanesque and Gothic buildings that have survived repeated attacks, while a Jewish community flourished here until its expulsion in 1492.

The Best...

➡ **Sight** Catedral de Girona

➡ **Place to Eat** El Celler de Can Roca (p222)

➡ **Place to Drink** Espresso Mafia (p222)

Top Tip

Soak up the city landscape on a walk along Girona's majestic medieval walls; there are several access points, including a lane east of the cathedral leading into the Jardins dels Alemanys.

Getting There & Away

➡ **Car** Take the AP7 (toll) motorway via Granollers.

➡ **Train** Frequent services to/from Barcelona (€11.25 to €31.30, 40 minutes to 1¼ hours, at least half-hourly).

Need to Know

➡ **Location** 100km northeast of Barcelona.

➡ **Oficina de Turisme de Girona** (☑972 01 00 01; www.girona.cat/turisme; Rambla de

⊙ SIGHTS & ACTIVITIES

Girona's exquisitely preserved **Call** (Jewish Quarter) – a labyrinth of low-slung stone arches and slender cobbled streets – flourished around narrow Carrer de la Força for six centuries, until relentless Christian persecution forced the Jews out of Spain.

For deeper insight into Girona, take a 90-minute walking tour (€12) offered daily (except Mondays) at noon by the Oficina de Turisme de Girona.

★**CATEDRAL DE GIRONA** CATHEDRAL
(www.catedraldegirona.cat; Plaça de la Catedral; adult/concession incl Basílica de Sant Feliu €7/5; ⊙10am-7.30pm Jul & Aug, to 6.30pm Apr-Jun, Sep & Oct, to 5.30pm Nov-Mar) Towering over a flight of 86 steps rising from Plaça de la Catedral, Girona's imposing cathedral is far more ancient than its billowing baroque facade suggests. Built over an old Roman forum, parts of its foundations date from the 5th century. Today, 14th-century Gothic styling – added over an 11th-century Romanesque church – dominates, though a beautiful, double-columned Romanesque **cloister** dates from the 12th century. With the world's second-widest Gothic nave, it's a formidable sight to explore; audio guides are provided.

★**MUSEU D'HISTÒRIA DELS JUEUS** MUSEUM
(www.girona.cat/call; Carrer de la Força 8; adult/child €4/free; ⊙10am-8pm Mon-Sat, to 2pm Sun Jul & Aug, 10am-6pm Tue-Sat, to 2pm Mon & Sun Sep-Jun) Until 1492, Girona was home to Catalonia's second-most-important medieval Jewish community, after Barcelona's, and one of the country's finest Jewish quarters. This excellent museum takes pride in this heritage, without shying away from less salubrious aspects such as Inquisition persecution and forced conversions. You also see a rare 11th-century *miqvé* (ritual bath) and a 13th-century Jewish house.

MUSEU D'ART DE GIRONA   GALLERY

(www.museuart.com; Pujada de la Catedral 12; €6, incl Catedral & Basílica de Sant Feliu €10; ⊙10am-7pm Tue-Sat May-Sep, to 6pm Oct-Apr, to 2pm Sun year-round) Next to the cathedral, in the 12th- to 16th-century Palau Episcopal, this art gallery impresses with the scale and variety of its collection. Around 8500 pieces of art, mostly from this region, fill its displays, which range from Romanesque woodcarvings and murals to paintings of the city by 20th-century Polish-French artist Mela Muter, early-20th-century sculptures by influential Catalan architect Rafael Masó i Valentí, and works by leading Modernista artist Santiago Rusiñol.

BASÍLICA DE SANT FELIU   BASILICA

(Plaça de Sant Feliu; adult/student incl Catedral €7/5; ⊙10am-5.30pm Mon-Sat, 1-5.30pm Sun) Just downhill from the cathedral stands Girona's second great church, with its landmark truncated bell tower. The nave is majestic with Gothic ribbed vaulting, while St Narcissus, the city's patron, is venerated in an enormous marble-and-jasper, late-baroque side chapel. To the right of the chapel is the saint's Gothic, 1328 sepulchre (which previously held his remains), displaying his reclining form and scenes from his life, including the conversion of women, martyrdom and expelling of an evil genie.

BANYS ÀRABS   RUINS

(www.banysarabs.org; Carrer de Ferran el Catòlic; adult/child €2/1; ⊙10am-7pm Mon-Sat Mar-Oct, to 6pm Mon-Sat Nov-Feb, to 2pm Sun year-round) Although modelled on earlier Islamic and Roman bathhouses, the Banys Àrabs are a finely preserved, 12th-century Christian affair in Romanesque style (restored in the 13th century). The baths contain an *apodyterium* (changing room), with a small octagonal pool framed by slender pillars, followed by a *frigidarium* and *tepidarium* (with respectively cold and warm water) and a *caldarium* (a kind of sauna) heated by an underfloor furnace.

MONESTIR DE SANT PERE
DE GALLIGANTS   MONASTERY

(www.mac.cat; Carrer de Santa Llúcia; adult/child incl Museu d'Arqueologia de Catalunya–Girona €6/4; ⊙10am-6pm Tue-Sat Oct-Apr, to 7pm Tue-Sat May-Sep, to 2pm Sun year-round) This beautiful 11th- and 12th-century Romanesque Benedictine monastery has a sublime bell tower and a splendid cloister featuring other-worldly animals and mythical creatures on the 60 capitals of its double columns; there are some great architectural features in the church too.

Spread across the monastery is the **Museu d'Arqueologia de Catalunya–Girona**, exhibiting artefacts dating from prehistoric to medieval times.

MUSEU D'HISTÒRIA DE GIRONA   MUSEUM

(www.girona.cat/museuhistoria; Carrer de la Força 27; adult/student/child €4/2/free; ⊙10.30am-5.30pm Tue-Sat Oct-Apr, to 6.30pm Tue-Sat May-Sep, to 1.30pm Sun year-round) Eighteenth-century cloisters lend an appropriately antique feel to this journey from Roman Girona to medieval times to the present day. The museum's highlights include an exhibition illuminating the 3rd-to 4th-century Can Pau Birol mosaic, which depicts a lively circus scene with charioteers, and an explanation of the 1808 to 1809 siege of Girona by Napoleonic troops. Many pieces on display are copies rather than originals. Spanish-, English- and French-language booklets help with the Catalan-only display labels.

✖ EATING & DRINKING

★ LA FÁBRICA   CAFE €

(www.lafabricagirona.com; Carrer de la Llebre 3; dishes €3-9; ⊙9am-3pm; 🛜🌙) 🌠 Girona's culinary talents morph into top-quality coffee and Catalan-inspired brunchy favourites starring local ingredients at this energetic, German-Canadian–owned, cycle-themed cafe. Pillowy artisan *torrades* (toasts) – perhaps topped with avocado, feta and peppers – arrive on wooden sliders and are washed down with expertly poured brews made with beans sourced from eco-conscious suppliers.

FEDERAL   CAFE €

(🌀872 26 45 15; www.federalcafe.es; Carrer de la Força 9; mains €7-14; ⊙8.30am-8pm Mon-Thu, to 10pm Fri & Sat, 9am-7pm Sun; 🛜🌙) The same creative team behind the much-loved Barcelona cafe (p197) has opened a Federal in the heart of Girona's old town. Market-fresh organic ingredients star in a menu of brunch classics, delicious sandwiches and hearty salads. You'll also find decadent pastries and perfectly pulled espressos (plus a first-rate flat white). Outdoor dining on the tree-shaded square in front.

FIGUERES & THE TEATRE MUSEU DALÍ
···

Fourteen kilometres inland from Catalonia's glistening Golf de Roses and 35km north-east of Girona lies Figueres, birthplace of Salvador Dalí. Whatever your feelings about this complex, egocentric surrealist and showman, his flamboyant theatre-museum here is worth every minute you can spare. Beyond its star attraction, busy Figueres is a lively place with good restaurants, pleasant shopping streets and a grand 18th-century fortress.

Figueres train station, 800m southeast of the centre, has half-hourly trains to/from Girona (€4.10 to €6.90, 30 to 40 minutes) and Barcelona (€12 to €16, 1¾ to 2½ hours). High-speed trains to Girona, Barcelona and into France depart from Figueres-Vilafant station, 1.5km west of central Figueres.

The first name that pops into your head when you lay eyes on the red, castle-like **Teatre-Museu Dalí** (www.salvador-dali.org; Plaça de Gala i Salvador Dalí 5; adult/child under 9yr €15/free; ☉9am-8pm Apr-Jul & Sep, 9am-8pm & 10pm-1am Aug, 9.30am-6pm Tue-Sun Oct & Mar, 10.30am-6pm Tue-Sun Nov-Feb), topped with giant eggs and stylised Oscar-like statues and studded with plaster-covered croissants, is Salvador Dalí. An entirely appropriate final resting place for the master of surrealism, it has assured his immortality. Exhibits range from enormous, impossible-to-miss installations – like *Taxi plujós* (Rainy Taxi), an early Cadillac surmounted by statues – to the more discreet, including a tiny, mysterious room with a mirrored flamingo.

Between 1961 and 1974, Dalí converted Figueres' former municipal theatre, destroyed by a fire in 1939 at the end of the civil war, into the Teatre-Museu Dalí. It's full of illusions, tricks and the utterly unexpected, and contains a substantial portion of Dalí's life's work, though his most famous pieces are scattered around the world. The Teatre-Museu is Spain's most visited museum outside Madrid, so it's worth double-checking opening hours (it's closed on Mondays from October to May) and reserving tickets online in advance.

For immersion in the Dalí legend, stay at the mid-19th-century **Hotel Duran** (☑972 50 12 50; www.hotelduran.com; Carrer de Lasauca 5; r €65-100; P❄🔊🏍) , where the artist and his wife often made appearances. There's a fitting blend of old-style elegance with contemporary design, surrealist touches, and photos of Dalí with the former hotel manager, whose descendants now proudly run the place. Rooms are bright and modern. The excellent, art-filled **restaurant** (mains €17-28; ☉12.45-4pm & 8-10.30pm) serves lightly creative Catalan fare.

A short stroll from the Teatre-Museu Dalí, cheery, casual **Integral** (☑972 51 63 34; www.facebook.com/integral.figueres; Carrer de la Jonquera 30; mains €10-15; ☉1-3.30pm Mon & Tue, 1-3.30pm & 8-10.30pm Wed-Sat; ☑) prepares some of the best vegetarian dishes for miles around. Perch at the marble-topped bar to see the chefs in action while tucking into ginger-and-leek dumplings, courgette carpaccio, shiitake risotto, crunchy polenta balls and other delicacies – all made from high-quality regional organic ingredients.

ROCAMBOLESC ICE CREAM €

(☑972 41 66 67; www.rocambolesc.com; Carrer de Santa Clara 50; ice cream €3-4.50; ☉11am-11pm Sun-Thu, to midnight Fri & Sat) Savour some of Spain's most lip-smackingly delicious ice cream at Rocambolesc, part of the world-famous El Celler de Can Roca culinary clan. Candy-striped decor sets the magical scene for creatively cool concoctions like baked-apple ice cream or mandarin sorbet sprinkled with passionfruit flakes.

CAFÉ LE BISTROT CATALAN €€

(☑972 21 88 03; www.lebistrot.cat; Pujada de Sant Domènec 4; mains €8.50-18; ☉1-4pm & 7-11pm) Walls are draped in jasmine and tables spill out onto stairs climbing to a 17th-century church at this local favourite. The classic bistro-style menu twins French and Catalan cuisine, with crêpes, pastas, meaty mains, '*pagès*' pizzas and a huge array of *amanides* (salads) plus local cheeses. Inside, the setting is subdued, with

WORTH A DETOUR

COSTA BRAVA

Stretching northeast from Barcelona to the Spain–France border, Catalonia's Costa Brava ('rugged coast') is undoubtedly the most beautiful of Spain's three main holiday coasts. Though there's plenty of tourism development, this wonderfully scenic region also unveils unspoiled coves, spectacular seascapes, wind-battered headlands, coast-hugging hiking paths, charming seaside towns and some of Spain's finest diving. A break here makes the perfect add-on to explorations of Barcelona.

Calella de Palafrugell & Llafranc The whitewashed buildings of Calella, an agreeably tucked-away town 4km southeast of Palafrugell, cluster Aegean-style around a bay of rocky points and small, pretty beaches, with a few fishing boats hauled up on the sand. Neighbouring upmarket Llafranc has a small aquamarine bay and a gorgeous long stretch of golden sand, cupped on either side by craggy pine-dotted outcrops. Family-owned **Casamar** (☑972 30 01 04; www.hotelcasamar. net; Carrer del Nero 3; r incl breakfast €120-160; ☺mid-Apr–Dec; ❖☎) is a favourite cliffside hotel with an excellent Michelin-starred restaurant.

Begur & Around Crowned by an 11th-century castle, with exquisite coast glistening in its surrounds, Begur is one of the most beautiful and sought-after spots along the Costa Brava. This fairy-tale town, 8km northeast of Palafrugell, has a tempting array of restaurants, beach-chic boutiques, soothing hotels, and Modernista mansions that add splashes of colour among the stone streets of its medieval centre. Stay in a revamped 1800 old-town mansion at boutiquey **Cluc Hotel** (☑972 62 48 59; www.cluc.cat; Carrer del Metge Pi 8; r incl breakfast €123-210; ❖☎).

Cadaqués This easygoing white-walled village gleams above the cobalt-blue waters of a rocky bay on Catalonia's most easterly outcrop and owes its allure in part to its windswept pebble beaches, meandering lanes, pretty harbour and the wilds of nearby Cap de Creus – but it was Salvador Dalí who truly gave Cadaqués its sparkle, living much of his later life at his other-worldly seaside home in nearby Port Lligat. A fabulous little boutique bolthole here is the minimalist-chic **Tramuntana Hotel** (☑972 25 92 70; www.hotel-tramuntana-cadaques.com; Carrer de la Torre 9; r incl breakfast €115-140; ☺Mar-Oct; ⓟ❖☎).

check-print tiles and an old-fashioned marble-topped bar.

★ EL CELLER DE CAN ROCA
CATALAN €€€

(☑972 22 21 57; www.cellercanroca.com; Carrer Can Sunyer 48; degustation menus €190-220, with wine pairing €265-330; ☺8-9.30pm Tue, 12.30-2pm & 8-9.30pm Wed-Sat) Ever-changing avant-garde takes on Catalan dishes have catapulted El Celler de Can Roca to global fame. Holding three Michelin stars, it was named one of the best restaurants in the world numerous times by The World's 50 Best. Each year brings new innovations, from molecular gastronomy to multi-sensory food-art interplay, all with mama's home cooking as the core inspiration.

Run by the three Girona-born Roca brothers, El Celler de Can Roca is set in a refurbished country house, 2km northwest of central Girona. Closed some holidays; check the website for availability. Book online 11 months in advance or join the standby list.

ESPRESSO MAFIA
COFFEE

Map p103 (www.espressomafia.cc; Carrer de la Cort Reial 5; ☺9am-7pm Mon-Thu, to 8pm Fri & Sat, 10am-4pm Sun; ☎) ✿ With stripped-back white-on-white decor and (nonsmoking) tables below moody stone arches, Espresso Mafia is your go-to caffeine-shot spot on Girona's growing coffee scene. From smooth espresso and art-adorned latte to good old *café amb llet* (coffee with milk), coffee creations here are based on sustainably sourced beans, and best enjoyed with a slab of homemade cake.

Montserrat

Explore

Montserrat, 50km northwest of Barcelona, is at the heart of Catalan identity for its mountain, monastery and natural park weaving among distinctive rock formations. Montserrat mountain is instantly recognisable, sculpted over millennia by wind and frost. Its turrets of rock, a coarse conglomerate of limestone and eroded fragments, extend like gnarled fingers from its 1236m-high bulk. More than halfway up the mountain lies the Benedictine Monestir de Montserrat, home to La Moreneta, one of Spain's most revered icons (Montserrat is often used interchangeably for the monastery and the mountain). Extending from this sacred spot is the **Parc Natural de la Muntanya de Montserrat**, superlative hiking terrain where brooks tumble into ravines and lookout points deliver panoramas of rocky pillars.

The Best...

➡ **Sight** Monestir de Montserrat

➡ **Walk** Sant Jeroni (p224)

➡ **Entertainment** Escolania de Montserrat (p224)

Top Tip

The monastery is a hugely popular day trip from Barcelona and throngs with visitors, but serenity can still be found on the mountain's walking trails (p224).

Getting There & Away

➡ **Car** By car, take the C16 northwest from Barcelona, then the C58 north shortly beyond Terrassa, followed by the C55 south to Monistrol de Montserrat. You can leave your vehicle at the free car park and take the *cremallera* up to the top, or drive up and park (cars €7).

➡ **Train** The R5 line trains operated by **FGC** (www.fgc.net) run half-hourly to hourly to/from Barcelona's Plaça d'Espanya station (one hour). Services start at 5.16am, but take the 8.36am train to connect with the first **AERI cable car** (☑938 35 00 05; www.aeridemontserrat.com; 1-way/return €7.50/11.50; ☺every 15min 9.40am-7pm Mar-Oct, to 5.15pm Nov-Feb, closed mid-late Jan) to

the monastery from the Montserrat Aeri stop. Alternatively, take the R5 to the next stop (Monistrol de Montserrat), from where **cremallera trains** (☑902 31 20 20; www.cremallerad*montserrat.com; 1-way/return €7.50/12.50; ☺every 20-40min 8.48am-6.15pm mid-Sep–Jun, to 8.15pm Easter & Jul–mid-Sep) run up to the monastery (15 minutes) every 20 to 40 minutes. There are various train/*cremallera* combo tickets available.

Need to Know

➡ **Location** 50km northwest of Barcelona

➡ **Oficina de Turisme** (☑938 77 77 01; www. montserratvisita.com; ☺9am-5.45pm Nov-Mar, to 6.45pm Apr-Jun, Sep & Oct, to 8pm Jul & Aug)

⊙ SIGHTS

★ MONESTIR DE
MONTSERRAT   MONASTERY
(www.abadiamontserrat.net) Catalonia's most renowned monastery was established in 1025 to commemorate local shepherds' visions of the Virgin Mary, accompanied by celestial light and a chorus of holy music. Today, a community of 55 monks lives here. The monastery complex encompasses two blocks: on one side, the basilica and monastery buildings, and on the other, tourist and pilgrim facilities. Admirable monastery architecture lining the main **Plaça de Santa Maria** includes elegant 15th-century cloisters and a gleaming late-19th-century facade depicting St George and St Benedict in relief.

With marbled floors and art nouveau-style frescoes visible between graceful archways, the open courtyard fronting Montserrat's **basilica** (☺7am-8pm) immediately sets an impressive tone. The basilica itself, consecrated in 1592, has a brick facade featuring carvings of Christ and the 12 Apostles, dating to the early 20th century. Beyond its heavy doors, the interior glitters with white marble and gold in Renaissance and Catalan Gothic styles.

The stairs to the intimate **Cambril de la Mare de Déu** (☺7-10.30am & noon-6.15pm) are to the right of the main basilica entrance. Here you can pay homage to the famous La Moreneta ('Little Brown One', or 'Black Virgin'), a revered 12th-century Romanesque wood-carved statue of the Virgin Mary with Jesus seated on her knee (and

MONTSERRAT WALKS

To experience Montserrat's calm side, leave the touristic hubbub of the monastery and basilica behind and head out along the web of tempting hillside walking trails. The tourist office has basic maps.

Take the 10-minute **Funicular de Sant Joan** (www.cremallerademontserrat.cat; 1-way/return €9.10/14; ⊙every 12min 10am-4.50pm Nov-Mar, to 5.50pm Apr-Jun & mid-Sep–Oct, to 6.50pm Jul–mid-Sep, closed 3 weeks Jan) for the first 250m uphill from the monastery; alternatively, it's a 45-minute walk along the road between the funicular's lower and upper stations. From the top, it's a 20-minute stroll (signposted) to the **Ermita de Sant Joan**, with fine westward views.

More exciting is the signposted 7.5km (2½-hour) loop walk from the Funicular de Sant Joan's upper station, northwest to Montserrat's highest peak, **Sant Jeroni** (1236m). The walk takes you across the upper part of the mountain, with a close-up experience of some of the rock pillars. Wear good walking boots, bring water, and, before setting out, check with the tourist office regarding weather and trail conditions.

Catalonia's official patroness since 1881). The room on the west side of the courtyard from the basilica entrance is filled with offbeat ex-voto gifts and thank-you messages to the Virgin, while the alley you wander down after exiting the Cambril is alight with flickering candles.

MUSEU DE MONTSERRAT　　MUSEUM
(www.museudemontserrat.com; Plaça de Santa Maria; adult/child €8/4; ⊙10am-5.45pm, to 6.45pm late-Jun–mid-Sep, plus Sat & Sun Apr-Oct) This museum has excellent displays, ranging from an archaeological section with an Egyptian mummy to Gothic altarpieces to fine canvases by Caravaggio, El Greco, Picasso and several impressionists (Monet, Degas), plus a comprehensive collection of 20th-century Catalan art, and some fantastic Orthodox icons.

ENTERTAINMENT

ESCOLANIA DE MONTSERRAT　　LIVE MUSIC
(www.escolania.cat; ⊙performances 1pm & 6.45pm Mon-Thu, 1pm Fri, 11am & 6.45pm Sun) The clear voices of one of Europe's oldest boys' choirs have echoed through the basilica since the 14th century. The choir performs briefly on most days (except school holidays), singing *Virolai*, written by Catalonia's national poet Jacint Verdaguer, and *Salve Regina*, as well as at Sunday Mass (at 11am). The 50 *escolanets*, aged between nine and 14, go to boarding school in Montserrat and must endure a two-year selection process to join the choir.

Sitges

Explore

Just 35km southwest of Barcelona, Sitges sizzles with beach life, late-night clubs and an enviable festival calendar. Sitges has been a resort town since the 19th century, and was a key location for the Modernisme movement, which paved the way for the likes of Picasso. These days it's Spain's most famous gay holiday destination. In July and August, Sitges cranks up the volume to become one big beach party, while **Carnaval** (www.visitsitges.com; ⊙Feb/Mar) unbridles the town's hedonistic side. But despite the bacchanalian nightlife, Sitges remains a classy destination: its array of galleries and museums belies its small size, there's a good choice of upmarket restaurants in its historic centre (which is lined with chic boutiques), and the October **film festival** (Festival Internacional de Cinema Fantàstic de Catalunya; www.sitgesfilmfestival.com; ⊙Oct) draws culture fiends from miles around. The town is quieter during low season, but you can still get a feel for it.

The Best...

➡ **Sight** Museu del Cau Ferrat
➡ **Place to Eat** El Cable
➡ **Place to Drink** La Sitgetana (p226)

Top Tip

A lovely 8km walk leads southwest along the coast, past several secluded coves, to

Vilanova i la Geltrú, from where there are frequent trains back to Sitges (or Barcelona).

Getting There & Away

➡ **Bus** Mon-Bus (p268) runs to Barcelona (€4.10, 50 minutes, every 15 to 50 minutes) and Barcelona airport (€7.10, 30 minutes, half-hourly to hourly).

➡ **Car** The best road from Barcelona is the C32 (toll) motorway. The C31, which hooks up with the C32 after Castelldefels, is more scenic but often busy.

➡ **Train** From 5am to 10pm, regular R2 *rodalies* trains run to Barcelona Passeig de Gràcia and Sants (€4.20, 40 minutes). For Barcelona airport (€4.20, 45 minutes), change at El Prat de Llobregat.

Need to Know

➡ **Location** 35km southwest of Barcelona

➡ **Oficina de Turisme Sitges** (☑938 94 42 51; www.sitgestur.cat; Plaça Eduard Maristany 2; ◷10am-2pm & 4-8pm Mon-Sat mid-Jun–mid-Oct, 10am-2pm & 4-6.30pm Mon-Sat mid-Oct–mid-Jun, 10am-2pm Sun year-round)

◉ SIGHTS

The most beautiful part of Sitges is the headland area, where noble Modernista palaces and mansions strike poses around the pretty 17th-century **Església de Sant Bartomeu i Santa Tecla** (Plaça de l'Ajuntament; ◷Mass 7.30pm Mon-Fri, 8pm Sat, 9am, 11am, 12.30pm & 7.30pm Sun, hours vary), with the sparkling-blue Mediterranean as a backdrop.

★**MUSEU DEL CAU FERRAT** MUSEUM
(www.museusdesitges.cat; Carrer de Fonollar; incl Museu de Maricel adult/child €10/free; ◷10am-8pm Tue-Sun Jul-Sep, to 7pm Mar-Jun & Oct, to 5pm Nov-Feb) Built in the 1890s as a house-studio by Catalan artist Santiago Rusiñol, a pioneer of the Modernisme movement, this seaside mansion is crammed with his own art and that of his contemporaries (including his friend Picasso), as well as his extensive private collection of ancient relics and antiques. The visual feast is piled high, from Grecian urns and a 15th-century baptismal font to 18th-century tilework that glitters all the way to the floral-painted wood-beamed ceiling.

 EATING & DRINKING

★**EL CABLE** TAPAS €
(☑938 94 87 61; www.facebook.com/elcable barsitges; Carrer de Barcelona 1; tapas €2-8; ◷7-11pm Mon-Fri, noon-3.30pm & 7-11pm Sat & Sun) Always packed, down-to-earth El Cable might just be Sitges' most loved tapas bar, rolling out classics like *patatas bravas* (often branded the best in town) alongside divine, inventive bite-sized creations.

MORENO MAJOR 17 TAPAS €€
(☑938 53 16 16; Carrer Major 17; sharing plates €7-16, mains €14-22; ◷noon-midnight) The family-run purveyor of high-quality charcuterie in Sitges' market has opened this outstanding tapas bar and restaurant, serving up some of the best market-fresh fare in town. Feast on delectable razor clams, oysters and Cantabrian anchovies, while eyeing the tantalising seafood

---

SITGES BEACHES

Dotted with *xiringuitos* (beach bars), Sitges' main beach is divided into nine sections (with different names) by a series of breakwaters and flanked by the attractive seafront Passeig Marítim. The most central beaches are lively **La Fragata**, just below Sant Bartomeu church, and **La Ribera**, immediately west. About 500m southwest of the centre, **L'Estanyol** has summer *xiringuitos* with sunbeds; 1.5km further southwest, **Les Anquines** and **Terramar** have paddleboat rental and deck chairs in summer. Northeast of the centre lie easy-access **Sant Sebastià**, sheltered **Balmins** (favoured by nudists; 1km northeast of town) and brown-sand **Aiguadolç** (500m further east). **Bassa Rodona**, immediately west of the centre, is Sitges' famous unofficial 'gay beach', though gay sunbathers are now spread out pretty evenly.

selections at the bar, or join the garrulous restaurant crowd over Iberian pork, grilled octopus and ingredient-packed goat's cheese salads.

NEM   FUSION €€

(☑938 94 93 32; www.nemsitges.com; Carrer de l'Illa de Cuba 9; tapas €5-7; ⊙7.30-11pm Tue-Fri, 1.30-3.30pm & 7.30-11pm Sat; 🔊) At this packed-out fusion tapas spot, Spanish and Asian flavours collide in short, often-changing menus of deliciously creative concoctions that might include sea-bream sashimi, roasted celery with gorgonzola and walnuts, and Thai curry roast beef. Dine in a semi-open space at cosy corner tables or at the bar.

LA SITGETANA   CRAFT BEER

(www.facebook.com/lasitgetanacraftbeer; Carrer de Sant Bartomeu 10; ⊙6.30-11.30pm Mon-Fri, noon-3pm & 6.30-11.30pm Sat & Sun; 🔊) Spy the on-site brewery out the back at this ambitious, modern-minimalist craft-beer pub, with six taps devoted to artisan brews (pints around €5). Try a refreshing Weiss Subur (a Hefeweizen), the well-balanced Mariceld (an American Pale Ale), or sip on Penedès wines by the glass.

Penedès Wine Country

Explore

Some of Spain's finest wines come from the Penedès plains west and southwest of Barcelona. Sleepy Sant Sadurní d'Anoia, 35km west of Barcelona, is the capital of *cava*, a sparkling, Champagne-style wine popular worldwide and across Spain. The attractive historical town of Vilafranca del Penedès, 12km further southwest and with uplifting medieval and Modernista architecture, is the heart of the Penedès Denominació d'Origen (DO; Denomination of Origin) region (www.dopenedes.cat), which produces noteworthy light whites and some very tasty reds.

The Best...

➡ **Sight** Codorníu
➡ **Place to Eat** Cal Ton

Top Tip

If you're intent on serious wine sampling, several companies run tours of the wineries direct from Barcelona. Catalunya Bus Turístic conducts day tours from Barcelona, with tastings at three wineries (€75).

Getting There & Away

➡ **Car** If you're driving from Barcelona, follow the A2 north, then the AP7 west.
➡ **Train** *Rodalies* trains run from Barcelona Sants to Sant Sadurní (€4.20, 42 minutes, half-hourly) and Vilafranca (€5, 52 minutes).

Need to Know

➡ **Location** Around 40km west of Barcelona
➡ **Oficina de Turisme de Vilafranca del Penedès** (☑938 18 12 54; www.turismevilafranca.com; Carrer Hermenegild Clascar 2; ⊙3-6pm Mon, 9.30am-1.30pm & 3-6pm Tue-Sat, 10am-1pm Sun)

⊙ SIGHTS

The Penedès region's more enthusiastic bodegas will unravel their winemaking history and unique architecture, show you how *cava* and/or other wines are made, and finish off with a glass or two. Tours generally last 1½ hours and advance booking is essential. Most run in Catalan, Spanish or English; other languages may be available. Browse www.dopenedes.es and www.enoturismepenedes.cat for wine-tourism options.

★CODORNÍU   WINERY

(☑938 91 33 42; www.visitascodorniu.com; Avinguda de Jaume Codorníu, Sant Sadurní d'Anoia; adult/child €16/12; ⊙tours 10am-5pm Mon-Fri, to 1pm Sat & Sun) There is no more glorious spot to sip *cava* than the vaulted interior of Codorníu's palatial Modernista headquarters, designed by Catalan architect Josep Puig i Cadafalch, just beyond the northeast edge of Sant Sadurní d'Anoia. Codorníu's winemaking activities are documented back to the 16th century.

Josep Raventós was the first to create sparkling Spanish wine by the Champagne method in 1872, while his son Manuel is credited with bringing this winemaker into the big time during the late 19th century. Book multilingual 1½-hour tours online.

★ TORRES WINERY

(☑938 17 74 00; www.torres.es; Pacs del Penedès; tours from €15; ⊙9am-6pm Mon-Sat, to noon Sun) ◢ Just 3km northwest of Vilafranca on the BP2121, this is the area's premier winemaker, with a family winemaking tradition dating from the 17th century and a strong emphasis on organic production and renewable energy.

Tours in a multitude of languages explore the vineyards and several bodegas.

FREIXENET WINERY

(☑938 91 70 96; www.freixenet.es; Carrer de Joan Sala 2, Sant Sadurní d'Anoia; adult/child €15/10; ⊙tours 9am-4pm Mon-Sat, to 1pm Sun) The biggest *cava*-producing company, easily accessible right next to Sant Sadurní's train station. Book ahead for 1½-hour multilingual tours of its 1920s cellar, including a spin around the property on the tourist train and samples of Freixenet *cava*.

JEAN LEÓN WINERY

(☑938 17 76 90; www.jeanleon.com; Chatêau Leon, Torrelavit; tours adult/child from €12/free; ⊙9am-6pm Mon-Fri, to 3pm Sat & Sun) Since 1963, this winery has been using cabernet sauvignon and other French varietals to create high-quality wines. Ninety-minute visits (in Catalan, Spanish or English) to the wonderfully scenic vineyard, 12km north of Vilafranca, include a tasting of three wines and must be booked in advance.

ESPAI XOCOLATA SIMÓN COLL SHOWROOM

(☑938 91 10 95; www.simoncoll.com; Carrer de Sant Pere 37; adult/child €5.50/4; ⊙9am-7pm Mon-Fri, to 3pm Sat & Sun; ◧) Chocolate lovers shouldn't miss a visit to this family-run, bean-to-bar *fabricant de xocolata* (chocolate maker), which has been going strong since 1840 in Sant Sadurní. A tour (available in English, Spanish and Catalan) touches on the history and culture of chocolate making – with memorable tastings along the way. Afterwards, you can browse the beautifully packaged, high-quality chocolates in the store.

EATING

CAL FIGAROT CATALAN €€

(☑936 53 63 39; www.calblay.com; Carrer del General Prim 11; mains €10-15, lunch menu €13; ⊙noon-midnight Wed-Mon) Inside an impressive Modernista building, this casual eatery serves up satisfying Catalan cooking at excellent prices. Standouts include scrambled eggs with truffle and foie gras, various casseroles (like meatballs and cuttlefish), classic tapas, and cheese and meat boards.

The setting is a big draw as this is the headquarters of the Castellers de Vilafranca, and you can watch the group building human towers from the back terrace on Monday and Wednesday (8pm to 10pm) as well as Friday (9.30pm to midnight).

EL CONVENT CATALAN €€

(☑931 69 43 84; www.facebook.com/elconvent1850; Carrer de la Fruita 12; mains €10-21; ⊙7pm-midnight Tue-Fri, 9am-4pm & 8pm-midnight Sat) This warren-like, modern-rustic tavern delivers well-executed Catalan specials such as Pyrenean entrecôte, wild-salmon carpaccio, goat's-cheese salad and fondues for two, along with oysters, steamed clams and tempting platters of cheese and charcuterie. It's friendly, low-key and very popular.

★ CAL TON CATALAN €€€

(☑938 90 37 41; www.restaurantcalton.com; Carrer Casal 8; mains €18-29, tasting menus €32-55; ⊙1-3.30pm Tue & Sun, 1-3.30pm & 8.30-10.30pm Wed-Sat; ☎) An evening of gastronomic wonder awaits at Cal Ton, going strong since 1982. From feather-light potato-and-prawn ravioli to oxtail in red wine with pears, meals at this crisp modern restaurant exhaust superlatives.

Tarragona

Explore

In this effervescent port city, Roman history collides with beaches, bars and a food scene that perfumes the air with freshly grilled seafood. The biggest lure is the wealth of ruins in

Spain's second-most important Roman site, including a mosaic-packed museum and a seaside amphitheatre. A roll-call of fantastic places to eat gives you good reason to linger in the knot of lanes in the attractive medieval centre, flanked by a towering cathedral with Romanesque and Gothic flourishes.

Tarragona is also a gateway to the Costa Daurada's sparkling beaches and the feast of Modernisme architecture in nearby Reus, home to the **Gaudí Centre** (www.gaudicentre.cat; Plaça del Mercadal 3; adult/child €9/5; ☺10am-8pm Mon-Sat mid-Jun–mid-Sep, 10am-2pm & 4-7pm Mon-Sat mid-Sep–mid-Jun, 10am-2pm Sun year-round).

The Best...

→ **Sight** Catedral de Tarragona
→ **Place to Eat** Mercat Central
→ **Place to Drink** El Tamboret

Top Tip

For the quintessential Tarragona seafood experience, head to **Serrallo**, the town's fishing port, where a dozen bars and restaurants sell the day's catch. Many of Tarragona's sights close on Monday and/or Sunday.

Getting There & Away

→ **Bus** The **bus station** (Plaça Imperial Tarraco) is 1.5km west of the old town along Rambla Nova. **Alsa** (www.alsa. es) destinations include Barcelona Nord (€9.05, 1½ to two hours, seven daily).

→ **Car** Take the C32 toll road along the coast via Castelldefels or the AP7 (toll) motorway.

→ **Train** The local train station, Tarragona (not to be confused with Camp de Tarragona), is a 10-minute walk south of

---

ⓘ EXPERIENCING HISTORY

The **Museu d'Història de Tarragona** (MHT; www.tarragona.cat/patrimoni/museu-historia; adult per site/4 sites/all sites €3.30/7.40/11.05, children free) consists of various Unesco World Heritage Roman sites, as well as some other historic buildings around town. A combined ticket covers the Pretori i Circ Romans, Amfiteatre Romà, Passeig Arqueològic Muralles and Fòrum de la Colònia. Get exploring!

---

the old town near the beach, with services to/from Barcelona (€8 to €21, one to 1½ hours, every 10 to 30 minutes).

Need to Know

→ **Location** 85km southwest of Barcelona
→ **Tarragona Turisme** (☑977 25 07 95; www.tarragonaturisme.es; Carrer Major 37; ☺10am-8pm late Jun–late Sep, 10am-2pm & 3-5pm Mon-Fri, 10am-2pm & 3-7pm Sat, 10am-2pm Sun late Sep-late Jun)

◉ SIGHTS & ACTIVITIES

Several private operators run guided tours of Tarragona's old town; the tourist office has a list. A good choice is efficient, long-running **Itinere** (☑977 23 96 57; www.turismedetarragona.com; Baixada del Roser 8; 2hr tour €90), whose knowledgeable multilingual guides lead in-depth two- or three-hour walks of the main sights in Catalan, Spanish, English, French, Italian and German.

★**CATEDRAL DE TARRAGONA**   CATHEDRAL
(www.catedraldetarragona.com; Plaça de la Seu; adult/child €5/3; ☺10am-8pm Mon-Sat mid-Jun–mid-Sep, to 7pm Mon-Sat mid-Mar–mid-Jun & mid-Sep–Oct, to 5pm Mon-Fri, to 7pm Sat Nov–mid-Mar) Crowning the town, Tarragona's cathedral incorporates both Romanesque and Gothic features, as typified by the main facade. The flower-filled cloister has Gothic vaulting and Romanesque carved capitals, one of which shows rats conducting a cat's funeral...until the cat comes back to life! Chambers off the cloister display the remains of a Roman temple (unearthed in 2015) and the **Museu Diocesà**, its collection extending from Roman hairpins to 13th- and 14th-century polychrome Virgin woodcarvings. Don't miss the east nave's 14th-century frescoes.

Detailed audio guides (€2 to €4) are available in six languages. Cathedral rooftop tours (€15) can be booked online.

MUSEU NACIONAL ARQUEOLÒGIC DE TARRAGONA   MUSEUM
(www.mnat.cat; Plaça del Rei 5) This excellent museum does justice to the cultural and material wealth of Roman Tarraco. The mosaic collection traces changing trends from simple black-and-white designs to complex full-colour creations; highlights include the

fine 2nd- or 3rd-century *Mosaic de la Medusa* and the large, almost complete 3rd-century *Mosaic dels peixos de la Pineda*, showing fish and sea creatures.

The museum is currently closed for renovations, and is slated to reopen in 2022. Until then, some of the most important pieces from the collection are on display in **Tinglado 4** (🖉977 23 62 09; Moll de Costa, Port de Tarragona; adult/child incl audio guide €4/free; ⊙9.30am-8pm Tue-Sat Jun-Sep, to 6pm Tue-Sat Oct-May, 10am-2pm Sun year-round) in Tarragona's port; bus 22 takes you there from a stop near the Portal del Roser.

AMFITEATRE ROMÀ RUINS

(Parc de l'Amfiteatre; adult/child €3.30/free; ⊙9am-9pm Tue-Sat Easter-Sep, to 7pm Tue-Sat Oct-Easter, to 3pm Sun year-round) Near the beach is Tarragona's well-preserved amphitheatre, dating from the 2nd century CE, where gladiators hacked away at each other or wild animals. In its arena are the remains of a 6th-century Visigothic church and a 12th-century Romanesque church, both built to commemorate Saint Fructuosus and two deacons, believed to have been burnt alive here in 259 CE. At the time of research, parts of the amphitheatre were undergoing restoration, though the upper viewing gallery was open (and admission free).

PRETORI I CIRC ROMÀ RUINS

(Plaça del Rei; adult/child €3.30/free; ⊙9am-9pm Tue-Sat, to 3pm Sun Apr-Sep, to 7pm Tue-Fri, 9.30am-6.30pm Sat, to 2.30pm Sun Oct-Mar) This sizeable complex with two separate entrances includes part of the vaults of Tarragona's well-preserved, late-1st-century **Roman circus**, where chariot races were once held, as well as the Plaça del Rei's **Pretori tower** (climb it for 360-degree city views) and part of the **provincial forum**, the political heart of Roman Tarraconensis province. The circus, over 300m long and accommodating 30,000 spectators, stretched from here to beyond Plaça de la Font to the west.

EATING

★ MERCAT CENTRAL MARKET €

(Plaza Corsini; ⊙8.30am-9pm Mon-Sat) In a striking Modernista building, this historic 1915 market is looking better than ever thanks to a €47 million renovation completed in 2017. Temptations abound, from delectable fruits to cheeses and bakery items, plus food counters doling out seafood, charcuterie, sushi and Catalan wines. There's also a supermarket hidden downstairs.

EL VERGEL VEGAN €€

(🖉877 06 48 50; www.elvergeltarragona.com; Carrer Major 13; 3-course set menu €12-18; ⊙1-11pm; 🛜🍴) 🌿 This fabulous, fashionable vegan spot turns out creative plant-based deliciousness in two- or three-course menus, between whitewashed walls offset by sage-green shutters, patterned tiles and original artwork.

ARCS RESTAURANT CATALAN €€€

(🖉977 21 80 40; www.restaurantarcs.com; Carrer de Misser Sitges 13; mains €18-24; ⊙1-4pm & 8.30-11pm Tue-Sat) Inside a medieval cavern decorated with bright contemporary art and original Gothic arches, dine on creative European cooking that follows the seasons. Sample fresh pasta stuffed with black truffle and mushrooms, lobster salad over squid-ink noodles, oxtail with Priorat wine reduction, or the always-excellent catch of the day.

EL TAMBORET WINE BAR

(Carrer de Santa Anna 10; ⊙7-11pm Tue, noon-3pm & 7-11pm Wed-Sat, noon-3pm Sun) Hidden along a narrow lane near the Plaça del Forum, this delightful jewel-box-sized wine bar serves up a well-curated selection of wines from across Catalonia. Try a luscious Artigas from Priorat country or a bubbly from *cava* luminaries like Miquel Pons. Selections change regularly, and the friendly French owner is happy to guide you towards something extraordinary.

🛏 Sleeping

Barcelona has an excellent range of accommodation, from budget-friendly hostels and boutique B&Bs in Modernista buildings to luxury hotels overlooking the waterfront and scattered good-value apartments. Wherever (and whenever) you stay, it's wise to book well ahead.

Hostels, Hostals & Pensions

Barcelona has some seriously stylish budget-friendly hostels. Depending on the season you can pay as little as €20 to €25 for a dorm bed, though during high season rates look more like €30 to €45. Alternatively, check out Barcelona's many *hostals* and (more basic) *pensions* – small, family-run hotels. Some are fleapits, others immaculately maintained gems. Your budget inevitably goes further outside the city centre.

You're looking at a minimum of €35/55 for basic *individual/doble* (single/double) rooms, mostly with shared bathrooms; the best-value rooms usually get snapped up well in advance. For a double bed (rather than two singles), ask for a *llit/cama matrimonial* (Catalan/Spanish). Some places, especially at the lower end, offer triples and quads.

Hotels

At the bottom end there is often little to distinguish hotels from *pensions,* and from there they run up the scale to all-out five-star luxury. Some of the better features to look out for include rooftop pools and lounges; views; in-house spas; and proximity to sights and restaurants. For around €100 to €170 there are good, comfortable and stylish doubles across a wide range of hotels and areas. The top-end category starts at €250 for a double, and can easily rise to €500 (and beyond for suites).

Apartment & Room Rentals

A cosier (and often more cost-effective) alternative to hotels is a short-term apartment rental. Many firms organise short lets across town and, of course, Airbnb is a big player – though Airbnb and other apartment rental agencies have been accused of fuelling Barcelona's overtourism problem (p77) and hiking prices for locals.

Typical prices start at around €80 to €100 for two people per night, while for four people you might be looking at an average of €160 a night – but rates soar for more upscale apartments. Options outside the Ciutat Vella can be a good way to get to know buzzy residential neighbourhoods like Poblenou, Poble Sec, Gràcia or La Zona Alta. Bargains are sometimes available, but be aware that these are often in less salubrious areas. Many old-town apartments lack washing machines.

Accessible Accommodation

Many hotels claim to be equipped for guests with disabilities, but the reality frequently disappoints. The situation is improving, though, particularly at the midrange and high-end levels. Many apartments and hotels in the old centre lack lifts. Check out www.barcelona-access.cat for further information.

Useful Websites

Booking.com and, controversially, Airbnb (p77) are of course popular accommodation-booking portals. For other options, see Need to Know, p16.

Lonely Planet's Top Choices

El Palace (p239) A dazzling century-old L'Eixample five-star.

Hotel Neri (p233) Historical Barri Gòtic charm meets contemporary luxury.

Casa Bonay (p239) Local design and L'Eixample architecture.

Hotel Brummell (p241) A fun Poble Sec boutique gem.

Praktik Rambla (p237) Style, charm and history in L'Eixample.

360 Hotel Arts & Culture (p235) Social, stylish hostel in La Ribera.

Best By Budget: €

Casa Gràcia (p240) Stylish hostel with white-and-gold rooms and social events.

360 Hostel Arts & Culture (p235) Buzzy scene in an art-filled, contemporary-design hostel.

Pensió 2000 (p235) Family-run guesthouse overlooking the Palau de la Música Catalana.

Pars Tailor's Hostel (p241) Budget-chic Sant Antoni choice with a vintage vibe.

TOC Hostel (p241) Modern dorms and private rooms, plus a fab dip pool, on the Eixample–Sant Antoni border.

Pars Teatro Hostel (p241) Theatrically decorated hostel on the edge of Poble Sec.

Best By Budget: €€

Praktik Rambla (p237) A 19th-century Eixample mansion turned boutique beauty.

Hotel Brummell (p241) Boutique bliss (pool, cafe, yoga) in Poble Sec.

Five Rooms (p238) Charming Eixample pick with beautifully designed rooms.

Casa Mathilda (p238) Intimate, styled-up 1920s building in northern L'Eixample.

Barceló Raval (p234) Design smarts and an appealing rooftop with terrace, bar and pool.

Hotel Market (p241) Stylish rooms in the very hot 'hood of Sant Antoni.

Best By Budget: €€€

El Palace (p239) A plushly updated grande dame of L'Eixample.

Casa Bonay (p239) Designer Catalan-inspired interiors in an 1896 Eixample building.

Hotel Neri (p233) Beautiful, historical hotel in the thick of the Barri Gòtic.

The Serras (p233) Sleek portside five-star with rooftop pool.

Hotel Arts Barcelona (p237) Glossy design; awe-inspiring Port Olímpic architecture; fabulous food.

Best For Style

Casa Bonay (p239) Subtle celebration of Catalan style in L'Eixample.

Hotel Brummell (p241) Head-turner in Poble Sec with artful creativity.

Hotel Neri (p233) An elegant fusion of historical architecture and luxe modern design.

Margot House (p239) Wes Anderson–inspired L'Eixample hideaway.

Soho House (p234) Tiles, antiques and vaulted ceilings bring Catalan flavour to this exclusive 19th-century building.

Pars Tailor's Hostel (p241) A taste of 1930s fashion in Sant Antoni, at budget rates.

NEED TO KNOW

Price Ranges
The following price ranges refer to a double room with private bathroom per night during high season, including tax.

€ less than €75

€€ €75–€200

€€€ more than €200

Room Tax
➡ All accommodation is subject to IVA, a 10% value-added tax.

➡ There's also a tourist tax of €0.72 to €2.48 per person per night, depending on luxury level; this is expected to rise to up to €4 per night in 2020.

➡ IVA is usually included in quoted rates; tourist tax may not be.

Seasonal Rates
Most hotel rates vary over high, mid- and low seasons. Low season is roughly November to Easter, except over Christmas and New Year (though many Barcelona hotels now have a shorter low season). Whenever there is a major trade fair (the Mobile World Congress in February/March causes the most problems), high-season prices generally apply. Business-oriented hotels often consider weekends and holidays low season.

Reservations
➡ Booking ahead is essential, especially during peak periods like summer (though August can be quite a slack month).

SLEEPING

Where to Stay

NEIGHBOURHOOD	FOR	AGAINST
La Rambla & Barri Gòtic	Great location, close to major sights; perfect for exploring on foot; good nightlife and dining	Very touristed; noisy; some rooms small and lacking windows
El Raval	Central option, with good local nightlife, shops and restaurants, and walkable access to sights; bohemian vibe with lots of locals	Can be noisy; seedy and run-down in parts; many fleapits best avoided; some streets feel unsafe at night
La Ribera & El Born	Great restaurant, bar and shopping scenes; neighbourhood exploring and walking; central; top sights including the Museu Picasso and the Palau de la Música Catalana	Can be noisy; overly crowded; touristed
Barceloneta, the Waterfront & El Poblenou	Excellent seafood restaurants; easygoing local vibe; handy access to the promenade and beaches; creative scene in El Poblenou	Few sleeping options; beyond Barceloneta can be far from the action and better suited to business travellers
L'Eixample	Wide range of options for all budgets; close to Modernista sights; good restaurants, nightlife and shops; prime LGBTIQ+ scene (in the 'Gaixample')	Can be very noisy with lots of traffic; some parts are far from the old city; not as walkable as the old city
Gràcia	Youthful, local scene with lively restaurants, bars and shops; village feel with squares; great hostels	Far from the old city and beaches; few formal options (but lots of rooms for rent)
Montjuïc, Poble Sec & Sant Antoni	Near the museums, gardens and views of Montjuïc; great bars and restaurants in Sant Antoni and Poble Sec; locations in Poble Sec/Sant Antoni are also convenient for El Raval	Somewhat out of the way; can be a bit charmless up by Sants train station
Pedralbes & La Zona Alta	Good nightlife and restaurants in parts; less touristed; easier access to green spaces like Tibidabo and Parc Natural de Collserola	Very far from the action; spread-out area requiring frequent metro travel; geared more towards business travellers

🛏 La Rambla & Barri Gòtic

ITACA HOSTEL
HOSTEL €

Map p292 (📞93 301 97 51; www.itacahostel.com; Carrer de Ripoll 21; dm €18-40, tr €88-130; 🛜; Ⓜ Jaume I) A cheerful, laid-back yet lively budget find near the cathedral, 1st-floor Itaca has spacious, fan-cooled mixed dorms (sleeping six, eight or 10) with spring colours, personal power outlets and lockers. Most rooms have balconies, and there's a well-equipped kitchen, cosy lounge and private triple. The friendly team organises pub crawls, sangria nights, walking tours and more, making it great for meeting people.

KABUL PARTY HOSTEL
HOSTEL €

Map p292 (📞93 318 51 90; www.kabul.es; Plaça Reial 17; dm from €18; ❄🛜; Ⓜ Liceu) If you're a light sleeper you can forget about nodding off before 4am, but for partiers centrally located Kabul is a top choice. Small fuss-free modern dorms sleep two to 22, with private lockers and power outlets. It's easy to meet other travellers, with nightly activities (pub crawls, club nights, walking tours), free simple breakfasts and lively common spaces (roof terrace, lounge, pool table).

CATALONIA PORTAL DE L'ÀNGEL
HOTEL €€

Map p292 (📞93 318 41 41; www.cataloniahotels. com; Avinguda Portal de l'Àngel 17; s €90-220, d €112-225; ❄🛜🏊; Ⓜ Catalunya) A sensitively updated 19th-century palace in the thick of Barcelona, set around a handsome interior courtyard and marble staircase. Behind the restored neoclassical facade, rooms are smartly done in contemporary style with grey or beige velvet pillows, writing desks and tea/coffee kits. Those at the back have balconies, while a small pool, gardens and a glassed-in breakfast pagoda grace the quiet terrace.

HOTEL CONTINENTAL
HOTEL €€

Map p292 (📞93 445 76 57; www.hotelconti nental.com; La Rambla 138; r €134-209; ❄🛜; Ⓜ Catalunya) The friendly, floral-walled Continental's soundproofed rooms are a little old-fashioned but quite cosy, with coral touches, carpeted floors, microwaves, hairdryers and fridge; some have small balconies overlooking La Rambla (€20 extra). In 1937 George Orwell stayed here on his return from the front during the Spanish Civil War, when Barcelona was tense with factional strife.

H10 RACÓ DEL PI
HOTEL €€

Map p292 (📞93 342 61 90; www.h10hotels.com; Carrer del Pi 7; r €96-172; ❄🛜; Ⓜ Liceu) This super-handy three-star was stylishly carved out of a historic Barri Gòtic building, and features 37 rooms with patterned wallpaper, parquet floors, fresh flowers, colourful mosaic-tiled bathrooms and full soundproofing. The rooms' aesthetic is modern: light colours blended with the occasional art print. The location is terrific, just off one of the Barri Gòtic's prettiest squares.

⭐ HOTEL NERI
BOUTIQUE HOTEL €€€

Map p292 (📞93 304 06 55; www.hotelneri.com; Carrer de Sant Sever 5; r from €280; ❄🛜🏊🐾; Ⓜ Liceu) Occupying two chicly reimagined palaces from the 12th and 18th centuries, backing onto Plaça de Sant Felip Neri, this tranquil designer beauty wins everyone over. Sandstone walls lend a sense of history, while the 22 cream-toned, minimal-plastic rooms flaunt Molton Brown toiletries, pillow menus, world-roaming photos and jazzy carpets by the owners, and cutting-edge technology like infrared lights in the stone-clad bathrooms.

Sister hotel **The Wittmore** (Map p292; 📞93 550 08 85; www.thewittmore.com; Carrer de Riudarenes 7; r €250-500; ❄🛜; Ⓜ Jaume I), in the southern Gòtic, is a moody adults-only, no-photos affair with a British-countryside feel, plush interior rooms, a graceful roof terrace and a cosy bar.

⭐ THE SERRAS
BOUTIQUE HOTEL €€€

Map p292 (📞93 169 18 68; www.hoteltheserras barcelona.com; Passeig de Colom 9; r €300-415, ste from €600; ❄🛜🏊🐾; Ⓜ Barceloneta) With terrific port views, this fresh five-star offers every comfort – including a restaurant under Michelin-starred chef Marc Gascons and a rooftop bar and plunge pool – but never feels stuffy. The 28 chic white balconied rooms, with outsized tile-patterned headboards, have thoughtful extras like yoga mats, hair tongs, rain showers and luxurious mattresses; brighter front rooms have better views (some from the bathtub!).

The 19th-century building, designed by Francesc Daniel Molina, was once the studio of a young Pablo Picasso.

SOHO HOUSE
BOUTIQUE HOTEL €€€

Map p292 (☏93 220 46 00; www.sohohouse
barcelona.com; Plaça del Duc de Medinaceli 4; r
€230-400; ❄️🛜🏊; MDrassanes) An elegant
outpost of the famous London members'
club, with luxuriously appointed rooms,
an exclusive bar peopled with celebs, yoga
classes, a 24-hour gym, a Cowshed spa and
a rooftop pool with candy-striped loungers and incredible sea views. Vaulted brick
ceilings, antique furniture and tiled floors
highlight the building's 19th-century origins. Italian restaurant Cecconi's (p76) is a
draw in its own right.

Soho House also runs beautifully boutiquey **Little Beach House** (☏93 522 15 52;
www.littlebeachhousebarcelona.com; Carrer Mirador del Port 1, Garraf; r €255-385; ☉Apr-Oct; ❄️
🛜; Renfe train R2): just 17 Mediterranean-
inspired rooms in a chicly reimagined
1950s sea-fronting hotel in Garraf, a former
fishing village 30km southwest of central
Barcelona.

DO REIAL
BOUTIQUE HOTEL €€€

Map p292 (☏93 481 36 66; www.hoteldoreial.com;
Plaça Reial 1; s €246-450, d €297-450; ❄️🛜🏊;
MLiceu) Overlooking the magnificent plaza
for which it is named, this 18-room property has handsomely designed rooms with
beamed ceilings, wooden floors, Molton
Brown toiletries and all-important sound-
proofing. The service is excellent and the facilities extensive, with a roof terrace (bar in
summer), dipping pool, solarium and spa.
Its excellent market-to-table restaurants
pull in visiting foodies.

HOTEL 1898
LUXURY HOTEL €€€

Map p292 (☏93 552 95 52; www.hotel1898.
com; La Rambla 109; r €135-500, ste from €410;
❄️🛜🏊; MCatalunya, Liceu) The former Com-
pañía de Tabacos Filipinas building has
been resurrected as a handsome luxury
hotel crowned by a sleek rooftop terrace,
La Isabela bar (p78) and pool. Rooms are
smartly updated without losing their old-
world elegance, with marble bathrooms,
hardwood floors, tasteful furniture and
rich red or navy walls; some are smallish,
but deluxes and suites have terraces. Spa,
gym and indoor pool.

MERCER BARCELONA
BOUTIQUE HOTEL €€€

Map p292 (☏93 310 74 80; www.mercerbarce
lona.com; Carrer dels Lledó 7; r €378-480, ste
from €530; P❄️🛜🏊; MJaume I) On a narrow medieval street, the Mercer is one of
the Gòtic's standout boutique hotels. Renowned Spanish architect Rafael Moneo
stayed true to the building's original Gothic
and even Roman elements while creating
snug, elegant rooms, some overlooking an
interior garden. Soothing common areas
include a lovely rooftop dipping pool and
garden, stylish cocktail lounge, tapas bar
and Mediterranean restaurant.

OHLA BARCELONA
LUXURY HOTEL €€€

Map p292 (☏93 341 50 50; www.ohlabarcelona.
com; Via Laietana 49; r from €250; P❄️🛜🏊;
MUrquinaona) Unfolding behind a Modernista facade dotted with metallic orbs,
this beautifully designed hotel gets almost
everything right, from the top-notch service to Romain Fornell's Michelin-starred
restaurant Caelis to the truly rooftop terrace with bar, glassed-in pool and twinkling
views of Montjuïc. The sleek modern rooms
have lavish fabrics, pendular lights, iPod
docks and, for most, in-room shower cubes
(lacking privacy).

🛏 El Raval

BARCELÓ RAVAL
DESIGN HOTEL €€

Map p296 (☏93 320 14 90; www.barcelo.com;
Rambla del Raval 17-21; d €100-260; ❄️🛜; MLiceu) Part of the city's plans to pull El Raval
up by the bootstraps, this cylindrical design
tower makes a 21st-century splash. The rooftop terrace, plunge pool and **360° bar** (Map
p296; ☉11am-1am) offer fabulous views, and
the B-Lounge bar-restaurant is a lively tapas, brunch and cocktail spot. The fashion-
forward rooms have slick aesthetics (white
with lime-green or ruby-red splashes), coffee machines and rain showers.

CHIC&BASIC RAMBLAS
DESIGN HOTEL €€

Map p296 (☏93 302 71 11; www.chicandbasic.
com; Passatge de Gutenberg 7; d €133-162, f
€170-210; ❄️🛜♿; MDrassanes) A couple of
blocks into El Raval (despite the misleading
name), this branch of the popular, excellent-
value Chic&Basic chain is the most riotous
to date, with quirky and colourful interiors
that hit you from the second you see the
vintage Seat 600 in the foyer. Stripped-
back, neutral-toned rooms are inspired by
1960s Barcelona life, most with balconies
and feature walls.

CHIC&BASIC LEMON
BOUTIQUE HOTEL €€

Map p296 (☑93 342 66 66; www.chicandbasic lemonhotel.com; Carrer de Pelai; r €120-140; ✱ ☎; Ⓜ Universitat) Leafy patterns and floral prints adorn doors, furniture and walls at this cheerful, super-central, tropical-inspired pick from the popular Chic&Basic chain. The 30 rooms have desks and smart bathrooms; those overlooking Carrer de Pelai feature little balconies, though back rooms are quieter. There's a sunny plant-sprinkled terrace, plus complimentary tea/coffee and a warm welcome. Breakfast costs €6.75.

HOSTAL GRAU
BOUTIQUE HOTEL €€

Map p296 (☑93 301 81 35; www.hostalgrau.com; Carrer de les Ramelleres 27; d €104-180, apt from €160; ✱ ☎ ☜ ✿; Ⓜ Catalunya) 🍃 A family *hostal* started in the 1860s, now thoughtfully reimagined, this 'small, urban, green' hideaway retains its original twirling tiled staircase but has chic, sparkling-white rooms with organic materials and other ecoconscious touches like timed lights. The design is calming and minimalist, with pops of colour and original decorative pieces. Some rooms have street-facing balconies; others overlook a vertical garden.

There are also three similarly stylish self-catering apartments sleeping four to six people.

HOTEL SANT AGUSTÍ
HOTEL €€

Map p296 (☑93 318 16 58; www.hotelsa.com; Plaça de Sant Agustí 3; r €140-180; ✱ ☎; Ⓜ Liceu) A quick stroll west of La Rambla on a curious square, this former 18th-century monastery opened as a hotel in 1840, making it the city's oldest. Library-print wallpaper lines the corridors, while the 77 fresh rooms contrast dark woods and chic whites with open-stone or exposed-brick walls; most are spacious and light-filled, though a few were awaiting an upgrade at research time.

CASA CAMPER
DESIGN HOTEL €€€

Map p296 (☑93 342 62 80; www.casacamper. com; Carrer d'Elisabets 11; incl breakfast s €149-220, d €165-245; ✱ ☎ ☜; Ⓜ Catalunya) 🍃 The massive foyer resembles a contemporary art museum, but the rooms, boldly decorated in red, black and white, are the real surprise. Most have a sleeping and bathroom area, where you can contemplate hanging gardens outside, plus a separate lounge with balcony, TV and hammock across the corridor. Get to the rooftop for sweeping cityscapes, sunbeds and a cool-off shower.

Downstairs is Albert Raurich's Michelin-starred, Japanese-rooted restaurant Dos Palillos.

HOTEL ESPAÑA
HOTEL €€€

Map p296 (☑93 550 00 00; www.hotelespanya. com; Carrer de Sant Pau 9-11; d €95-290, f €155-280; ✱ ☎ ☜; Ⓜ Liceu) Known for its wonderful Modernista interiors in the dining rooms and bar, in which architect Domènech i Montaner, sculptor Eusebi Arnau and painter Ramon Casas had a hand, this hotel offers plush, contemporary rooms in a building that still manages to ooze a little history. There's a plunge pool and sundeck on the roof, along with a bar.

🛏️ La Ribera & El Born

★360 HOSTEL ARTS & CULTURE
HOSTEL €

Map p300 (☑93 530 56 77; https://360hostel arts.com; Ronda de Sant Pere 56; dm €27-55; ✱ ☎; Ⓜ Arc de Triomf) Loved for its lively social scene, 360 occupies the 1st floor of a lovely, bright, tile-floored old building near the Arc de Triomf. Comfortable, contemporary mixed dorms sleep six, eight or 16, with personal power outlets and lockers. Walls are adorned with art and there's a sunny terrace plus a well-equipped kitchen, daily walking tours and dinners, summer beach volleyball and more.

PENSIÓ 2000
PENSION €

Map p300 (☑93 310 74 66; www.pensio2000. com; Carrer de Sant Pere més Alt 6; d €60-100; ✱ ☎; Ⓜ Urquinaona) Right opposite the anything-but-simple Palau de la Música Catalana, this family-run, good-value 1st-floor guesthouse (no lift) has seven spacious rooms with mosaic-tiled floors and large shuttered windows in a charmingly updated 18th-century building. Thoughtful extras from welcoming owners Orlando and Manuela include water refills, hairdryers, board games, complimentary tea and coffee and a quiet courtyard.

HOTEL BANYS ORIENTALS
BOUTIQUE HOTEL €€

Map p300 (☑93 268 84 60; www.hotelbanysor ientals.com; Carrer de l'Argenteria 37; s/d €160/180; ✱ ☎; Ⓜ Jaume I) Book well ahead for this magnetically popular, clean-lined designer haunt: a glammed-up 19th-century travellers' inn with a quiet, boutiquey charm, attached to a good Catalan restaurant. Soft pastels and sleek monochrome combine with dark-hued floors; rooms, though on the small side, look onto the street or back lanes and have queen-sized beds and Rituals toiletries.

CHIC&BASIC BORN
HOTEL €€

Map p300 (☎93 295 46 52; www.chicandbasic. com; Carrer de la Princesa 50; s €110, d €123-132; ✳🛜; ⓂJaume I) Contemporary all-white style blends with soaring ceilings, decorative fairy lights and period trim across the 31 smallish rooms at this is very cool hotel, just over the road from the Parc de la Ciutadella. Many of the building's beautiful old features have been retained, such as the marble staircase; most rooms have balconies; and there are bikes to borrow.

YURBBAN PASSAGE
DESIGN HOTEL €€€

Map p300 (☎93 882 89 77; www.yurbbanpas sage.com; Carrer de Trafalgar 26; r €170-310; ✳🛜⛱; ⓂUrquinaona) A soothing stripped-back designer look runs through this four-star boutique-feel newcomer, perched across the 1878 Passatge de les Manufactures in a reimagined textiles factory. The attractive, minimalist, good-value rooms have capsule-coffee kits, desks, kettles, rain showers, yoga mats and, for some, private terraces. A pale-turquoise pool and relaxed bar crown the rooftop terrace, while downstairs lies an adults-only vegan spa.

Sister hotel **Yurbban Trafalgar** (Map p300; ☎93 268 07 27; www.yurbbantrafalgar. com; Carrer de Trafalgar 30; s €85-190, d €96-220; ✳🛜⛱; ⓂUrquinaona) next door is also hugely popular, with sharply styled dove-grey rooms (some with terraces) and a roof-terrace plunge pool and cocktail bar.

GRAND HOTEL CENTRAL
LUXURY HOTEL €€€

Map p300 (☎93 295 79 00; www.grandhotel central.com; Via Laietana 30; d €250-330, ste from €430; 🅿✳🛜⛱; ⓂJaume I) With super-soundproofed rooms, a warm professional welcome, an in-house spa and a fabulous rooftop infinity pool and all-day sky bar, this soothingly styled five-star is a standout along Via Laietana. Rooms are smartly decorated in whites, greys, blacks and beiges, with high ceilings, dark wooden floors and subtle lighting, in keeping with the building's art deco flair.

BARCELONA EDITION
DESIGN HOTEL €€€

Map p300 (☎93 626 33 30; www.editionhotels. com; Avinguda de Francesc Cambó 14; d €270-500; ⓂJaume I) Overlooking the Mercat de Santa Caterina, Ian Schrager's much-anticipated five-star Edition sees elegant, tech-forward rooms dressed in walnut wood, Spanish leather and natural tones, along with a superb rooftop bar, The Roof (p111), and plunge pool with wraparound views. Enjoy gourmet Mediterranean cuisine at Bar Veraz, speciality cocktails at the speakeasy-inspired Punch Room, and wild dinner shows at clandestine Cabaret in the basement.

🛏 Barceloneta, the Waterfront & El Poblenou

AMISTAT BEACH HOSTEL
HOSTEL €

Map p304 (☎93 221 32 81; www.amistatbeach hostel.com; Carrer de l'Amistat 21-23; dm/d from €22/102; ✳🛜; ⓂPoblenou) A stylish Poblenou budget find, Amistat has sociable common areas including a beanbag-filled lounge with DJ set-up, low-lit TV room, terrace and guest kitchen. Dorms (including one for women only, aside from a splash of colour on the ceilings; the two doubles have private bathrooms. Upbeat staff organise club nights and other events.

POBLENOU BED & BREAKFAST
GUESTHOUSE €€

Map p304 (☎93 221 26 01; www.hostalpoblenou. com; Carrer del Taulat 30; s/d from €76/100; ✳🛜; ⓂLlacuna) A five-minute walk from Bogatell beach and steps from Rambla del Poblenou, this 1930s house, with original high ceilings and beautifully tiled floors, conceals six individually styled rooms named for Spanish artists. All have a fresh feel, light colours, potted plants, comfortable beds and beach towels in palm bags; some have tiny balconies. Breakfast (€10) is on the flower-filled terrace.

HOTEL 54
HOTEL €€

Map p302 (☎93 225 00 54; www.hotel54barce loneta.es; Passeig de Joan de Borbó 54; s/d from €155/165; ✳🛜; ⓂBarceloneta) It's all about location at this sparkling three-star in the thick of Barceloneta. Modern rooms have dark tiled floors, stylish bathrooms and splashes of turquoise. Most sought-after are those with marina and sunset views from their little bougainvillea-adorned balconies; others look out over Barceloneta's lanes. Up on the roof there's a sleek terrace enjoying panoramas over the city and harbour.

BED & BEACH
GUESTHOUSE **€€**

Map p304 (📞630 528156; www.bedandbeach barcelona.com; Pasaje General Bassols 26; d €60-130; ☺Easter-Oct; ✳🛜; Ⓜ Bogatell) Just 200m west of Platja de la Nova Icària on a quiet street, this warm guesthouse with a boho touch has eight cosy, spotless contemporary rooms in a refurbished 1902 building. Some lack natural light and/or share bathrooms, while others are bright and spacious, with in-room kitchens. There's also a communal kitchen, plus a rooftop terrace that's fabulous for a sunset drink.

MELIÁ SKY BARCELONA
HOTEL **€€**

Map p304 (📞93 367 20 50; www.melia.com; Carrer de Pere IV 272-286; d/ste from €150/190; Ⓟ✳🛜♿; Ⓜ Poblenou) Created by Dominique Perrault, the slim Meliá tower is made from two filigree glass slabs, overlooking Jean Nouvel's Parc del Centre del Poblenou. Rooms in bright metallic design have city or sea views and ecofriendly toiletries; five-star Level rooms get extra perks like an all-day snack/drinks lounge. Extensive facilities include an inviting pool, a spa and bars and terraces.

⭐HOTEL ARTS BARCELONA
LUXURY HOTEL **€€€**

Map p304 (📞93 221 10 00; www.ritzcarlton.com; Carrer de la Marina 19-21; d/ste from €295/445; Ⓟ✳@🛜♿; Ⓜ Ciutadella Vila Olímpica) A sky-high tower by Bruce Graham, looming above the Port Olímpic, the swish Arts is one of Barcelona's most fashionable hotels. Its 483 rooms are kitted out with high-end features, soaking tubs and unbeatable views; public spaces are graced by designer flowers and original artwork. Services range from the seductive top-floor spa (p137) and adults-only infinity pool to six restaurants, including two-Michelin-star Enoteca.

W BARCELONA
DESIGN HOTEL **€€€**

Map p302 (📞93 295 28 00; www.marriott.com; Plaça de la Rosa dels Vents 1; r/ste from €260/370; Ⓟ✳🛜♿; 🚌V15, V19, Ⓜ Barceloneta) Designed by Barcelona-born architect Ricardo Bofill in 2009, this glinting, spinnaker-shaped glass tower is a coastal landmark. Inside are 473 contemporary-chic, tech-forward rooms, most with coastal panoramas. Guests can flit between the gym, spa, infinity pool (with bar) and beach loungers, before sipping cocktails at the 26th-floor Eclipse bar and a seafood dinner at star chef Carles Abellán's La Barra (p128).

H10 PORT VELL
HOTEL **€€€**

Map p302 (📞93 310 30 65; www.h10hotels.com; Pas de Sota Muralla 9; s/d from €120/150; ✳🛜♿; Ⓜ Barceloneta) The location is excellent at this 58-room four-star hotel within a short stroll of El Born and Barceloneta. Smart, modern, neutral-toned rooms have a trim, minimalist design with black-and-white bathrooms, rain showers and coffee kits; the best have tiny balconies with views over the marina. But the big draw is the rooftop terrace, with sunloungers, a plunge pool and evening cocktails.

PULLMAN BARCELONA SKIPPER
LUXURY HOTEL **€€€**

Map p304 (📞93 221 65 65; https://pullman.accor.com; Avinguda del Litoral 10; r/ste from €250/440; Ⓟ✳🛜♿🛗♿; Ⓜ Ciutadella Vila Olímpica) Mesmerising views of Frank Gehry's shimmering Peix (p124) sculpture unfold from the rooftop infinity pool at this five-star hotel (with spa) and from some of the 241 rooms, which are decorated in sleek timbers (some open to terraces). There's a second swimming pool at the base of the winged statue of fish in the courtyard. Family-friendly facilities include interconnecting rooms and cots.

🛏 L'Eixample

ROCK PALACE HOSTEL
HOSTEL **€**

Map p306 (📞93 453 32 81; www.santjordihostels.com; Carrer de Balmes 75; dm/d from €25/35; ✳@🛜♿; Ⓜ Passeig de Gràcia) In a prime night-out-in-L'Eixample spot, this modern hostel is known for its sociable vibe, rooftop dip pool and buzzy club- and music-themed communal spaces. Well-kept mixed dorms with tiled floors, uncluttered white-and-green decor and personal lights, shelves, lockers and power outlets sleep three to 14; there are private doubles too. The Sant Jordi chain also has Sagrada Família and Gràcia branches.

Private double rooms are only available outside of high season.

⭐PRAKTIK RAMBLA
BOUTIQUE HOTEL **€€**

Map p306 (📞93 343 66 90; www.hotelpraktikrambla.com; Rambla de Catalunya 27; s/d/tr from €122/135/169; ✳🛜; Ⓜ Passeig de Gràcia) 🌿 On a leafy boulevard, this 19th-century gem of a mansion hides a gorgeous little boutique number designed by beloved local interior designer Lázaro Rosa-Violán.

While high ceilings, patterned walls and original tiles have been maintained, the 43 rooms have bold ceramics, spot lighting and contemporary art. The relaxed library and back terrace are perfect for enjoying the complimentary coffee and croissants.

This is Praktik's flagship, but it also runs other equally enticing properties across L'Eixample: Praktik Bakery (with in-house bakery), Praktik Garden (filled with plants), Praktik Vinoteca (wine-inspired) and Praktik Èssens (perfume-themed).

FIVE ROOMS
BOUTIQUE HOTEL €€

Map p310 (☑93 342 78 80; www.thefiverooms. com; Carrer de Pau Claris 72; s/d/ste/apt incl breakfast from €129/150/160/200; ﹡☎; MⓂUrquinaona) Thoughtfully expanded from its origins, the cosy-chic Five Rooms now hosts 12 rooms across a turn-of-the-century building on the southern edge of L'Eixample. Each minimal-design room is different (some with balconies), but all have open-brick walls, soothing tones, firm beds, restored tiles and stylish bathrooms. Breakfast is served in a book-lined lounge. Two kitchen-equipped, four-person apartments await just down the street.

CASA MATHILDA
BOUTIQUE HOTEL €€

Map p310 (☑93 532 16 00; https://casa mathilda.com; Carrer de Roger de Llúria 125-127; r €80-200; ﹡☎; MⓂDiagonal) Named after welcoming owner Assumpta Baldó's mother, this stylishly homey 14-room boutique gem meanders across a beautiful 1920s building to an intimate terrace overlooking a classic L'Eixample courtyard. Each room is thoughtfully and individually styled in calming shades of purple, grey or green, with gorgeous tiling (some original, others custommade), local artwork, in-room sinks and chic modern bathrooms with rain showers.

CAMI BED & GALLERY
BOUTIQUE HOTEL €€

Map p310 (☑671 436822; www.camibedandgal lery.com; Carrer de Casp 22; r without/with bathroom from €103/111; ﹡☎; MⓂCatalunya) Just footsteps from the Plaça de Catalunya, this handsome and central Modernista building was reimagined by artist and designer Camila Vega and doubles as a gallery, staging exhibitions and cultural events. The seven airy and high-ceilinged, art-themed rooms are each slightly different in character and have oak or ceramic floors, coffee sets, hairdryers and bathrobes; some share bathrooms.

ANAKENA HOUSE
BOUTIQUE HOTEL €€

Map p306 (☑93 467 36 15; www.anakenahouse. com; Carrer del Consell de Cent 276; r €150-170; ﹡☎; MⓂPasseig de Gràcia) The 1st floor of this Modernista building designed by Catalan architect Enric Sagnier i Villavecchia has been transformed into an intimate, elegant boutique property filled with original tilework. The nine rooms are styled in calming olive tones, with antique furniture, feathered lamps, rain showers and designer lighting. All but the two interiors have street views, most from little balconies.

ROOM MATE PAU
HOTEL €€

Map p310 (☑93 343 63 00; www.room-mate hotels.com; Carrer de Fontanella 7; r/ste from €157/218; ﹡☎; MⓂCatalunya) 🖉 Just off Plaça de Catalunya, the most central of fun, eco-conscious Room Mate's properties blends upscale hostel and boutique hotel. The 66 bright-white rooms are cleverly configured with designer furnishings, plump mattresses, colourful carpets, USB-connected TVs and tea/coffee kits. The two top-floor suites with terrace, bath and twin showers are popular, and there's a striking courtyard with a living wall.

Room Mate has a clutch of other much-loved, sensibly priced hotels in L'Eixample: Anna, Emma, Carla and Gerard (the last is the glossiest).

RETROME
BOUTIQUE HOTEL €€

Map p310 (☑93 174 40 37; www.retrome.net; Carrer de Girona 81; r incl breakfast €125-160; ﹡☎; MⓂGirona) Tucked into the quieter (eastern) side of La Dreta de L'Eixample, wonderfully original Retrome has a cosy, homey, retro-chic feel. The 15 stylishly antique-y rooms (king-sized beds, balconies, record players) are spread across two late-19th-century town houses, with original features such as floor tiles offsetting vintage furnishings from the 1960s and 1970s. There's complimentary coffee plus a cafe-reception where staff dish out advice.

HOTEL CONSTANZA
BOUTIQUE HOTEL €€

Map p310 (☑93 270 19 10; www.hotelconstanza. com; Carrer del Bruc 33; s/d/f from €93/101/171; ﹡☎🖐; MⓂUrquinaona) With glossy design elements and charming little details such as flowers in the bathroom, this 46-room gem has stolen many a heart. The enticing rooms have velvet headboards, rain showers and chocolate-brown decor, plus some have balconies; family rooms come with fold-out couches. Strewn with white sofas, the stylish roof terrace looks over L'Eixample's rooftops.

AXEL HOTEL
HOTEL €€

Map p306 (☑93 323 93 93; www.axelhotels. com; Carrer d'Aribau 33; r from €150; ❄️🛜🏊; MUniversitat) A sizzling hub of Barcelona's gay scene, all-welcoming Axel occupies a sleek corner block with a wrought-iron and stained-glass canopied entrance. Its 101 smartly contemporary rooms have sound-proofing, king-sized beds and tea/coffee sets; Premium Superior rooms have lovely stained-glass galleries. Take a break in the rooftop pool or cocktail bar, the Finnish sauna or the spa. Also runs gay-oriented hotel TWO in Sant Antoni.

HOSTAL OLIVA
HOSTAL €€

Map p310 (☑93 488 01 62; www.hostaloliva.com; Passeig de Gràcia 32; r €71-125; ❄️🛜; MPasseig de Gràcia) A picturesque antique lift wheezes its way up to this 4th-floor, 15-room *hostal*, a terrific cheapie in one of Barcelona's most expensive neighbourhoods, going strong since 1931. Some of the singles barely fit a bed, but doubles are bright and spacious (some with tiled floors, others parquet). A few rooms overlook Passeig de Gràcia; the most affordable share bathrooms.

⭐EL PALACE
HISTORIC HOTEL €€€

Map p310 (☑93 510 11 30; www.hotelpalace barcelona.com; Gran Via de les Corts Catalanes 668; d/ste from €260/380; 🅿️❄️@🛜🏊🛁; MPasseig de Gràcia) Launched in 1919 as the Ritz (with Paris, London and Madrid), Barcelona's dazzling luxury original continues to wow a century later. The 120 exquisitely updated rooms retain their historic charm; the six top-tier suites are styled for celebrity guests. It's all complemented by state-of-the-art facilities including a Mayan-inspired spa and Modernista-style rooftop gardens with pool, restaurant and bar basking in 360-degree views.

⭐CASA BONAY
BOUTIQUE HOTEL €€€

Map p310 (☑93 545 80 70; www.casabonay.com; Gran Via de les Corts Catalanes 700; d/f from €150/224; ❄️🛜; MTetuan) 🍃 A beautifully revamped 1896 building laid with original tiles, Casa Bonay feels like a wonderfully chic friend's home. The minimalist-design rooms have been conceived working with local designers, from handmade throws to Santa & Cole lighting; some have glassed-

in balconies, others terraces and outdoor showers. A summer *xiringuito* graces the rooftop terrace, which also hosts a herb garden and cool-off shower.

Other perks range from free bikes, yoga mats and SUP boards to fashionable Catalan-Asian fusion restaurant King Kong Lady, speciality cafe Satan's Coffee Corner (p161) and moody cocktail/DJ bar Libertine.

⭐MARGOT HOUSE
BOUTIQUE HOTEL €€€

Map p310 (☑93 272 00 76; www.margothouse. es; Passeig de Gràcia 46; d/ste from €210/265; ❄️@🛜; MPasseig de Gràcia) In the thick of L'Eixample, this elegant, intimate, supremely peaceful nine-room designer bolthole is styled in fresh minimalist whites and natural woods. Textiles, lamps and furniture come from Catalan designers, while Aesop toiletries grace the sleek bathrooms; the four light-bathed suites overlook Passeig de Gràcia, with freestanding tubs. The book-filled lounge has coffee and an honesty bar; there's a fabulous gourmet breakfast.

COTTON HOUSE
LUXURY HOTEL €€€

Map p310 (☑93 450 50 45; www.hotelcotton house.com; Gran Via de les Corts Catalanes 670; d/ste from €250/460; ❄️🛜🏊; MUrquinaona) An exquisite 1879 building awash with wooden floors, carved ceilings and a roof-top pool, this splendid address occupies the former headquarters of the Cottonmakers' Guild, which you'll notice from the lobby's huge sprays of cotton bolls to the room names (Damask, Egyptian, Taffeta). All-white rooms are elegantly styled, with wide beds, rain showers and Ortigia toiletries; back rooms have balconies.

ALMA
DESIGN HOTEL €€€

Map p310 (☑93 216 44 90; https://almahotels. com; Carrer de Mallorca 271; r from €300; ❄️🛜; MDiagonal) It's all about stripped-back, straight-lined luxury, sober-toned minimalism and spot-on service at this calming five-star beauty, with 72 tech-forward rooms in an early-20th-century building that marries original architecture with contemporary design. An all-white basement spa with pool, sauna and gym awaits, and the summer-only roof terrace gazes out on L'Eixample's sights, though the leafy hidden garden is the show-stealer.

SIR VICTOR
DESIGN HOTEL €€€

Map p310 (☑93 271 12 44; www.sirhotels.com; Carrer del Rosselló 265; r from €240; ❄️🛜🏊;

MDiagonaI) Named for Catalan author Caterina Albert i Paradís, who published as Victor Català, this rippling building has been plushly reincarnated by forward-thinking Amsterdam-born boutique chain Sir Hotels. Stylish rooms have coffee machines, balconies and works by emerging local artists. Other perks include excellent steak restaurant Mr Porter, a rooftop pool and bar, a luxe spa and a library spotlighting female writers.

THE ONE BARCELONA   LUXURY HOTEL €€€
Map p310 (☑93 214 20 70; www.hotelstheone.com; Carrer de Provença 277; r/ste from €244/364; ❄🛜🏊; MDiagonaI) Designed by interiorist Jaime Beriestain, this five-star stunner has 89 light-filled, gold-and-cream rooms (corner suites like 203 are lovely). Works by Catalan artists, including Miró and Tàpies, adorn public spaces; rooms feature pieces by Chilean artist Fernando Prats. A panoramic roof terrace, bar-restaurant and plunge pool, a spa (indoor pool, sauna) and a 24-hour gym are among the facilities.

MANDARIN ORIENTAL   LUXURY HOTEL €€€
Map p310 (☑93 151 88 88; www.mandarinoriental.com; Passeig de Gràcia 38-40; d/ste from €475/995; P❄🛜🏊; MPasseig de Gràcia) At this imposing former bank, the 98 rooms channel contemporary designer style (straight lines, muted colour schemes), while fabulous views unfurl from the roof terrace, its stunning black-tiled pool and its Peruvian fusion bar-restaurant. Many standard rooms have deep bathtubs; all overlook Passeig de Gràcia or an interior sculpted garden. Also here is double-Michelin-starred restaurant Moments, along with a swish spa.

HOTEL PULITZER   HOTEL €€€
Map p306 (☑93 481 67 67; www.hotelpulitzer.es; Carrer de Bergara 8; r from €170; ❄🛜🏊; MCatalunya) 🍃 Elegant bathrooms are tiled in beachy turquoise, carpets are stamped with zebra prints and there's a touch of tropical style at the Pulitzer, loved locally for its leafy, vibrant roof-terrace bar (p160) and central location. Rooms with sustainable technology flaunt a minimalist-chic vibe courtesy of *barcelonin* designer Lázaro Rosa-Violán: monochrome decor, dark-wood furniture (including some four-poster beds), leather flourishes, recycled materials.

MAJÈSTIC HOTEL & SPA   LUXURY HOTEL €€€
Map p310 (☑93 488 17 17; www.hotelmajestic.es; Passeig de Gràcia 68; d/apt/ste from €270/330/480; P❄🛜🏊🏋; MPasseig de Gràcia) The rooftop pool and bar at this grand, sprawling 1918 old-timer are superb for views and cocktails, or you can pamper yourself at the spa or one of the graceful restaurants. A subtly updated, warm-toned classic look runs through the 271 rooms, which have white-marble bathrooms and other plush touches by Mallorcan designer Antonio Obrador. Standard rooms are smallish but comfortable.

🛏 Gràcia

★ CASA GRÀCIA   HOSTEL €
Map p312 (☑93 174 05 28; www.casagraciabcn.com; Passeig de Gràcia 116; dm/s/d/tr/apt from €31/110/120/145/162; ❄@🛜; MDiagonaI) Set across two reimagined historic buildings, Casa Gràcia raised the bar for Barcelona budget accommodation. Crisp white-design dorms sleeping four or six (with women-only options) have individual power outlets, lights and lockers. The best, brightest doubles face the street. Services include a leafy terrace, fully-equipped kitchen and arty library lounge, a popular restaurant and DJ-fuelled bar, plus free yoga and walking tours.

YEAH HOSTEL   HOSTEL €
(☑93 531 01 35; www.yeahhostels.com; Carrer de Girona 176; dm €30-45, d €120-130; ❄🛜🏊; MVerdaguer) A lively, contemporary-design hostel with wood-and-white dorms for four or six (some for women only), a cosy communal lounge, a well-equipped kitchen and, best of all, a chilli-red pool on the roof. Dorm beds have curtains, lockers and power outlets, while the handful of private 'suites' sleeping two or four come with little balconies. Cheery staff arrange walking tours and group dinners.

GENERATOR BARCELONA   HOSTEL €
Map p312 (☑93 220 03 77; https://staygenerator.com; Carrer de Còrsega 373; dm/d/q/penthouse from €30/110/140/315; MDiagonaI) Part of the world-roaming, design-forward Generator brand, this stylish budget pick has much to recommend it, including a festival-inspired bar made from reclaimed lumber and recycled elevator parts, festooned with an explosion of paper lanterns. Fresh-white dorms are for six or eight people, with women-

only rooms, and have personal shelves, lights, power outlets and under-bed lockers. Private twins are simple but modern.

JAM HOSTEL
HOSTEL €

Map p312 (☑93 315 53 38; www.jamhostelbarcelona.com; Carrer de Montmany 38-42; dm €20-35, d €90; ❄☎; ⓂJoanic) ✈ This welcoming, original ecoconscious operation is a powerhouse of sustainable tourism, working with responsible local companies and using renewable energy, upcycled materials and fair-trade coffee. Minimalist dorms for four, eight or nine have personal power outlets, shelves and lockers; shared bathrooms are thoughtfully designed, with spacious showers and hairdryers. There are also private doubles, bike tours, yoga (€5) and an enormous terrace.

★HOTEL CASA FUSTER
LUXURY HOTEL €€€

Map p312 (☑93 255 30 00; www.hotelcasafuster.com; Passeig de Gràcia 132; d/ste from €250/350; Ⓟ❄❄☎❄; ⓂDiagonal) Designed by Domènech i Montaner from 1908 to 1911, this sumptuous Modernista mansion is one of Barcelona's most luxurious addresses. Rooms are individual and plush (though standards are small), with chocolate-brown or soft-beige decor and marble bathrooms. Period features have been thoughtfully restored and complemented by hydromassage tubs and king-sized beds. The rooftop terrace (with pool and summer bar) offers spectacular views.

🛏 Montjuïc, Poble Sec & Sant Antoni

★PARS TAILOR'S HOSTEL
HOSTEL €

Map p314 (☑93 250 56 84; www.parshostels.com; Carrer de Sepúlveda 146; dm €25-32; ❄☎; ⓂUrgell) Decorated like a 1930s tailor's shop, this lively, friendly, budget-chic hostel is filled with old sewing machines, battered suitcases and other vintage pieces collected from around Barcelona. Fabric-themed dorms (including a women-only room) sleep six, eight or 12, with personal power outlets and lockers. You can relax in the comfy lounge or back terrace, cook in the well-equipped kitchen and join organised activities.

TOC HOSTEL
HOSTEL €

Map p314 (☑93 453 44 25; https://tochostels.com; Gran Via de les Corts Catalanes 580; dm/d from €36/140; ❄☎❄; ⓂUniversitat) Inhabiting a graceful old building on the southern fringes of L'Eixample, TOC appeals with its sun-soaked back terrace and pool, stylish communal spaces (bar, kitchen, lounge), lively events and rotating art exhibitions. Bright, spacious dorms (including female-only ones), some overlooking Gran Via, for six or eight have personal plugs, lights, lockers and curtains. Private doubles have queen-sized beds and, for some, terraces.

PARS TEATRO HOSTEL
HOSTEL €

Map p314 (☑93 443 94 66; www.parshostels.com; Carrer d'Albareda 12; dm €25-44; ☎; ⓂDrassanes) True to its name, this wonderfully original, theatrically styled hostel takes its inspiration from Poble Sec's arty history. Photos of bygone actors hang above a row of red-velvet theatre seats in the vintage-filled main lounge. White-themed dorms, for four, six or 10, are more restrained, with individual power outlets, lockers and reading lights. Helpful staff organise dinners, parties and activities.

★HOTEL BRUMMELL
BOUTIQUE HOTEL €€

Map p314 (☑93 125 86 22; www.hotelbrummell.com; Carrer Nou de la Rambla 174; r from €150; ❄☎❄; ⓂParal·lel) With a creative soul, fun atmosphere and custom-designed furniture alongside European and Sri Lankan antiques, this thoughtfully styled Poble Sec boutique continues to turn heads. The 20 bright, bespoke rooms have minimalist design, rain showers and yoga mats; the best have terraces with views and outdoor tubs. Kind-hearted staff share tips, and there's a great restaurant-cafe plus a terrace with dip pool.

HOTEL MARKET
BOUTIQUE HOTEL €€

Map p314 (☑93 325 12 05; www.hotelmarketbarcelona.com; Carrer del Comte Borrell 68; d/ste from €150/170; ❄☎; ⓂSant Antoni) Attractively located in a renovated building just north of the Mercat de Sant Antoni, this chic boutique spot has 68 black-and-white-toned, contemporary-design rooms with wide-plank floors, oversized armoires, bold art prints and carefully designed bathrooms (stone basins, rain showers). Some have tiny (two-seat) balconies; suites come with terraces. Downstairs are a smart Mediterranean restaurant and cocktail bar.

CASA VAGANTO
BOUTIQUE HOTEL €€

Map p314 (📞93 027 27 27; www.vagantohotel.
com; Carrer d'En Fontrodona 1; r incl breakfast
€150-209; ❄🛜; MParal·lel) Set in an elegant
19th-century building, this colourfully and
chicly styled boutique find is inspired by
travel and dressed with warm woods, textured surfaces, tropical prints, feature walls
and sprinkled terracotta-pot plants. The
19 contemporary-design rooms have rain
showers, prettily tiled bathrooms (some
with in-room sinks) and blackout blinds,
and there's complimentary tea, coffee and
a glass of wine.

HOSTAL CÈNTRIC
HOSTAL €€

Map p314 (📞93 426 75 73; www.hostalcentric.
com; Carrer de Casanova 13; s/d from €116/140;
❄🛜; MUrgell) Done out in light timbers and
fabrics, Hostal Cèntric has an appealing
central location just west of the northern
Raval. Rooms are simply but smartly updated and brilliantly maintained, and some
have tiny balconies. Head to higher floors
to avoid street noise. Staff go out of their
way to help.

NOBU BARCELONA
LUXURY HOTEL €€€

Map p314 (📞93 493 60 26; https://barcelona.
nobuhotels.com; Avinguda de Roma 2-4; r incl
breakfast from €250; ❄🛜; MSants Estació, Tarragona) The luxe 2019-launched Nobu, opposite Sants station, has fabulous views across
Barcelona, especially from the excellent
23rd-floor signature restaurant and sushi
bar. A sleek fusion of Catalan and Japanese
design infuses the soothing rooms, which
feature swirling blues, lots of natural light
and, for some, custom-made bedheads and
wooden *ofuro* tubs; the best enjoy city panoramas from the bath.

A spa is in the works for 2020, and there's
also a stylish lobby cocktail bar.

🛏 Pedralbes
& La Zona Alta

POL & GRACE
BOUTIQUE HOTEL €€

Map p317 (📞93 415 40 00; www.polgracehotel.
es; Carrer de Guillem Tell 49; s €100-180, d €140-
200; P❄🛜; ℝFGC Molina, Sant Gervasi) 🌿
At this stylish, ultracontemporary hotel, the
60 uniquely designed white-on-white rooms
revolve around Barcelona themes (Gaudí,
the Museu del Disseny, Catalan festivals and
gastronomy) and are gradually being jazzed
up with original artwork. All are decently

sized and have ecofriendly toiletries; singles
have small double beds. Neon-painted pillars, sunbeds, a shower and an organic garden dot the view-laden roof terrace.

ANITA'S B&B
B&B €€

Map p318 (📞670 064258; www.anitasbarcelona.
com; Carrer d'August Font 24; r incl breakfast from
€95; 🛜; 🚌124) Soul-stirring views of the
city and the Mediterranean beyond sparkle from this sweet, family-owned hillside
B&B on Tibidabo's lower slopes. The three
fan-cooled rooms are generously sized, with
sitting areas, tea/coffee kits and a cosy at-
home feel; two share a terrace with sweeping panoramas. A 3.5km (one-hour) uphill
hike leads to the top of Tibidabo.

WILSON BOUTIQUE HOTEL
BOUTIQUE HOTEL €€

Map p317 (📞93 209 25 11; www.wilsonbcn.com;
Avinguda Diagonal 568; d/ste/f from €150/228/
248; ❄🛜🛗; MDiagonal, Hospital Clínic) On
the northwestern fringes of L'Eixample,
this four-star hotel's 54 contemporary-style
rooms are spread over eight floors and well
soundproofed, cutting out busy Avinguda
Diagonal noise. Each is painted in strong
accent colours, with a kettle and desk, and
some open to terraces. Family rooms sleep up
to four people, with cots on request.

★GRAN HOTEL
LA FLORIDA
HISTORIC HOTEL €€€

Map p318 (📞93 259 30 00; www.hotellaflorida.
com; Carretera de Vallvidrera al Tibidabo 83-93;
d/f/ste from €235/345/495; P❄🛜🛗; 🚌111)
Hemingway is among the former guests of
this magnificent 1920s-built property atop
Tibidabo, which had a designer makeover
this century. Vibrant red sunbeds offset
a metallic infinity pool with spectacular
views across Barcelona, while other facilities include an indoor pool, a L'Occitane
spa and three restaurants. The 70 elegant
rooms are styled with soothing neutrals
and Modernista touches.

ABAC BARCELONA
BOUTIQUE HOTEL €€€

Map p318 (📞93 319 66 00; www.abacbarce
lona.com; Avinguda del Tibidabo 1; r from €350;
❄🛜🛗; ℝFGC Avinguda Tibidabo) A listed
1890-built private mansion now houses
this ultrastylish 15-room five-star. Chicly
designed rooms are kitted out with rainfall
showers, luxury bed linens and calming
cream tones; some open to private terraces
with hot tubs. Also here are a lovely spa and
pool, and one of the city's top restaurants
(p<OV>), with two Michelin stars.

Understand Barcelona

Above: Camp Nou (p206), home of FC Barcelona

History

The settlement of Barcelona has seen waves of immigrants and conquerors over its 2000-plus years, including Romans, Visigoths and Franks. Barcelona's fortunes have risen and fallen: from the golden era of princely power in the 14th century to the dark days of the Franco regime. An independent streak has always run through this city, often leading to conflict with the Kingdom of Castile – an antagonism that continues today, with a desire for more autonomy, or, increasingly, full independence, from Spain.

The Romans

Barcelona's recorded history really begins with the Romans when Barcino (much later Barcelona) was founded in the reign of Caesar Augustus. The Romans were attracted to the location for the possibility of building a port here.

Rome's legacy was huge, giving Hispania (as the Iberian Peninsula was known to the Romans) a road system, aqueducts, temples and the religion that still predominates today, Christianity. Before Rome embraced this monotheistic tradition, however, there were waves of persecution of early Christians. Emperor Constantine declared Christianity the official religion in 312 CE.

In 1991 the remains of 25 corpses, dating from 4000 BCE, were found in Carrer de Sant Pau in El Raval. In those days much of El Raval was a bay and the hillock (Mont Tàber) next to Plaça de Sant Jaume may have been home to a Neolithic settlement.

Guifré el Pelós & the Catalan Golden Age

In the 9th century CE, when much of Spain was ruled by the Moors, Louis the Pious – the son of Charlemagne and the future Frankish ruler – conquered Barcelona and claimed it as part of his empire. Barcelona in those days was a frontier town in what was known as the Frankish or Spanish March – a rough-and-ready buffer zone between the Pyrenees and the Moors, who had conquered most of the lands to the south.

The March was under nominal Frankish control, but the real power lay with local potentates who ranged across the territory. One of these rulers went by the curious name of Guifré el Pelós (Wilfred the Hairy). According to legend, old Guifré had hair in parts most people do not

TIMELINE	c 4000 BCE	218 BCE	415 CE
	A Neolithic settlement may have thrived around the present-day Plaça de Sant Jaume at this time, as indicated by jasper implements discovered around Carrer del Paradís.	In a move to block supplies to the Carthaginian general Hannibal, Roman troops under Scipio land at Empúries, found Tarraco (Tarragona) and take control of the Catalan coast.	Visigoths under Ataülf, with captured Roman empress Galla Placidia as his wife, make Barcino their capital. With several interruptions, it remains so until the 6th century.

(exactly which parts was never specified!). He and his brothers gained control of most of the Catalan counties by 878 and Guifré entered the folk mythology of Catalonia.

Guifré consolidated power over Catalonia and ushered in an era of early building projects. He endowed churches and had a new palace built for himself in Barcelona (of which nothing remains). His achievements were later described by medieval monks and Romantic poets, who credit him with transforming a minor town into the future seat of an empire. If Catalonia can be called a nation, then its 'father' was the hirsute Guifré. He founded a dynasty that lasted nearly five centuries, and which developed almost independently from the Reconquista wars that were playing out in the rest of Iberia.

Romanesque Beauties

At the beginning of the 2nd millennium, Catalan culture entered a rich new age. Romanesque churches in the countryside fostered a powerful new style of architecture. Inside lay richly painted frescoes created with the finest pigments and bearing notable Byzantine influences. Some of these works – rescued from churches that later fell into ruin (though some have now been restored) – are beautifully preserved inside the Museu Nacional d'Art de Catalunya (MNAC; p189) on Montjuïc. Commerce was also on the rise, fuelled by a new class of merchants and tradespeople.

A Growing Empire

Shipbuilding, textiles and farming (grain and grapes) helped power expansion. An even bigger catalyst to Catalonia's growth came in 1137 when Ramon Berenguer IV, the Count of Barcelona, became engaged to Petronila, heir to the throne of neighbouring Aragón, thus creating a joint state that set the scene for Barcelona's golden age.

In the following centuries the regime became a flourishing merchant empire, seizing Valencia and the Balearic Islands from the Moors, and later taking territories as far flung as Sardinia, Sicily and parts of Greece.

Barcelona's Golden Age

The 14th century marked the golden age of Barcelona. Its trading wealth paid for the great Gothic buildings that bejewel the city to this day. La Catedral (p62), the Capella Reial de Santa Àgata (inside the Museu d'Història de Barcelona, p67) and the churches of Santa Maria del Pi (p66) and Santa Maria del Mar (p101) were all completed during

HISTORY ROMANESQUE BEAUTIES

In Catalan folklore, the idea for the Catalan flag – alternating red and yellow bars – was born when, during battle, King Louis the Pious dipped four fingers into the wound of a dying Wilfred the Hairy, and ran them across Wilfred's golden shield. Never mind the fact that Louis died long before Wilfred was born.

According to a medieval legend, Barcelona was founded by Hercules himself. Although versions differ, all tell of nine *barcas* (boats), one of which separates from the others in a storm, and is piloted by Hercules to a beautiful coastal spot where he founds a city, naming it Barca Nona (Ninth Boat).

878	985	1060	1137
Wilfred the Hairy consolidates power throughout Catalonia and founds a long-lasting dynasty with his capital in Barcelona.	Al-Mansur (the Victorious) rampages across Catalan territory and devastates Barcelona in a lightning campaign. Much of the population is taken as slaves to Córdoba.	Some 150 years before the Magna Carta, Count Ramon Berenguer I approves the 'Usatges de Barcelona', a bill of rights establishing all free men as equal before the law.	Count Ramon Berenguer IV is betrothed to one-year-old Petronila, daughter of the king of Aragón, creating a new combined state that becomes known as the Corona de Aragón.

this time. King Pere III (1336–87) later created the breathtaking Reials Drassanes (Royal Shipyards; now the Museu Marítim, p120) and extended the city walls yet again, this time to include El Raval to the west.

Black Death & Pogroms

Preserving the empire began to exhaust Catalonia. Sea wars with Genoa, resistance in Sardinia, the rise of the Ottoman Empire and the loss of the gold trade all drained the city's coffers. Commerce collapsed. The Black Death and famines killed about half of Catalonia's population in the 14th century. Barcelona also lost some of its best merchants when bloodthirsty mobs attacked Jewish businesses and homes in 1391.

The Peasants' Revolt

After the last of Guifré el Pelós' dynasty, Martí I, died heirless in 1410, Barcelona saw its star diminish when Catalonia effectively became part of the Castilian state, under the rule of Fernando from the Aragonese throne and Isabel, queen of Castilla (the Reyes Católicos, or Catholic Monarchs). Impoverished and disaffected by ever-growing financial demands from the crown, Catalonia revolted in the 17th century when Catalan peasants gathered on La Rambla outside the walls of the city and began rioting.

They murdered the Viceroy, Dalmau de Queralt, and sacked and burned his ministers' houses in what was later known as the Guerra dels Segadors (Reapers' War). Under French protection, Catalonia declared itself to be an independent 'republic'. Anarchy ruled over the next few years, until Barcelona was finally besieged into submission by Castilla.

Little was gained from the effort, though the event was later commemorated as the first great Catalan drive towards independence. The song 'Els Segadors', written down in the 19th century (but with an oral tradition dating back to the 1600s), officially became Catalonia's 'national anthem' in 1993.

War of the Spanish Succession

Although Catalonia had only limited autonomy in the late 1600s, things grew worse at the turn of the 18th century when it supported the losing side in the War of the Spanish Succession. Barcelona, under the auspices of British-backed archduke Charles of Austria, fell after an 18-month siege on 11 September 1714 to the forces of Bourbon king Felipe V, who established a unitary Castilian state.

Barcelona's first patron saint, Santa Eulàlia (290–304 CE), was martyred for her faith during the persecutory reign of Diocletian. Her death involved 13 tortures (one for each year of her life), including being rolled in a glass-filled barrel, having her breasts cut off, and crucifixion. The 13 geese that wander La Catedral's cloister are linked to her, and there is a major festival (p24) in her name each February.

1225–29	1283	1323	1348
At age 18 Jaume I takes command; four years later he conquers Muslim-held Mallorca, the first of several dazzling conquests that lead him to be called El Conqueridor (the Conqueror).	The Corts Catalanes, a legislative council for Catalonia, meets for the first time and begins to curtail unlimited powers of sovereigns in favour of nobles and the powerful trading class.	Catalan forces land in Sardinia and launch a campaign of conquest that will not end until 1409. Their fiercest enemy is Eleonora de Arborea, a Sardinian Joan of Arc.	Plague devastates Barcelona. Over 25% of the city's population dies. Further waves of the Black Death, a plague of locusts in 1358 and an earthquake in 1373 deal further blows.

Catalonia under a Repressive Regime

Angered at Catalonia's perceived treachery, the new king abolished the Generalitat and levelled a whole district of medieval Barcelona to make way for a huge fort (the Ciutadella) to watch over the city. The excavated ruins beneath the Born Centre de Cultura i Memòria (p104), which opened in 2013, show what life was like for those living in the 1700s on the future site of the Ciutadella. Their lives changed irrevocably as their homes were destroyed and they were relocated to the new, soulless geometric grid of Barceloneta. Not surprisingly, the citadel became the city's most hated symbol for most Catalans.

Teaching and writing in Catalan was banned, as Felipe V proceeded with a widespread plan of 'Castilianisation', in hopes of crushing future dissent. What was left of Catalonia's possessions were farmed out to the great powers.

A New Boom

After the initial shock, Barcelona found the Bourbon rulers to be comparatively light-handed in their treatment of the city. The big break came in 1778, when the ban on trade with the Spanish American colonies was lifted. In Barcelona itself, growth was modest but sustained; small-scale manufacturing provided employment and profit, and wages began to rise.

Barcelona's growth was briefly slowed by the French invasion in 1808, but gradually returned after Napoleon's defeat in 1814. The cotton trade with America helped fuel the boom. In the 1830s, the first steam-driven factories opened in Barcelona, heralding a wave of development that would last for most of the century. Wine, cork and iron industries flourished. From the mid-1830s onwards, steamships were launched off the slipways. In 1848, Spain's first railway line was opened between Barcelona and Mataró.

A Dramatic Redesign

Creeping industrialisation and prosperity for the business class did not work out so well down the line. Working-class families lived in increasingly putrid and cramped conditions. Poor nutrition, bad sanitation and disease were the norm in workers' districts, and riots, predictably, resulted. As a rule they were put down with little ceremony – the 1842 rising was bombarded into submission from the Castell de Montjuïc.

In 1869 a plan to expand the city was begun. Ildefons Cerdà designed L'Eixample (the Expansion) as a grid, broken up with gardens and parks and grafted on to the old city, beginning at Plaça de Catalunya. The

Although 11 September reflects the tragic fall of Barcelona in 1714, the day is still commemorated as the Diada, the National Day of Catalonia – often a day of political rallies and demonstrations, with independence very much on the agenda.

HISTORY CATALONIA UNDER A REPRESSIVE REGIME

Many Gothic masterpieces were built in the mid-14th century, simultaneously a time of great suffering in Barcelona. When a wheat crop failed in 1333, the resulting famine killed 10,000 people (a quarter of the city's population). In the 1340s, plague killed four of its five councillors, along with many others.

1383	1387	1469	1478
After 50 or so years of frenzied construction, the massive Santa Maria del Mar church rises above La Ribera – one of many Gothic architectural gems completed in the 14th century.	During the reign of Juan I, Barcelona hosts its first bullfight (according to the city's historical archive). It isn't until the 19th century, however, that bullfighting gains widespread popularity.	Isabel, heir to the Castilian throne, marries Aragonese heir Fernando, uniting two of Spain's most powerful monarchies and effectively subjugating Catalonia to the Castilian state.	Isabel and Fernando, the Reyes Católicos (Catholic Monarchs), stir up religious bigotry and establish the Spanish Inquisition, which sees thousands killed until it's finally abolished in 1834.

plan was revolutionary. Until then it had been illegal to build on the plains between Barcelona and Gràcia, as the area was a military zone. The flourishing bourgeoisie paid for lavish, ostentatious buildings, many of them in the unique Modernista style, designed by the great Antoni Gaudí (p166) and his contemporaries.

The 19th-Century Renaissance

Barcelona was comparatively peaceful for most of the second half of the 19th century but far from politically inert. The relative calm and growing wealth that came with commercial success helped revive interest in all things Catalan.

The Renaixença (Renaissance) reflected the feeling of renewed self-confidence in Barcelona. Politicians and academics increasingly studied and demanded the return of former Catalan institutions and legal systems. The Catalan language was readopted by the middle and upper classes and new Catalan literature emerged.

In 1892, the Unió Catalanista (Catalanist Union) demanded the re-establishment of the Corts in a document known as the *Bases de Manresa*. In 1906 the suppression of Catalan news sheets was greeted by the formation of Solidaritat Catalana (Catalan Solidarity; a nationalist movement), which attracted a broad band of Catalans, not all of them nationalists.

Perhaps the most dynamic expression of the Catalan Renaissance occurred in the world of art. Barcelona was the home of Modernisme, or Catalan art nouveau. While the rest of Spain stagnated, Barcelona was a hotbed of artistic activity – an avant-garde base with close links to Paris. The young Picasso spread his artistic wings here and drank in the artists' hang-out of Els Quatre Gats, and work on Gaudí's great opus, La Sagrada Família (p140), began in 1882.

An unpleasant wake-up call came with Spain's short, futile war with the USA in 1898, in which it lost not only its entire navy but also its last colonies (Cuba, Puerto Rico and the Philippines). The blow to Barcelona's trade was enormous.

Working-Class Turmoil

Barcelona's total population grew from 115,000 in 1800 to more than 500,000 by 1900 and over one million by 1930 – boosted, in the early 19th century, by poor immigrants from rural Catalonia and, later, from other regions of Spain. All this made Barcelona ripe for unrest.

The city became a swirling vortex of poor workers, Republicans, bourgeois regionalists, gangsters, anarchists and hired *pistolers* (gunmen). Among the underclasses, who lived in some of the most abysmal

History Sights

Museu d'Història de Barcelona (La Rambla & Barri Gòtic)

Museu d'Història de Catalunya (Barceloneta, the Waterfront & El Poblenou)

Via Sepulcral Romana (La Rambla & Barri Gòtic)

Museu Marítim (Barceloneta, the Waterfront & El Poblenou)

Born Centre de Cultura i Memòria (La Ribera & El Born)

1640–52	1714	1770	1808
Catalan peasants, angered at having to quarter Castilian troops during the Thirty Years War, declare their independence under French protection. Spain eventually crushes the rebellion.	Barcelona loses all autonomy after surrendering to the Bourbon king, Felipe V, on 11 September at the end of the War of the Spanish Succession.	A freak hurricane strikes Barcelona, causing considerable damage. Among other things, the winds destroy more than 200 of the city's 1500 gaslight street lamps.	In the Battle of Bruc, Catalan militiamen defeat occupying Napoleonic units, yet Barcelona, Figueres and the coast remain under French control until Napoleon's retreat in 1814.

conditions in Europe, there was a deep undercurrent of discontent towards the upper classes, the state and the Catholic Church (which had long been viewed as an ally to the rich and powerful).

Anarchist Bombings & the Tragic Week

When the political philosophy of anarchism began spreading through Europe, it was embraced by many industrial workers in Barcelona, who embarked on a road to social revolution through violent means.

One anarchist bomb at the Liceu opera house (p79) on La Rambla in the 1890s killed 22 people. Anarchists were also blamed for the Setmana Tràgica (Tragic Week) in July 1909 when, following a military call-up for Spanish campaigns in Morocco, mobs wrecked 70 religious buildings and workers were shot on the street in reprisal.

Class Struggle & the Coming War

In the post-WWI slump, trade unionism took hold. This movement was led by the anarchist Confederación Nacional del Trabajo (CNT; National Labour Confederation), which embraced 80% of the city's workers. During a wave of strikes in 1919 and 1920, employers hired assassins to eliminate union leaders. The 1920s dictator General Miguel Primo de Rivera opposed bourgeois-Catalan nationalism and working-class radicalism, banning the CNT and even closing Barcelona's football club, a potent symbol of Catalanism. But he did support the staging of a second world fair in Barcelona, the Montjuïc World Exhibition of 1929.

Rivera's repression succeeded only in uniting, after his fall in 1930, Catalonia's radical elements. Within days of the formation of Spain's Second Republic in 1931, leftist Catalan nationalists of the Esquerra Republicana de Catalunya (ERC; Republican Left of Catalonia), led by Francesc Macià and Lluís Companys, proclaimed Catalonia a republic within an imaginary 'Iberian Federation'. Madrid pressured them into accepting unitary Spanish statehood, but after the leftist Popular Front victory in the February 1936 national elections, Catalonia briefly won genuine autonomy, with Companys as president.

But things were racing out of control. The left and the right across Spain were shaping up for a showdown.

Civil War Erupts

On 17 July 1936, an army uprising in Morocco, led by General Francisco Franco and other rebels, kick-started the Spanish Civil War. The main players in the conflict were the Nationalists and the Republicans. The Nationalists were allied with conservatives (and the Church). Angry at

Barcelona nearly staged the Olimpíada Popular (People's Olympiad) in 1936, an alternative to the Olympics being held in fascist Germany. Around 6000 athletes from 23 countries registered. However, the civil war erupted just before the start. Some athletes who arrived stayed on and joined militias to help defend the republic.

1869	1873	1888	1898
Ildefons Cerdà designs L'Eixample (the Expansion) district with wide boulevards and a grid pattern. Modernista architects of the day showcase their creations here.	Antoni Gaudí, 21 years old and in Barcelona since 1869, enrols in architecture school, from which he graduates five years later, having already designed the street lamps in Plaça Reial.	Showcasing the grand Modernista touches of recent years (including L'Eixample), Barcelona hosts Spain's first International Exposition, held in the new, manicured Parc de la Ciutadella.	Spain loses its entire navy and last remaining colonies (the Philippines, Cuba and Puerto Rico) in two hopeless campaigns against the USA, dealing a heavy blow to Barcelona businesses.

the new leftist direction in which Spain was heading, they staged a coup and quickly gained the following of most of the army. On the opposite side was the Republican government, which was supported by those loyal to Spain's democratically elected government. Republican supporters were a loose coalition of workers' parties, socialists, anarchists, communists and other left-wing groups.

Barcelona's army garrison attempted to take the city for General Franco, but was defeated by anarchists and police loyal to the government. Franco's Nationalist forces quickly took hold of most of southern and western Spain; Galicia and Navarra in the north were also his. Most of the east and industrialised north stood with Madrid. Initial rapid advances on Madrid were stifled and the two sides settled in for almost three years of misery.

Historical Reads

Barcelona: The Great Enchantress (Robert Hughes)

Barcelona – A Thousand Years of the City's Past (Felipe Fernández Armesto)

Homage to Catalonia (George Orwell)

Homage to Barcelona (Colm Tóibín)

The Shadow of the Wind (Carlos Ruiz Zafón)

The Struggle for Catalonia (Raphael Minder)

Life Under the Anarchists

For nearly a year, Barcelona was run by anarchists and the Trotskyist militia of the Partido Obrero de Unificación Marxista (POUM; Workers' Marxist Unification Party), with Companys president only in name. Factory owners and rightists fled the city. Trade unions took over factories and public services, hotels and mansions became hospitals and schools, everyone wore workers' clothes (in something of a foretaste of what would later happen in Mao's China), bars and cafes were collectivised, trams and taxis were painted red and black (the colours of the anarchists), and one-way streets were ignored as they were seen to be part of the old system.

The anarchists were a disparate lot, ranging from gentle idealists to hardliners, who drew up death lists, held kangaroo courts, shot priests, monks and nuns (more than 1200 of whom were killed in Barcelona province during the civil war), and also burnt and wrecked churches – which is why so many of Barcelona's churches are today oddly plain inside. They in turn were shunted aside by the communists (directed by Stalin from Moscow) after a bloody internecine battle in Barcelona that left over 1000 dead in May 1937.

Barcelona also suffered aerial bombing raids carried out by Italian bombers sympathetic to Franco. The pockmarked walls around Plaça de Sant Felip Neri (p68) still bear the scars of one particularly gruesome day of bombardment when dozens of civilians – many of them children from the square's school – were killed here.

Barcelona became the Republicans' national capital in autumn 1937. The Republican defeat in the Battle of the Ebro in southern Catalonia the following summer left Barcelona undefended. Republican resistance crumbled, in part due to exhaustion, in part due to disunity. In

July 1909	1914	1923	July 1936
After the call-up of reserve troops to fight a war in Morocco, *barcelonins* riot. Over 100 are reportedly killed in what's later known as Setmana Tràgica (Tragic Week).	The Mancomunitat de Catalonia, a first timid attempt at self-rule (restricted largely to administrative matters) and headed by Catalan nationalist Enric Prat de la Riba, is created in April.	Dictator Primo de Rivera takes power and, as part of his repressive measures, bans FC Barça.	General Franco launches the Spanish Civil War in Morocco. General Goded leads army units to take Barcelona for Franco, but is defeated by left-wing militia, workers and loyalist police.

1938 Catalan nationalists started negotiating separately with the Nationalists. The city fell to Franco's forces in January 1939.

Franco Takes the City

Franco's tanks rolled into a strangely silent and empty city on 26 January 1939. Almost half a million people had fled to the north, with 460,000 people crossing into France by 10 February. The first few months of occupation were a strange hiatus before the onset of the full machinery of oppression. Within two weeks of the city's fall a dozen cinemas were in operation, and the following month Hollywood comedies were being shown between rounds of Nationalist propaganda. The people were even encouraged to dance the *sardana,* Catalonia's national dance, in public (the Nationalists thought such folkloric generosity might endear them to the people of Barcelona).

On the other hand, the city presented an exhausted picture. The metro was running, but there were no buses (they had all been used on the front). Virtually all the animals in the city zoo had died of starvation or wounds. There were frequent blackouts, and would be for years.

Round-Ups & Executions

By 1940, with WWII raging across Europe, Franco had his regime more firmly in place and things turned darker for many. Catalan Francoists led the way in rounding up anarchists and former Republican supporters; up to 35,000 people were shot in purges. At the same time, small bands of resistance fighters continued to harry the Nationalists in the Pyrenees through much of the 1940s. Catalonia's president, Lluís Companys, was arrested in France by the Gestapo in August 1940, handed over to Franco, and shot on 15 October on Montjuïc.

The executions continued into the 1950s. Most people accepted the situation and tried to get on with living, while some leapt at opportunities, occupying flats abandoned by 'Reds' who had been forced to flee. Speculators and industrialists allied with Franco were able to earn a lucrative income, but the majority of *barcelonins* were affected by nationwide poverty.

Life Under Franco

Franco took a particularly hard line against Barcelona. Catalan monuments in the city were dismantled. He banned public use of Catalan, and had all town, village and street names rendered in Spanish (Castilian). Education, radio, TV and the daily press would henceforth be in

Ever at the vanguard, Barcelona had the first daily newspaper printed in Spain, plus its first cinema, public phone and airline (to Mallorca). It also built the world's second metropolitan railway (London was first).

March 1938	1939	1940	1957
In just three days of day-and-night air raids on Barcelona carried out by fascist Italian bombers based in Franco-controlled Mallorca, 979 people are killed and 1500 wounded.	The first of Franco's troops, along with Italian tanks, roll into Barcelona and parade down Avinguda Diagonal. Thousands flee the city towards the French border.	Hitler's henchman and chief of the SS, Heinrich Himmler, visits Barcelona, stays at the Ritz, enjoys a folkloric show at the Poble Espanyol and has his wallet stolen.	The Francoist Josep Maria de Porcioles becomes mayor of Barcelona and remains in charge until 1973. He presides over a willy-nilly building spree in the city.

Spanish. Independent political activity was banned, as was the celebration of traditional Catalan holidays.

In Barcelona, the Francoist Josep Maria de Porcioles became mayor in 1957, a post he held until 1973. That same year he obtained for the city a 'municipal charter' that expanded the mayor's authority and the city's capacity to raise and spend taxes, manage urban development and, ultimately, widen the city's metropolitan limits to absorb neighbouring territory. He was responsible for such monstrosities as the concrete municipal buildings on Plaça de Sant Miquel in the Barri Gòtic. His rule marked a grey time for Barcelona.

Films Set in Franco's Spain

El Laberinto del Fauno (Pan's Labyrinth; 2006)

El Espíritu de la Colmena (The Spirit of the Beehive; 1973)

¡Bienvenido, Mr Marshall! (Welcome, Mr Marshall!; 1952)

Las 13 Rosas (The 13 Roses; 2007)

Soldados de Salamina (Soldiers of Salamis; 2003)

Immigrants Pour into Barcelona

Under Franco a flood of 1.5 million immigrants from poorer parts of Spain – chiefly Andalucía, Extremadura and the northwest – poured into Catalonia (750,000 of them to Barcelona) in the 1950s and '60s looking for work. Many lived in appalling conditions. While some made the effort to learn Catalan and integrate as fully as possible into local society, the majority came to form Spanish-speaking pockets in the poorer working-class districts of the city and in a ring of satellite towns. Even today, the atmosphere in many of these towns is more Andalucian than Catalan. Catalan nationalists believe it was all part of a Francoist plot to undermine the Catalan identity.

The Road to Democracy

When the death of Franco was announced in 1975, *barcelonins* took to the streets in celebration. The next five years saw the gradual return of democracy. In 1977 Josep Tarradellas, who was head of Catalonia's government in exile, returned to Barcelona and was officially recognised by the Spanish government as head of a new Catalan coalition. *Barcelonins* who lived during that time will likely recall Tarradellas' historic words given from the balcony of the Palau de la Generalitat. Before a huge crowd gathered on Plaça de Sant Jaume, he said, *'Ciutadans de Catalunya, ja sóc aquí!'* (Citizens of Catalonia, I am here!).

Twenty years after his stint in Franco's jails, Jordi Pujol (an early ringleader in protests against the Francoists) was elected president of Catalonia in 1980. These were the first free regional elections since before the civil war. A wily antagonist of the central authorities in Madrid, Pujol waged a quarter-century war of attrition, eking out greater fiscal and policy autonomy and vigorously promoting a re-Catalanisation programme, with uneven success.

1975	1980	1992	2003
The death of Franco is greeted with mass jubilation, and followed by general elections two years later.	Right-wing Catalan nationalist Jordi Pujol is elected president of the resurrected Catalan regional government at the head of the nationalist CiU coalition; he remains in power until 2003.	Barcelona takes centre stage as it hosts the summer Olympic Games. In preparation the city undergoes a radical renovation program, the momentum of which continues today.	Popular former mayor of Barcelona Pasqual Maragall becomes the first socialist president of Catalonia in tight elections after Pujol steps aside in favour of CiU's Artur Mas.

Barcelona's Olympian Moment

Politics aside, the big event in post-Franco Barcelona was the successful 1992 Olympic Games, planned under the guidance of the popular Socialist mayor Pasqual Maragall. The games spurred a burst of public works and art and brought new life to areas such as Montjuïc, where the major events were held. The once-shabby waterfront was transformed with promenades, beaches, marinas, restaurants, leisure attractions, sculpture and new housing.

Urban Renewal

After the turn of the millennium, Barcelona continued to invest in urban renewal, with ambitious projects such as the 22@ high-tech zone in the once-industrial El Poblenou district, the major development around new trade conference grounds between the city and the airport, and the Diagonal Mar waterfront development around the Parc del Fòrum at the northeast tip of the city.

A Move Towards Independence

Since the demise of Franco, Spain has devolved considerable powers to its 17 regions, which are officially known as *comunidades autónomas* (*comunitats autònomes* in Catalan; autonomous communities). Catalans approved a new Estatut in a referendum in 2006, but within months the right-wing Partido Popular (warning of the 'Balkanistation' or break-up of Spain) launched an appeal in the Constitutional Court against the Estatut, which it claimed granted too much autonomy.

After four years of wrangling, in 2010 the court delivered a verdict, ruling that 14 of the articles were unconstitutional – including areas of language, taxes, the judiciary and self-recognition as a 'nation'. Catalans converged on the streets en masse to protest the decision, which was widely hailed as one more blow to relations between Barcelona and Madrid.

Separatism on the Rise

Over the last decade or so, the idea that Catalonia could break away from Spain as a sovereign republic has gained so much traction that it dominates the political landscape both regionally and nationally. Fuelled in no small part by soaring unemployment and painful austerity measures in the wake of the 2008 financial crisis – not to mention Catalonia's heavy tax burden – the fervour to secede has only grown in the last few years.

2006	2010	2010	2014
The Catalan government negotiates a new autonomy statute with Madrid in a compromise that leaves many unsatisfied and ultimately leads to the fall of Maragall.	Pope Benedict XVI consecrates the basilica of La Sagrada Família before an audience of 6500, including former King Juan Carlos I and Queen Sofía.	Hot on the heels of its victory in the European football championship in 2008, Spain defeats the Netherlands in the World Cup held in South Africa, its first-ever World Cup title.	Six months after a human chain stretches 400km across the region, Spanish judges declare Catalonia's planned referendum on independence unconstitutional. Secessionists vow to proceed regardless.

A GREENER FUTURE

Over the last decade, Barcelona has undergone great transformations, with an eye towards sustainability. Since 2000 the city has required all new buildings to install solar panels to provide most of their hot water. The massive solar panel near the Parc del Fòrum is the largest of any city in Europe. Barcelona's shared bike programme for residents, Bicing, launched in 2007, has helped reduce traffic on the road, with some 104,000 subscribers in 2019 (saving around 7 million kg of CO_2 per year). The city also has one of the cleanest bus fleets in Europe, and has become a leader in the realm of electric vehicles, with more than 300 charging stations.

Films in Barcelona

All About My Mother (1999)

Vicky Cristina Barcelona (2008)

L'Auberge Espagnole (2002)

Barcelona (1994)

In September 2017, former Catalan president Carles Puigdemont (now in exile in Belgium) pushed a referendum law through the regional parliament, and the vote (deemed illegal by Spain's constitutional court) went ahead a couple of weeks later. According to the Catalan government, of the 43% of potential voters who took part, 90% voted for independence. There were some scenes of violence at polling stations involving the Policía Nacional, sent in by the Spanish government, under Mariano Rajoy of the Partido Popular (PP; People's Party). Independence was declared by the Catalan government days later, and immediately quashed by Madrid, with several high-profile Catalan leaders arrested and jailed on charges of rebellion and sedition.

A minor thawing of relations came with a vote of no confidence in Rajoy, who was replaced by Partido Socialista Obrero Español (PSOE; Spanish Socialist Workers' Party) leader Pedro Sánchez in May 2018. During Spain's April 2019 general election, which initially failed to establish a majority government, Catalonia's drive for independence was a core issue; following the ensuing November 2019 election, Sánchez formed a coalition government with Unidas Podemos. Meanwhile, in October 2019, nine separatist Catalan leaders were jailed for sedition for between nine and 13 years. Thousands took to the streets of Barcelona in protest, and there were violent clashes between police and the public, including at Barcelona airport. In June 2021, Sánchez officially pardoned the nine jailed leaders, who were then released.

At the time of writing, Catalonia's largest separatist party, the Esquerra Republicana de Catalunya (ERC; Republican Left of Catalonia; currently in power along with pro-independence Junts per Catalunya), had supported the new Sánchez-led coalition government in the national parliament. The PSOE, meanwhile, had agreed to set up negotiations to resolve the conflict over Catalonia's future between Spain's central government and the Catalan government, but how it all shakes out is anybody's guess..

2015	2017	October 2019	2026
After elections, separatists take control of Catalonia's government, laying out a route to independence within 18 months. Ada Colau becomes Barcelona's first woman mayor.	Catalonia's referendum goes ahead in October. Independence is declared, former Spanish Prime Minister Mariano Rajoy imposes direct rule and Catalan leader Carles Puigdemont flees to Belgium.	Nine separatist Catalan politicians are sentenced to nine to 13 years' jail for their role in the referendum, leading to protests. In June 2021, all nine are pardoned by Spanish Prime Minister Pedro Sánchez and released.	Builders aim to finish La Sagrada Família on the centenary of the death of its creator, Gaudí (1852–1926), though the COVID-19 pandemic has inevitably delayed things.

Catalan Culture

The fortunes of Catalonia have risen and fallen over the years, as Barcelona has gone from wealthy mercantile capital to a city of repression under the Franco regime, followed by a growing push for independence in recent years. Despite today's challenges, Catalan culture continues to flourish, with a lively festival calendar and abundant civic pride manifested in aspects from the language spoken on the streets to Barcelona's much-loved football team.

Language

Throughout the region, born-and-bred locals proudly speak Catalan, a Romance language related to French, Spanish (Castilian) and Italian, and also spoken in Andorra, the Balearics and Valencia. It was only relatively recently, however, that Catalan was deemed 'legitimate'. After Barcelona was crushed in the War of the Spanish Succession in 1714, the use of Catalan was repeatedly banned or at least frowned upon. Franco was the last

Above: *Correfoc* (fire running), Gràcia

of Spain's rulers to clamp down on its public use. All that changed in 1980, when the first autonomous regional parliament was assembled and adopted new laws towards *normalització lingüística* (linguistic normalisation).

Today Catalonia's state school system uses Catalan as the language of instruction, though most Catalan speakers end up bilingual, particularly in urban areas. Around town, Catalan is the lingua franca: advertising and road signs are in Catalan, while newspapers, magazines and other publications can be found in both Catalan and Spanish. There's also a mix of Catalan and Spanish programming on radio and TV stations.

> Catalan is spoken by over 10 million people, with around 73% of Catalonia's population able to speak it and 95% understanding it.

Folk Dancing

On weekends year-round, devotees of the folk dance *sardana* gather in town squares, while a small band puts everyone in motion. Catalans of all ages come out for the dance, which takes place in a circle with dancers holding hands. Together they move right, back and then left, hopping, raising their arms and generally building momentum as the tempo picks up. All are welcome to join in, though you'll have to watch a few rounds to get the hang of it.

Festivals

Catalonia's best celebrations tend to revolve around religious holidays, and feature abundant merrymaking. You'll see plenty of *sardana* dancing and *castell* (human-castle) building, as well as *gegants* (papier-mâché giants: lords, princesses, sultans, fishers, and historic and contemporary figures, often 'dancing' in pairs) and *capgrossos* (oversized heads worn by actors).

Another feature of these Catalan festivals is the *correfoc* (fire running): horned devils brandishing firework-spouting pitchforks wreak mayhem in the streets, sometimes accompanied by fire-breathing dragons, or even wooden carts that are set alight. Full coverings (hats, gloves, goggles, long sleeves) are highly recommended for anyone who wants to get near.

Castells

One of the big highlights of any traditional Catalan festival is the building of human *castells*, a Catalan tradition born in the 18th century in the town of Valls near Tarragona. Teams from across the region compete to build human towers up to 10 storeys tall. These usually involve levels of three to five people standing on each other's shoulders. A crowd of teammates forms a supporting scrum around the strong team members at the base. To successfully complete the castle, a small child called the *enxaneta* must reach the top and signal with his or her hand.

> At Christmas some rather unusual Catalan characters appear. The *caganer* (crapper) is a chap with dropped pants who balances over his unsightly offering (a symbol of fertility for the coming year). There's also the *caga tío* (poop log), which on Christmas Day is supposed to *cagar* (crap) out gifts.

FC Barcelona

One of the city's best-loved names is FC Barça, which is deeply associated with Catalans and even Catalan nationalism. The team was long a rallying point for Catalans when other aspects of Catalan culture were suppressed. The club openly supported Catalonia's drive towards autonomy in 1918, and in 1921 the club's statutes were drafted in Catalan. The pro-Catalan leanings of the club and its siding with the republic during the Spanish Civil War earned reprisals from the government. Club president Josep Sunyol was murdered by Franco's soldiers in 1936, and the club building was bombed in 1938.

In 1968 club president Narcís de Carreras uttered the now famous words, *El Barça: més que un club* ('more than a club'), which became the team's motto – and emphasised its role as an anti-Franco symbol and a catalyst for change in the province and beyond. Today FC Barça is one of the world's most admired teams, with membership at over 143,000 in recent years. Barcelona's other football team, RCD Espanyol, is traditionally associated with immigrants from elsewhere in Spain.

Fantastic Architecture

Famed for its architectural treasures, Barcelona is dotted with striking Gothic cathedrals, fantastical Modernista creations and avant-garde works. Building first boomed in the late Middle Ages, when Barcelona was the seat of the Catalan empire. In the late 19th century, the city broke its medieval confines and was transformed through whimsical Modernisme. The third notable era of design began in the late 1980s and continues today.

The Gothic Period

Barcelona's original building boom arrived at the height of the Middle Ages, when its imposing Gothic churches, mansions and shipyards were raised, together creating what survives to this day as one of the most extensive Gothic quarters in Europe. Most of these architectural treasures lie within the boundaries of the Ciutat Vella (Old City), but a few examples can be found beyond, notably the Reial Monestir de Santa Maria de Pedralbes (p207).

Historical Roots

The soaring Gothic style took off in France in the 12th century and spread across Europe. Its emergence coincided with Jaume I's march into Valencia and the annexation of Mallorca and Ibiza, accompanied by the rise of a trading class and a burgeoning mercantile empire. The enormous cost of building these grand new monuments could thus be covered by the steady increase in the city's wealth.

Perhaps the single greatest building spurt came under Pere III (1319–87). This is odd in a sense because, as Dickens might have observed, it was not only the best of times, but also the worst. By the mid-14th century, when Pere III was in command, Barcelona had been pushed to the ropes by a series of disasters: famine, repeated plagues and pogroms.

Maybe he didn't notice. He built, or began to build, much of La Catedral, the Drassanes, the Llotja stock exchange, the Saló del Tinell within the Palau Reial Major, the Casa de la Ciutat – which now houses the Ajuntament (town hall; p65) – and numerous lesser buildings, not to mention part of the city walls. The churches of Santa Maria del Pi (p66) in the Barri Gòtic and Santa Maria del Mar (p101) in El Born were completed by the end of the 14th century.

Architectural Features

The style of church architecture reflected the development of building techniques. The introduction of buttresses, flying buttresses and ribbed vaulting in ceilings allowed engineers to raise edifices that were loftier and seemingly lighter than ever before. The pointed arch became standard and great rose windows were added as the source of light inside these enormous spaces.

Think about the hovels that labourers on such projects lived in and the primitive nature of building materials available, and you get an idea of the awe such churches, once completed, must have inspired. And they

Catalonia's vast 14th-century mercantile empire fuelled Barcelona's boom. All manner of goods flowed to and from Sardinia, Flanders, North Africa and other places, with Catalan Jews carrying out much of this trade. The later pogroms, Inquisition and expulsion of Jews had devastating financial consequences and contributed to reducing Barcelona to penury.

were not built in a day. It took more than 160 years, a fairly typical time frame, to finish La Catedral, although its facade was not erected until the 19th century. Its rival, the Basílica de Santa Maria del Mar, was one for the record books, taking only 54 years to build.

Gothic Masterpieces

La Catedral (La Rambla & Barri Gòtic)
....
Basílica de Santa Maria del Mar (La Ribera & El Born)
....
Basílica de Santa Maria del Pi (La Rambla & Barri Gòtic)
....
Saló del Tinell (in Museu d'Història de Barcelona; La Rambla & Barri Gòtic)
....
The Drassanes (Museu Marítim; Barceloneta, the Waterfront & El Poblenou)
....
Reial Monestir de Santa Maria de Pedralbes (Camp Nou, Pedralbes & La Zona Alta)

Catalan Gothic

Catalan Gothic did not follow the same course as the style typical of northern Europe. Its decoration tends to be more sparing and the most obvious defining characteristic is the triumph of breadth over height. While northern European cathedrals reach for the sky, Catalan Gothic has a tendency to push to the sides, stretching its vaulting design to the limit.

The Palau Reial Major's Saló del Tinell (p67), with a parade of 15m arches (among the largest ever built without reinforcement) holding up the roof, is a perfect example of Catalan Gothic. Another is the present home of the Museu Marítim (p120), the Drassanes, Barcelona's medieval shipyards. In their churches, too, the Catalans opted for a more robust shape and lateral space – step into the Basílica de Santa Maria del Mar or the Basílica de Santa Maria del Pi and you'll soon get the idea. The three-tiered cloister and sober church of the Reial Monestir de Santa Maria de Pedralbes (p207) are also prime examples of Catalan Gothic.

Another notable departure from what you might have come to expect of Gothic north of the Pyrenees is the lack of spires and pinnacles. Bell towers tend to terminate in a flat or nearly flat roof. Occasional exceptions prove the rule – the main facade of Barcelona's La Catedral, with its three gnarled and knobbly spires, does vaguely resemble the outline that confronts you in cathedrals in Chartres or Cologne. But then it was a 19th-century addition, admittedly to a medieval design.

Late Gothic

Gothic had a longer use-by date in Barcelona than in many other European centres. By the early 15th century, the Generalitat still didn't have a home worthy of its name, and architect Marc Safont set to work on the facade of the present building (p65) on Plaça de Sant Jaume. Even renovations carried out a century later were largely in the Gothic tradition, although some Renaissance elements eventually snuck in.

Carrer de Montcada (p103), in La Ribera, was the result of a late-medieval act of town planning. Eventually mansions belonging to the moneyed classes of 15th- and 16th-century Barcelona were built along it. Most of them went through a gentle baroque makeover in later years, and many now house museums and art galleries among their pleasing courtyards and decorated staircases.

The Arabs invented the ancient technique of *trencadís*, but Gaudí was the first architect to revive it. The procedure involves taking ceramic tiles or fragments of broken pottery or glass and creating a mosaic-like sheath on roofs, ceilings, chimneys, benches, sculptures or any other surface.

Modernisme

Barcelona's flamboyant Modernisme (p166) buildings emerged during the late 19th century, a period of great artistic and political fervour deeply connected to Catalan identity, and which transformed early-20th-century Barcelona into a showcase for avant-garde architecture. Aiming to establish a new Catalan archetype, Antoni Gaudí and other visionary architects drew inspiration from the past, using elements from the Spanish vernacular – shapes, details and brickwork reminiscent of Islamic, Gothic and Renaissance designs.

The Modernistas also revived traditional artisan trades, which you can see in the exquisite stonework and stained-glass windows, and in their artful use of wrought iron, ceramics and mosaic tiles. Nature was celebrated and imitated to perfection in Gaudí's organic forms: leaning

MODERNISME & CATALAN IDENTITY

Modernisme did not appear in isolation in Barcelona. To the British and French the style was art nouveau; to the Italians, Lo Stile Liberty; the Germans called it Jugendstil (Youth Style); and the Austrians, Sezession (Secession). Its vitality and rebelliousness can be summed up in those epithets: modernity, novelty, liberty, youth and secession. A key uniting element was the sensuous curve, implying movement, lightness and vitality. It touched painting, sculpture and the decorative arts, as well as architecture. This leitmotif informed much art-nouveau thinking, in part inspired by long-standing tenets of Japanese art.

There is something misleading about the name Modernisme. From Gaudí down, Modernista architects looked to the past (rather than the future) for inspiration. Gothic, Islamic and Renaissance design all had something to offer. At its most playful, Modernisme was able to intelligently flout the rule books of these styles and create exciting new visions.

Aesthetics aside, the political associations are significant, as Modernisme became a means of expression for Catalan identity. It barely touched the rest of Spain; where it did (such as in the seaside town of Comillas in Cantabria), one frequently finds the involvement of Catalan architects (in Comillas' case, Gaudí, Martorell and Domènech i Montaner all contributed). As many as 2000 buildings in Barcelona and throughout Catalonia display Modernista traces. Buildings from rich bourgeois mansion blocks to churches, from hospitals to factories, went up in this 'style', a word too constraining to adequately describe the flamboyant breadth of eclecticism inherent in it.

treelike columns, walls that undulate like the sea, and the use of native plants as decorative elements. Inside these buildings, the artistry and imaginative design continues.

For many, Modernisme is synonymous with Gaudí (p166; 1852–1926), but he was by no means alone. Lluís Domènech i Montaner (p169; 1850–1923) and Josep Puig i Cadafalch (p170; 1867–1956) left a wealth of remarkable buildings across Barcelona. The Rome-trained sculptor Eusebi Arnau (1863–1933) was one of the most popular figures called upon to decorate Barcelona's Modernista piles. The appearance of the Hospital de la Santa Creu i de Sant Pau (now called the Recinte Modernista de Sant Pau; p151) is one of his legacies and he also had a hand in the Palau de la Música Catalana (p102) and Casa Amatller (p148).

Olympic & Contemporary Architecture

Barcelona's latest architectural revolution began in the 1980s. The appointment then of Oriol Bohigas, still regarded as an elder statesman of architecture, as head of urban planning by the ruling Socialist party marked a new beginning. The city set about its biggest phase of renewal since the heady days of L'Eixample and Modernisme.

The Olympic Games Building Boom

The biggest urban makeover in 100 years happened in the run-up to the 1992 Olympics, when more than 150 architects beavered away on almost 300 building and design projects. The city saw dramatic transformations, including the construction of huge arterial highways and the refurbishment of whole neighbourhoods in dire need of repair. In a rather crafty manoeuvre, the city government used national monies to fund urban improvements the capital would never normally have approved. Several kilometres of waterfront wasteland that included the Port Vell was beautifully transformed into sparkling new beaches

Modernista Masterpieces

Casa Batlló
(L'Eixample)

La Sagrada Família
(L'Eixample)

Palau de la Música Catalana
(La Ribera & El Born)

La Pedrera
(L'Eixample)

Palau Güell (El Raval)

Casa Amatller
(L'Eixample)

Recinte Modernista de Sant Pau
(L'Eixample)

Colònia Güell
(outside Barcelona)

(suddenly Barcelona had prime beachfront real estate) and public art-works such as Frank Gehry's *Peix* (p124) were commissioned. The long road to resurrecting Montjuïc took off with the refurbishment of the Olympic stadium (p194) and the creation of landmarks like Santiago Calatrava's Torre Calatrava.

Post-1992, landmark buildings still went up in strategic spots, usual-ly with the ulterior motive of trying to pull the surrounding area up by its bootstraps. One of the most emblematic of these projects is El Raval's gleaming white Museu d'Art Contemporani de Barcelona, better known as MACBA (p86), which opened in 1995. The museum was designed by Richard Meier and incorporates the characteristic elements for which the American architect is so well known – the geometric minimalism and the pervasive use of all white with glass and steel.

Arousing more than a little architectural debate, as with so many of architect Ricardo Bofill's projects, the Teatre Nacional de Catalunya (p134), which opened in 1996, is a blend of the neoclassical and the modern. Framed by 26 columns with a single gabled roof and grand entrance steps, the theatre takes the form of a Greek temple, though its all-glass exterior gives it a light and open appearance.

Henry Cobb's World Trade Center, at the tip of a quay jutting out into the waters of Port Vell, has been overshadowed by Ricardo Bofill's W Barcelona (p237) hotel, whose spinnaker-like front looks out to sea from the southern end of La Barceloneta's beach strip.

The New Millennium

One of the first big Barcelona projects of the 21st century occurred around Diagonal Mar. A whole district has been built in the northeast-ern coastal corner of the city, where before there was a void. High-rise apartments, waterfront office towers and five-star hotels – among them the eye-catching Meliá Sky Barcelona (p237) hotel, completed in 2008 by Dominique Perrault – mark this regenerated district. The hovering blue, triangular Edifici Fòrum by Swiss architects Herzog & de Meu-ron, which hosts the Museu Blau (p124), is the most striking landmark here, along with a gigantic photovoltaic panel that provides some of the area's electricity.

Much of the district was completed in 2004, though the area contin-ues to evolve as new buildings are added to the mix. Among the most notable additions of the past decade are a 24-storey whitewashed trap-ezoidal prism that serves as the headquarters for the national telephone company, Telefónica. Designed by Enric Massip-Bosch and dubbed the Diagonal 00, it has a deceivingly two-dimensional appearance upon initial approach. Shortly after its completion in 2011, the Torre was awarded the respected Leading European Architects Forum (LEAF) award for commercial building of the year.

Another prominent addition to the skyline came in 2005. The shim-mering, cucumber-shaped Torre Glòries (p126) is a product of French architect Jean Nouvel, emblematic of the city's desire to make the devel-oping high-tech zone of 22@ a reality.

Southwest, on the way to the airport, the Fira M2 trade fair along Gran Via de les Corts Catalanes is now marked by red twisting twin landmark towers (one the Hotel Santos Porta Fira, the other offices) de-signed by Japanese star architect and self-confessed Gaudí fan Toyo Ito.

The heart of La Ribera got a fresh look in 2005 with the renovated Mercat de Santa Caterina (p104). The market is quite a sight, with its wavy ceramic roof and tubular skeleton, designed by Enric Miralles, one of the most promising names in Catalan architecture until his pre-mature death (sadly before the market renovations were completed).

Contem-porary Buildings

Torre Glòries (Barceloneta, the Waterfront & El Poblenou)

Teatre Nacional de Catalunya (Barceloneta, the Waterfront & El Poblenou)

Mercat de Santa Caterina (La Rib-era & El Born)

MACBA (El Raval)

Edifici Fòrum (Barceloneta, the Waterfront & El Poblenou)

W Barcelona (Barceloneta, the Waterfront & El Poblenou)

Les Arenes (Plaça d'Espanya; Montjuïc, Poble Sec & Sant Antoni)

Torre de Collse-rola (Camp Nou, Pedralbes & La Zona Alta)

Hotel Santos Porta Fira (Llo-bregat)

Miralles' Edifici de Gas Natural (p122), a 100m glass tower near the waterfront in La Barceloneta, is extraordinary for its mirrorlike surface and weirdly protruding adjunct buildings, which could be giant glass cliffs bursting from the main tower's flank.

The City of Tomorrow

Big projects have slowly taken shape around the city. The redevelopment of the area near Plaça de les Glòries Catalanes is one of the latest completions, with the goal of revitalising the Poblenou neighbourhood and making it a draw for visitors.

The centrepiece, completed in 2013, is the Museu del Disseny (p123), which incorporates sustainable features in its cantilevered, metal-sheathed building. Vaguely futuristic (though some say it looks like a stapler), it has a rather imposing, anvil-shaped presence over the neighbourhood.

Nearby stands Mercat dels Encants (p135), the 'Charms' flea market, which was given a dramatic new look by local architecture firm b720 Fermín Vázquez Arquitectos. Traders now sell their wares beneath a giant, mirrored canopy made up of geometric panels and held aloft with long, slender poles. The adjacent traffic-choked roundabout and road is gradually being turned into a park (with some sections already open).

In a rather thoughtful bit of recycling, British architect Lord Richard Rogers transformed the former Les Arenes (p203) bullring on Plaça d'Espanya into a singular, circular leisure complex, with shops, cinemas and more, which opened in 2011. He did so while maintaining its red-brick, 19th-century Moorish-looking facade. Perhaps its best feature is the rooftop with 360-degree views from the open-air promenade, cafes and restaurants.

In the Ciutat Vella (Old City), El Raval has been the latest focal point for urban renewal. The Filmoteca de Catalunya (p94) is a hulking, rather brutalist building of concrete and glass, with sharp angles. It was designed by Catalan architect Josep Lluís Mateo, completed in 2011, and sits near the Richard Meier–designed MACBA.

No one longs for the pre-Olympic days when the waterfront was a dangerous and polluted wasteland. However, some old-timers still bemoan the loss of its old rickety restaurant shacks, which sat on stilts over the water and served delectable if utterly unfussy seafood.

FANTASTIC ARCHITECTURE THE CITY OF TOMORROW

ESKYSTUDIO/SHUTTERSTOCK ©

Facade of Las Arenas (p203), in a former bullring

Picasso, Miró & Dalí

Three of Spain's greatest 20th-century artists have deep connections to Barcelona. Picasso spent his formative years in the city and maintained lifelong friendships with Catalans; indeed, it was Picasso's own idea to create a museum of his works here. Joan Miró is one of Barcelona's most famous native sons and his instantly recognisable style can be seen in public installations across the city. Although Salvador Dalí is more commonly associated with Figueres, Barcelona was a great source of inspiration for him, particularly the fantastical architectural works of Antoni Gaudí.

Pablo Picasso

Born in Málaga (Andalucía), Pablo Ruiz Picasso (1881–1973) was sketching by the age of nine. As a young boy, he lived briefly in A Coruña (in Galicia), before landing in Barcelona in 1895. His father had obtained a post teaching art at the La Llotja school of fine arts and enrolled his son there. It was in Barcelona and Catalonia that Picasso matured, spending his time ceaselessly drawing and painting.

After a stint at the Real Academia de Bellas Artes de San Fernando in Madrid in 1897, Picasso spent six months with his friend Manuel Pallarès in bucolic Horta de Sant Joan, in western Catalonia – he would later claim that it was there he learned everything he knew. In Barcelona, Picasso lived and worked in the Barri Gòtic and El Raval (where he was introduced to the seamier side of life in the Barri Xinès).

By the time Picasso moved to France in 1904, he had explored his first highly personal style. In this so-called Blue Period, his canvases have a melancholy feel heightened by the trademark dominance of dark blues. Some of his portraits and cityscapes from this period were created in and inspired by what he saw in Barcelona. A number of Blue Period pieces hang in Barcelona's Museu Picasso (p99).

By the mid-1920s, he was dabbling with surrealism. His best-known work is *Guernica* (displayed in Madrid's Museo Nacional Centro de Arte Reina Sofía), a complex painting portraying the horror of war, inspired by the German aerial bombing of the Basque town Guernica (Gernika) in 1937.

Joan Miró

The Fundació Joan Miró (p188), housed in an extensive, elegant all-white gallery atop Montjuïc, hosts the single largest collection of Miró's work in the world today.

At the time the 13-year-old Picasso arrived in Barcelona, his near contemporary, Joan Miró (1893–1983), was still learning to crawl in the Barri Gòtic, where he was born. He spent a third of his life in Barcelona but later divided his time between France, the Tarragona countryside and the island of Mallorca, where he ended his days.

Like Picasso, Miró attended La Llotja. He was initially uncertain about his artistic vocation – in fact, he studied commerce. In Paris from 1920, he mixed with Picasso, Hemingway, Joyce and friends, and made his own mark, after several years of struggle, with an exhibition in 1925.

It was during WWII, while living in seclusion in Normandy, that Miró's definitive leitmotifs emerged. Among the most important im-

ART ON THE STREETS

Barcelona hosts an array of intriguing street sculpture, such as Miró's 1983 *Dona i ocell* (Woman and Bird; p195), in the park dedicated to the artist, and *Peix* (Fish; p124), Frank Gehry's shimmering, bronze-coloured headless fish facing the Port Olímpic. Halfway along La Rambla, at Plaça de la Boqueria, you can walk all over Miró's mosaic (p60).

Picasso left an open-air mark with his design on the facade of the Col·legi d'Arquitectes de Catalunya (p69), opposite La Catedral in the Barri Gòtic. Other works include *El cap de Barcelona* (The Barcelona Head; p122) by Roy Lichtenstein at the Port Vell end of Via Laietana and Fernando Botero's rotund *El gat* on Rambla del Raval (p88).

Wander down to the Barceloneta seaside for a peek at Rebecca Horn's 1992 tribute to the old shacks that used to line the waterfront, the precarious *L'estel ferit* (The Wounded Shooting Star; p122). A little further south is the 2003 *Homenatge a la natació* (Homage to Swimming; p125), a complex metallic rendition of swimmers and divers in the water by Alfredo Lanz.

Heading a little further back in time, in 1983 Antoni Tàpies constructed *Homenatge a Picasso* (Tribute to Picasso; p103) on Passeig de Picasso – essentially a glass cube set in a pond and filled with, well, junk. Antoni Llena's *David i Goliat* (David and Goliath), a massive sculpture of tubular and sheet iron, in the Parc de les Cascades near the Port Olímpic's two skyscrapers, looks like an untidy kite inspired by Halloween. Beyond this, Avinguda d'Icària is lined by architect Enric Miralles' so-called *Pergoles* – bizarre, twisted metal contraptions.You'll see some of Barcelona's best street art over in El Raval, Poble Sec and Sant Antoni.

ages that appear frequently throughout his work are women, birds (the link between Earth and the heavens), stars (the unattainable heavenly world, the source of imagination) and a sort of net entrapping all these levels of the cosmos. The Miró works that most people are acquainted with emerged from this time – arrangements of lines and symbolic figures in primary colours, with shapes reduced to their essence.

From 1956 until his death in 1983, Miró lived in Mallorca, home of his wife, Pilar Juncosa.

Salvador Dalí

The great Catalan artist Salvador Dalí i Domènech (1904–89) was born and died in Figueres, where he left his single greatest artistic legacy, the Teatre-Museu Dalí (p221). Although few of his famed works reside in Barcelona, the city was a stimulating atmosphere for Dalí, and places like Park Güell, with its surrealist-like aspects, had a powerful effect on him.

Prolific painter, showman, shameless self-promoter or just wildly eccentric, Dalí was nothing if not a character – probably a little too much for the conservative small-town folk of Figueres.

Dalí's big life change came in 1929, when the French poet Paul Éluard visited Cadaqués (on the north Catalan coast) with his Russian wife, Gala. The rest, as they say, is histrionics. Dalí shot off to Paris to be with Gala and plunged into the world of surrealism. In the 1930s, Salvador and Gala returned to live at Port Lligat near Cadaqués, where they played host to a long list of fashionable and art-world guests until the war years – the parties were by all accounts memorable.

The 1960s saw Dalí painting pictures on a grand scale, including his 1962 reinterpretation of Marià Fortuny's *Batalla de Tetuán*. On his death in 1989, he was buried (according to his own wishes) in the Teatre-Museu he had created on the site of the old theatre in central Figueres, which today also houses the world's best Dalí collection.

Rhythms of Barcelona

Barcelona's vibrant music and dance scene has been shaped by artists both traditional and cutting edge. From Nova Cançó, composed during the dark years of the dictatorship, to the hybridised Catalan rumba and hands-in-the air rock ballads of the 1970s and '80s, Barcelona's music evolves constantly. Today's groups continue to push musical boundaries, blending rhythms from all corners of the globe. In the realm of dance, flamenco has a small, loyal following, while the old-fashioned folk dance *sardana* continues to attract growing numbers.

Contemporary Music

Nova Cançó

Curiously, it was probably the Francoist repression that most helped foster a vigorous local music scene in Catalan. In the dark 1950s, the Nova Cançó (New Song) movement was born to resist linguistic oppression with music in Catalan (getting air time on the radio was long close to impossible), throwing up stars that in some cases won huge popularity throughout Spain, such as Valencia-born Raimon.

More specifically loved in Catalonia as a Bob Dylan–style 1960s protest singer-songwriter was Lluís Llach, much of whose music was more or less antiregime. Joan Manuel Serrat is another legendary figure, whose appeal stretches from Barcelona to Buenos Aires. Born in the Poble Sec district, this poet-singer is equally at ease in Catalan and Spanish. In 1968 he refused to represent Spain at the Eurovision Song Contest unless he was allowed to sing in Catalan. Accused of being anti-Spanish, he was long banned from performing in Spain.

Talented Mallorca-born singer Maria del Mar Bonet arrived in Barcelona in 1967. She sings in Catalan, and many of her searing and powerful songs were banned by the dictatorship. Through concert tours abroad she has attracted worldwide attention, and has performed with distinguished groups and soloists across the globe.

Around the same time Nova Cançó singers were taking aim at the Franco regime, folk singers from Latin America were decrying their own corrupt military dictatorships. Songs by Víctor Jara of Chile, Mercedes Sosa of Argentina and Chico Buarque of Brazil helped unite people in the fight against oppression.

Rock, Pop & Beyond

A specifically local strand of rock emerged in Barcelona after the 1980s. Rock Català (Catalan rock) is not essentially different to rock from anywhere else, except that it is sung in Catalan by local bands that appeal to local tastes. Among the most popular groups of years past include Sau, Els Pets, Lax'n'Busto and Valenciano band Obrint Pas.

Far greater success across Spain has gone to Estopa, a male rock duo from Cornellà, a satellite suburb of Barcelona. These guitar-wielding brothers sing a clean Spanish rock, occasionally with a vaguely flamenco flavour. In the same vein, Barcelona hit trio Pastora peddles a successful brand of Spanish pop, mixing electric sounds with a strong acoustic element.

Towards the end of the 1990s a very different Barcelona music style emerged, typified by the eclectic sounds of Manu Chao and Ojos de Brujo, both of which had international success. A Barcelona band with

LONGING FOR CUBA

The oldest musical tradition to have survived to some degree in Catalonia is that of the *havaneres* (from Havana) – nostalgic songs and melancholy sea shanties brought back from Cuba by Catalans who lived, sailed and traded there in the 19th century. Even after Spain lost Cuba in 1898, the *havanera* tradition (a mix of European and Cuban rhythms) continued. A magical opportunity to enjoy these songs is the **Cantada d'Havaneres** (www.havanerescalella.cat), a one-day festival held at Calella de Palafrugell on the Costa Brava in early July. Otherwise you may stumble across performances elsewhere along the coast or even in Barcelona, but there is no set programme.

similar flavours is Macaco, formed by former Ojos de Brujo singer Dani Carbonell. All three acts switch between languages – Catalan, Spanish, English and Portuguese among others – and blend Latin rhythms with flamenco, ska, electronica and many more. When people talk about the 'Raval sound' (after the name of the still somewhat seedy old-city district), this is the kind of thing they mean.

Born in El Raval, Cabo San Roque is an even more experimental group, incorporating huge soundscapes, powerful rhythms and mechanical accents often using non-traditional John Cage–style instruments in their avant-garde performances.

Another key name on El Raval's scene is 08001 (which is the area's postcode). This ever-evolving collective brings together musicians from across the globe, fusing unusual sounds from hip-hop, flamenco, reggae and rock to styles from Morocco, West Africa, the Caribbean and beyond. Its last album *No Pain No Gain* came out in 2013, but the artists continue to work together.

Hailing from Barcelona, Mishima is an indie pop band that has recorded a mix of albums in English and Catalan. They remained largely obscure prior to the release of their 2007 album *Set tota la vida,* which earned accolades across the music industry. Barcelona duo The Pinker Tones attained international success with an eclectic electronic mix of music. Electro group Love of Lesbian is another festival favourite, as is Catalan techno DJ John Talabot.

Catalonia's most recent breakout star, however, is singer-songwriter Rosalía, who was born in 1993 in Sant Esteve Sesrovires just outside Barcelona. Rosalía made her name on the Spanish flamenco scene before becoming an international sensation for her creative flamenco-pop, including collaborations with top reggaeton and pop stars and even a cameo in Pedro Almodóvar's award-winning 2019 film *Dolor y gloria.*

Classical, Opera & Baroque

Spain's contribution to the world of classical music has been modest, but Catalonia has produced a few exceptional composers. Best known is Camprodon-born Isaac Albéniz (1860–1909), a gifted pianist who later turned his hand to composition. Among his best-remembered works is the *Iberia* cycle.

The late Montserrat Caballé (1933–2018) was Barcelona's most successful recent voice. Born in Gràcia, the soprano made her debut in 1956 in Basel (Switzerland). Her home-town launch came four years later in the Gran Teatre del Liceu. In 1965 she performed to wild acclaim at New York's Carnegie Hall and went on to become one of the world's finest 20th-century sopranos. Her daughter, Montserrat Martí, is also a singer and they occasionally appeared together. Another fine Catalan

Top Albums

Barí, Ojos de Brujo

Anells d'aigua, Maria del Mar Bonet

Verges 50, Lluís Llach

Wild Animals, The Pinker Tones

Set tota la vida, Mishima

Vorágine, 08001

Rey de la rumba, Peret

X Anniversarium, Estopa

EnLorquecido, Miguel Poveda

soprano was Victoria de los Ángeles (1923–2005), while Catalonia's other world-class opera star is renowned tenor Josep (José) Carreras.

Catalan conductor Jordi Savall has assumed the task of rediscovering a European heritage in music that predates the era of the classical greats. He and his late wife, soprano Montserrat Figueras, have, along with musicians from other countries, been largely responsible for resuscitating the beauties of medieval, Renaissance and baroque music. In 1987 Savall founded La Capella Reial de Catalunya and two years later he formed the baroque orchestra Le Concert des Nations. You can sometimes catch their recitals in locations such as the Gran Teatre del Liceu or the Basílica de Santa Maria del Mar.

Dance

Flamenco

For those who think that the passion of flamenco is the preserve of the south, think again. The Roma people get around, and some of the big names of the genre come from Catalonia. They were already in Catalonia long before the massive migrations from the south of the 1960s, but with these waves came an exponential growth in flamenco bars as Andalucians sought to recreate a little bit of home.

First and foremost, one of the greatest *bailaoras* (flamenco dancers) of all time, Carmen Amaya (1913–63), was born in what is now the Port Olímpic. She danced to her father's guitar in the streets and bars around La Rambla in the years before the civil war. Much to the bemusement of purists from the south, not a few flamenco stars today have at least trained in flamenco schools in Barcelona – dancers Antonio Canales and Joaquín Cortés are among them.

Other Catalan stars of flamenco include *cantaores* (singers) Juan Cortés Duquende and Miguel Poveda, a boy from Badalona (just north of Barcelona), who took an original step in 2005 by releasing a flamenco album, *Desglaç,* in Catalan. Another interesting flamenco voice in Catalonia is Ginesa Ortega Cortés, actually born in France. She masters traditional genres ably but loves to experiment. In her 2002 album, *Por los espejos del agua* (Through the Water's Mirrors), she does a reggae version of flamenco and she has sung flamenco versions of songs by Joan Manuel Serrat and Billie Holiday.

The seven-man, one-woman group Ojos de Brujo (Wizard's Eyes) melded flamenco and rumba with rap, ragga and electronic music. The band split up in 2013, with lead singer Marina setting off to pursue a reasonably successful solo career as 'Marinah' and Dani Carbonell forming Macaco.

Sardana

The Catalan dance par excellence is the *sardana,* whose roots lie in the far northern Empordà region of Catalonia. Compared with flamenco it is sober indeed, but not unlike a lot of other Mediterranean folk dances.

The dancers hold hands in a circle and wait for the 10 or so musicians to begin. The performance starts with the piping of the *flabiol,* a little wooden flute. When the other musicians join in, the dancers start – a series of steps to the right, one back and then the same to the left. As the music 'heats up' the steps become more complex, the leaps are higher and the dancers lift their arms. Then they return to the initial steps and continue. If newcomers wish to join in, space is made for them as the dance continues and the whole thing proceeds in a more or less seamless fashion.

A reliable spot to see *sardana* is outside La Catedral (p62) in the Barri Gòtic on Saturday at 6pm and Sunday at 11am.

RHYTHMS OF BARCELONA DANCE

Born in Catalonia, Pau Casals (1876–1973) was one of the greatest cellists of the 20th century. Living in exile in southern France, he declared he would not play in public as long as Western democracies continued to tolerate Franco's regime. In 1958 he was a candidate for the Nobel Peace Prize.

Survival Guide

Cable car (p270) over Barcelona

Transport

ARRIVING IN BARCELONA

Most travellers arrive in Barcelona through El Prat airport. Some budget airlines use Girona-Costa Brava airport or Reus airport.

By train, the high-speed TGV takes 6½ hours from Paris to Barcelona. Long-distance trains arrive into Estació Sants, 2.5km west of La Rambla.

Most long-haul buses operate from the **Estació d'Autobusos Barcelona Nord** (Estació del Nord; Map p310; ☑93 706 53 66; www. barcelonanord.cat; Carrer d'Alí Bei 80; MArc de Triomf) in El Fort Pienç, near the Arc de Triomf; international buses also use the **Estació d'Autobusos de Sants** (Map p314; Carrer de Viriat; MSants Estació).

Barcelona also has ferry connections to the Balearic Islands with **Trasmediterránea** (Map p302; ☑902 454645; www.trasmediterranea.es; Moll de Barcelona; MDrassanes), as well as links to/from Italy. Boats depart from the Moll de Barcelona port just south of the old city.

Air

Aeroport de Barcelona–El Prat

Barcelona–El Prat Airport (☑91 321 10 00; www. aena.es; ☎) lies 15km south-west of Plaça de Catalunya at El Prat de Llobregat. It has two terminals: T1 and older T2, itself divided into three areas (A, B and C).

Tourist Information The main **tourist office** (☑93 285 38 32; www.barcelonaturisme. com; Aeroport de Barcelona–El Prat, Terminal 2; ☺8.30am-8.30pm) is on the ground floor of Terminal 2B; another in T1 operates the same hours.

Left luggage Offices in both terminals.

BUS

The **A1 Aerobús** (Map p314; ☑902 100104; www. aerobusbcn.com; 1 way/return €5.90/10.20; ☺5.05am-12.35am; MEspanya) runs from T1 to Plaça de Catalunya (30 to 40 minutes depending on traffic) via Plaça d'Espanya, Gran Via de les Corts Catalanes (corner of Carrer del Comte d'Urgell) and Plaça de la Universitat every five to 10 minutes from 5.35am to 1.05am. Buses from Plaça de Catalunya to the airport run every five to 10 minutes from 5am to 12.30am, stopping at the corner of Carrer de Sepúlveda and Carrer del Comte d'Urgell, and at Plaça d'Espanya.

The **A2 Aerobús** from T2 (stops outside terminal areas A, B and C) to Plaça de Catalunya runs from 5.35am to 1am every 10 minutes, following the same route as the A1 Aerobús; in the reverse direction it's every 10 minutes 5am to 12.30am. Fares on both services are €5.90/10.20 single/return. Buy tickets online, at the bus (cash only) or from the tourist office.

Slower local buses (such as route 46 to/from Plaça d'Espanya and routes 165 and N17 to/from Plaça de Catalunya) also serve T1 and/or T2.

Mon-Bus (www.monbus.cat) Regular direct buses between T1 only and Sitges (€8, 25 minutes, half-hourly 6.50am to 8.50pm, hourly 9.50pm to 11.50pm); the stop in Sitges is on Passeig de Vilafranca.

Bus Plana (☑977 553680; www.busplana.com) Services between El Prat airport and Tarragona (1 way/return €15/25, one to 1¼ hours), along with Reus and Costa Daurada destinations.

Sagalés (☑902 130014; www. sagales.com) Buses from El Prat airport to Girona (€19, 2¼ hours, five daily), Girona airport (€17, two hours, two daily) and Figueres (€25, 2½ to three hours, four daily).

METRO

Línia 9 Sud (L9S) connects T1 and T2 with Zona Universitària (32 minutes) every seven minutes from 5am to midnight Sunday to Thursday, 5am to 2am on Friday and 24 hours on Sunday; change lines en route for Barcelona city centre (€5.15).

TAXI

Taxis between either terminal and the city centre (around 30 minutes depending on traffic) cost €25 to €35. There can be long queues for taxis in high season.

TRAIN

From 5.42am to 11.38pm, Renfe (www.renfe.com) runs the half-hourly R2 Nord train line from the airport via several stops to Barcelona's main train station, Estació Sants (20 minutes), and Passeig de Gràcia (27 minutes) in central Barcelona, after which it heads northwest out of the city. The first service for the airport from Passeig de Gràcia leaves at 5.08am and the last at 11.06pm; all pass through Estació Sants around five minutes later. One-way tickets cost €4.20.

The airport train station is a five-minute, 200m walk from T2. Free 24-hour shuttle buses (allow 10 to 20 minutes) link the train station and T2 with T1 every five to 15 minutes.

Aeroport Girona-Costa Brava

Girona-Costa Brava airport (www.aena.es), 13km southwest of Girona and 92km northeast of Barcelona, is served by flights from across Europe, mostly with Ryanair (www.ryanair.com).

BUS

The **Sagalés Airport Line** (☑902 130014; www.sagales airportline.com; 1 way/return €16/25; ⓜArc de Triomf) runs direct between Girona-Costa Brava airport and Barcelona's Estació del Nord bus station (€16, 1¼ hours, three to four daily), as well as between Girona airport and Barcelona's El Prat airport (€17, two hours, two daily). Sagalés also connects Girona airport to Girona's bus/train station (€2.75, 20 to 30 minutes, hourly).

TRAIN

Regular Renfe trains run between Girona and Barce-

lona (€8.40 to €12.25, 1¼ to two hours). Speedier Avant trains (€17.40) get there in 38 minutes.

Aeroport de Reus

Reus airport (☑91 321 10 00; www.aena.es), 13km west of Tarragona and 108km southwest of Barcelona, has flights from across Europe with airlines such as Ryanair and easyJet (www.easyjet.com).

Bus

➡ Much of the Pyrenees and the entire Costa Brava are served only by buses, with train services limited to important railheads such as Girona.

➡ Most bus companies operating across Catalonia use the **Estació del Nord** (Estació del Nord; Map p310; ☑93 706 53 66; www.barcelonanord.cat; Carrer d'Alí Bei 80; ⓜArc de Triomf) in El Fort Pienç, though **Hispano-Igualadina** (Map p314; ☑93 339 73 29; www. igualadina.com; Carrer de Viriat; ⓜSants Estació) and **TEISA** (Map p310; ☑93 215 35 66; www.teisa-bus.com; Carrer de Pau Claris 117; ⓜPasseig de Gràcia) use the Estació de Sants and Carrer de Pau Claris in L'Eixample, respectively.

➡ Long-distance national buses operate from the Estació del Nord, many under the umbrella of **ALSA** (☑902 422242; www. alsa.es). There are frequent services to Madrid (seven to eight hours), Valencia (four to 5½ hours) and Zaragoza (3½ hours), and several daily departures to distant destinations such as Burgos, Santiago de Compostela and Seville.

➡ **Eurolines** (www.eurolines. es) is the main international bus carrier, serving Europe and Morocco from the Estació del Nord and the **Estació d'Autobusos de Sants**.

Train

➡ Train is the most convenient overland option for reaching Barcelona from major Spanish centres like Madrid and Valencia

➡ A network of *rodalies/ cercanías* run by Renfe serves towns around Barcelona.

➡ Frequent high-speed Tren de Alta Velocidad Española (AVE) trains between Madrid and Barcelona run daily in each direction, several in under three hours. After the AVE, Euromed and other similarly modern trains, the most common long-distance trains are the slower, all-stops Talgo.

GETTING AROUND

Metro

Transports Metropolitans de Barcelona (TMB) metro system (www.tmb.cat) has 11 numbered and colour-coded lines. It runs from 5am to midnight Sunday to Thursday and holidays, from 5am to 2am on Friday and days immediately preceding holidays, and 24 hours on Saturday. Ongoing work to expand the metro continues on several lines.

Train

Suburban trains run by the **Ferrocarrils de la Generalitat de Catalunya** (FGC; www.fgc.net) include useful city lines. All lines heading north from Plaça de Catalunya stop at Carrer de Provença and Gràcia; L7 goes to near Tibidabo and L6 goes to Reina Elisenda, near the Monestir de Pedralbes. Most trains from Plaça de Catalunya continue beyond Barcelona to Sant Cugat, Sabadell and Terrassa. Other FGC lines head west from Plaça d'Espanya, including R5 towards Manresa, which is handy for day-tripping to Montserrat (p223).

TICKETS & PASSES

The metro, FGC trains, *rodalies/cercanías* (Renfe-run local trains) and buses come under a combined system. Single-ride tickets on all transport within Zone 1 cost €2.40. Multitrip prices (Zone 1) include.

➡ **Targeta T-Casual** (€11.35) – 10 rides on the metro, buses, FGC trains and *rodalies*.

➡ **T-Usual** (€40) – 30 days' unlimited public transport.

➡ **Targeta T-DIA** (€8.60) – one day unlimited travel.

➡ **Two-/three-/four-/five-day Hola Barcelona tickets** (€15.20/22.20/28.80/35.40) – unlimited travel on all transport except the Aerobús.

➡ **T-Jove** (€105) Unlimited travel for 90 days for those aged under 25.

FGC trains run from about 5am (with only one or two services before 6am) to 11pm or midnight Sunday to Thursday, and from 5am to about 1am on Friday and Saturday.

Bus

Transports Metropolitans de Barcelona (www.tmb. cat) buses run along most city routes every few minutes from between 5am and 6.30am to around 10pm or 11pm. Many routes pass through Plaça de Catalunya and/or Plaça de la Universitat.

After 11pm, **Nitbus** (www. ambmobilitat.cat) runs a reduced network of 17 yellow night buses until 3am or 5am (including N17 to/from the airport).

Taxi

Taxis charge €2.25 flag fall plus meter charges of €1.18 per kilometre (€1.41 from 8pm to 8am and all day on weekends). A further €4.30 is added for all trips to/from the airport and €2.50/4.30 for journeys starting from Estació Sants/the port. The 3km trip from Estació Sants to Plaça de Catalunya costs about €11. You can flag a taxi down, call one or book through a wealth of app- and/or website-based

companies. The usual call-out charge is €3.40 (€4.20 at night and on weekends).

Fonotaxi (📞93 300 11 00; www.fonotaxi.net)

Greentaxi (📞900 827900; www.greentaxi.es) Wheelchair accessible.

Ràdio Taxi 033 (📞93 303 30 33; www.radiotaxi033.com)

Taxi Amic (📞93 420 80 88; www.taxi-amic-adaptat.com) For people with disabilities or requiring additional space; book at least 24 hours ahead.

Taxi Ecològic (📞93 278 30 00; http://taxiecologic.com) 🔋 Electric or hybrid cars.

Taximés (📞93 330 03 00; www.taximes.com)

Tram

There are six **tram lines** (📞900 701181; www.tram.cat) in Barcelona, on which all standard transport passes are valid.

T1, T2 and T3 Into the western suburbs from Plaça de Francesc Macià (where Sant Gervasi, western L'Eixample and Les Corts meet).

T4 From behind the zoo (near the Ciutadella Vila Olímpica metro stop) to Sant Adrià via Glòries and El Fòrum.

T5 Between Glòries and Badalona (Gorg stop).

T6 Between Glòries and Sant Adrià.

Cable Car

Telefèric del Port (Map p302; www.telefericodebarcelona. com; Passeig de Joan de Borbó; 1 way/return €11/16.50; ⏱10.30am-8pm Jun-early Sep, shorter hours early Sep-May; 🚌V15, V19, Ⓜ️Barceloneta) Runs between the waterfront southwest of Barceloneta and Montjuïc.

Telefèric de Montjuïc (p192).

Bicycle

An extensive, ever-growing network of bike lanes has been laid out across Barcelona Numerous companies hire bicycles and run cycling tours. Barcelona's main bikeshare scheme Bicing (www. bicing.barcelona) is, for now, geared towards residents rather than tourists.

Cruising Barcelona (p96)

Fat Tire Tours (p83)

Pedal Bike Rental (p136)

Terra Bike Tours (p165)

Car & Motorcycle

With the convenience of public transport, the pleasure of exploring on foot and the high price of parking, it's unwise to drive in Barcelona. However, if you're planning a road trip outside the city, a car is handy, and scooters are popular for zipping around town.

Avis, Europcar, National/ Atesa and Hertz have desks at El Prat airport, and most at the Estació Sants and Estació del Nord. Outlets in central Barcelona include **Enterprise** (📞93 323 07 01; www.enterprise.es; Carrer de Muntaner 45; ⏱8am-8pm Mon-Fri, 9am-1pm Sat; Ⓜ️Universitat) for electric cars, bicycles and scooters.

Directory A–Z

Accessible Travel

All buses in Barcelona are wheelchair accessible, as are most metro stations (generally by lift, though there have been complaints that these are only good for people with prams); of 160 stations, all but 14 are adapted (check www.tmb.cat/en/transport-accessible). Ticket vending machines in metro stations are adapted for travellers with disabilities and have Braille options for those with visual impairments. Punt TMB info points at Diagonal and Universitat metro stations provide embossed maps and metro guides in Braille.

Most hotels and public institutions have wheelchair access, and most street crossings in central Barcelona are wheelchair-friendly. **Barcelona Turisme** (Map p310; ☑93 285 38 34; www.barcelonaturisme.com; Plaça de Catalunya 17-S, underground; ⊙8.30am-9pm; ⓂCatalunya) provides details of accessible hotels online, and also runs a wheelchair-accessible **tour** (Map p306; ☑93 285 38 32; www.barcelonaturisme.com; Plaça de Catalunya 17; ⓂCatalunya) of the Barri Gòtic.

Several taxi companies have adapted vehicles, including **Taxi Amic** (☑93 420 80 88; www.taxi-amic-adaptat.com) and **Greentaxi** (☑900 827900; www.greentaxi.es).

From July to mid-September and on weekends in June, volunteers at several beaches including Nova Icària and Barceloneta provide amphibious chairs and assistance, usually from around 11am to 2pm and 4pm to 7pm.

Discount Cards

The ISIC (International Student Identity Card; www.isic.org) and the European Youth Card (www.eyca.org) allow discounted access to some sights. Students generally pay a little more than half of adult admission prices, as do children aged under 12 and senior citizens (aged 65 and over) with appropriate ID. Some sights offer slightly reduced rates for the under-30s, too.

Possession of a **Bus Turístic** (☑93 298 70 00; www.barcelonabusturistic.cat; adult/child 1-day pass €30/16, 2-day pass €40/21; ⊙9am-8pm mid-Apr–Oct, to 7pm Nov–mid-Apr) ticket entitles you to discounts at some museums.

Articket BCN (www.articketbcn.org) Gives admission to six art galleries for €35 and is valid for six months; buy online, at tourist offices or at the museums themselves. The six sights are the Museu Picasso, Museu Nacional d'Art de Catalunya (MNAC), Museu d'Art Contemporani de Barcelona (MACBA), Fundació Antoni Tàpies, Centre

de Cultura Contemporània de Barcelona (CCCB) and Fundació Joan Miró.

Arqueoticket (www.barcelonaturisme.com) This ticket (€14.50) grants free admission to the Museu d'Arqueologia de Catalunya, Museu Egipci, Museu d'Història de Barcelona and Born Centre de Cultura i Memòria.

Barcelona Card (www.barcelonacard.com) It costs €20/46/56/61 for two/three/four/five days, and you get free transport as well as discounted admission (up to 60% off) or free entry to many sights. Children aged four to 12 pay around 50% less.

Ruta del Modernisme (www.rutadelmodernisme.com) Modernista sights at discounted rates; costs €12.

Emergency & Important Numbers

Ambulance	☑061
EU standard emergency number	☑112
Country code	☑34
International access code	☑00
Guàrdia Urbana	☑092

Electricity

Spain uses 230V/50Hz, like the rest of continental Europe.

Type C
230V/50Hz

Type F
230V/50Hz

Internet Access

Most hotels, cafes, bars and restaurants offer free wi-fi, of varying quality. The city also has dozens of free public wi-fi hotspots, though signal is often weak (www.bcn.cat/barcelonawifi).

Money

ATMs are widely available. Credit and debit cards are accepted in most hotels, shops, restaurants and taxis.

Credit Cards

Major cards (Visa, Master-Card, Maestro, Cirrus) are accepted across Barcelona, though there may be a mini-mum spend of €5 or €10. When paying by credit card, photo ID is often required, even for chip cards (for US travellers without chip cards, just indicate that you'll give a signature).

Opening Hours

Restaurants 1pm–4pm and 8.30pm–midnight; some open all day

Shops 9am or 10am–1.30pm or 2pm and 4pm or 4.30pm–8pm or 8.30pm Monday to Saturday

Bars 6pm–2am (to 3am weekends)

Clubs Midnight–6am Thursday to Saturday

Banks 8.30am–2pm Monday to Friday; some also 4pm–7pm Thursday or 9am–1pm Saturday

Museums & art galleries Vary considerably; generally 10am–8pm (though some shut for lunch around 2pm–4pm). Many close all day Monday and from 2pm Sunday.

Public Holidays

New Year's Day (Any Nou/Año Nuevo) 1 January

Epiphany/Three Kings' Day (Epifanía or El Dia dels Reis/Día de los Reyes Magos) 6 January

Good Friday (Divendres Sant/Viernes Santo) March/April

Easter Monday (Dilluns de Pasqua Florida/Lunes de Pascua) March/April

Labour Day (Dia del Treball/Fiesta del Trabajo) 1 May

Day after Pentecost Sunday (Dilluns de Pasqua Granada) May/June

Feast of St John the Baptist (Dia de Sant Joan/Día de San Juan Bautista) 24 June

Feast of the Assumption (L'Assumpció/La Asunción) 15 August

Catalonia's National Day (Diada Nacional de Catalunya) 11 September

Festes de la Mercè 24 September

Spanish National Day (Festa de la Hispanitat/Día de la Hispanidad) 12 October

All Saints Day (Dia de Tots Sants/Día de Todos los Santos) 1 November

Constitution Day (Dia de la Constitució/Día de la Constitución) 6 December

Feast of the Immaculate Conception (La Immaculada Concepció/La Inmaculada Concepción) 8 December

Christmas (Nadal/Navidad) 25 December

Boxing Day/St Stephen's Day (Dia de Sant Esteve) 26 December

Safe Travel

Spain has been particularly hard hit by the COVID-19 pandemic, especially in cities such as Madrid, Barcelona and Zaragoza, with tight lockdown restrictions in place on and off throughout 2020 and 2021. At the time of writing, however, Spain had one of the world's highest COVID-19 vaccination rates, and required proof of full vaccination (or a recent negative test) for anyone wishing to enter the country. Travellers should abide by all local safety regulations and entry requirements.

Taxes & Refunds

Value-added tax (VAT) is known as IVA (*impuesto sobre el valor añadido;* pronounced '*ee*-ba'). IVA is 10% on accommodation and restaurant prices and is usually – but not always – included in quoted prices. On most retail goods the IVA is 21%. IVA-free shopping is available in duty-free shops at all airports for people travelling between EU countries.

Non-EU residents are entitled to a refund of the 21% IVA on purchases from any shop, if the goods are taken out of the EU within three months. Ask the shop for a DIVA tax-free electronic form, then scan the form at the automatic DIVA machines when you depart from Spain (or at custom booths elsewhere in the EU). You will need your passport and a boarding card that shows you are leaving the EU, and your luggage and goods (so do this before checking in bags). The machine (or officer) will approve the invoice and you can then collect the refund from Tax Free offices at the airport or port.

Telephone

Local SIM cards can generally be used in unlocked European, Australian and North American phones (but may not be compatible with the Japanese system). Travellers with phones from within the EU have free roaming.

Mobile Phones

➡ Mobile-phone numbers start with 6 or 7.

➡ You can buy SIM cards and prepaid data and call time in Spain for your own mobile phone (provided you own an unlocked phone that is compatible – these days most are compatible).

➡ You will need your passport to open any kind of mobile-phone account, prepaid or otherwise.

Time

➡ Spain is on CET, one hour ahead of GMT/UTC during winter, and two hours ahead during daylight saving (the last Sunday in March to the last Sunday in October).

➡ Spaniards use the 24-hour clock for official business (timetables etc) but generally switch to the 12-hour version in daily conversation.

Tourist Information

A couple of general tourist information phone numbers are 010 (for Barcelona) and 012 (for all Catalonia, run by the Generalitat).

Plaça de Catalunya (Map p310; 93 285 38 34; www.barcelonaturisme.com; Plaça de Catalunya 17-S, underground; 8.30am-9pm; Catalunya)

Plaça Sant Jaume (Map p292; 93 285 38 34; www.barcelonaturisme.com; Plaça de Sant Jaume; 8.30am-8pm Mon-Fri, 9am-3pm Sat & Sun; Catalunya)

Catedral (Map p292; 93 368 97 00; www.barcelonaturisme.com; Plaça Nova, Col·legi d'Arquitectes; 9am-7pm Mon-Sat, to 3pm Sun)

Estació Sants (Map p314; 93

285 38 34; www.barcelona turisme.com; Barcelona Sants; 8.30am-8.30pm daily Apr-Oct, 8.30am-8.30pm Mon-Fri, to 2.30pm Sat & Sun Nov-Mar; Sants Estació)

Palau Moja (Barri Gòtic) (Map p292; 93 285 38 34; www.barcelonaturisme.com; Carrer de la Portaferrisa 1; 10am-9pm; Liceu)

Aeroport del Prat (93 285 38 32; www.barcelonaturisme.com; Aeroport de Barcelona–El Prat, Terminal 2; 8.30am-8.30pm)

Oficina de Turisme de Catalunya (Regional Tourist Office; Map p306; 93 238 80 91; https://escasateva.catalunya.com; Passeig de Gràcia 107, Palau Robert; 9am-8pm Mon-Sat, to 2.30pm Sun; Diagonal)

Visas

Spain is one of 26 member countries of the Schengen Agreement, under which 22 EU countries (all but Bulgaria, Cyprus, Croatia, Ireland and Romania) plus Iceland, Norway, Liechtenstein and Switzerland have abolished checks at common borders.

The visa situation for entering Spain is as follows:

Citizens or residents of EU & Schengen countries No visa required.

Citizens or residents of the UK, Australia, Canada, Israel, Japan, New Zealand & the USA From late 2022 or early 2023, nationals of these countries will require prior authorisation to enter Spain under the new European Travel Information and Authorisation System (ETIAS; www.etias.com). With ETIAS pre-authorisation (valid for three years), travellers can stay in Spain visa-free for 90 days within any given 180-day period.

Other countries Check with a Spanish embassy or consulate.

To work or study in Spain A special visa may be required – contact a Spanish embassy or consulate before travel.

Women Travellers

Spain is a generally safe and progressive country, and travelling here as a woman is as easy and safe as anywhere else in the western world; in Barcelona your biggest concern is likely to be pickpockets. That said, stick to your usual instincts and common sense: avoid empty city streets at night, let someone know where you are, choose accommodation carefully, etc.

Topless bathing is common at beaches and pools across Spain, and, when it comes to clothing, in Barcelona anything goes.

Ca la Dona (Map p292; ☑93 412 71 61; https://caladona.org; Carrer de Ripoll 25; ☉10am-1pm & 5-8pm Mon-Thu; ⓂJaume I) The nerve centre of the region's feminist movement, with diverse women's groups.

Institut Català de les Dones (http://dones.gencat.cat) Can point you in the right direction for information on marriage, divorce, rape/assault counselling and related issues. The 24-hour hotline for victims of assault is 900 900120.

RESPONSIBLE TRAVEL

Barcelona's struggle with overtourism has hit headlines in recent years and the Catalan authorities are working hard to push forward a more sustainable tourism model. There are many ways travellers can explore more responsibly here.

Overtourism

➡ Travel off-season (outside May to September and Easter) and mid-week.

➡ Tourist apartments and illegal lets are driving up rents for the local population. Check you're staying in official registered accommodation (www.fairtourism.barcelona).

➡ Combine your Barcelona trip with exploring other parts of Catalonia: soulful Girona, Roman Tarragona, the spectacular Pyrenees.

➡ Read up on Barcelona's ongoing sustainable tourism projects and responsible travel tips (https://meet.barcelona.cat).

Support Local & Give Back

➡ Join one of Barcelona's many volunteering projects (https:// www.barcelona.cat/en/getinvolved) or beach clean-ups (https://cleanbeachinitiative.org).

➡ Enjoy a guided tour to support local experts, from historians to architects. **Hidden City Tours** (www.hiddencity tours.com; tour per person €21.50) ✐ works with guides who have been part of the city's homeless community.

➡ Rising rents have closed down some of Barcelona's best-known traditional shops; help by shopping at long- established favourites with special preservation status (p48).

➡ Support hospitality-training programs for those struggling to access the job market (including undocumented migrants) at **Espai Mescladís** (☑93 319 87 32; www.facebook.com/mescladis; Carrer dels Carders 35; dishes €3-8; ☉10am-8.30pm; ⚲) ✐, a lovely El Born cafe run by not-for-profit organisation Mescladís.

Leave a Light Footprint

➡ While Barcelona's bike-share scheme Bicing isn't currently aimed at tourists, there are plenty of local bike-rental operators (p270).

➡ Tap into the city's excellent public transport system (p269).

Language

Catalan (català) and Spanish (español, more precisely known as castellano, or Castilian) both have official-language status in Catalonia. Aranese (aranés), which is a dialect of Gascon, is also an official language in the Val d'Aran. In Barcelona, you'll hear as much Spanish as Catalan, so we've provided some Spanish as well as Catalan basics here to get you started.

Most Spanish sounds are pronounced the same as their English counterparts. If you follow our coloured pronunciation guides, you'll be understood. Note that the kh is a throaty sound (like the 'ch' in the Scottish loch), ly is pronounced as the 'lli' in 'million', ny as the 'ni' in 'onion', th is pronounced with a lisp, and r is strongly rolled. In our pronunciation guides, the stressed syllables are in italics.

Where necessary, masculine and feminine forms are given for the words and phrases in this chapter, separated by a slash and with the masculine form first, eg perdido/a (m/f). Where both polite and informal options are given, they are indicated by the abbreviations 'pol' and 'inf' respectively.

BASICS

Hello.	Hola.	o·la
Goodbye.	Adiós.	a·dyos
How are you?	¿Qué tal?	ke tal
Fine, thanks.	Bien, gracias.	byen gra·thyas
Excuse me.	Perdón.	per·don
Sorry.	Lo siento.	lo see·en·to
Yes./No.	Sí./No.	see/no

WANT MORE?

For in-depth language information and handy phrases, check out Lonely Planet's Spanish phrasebook. You'll find it at shop.lonelyplanet.com, or you can buy Lonely Planet's iPhone phrasebooks at the Apple App Store.

Please.	Por favor.	por fa·vor
Thank you.	Gracias.	gra·thyas
You're welcome.	De nada.	de na·da

My name is ...
Me llamo ...   me lya·mo ...

What's your name?
¿Cómo se llama Usted?   ko·mo se lya·ma oo·ste (pol)
¿Cómo te llamas?   ko·mo te lya·mas (inf)

Do you speak (English)?
¿Habla (inglés)?   a·bla (een·gles) (pol)
¿Hablas (inglés)?   a·blas (een·gles) (inf)

I (don't) understand.
Yo (no) entiendo.   yo (no) en·tyen·do

ACCOMMODATION

I'd like to book a room.
Quisiera reservar una habitación.   kee·sye·ra re·ser·var oo·na a·bee·ta·thyon

How much is it per night/person?
¿Cuánto cuesta por noche/persona?   kwan·to kwes·ta por no·che/per·so·na

Does it include breakfast?
¿Incluye el desayuno?   een·kloo·ye el de·sa·yoo·no

hotel	hotel	o·tel
guesthouse	pensión	pen·syon
youth hostel	albergue juvenil	al·ber·ge khoo·ve·neel

I'd like a ... room.	Quisiera una habitación ...	kee·sye·ra oo·na a·bee·ta·thyon ...
single	individual	een·dee·vee·dwal
double	doble	do·ble

air-con	aire acondicionado	ai·re a·kon·dee·thyo·na·do
bathroom	baño	ba·nyo
window	ventana	ven·ta·na

KEY PATTERNS

To get by in Spanish, mix and match these simple patterns with words of your choice:

When's (the next flight)?
¿Cuándo sale *kwan*·do sa·le
(el próximo vuelo)? (el prok·see·mo vwe·lo)

Where's (the station)?
¿Dónde está *don*·de es·ta
(la estación)? (la es·ta·thyon)

Where can I (buy a ticket)?
¿Dónde puedo *don*·de pwe·do
(comprar (kom·prar
un billete)? oon bee·lye·te)

Do you have (a map)?
¿Tiene (un mapa)? *tye*·ne (oon ma·pa)

Is there (a toilet)?
¿Hay (servicios)? ai (ser·vee·thyos)

I'd like (a coffee).
Quisiera (un café). kee·sye·ra (oon ka·fe)

I'd like (to hire a car).
Quisiera (alquilar kee·sye·ra (al·kee·lar
un coche). oon ko·che)

Can I (enter)?
¿Se puede (entrar)? se pwe·de (en·trar)

Could you please (help me)?
¿Puede (ayudarme), pwe·de (a·yoo·dar·me)
por favor? por fa·vor

Do I have to (get a visa)?
¿Necesito ne·the·see·to
(obtener (ob·te·ner
un visado)? oon vee·sa·do)

DIRECTIONS

Where's ...?
¿Dónde está ...? *don*·de es·ta ...

What's the address?
¿Cuál es la dirección? kwal es la dee·rek·thyon

Could you please write it down?
¿Puede escribirlo, pwe·de es·kree·beer·lo
por favor? por fa·vor

Can you show me (on the map)?
¿Me lo puede indicar me lo pwe·de een·dee·kar
(en el mapa)? (en el ma·pa)

at the corner	en la esquina	en la es·kee·na
at the traffic lights	en el semáforo	en el se·ma·fo·ro
behind	detrás de	de·tras de
far (away)	lejos	le·khos
in front of	enfrente de	en·fren·te de
left	izquierda	eeth·kyer·da
near	cerca	ther·ka
next to	al lado de	al la·do de
opposite	frente a	fren·te a
right	derecha	de·re·cha
straight ahead	todo recto	to·do rek·to

EATING & DRINKING

I'd like to Quisiera kee·sye·ra
book a table reservar una re·ser·var oo·na
for ... mesa para ... me·sa pa·ra ...

(eight) o'clock las (ocho) las (o·cho)

(two) people (dos) (dos)
personas per·so·nas

What would you recommend?
¿Qué recomienda? ke re·ko·myen·da

What's in that dish?
¿Que lleva ese plato? ke lye·va e·se pla·to

I don't eat ...
No como ... no ko·mo ...

Cheers!
¡Salud! sa·loo

That was delicious!
¡Estaba buenísimo! es·ta·ba bwe·nee·see·mo

Please bring the bill.
Por favor nos trae por fa·vor nos tra·e
la cuenta. la kwen·ta

Key Words

appetisers	aperitivos	a·pe·ree·tee·vos
bar	bar	bar
bottle	botella	bo·te·lya
bowl	bol	bol
breakfast	desayuno	de·sa·yoo·no
cafe	café	ka·fe
children's menu	menú infantil	me·noo een·fan·teel
(too/very) cold	(muy) frío	(mooy) free·o
dinner	cena	the·na
food	comida	ko·mee·da
fork	tenedor	te·ne·dor
glass	vaso	va·so
highchair	trona	tro·na
hot (warm)	caliente	ka·lyen·te
knife	cuchillo	koo·chee·lyo
lunch	comida	ko·mee·da
main course	segundo plato	se·goon·do pla·to
market	mercado	mer·ka·do
menu (in English)	menú (en inglés)	oon me·noo (en een·gles)

CATALAN

The recognition of Catalan as an official language in Spain is the end result of a regional government campaign that began when the province gained autonomy at the end of the 1970s. Until the Battle of Muret in 1213, Catalan territory extended across southern France, taking in Roussillon and reaching into Provence. Catalan was spoken, or at least understood, throughout these territories and in what is now Catalonia and Andorra. In the couple of hundred years that followed, the Catalans spread their language south into Valencia, west into Aragón and east to the Balearic Islands. The language also reached Sicily and Naples, and the Sardinian town of Alghero is still a partly Catalan-speaking outpost today. Catalan is spoken by up to 10 million people in Spain.

In Barcelona you'll hear as much Spanish as Catalan. Your chances of coming across English speakers are also good. Elsewhere in the province, don't be surprised if you get replies in Catalan to your questions in Spanish. However, you'll find that most Catalans will happily speak to you in Spanish, especially once they realise you're a foreigner. This said, the following Catalan phrases might win you a few smiles and perhaps help you make some new friends.

Hello.	*Hola.*	**Monday**	*dilluns*
Goodbye.	*Adéu.*	**Tuesday**	*dimarts*
Yes.	*Sí.*	**Wednesday**	*dimecres*
No.	*No.*	**Thursday**	*dijous*
Please.	*Sisplau./Si us plau.*	**Friday**	*divendres*
Thank you (very much).	*(Moltes) gràcies.*	**Saturday**	*dissabte*
You're welcome.	*De res.*	**Sunday**	*diumenge*
Excuse me.	*Perdoni.*		
May I?/Do you mind?	*Puc?/Em permet?*	1	*un/una (m/f)*
I'm sorry.	*Ho sento./Perdoni.*	2	*dos/dues (m/f)*
		3	*tres*
What's your name?	*Com et dius?* (inf)	4	*quatre*
	Com es diu? (pol)	5	*cinc*
My name is ...	*Em dic ...*	6	*sis*
Where are you from?	*D'on ets?*	7	*set*
Do you speak English?	*Parla anglès?*	8	*vuit*
I understand.	*Ho entenc.*	9	*nou*
I don't understand.	*No ho entenc.*	10	*deu*
Could you speak in	*Pot parlar castellà*	11	*onze*
Castilian, please?	*sisplau?*	12	*dotze*
How do you say ... in	*Com es diu ... en*	13	*tretze*
Catalan?	*català?*	14	*catorze*
		15	*quinze*
I'm looking for ...	*Estic buscant ...*	16	*setze*
How do I get to ...?	*Com puc arribar a ...?*	17	*disset*
Turn left.	*Giri a mà esquerra.*	18	*divuit*
Turn right.	*Giri a mà dreta.*	19	*dinou*
near	*a prop de*	20	*vint*
far	*a lluny de*	100	*cent*

Signs

Abierto	Open
Cerrado	Closed
Entrada	Entrance
Hombres	Men
Mujeres	Women
Prohibido	Prohibited
Salida	Exit
Servicios/Aseos	Toilets

plate	plato	pla·to
restaurant	restaurante	res·tow·ran·te
spoon	cuchara	koo·cha·ra
supermarket	supermercado	soo·per·mer·ka·do
vegetarian food	comida vegetariana	ko·mee·da ve·khe·ta·rya·na
with/without	con/sin	kon/seen

Meat & Fish

beef	carne de vaca	kar·ne de va·ka
chicken	pollo	po·lyo
duck	pato	pa·to
lamb	cordero	kor·de·ro
lobster	langosta	lan·gos·ta
pork	cerdo	ther·do
prawns	camarones	ka·ma·ro·nes
tuna	atún	a·toon
turkey	pavo	pa·vo
veal	ternera	ter·ne·ra

Fruit & Vegetables

apple	manzana	man·tha·na
apricot	albaricoque	al·ba·ree·ko·ke
artichoke	alcachofa	al·ka·cho·fa
asparagus	espárragos	es·pa·ra·gos
banana	plátano	pla·ta·no
beans	judías	khoo·dee·as
beetroot	remolacha	re·mo·la·cha
cabbage	col	kol
carrot	zanahoria	tha·na·o·rya
celery	apio	a·pyo
cherry	cereza	the·re·tha
corn	maíz	ma·eeth
cucumber	pepino	pe·pee·no
fruit	fruta	froo·ta
grape	uvas	oo·vas

lemon	limón	lee·mon
lentils	lentejas	len·te·khas
lettuce	lechuga	le·choo·ga
mushroom	champiñón	cham·pee·nyon
nuts	nueces	nwe·thes
onion	cebolla	the·bo·lya
orange	naranja	na·ran·kha
peach	melocotón	me·lo·ko·ton
peas	guisantes	gee·san·tes
(red/green) pepper	pimiento (rojo/verde)	pee·myen·to (ro·kho/ver·de)
pineapple	piña	pee·nya
plum	ciruela	theer·we·la
potato	patata	pa·ta·ta
pumpkin	calabaza	ka·la·ba·tha
spinach	espinacas	es·pee·na·kas
strawberry	fresa	fre·sa
tomato	tomate	to·ma·te
vegetable	verdura	ver·doo·ra
watermelon	sandía	san·dee·a

Other

bread	pan	pan
butter	mantequilla	man·te·kee·lya
cheese	queso	ke·so
egg	huevo	we·vo
honey	miel	myel
jam	mermelada	mer·me·la·da
oil	aceite	a·they·te
pasta	pasta	pas·ta
pepper	pimienta	pee·myen·ta
rice	arroz	a·roth
salt	sal	sal
sugar	azúcar	a·thoo·kar
vinegar	vinagre	vee·na·gre

Drinks

beer	cerveza	ther·ve·tha
coffee	café	ka·fe
(orange) juice	zumo (de naranja)	thoo·mo (de na·ran·kha)
milk	leche	le·che
tea	té	te
(mineral) water	agua (mineral)	a·gwa (mee·ne·ral)
(red) wine	vino (tinto)	vee·no (teen·to)
(white) wine	vino (blanco)	vee·no (blan·ko)

EMERGENCIES

| Help! | ¡Socorro! | so·ko·ro |
| Go away! | ¡Vete! | ve·te |

Call ...!	¡Llame a ...!	lya·me a ...
a doctor	un médico	oon me·dee·ko
the police	la policía	la po·lee·thee·a

I'm lost.
Estoy perdido/a. es·*toy* per·*dee*·do/a (m/f)

I had an accident.
He tenido un e te·*nee*·do oon
accidente. ak·thee·*den*·te

I'm ill.
Estoy enfermo/a. es·*toy* en·*fer*·mo/a (m/f)

It hurts here.
Me duele aquí. me dwe·le a·*kee*

I'm allergic to (antibiotics).
Soy alérgico/a a soy a·*ler*·khee·ko/a a
(los antibióticos). (los an·tee·*byo*·tee·kos) (m/f)

SHOPPING & SERVICES

I'd like to buy ...
Quisiera comprar ... kee·*sye*·ra kom·*prar* ...

I'm just looking.
Sólo estoy mirando. so·lo es·*toy* mee·*ran*·do

Can I look at it?
¿Puedo verlo? pwe·do ver·lo

I don't like it.
No me gusta. no me *goos*·ta

How much is it?
¿Cuánto cuesta? kwan·to *kwes*·ta

That's too expensive.
Es muy caro. es mooy *ka*·ro

Can you lower the price?
¿Podría bajar un po·*dree*·a ba·*khar* oon
poco el precio? po·ko el *pre*·thyo

There's a mistake in the bill.
Hay un error en ai oon e·*ror* en
la cuenta. la *kwen*·ta

ATM	cajero	ka·*khe*·ro
	automático	ow·to·ma·tee·ko
internet cafe	cibercafé	thee·ber·ka·*fe*
post office	correos	ko·*re*·os
tourist office	oficina	o·fee·*thee*·na
	de turismo	de too·*rees*·mo

TIME & DATES

What time is it?
¿Qué hora es? ke o·ra es

It's (10) o'clock.
Son (las diez). son (las dyeth)

Half past (one).
Es (la una) es (la oo·na)
y media. ee me·dya

morning	mañana	ma·*nya*·na
afternoon	tarde	*tar*·de
evening	noche	*no*·che
yesterday	ayer	a·*yer*
today	hoy	oy
tomorrow	mañana	ma·*nya*·na

Monday	lunes	*loo*·nes
Tuesday	martes	*mar*·tes
Wednesday	miércoles	*myer*·ko·les
Thursday	jueves	*khwe*·bes
Friday	viernes	*vyer*·nes
Saturday	sábado	*sa*·ba·do
Sunday	domingo	do·*meen*·go

January	enero	e·*ne*·ro
February	febrero	fe·*bre*·ro
March	marzo	*mar*·tho
April	abril	a·*breel*
May	mayo	*ma*·yo
June	junio	*khoo*·nyo
July	julio	*khoo*·lyo
August	agosto	a·*gos*·to
September	septiembre	sep·*tyem*·bre
October	octubre	ok·*too*·bre
November	noviembre	no·*vyem*·bre
December	diciembre	dee·*thyem*·bre

TRANSPORT

boat	barco	*bar*·ko
bus	autobús	ow·to·*boos*
plane	avión	a·*vyon*
train	tren	tren

first	primer	pree·*mer*
last	último	*ool*·tee·mo
next	próximo	*prok*·see·mo

Question Words		
What?	¿Qué?	ke
When?	¿Cuándo?	*kwan*·do
Where?	¿Dónde?	*don*·de
Who?	¿Quién?	kyen
Why?	¿Por qué?	por ke

I want to go to ...
Quisiera ir a ...   kee·sye·ra eer a ...

What time does it arrive/leave?
¿A qué hora llega/sale?   a ke o·ra lye·ga/sa·le

Does it stop at ...?
¿Para en ...?   pa·ra en ...

Can you tell me when we get to ...?
¿Puede avisarme   pwe·de a·vee·sar·me
cuando lleguemos a ...?   kwan·do lye·ge·mos a ...

What stop is this?
¿Cuál es esta parada?   kwal es es·ta pa·ra·da

I want to get off here.
Quiero bajarme aquí.   kye·ro ba·khar·me a·kee

a ... ticket	un billete de ...	oon bee·lye·te de ...
1st-class	primera clase	pree·me·ra kla·se
2nd-class	segunda clase	se·goon·da kla·se
one-way	ida	ee·da
return	ida y vuelta	ee·da ee vwel·ta
aisle seat	asiento de pasillo	a·syen·to de pa·see·lyo
cancelled	cancelado	kan·the·la·do
delayed	retrasado	re·tra·sa·do
platform	plataforma	pla·ta·for·ma
ticket office	taquilla	ta·kee·lya
timetable	horario	o·ra·ryo
train station	estación de trenes	es·ta·thyon de tre·nes
window seat	asiento junto a la ventana	a·syen·to khoon·to a la ven·ta·na
I'd like to hire a ...	Quisiera alquilar ...	kee·sye·ra al·kee·lar ...
bicycle	una bicicleta	oo·na bee·thee·kle·ta
car	un coche	oon ko·che
motorcycle	una moto	oo·na mo·to

Numbers		
1	uno	oo·no
2	dos	dos
3	tres	tres
4	cuatro	kwa·tro
5	cinco	theen·ko
6	seis	seys
7	siete	sye·te
8	ocho	o·cho
9	nueve	nwe·ve
10	diez	dyeth
20	veinte	veyn·te
30	treinta	treyn·ta
40	cuarenta	kwa·ren·ta
50	cincuenta	theen·kwen·ta
60	sesenta	se·sen·ta
70	setenta	se·ten·ta
80	ochenta	o·chen·ta
90	noventa	no·ven·ta
100	cien	thyen
1000	mil	meel

diesel	gasóleo	ga·so·lyo
helmet	casco	kas·ko
mechanic	mecánico	me·ka·nee·ko
petrol/gas	gasolina	ga·so·lee·na
service station	gasolinera	ga·so·lee·ne·ra

(How long) Can I park here?
¿(Por cuánto tiempo)   (por kwan·to tyem·po)
Puedo aparcar aquí?   pwe·do a·par·kar a·kee

The car has broken down.
El coche se ha averiado.   el ko·che se a a·ve·rya·do

I have a flat tyre.
Tengo un pinchazo.   ten·go oon peen·cha·tho

I've run out of petrol.
Me he quedado sin   me e ke·da·do seen
gasolina.   ga·so·lee·na

GLOSSARY

Items listed below are in Catalan/Spanish (Castilian) where they start with the same letter. Where the two terms start with different letters, or where only the Catalan or the Spanish term is provided, they are listed separately and marked (C) for Catalan or (S) for Spanish. If an entry is not marked at all, it is because it takes the same form in both languages.

ajuntament/ayuntamiento – town hall

artesonado (S) – Mudéjar wooden ceiling with interlaced beams leaving a pattern of spaces for decoration

avinguda (C) – avenue

barcelonin (C) – inhabitant/native of Barcelona

Barcino – Roman name for Barcelona

barri/barrio – neighbourhood, quarter of Barcelona

caganer (C) – the crapper, a character appearing in Catalan nativity scenes

capella/capilla – chapel

carrer/calle – street

casa – house

castellers (C) – human-castle builders

cercanías (S) – local trains serving Barcelona's airport, suburbs and some outlying towns

comte/conde – count

correfoc (C) – appearance of firework-spouting devils at festivals; literally 'fire runs'

El Call (C) – the Jewish quarter in medieval Barcelona

església (C) – church

farmàcia/farmacia – pharmacy

festa/fiesta – festival, public holiday or party

FGC (C) – Ferrocarrils de la Generalitat de Catalunya; local trains operating alongside the metro in Barcelona

fundació/fundación – foundation

garum – a spicy sauce made from fish entrails, found throughout the Roman Empire

gegants – huge figures paraded at *festes*

Generalitat (C) – Catalan regional government

guiri – foreigner (somewhat pejorative)

hostal – commercial establishment providing one- to three-star accommodation

iglesia (S) – church

IVA – *impost sobre el valor afegit/impuesto sobre el valor añadido;* value-added tax

masia – Catalan country farmhouse

mercat/mercado – market

Modernisme (C) – the turn-of-the-19th-century artistic style, influenced by art nouveau, whose leading practitioner was Antoni Gaudí

Modernista – an exponent of Modernisme

Mudéjar (S) – a Muslim living under Christian rule in medieval Spain; also refers to their decorative style of architecture

palau (C) – palace

passatge (C) – laneway

pensió/pensión – commercial establishment providing one- to three-star accommodation

plaça/plaza – plaza

platja/playa – beach

Renaixença – rebirth of interest in Catalan literature, culture and language in the second half of the 19th century

rodalies (C) – see *cercanías*

saló (C) – hall

sardana – traditional Catalan folk dance

s/n (S) – *sin número* (without number)

tablao – restaurant where flamenco is performed

teatre – theatre

terrassa/terazza – terrace; often means a cafe or bar's outdoor tables

trencadís – a Modernista style of mosaic, created using broken tiles

turista – 2nd class; economy class

Behind the Scenes

SEND US YOUR FEEDBACK

We love to hear from travellers – your comments keep us on our toes and help make our books better. Our well-travelled team reads every word on what you loved or loathed about this book. Although we cannot reply individually to your submissions, we always guarantee that your feedback goes straight to the appropriate authors, in time for the next edition. Each person who sends us information is thanked in the next edition – the most useful submissions are rewarded with a selection of digital PDF chapters.

Visit **lonelyplanet.com/contact** to submit your updates and suggestions or to ask for help. Our award-winning website also features inspirational travel stories, news and discussions.

Note: We may edit, reproduce and incorporate your comments in Lonely Planet products such as guidebooks, websites and digital products, so let us know if you don't want your comments reproduced or your name acknowledged. For a copy of our privacy policy visit lonelyplanet.com/privacy.

WRITER THANKS

Isabella Noble

An enormous *gràcies* to everyone who helped out on all things Barcelona: Sally Davies, Esme Fox, Marwa El-Hennawey Preston, Tom Stainer, the Devour team, Clementina Milà, Joan Pau Aragón, María del Río, Vera de Frutos, Suzy Taher, Isabelle Kliger, Nigel Haywood, Alex Pérez, Lorna Turnbull, José Fabra and friends, Pau Gavaldà, David Doyes, and Ariadna and family. As always, the biggest thanks (and *salut!*) to my loyal research assistants Jack Noble, John Noble and Andrew Brannan.

Regis St Louis

I'm indebted to countless locals, expats and fellow travellers who shared tips and cultural insight along the way. *Besos* to Cassandra, Magdalena and Genevieve for the warm homecoming.

ACKNOWLEDGEMENTS

Cover photograph: Basílica del Sagrat Cor de Jesús, Tibidabo, Andrii Zabolotnyi/Shutterstock ©
Illustration p142-3 by Javier Zarracina.

THIS BOOK

This 12th edition of Lonely Planet's *Barcelona* guidebook was researched and written by Isabella Noble and Regis St Louis. The previous edition was written by Isabella, Sally Davies and Catherine Le Nevez. This guidebook was produced by the following:

Senior Product Editors
Sandie Kestell, Jess Ryan, Angela Tinson

Senior Cartographer
Anthony Phelan

Product Editors
James Appleton, Will Allen, Paul Harding

Book Designers
Catalina Aragón, Gwen Cotter

Assisting Editors
Sarah Bailey, Imogen Bannister, Melanie Dankel, Carly Hall, Lorna Parkes

Cover Researcher
Brendan Dempsey-Spencer

Thanks to
Ronan Abayawickrema, Fergal Condon, Harsha Maheshwari, Karen Henderson, Darren O'Connell, Genna Patterson, Nick Wood

See also separate subindexes for:

✗ **EATING P286**

🍷 **DRINKING & NIGHTLIFE P287**

☆ **ENTERTAINMENT P288**

🛍 **SHOPPING P288**

🛏 **SLEEPING P289**

🏃 **SPORTS & ACTIVITIES P289**

Index

Barcelona Maps

Sights

- Beach
- Bird Sanctuary
- Buddhist
- Castle/Palace
- Christian
- Confucian
- Hindu
- Islamic
- Jain
- Jewish
- Monument
- Museum/Gallery/Historic Building
- Ruin
- Shinto
- Sikh
- Taoist
- Winery/Vineyard
- Zoo/Wildlife Sanctuary
- Other Sight

Activities, Courses & Tours

- Bodysurfing
- Diving
- Canoeing/Kayaking
- Course/Tour
- Sento Hot Baths/Onsen
- Skiing
- Snorkelling
- Surfing
- Swimming/Pool
- Walking
- Windsurfing
- Other Activity

Sleeping

- Sleeping
- Camping
- Hut/Shelter

Eating

- Eating

Drinking & Nightlife

- Drinking & Nightlife
- Cafe

Entertainment

- Entertainment

Shopping

- Shopping

Information

- Bank
- Embassy/Consulate
- Hospital/Medical
- Internet
- Police
- Post Office
- Telephone
- Toilet
- Tourist Information
- Other Information

Geographic

- Beach
- Gate
- Hut/Shelter
- Lighthouse
- Lookout
- Mountain/Volcano
- Oasis
- Park
- Pass
- Picnic Area
- Waterfall

Population

- Capital (National)
- Capital (State/Province)
- City/Large Town
- Town/Village

Transport

- Airport
- Border crossing
- Bus
- Cable car/Funicular
- Cycling
- Ferry
- Metro station
- Monorail
- Parking
- Petrol station
- S-Bahn/Subway station
- Taxi
- T-bane/Tunnelbana station
- Train station/Railway
- Tram
- U-Bahn/Underground station
- Other Transport

Routes

- Tollway
- Freeway
- Primary
- Secondary
- Tertiary
- Lane
- Unsealed road
- Road under construction
- Plaza/Mall
- Steps
- Tunnel
- Pedestrian overpass
- Walking Tour
- Walking Tour detour
- Path/Walking Trail

Boundaries

- International
- State/Province
- Disputed
- Regional/Suburb
- Marine Park
- Cliff
- Wall

Hydrography

- River, Creek
- Intermittent River
- Canal
- Water
- Dry/Salt/Intermittent Lake
- Reef

Areas

- Airport/Runway
- Beach/Desert
- Cemetery (Christian)
- Cemetery (Other)
- Glacier
- Mudflat
- Park/Forest
- Sight (Building)
- Sportsground
- Swamp/Mangrove

Note: Not all symbols displayed above appear on the maps in this book

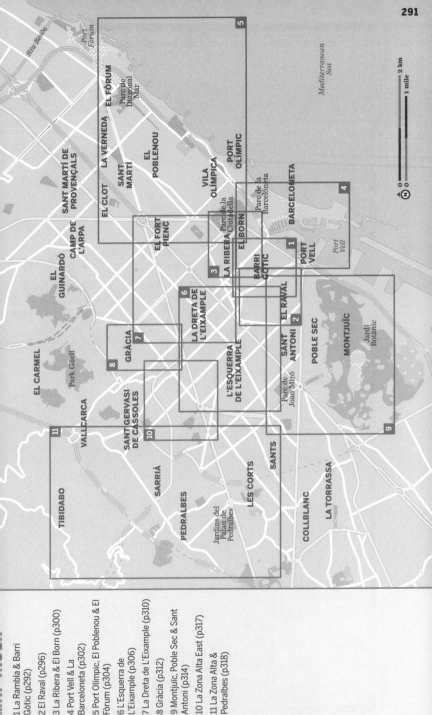

LA RAMBLA & BARRI GÒTIC

Key on p294

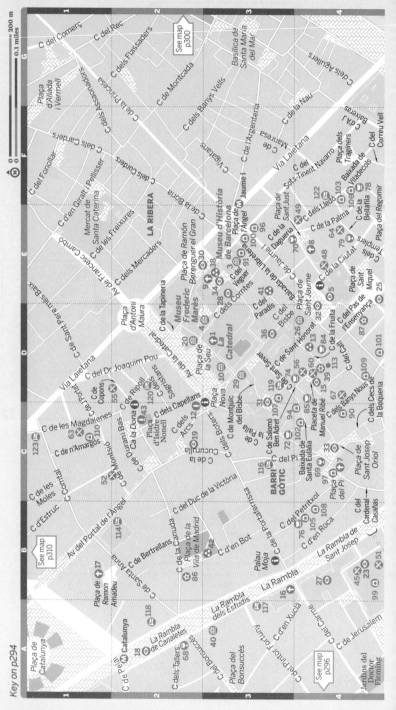

0.1 miles
200 m

See map p300
See map p310
See map p296

Plaça de Catalunya

La Rambla de Canaletes

La Rambla dels Estudis

La Rambla de Sant Josep

La Rambla

Plaça del Bonsuccès

Plaça de Ramon Amadeu

Plaça de la Vila de Madrid

Plaça d'Isidre Nonell

Plaça Nova

Plaça de la Seu

La Catedral

Plaça del Pi

Plaça de Sant Josep Oriol

Plaça de Sant Jaume

Plaça de Sant Just

Plaça de Sant Miquel

Plaça de l'Àngel

Plaça de Ramon Berenguer el Gran

Museu d'Història de Barcelona

Museu Frederic Marès

Plaça d'Antoni Maura

Mercat de Santa Caterina

Plaça d'Allada i Vermell

Basílica de Santa Maria del Mar

Plaça dels Traginers

Plaça del Regomir

Jardins del Doctor Fleming

BARRI GÒTIC

LA RIBERA

C del Comerç
C del Rec
C dels Flassaders
C de la Princesa
C de Montcada
C dels Banys Vells
C de la Nau
C dels Agullers
C d'A Baixeras
Correu Vell
C del Sots-Tinent Navarro
C dels Lledó
Baixada de Viladecols
C de la Bellafila
Plaça del Regomir
C de la Ciutat
C de la Palma
C de la Daguería
C de Manresa
C de l'Argentería
C dels Cardérs
C d'en Giralt i Pellisser
C dels Cordérs
C de les Freixures
C dels Mercaders
Av de Francesc Cambó
C del Fonollar
C de Sant Pere més Baix
Via Laietana
C del Dr Joaquim Pou
C de Copons
C de Ripoll
C de les Magdalenes
C de n'Amargós
C dels Sagristans
C de la Catedral
Av de la Catedral
C de la Tapinería
C dels Comtes
C de la Llibretería
Baixada de la Llibretería
C del Veguer
Baixada de Santa Clara
C del Paradís
C del Bisbe
C de Sant Honorat
C de Sant Sever
C de Sant Jaume
Plaça de Sant Jaume
C de la Fruita
C del Pas de l'Ensenyança
C del Cós
C dels Banys Nous
C dels Cecs de la Boquería
C de Manuel Ribé
Placeta de Manuel Ribé
C de Salomó Ben Adret
Baixada de Santa Eulàlia
C del Call
C de Sant Domènec del Call
C de Montjuïc del Bisbe
C de la Palla
C dels Boters
C de la Cucurulla
C dels Arcs
C dels Capellans
C de Durban i Bas
C de Ca la Dona
C de Montsió
C Duran i Bas
C Comtal
C de les Moles
C d'Estruc
Av del Portal de l'Angel
C de Santa Anna
C de Bertrellans
C de la Canuda
C d'en Bot
C del Duc de la Victòria
C de la Portaferrissa
C del Pi
C del Petritxol
C d'en Roca
C del Cardenal Casañas
C del Pintor Fortuny
C d'en Xuclà
C del Carme
C de Jerusalem
C Pelai
C dels Tallers
C del Bonsuccès
Palau Moja
Palau de la Virreina

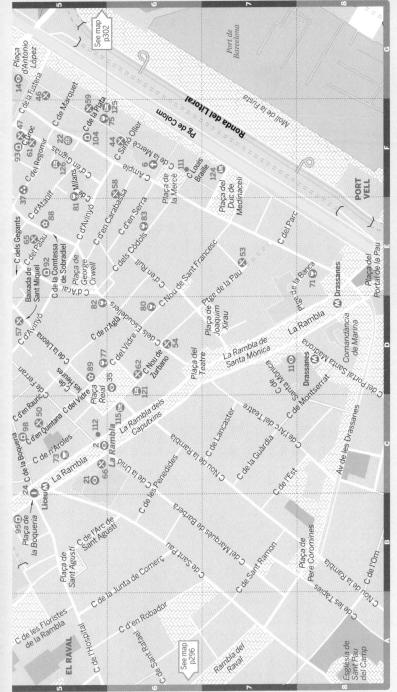

See map p302

See map p296

Port de Barcelona

Ronda del Litoral

Moll de la Fusta

PORT VELL

Plaça del Portal de la Pau

Pg de Colom

Plaça d'Antonio López

C de la Fusteria

C de Marquet

C de la Plata

C Simó Oller

C de la Mercè

C Ample

Plaça de la Mercè

C Louis Braille

Plaça del Duc de Medinaceli

Groc

C del Regomir

C d'en Gignàs

C d'Atauif

C d'Avinyó

C d'en Carabassa

C d'en Serra

C dels Còdols

Plaça de George Orwell

C d'Arai

C de la Comtessa de Sobradiel

C dels Gegants

C del Pau

Baixada de Sant Miquel

C en Rull

C Nou de Sant Francesc

Ptge de la Pau

C del Parc

Plaça de la Banca

Pg de la Banca

Drassanes

Plaça Joaquim Xirau

C d'Avinyó

C de la Lleona

C de n'Aglà

C dels Escudellers

La Rambla de Santa Mònica

La Rambla

Comandància de Marina

C del Vidre

C Nou de Zurbano

Plaça del Teatre

C de Santa Mònica

Drassanes

C del portal Santa Madrona

Plaça Reial

C de les Heures

C d'en Rauric

C d'en Quintana

C del Vidre

La Rambla dels Caputxins

C de Lancaster

C de l'Arc del Teatre

C de Montserrat

Av de les Drassanes

C de la Boqueria

C d'en Aroles

La Rambla

C Nou de la Rambla

C de la Guàrdia

Liceu

Plaça de la Boqueria

C de la Unió

C de les Penedides

C de l'Est

Plaça de Sant Agustí

C de l'Arc de Sant Agustí

C del Marquès de Barberà

C de Sant Ramon

Plaça de Pere Coromines

EL RAVAL

C de l'Hospital

C de la Junta de Comerç

C de Sant Pau

C de Sant Rafael

C d'en Robador

Rambla del Raval

C de les Tàpies

C Nou de la Rambla

C de l'Om

Església de Sant Pau del Camp

C de les Floristes de la Rambla

BARRI GÒTIC

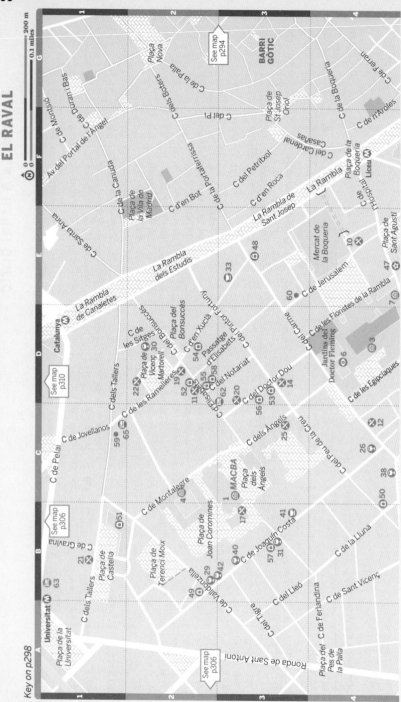

EL RAVAL

Key on p298

0   200 m
0   0.1 miles

See map p294

See map p310

See map p306

See map p306

BARRI GÒTIC

Plaça Nova

C de Montsió
C de Durant i Bas
Av del Portal de l'Àngel
C dels Boters
C de la Palla
C del Pi
C de la Boqueria
C de n'Aroles
C de Ferran

Plaça de St Josep Oriol
C del Cardenal Casañas

C de la Canuda
Plaça de la Vila de Madrid
C d'en Bot
C de la Portaferrissa
C del Petritxol
C d'en Roca
La Rambla de Sant Josep
La Rambla

C de Santa Anna
La Rambla dels Estudis

La Rambla de Canaletes

Plaça de la Boqueria
Liceu
C de l'Hospital
Plaça de Sant Agustí

Catalunya

C de Pelai
C de Jovellanos

C de les Sitges
C de les Ramelleres
Plaça de Vicenç Martorell
C del Bonsuccés
C d'en Xuclà
C del pintor Fortuny
Plaça del Bonsuccés
Passatge d'Elisabets
C del Notariat
C d'Elisabets
C del Doctor Dou
C de les Egipcíaques

C del Carme
Mercat de la Boqueria
C de Jerusalem
C de les Floristes de la Rambla
Jardins del Doctor Fleming

Universitat

Plaça de la Universitat
C dels Tallers
C de Gravina
C de les Tallers
Plaça de Castella
Plaça de Terenci Moix
Plaça de Joan Corominas
C de Montalegre
MACBA
Plaça dels Àngels
C dels Àngels
C del Peu de la Creu
C de Joaquín Costa
C de Valldonzella
C del Tigre
C de Ferlandina
C del Lleó
C de la Lluna
C de Sant Vicenç

Ronda de Sant Antoni
Plaça del Pes de la Palla

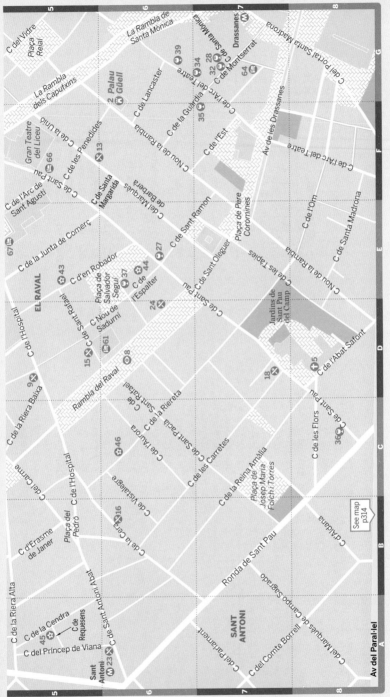

EL RAVAL

LA RIBERA & EL BORN *Map on p300*

Key on p299

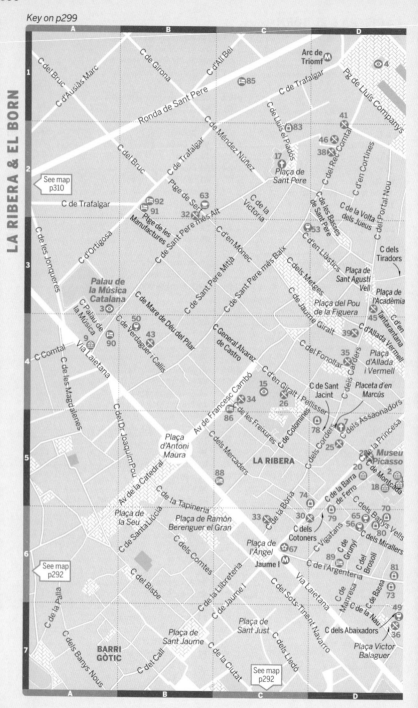

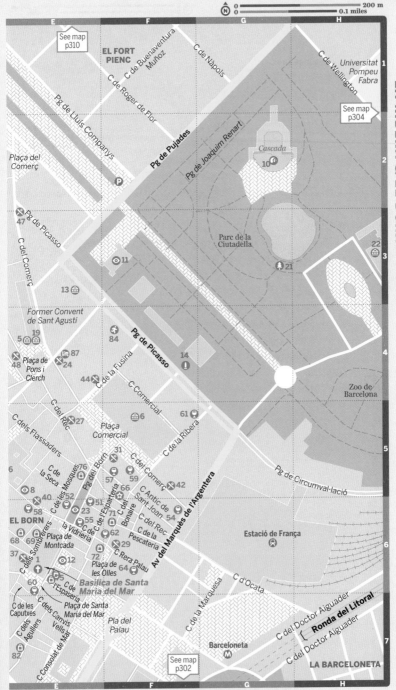

0 — 200 m
0 — 0.1 miles

EL FORT PIENC

C de Buenaventura Muñoz

C de Nápols

C de Roger de Flor

C de Wellington

Universitat Pompeu Fabra

See map p310

Pg de Lluís Companys

Pg de Pujades

Pg de Joaquim Renart

See map p304

Plaça del Comerç

Cascada

10

Parc de la Ciutadella

22

Pg de Picasso

47

C del Comerç

11

Zoo de Barcelona

21

13

Former Convent de Sant Agustí

19
5

84

Pg de Picasso

14

48 Plaça de Pons i Clerch

87
24

44

C de la Fusina

C Comercial

27

C dels Flassaders

C del Rec

Plaça Comercial

6

61

C de la Ribera

31

Pg de Circumval·lació

C de la Seca

76

C del Comerç

8
40

57

59

42

52

66

C Antic de Sant Joan

C de l'Esparteria

C del Bonaire

51

71

23

54

C del Rec

Av del Marquès de l'Argentera

55

58

Estació de França

EL BORN

62

C de la Pescateria

68

69

Plaça de Montcada

29

72

Pla del Palau

37

1

12

Plaça de les Olles

C Rera Palau

64

C d'Ocata

60

C de l'Espaseria

Basílica de Santa Maria del Mar

Plaça de Santa Maria del Mar

C de la Marquesa

C dels Canvis Vells

Pla del Palau

C de les Caputxes

C dels Aguilers

C de Consolat de Mar

82

Barceloneta

See map p302

C del Doctor Aiguader

Ronda del Litoral

C del Doctor Aiguader

LA BARCELONETA

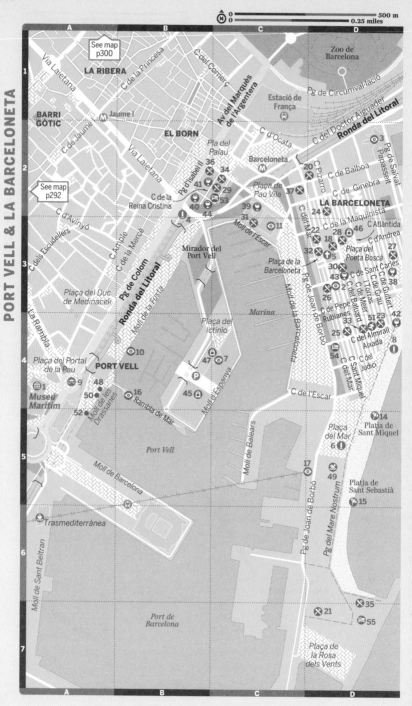

PORT VELL & LA BARCELONETA

0 — 500 m
0 — 0.25 miles

See map p300

See map p292

La Ribera

Barri Gòtic

C del Correr
C de la Princesa
Via Laietana
C del Marqués de l'Argentera
Av del Marqués de l'Argentera

Zoo de Barcelona

Pg de Circumval·lació

Estació de França

Ronda del Litoral
C del Doctor Aiguader

El Born

Pla del Palau

Barceloneta

C d'Ocata

Pg de Salvat Papasseit

La Barceloneta

Plaça de Pau Vila

C de la Reina Cristina

Pg d'Isabel II

36
34
41
29
53
40
44
39
31
11
4

20
37
24
3

C Pizarro
C de Balboa
C de Ginebra
C de la Maquinista
C Atlàntida
28
46
22
18
C d'Andrea
32
5
Plaça del Poeta Bosca
27
30
43
2
C de Sant Carles
C de Guitert
38
26
C de Meer
C de Grau
C Baluard
51
23
42
33
25
C del Almirall Aixada
8

C de Pepe Rubianes

C Ample
C de la Mercè
Pg de Colom
Ronda del Litoral
Moll de la Fusta

C d'Avinyó
C dels Escudellers
La Rambla

Plaça del Duc de Medinaceli

Mirador del Port Vell

Plaça de l'Ictíni

Marina

Moll de la Barceloneta
Pg de Joan de Borbó

Plaça de la Barceloneta

54

C del Judici
C de Sant Miquel
C del Mar

Plaça del Portal de la Pau

Port Vell

10
9
48
50
16
52
1
Museu Marítim

Moll de les Drassanes
Rambla de Mar

47
7
45

Moll d'Espanya

Moll de Balears

Port Vell

C de l'Escar

Plaça del Mar
6

14
Platja de Sant Miquel

17
49

15
Platja de Sant Sebastià

Moll de Barcelona

Trasmediterránea

Moll de Sant Beltran

Port de Barcelona

Pg de Joan de Borbó
Pg del Mare Nostrum

35
21
55

Plaça de la Rosa dels Vents

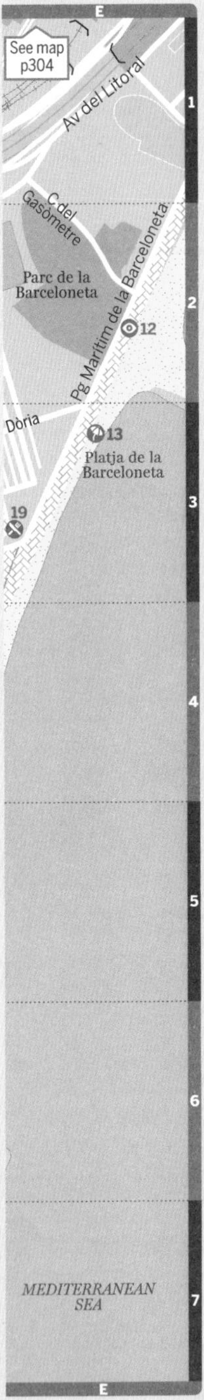

E
See map p304
Av del Litoral
C del Gasòmetre
Parc de la Barceloneta
Pg Marítim de la Barceloneta
12
Dòria
13
Platja de la Barceloneta
19
MEDITERRANEAN SEA
1
2
3
4
5
6
7
E

Top Experiences **p119**

1 Museu Marítim A4

Sights **p121**

2 Casa de la Barceloneta D3
3 Edifici de Gas Natural D2
4 El Cap de Barcelona B2
5 Església de Sant Miquel del Port D3
6 Homenatge a la Natació D5
7 L'Aquàrium C4
8 L'Estel Ferit D4
9 Mirador de Colom A4
Museu d'Història de Catalunya .... (see 11)
10 Pailebot de Santa Eulàlia B4
11 Palau de Mar C3
12 Passeig Marítim de la Barceloneta E2
13 Platja de la Barceloneta E3
14 Platja de Sant Miquel D5
15 Platja de Sant Sebastià D5
16 Rambla de Mar B4
17 Telefèric del Port D5

Eating **p126**

1881 .... (see 11)
18 Baluard Barceloneta D3
19 Barraca E3
20 Bitácora D2
21 Blue Spot D7
22 Bodega La Peninsular D3
23 Can Majó D4
24 Can Maño D2
25 Can Ros D4
26 Can Solé D3
27 El Filferro D3
28 El Guindilla D3
29 Green Spot C2
La Barra de Carles Abellán .... (see 55)
30 La Cova Fumada D3
31 La Gavina C3
32 L'Òstia D3
33 NAP Mar D4
34 Oaxaca C2
35 Pez Vela D6
36 Restaurant 7 Portes B2
37 Vaso de Oro C2

Drinking & Nightlife **p131**

38 Absenta D3
Bar Leo .... (see 38)
39 BlackLab C2
40 Bodega Vidrios y Cristales B2
41 Can Paixano B2
42 La Deliciosa D4
43 La Violeta D3
44 Perikete B2
Santa Marta .... (see 23)
The Mint .... (see 40)

Shopping **p135**

45 Maremàgnum B4
Mercat de Colom .... (see 9)
46 Mercat de la Barceloneta D3
47 Mercat de Pintors C4

Sports & Activities **p136**

48 BCNaval Tours A4
49 Club Natació Atlètic-Barceloneta D5
50 Las Golondrinas A4
51 Molokai SUP Center D4
52 Orsom A5

Sleeping **p236**

53 H10 Port Vell C2
54 Hotel 54 .... D4
55 W Barcelona D7

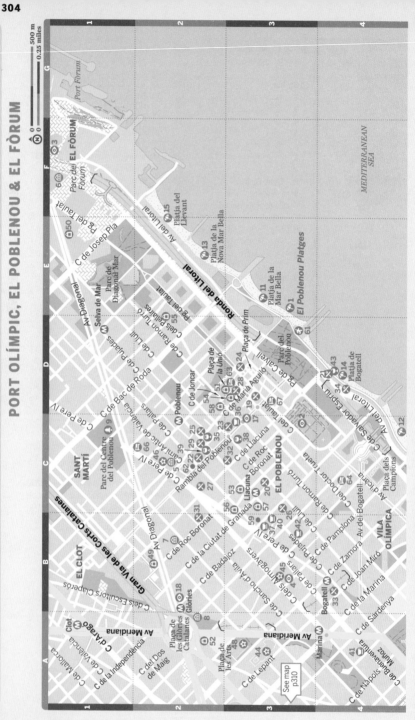

PORT OLÍMPIC, EL POBLENOU & EL FÒRUM

Key on p308

L'ESQUERRA DE L'EIXAMPLE

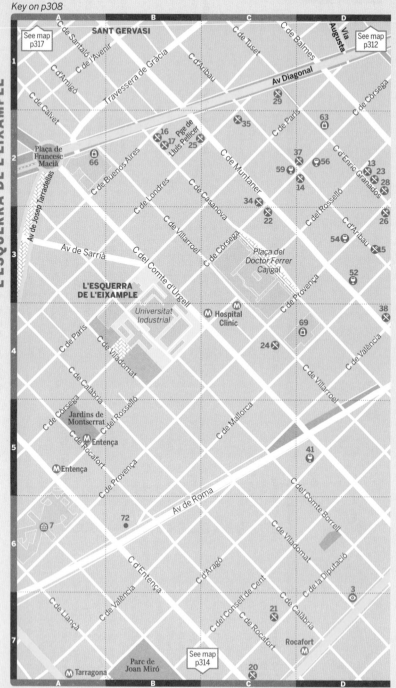

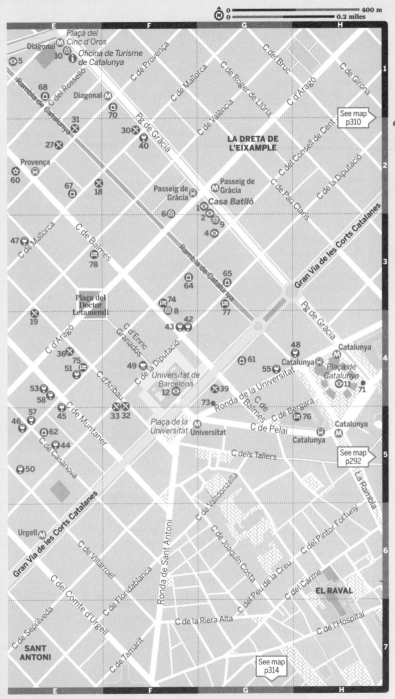

L'ESQUERRA DE L'EIXAMPLE *Map on p306*

LA DRETA DE L'EIXAMPLE *Map on p310*

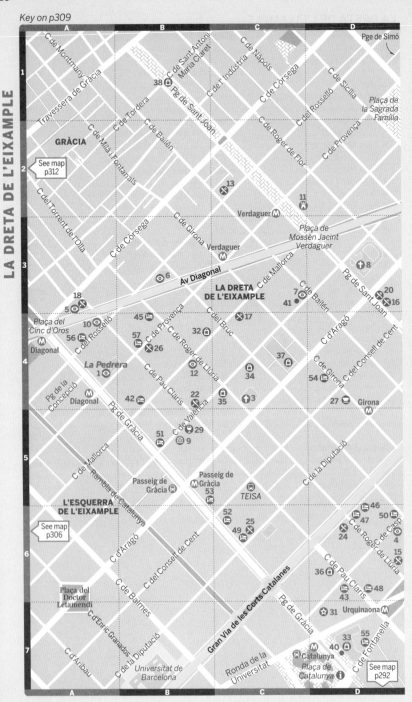

LA DRETA DE L'EIXAMPLE

GRÀCIA

See map p312

LA DRETA DE L'EIXAMPLE

L'ESQUERRA DE L'EIXAMPLE

See map p306

See map p292

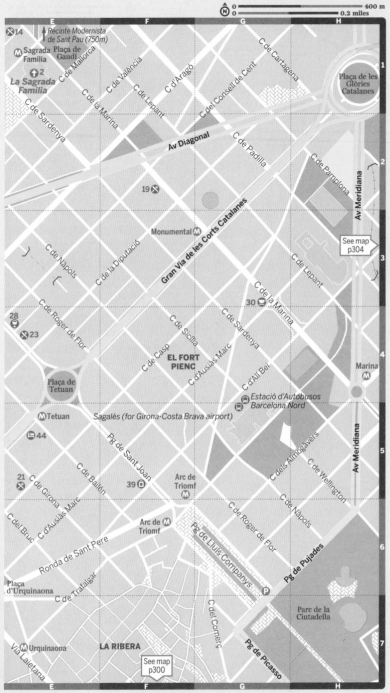

0 — 400 m
0 — 0.2 miles

14

Recinte Modernista
de Sant Pau (750m)

Sagrada
Família

Plaça de
Gaudí

C de Mallorca

C de València

C d'Aragó

C de Cartagena

Plaça de les
Glòries
Catalanes

La Sagrada
Família

2

C de la Marina

C de Lepant

C del Consell de Cent

C de Sardenya

Av Diagonal

C de Padilla

C de Pamplona

Av Meridiana

19

Monumental

Gran Via de les Corts Catalanes

C de Nàpols

C de la Diputació

See map
p304

C de Lepant

30

C de la Marina

28

C de Roger de Flor

23

C de Sicília

C de Sardenya

C de Casp

EL FORT
PIENC

C d'Ausiàs Marc

C d'Alí Bei

Marina

Plaça de
Tetuan

C d'Ausiàs Marc

Estació d'Autobusos
Barcelona Nord

Tetuan

Sagalés (for Girona-Costa Brava airport)

44

Pg de Sant Joan

C dels Almogàvers

C de Wellington

21

C de Girona

C de Bailèn

39

Arc de
Triomf

C de Nàpols

Av Meridiana

C del Bruc

C d'Ausiàs Marc

Arc de
Triomf

Pg de Lluís Companys

C de Roger de Flor

Pg de Pujades

Ronda de Sant Pere

Plaça
d'Urquinaona

C de Trafalgar

P

Parc de la
Ciutadella

Urquinaona

LA RIBERA

C del Comerç

Pg de Picasso

Via Laietana

See map
p300

Travessera de Dalt

Park Güell
(see inset; 600m)

Bunkers del Carmel
(see inset; 1.5km);
Can Travi Nou (3.5km)

25

C de Sant Salvador

C de Rabassa

C de Martí

Plaça de
Rovira i Trias

Inset

Park
Güell

28

Túnel de la Rovira

Travessera
de Dalt

To Main
Map

GRÀCIA

C de Verdi

C de Verntallat

54

31

63

C del Torrent de les Flors

C de Sant Lluís

Joanic

C de Topazi

12

C del Robí

4

C d'Astúries

10

C del Torrent d'En Vidalet

30

C de Joan Blanques

C de Montmany

77

45

73

17

71

Plaça de
la Virreina

42

Casa Vicens
(150m)

20

C del Torrent de l'Olla

Plaça del
Diamant

C de l'Or

C de Verdi

53

70

C de la Perla

55

C de les
Guilleries

36

C de Vallfogona

C de Torrijos

38

40

C de Ramón y Cajal

C de Bailén

Fontana

C d'Astúries

52

C de Terol

8

Plaça de la Revolució
de Setembre de 1868

56

43

33

66

C de Montseny

C de Ros de Olano

C de Pere Serafí

57

Plaça del
Sol

11

C del Planeta

C de Maspons

23

C de la Mare de Deu
dels Desamparats

51

C de Puigmartí

C de Siracusa

Plaça de
Raspall

C de Milà i Fontanals

19

C Gran de Gràcia

Travessera de Gràcia

46

C del Torrent de l'Olla

C de Progrés

49

C de
Tordera

Yeah Hostel
(100m)

See map
p310

C de Berga

65

16

58

18

72

44

9

C de Martínez de la Rosa

Plaça de la
Llibertat

7

67

64

Plaça de la
Vila de Gràcia

C de Sant
Domènec

C de Goya

24

37

C de Francesc Giner

22

41

35

C de la Llibertat

61

C del Perill

75

27

69

39

21

C de Mozart

C de Ferrer
de Blanes

32

13

62

C de Vic

C de Lluís Antúnez

C Gran de Gràcia

C de Bonavista

C de Santa Teda

26

C de Còrsega

C de Roger
de Llúria

50

76

59

60

68

47

14

48

C de Santa
Teresa

C de Pau Claris

Via Augusta

See map
p317

Plaça de
Narcís
Oller

34

C de Sèneca

C de Sant Miquel

C de la Riera de Sant Miquel

Pg de Gràcia

74

15

29

See map
p306

Plaça del
Cinc d'Oros

Av Diagonal

LA DRETA DE
L'EIXAMPLE

C de Balmes

Diagonal

Key on p316

MONTJUÏC, POBLE SEC & SANT ANTONI

See map p306

SANTS

Sants Estació

Plaça dels Països Catalans

Av de Roma

C de Llançà

C de València

Estació d'Autobusos de Sants

Hispano-Igualadina

85

C d'Aragó

C del Consell de Cent

C de la Diputació

C de Calàbria

Rocafort

Estació Sants

Tarragona

Parc de Joan Miró

22

C d'Enterça

Plaça de Joan Peiró

Pg de Sant Antoni

C del Rector Triadó

C de Béjar

C de Tarragona

Dona i Ocell

Gran Via de les Corts Catalanes

C de Rocafort

Parc de l'Espanya Industrial

C de Mundadas

Plaça d'Osca

77

Av de Mistral

C de Sepúlveda

C de Sants

Hostafrancs

C de la Creu Coberta

25

Av del Paral·lel

Plaça d'Espanya

36

C de la Font Honrada

C de la Bordeta

Espanya

Plaça de l'Univers

C de Lleida

C de Mèxic

Av de la Reina Maria Cristina

C de Gavà

Av de Rius i Taulet

Gran Via de les Corts Catalanes

3

6

23

Plaça del Marquès de Foronda

Magòria La Campana

C de Sant Fructuós

C de la Dàlia

C de Francesc Ferrer i Guàrdia

26

7

64

Pg de les Cascades

20

17

2

15

Mirador del Palau Nacional

Museu Nacional d'Art de Catalunya

Av dels Montanyans

Plaça de Sant Jordi

Antic Jardí Botànic

Jardins de Joan Maragall

10

Av de l'Estadi

Inset

0   200 m
0   0.1 miles

80

Antic Jardí d'Aclimatació

Gran Via de les Corts Catalanes

88

C de Muntaner

Pg de Minici Natal

Plaça de Nèmesi Ponsatí

5

34

C de Casanova

Ronda de Sant Antoni

Plaça d'Europa

Anella Olímpica

Pg de Pierre de Coubertin

40

29

C de Villarroel

C de Sepúlveda

82

41

Palau Sant Jordi

73

C de Floridablanca

86

Pg Olímpic

C dels Jocs de 92

Pg de la Zona Franca

Parc del Migdia

Carrer de la Mare de Déu de Port

Cementiri de Montjuïc Entrance (1.2km); Col·lecció de Carrosses Fúnebres (1.2km)

Cementiri de Montjuïc

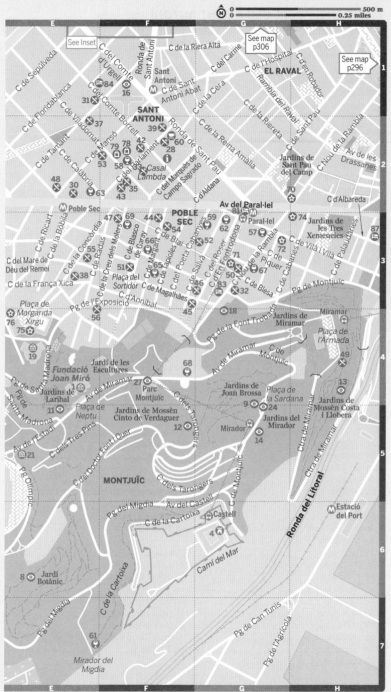

MONTJUÏC, POBLE SEC & SANT ANTONI *Map on p314*

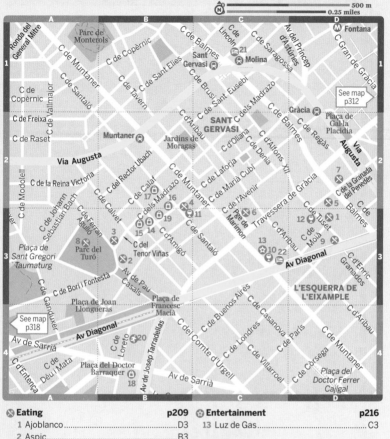

LA ZONA ALTA & PEDRALBES

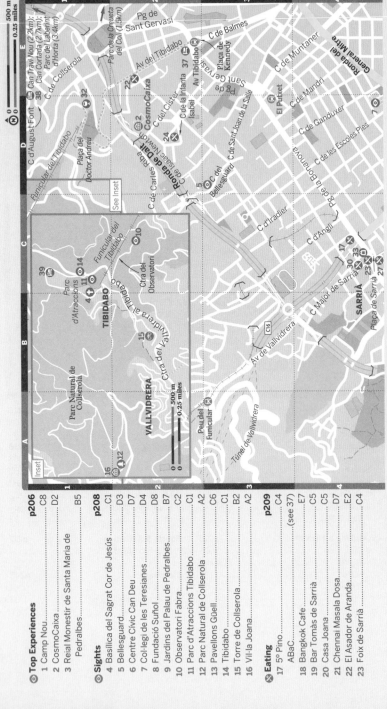

See map p317

Our Story

A beat-up old car, a few dollars in the pocket and a sense of adventure. In 1972 that's all Tony and Maureen Wheeler needed for the trip of a lifetime – across Europe and Asia overland to Australia. It took several months, and at the end – broke but inspired – they sat at their kitchen table writing and stapling together their first travel guide, *Across Asia on the Cheap*. Within a week they'd sold 1500 copies. Lonely Planet was born.

Today, Lonely Planet has offices in the US, Ireland and China, with more than 2000 contributors around the globe. We share Tony's belief that 'a great guidebook should do three things: inform, educate and amuse'.

Our Writers

Isabella Noble

Plan Your Trip, Explore Barcelona, Understand Barcelona, Survival Guide
English-Australian on paper and Spanish at heart, travel journalist Isabella has been wandering the globe since her first round-the-world trip as a one-year-old. Having grown up in an Andalucian village, she is a Spain specialist, and also writes extensively about India, Thailand, Greece, the UK and beyond for Lonely Planet, the *Telegraph*, Condé Nast Traveller, the *Guardian*, GeoPlaneta, Ink magazines, BA High Life and others. Isabella has written many Lonely Planet guides to Spain (from *Andalucía* to *Pocket Ibiza* and *Pocket Barcelona*), is a Telegraph Travel Spain expert and writes in Spanish too. She has also contributed to Lonely Planet *India, South India, Thailand, Thailand's Islands & Beaches, Southeast Asia on a Shoestring, Great Britain, Greece* and *Greek Islands,* and authored *Pocket Phuket.* Find Isabella on Twitter and Instagram (@isabellamnoble) or at https://isabellanoble.com.

Regis St Louis

Day Trips from Barcelona Regis grew up in a small town in the American Midwest – the kind of place that fuels big dreams of travel –and he developed an early fascination with foreign dialects and world cultures. He spent his formative years learning Russian and a handful of Romance languages, which served him well on journeys across much of the globe. Regis has contributed to more than 50 Lonely Planet titles, covering destinations across six continents. His travels have taken him from the mountains of Kamchatka to remote island villages in Melanesia, and to many grand urban landscapes. When not on the road, he lives in New Orleans.

Published by Lonely Planet Global Limited
CRN 554153
12th edition – May 2022
ISBN 978 1 78701 528 9
© Lonely Planet 2022 Photographs © as indicated 2022
10 9 8 7 6 5 4 3 2 1
Printed in China